# The Complete

# Chi's Sweet Home

## Part 3

### Konami Kanata

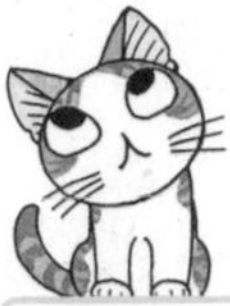

# contents

## homemade 111 ~ 164 + + 

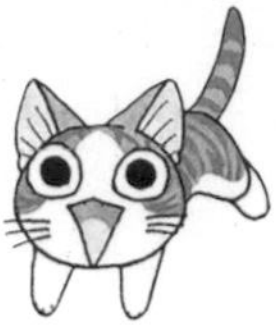

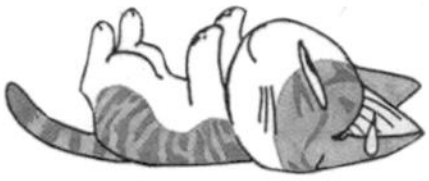



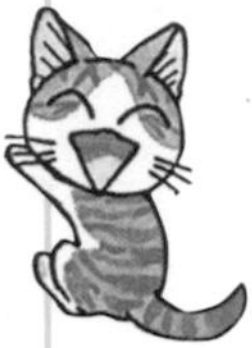

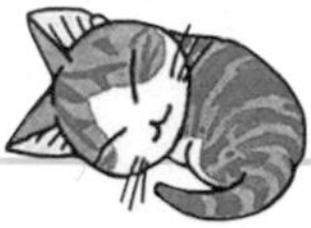

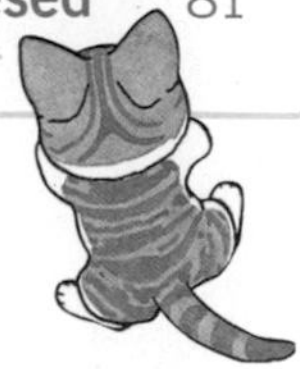

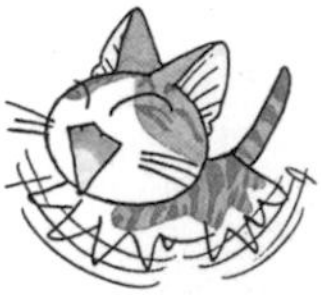

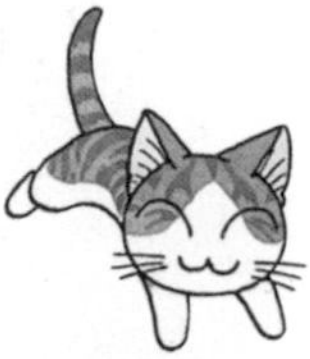

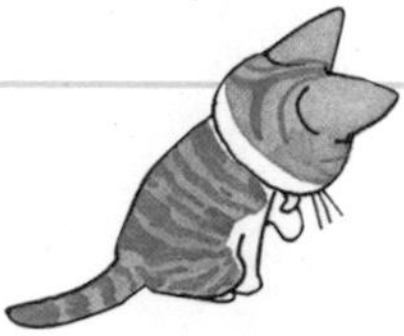

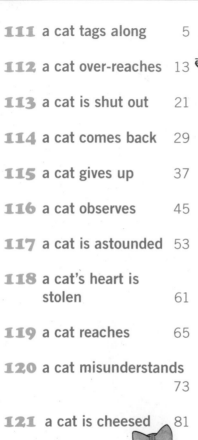

# homemade 111: a cat tags along

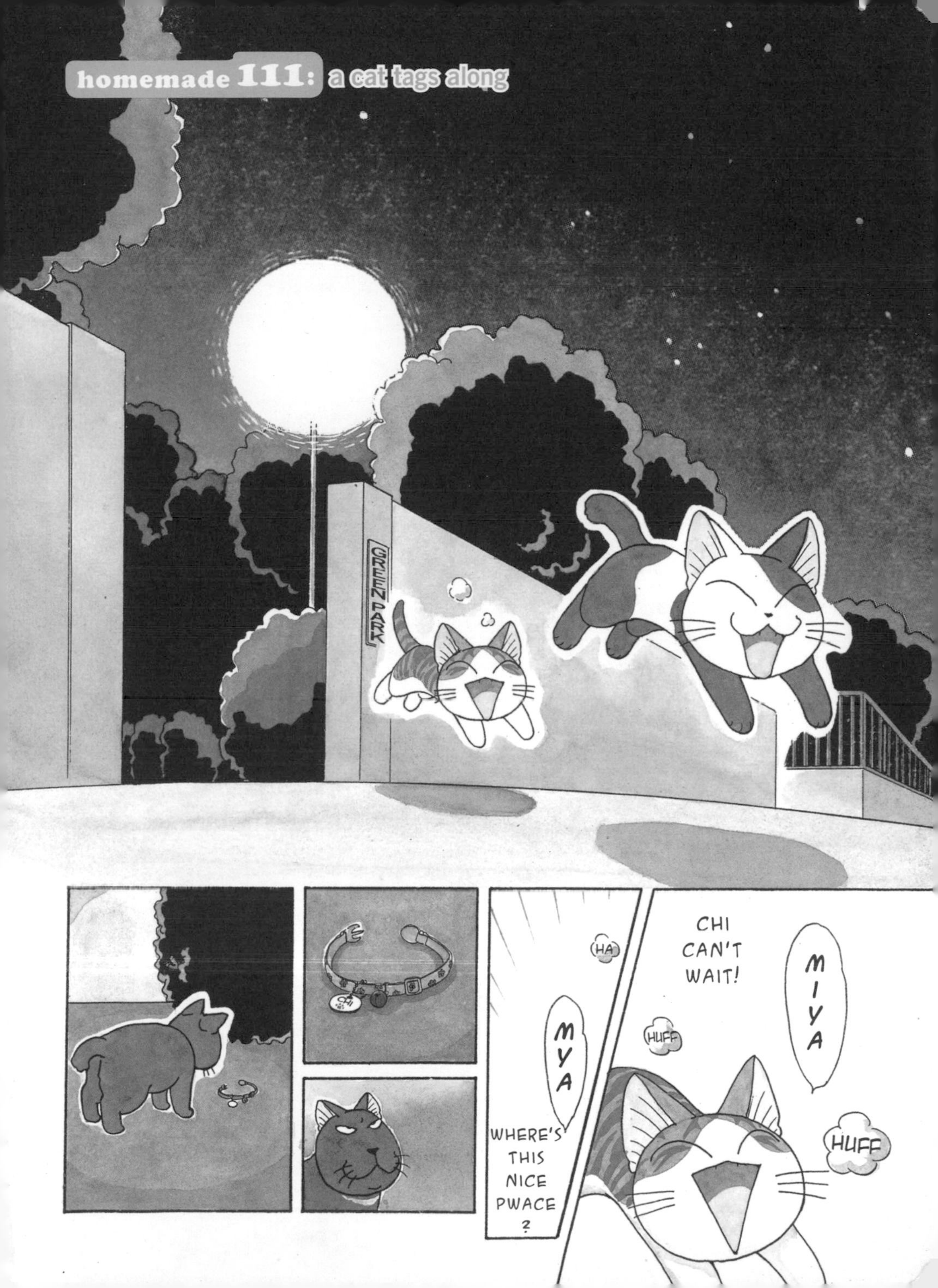
GREEN PARK
CHI
HA
MYA
WHERE'S THIS NICE PWACE?
CHI CAN'T WAIT!
MIYA
HUFF
HUFF

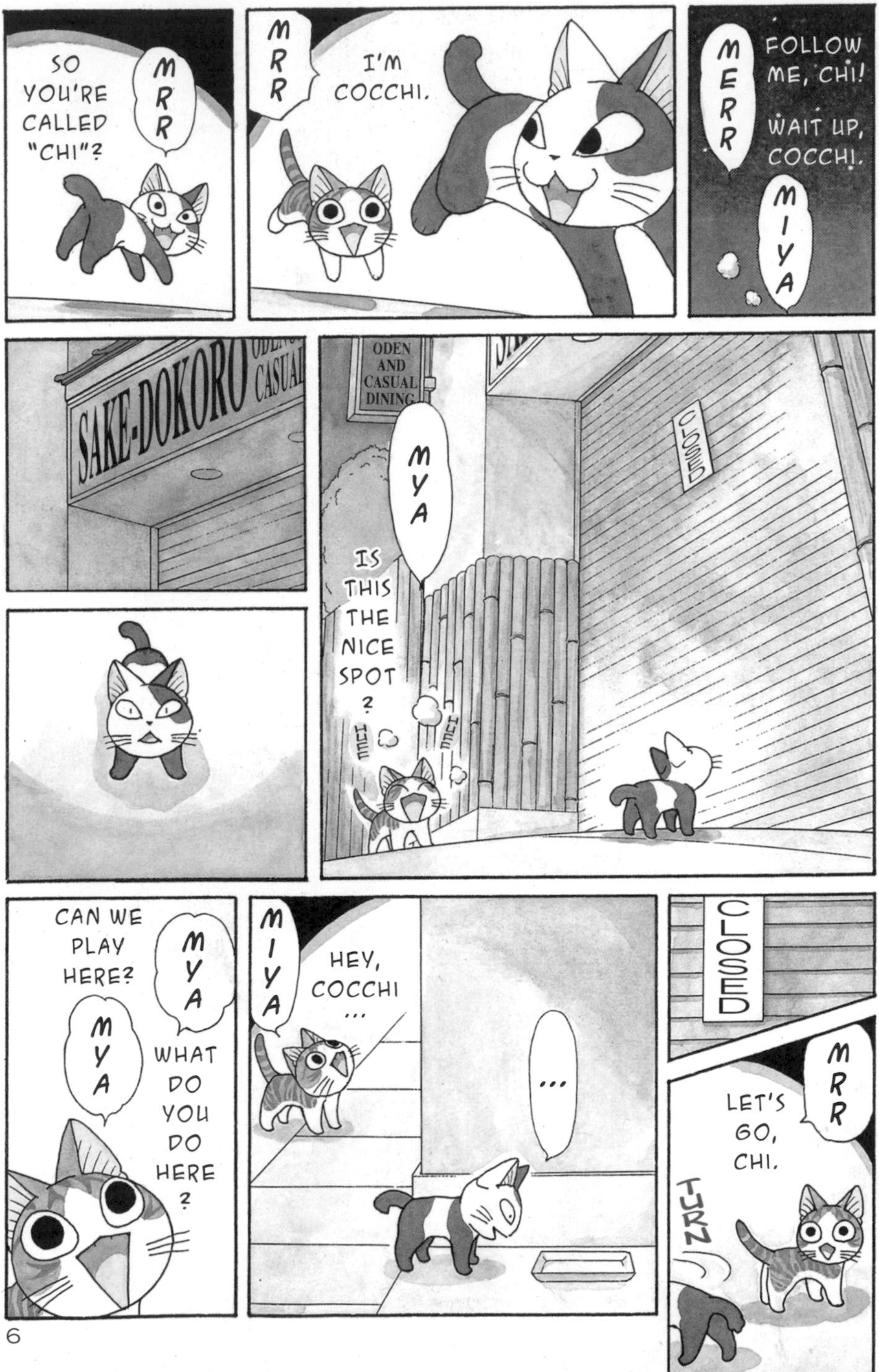
SO YOU'RE CALLED "CHI"?
MRR
MRR
I'M COCCHI.
MERR
FOLLOW ME, CHI!
WAIT UP, COCCHI.
MIYA
SAKE-DOKORO
ODEN AND CASUAL DINING
MYA
IS THIS THE NICE SPOT?
HUFF
HUFF
CLOSED
CAN WE PLAY HERE?
MYA
MYA
WHAT DO YOU DO HERE?
MIYA
HEY, COCCHI...
...
CLOSED
MRR
LET'S GO, CHI.
TURN

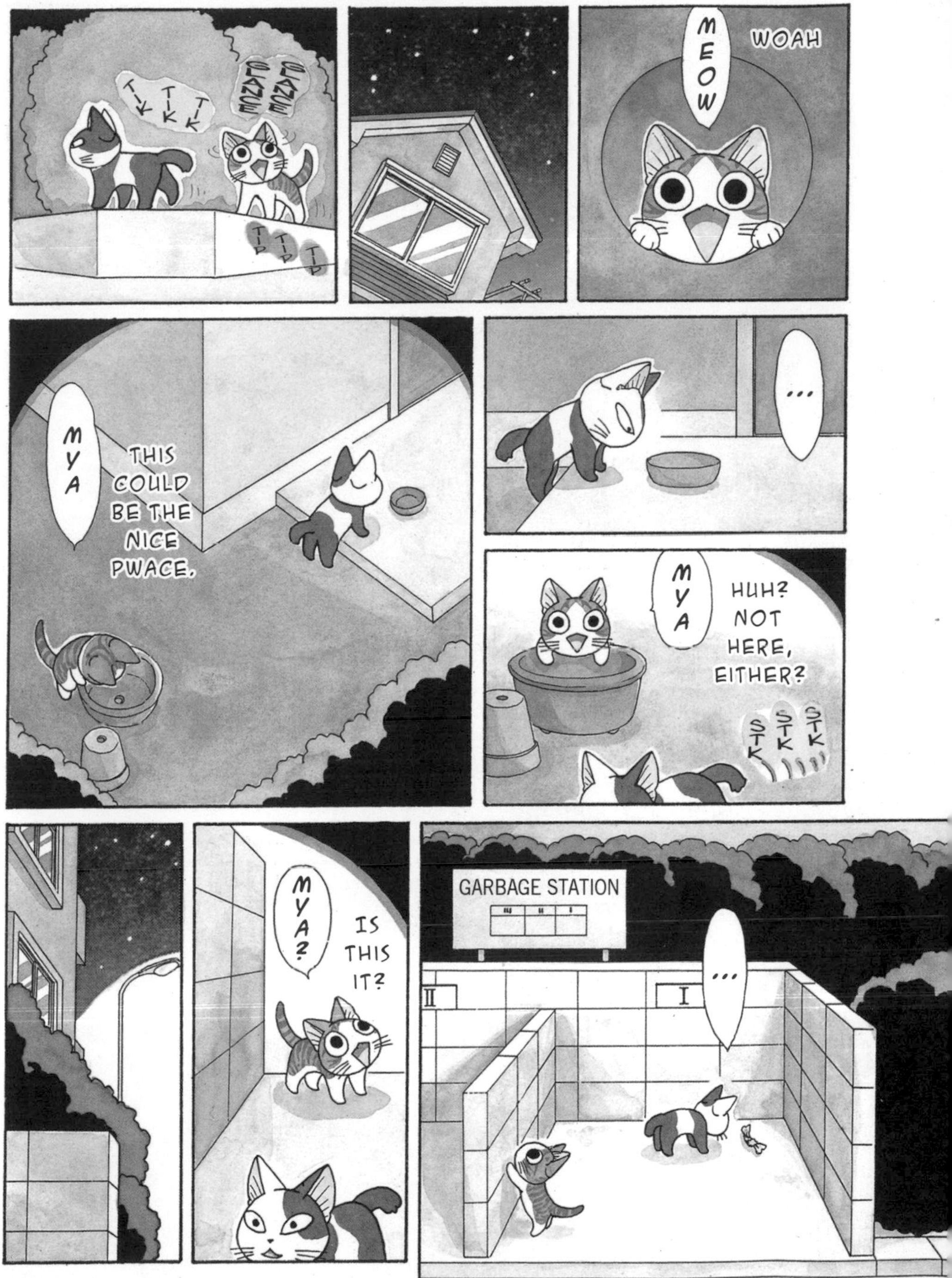
TIK TIK TIK
GLANCE GLANCE
TIP TIP TIP
MEOW
WOAH
MYA
THIS COULD BE THE NICE PWACE.
...
MYA
HUH? NOT HERE, EITHER?
STK STK STK
MYA?
IS THIS IT?
GARBAGE STATION
II
I
...

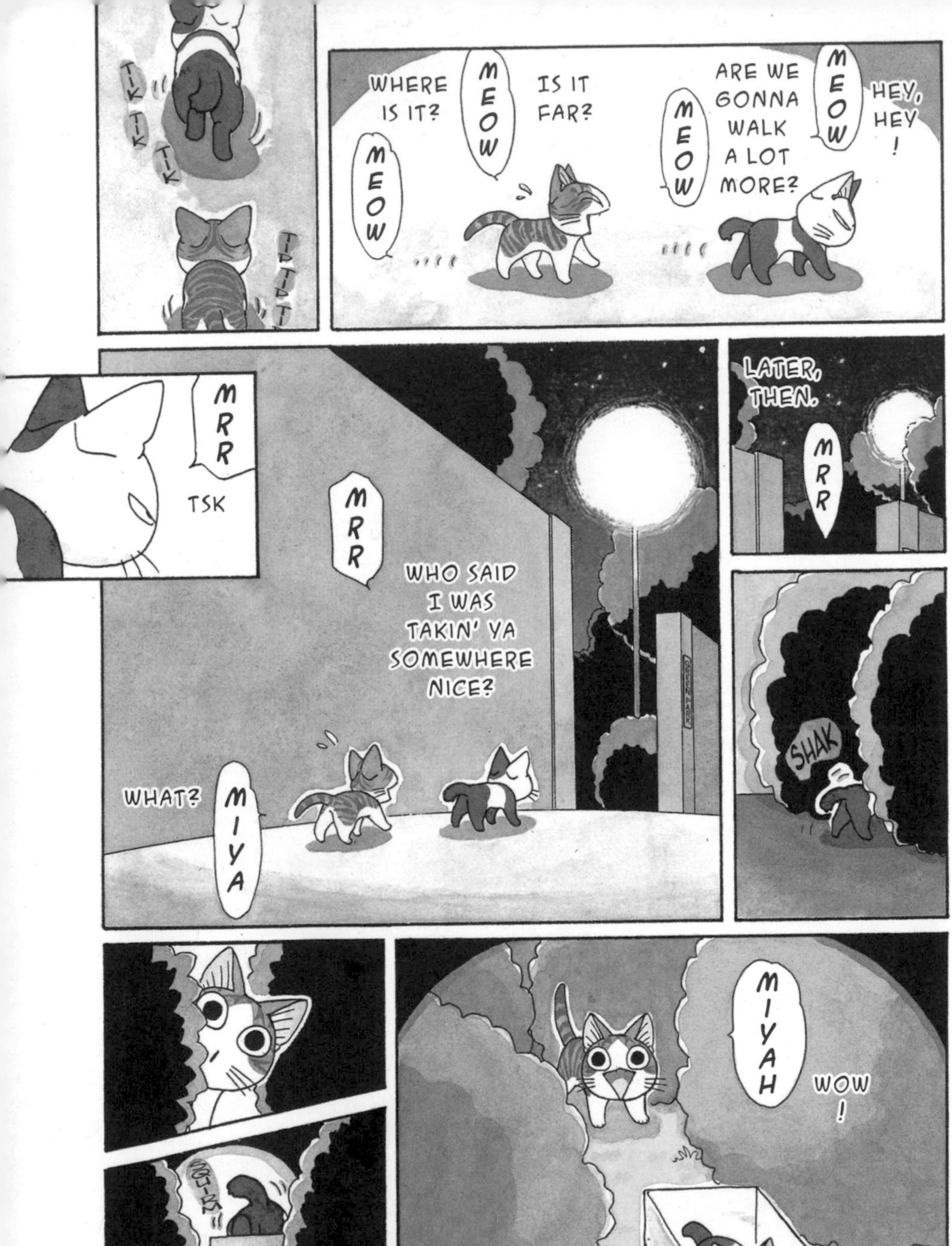
TIK TIK TIK
TIP TIP TIP
MEOW
WHERE IS IT?
MEOW
IS IT FAR?
MEOW
ARE WE GONNA WALK A LOT MORE?
MEOW
HEY, HEY!
MRR
TSK
MRR
WHO SAID I WAS TAKIN' YA SOMEWHERE NICE?
WHAT?
MIYA
LATER, THEN.
MRR
SHAK
SQUIRM
MIYAH
WOW!

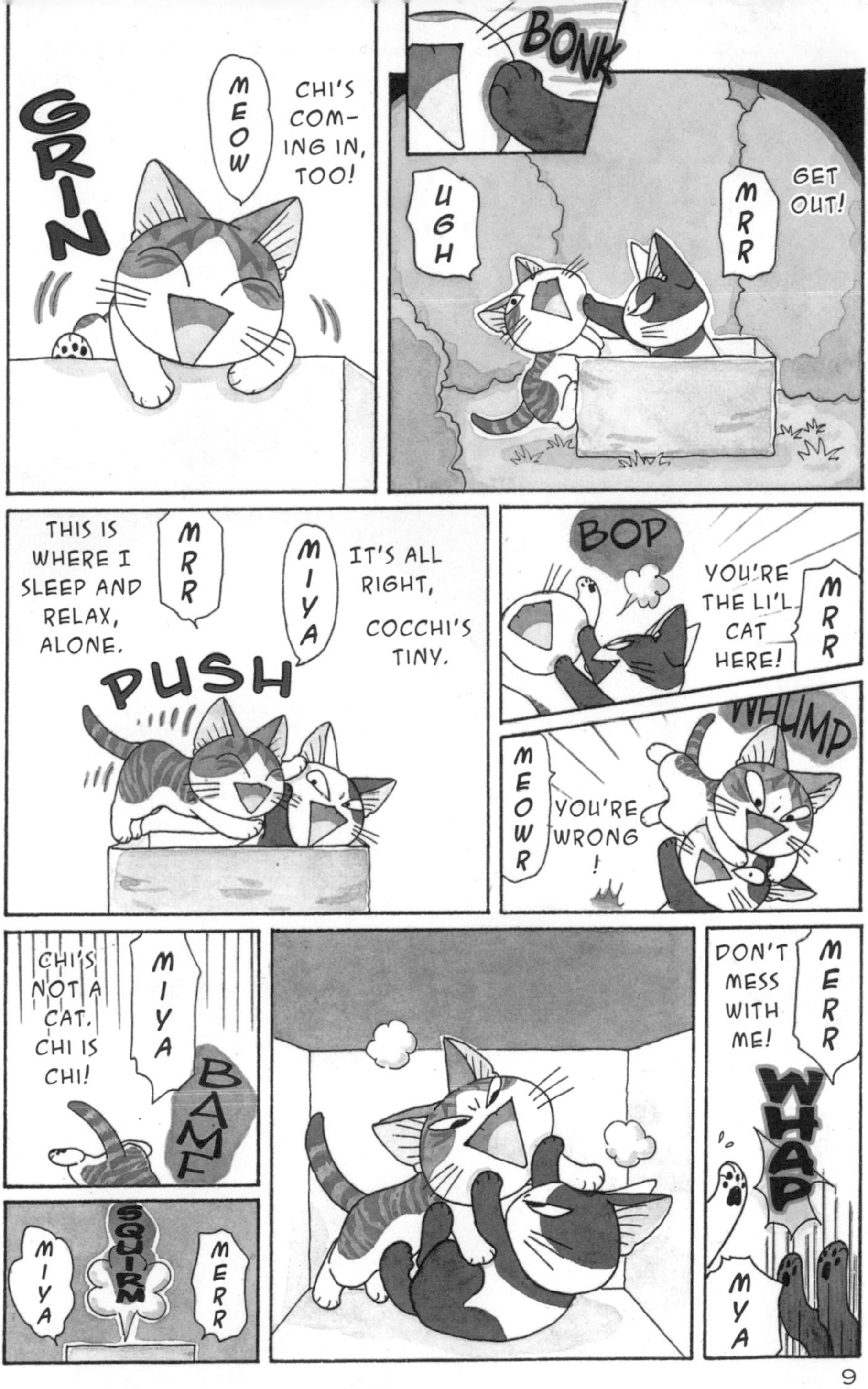
GRIN
MEOW
CHI'S COMING IN, TOO!
BONK
UGH
MRR
GET OUT!
THIS IS WHERE I SLEEP AND RELAX, ALONE.
MRR
MIYA
IT'S ALL RIGHT, COCCHI'S TINY.
PUSH
BOP
YOU'RE THE LI'L CAT HERE!
MRR
WHUMP
MEOWR
YOU'RE WRONG!
CHI'S NOT A CAT. CHI IS CHI!
MIYA
BAMF
MIYA
SQUIRM
MERR
DON'T MESS WITH ME!
MERR
WHAP
MYA

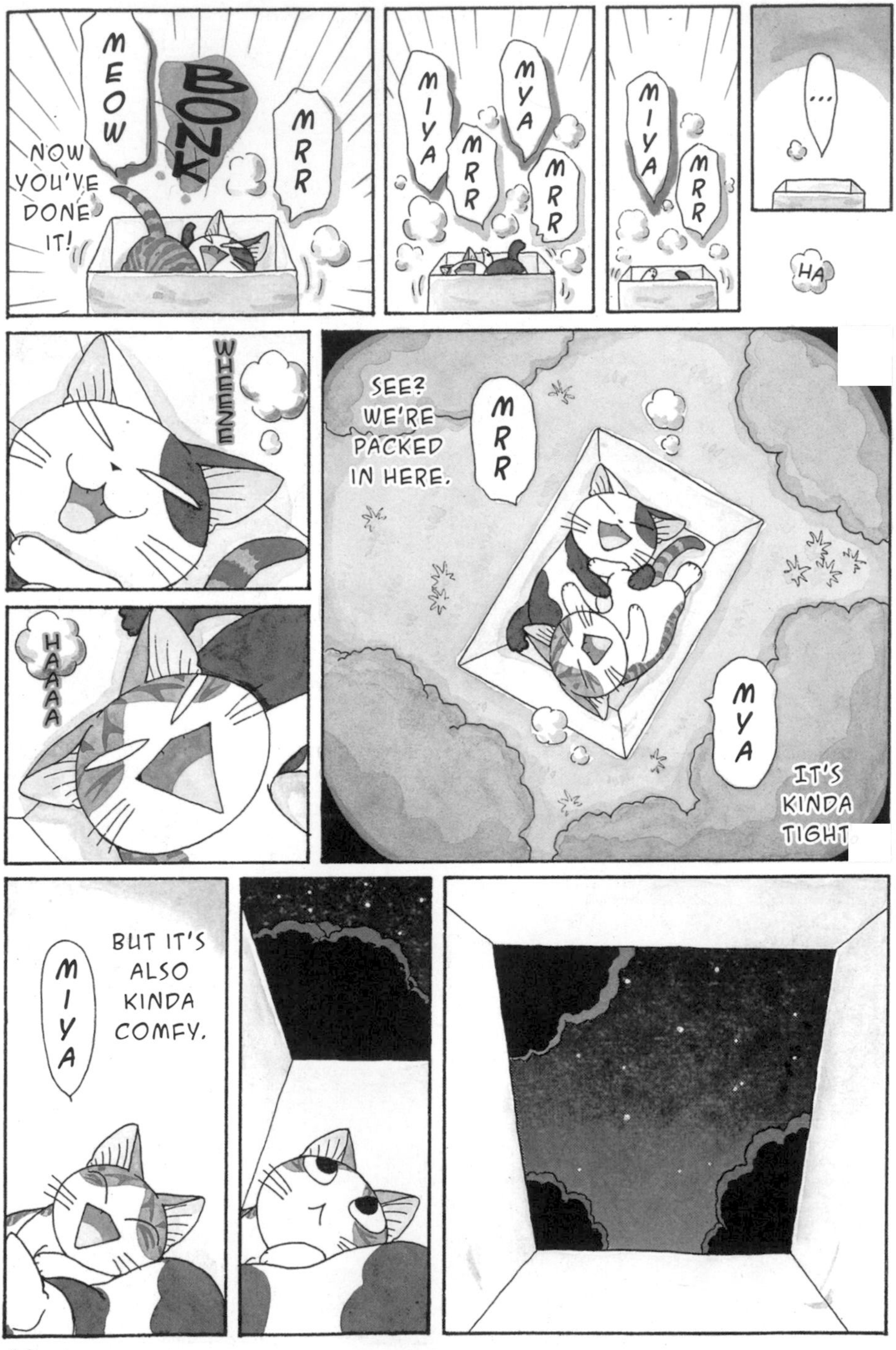
MEOW
BONK
MRR
NOW YOU'VE DONE IT!
MIYA
MRR
MYA
MRR
MIYA
MRR
...
HA
WHEEZE
HAAAAA
SEE? WE'RE PACKED IN HERE.
MRR
MYA
IT'S KINDA TIGHT
MIYA
BUT IT'S ALSO KINDA COMFY.

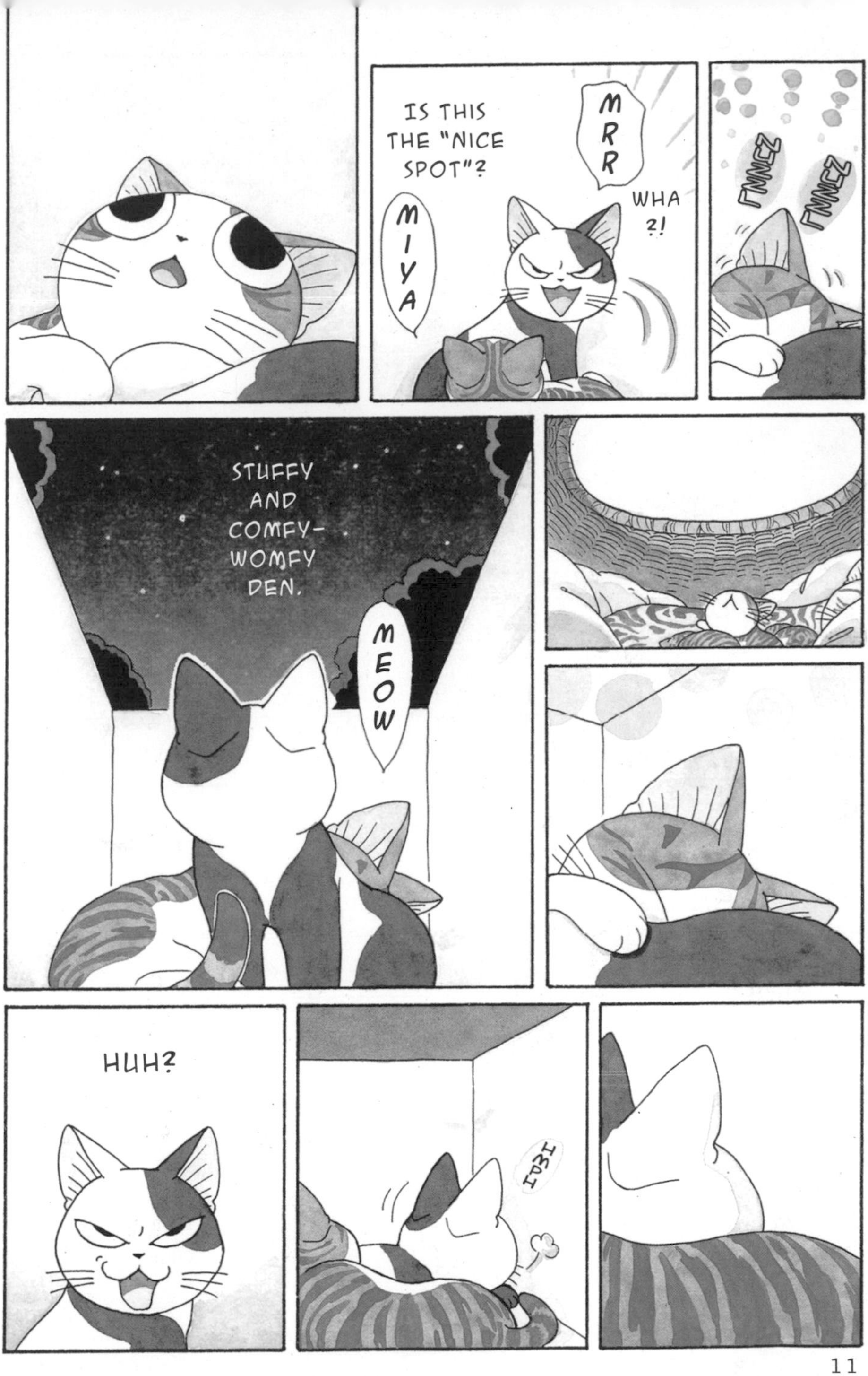
IS THIS THE "NICE SPOT"?
MRR
MIYA
WHA ?!
STUFFY AND COMFY-WOMFY DEN.
MEOW
HUH?

STUFFY AND COMFY ...

AND WARM.

TSK

ГMNNCZ

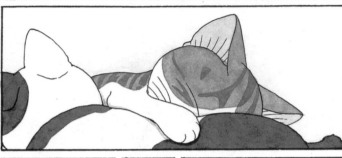

CHI DOESN'T KNOW THIS SMELL.

I KNOW THIS SMELL

FROM SOMETIME, SOMEWHERE.

BUT

IT'S STWANGE ...

**the end**

# homemade 112: a cat over-reaches

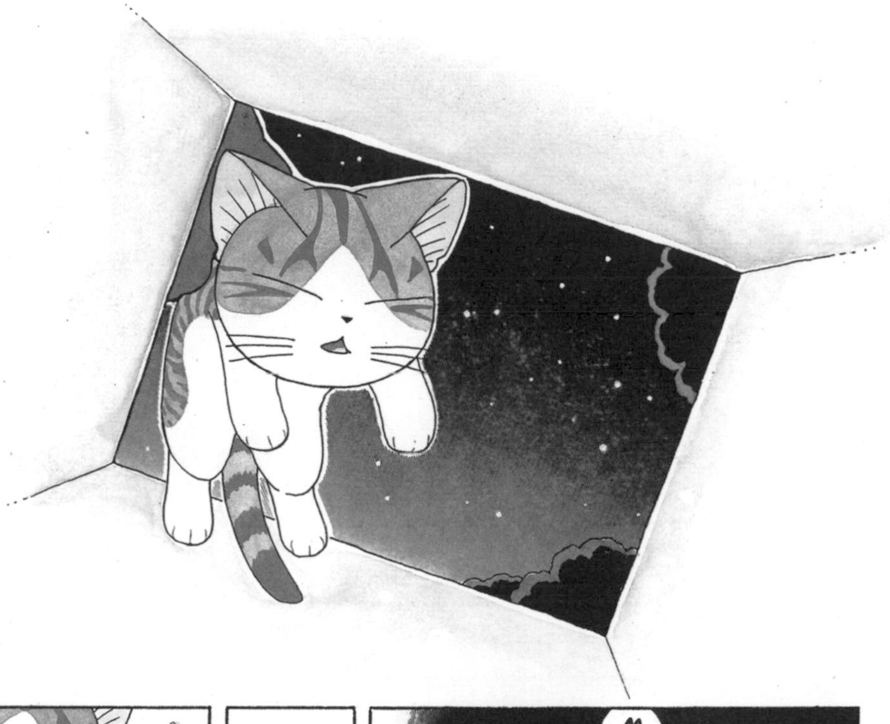

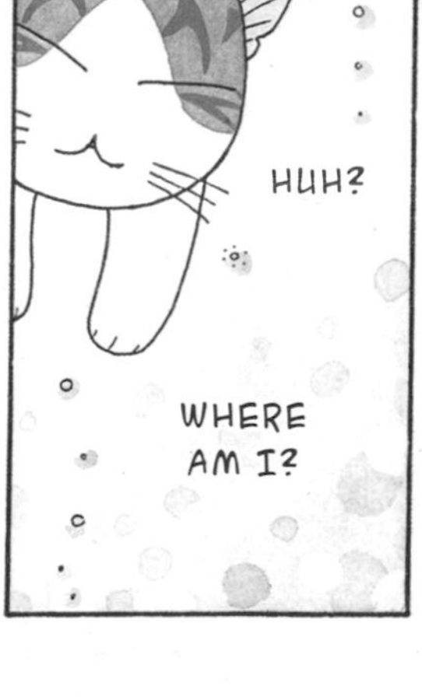

HUH?
WHERE AM I?

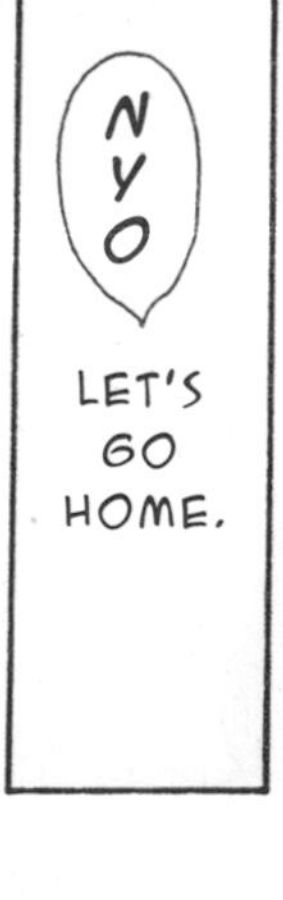

NYO
LET'S GO HOME.

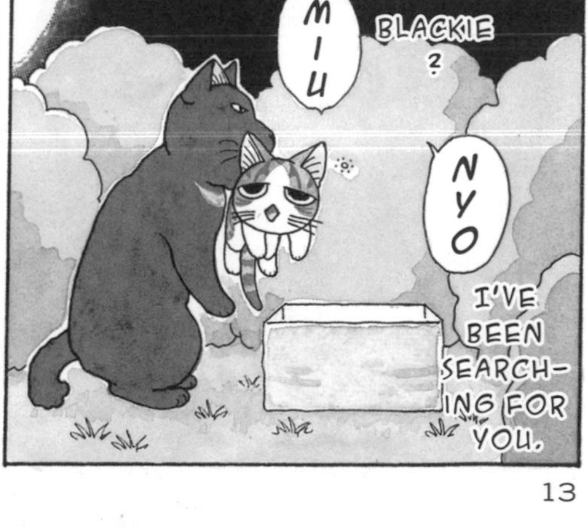

MIU
BLACKIE?
NYO
I'VE BEEN SEARCHING FOR YOU.

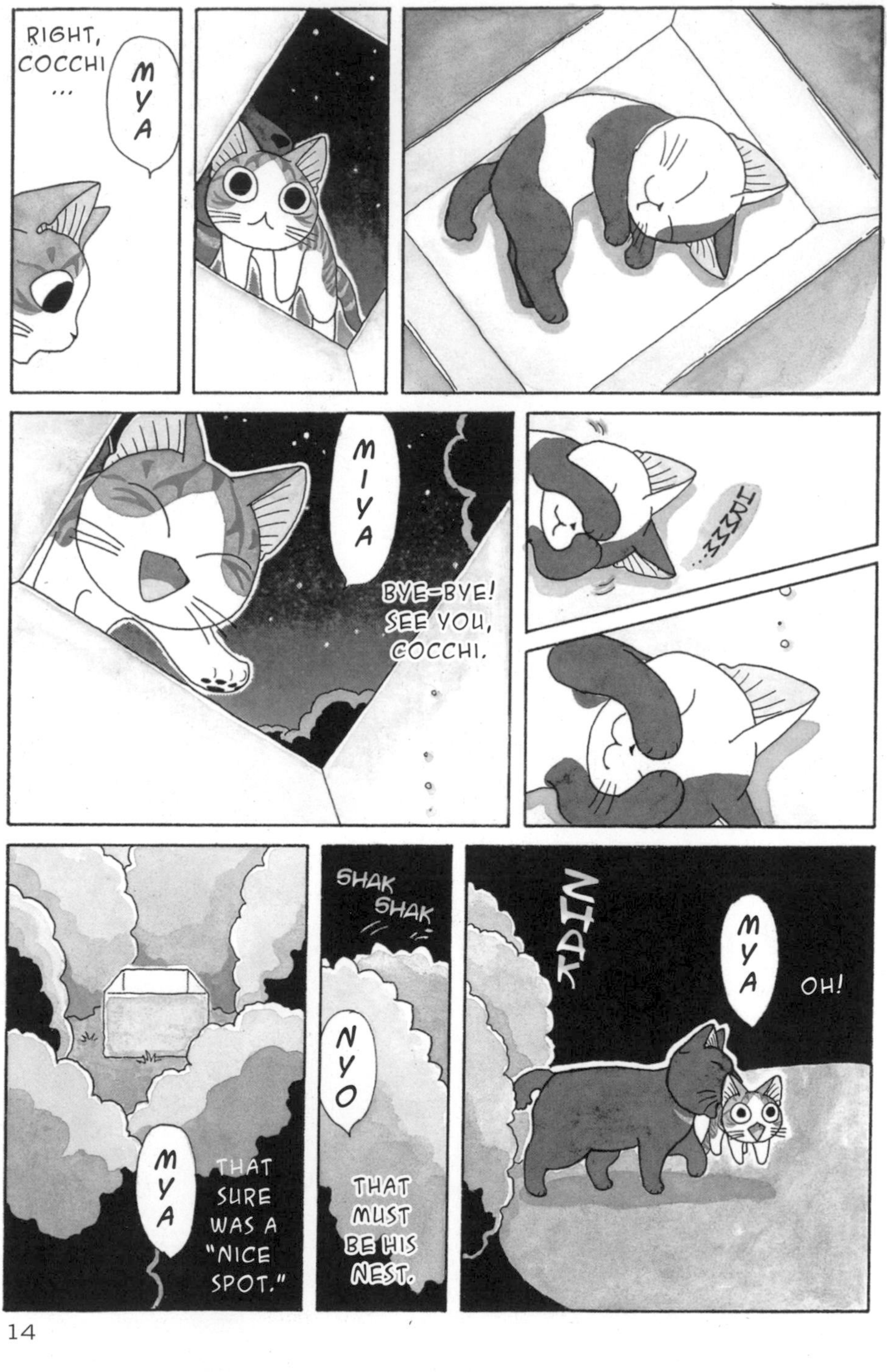
RIGHT, COCCHI...
MYA
MIYA
BYE-BYE! SEE YOU, COCCHI.
MYA
THAT SURE WAS A "NICE SPOT."
SHAK SHAK
NYO
THAT MUST BE HIS NEST.
MYA
OH!

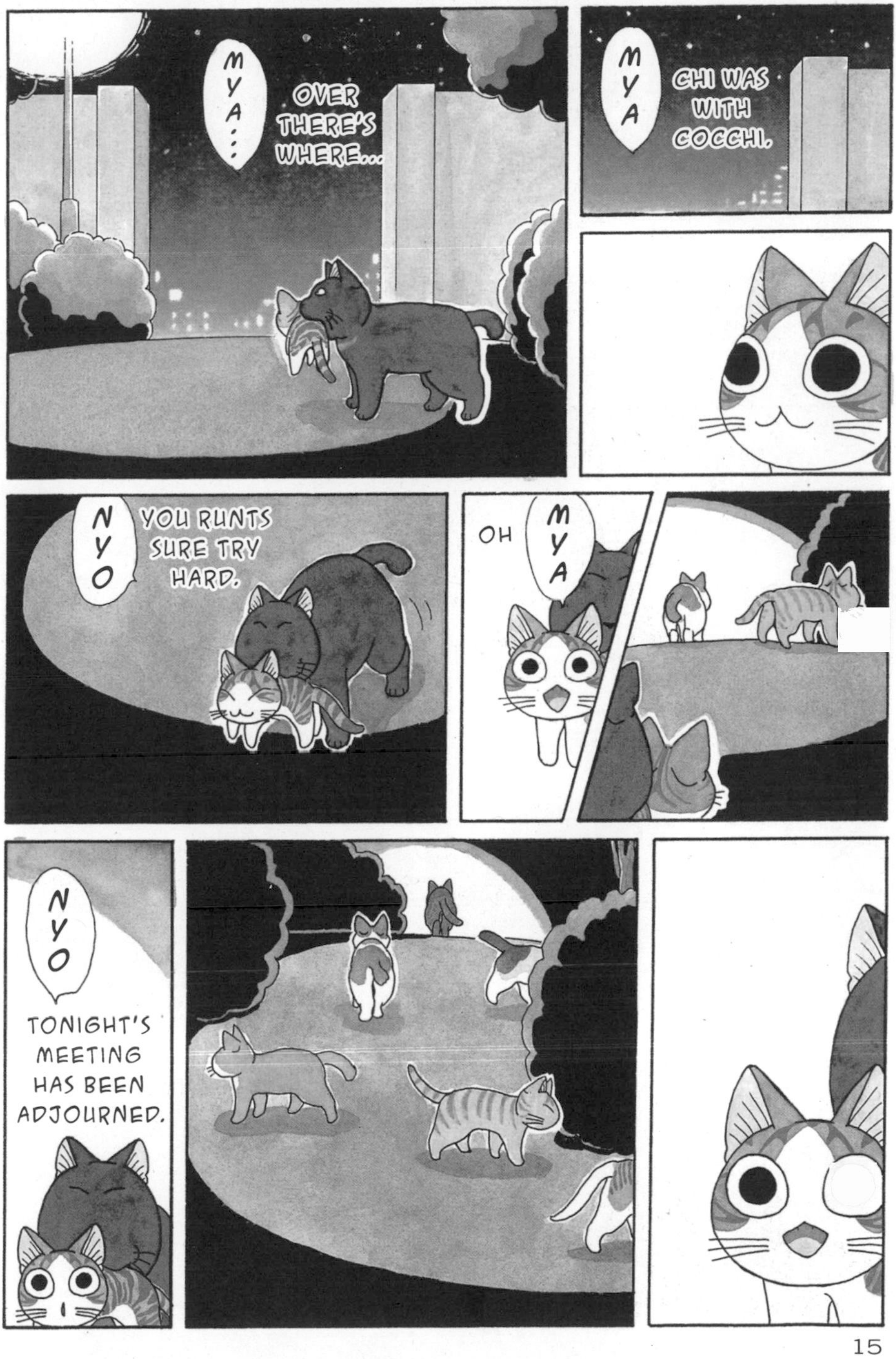
MYA...
OVER THERE'S WHERE...
MYA
CHI WAS WITH COCCHI.
NYO
YOU RUNTS SURE TRY HARD.
OH
MYA
NYO
TONIGHT'S MEETING HAS BEEN ADJOURNED.

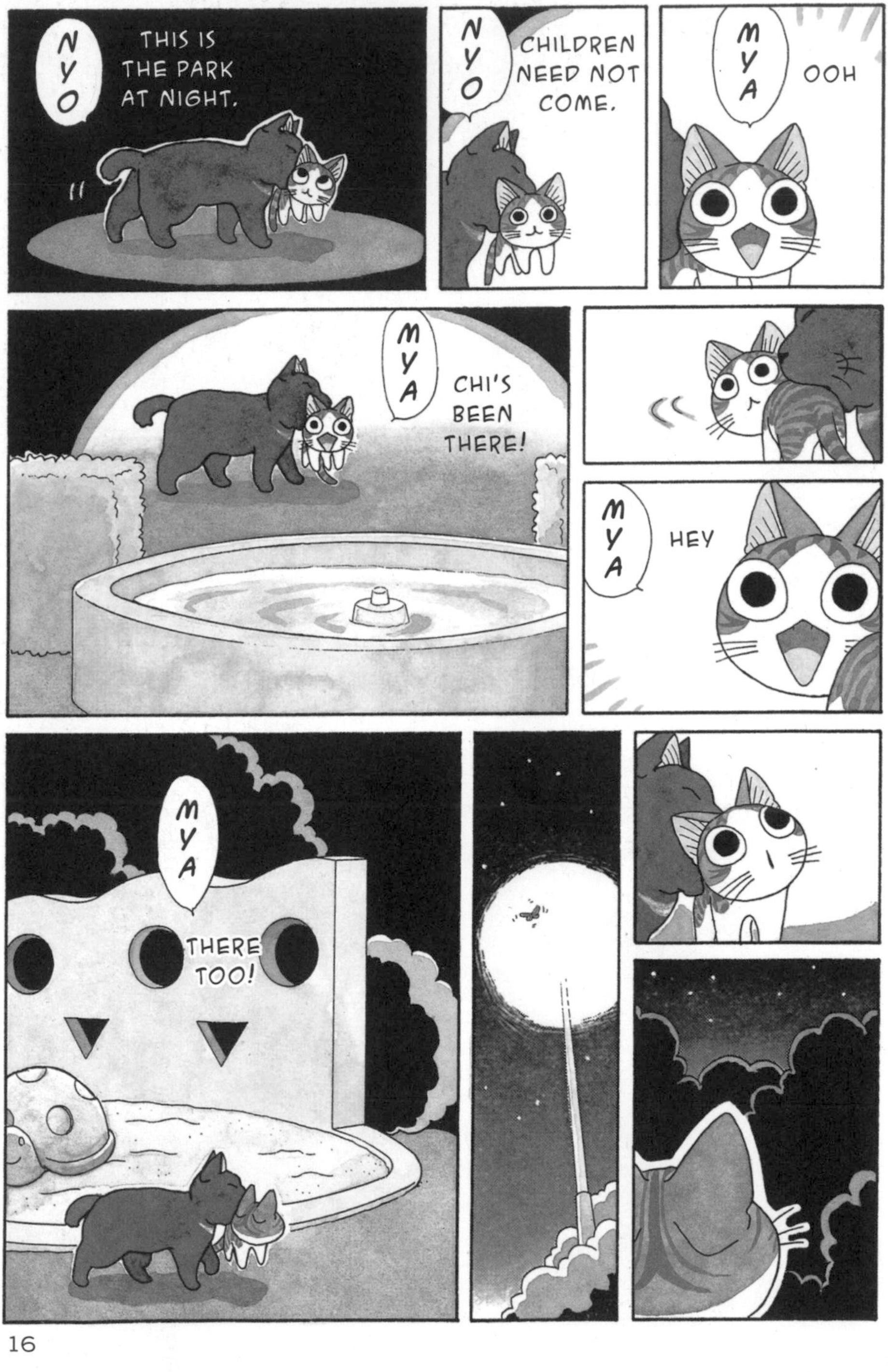
NYO
THIS IS THE PARK AT NIGHT.
NYO
CHILDREN NEED NOT COME.
MYA
OOH
MYA
CHI'S BEEN THERE!
MYA
HEY
MYA
THERE TOO!

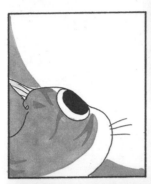

MIYA

CHI CAN WALK ON HER OWN.

THE PARK AT NIGHT.

HEH

LET'S GO HOME, BLACK-IE!

MYA!

NYO

YEAH

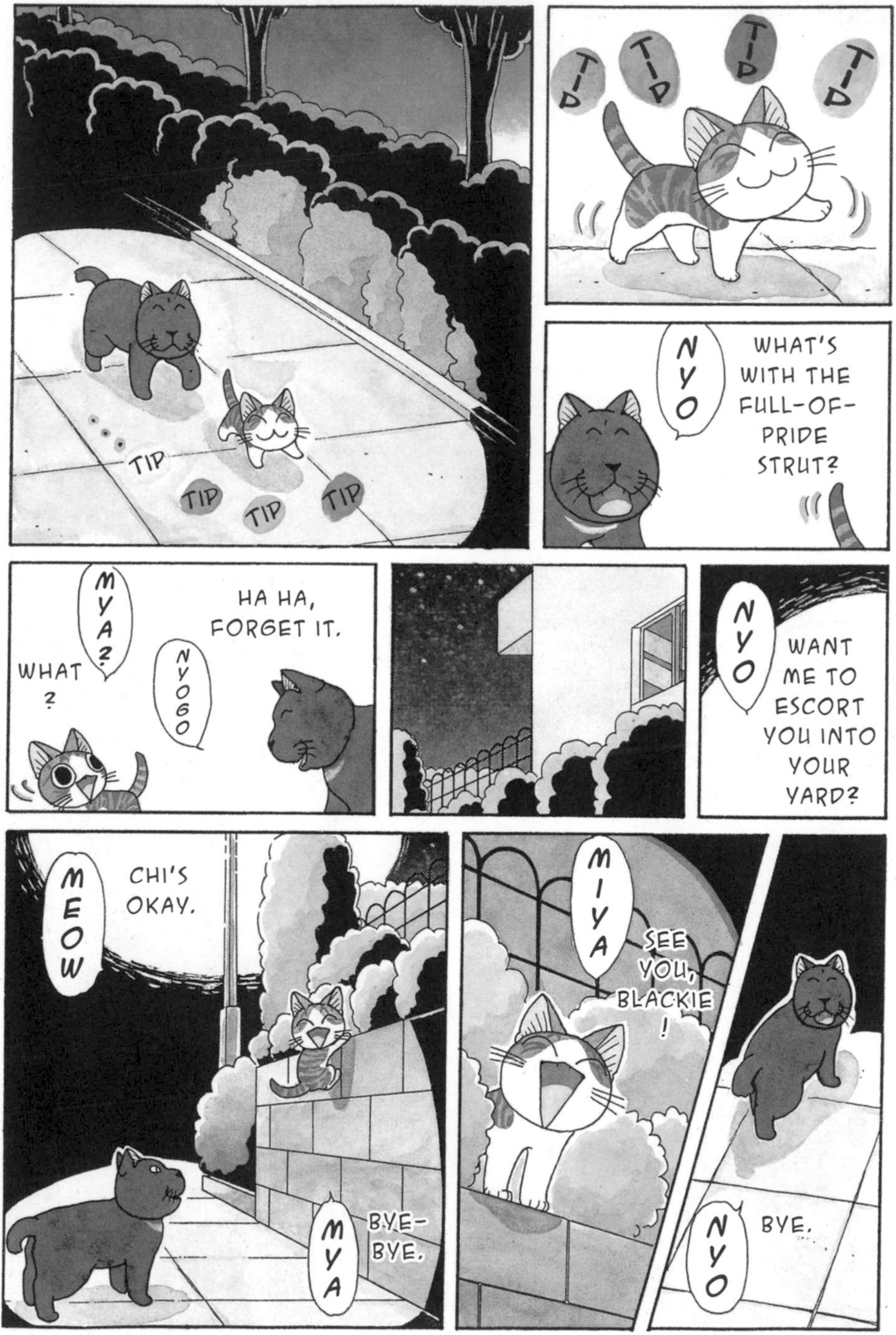
TIP
TIP
TIP
TIP
TIP
TIP
TIP
TIP
NYO
WHAT'S WITH THE FULL-OF-PRIDE STRUT?
MYA?
WHAT?
NYOGO
HA HA, FORGET IT.
NYO
WANT ME TO ESCORT YOU INTO YOUR YARD?
MEOW
CHI'S OKAY.
MYA
BYE-BYE.
MIYA
SEE YOU, BLACKIE!
NYO
BYE.

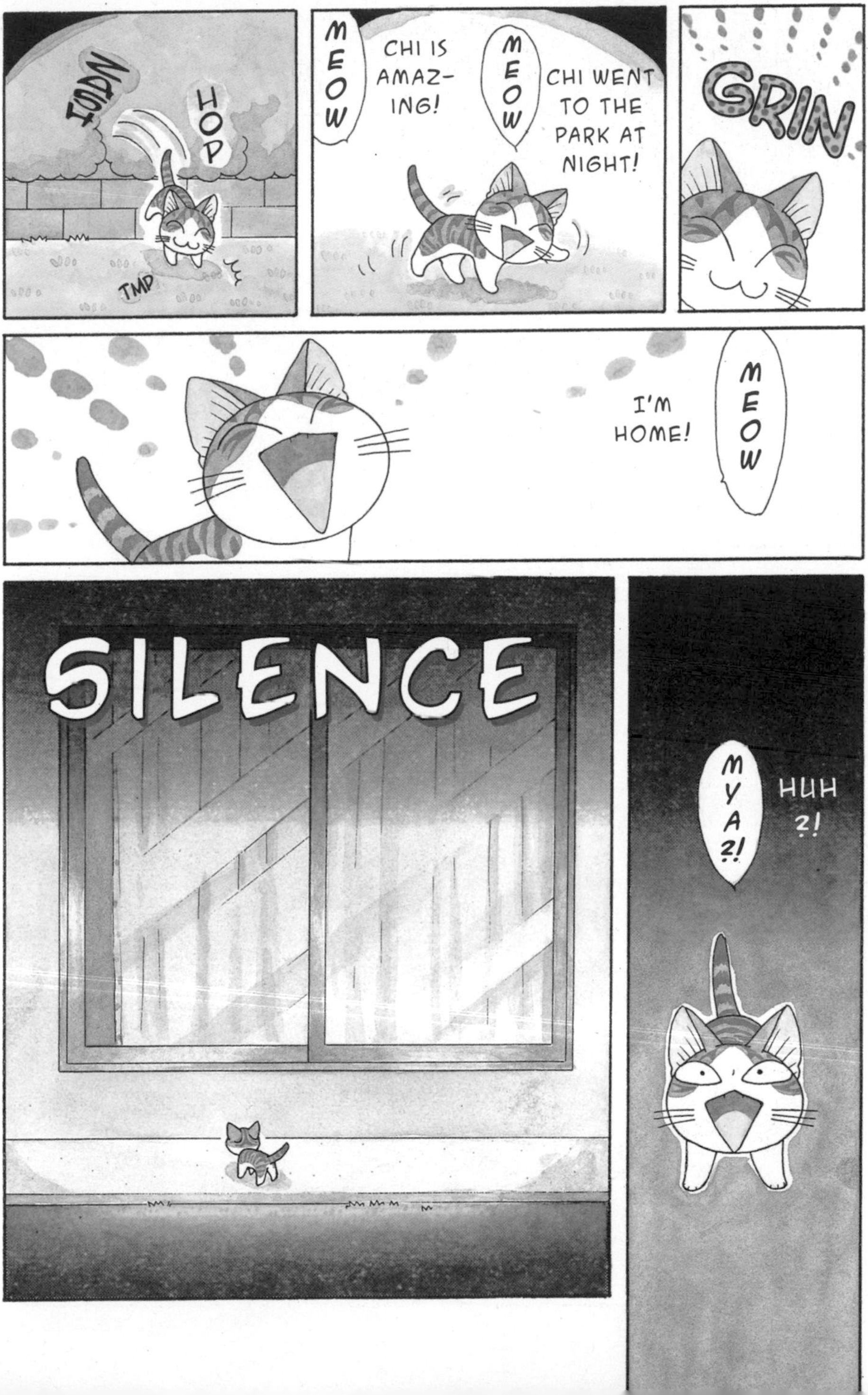
HOP
TMP
MEOW
CHI IS AMAZ-ING!
MEOW
CHI WENT TO THE PARK AT NIGHT!
GRIN
I'M HOME!
MEOW
SILENCE
MYA?!
HUH?!

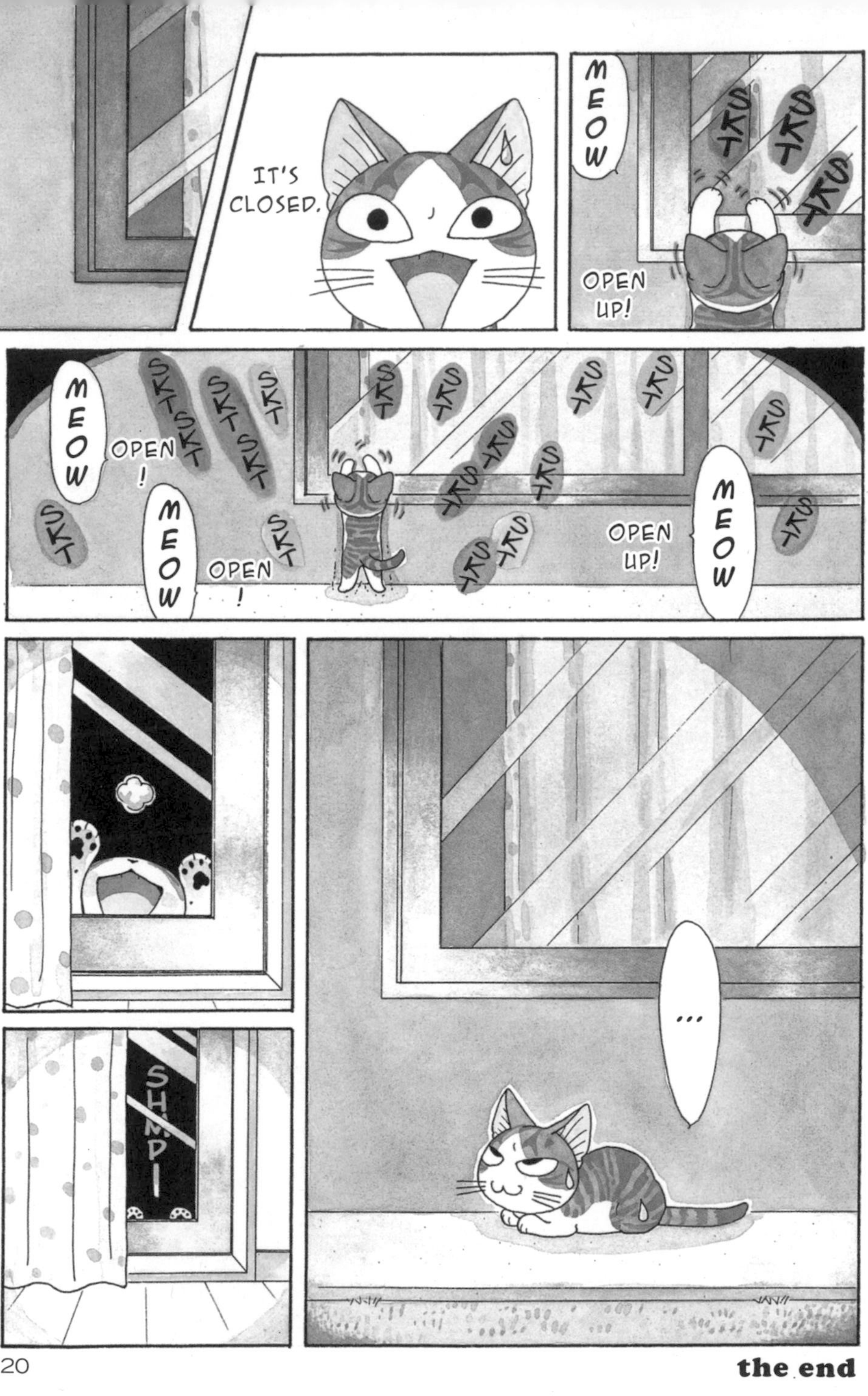

IT'S CLOSED.
MEOW
SKT
SKT
SKT
OPEN UP!
MEOW
SKT
SKT SKT
SKT SKT
SKT
OPEN!
SKT
MEOW
OPEN!
SKT
SKT
SKT
SKT SKT
SKT SKT
SKT
SKT
SKT
SKT
SKT
OPEN UP!
MEOW
SHMPI
...


the end

## homemade 113: a cat is shut out

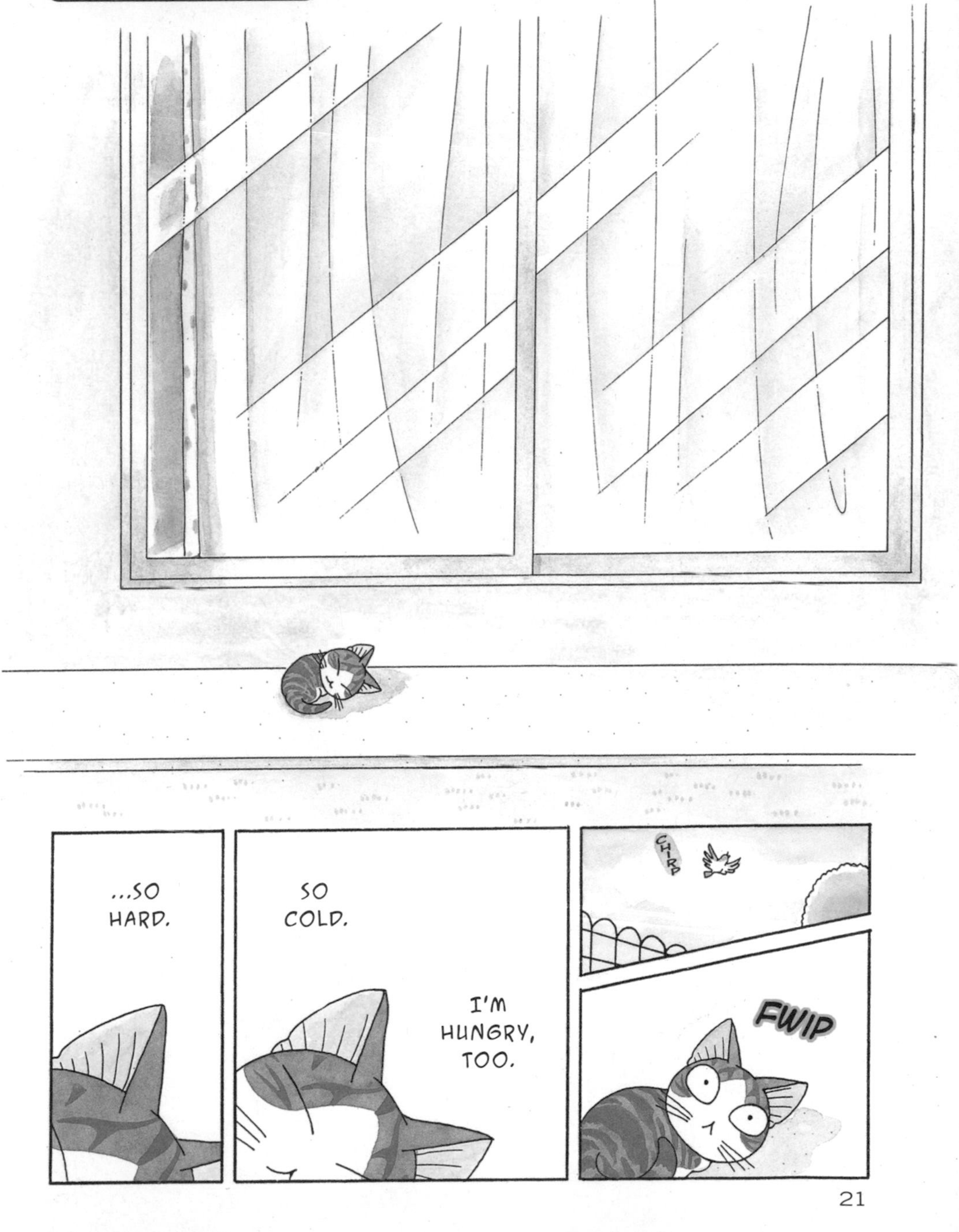

...SO HARD.
SO COLD.
I'M HUNGRY, TOO.
CHIRP
FWIP

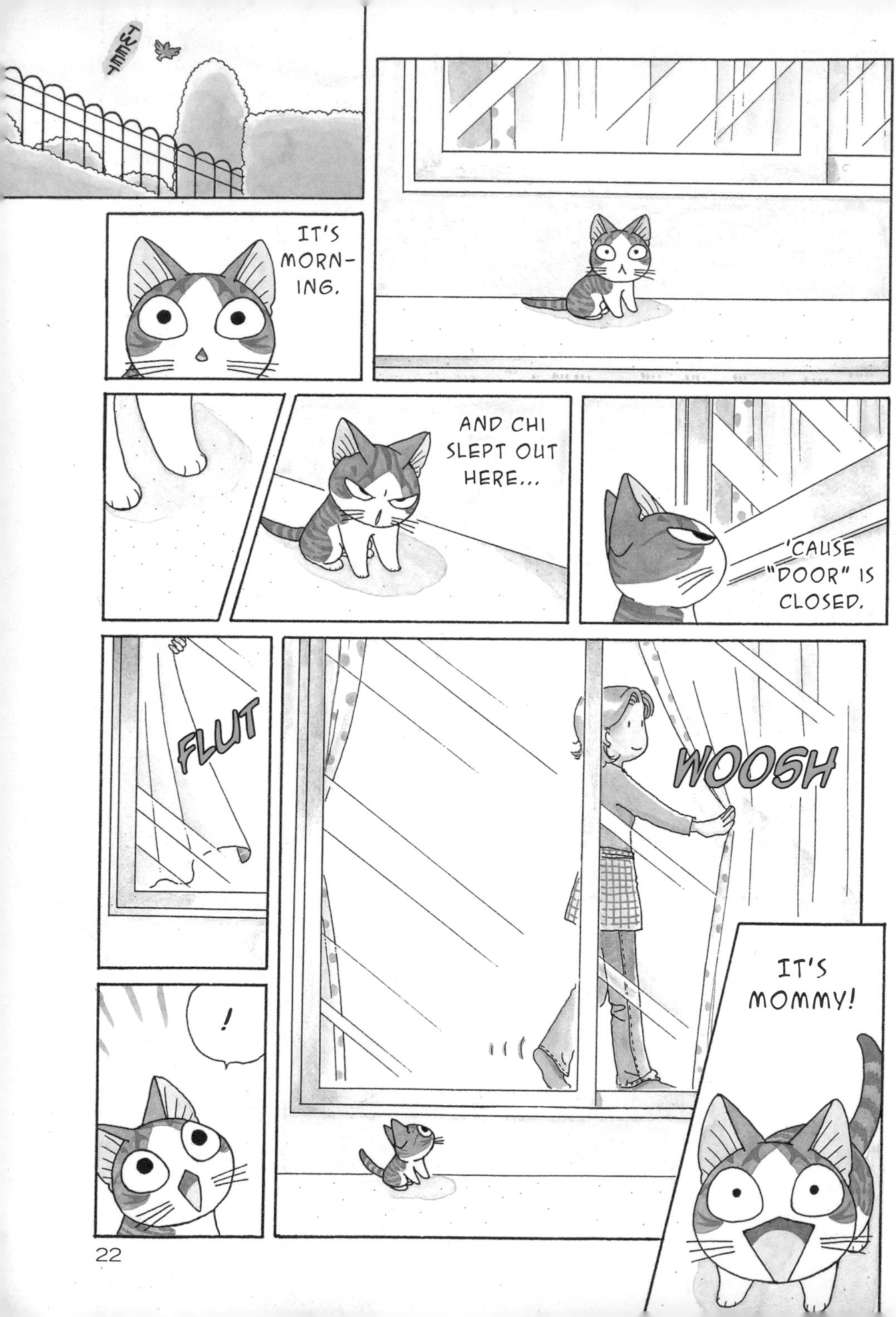
TWEET
IT'S MORNING.
AND CHI SLEPT OUT HERE...
'CAUSE "DOOR" IS CLOSED.
FLUT
WOOSH
!
IT'S MOMMY!

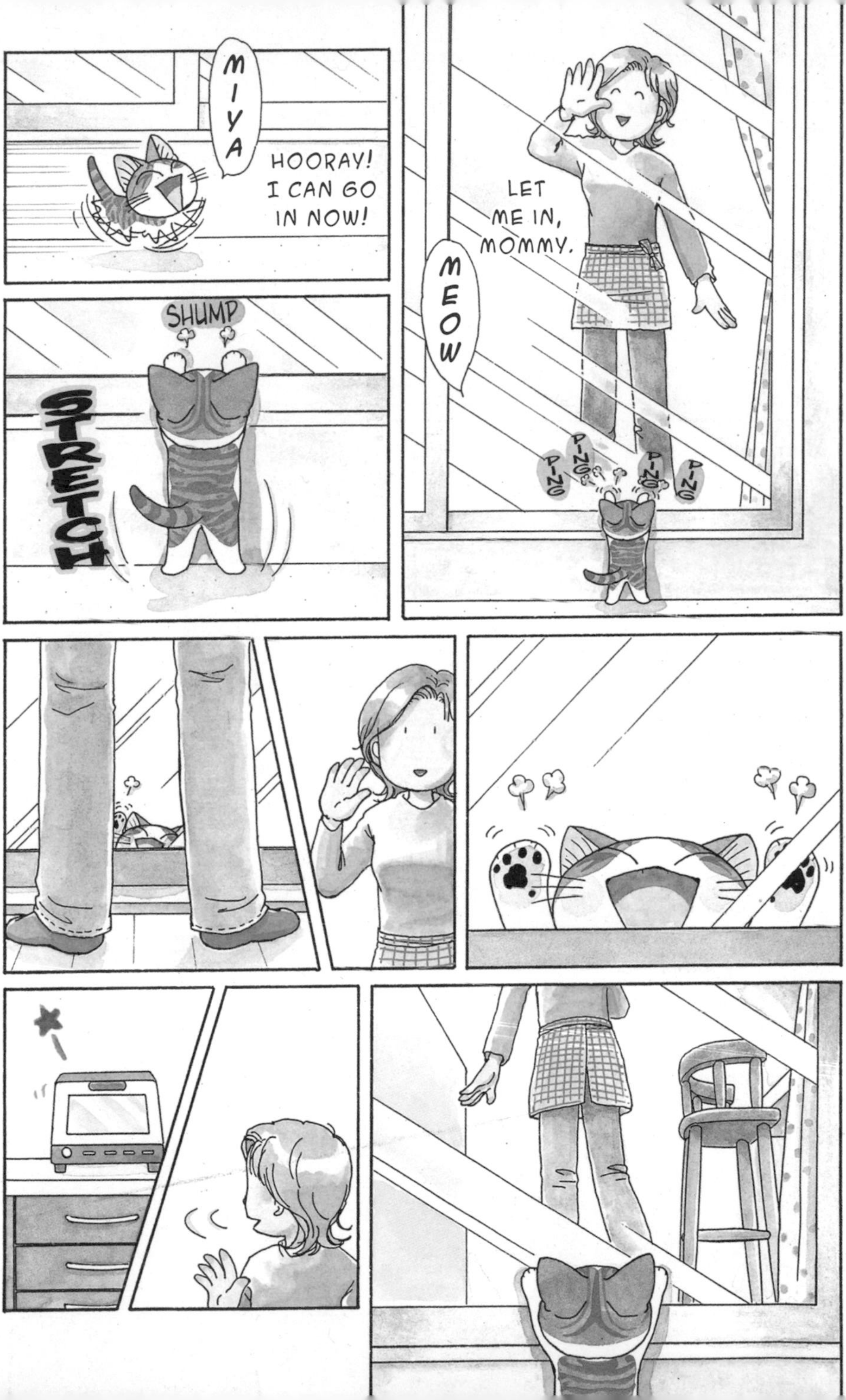
MIYA
HOORAY! I CAN GO IN NOW!
SHUMP
STRETCH
LET ME IN, MOMMY.
MEOW
PING
PING
PING
PING

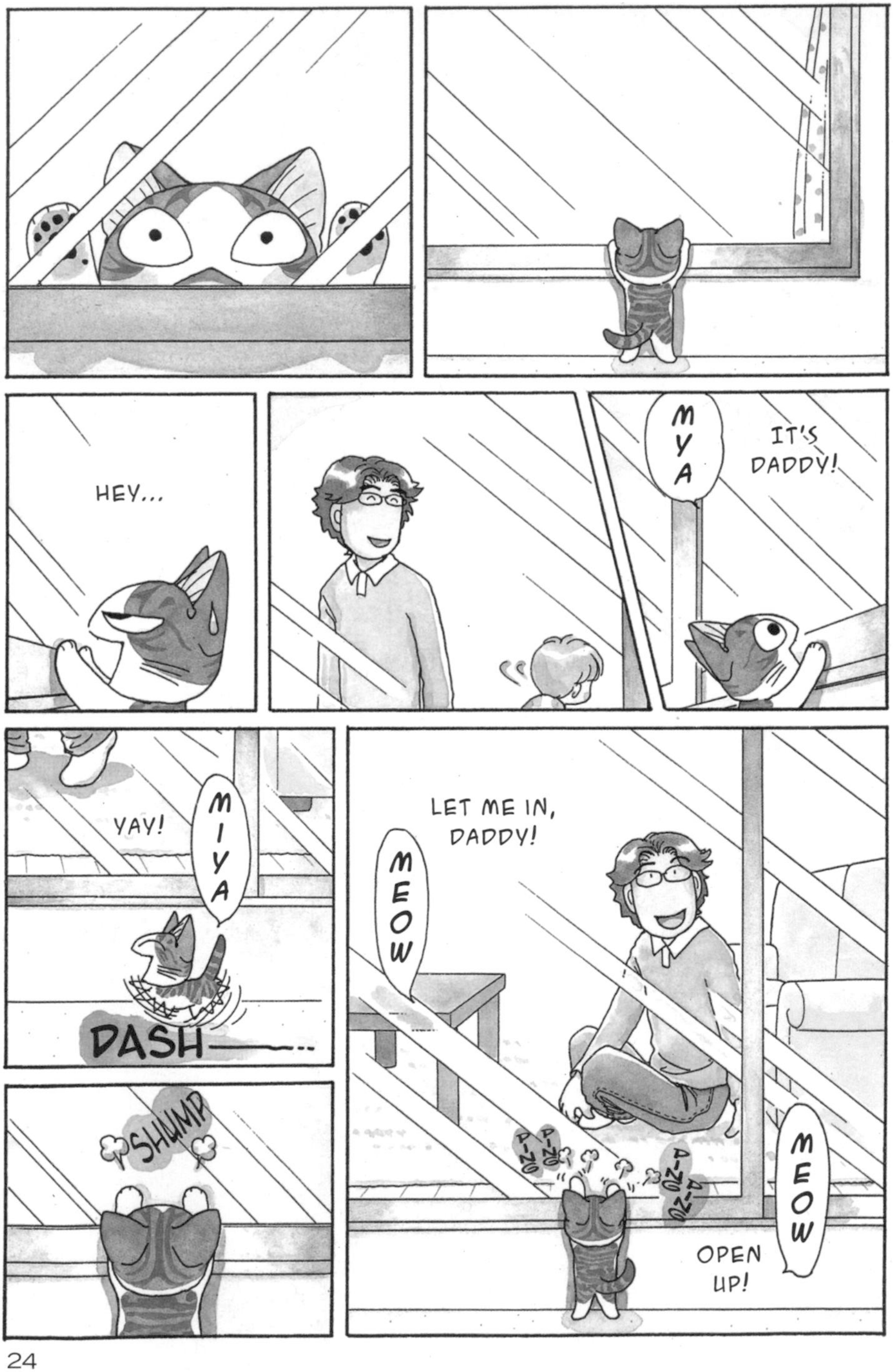
HEY...
MYA
IT'S DADDY!
YAY!
MIYA
DASH
SHUMP
LET ME IN, DADDY!
MEOW
PING PING
PING PING
MEOW
OPEN UP!

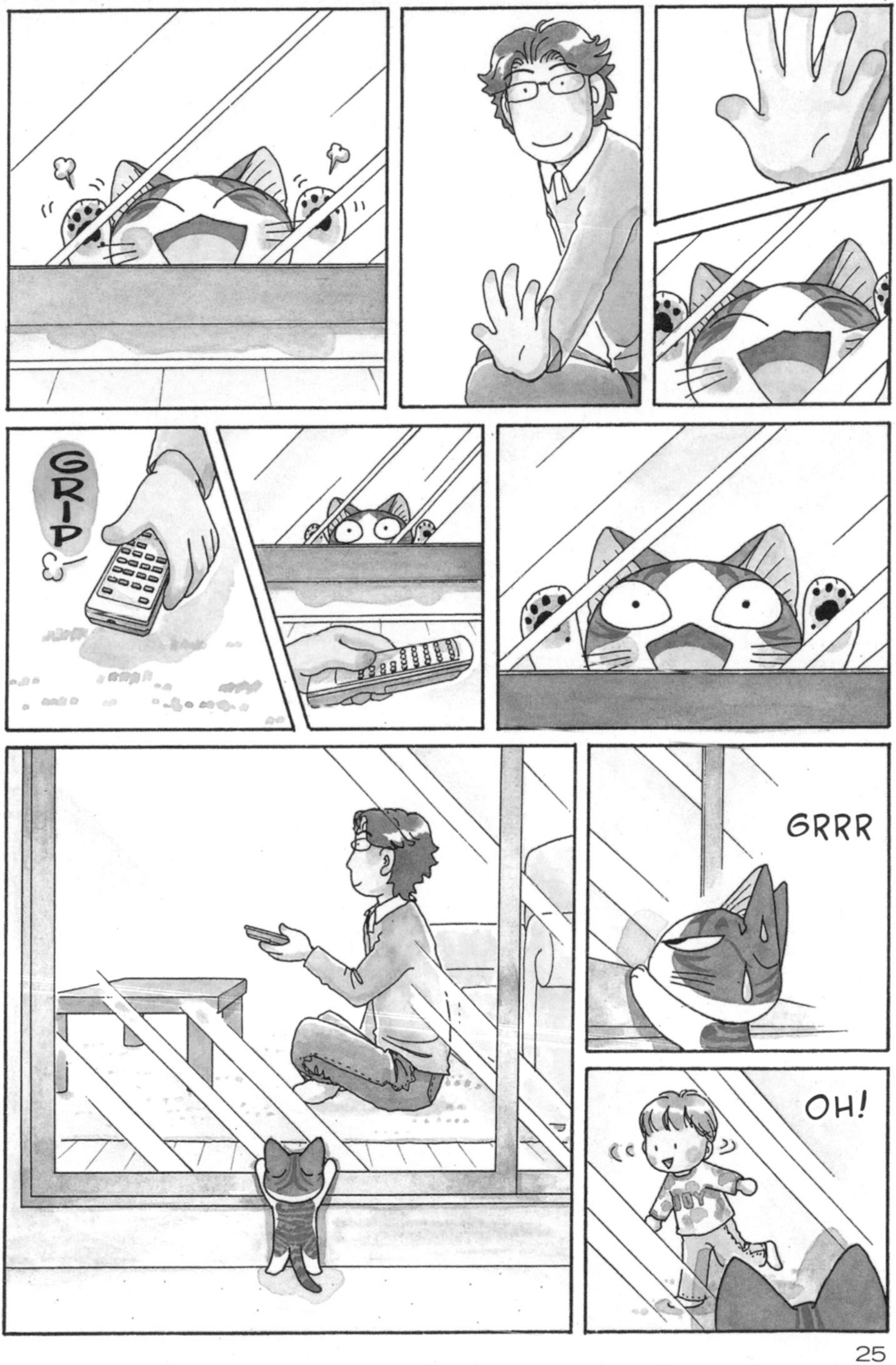
GRIP
GRRR
OH!

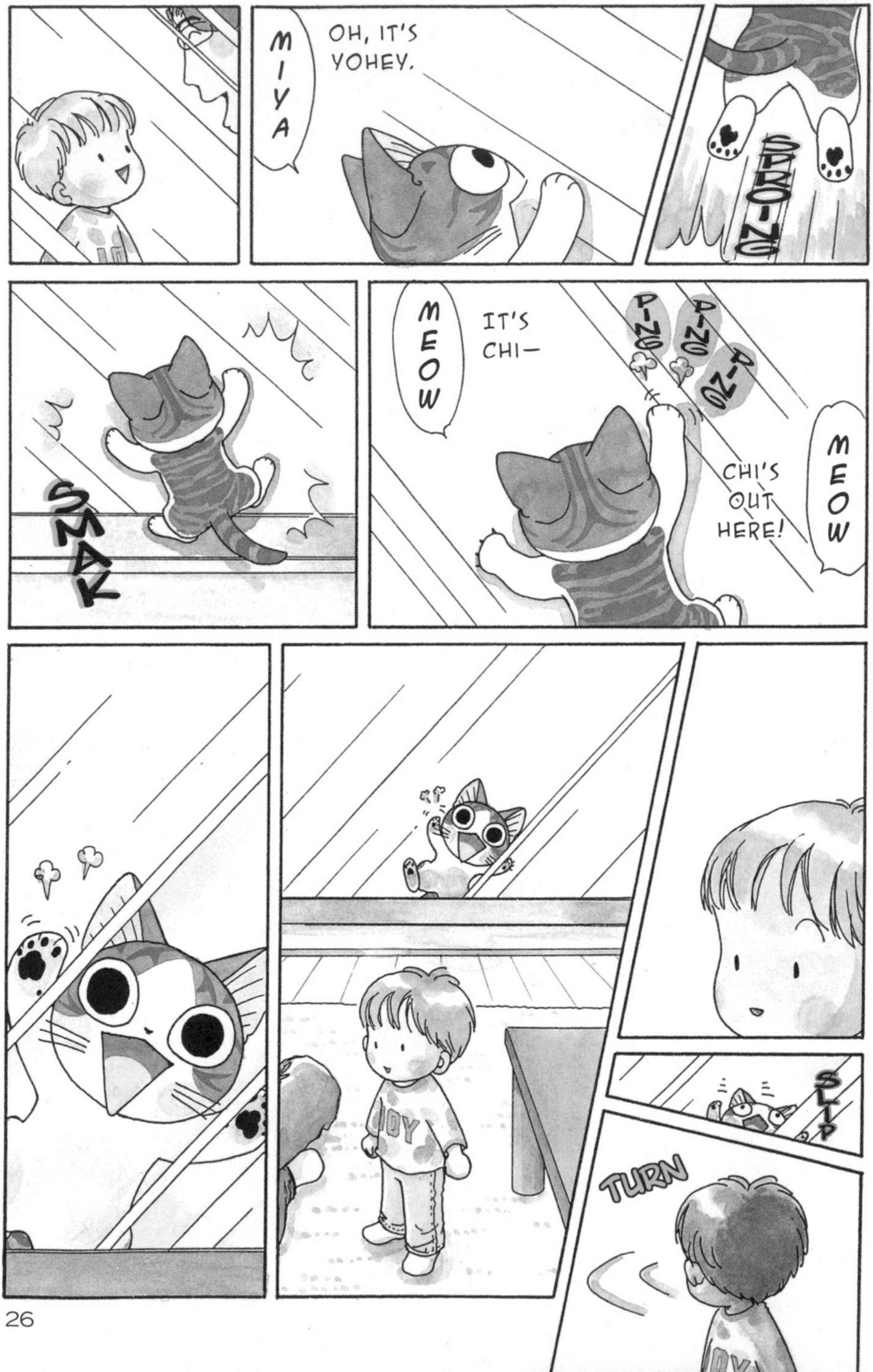
MIYA
OH, IT'S YOHEY.
SPROING
SMAK
MEOW
IT'S CHI—
PING PING PING
MEOW
CHI'S OUT HERE!
SLIP
TURN

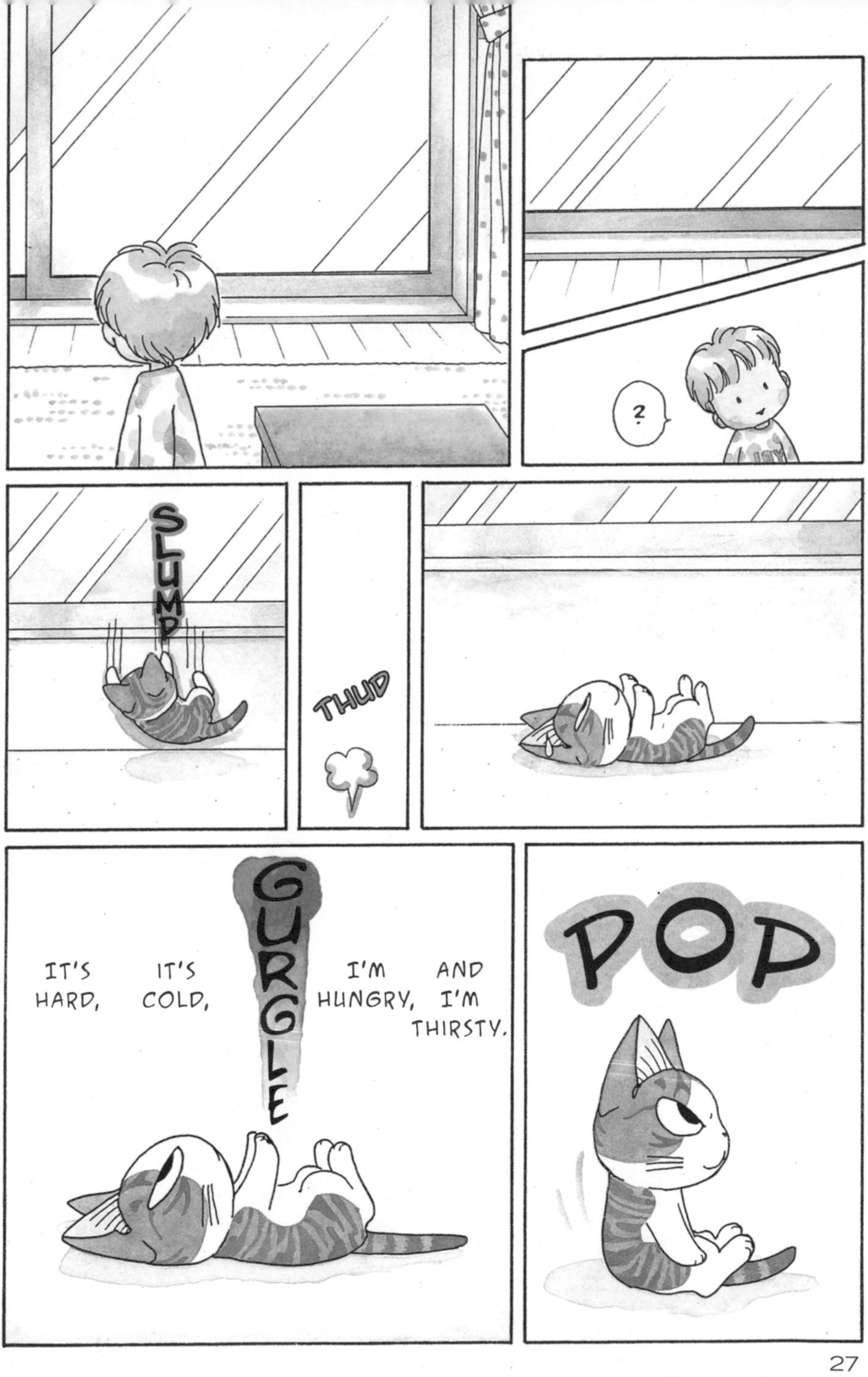
?
SLUMP
THUD
IT'S HARD,
IT'S COLD,
GURGLE
I'M HUNGRY,
AND I'M THIRSTY.
POP

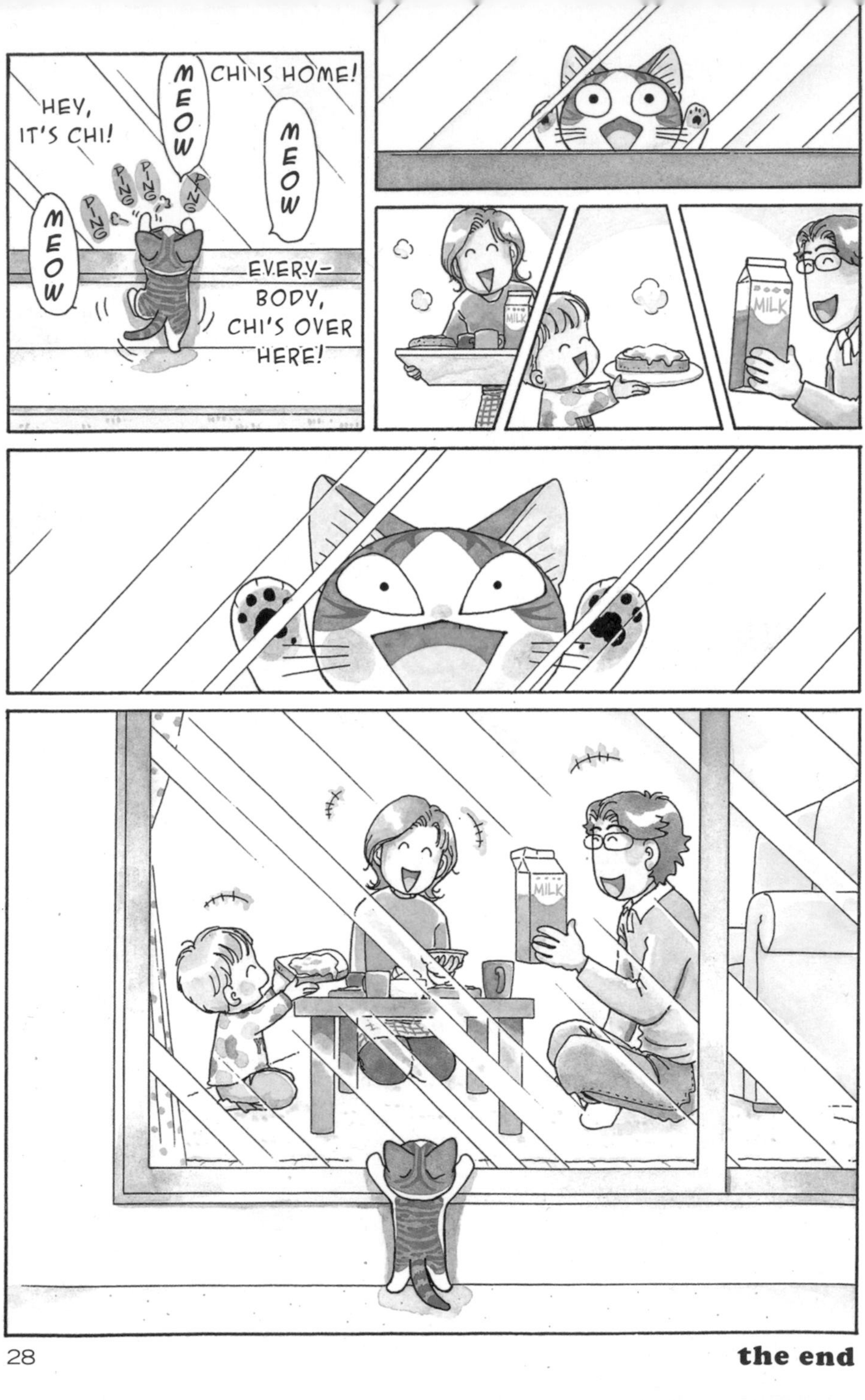
HEY, IT'S CHI!
MEOW
CHI'S HOME!
MEOW
MEOW
PING PING PING PING
EVERY-BODY, CHI'S OVER HERE!



the end

# homemade 114: a cat comes back

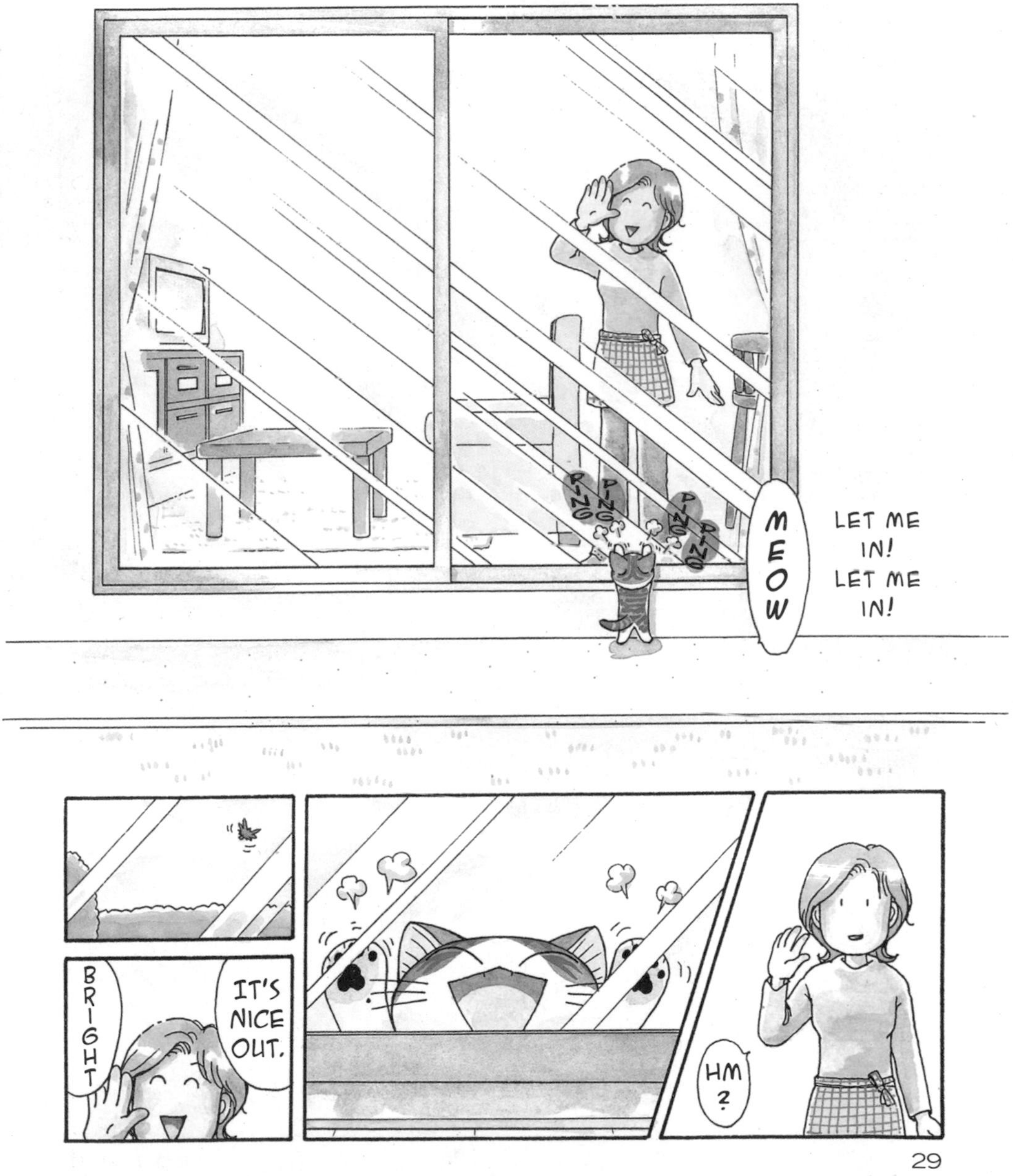
PING
PING
PING
PING
MEOW
LET ME IN! LET ME IN!
BRIGHT
IT'S NICE OUT.
HM?

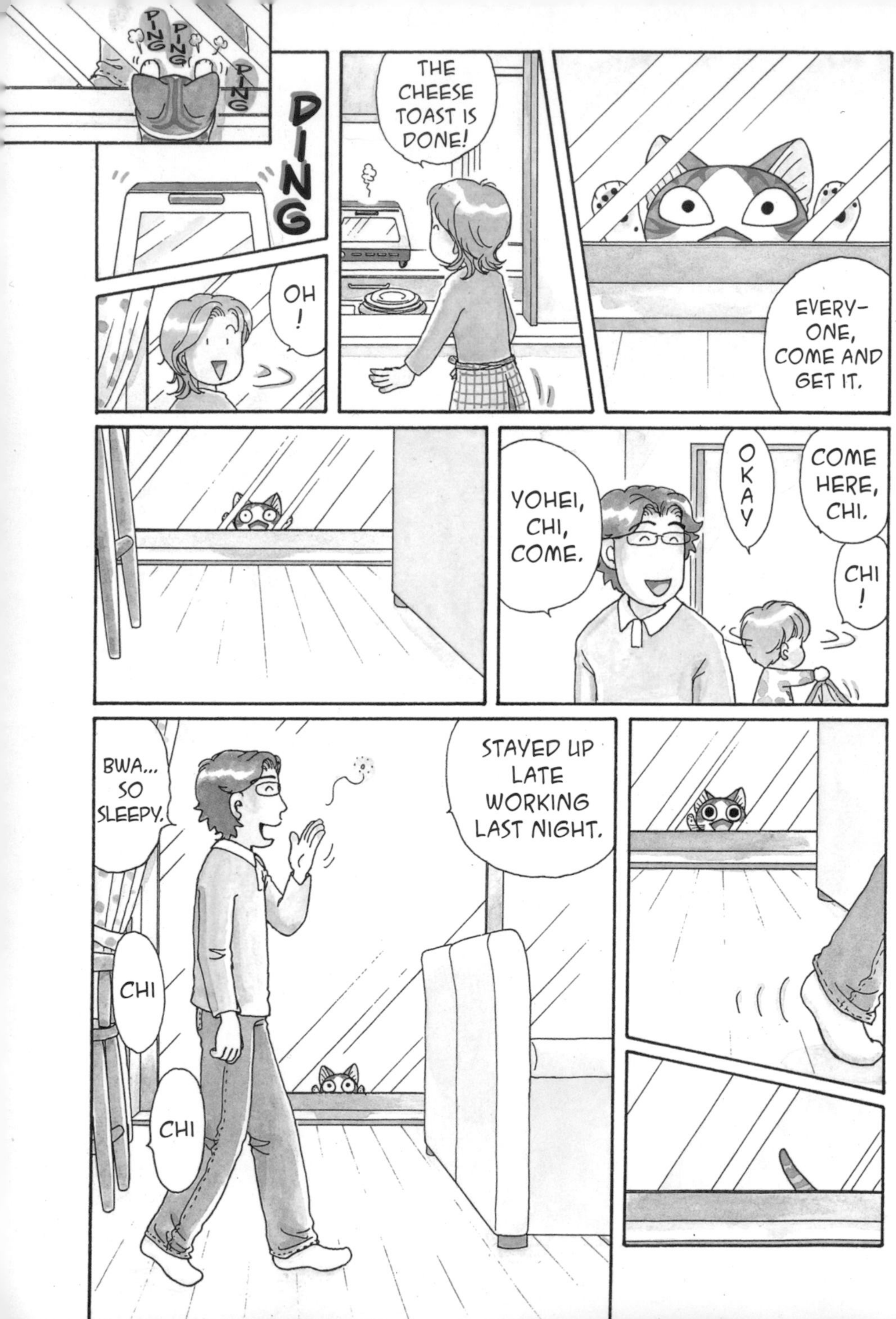
PING
PING
PING
PING
DING
OH!
THE CHEESE TOAST IS DONE!
EVERY-ONE, COME AND GET IT.
YOHEI, CHI, COME.
OKAY
COME HERE, CHI.
CHI!
BWA... SO SLEEPY.
CHI
CHI
STAYED UP LATE WORKING LAST NIGHT.

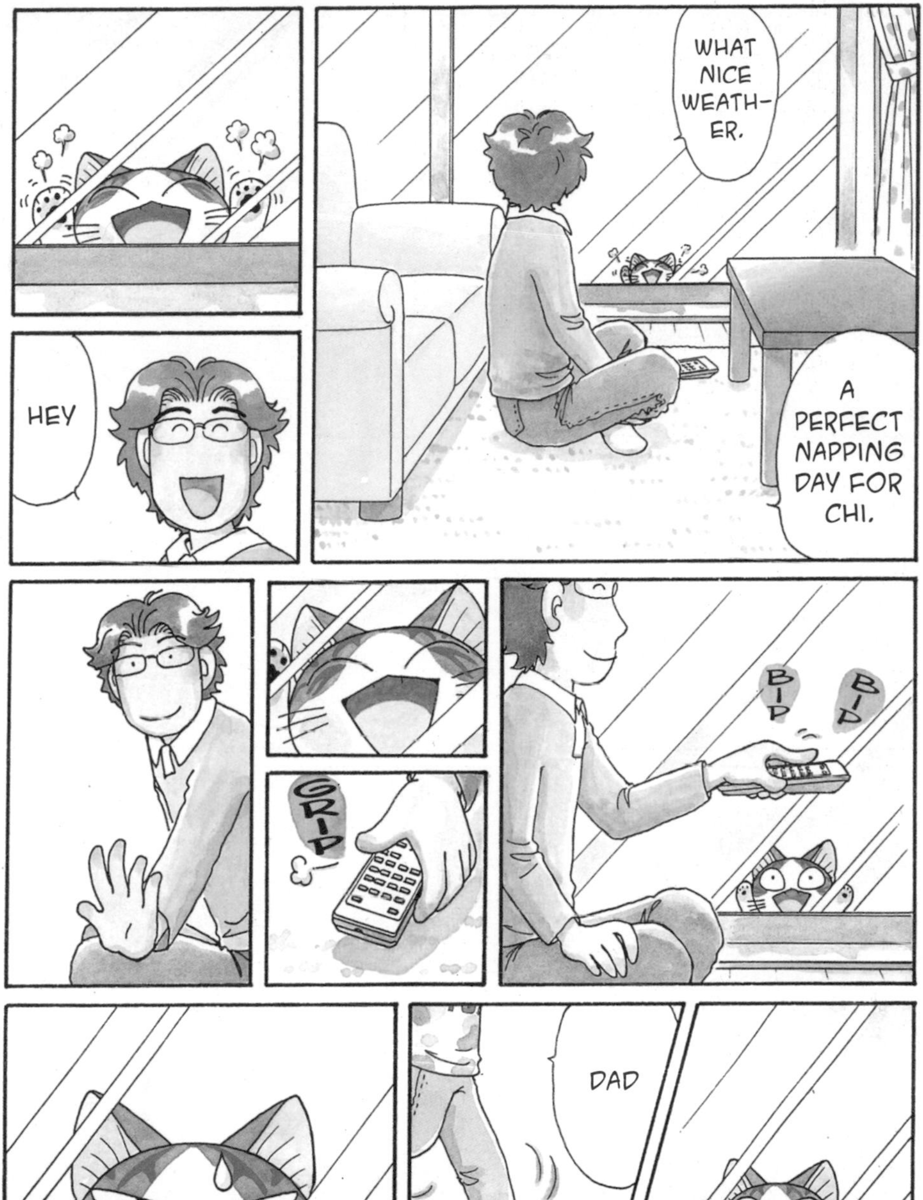
WHAT NICE WEATH- ER.
A PERFECT NAPPING DAY FOR CHI.
HEY
GRIP
BIP BIP
DAD
TMP TMP TMP

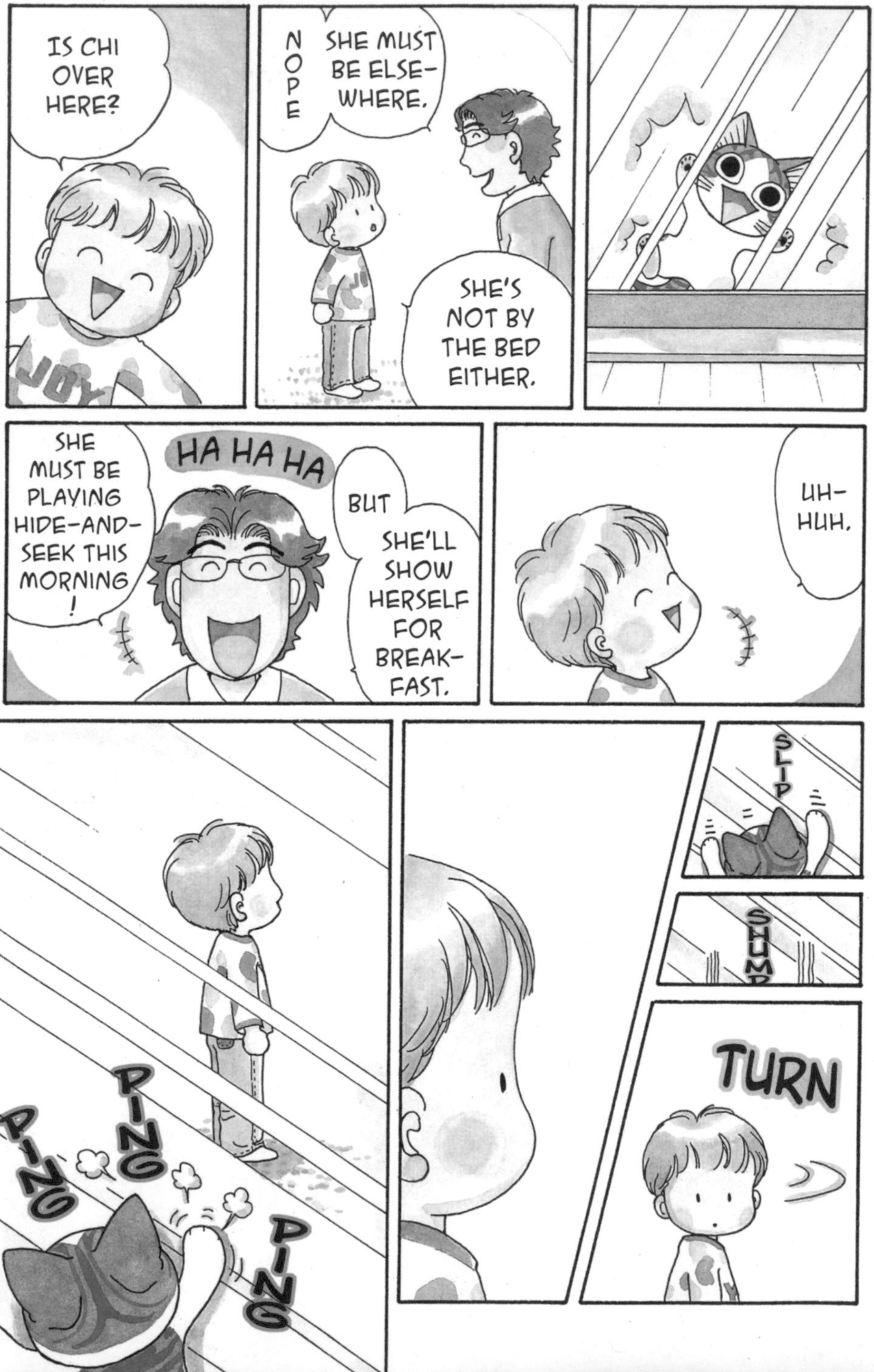
IS CHI OVER HERE?
NOPE
SHE MUST BE ELSE-WHERE.
SHE'S NOT BY THE BED EITHER.
SHE MUST BE PLAYING HIDE-AND-SEEK THIS MORNING!
HA HA HA
BUT
SHE'LL SHOW HERSELF FOR BREAK-FAST.
UH-HUH.
PING
PING
PING
SLIP
SHUMP
TURN

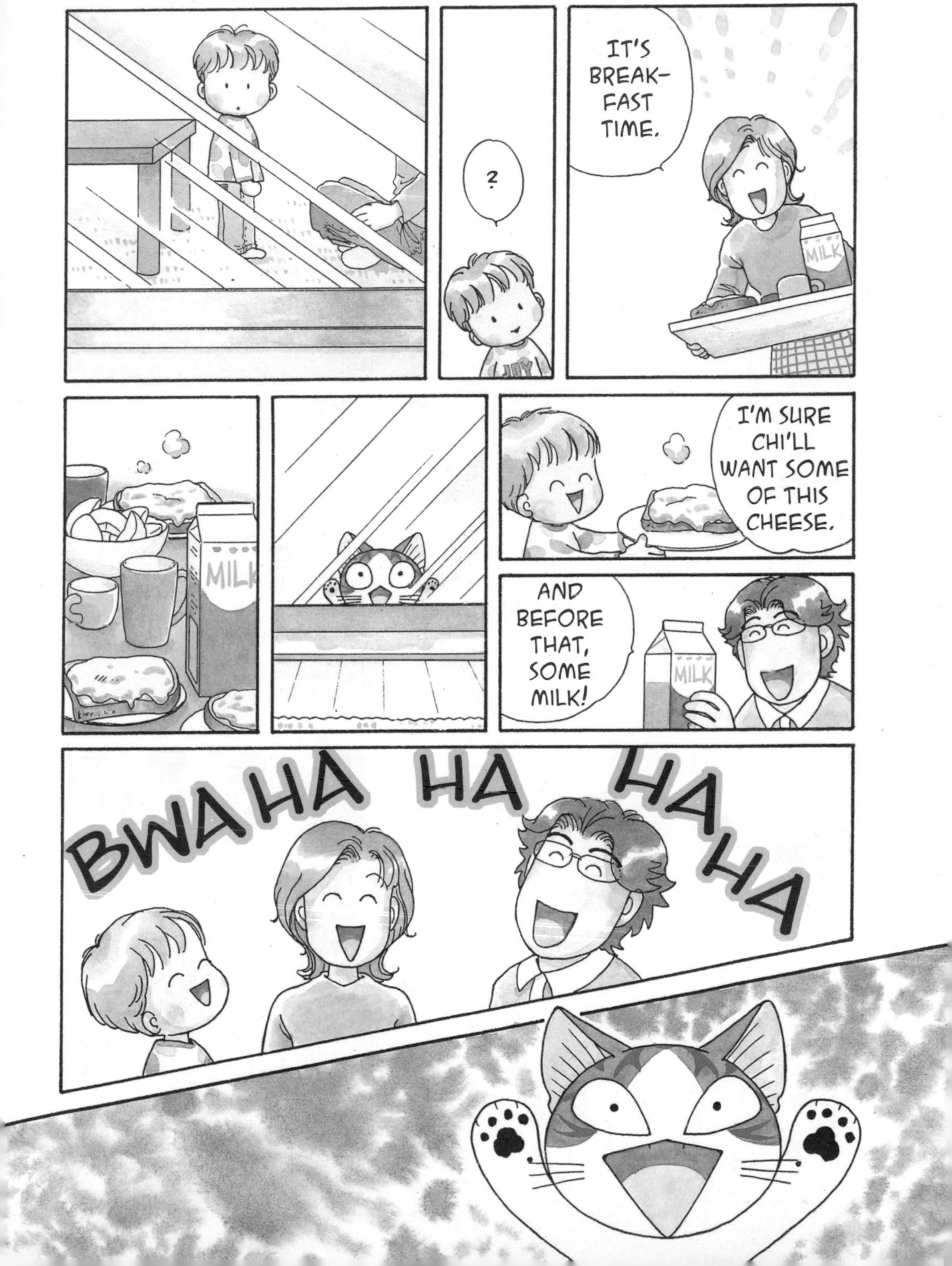
?
IT'S BREAK-FAST TIME.
I'M SURE CHI'LL WANT SOME OF THIS CHEESE.
AND BEFORE THAT, SOME MILK!
BWA HA HA HA HA HA

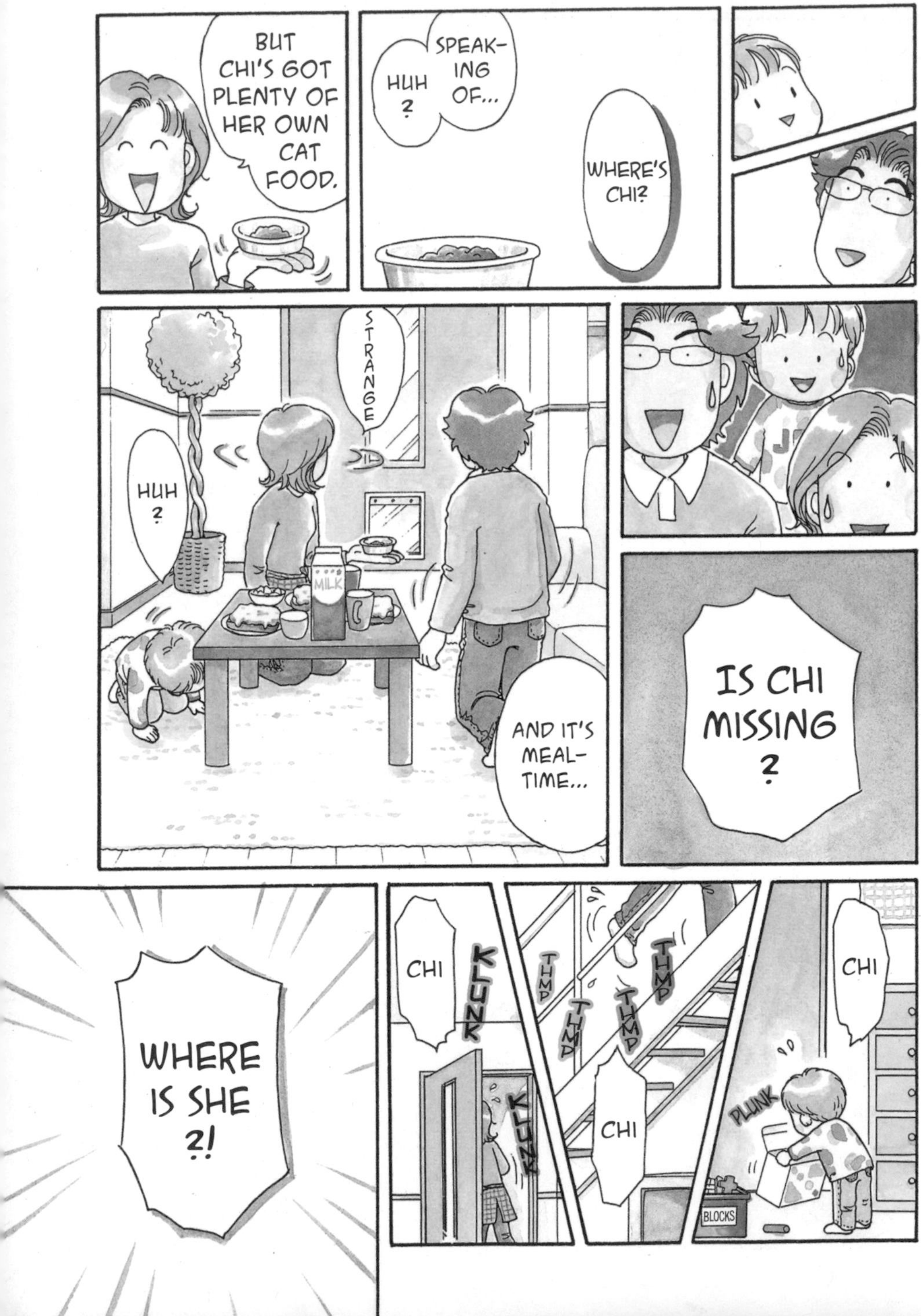
BUT CHI'S GOT PLENTY OF HER OWN CAT FOOD.
HUH?
SPEAKING OF...
WHERE'S CHI?
STRANGE
HUH?
AND IT'S MEALTIME...
IS CHI MISSING?
WHERE IS SHE?!
CHI
KLUNK
KLUNK
THMP
THMP
THMP
THMP
CHI
CHI
PLUNK
BLOCKS

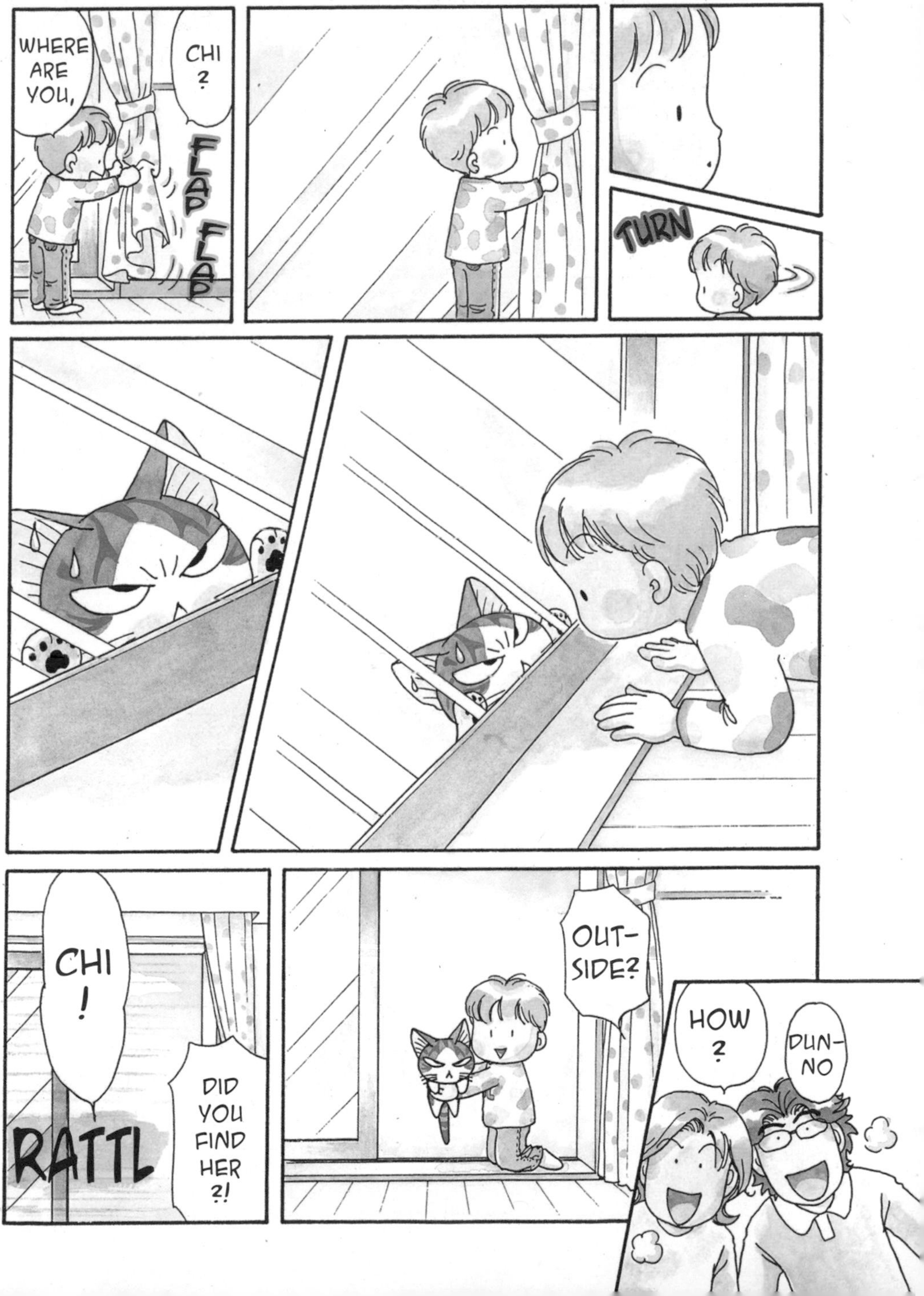
WHERE ARE YOU,
CHI?
FLAP FLAP
TURN
CHI!
RATTL
DID YOU FIND HER?!
OUT-SIDE?
HOW?
DUN-NO

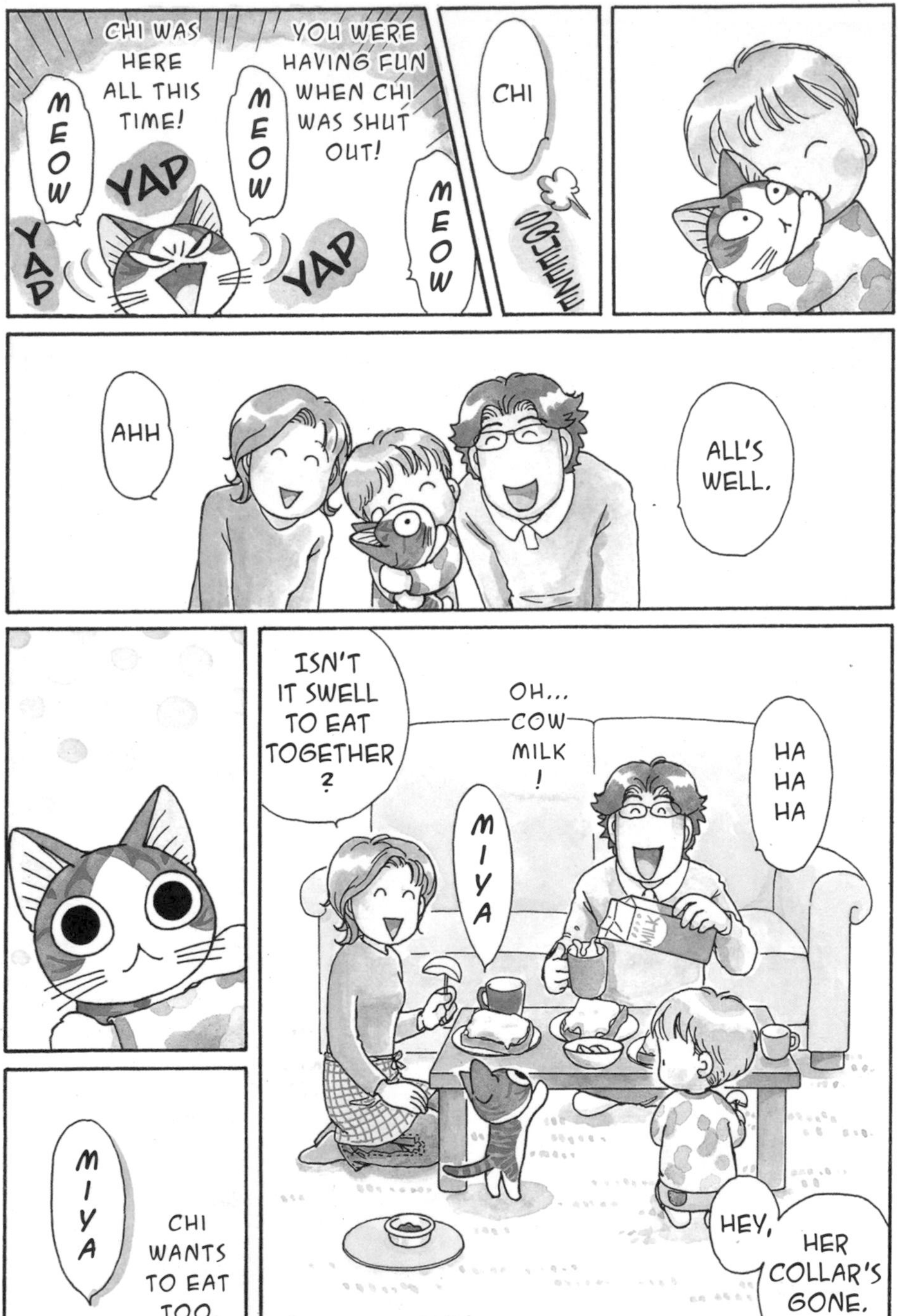
MEOW
CHI WAS HERE ALL THIS TIME!
YAP
YAP
MEOW
YOU WERE HAVING FUN WHEN CHI WAS SHUT OUT!
YAP
CHI
MEOW
AHH
ALL'S WELL.
MIYA
ISN'T IT SWELL TO EAT TOGETHER?
MIYA
OH... COW MILK!
HA HA HA
MILK
CHI WANTS TO EAT TOO.
HEY, HER COLLAR'S GONE.



**the end**

# homemade 115: a cat gives up

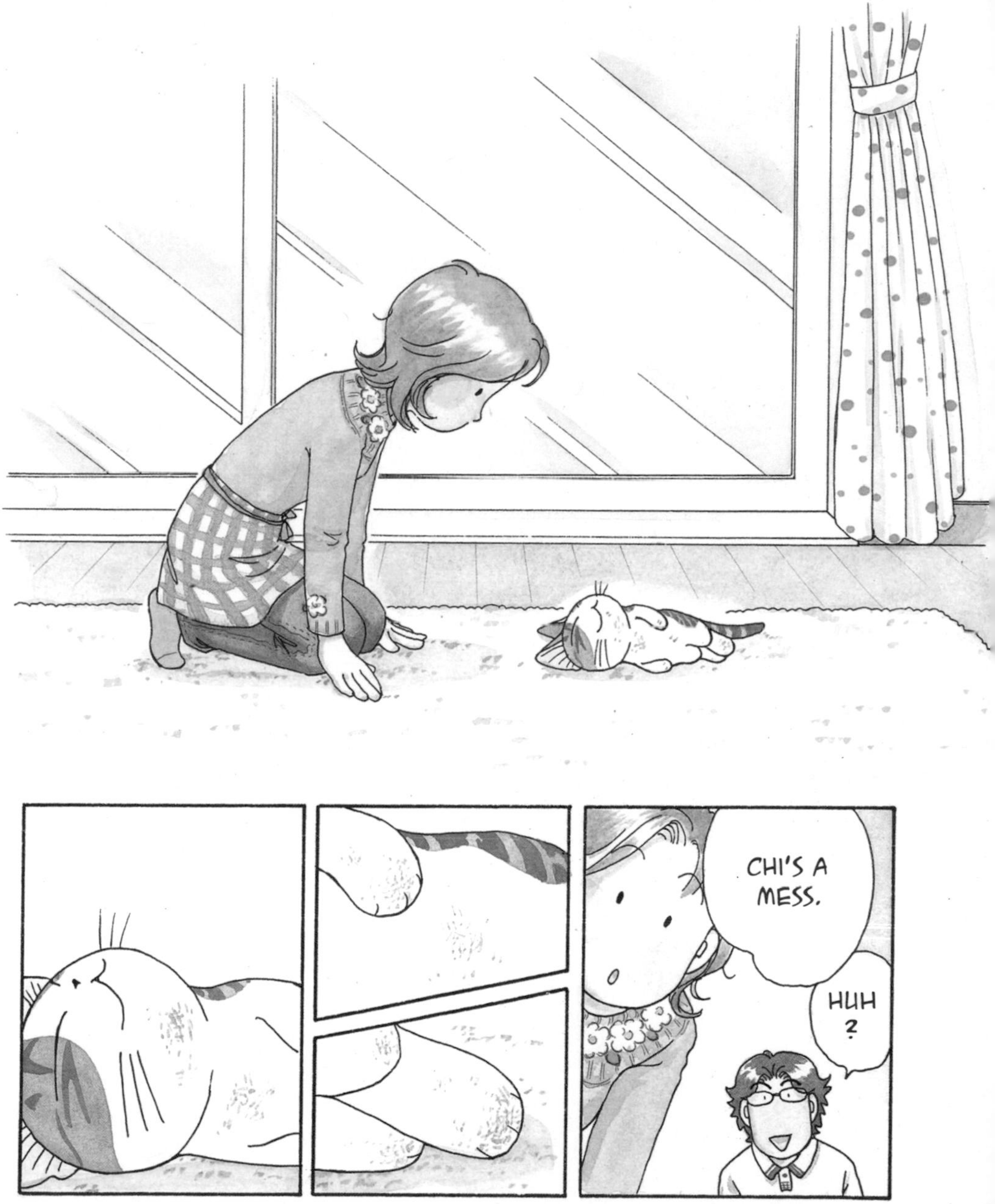
CHI'S A MESS.
HUH ?

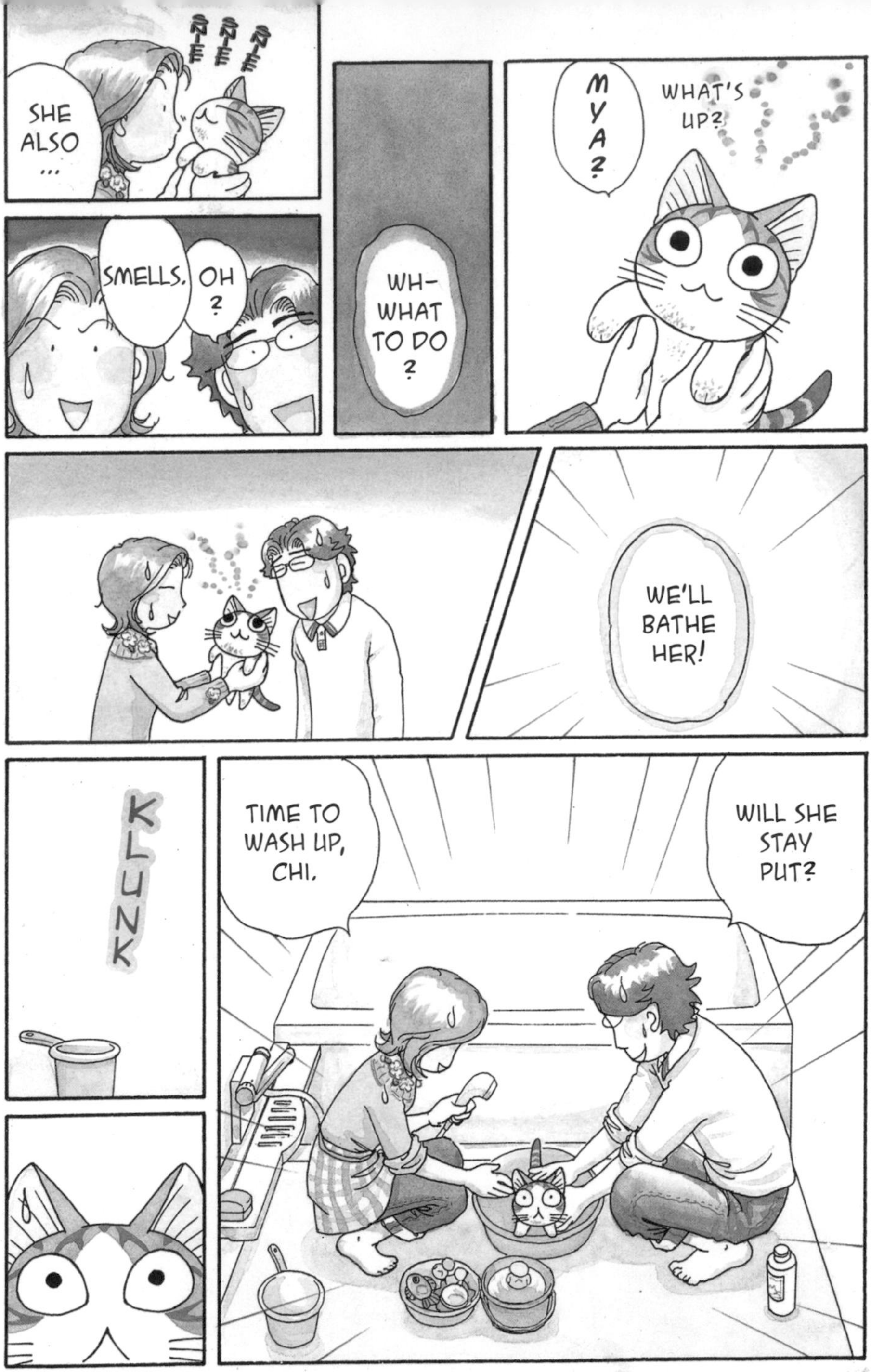
SNIFF SNIFF SNIFF
SHE ALSO ...
SMELLS.
OH ?
WH- WHAT TO DO ?
MYA ?
WHAT'S UP?
WE'LL BATHE HER!
KLUNK
TIME TO WASH UP, CHI.
WILL SHE STAY PUT?

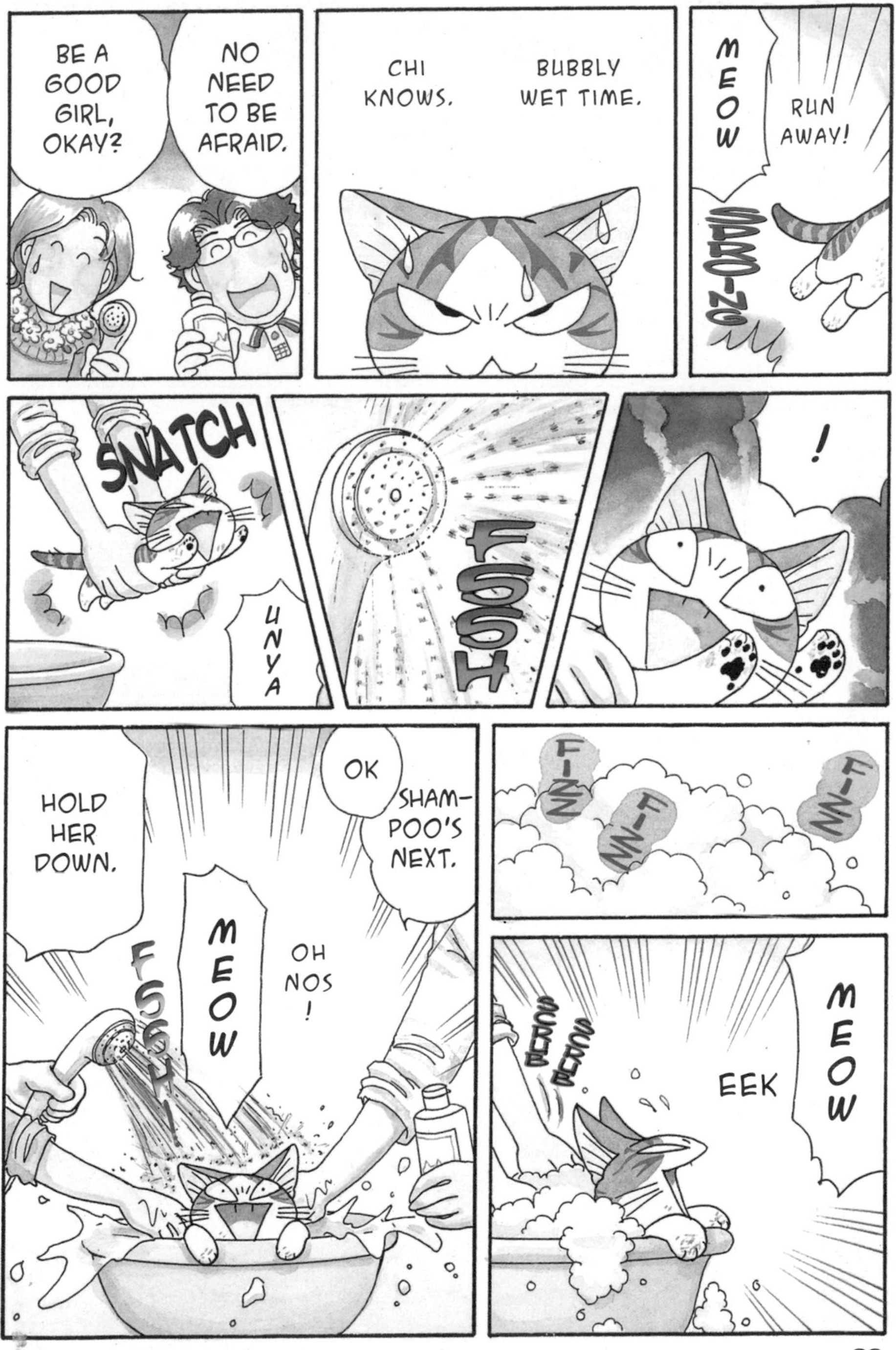
BE A GOOD GIRL, OKAY?
NO NEED TO BE AFRAID.
CHI KNOWS.
BUBBLY WET TIME.
MEOW
RUN AWAY!
SPROING
SNATCH
UNYA
FSSH
!
HOLD HER DOWN.
OK
SHAM-POO'S NEXT.
FSSH!
MEOW
OH NOS!
FIZZ
FIZZ
FIZZ
SCRUB
SCRUB
EEK
MEOW

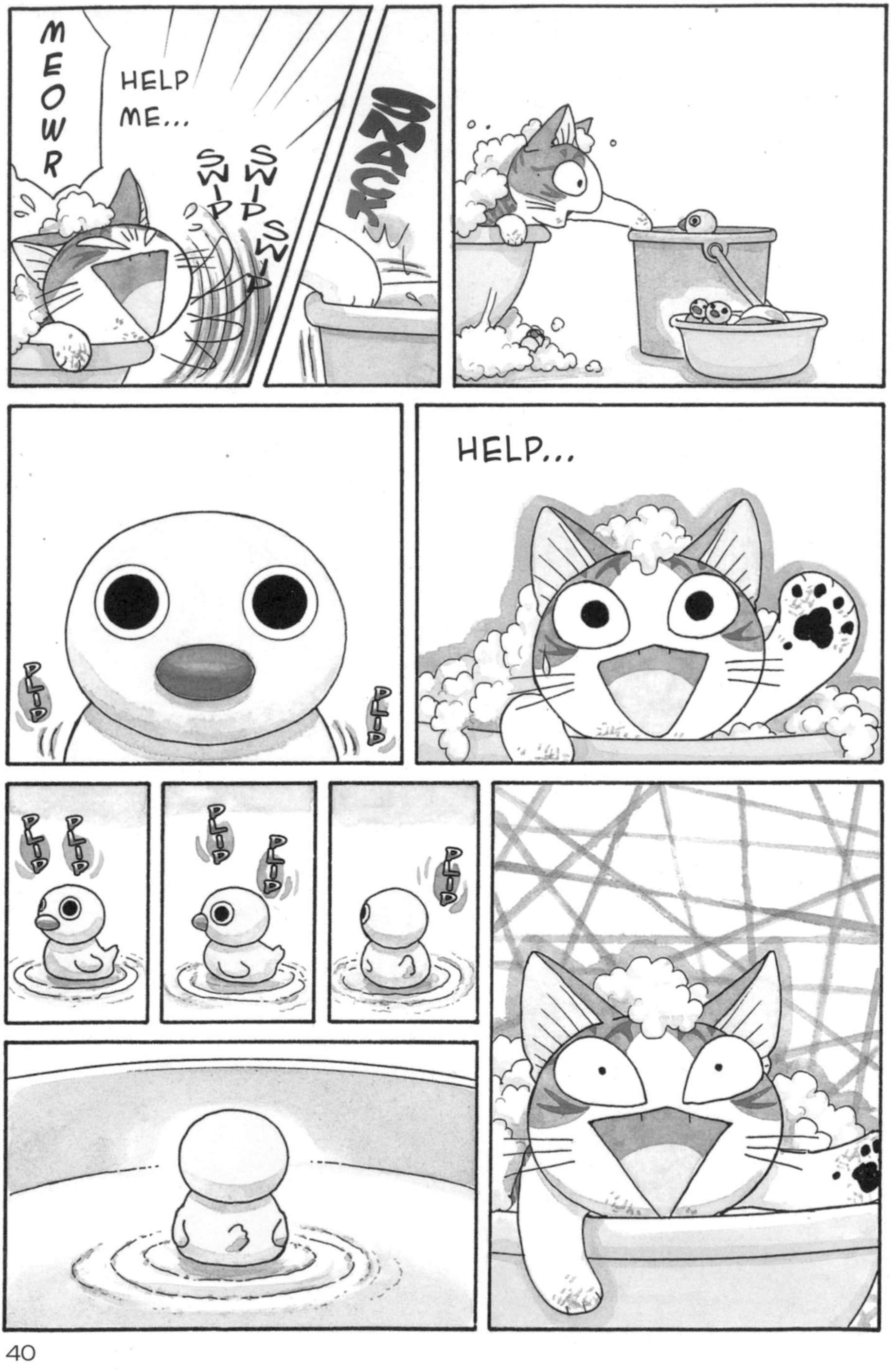
MEOWR
HELP ME...
SWIP SWIP SWIP
SMACK
HELP...
PLIP PLIP
PLIP PLIP
PLIP PLIP
PLIP

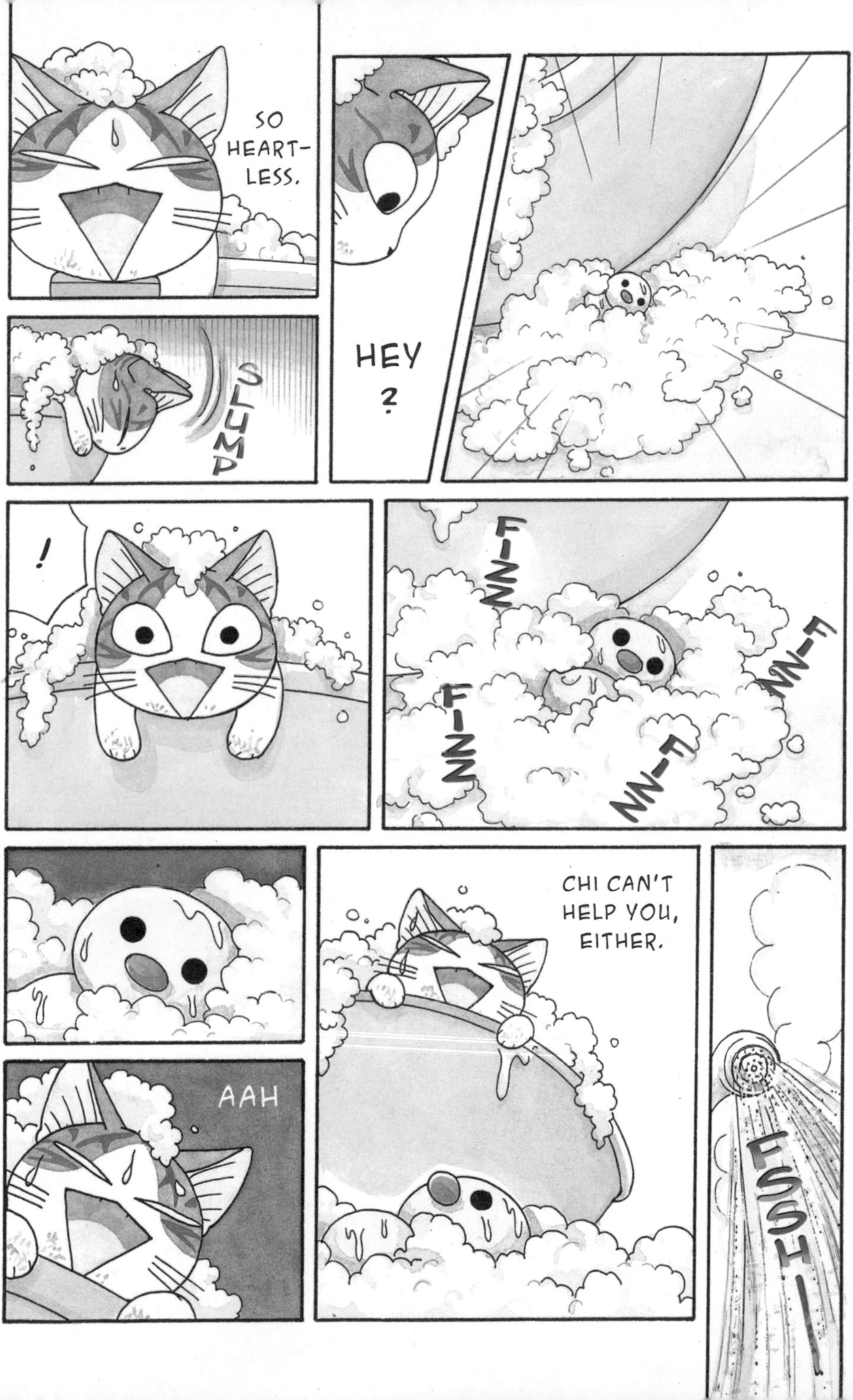
SO HEART-LESS.
SLUMP
HEY?
!
FIZZ FIZZ
NN-FI NN-FI
AAH
CHI CAN'T HELP YOU, EITHER.
FSSH

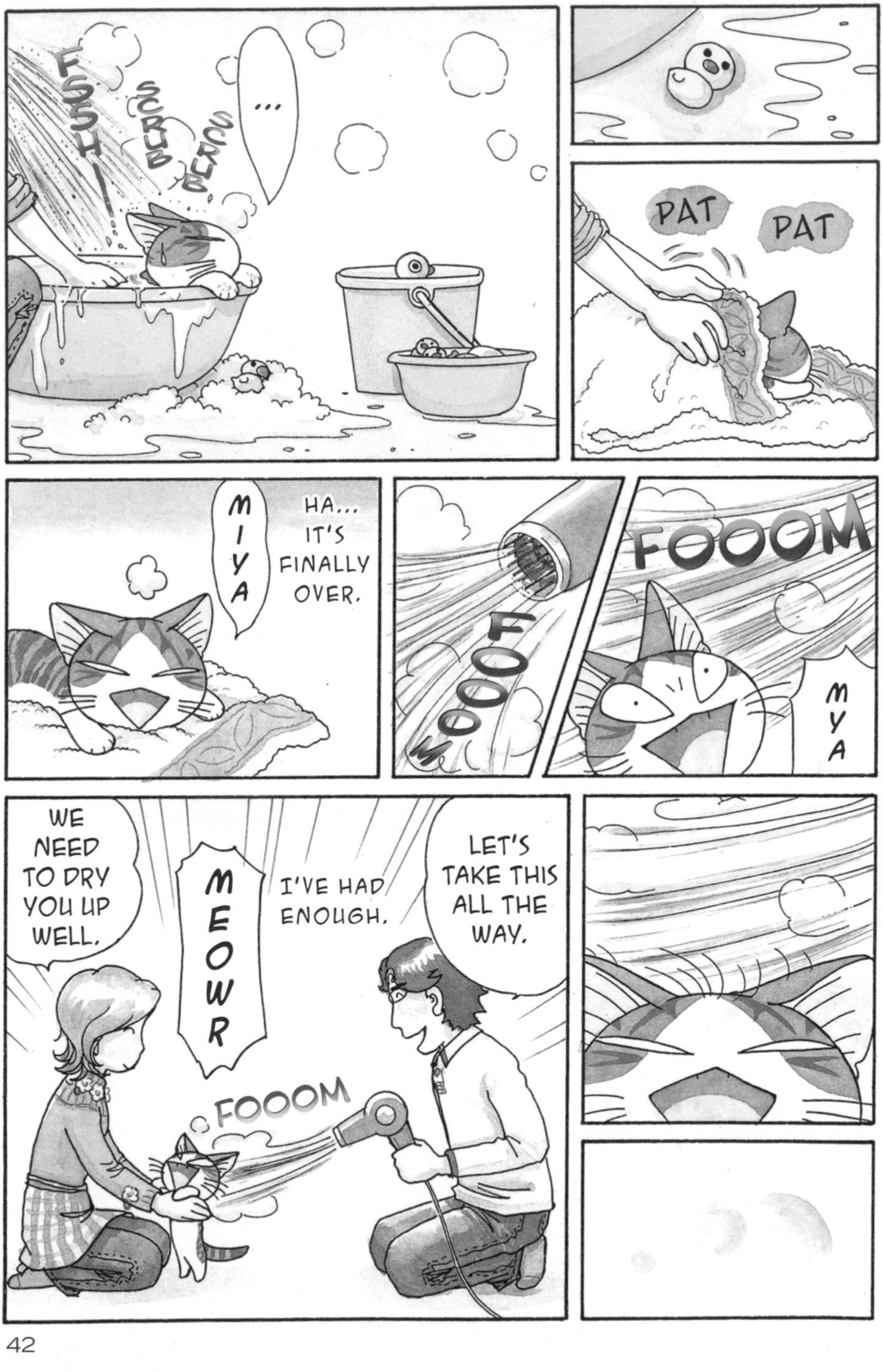
FSSSH!
SCRUB
SCRUB
...
PAT
PAT
MIYA
HA... IT'S FINALLY OVER.
FOOOM
FOOOM
MYA
WE NEED TO DRY YOU UP WELL.
MEOWR
I'VE HAD ENOUGH.
LET'S TAKE THIS ALL THE WAY.
FOOOM

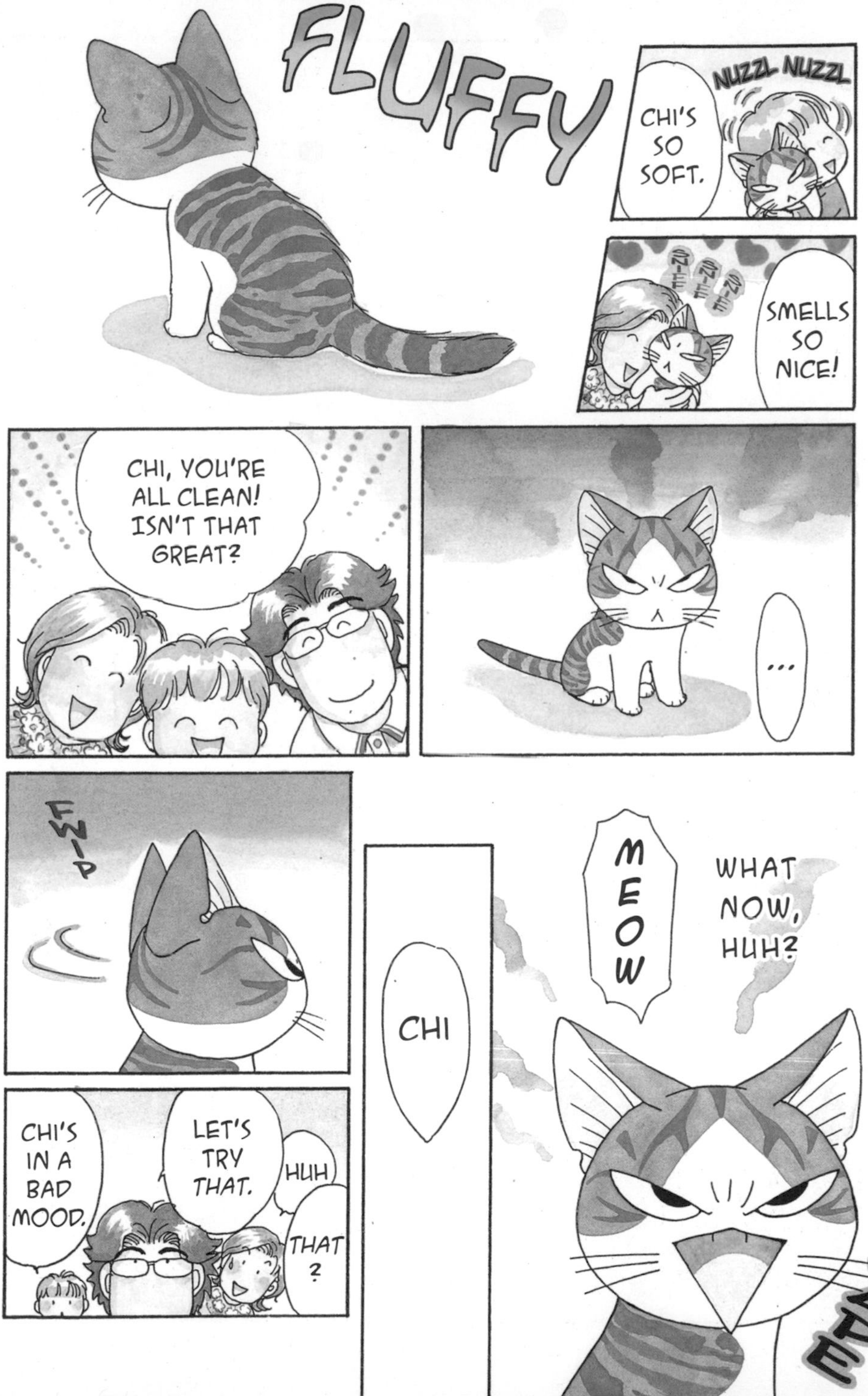
FLUFFY
CHI'S SO SOFT.
NUZZL NUZZL
SNIFF SNIFF SNIFF
SMELLS SO NICE!
CHI, YOU'RE ALL CLEAN! ISN'T THAT GREAT?
...
FWIP
CHI'S IN A BAD MOOD.
LET'S TRY THAT.
HUH
THAT?
CHI
MEOW
WHAT NOW, HUH?
GAPE

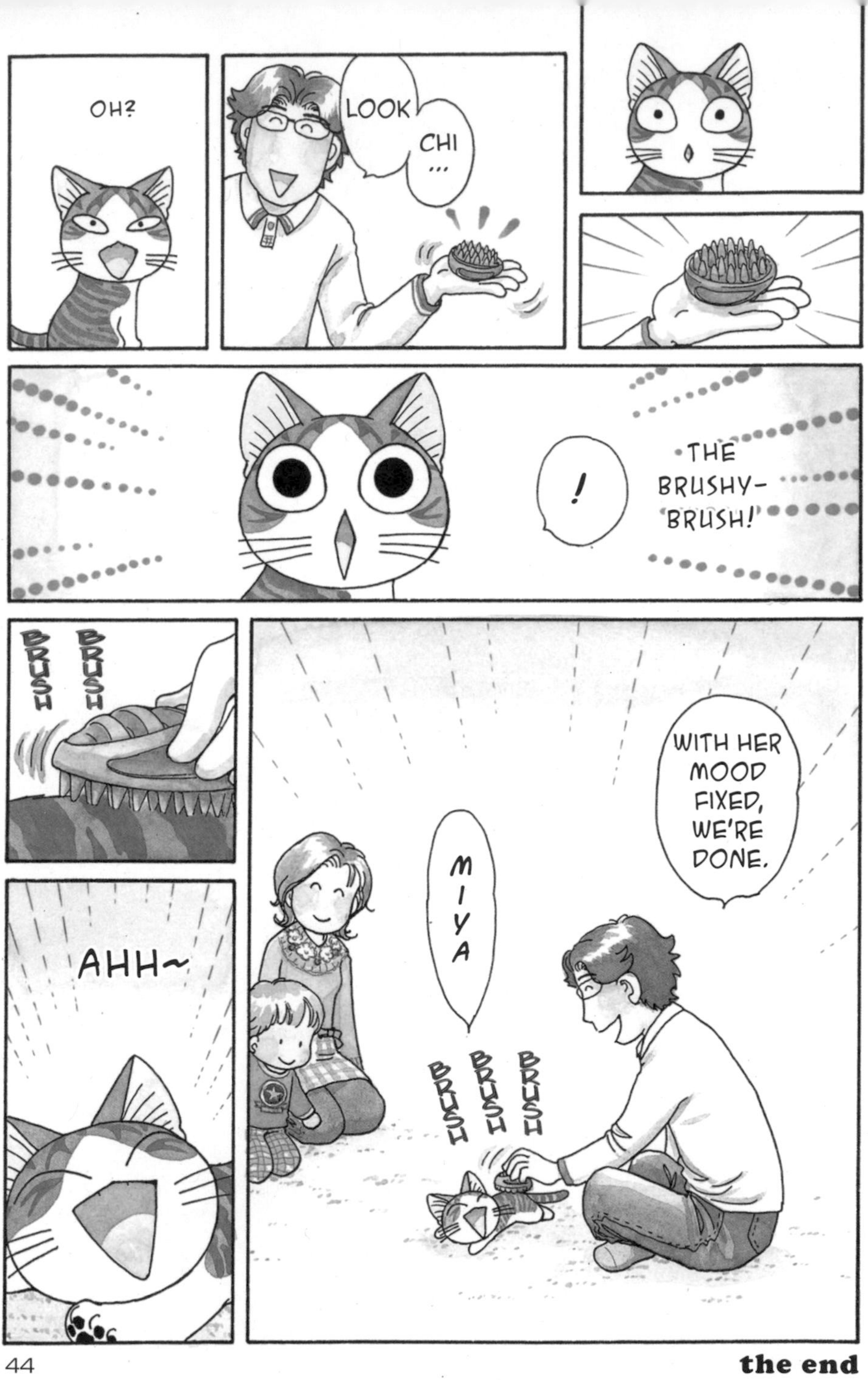
OH?
LOOK
CHI
...
THE BRUSHY-BRUSH!
!
BRUSH BRUSH
WITH HER MOOD FIXED, WE'RE DONE.
MIYA
BRUSH BRUSH BRUSH
AHH~

the end

## homemade 116: a cat observes

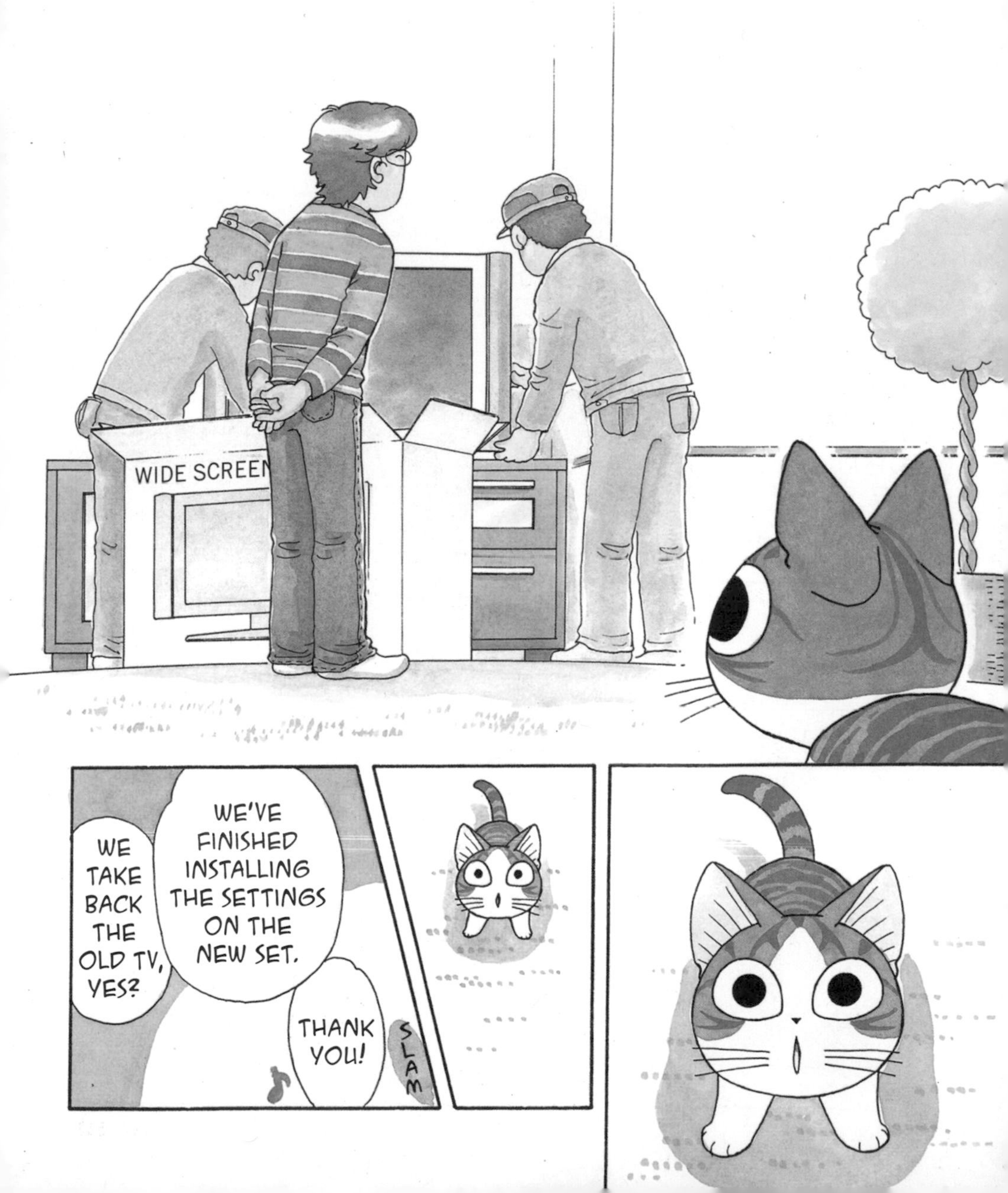
WIDE SCREEN
WE TAKE BACK THE OLD TV, YES?
WE'VE FINISHED INSTALLING THE SETTINGS ON THE NEW SET.
THANK YOU!
SLAM

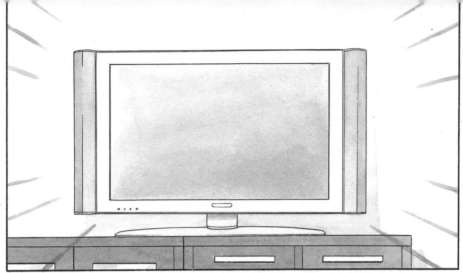

IT'S SO THIN! AND WHAT A BIG SCREEN.

IT'S SO COOL!

YUP

YUP

THERE ARE SO MANY BUTTONS, HDTV, SATELLITE...

IT'S DIGITAL SO THERE'S EVEN A PROGRAMMING GUIDE.

STARE

WHAT'S THAT?

MIYA

POWER ON!

BIP

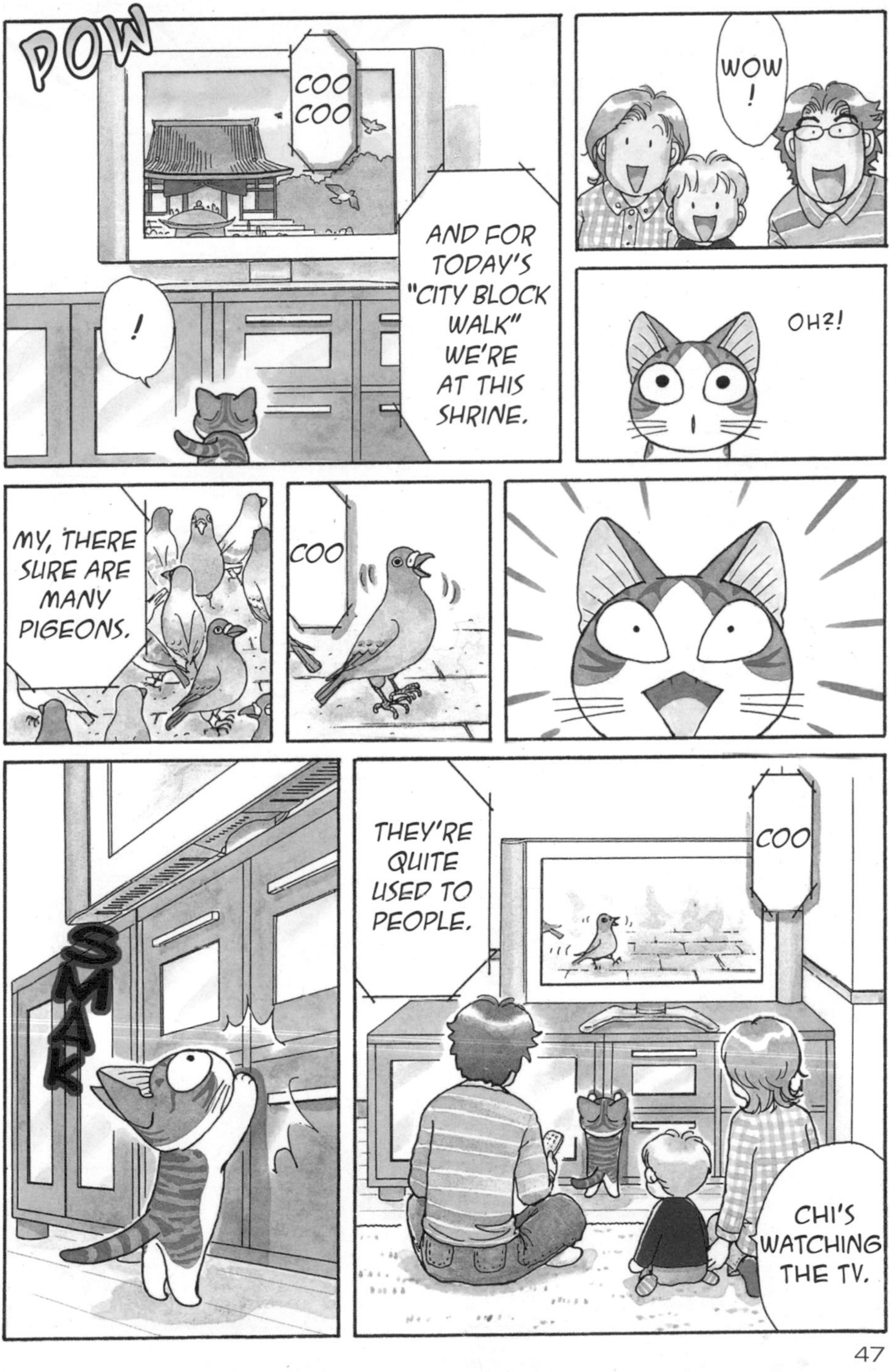
POW
COO COO
AND FOR TODAY'S "CITY BLOCK WALK" WE'RE AT THIS SHRINE.
!
WOW!
OH?!
MY, THERE SURE ARE MANY PIGEONS.
COO
SMAK
THEY'RE QUITE USED TO PEOPLE.
COO
CHI'S WATCHING THE TV.

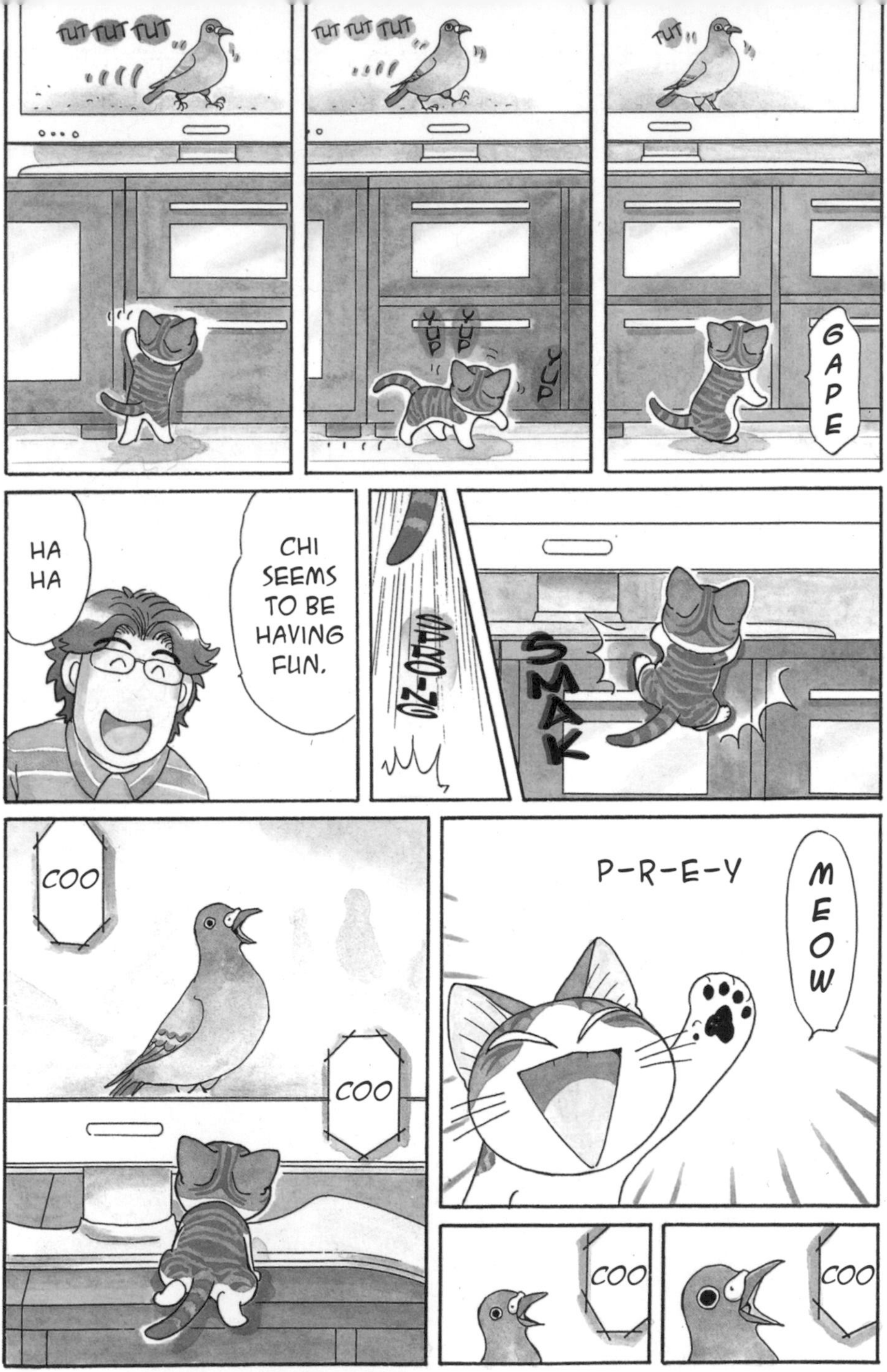
TUT TUT TUT
TUT TUT TUT
YUP
YUP
YUP
TUT
GAPE
HA HA
CHI SEEMS TO BE HAVING FUN.
SPRO-NG
SMAK
COO
COO
P-R-E-Y
MEOW
COO
COO

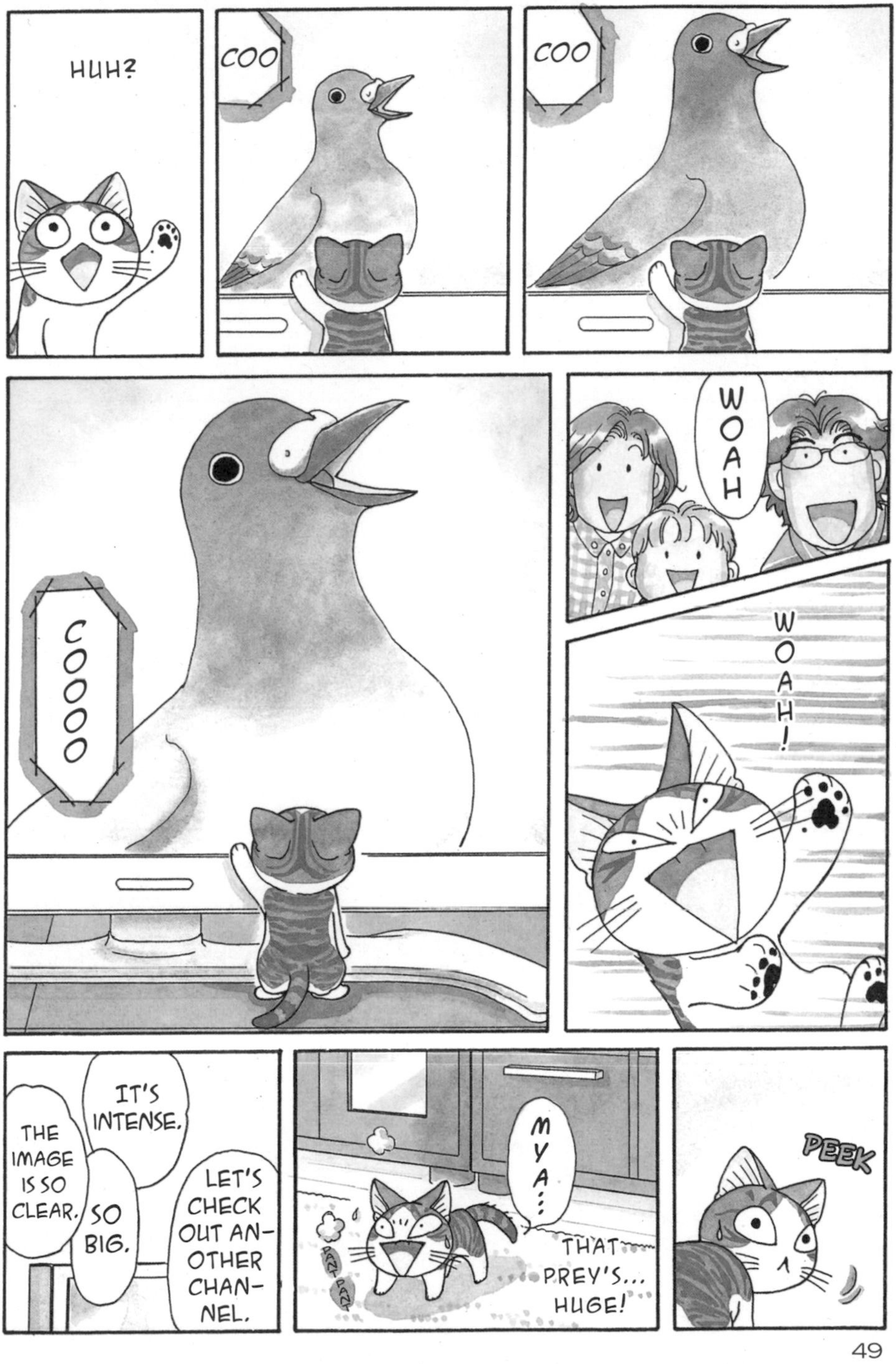
HUH?
COO
COO
COOOOO
WOAH
WOAH!
IT'S INTENSE.
THE IMAGE IS SO CLEAR.
SO BIG.
LET'S CHECK OUT AN-OTHER CHAN-NEL.
MYA...
PANT PANT
THAT PREY'S... HUGE!
PEEK

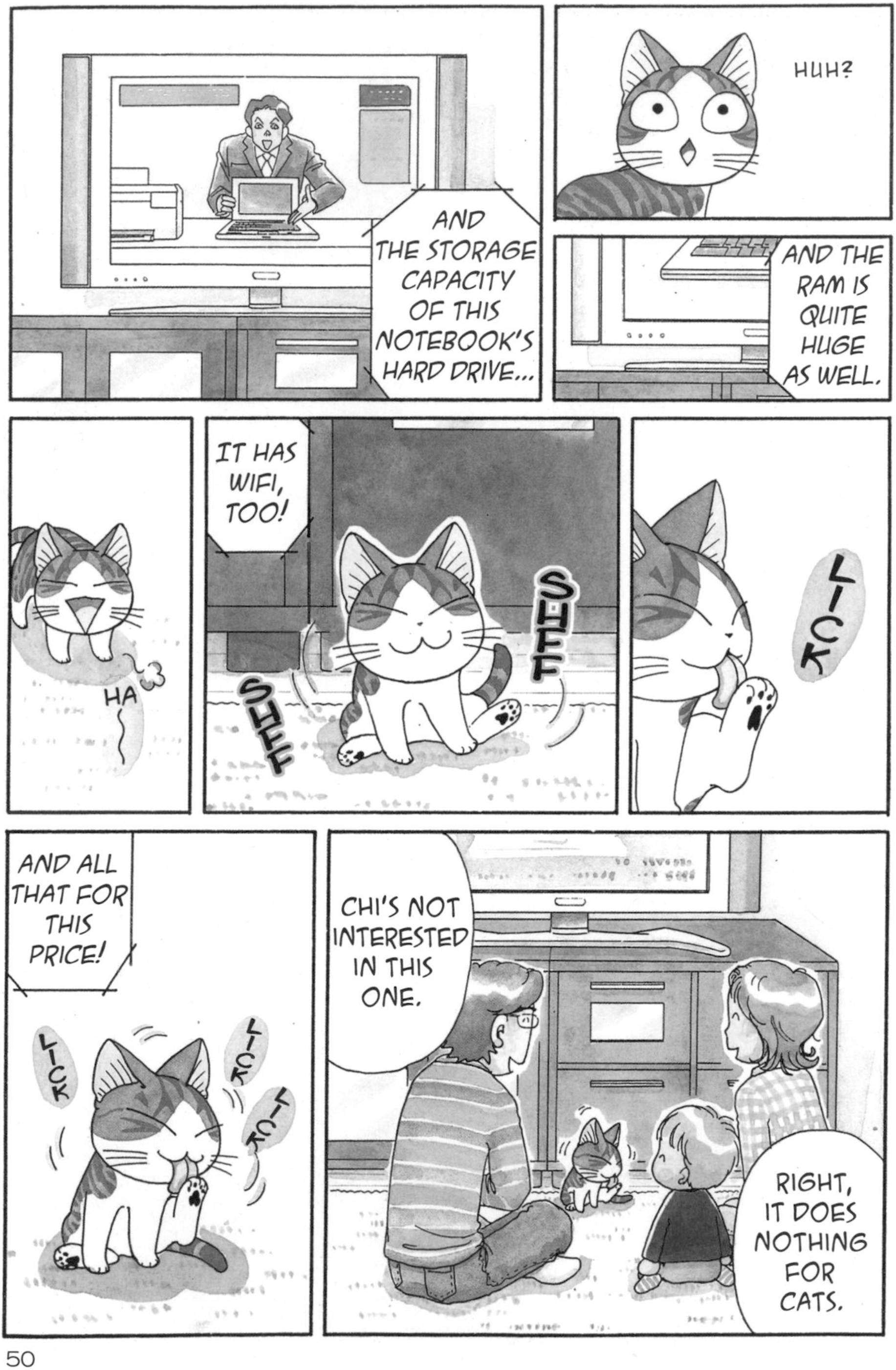
AND THE STORAGE CAPACITY OF THIS NOTEBOOK'S HARD DRIVE...
HUH?
AND THE RAM IS QUITE HUGE AS WELL.
HA
IT HAS WIFI, TOO!
SHFF
SHFF
LICK
AND ALL THAT FOR THIS PRICE!
LICK
LICK
LICK
CHI'S NOT INTERESTED IN THIS ONE.
RIGHT, IT DOES NOTHING FOR CATS.

HEH

HOW ABOUT ANOTHER CHANNEL?

THERE! A SCHOOL OF MACKEREL!

OH

CHI'S GONNA LIKE THIS!

HERE, CHI...

HILIP

PLUNK

CHECK IT OUT.

LOOK, CHI... FISH!

HMM?

WHAT DO YOU THINK? FUN, HUH?

PLOOP

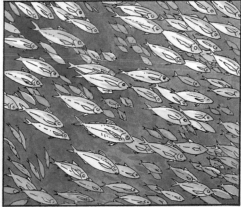

51

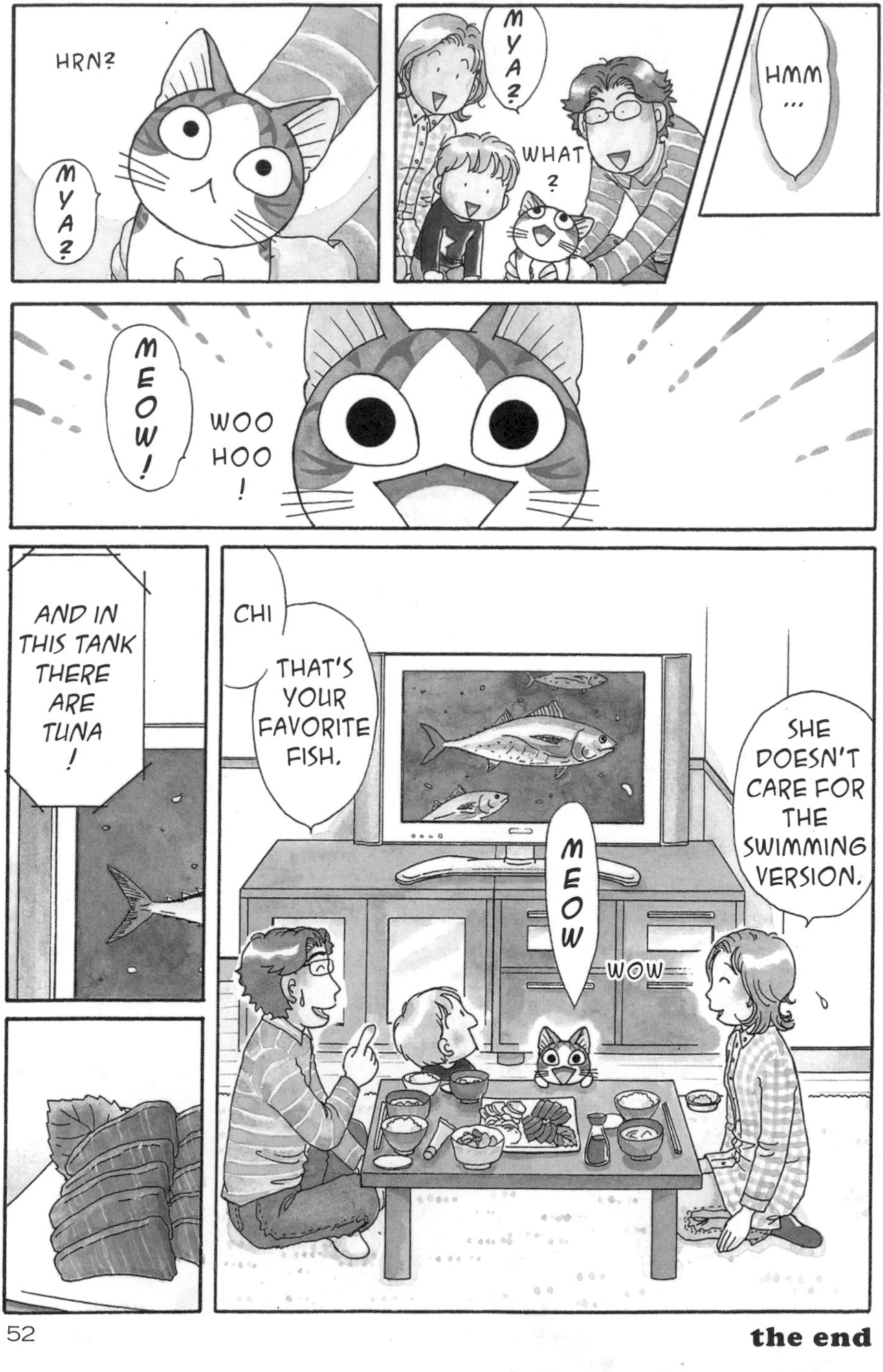
HRN?
MYA?
MYA?
WHAT?
HMM...
MEOW!
WOO HOO!
AND IN THIS TANK THERE ARE TUNA!
CHI
THAT'S YOUR FAVORITE FISH.
MEOW
SHE DOESN'T CARE FOR THE SWIMMING VERSION.
WOW

**the end**

# homemade 117: a cat is astounded

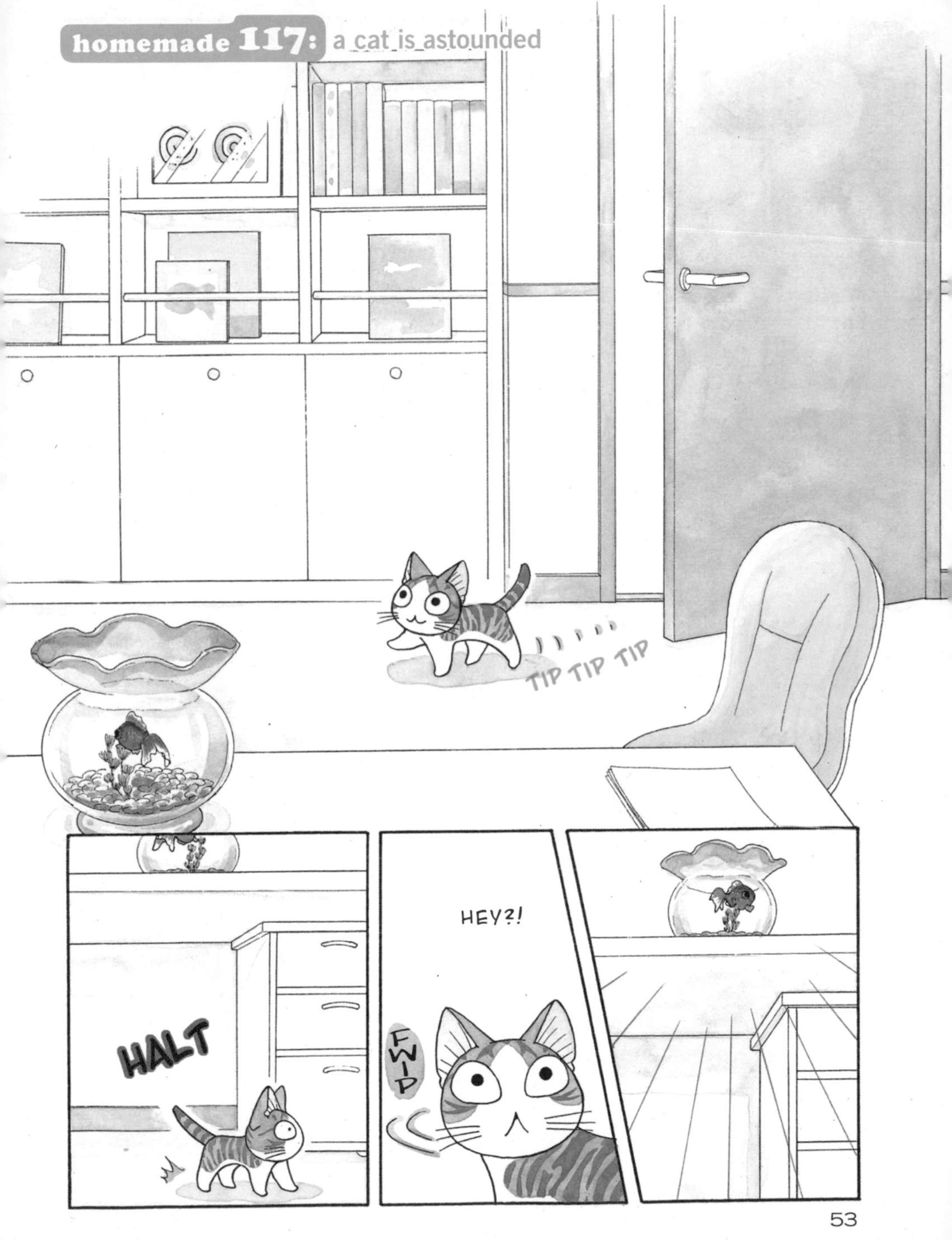
TIP TIP TIP
HALT
HEY?!
FWIP

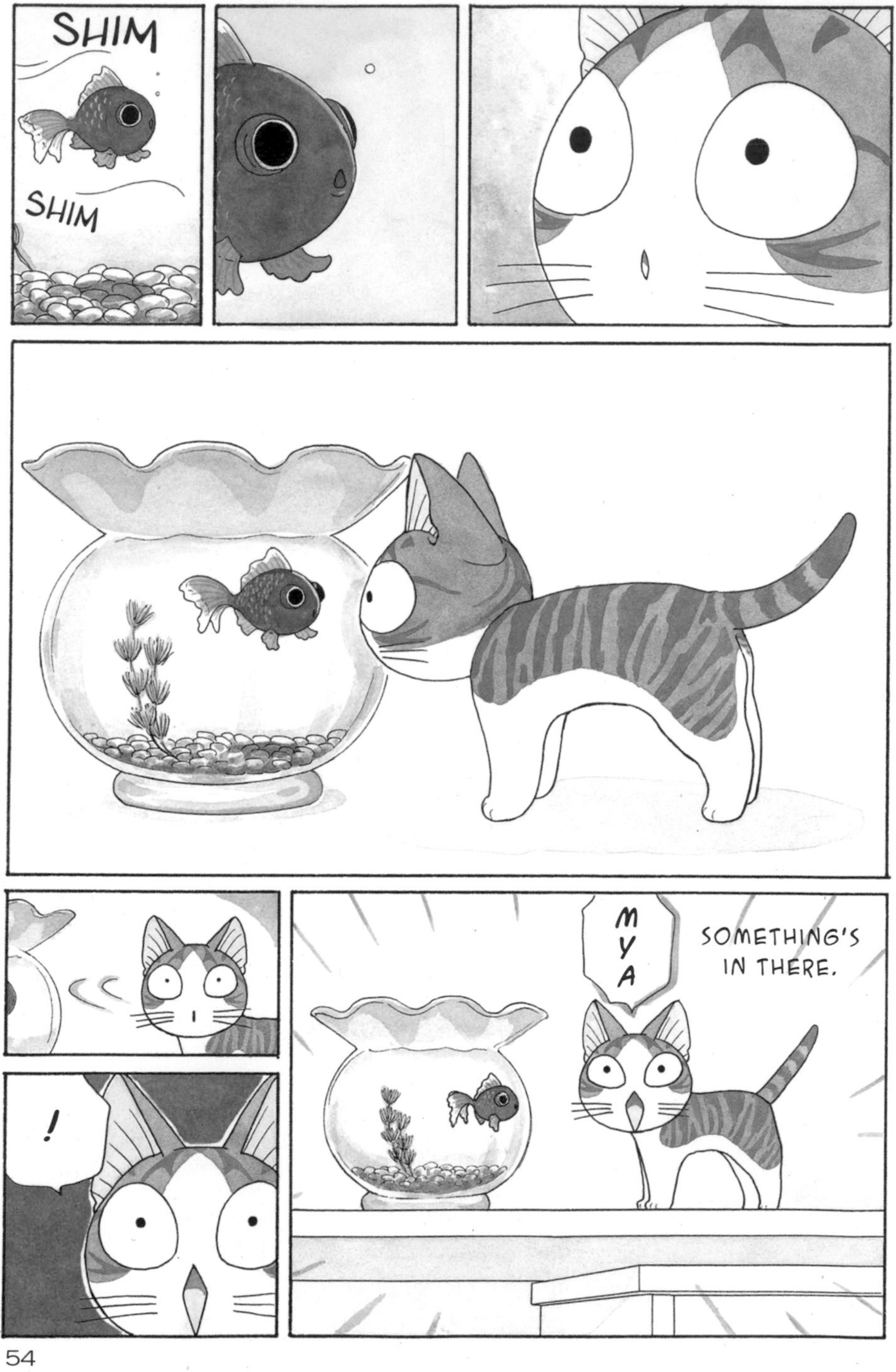
SHIM
SHIM
!
MYA
SOMETHING'S IN THERE.

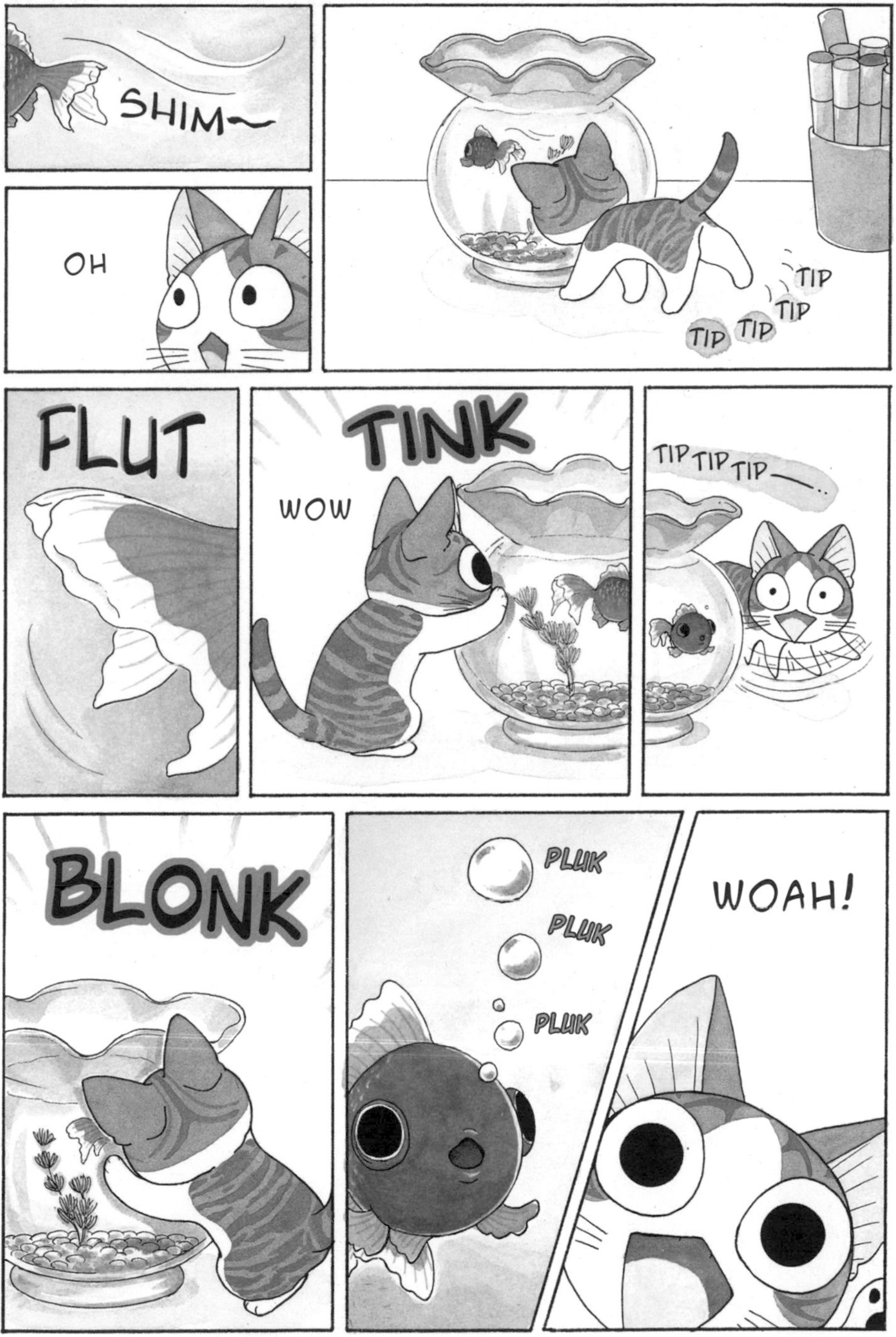

SHIM~
OH
TIP
TIP
TIP
TIP
FLUT
TINK
WOW
TIP TIP TIP——..
BLONK
PLUK
PLUK
PLUK
WOAH!

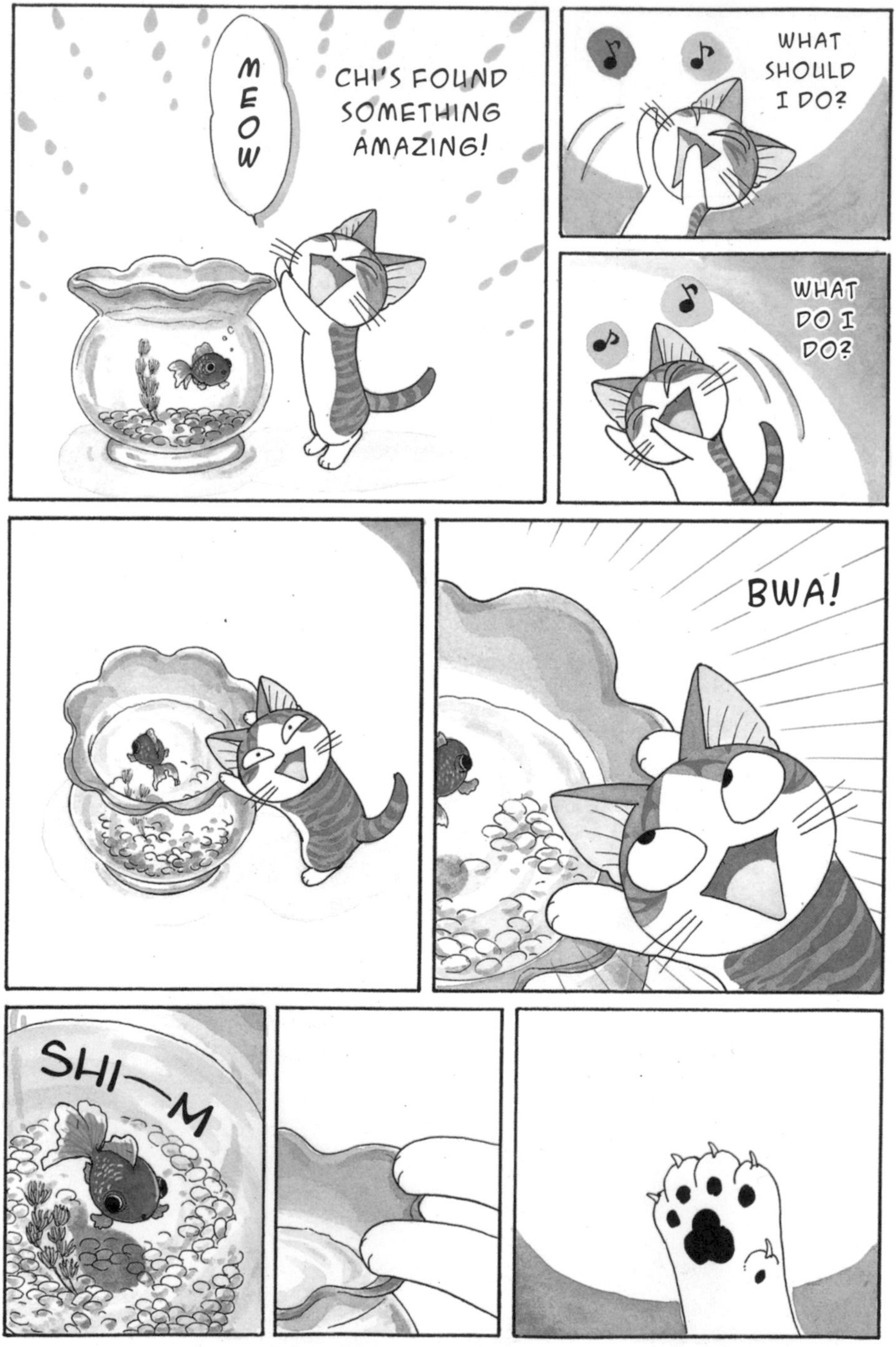
MEOW
CHI'S FOUND SOMETHING AMAZING!
WHAT SHOULD I DO?
WHAT DO I DO?
BWA!
SHI—M

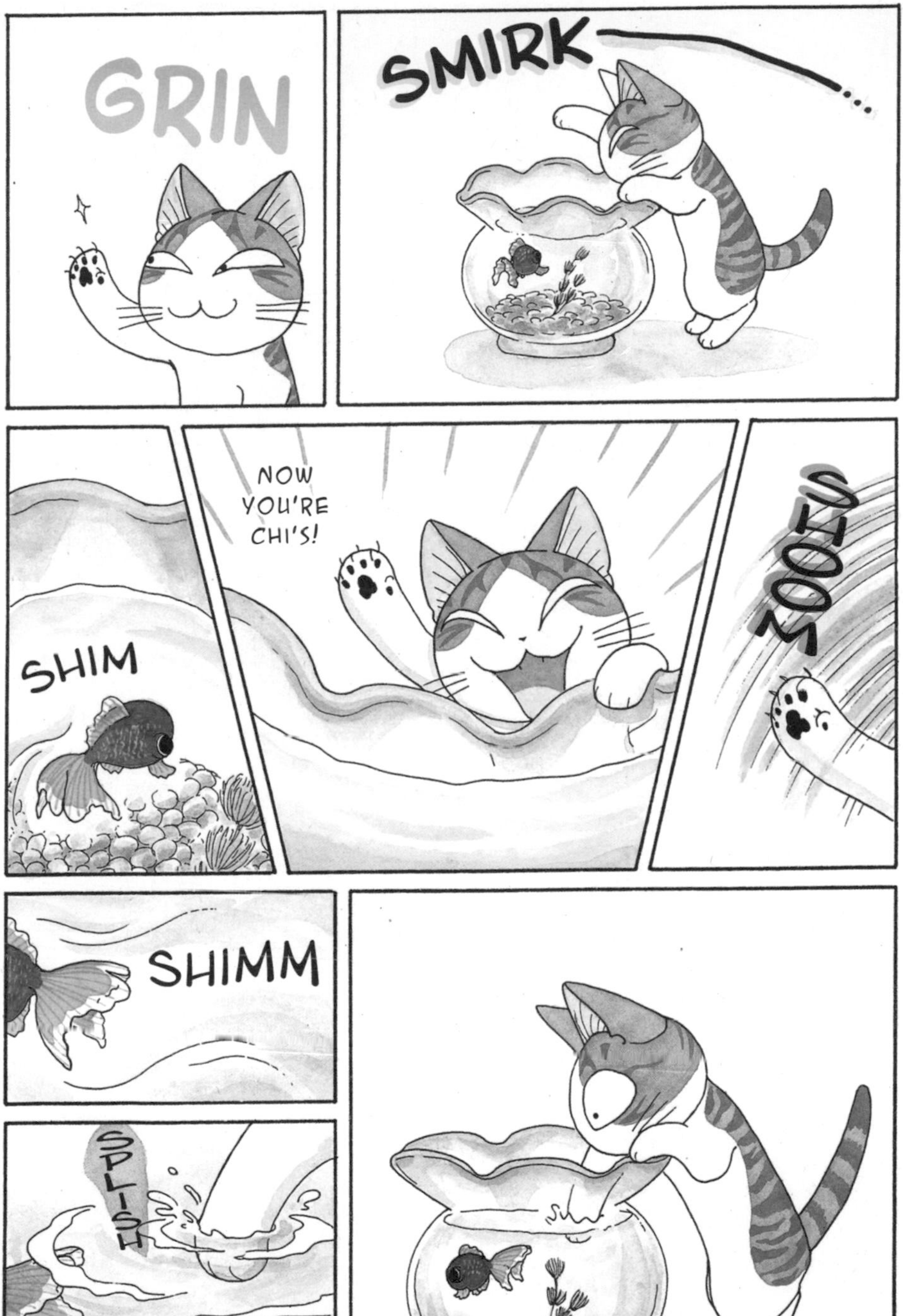
GRIN
SMIRK...
SHIM
NOW YOU'RE CHI'S!
SWOOP
SHIMM
SPLISH

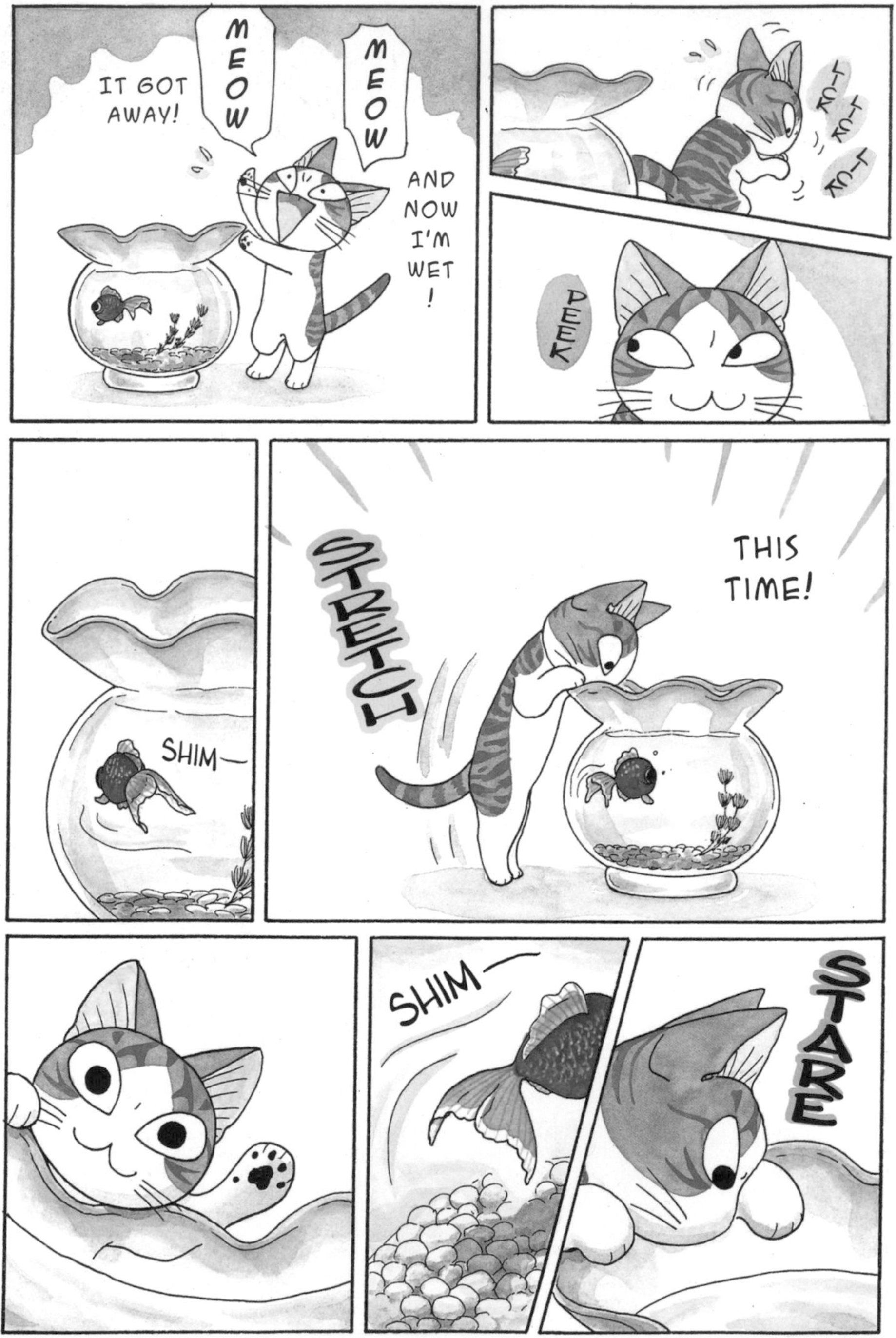
IT GOT AWAY!
MEOW
MEOW
AND NOW I'M WET!
LICK LICK
PEEK
SHIM—
STRETCH
THIS TIME!
SHIM—
STARE

STARE

HALT

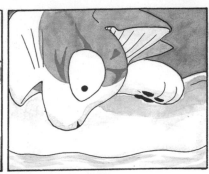

WOOSH

NOW!

WHAT?

CHI'S GONE UPSTAIRS?

YUP

SHE WAS JUST CLIMBING UP THE STAIRS.

THIS IS BAD!

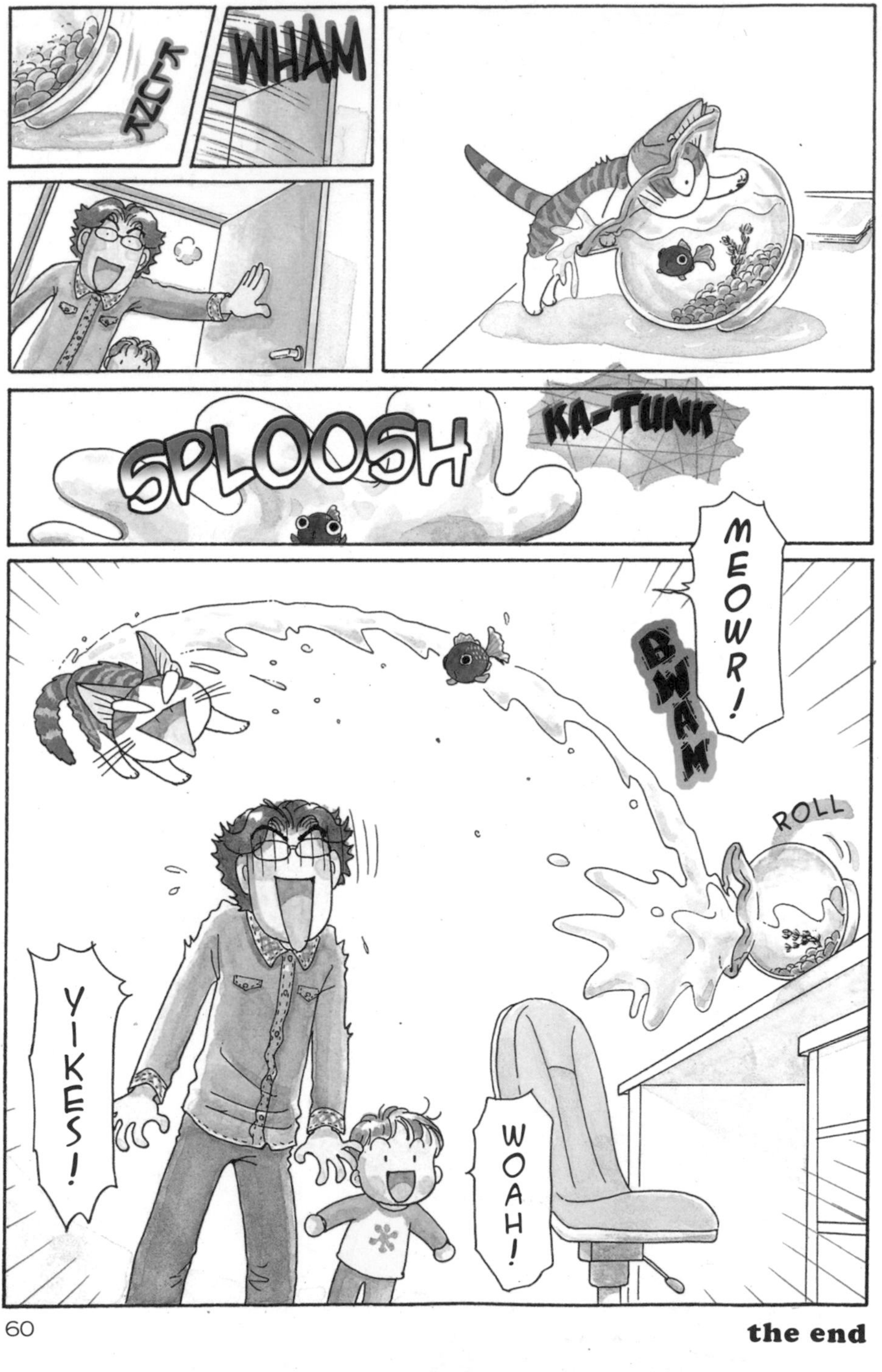
WHAM
SPLOOSH
KA-TUNK
MEOWR!
BWAM
ROLL
YIKES!
WOAH!



**the end**

## homemade 118: a cat's heart is stolen

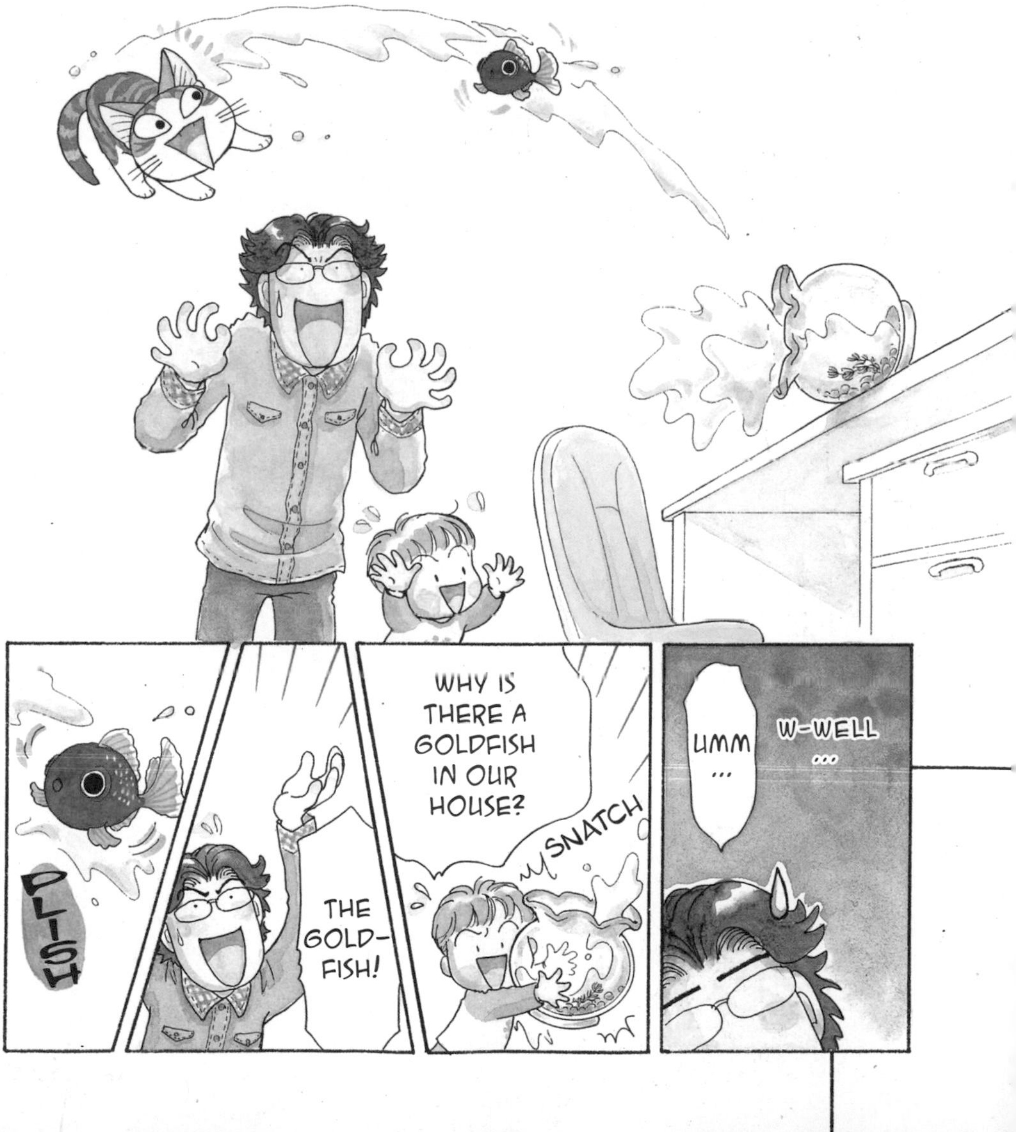
PLISH
THE GOLD-FISH!
WHY IS THERE A GOLDFISH IN OUR HOUSE?
SNATCH
UMM ...
W-WELL ...

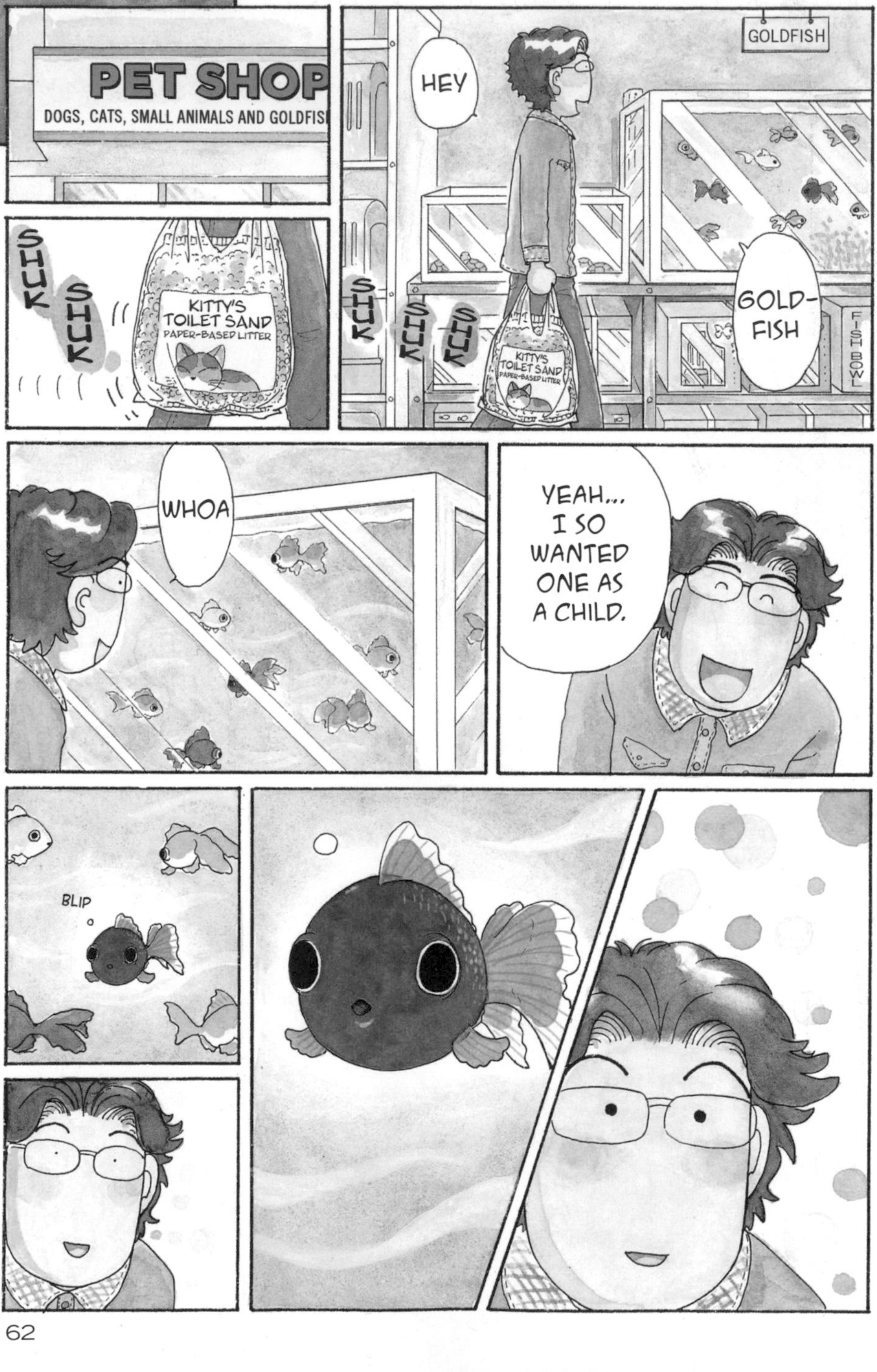
PET SHOP
DOGS, CATS, SMALL ANIMALS AND GOLDFIS
GOLDFISH
HEY
SHUK SHUK
KITTY'S TOILET SAND PAPER-BASED LITTER
SHUK SHUK SHUK
KITTY'S TOILET SAND PAPER-BASED LITTER
GOLD-FISH
FISH BOWL
WHOA
YEAH... I SO WANTED ONE AS A CHILD.
BLIP

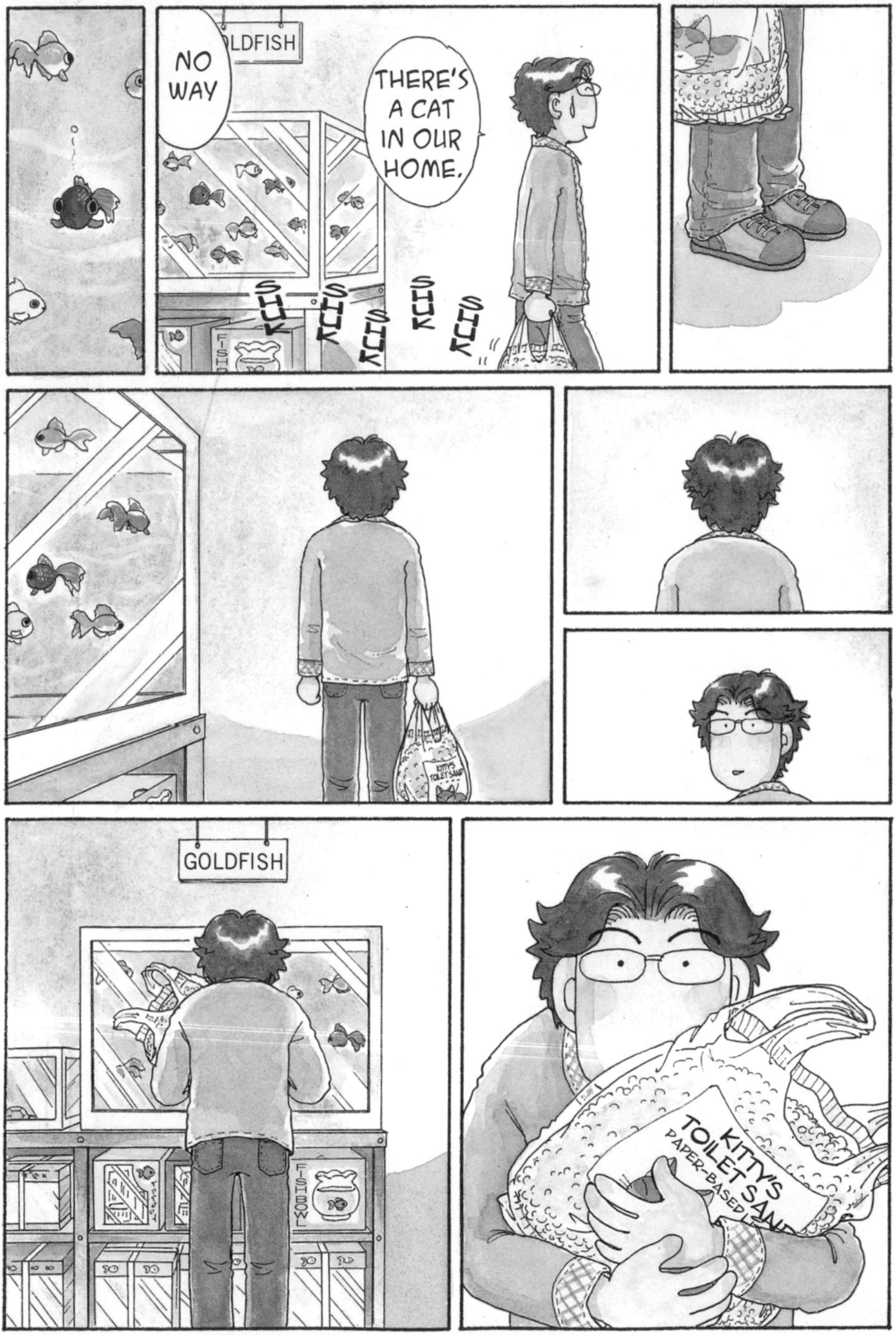
GOLDFISH
NO WAY
THERE'S A CAT IN OUR HOME.
SHUK SHUK SHUK SHUK SHUK
FISH
KITTY'S TOILET SAND
GOLDFISH
FISHBOWL
KITTY'S TOILET SAND
PAPER-BASED

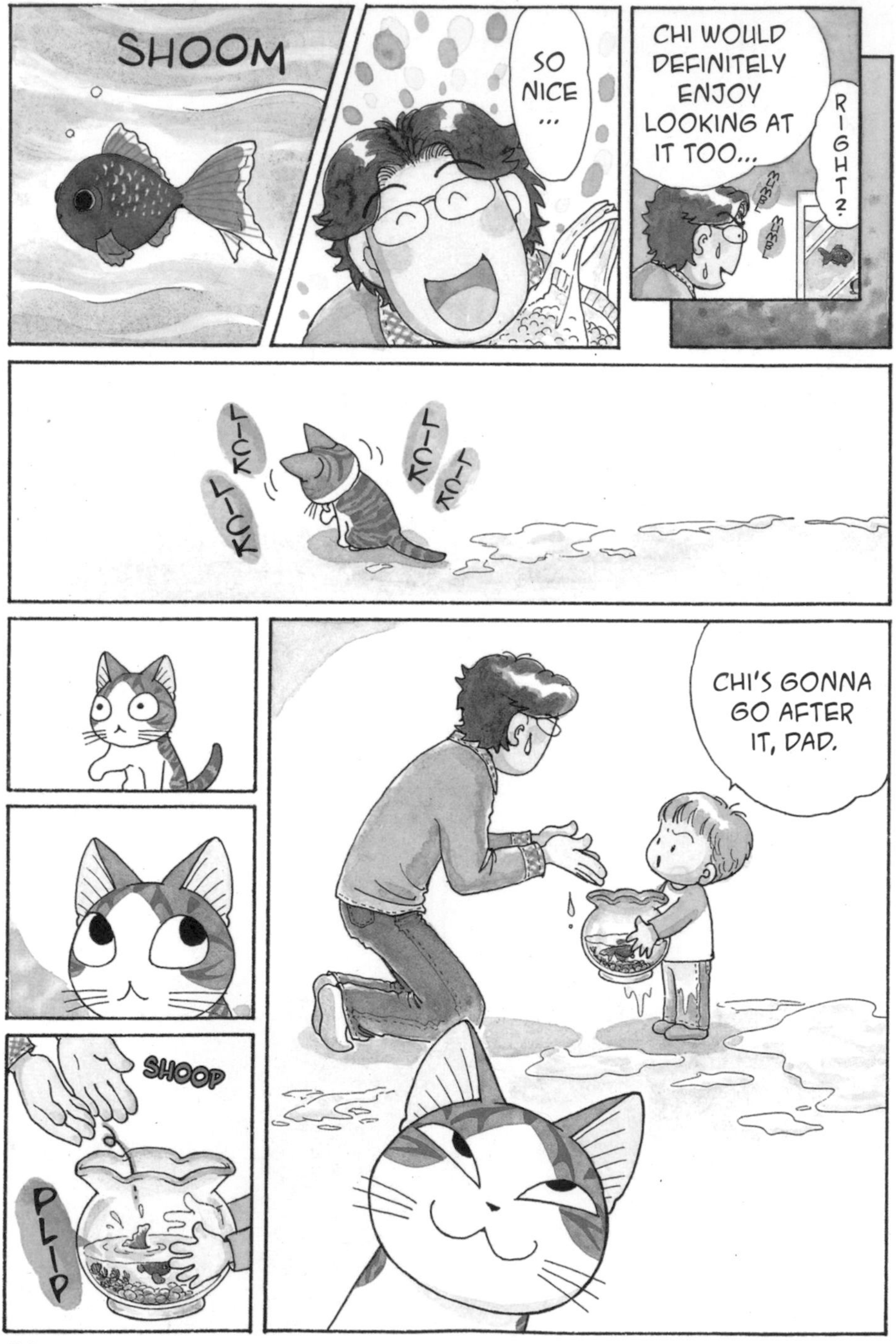
SHOOM
SO NICE ...
CHI WOULD DEFINITELY ENJOY LOOKING AT IT TOO...
RIGHT?
MUMBL MUMBL
LICK LICK
LICK LICK
SHOOP
PLIP
CHI'S GONNA GO AFTER IT, DAD.



**the end**

## homemade 119: a cat reaches

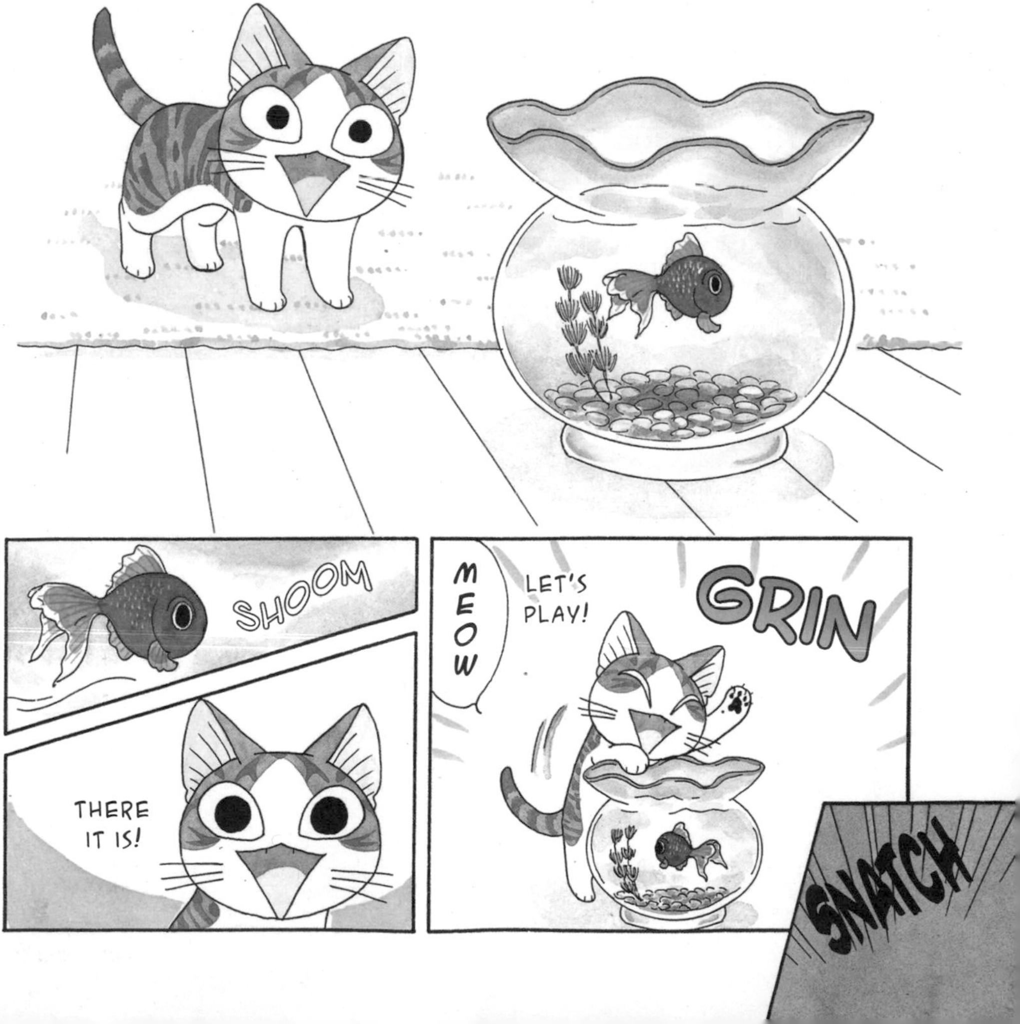
SHOOM
THERE IT IS!
MEOW
LET'S PLAY!
GRIN
SNATCH

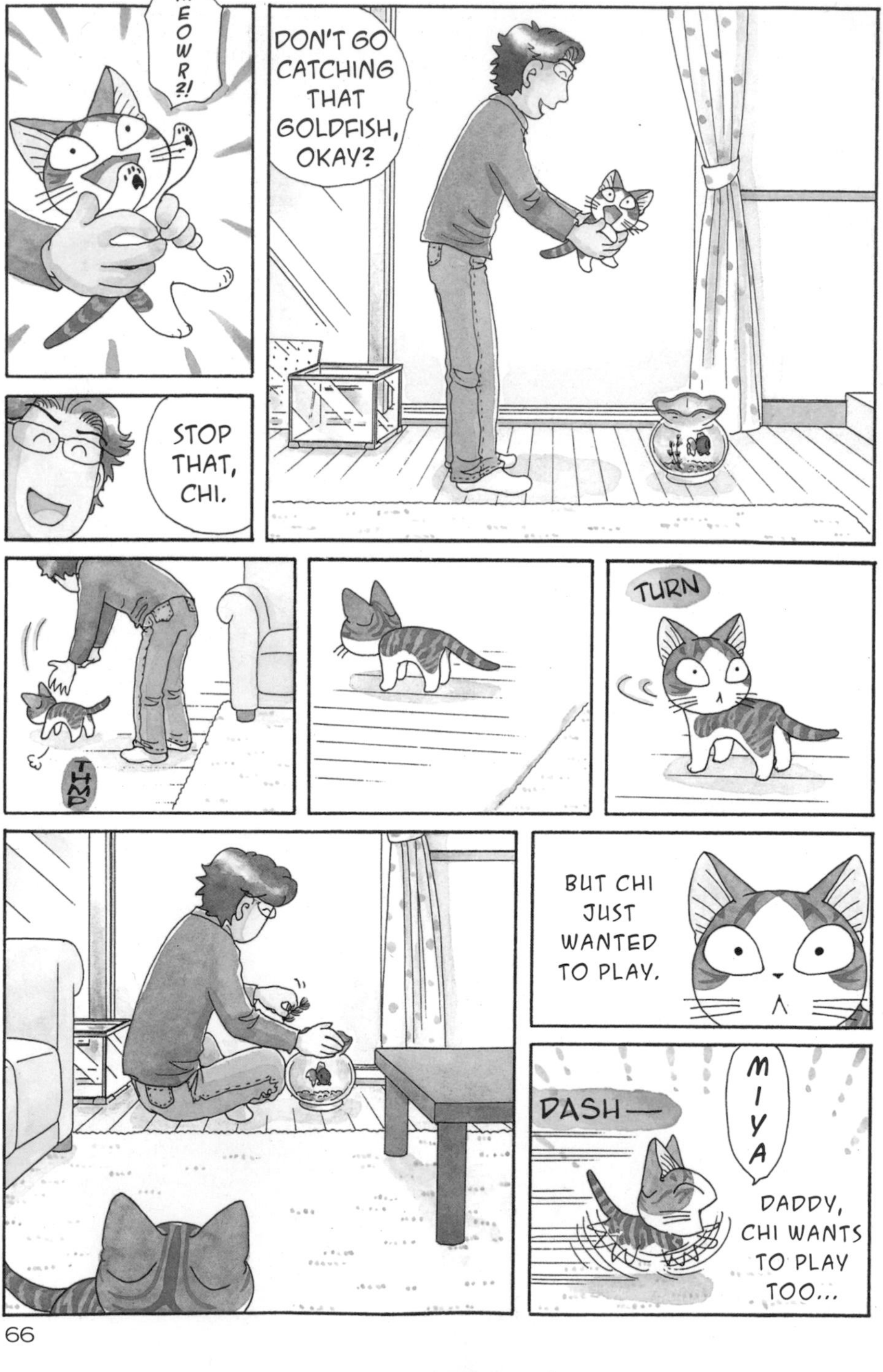

MEOWR?!
DON'T GO CATCHING THAT GOLDFISH, OKAY?
STOP THAT, CHI.
THMP
TURN
BUT CHI JUST WANTED TO PLAY.
DASH—
MIYA
DADDY, CHI WANTS TO PLAY TOO...

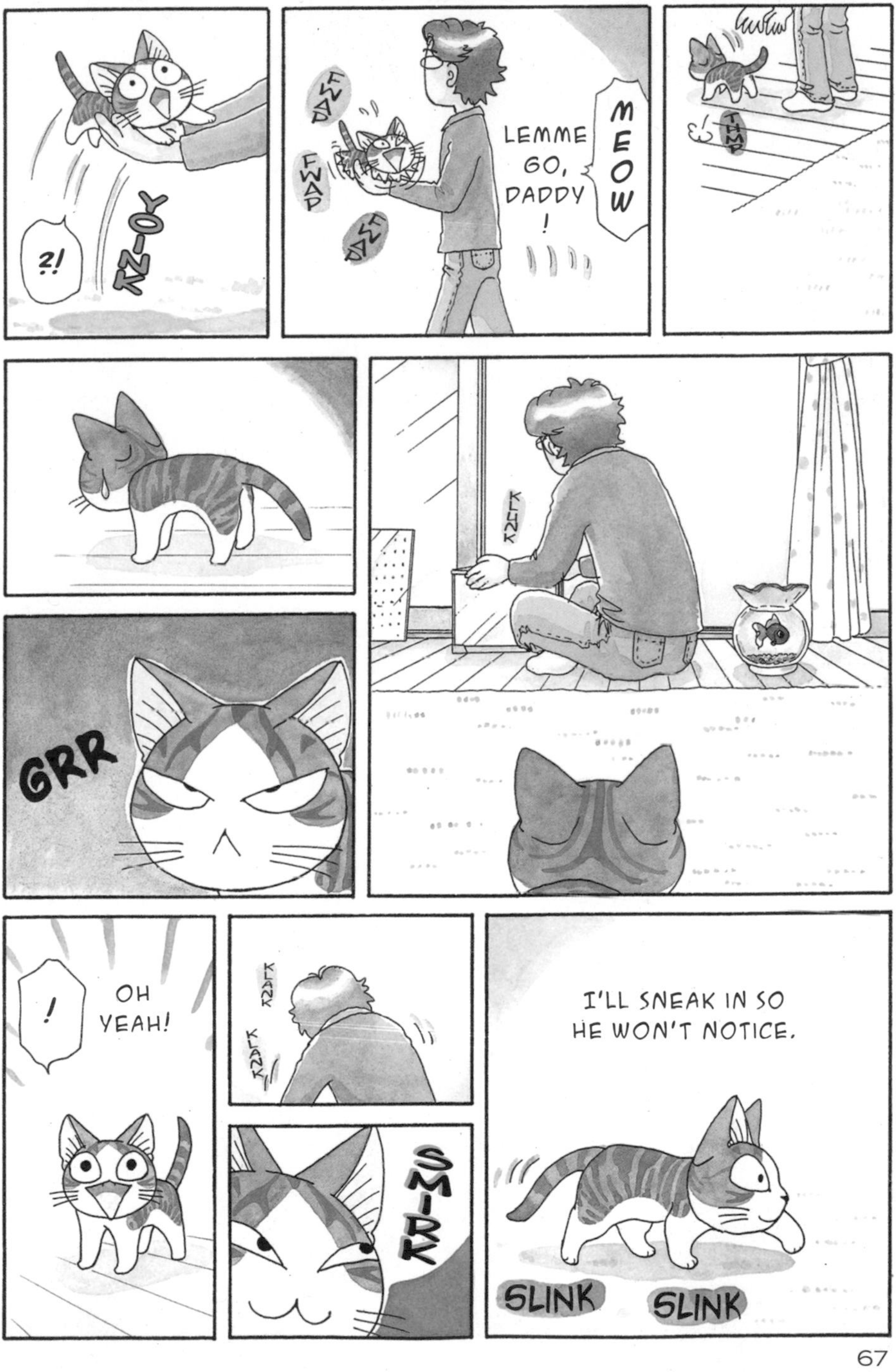
?!
YOINK
FWAP
FWAP
FWAP
LEMME GO, DADDY!
MEOW
THMP
GRR
KLUNK
!
OH YEAH!
KLANK
KLANK
SMIRK
I'LL SNEAK IN SO HE WON'T NOTICE.
SLINK
SLINK

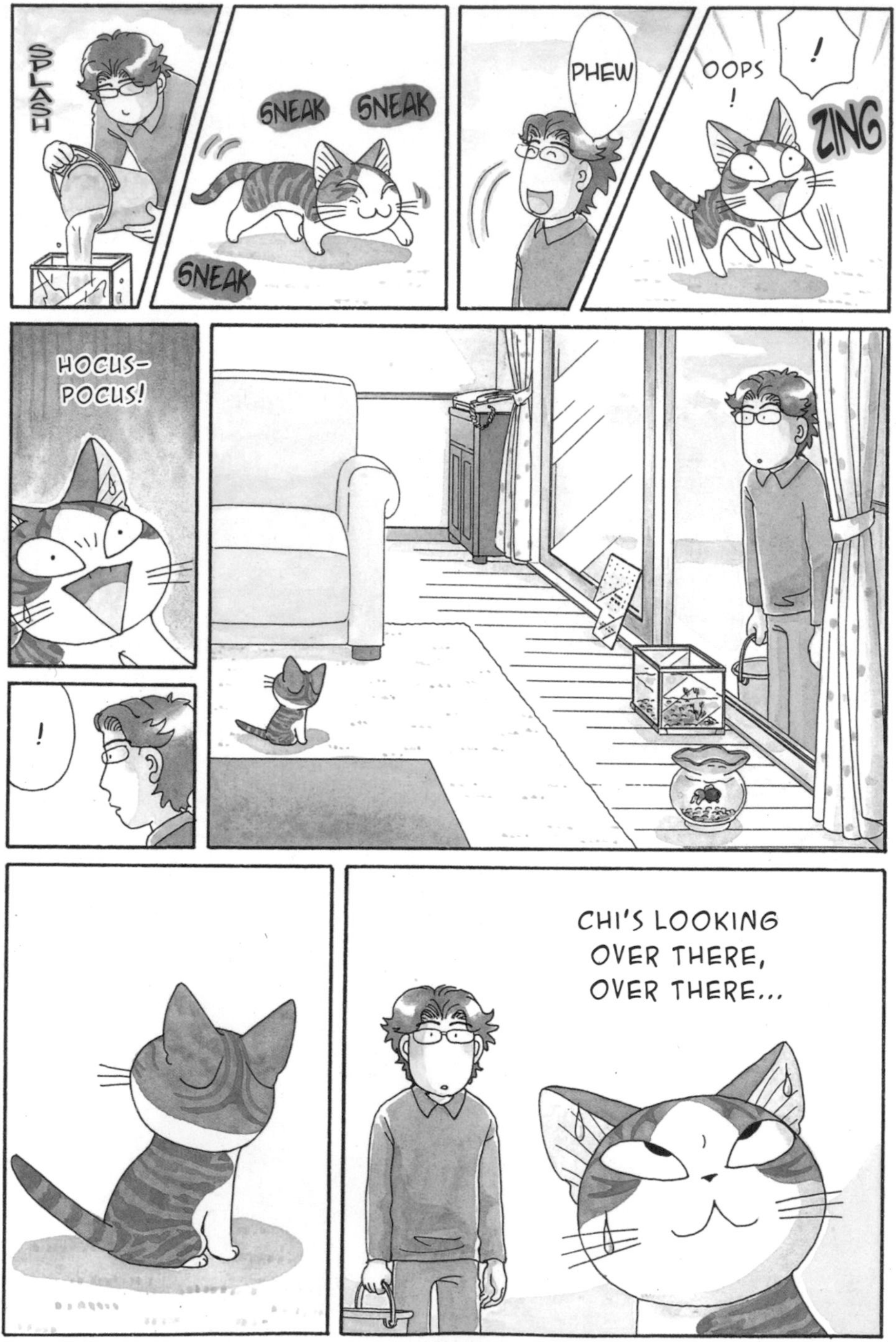
SPLASH
SNEAK SNEAK
SNEAK
PHEW
OOPS!
!
ZING
HOCUS-POCUS!
!
CHI'S LOOKING OVER THERE, OVER THERE...

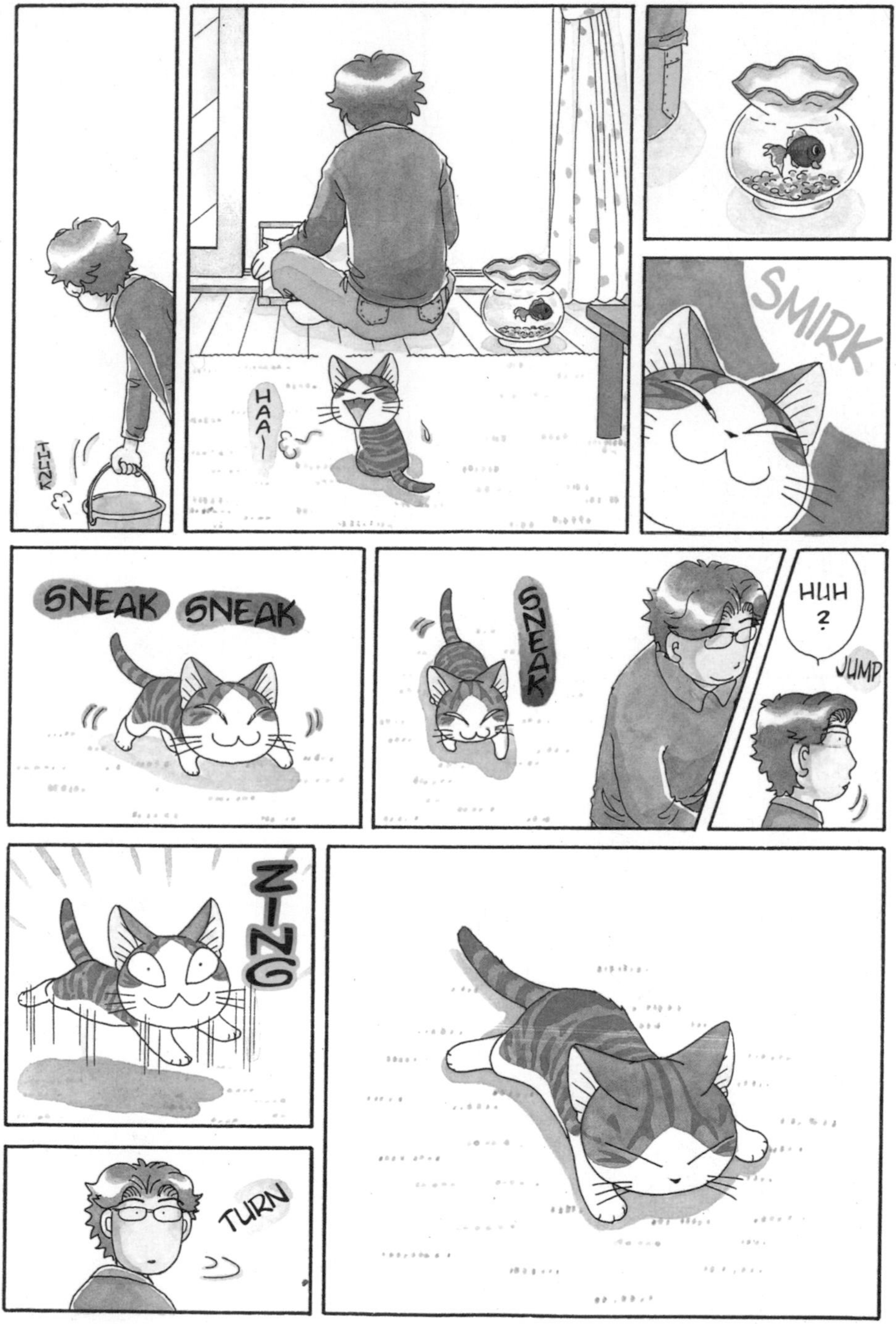
THUNK
HAAA
SMIRK
SNEAK SNEAK
SNEAK
HUH?
JUMP
ZING
TURN

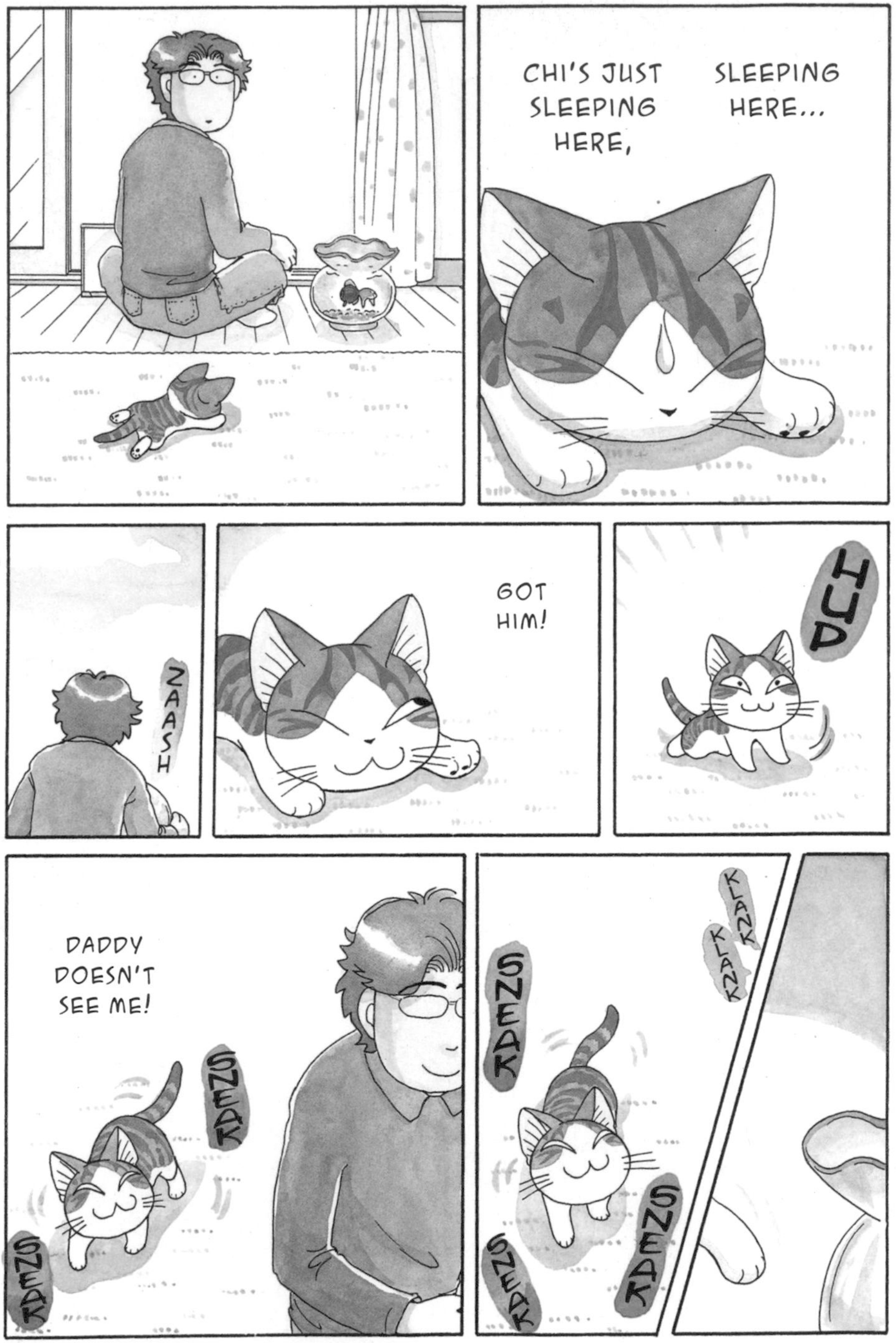
CHI'S JUST SLEEPING HERE,
SLEEPING HERE...
ZAASH
GOT HIM!
HUD
DADDY DOESN'T SEE ME!
SNEAK
SNEAK
SNEAK
SNEAK
SNEAK
KLANK
KLANK

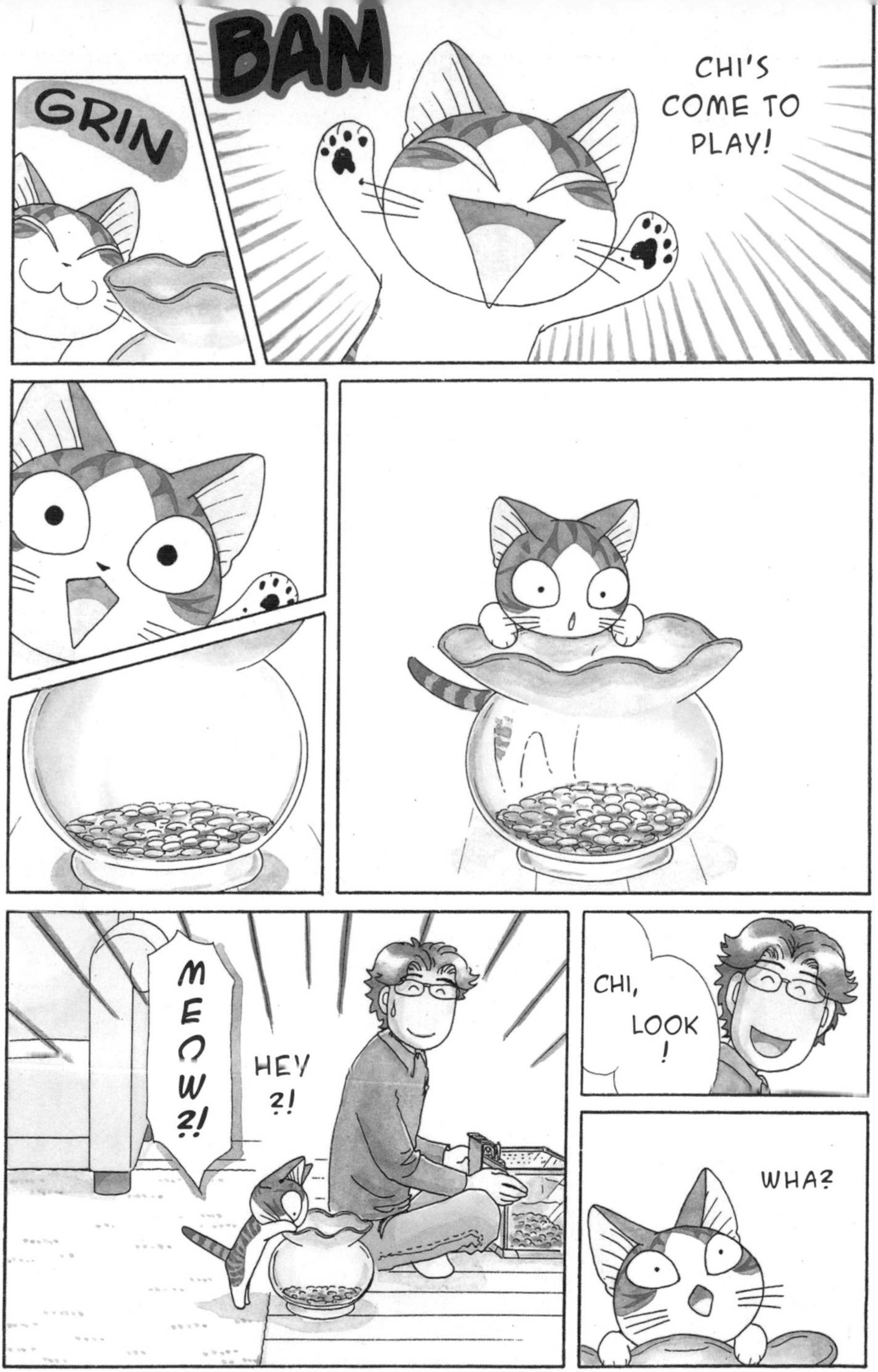
GRIN
BAM
CHI'S COME TO PLAY!
MEOW?!
HEY?!
CHI, LOOK!
WHA?

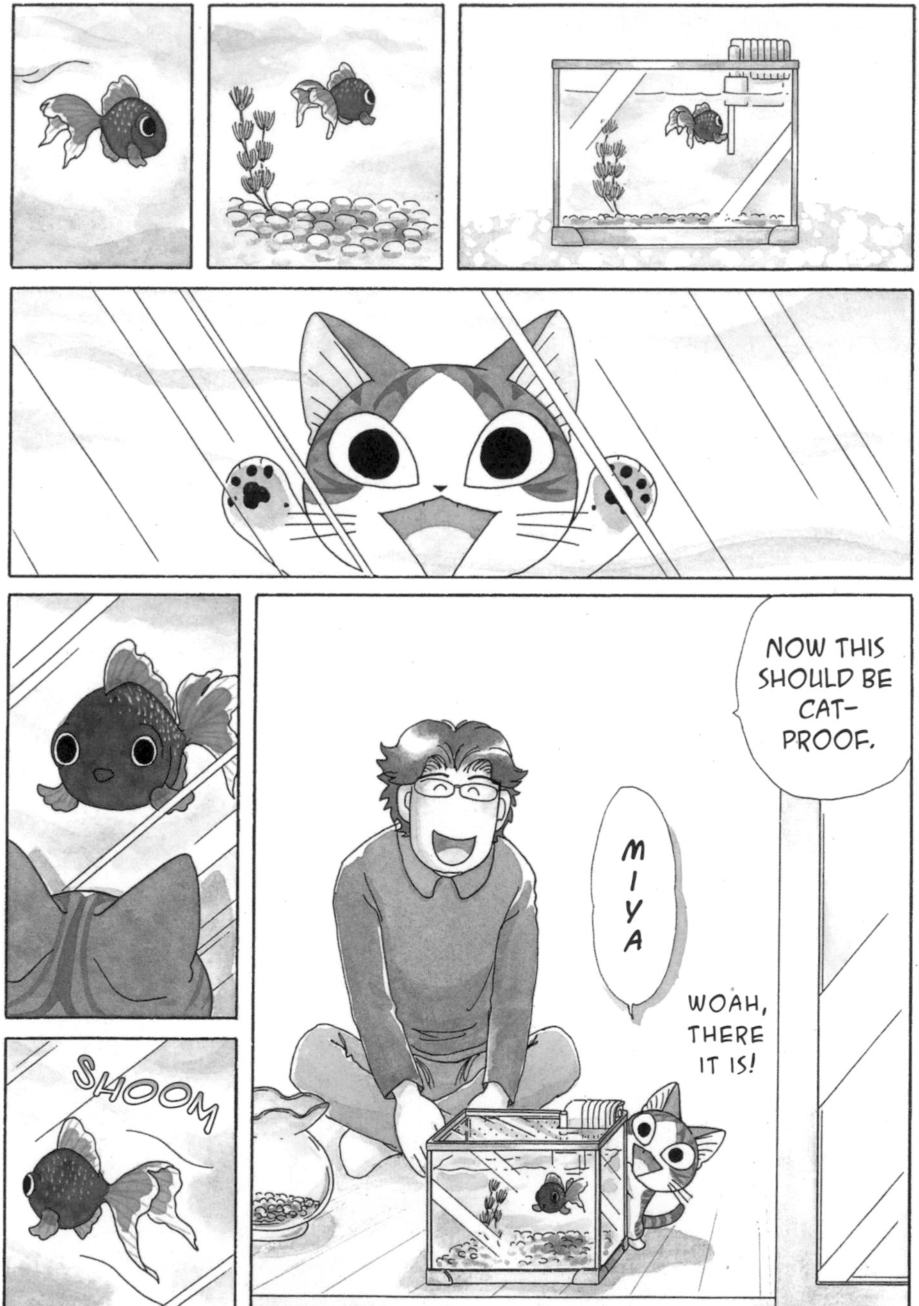
SHOOM
NOW THIS SHOULD BE CAT-PROOF.
MIYA
WOAH, THERE IT IS!



**the end**

## homemade 120: a cat misunderstands

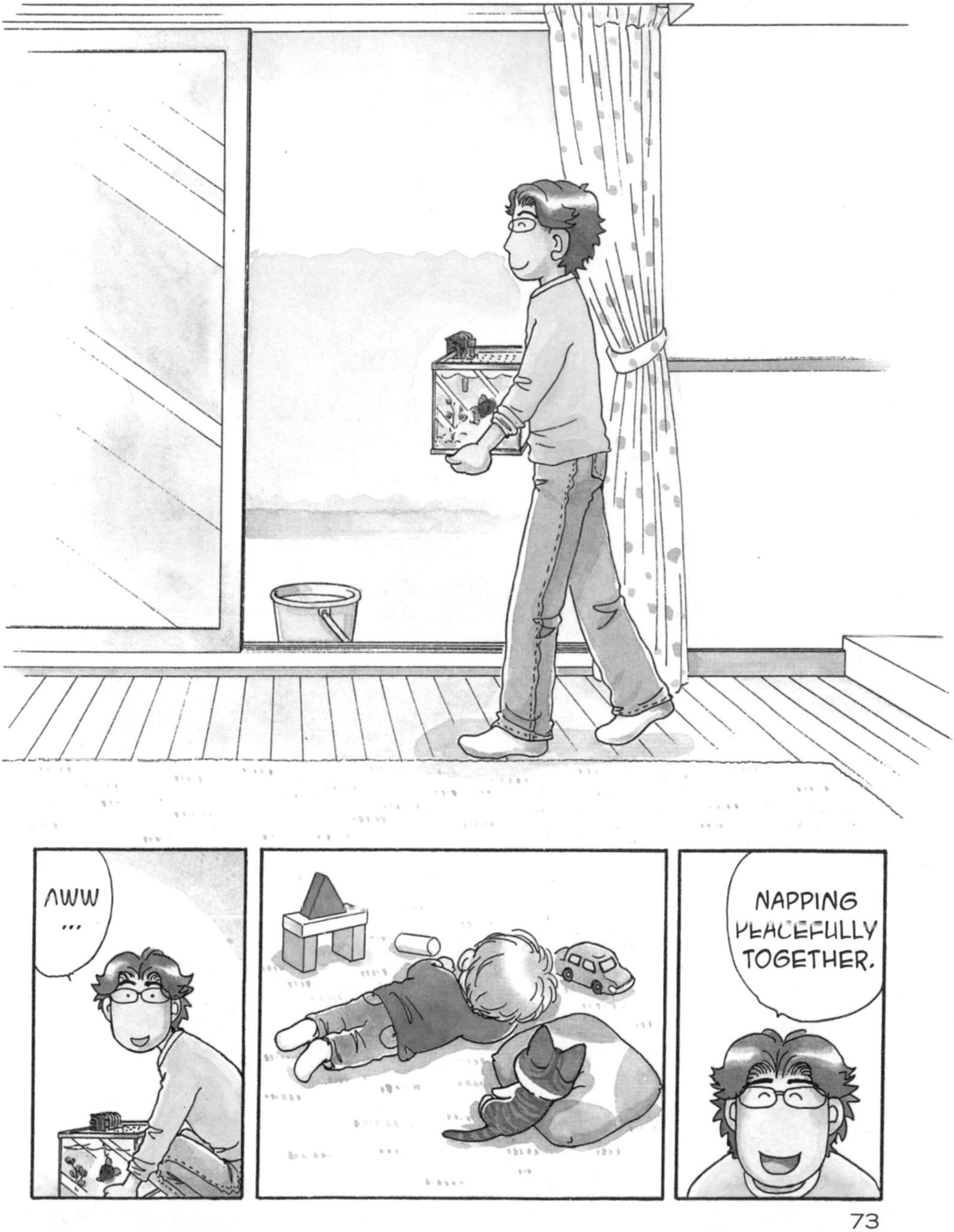
AWW ...
NAPPING PEACEFULLY TOGETHER.

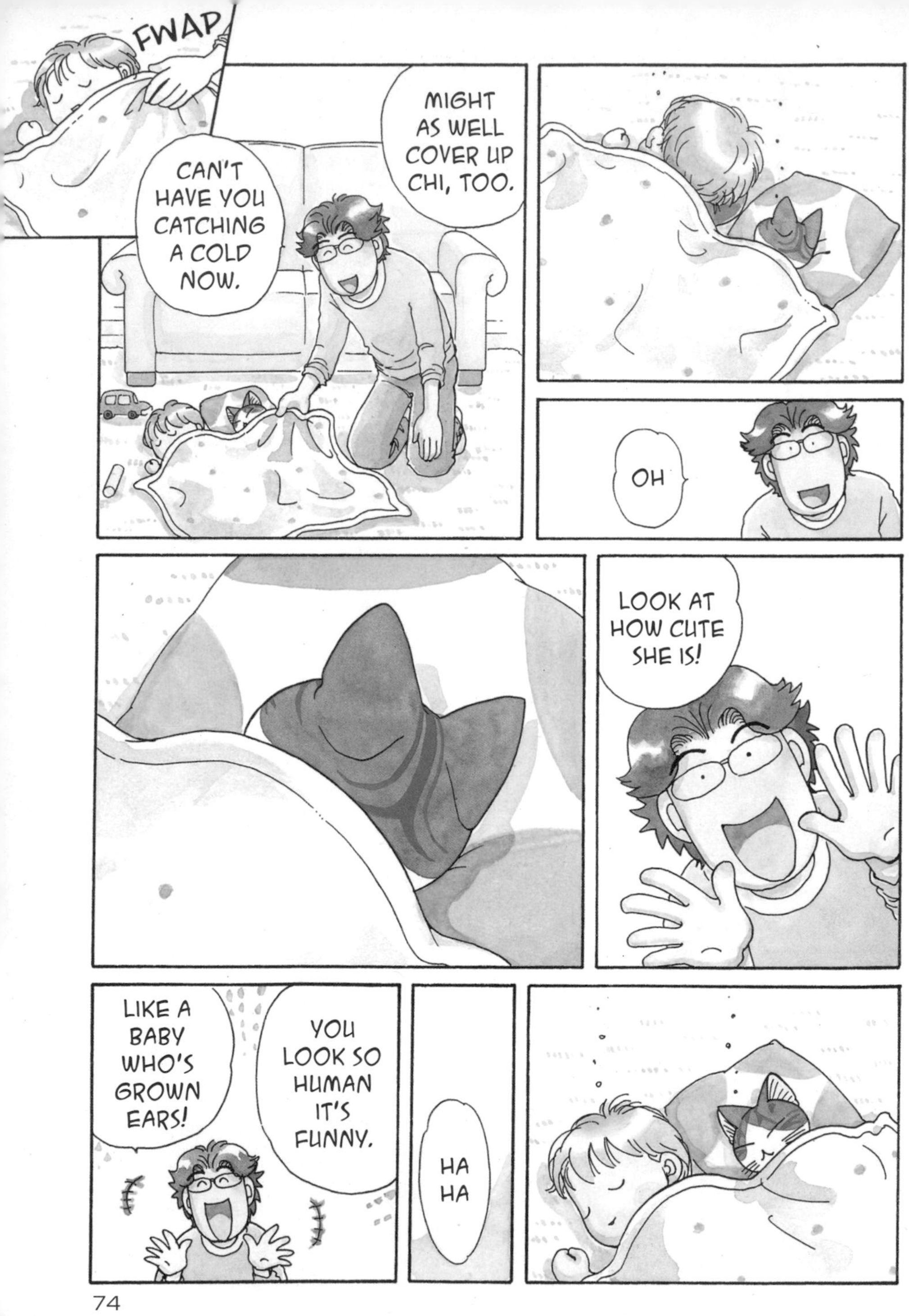
FWAP
CAN'T HAVE YOU CATCHING A COLD NOW.
MIGHT AS WELL COVER UP CHI, TOO.
OH
LOOK AT HOW CUTE SHE IS!
LIKE A BABY WHO'S GROWN EARS!
YOU LOOK SO HUMAN IT'S FUNNY.
HA HA

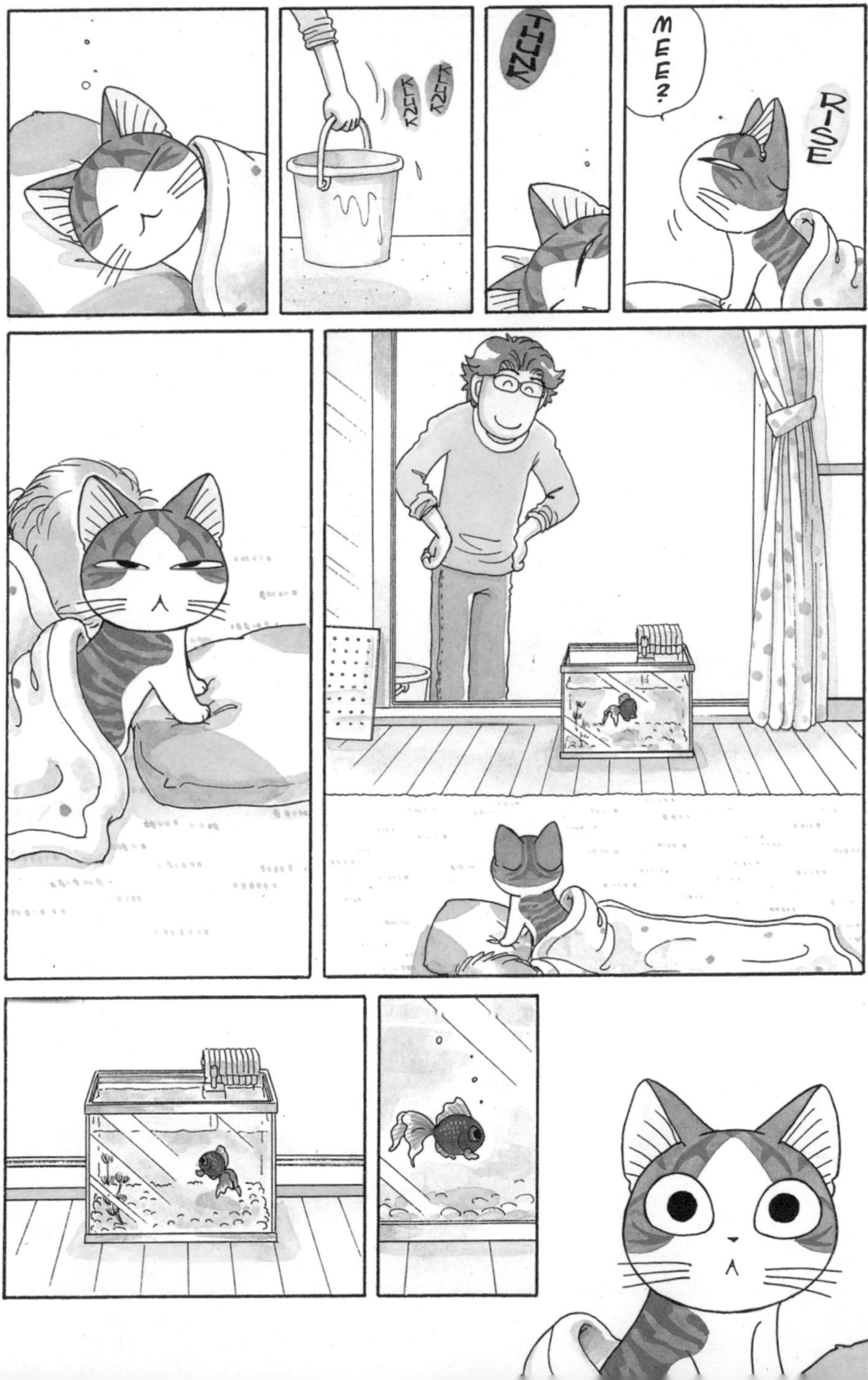
KLUNK
KLUNK
THUNK
MEEE?
RISE

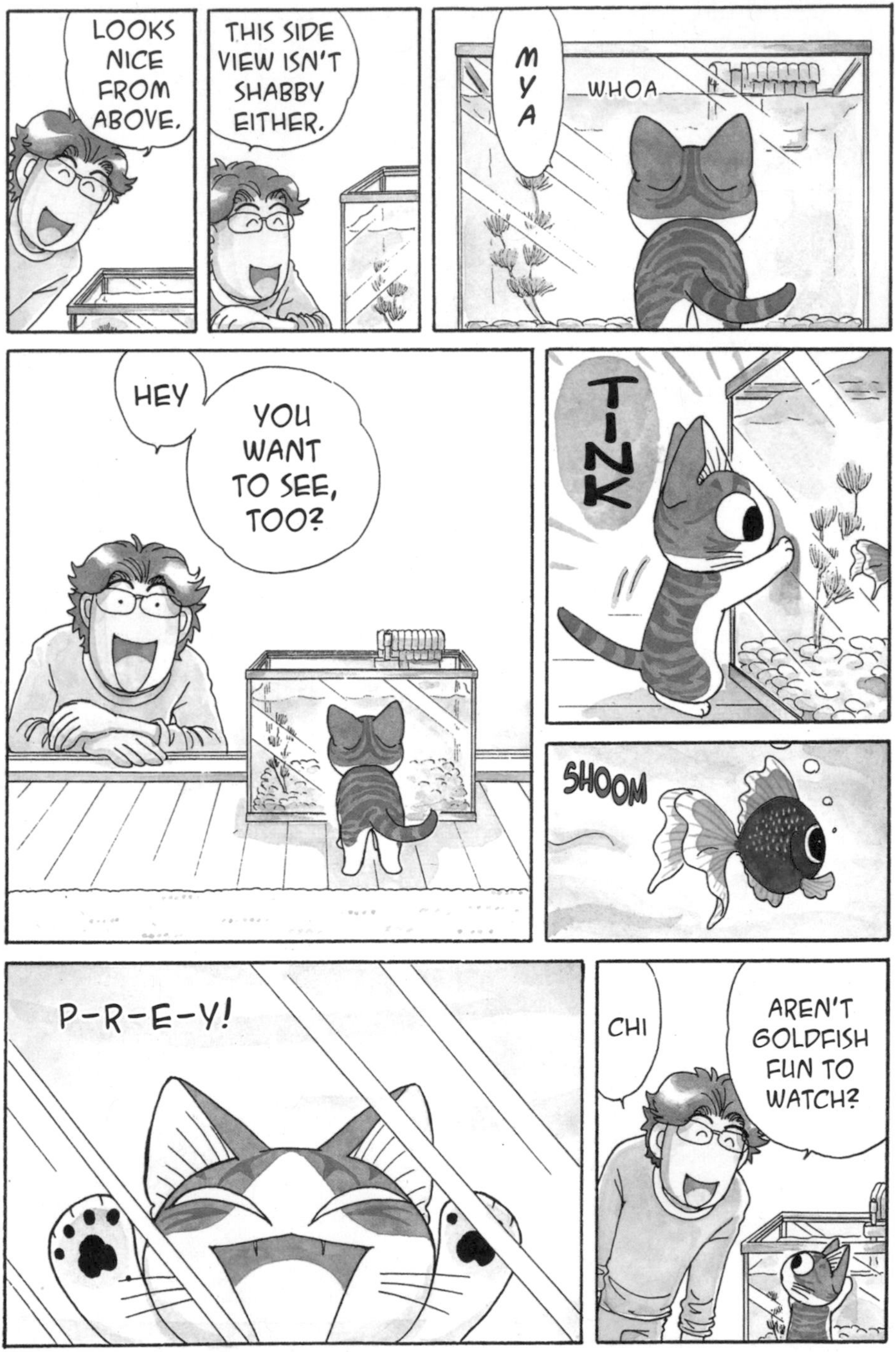
LOOKS NICE FROM ABOVE.
THIS SIDE VIEW ISN'T SHABBY EITHER.
MYA
WHOA
HEY
YOU WANT TO SEE, TOO?
TINK
SHOOM
P-R-E-Y!
CHI
AREN'T GOLDFISH FUN TO WATCH?

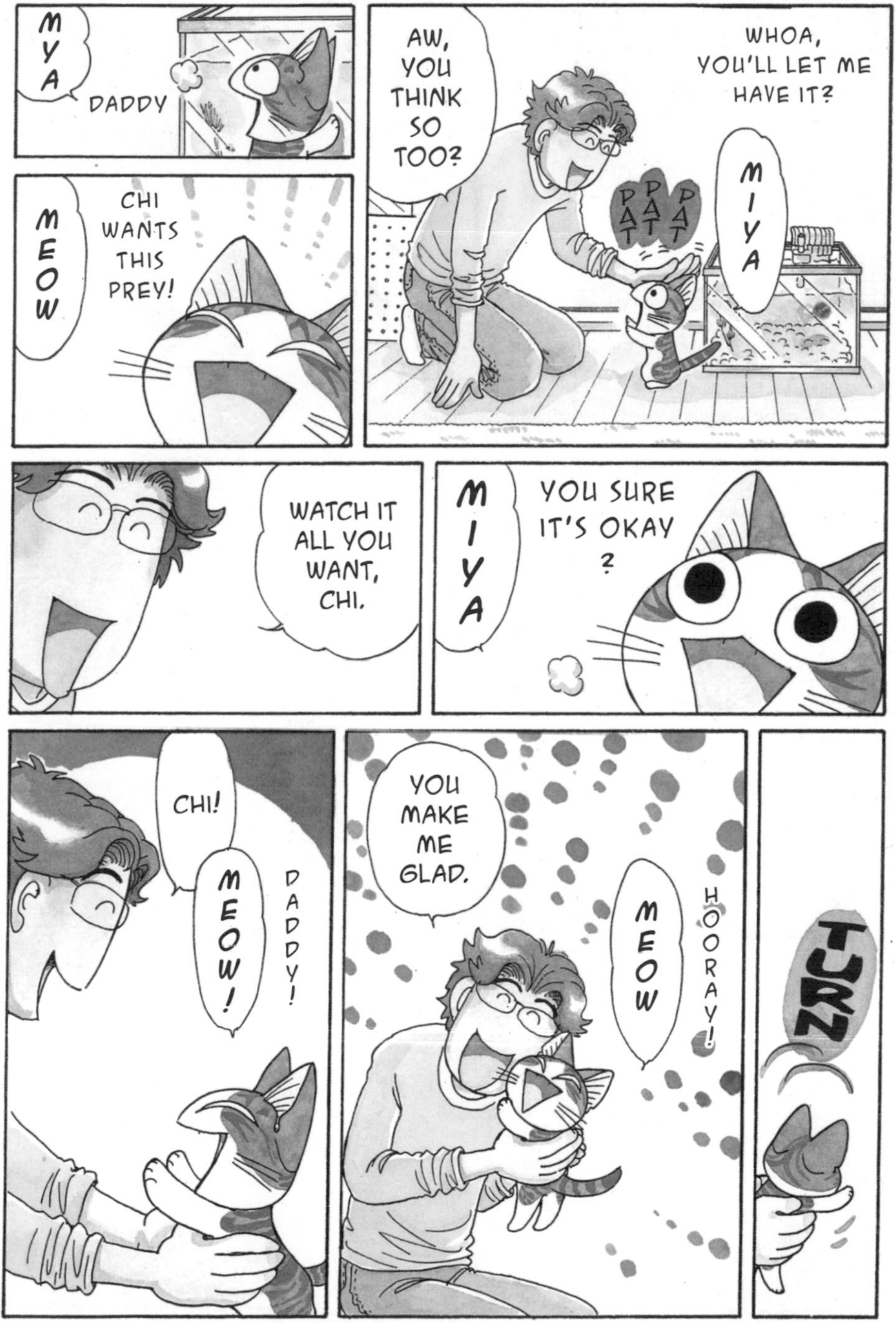
MYA
DADDY
MEOW
CHI WANTS THIS PREY!
AW, YOU THINK SO TOO?
WHOA, YOU'LL LET ME HAVE IT?
PAT PAT PAT
MIYA
WATCH IT ALL YOU WANT, CHI.
MIYA
YOU SURE IT'S OKAY?
CHI!
MEOW!
DADDY!
YOU MAKE ME GLAD.
MEOW
HOORAY!
TURN

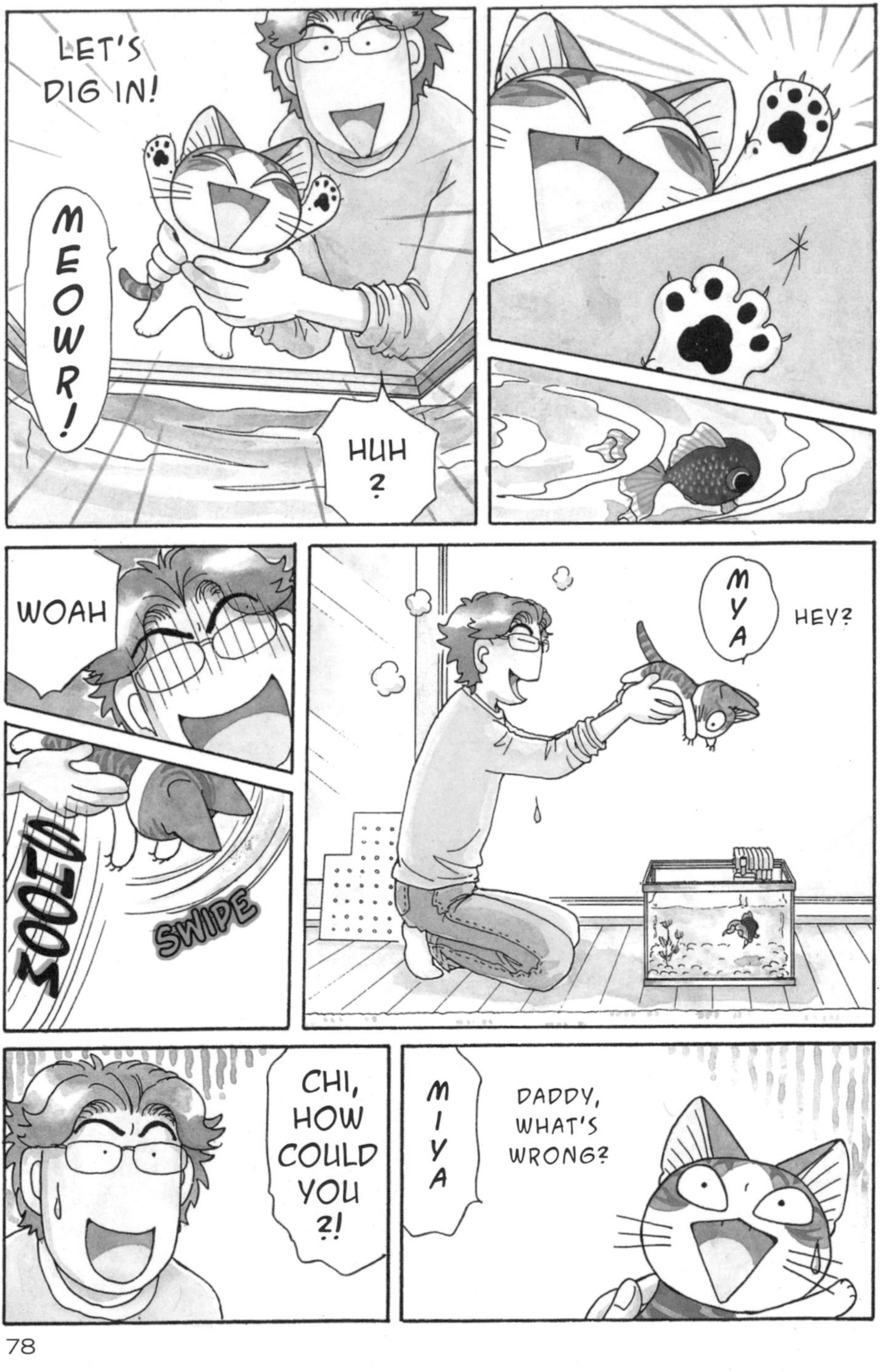
LET'S DIG IN!
MEOWR!
HUH?
WOAH
SWIPE
MYA
HEY?
CHI, HOW COULD YOU?!
MIYA
DADDY, WHAT'S WRONG?

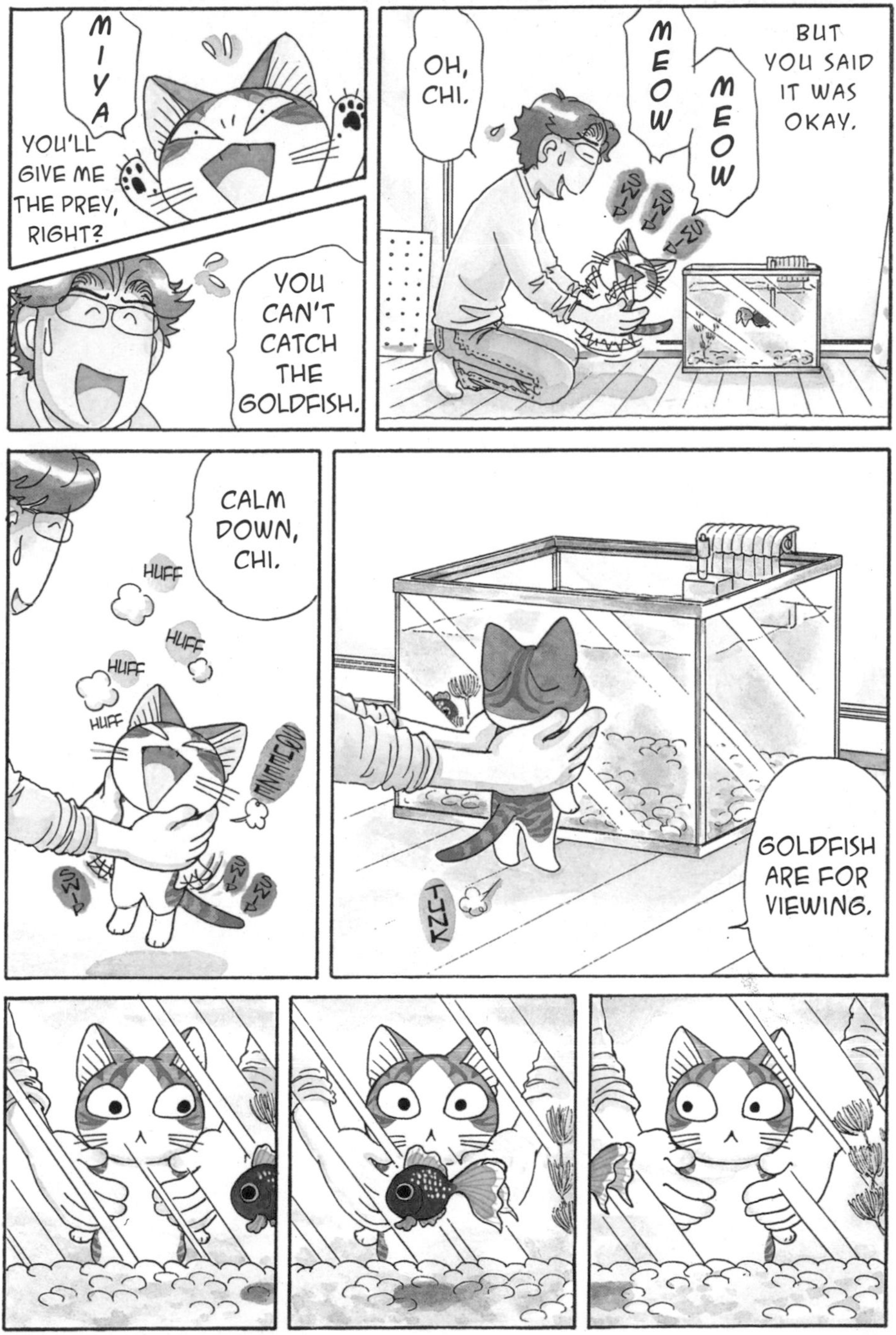
MIYA
YOU'LL GIVE ME THE PREY, RIGHT?
YOU CAN'T CATCH THE GOLDFISH.
OH, CHI.
MEOW
MEOW
BUT YOU SAID IT WAS OKAY.
SWIP
SWIP
SWIP
CALM DOWN, CHI.
HUFF
HUFF
HUFF
HUFF
SWIP
SWIP
SWIP
GOLDFISH ARE FOR VIEWING.
TUNK

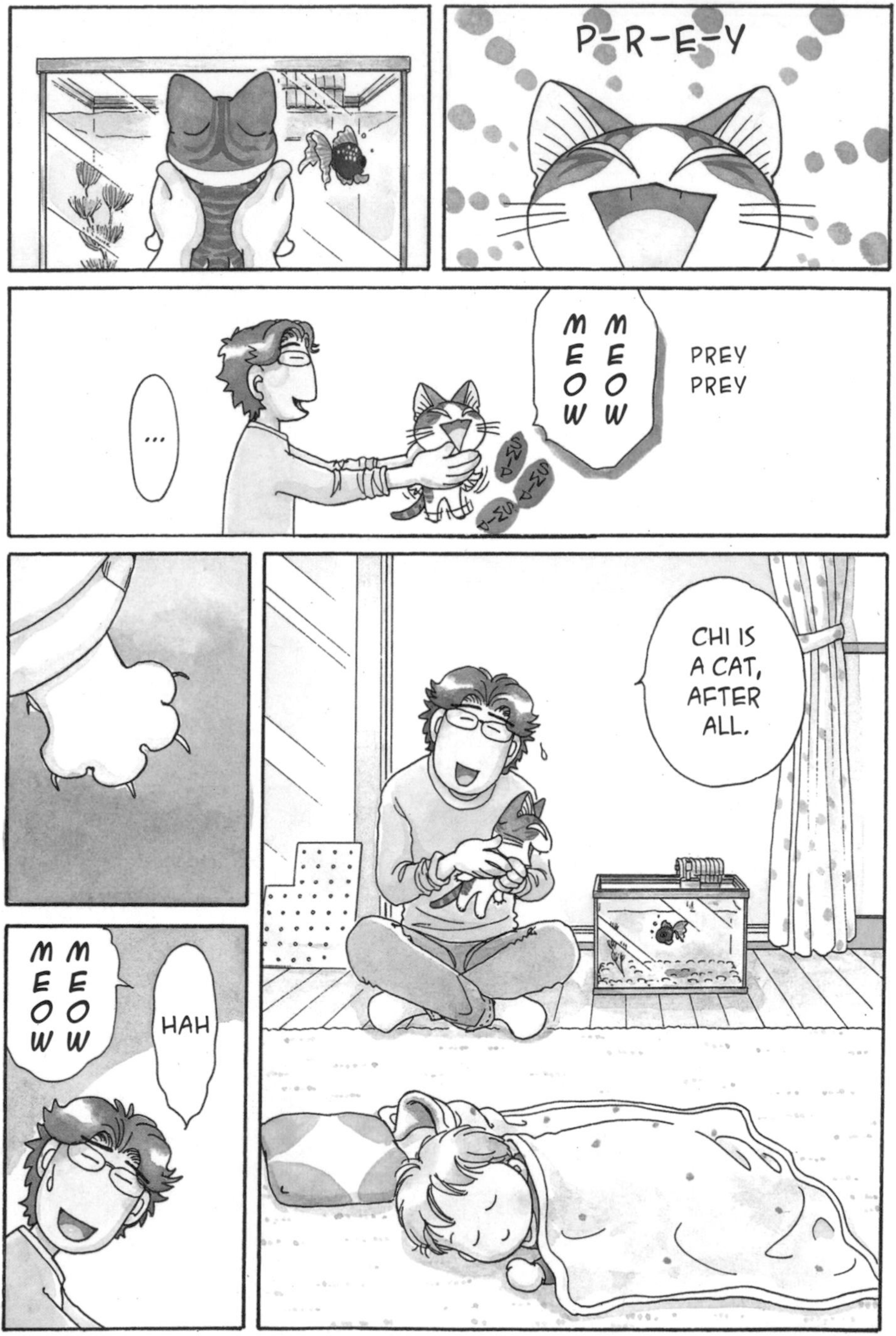
P-R-E-Y
...
MEOW MEOW
PREY PREY
MEOW MEOW
HAH
CHI IS A CAT, AFTER ALL.

**the end**

# homemade 121: a cat is cheesed

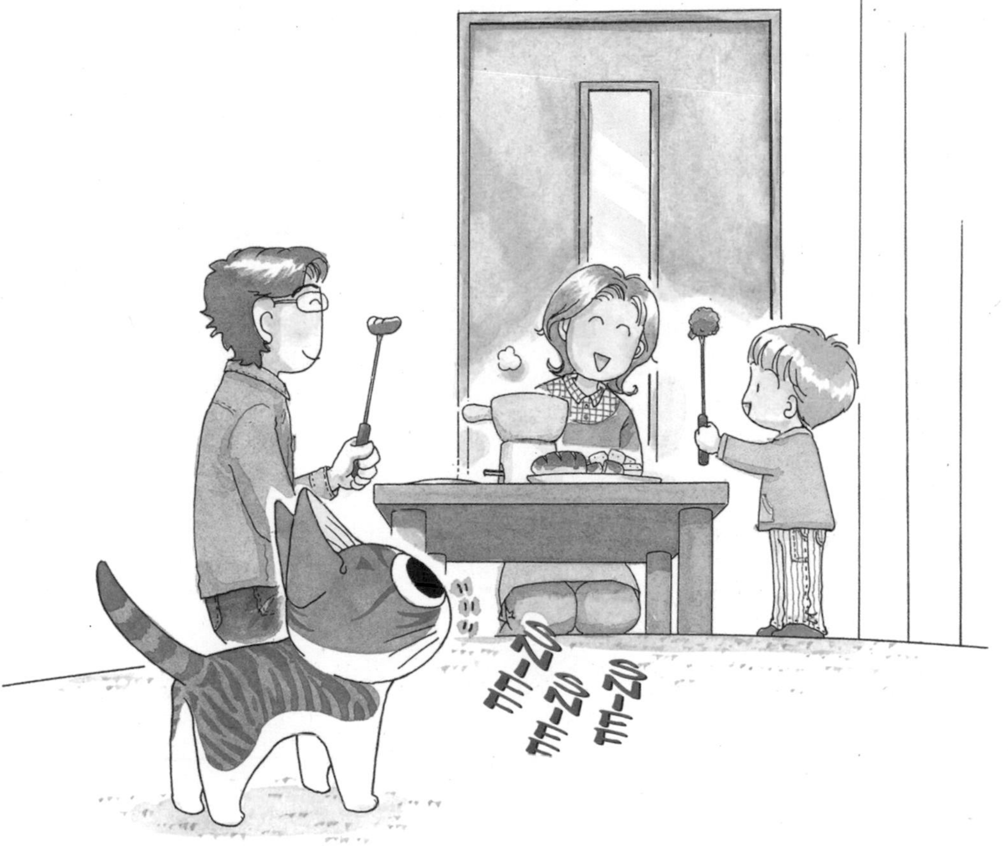
SU-TTT
SU-TTT
SU-TTT

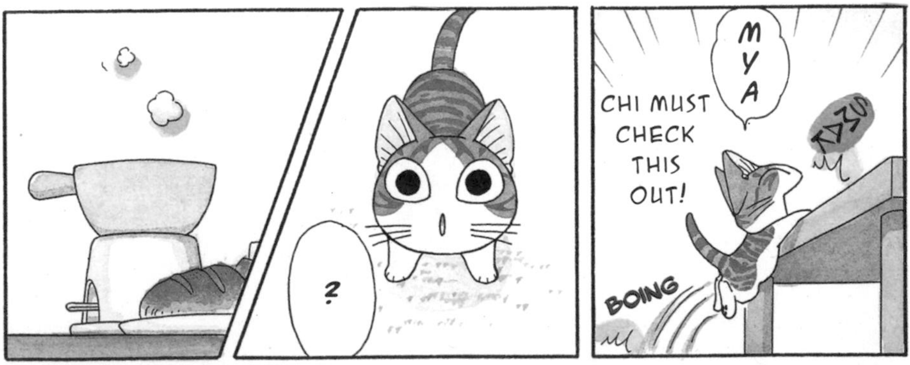
?
MYA
CHI MUST CHECK THIS OUT!
BOING

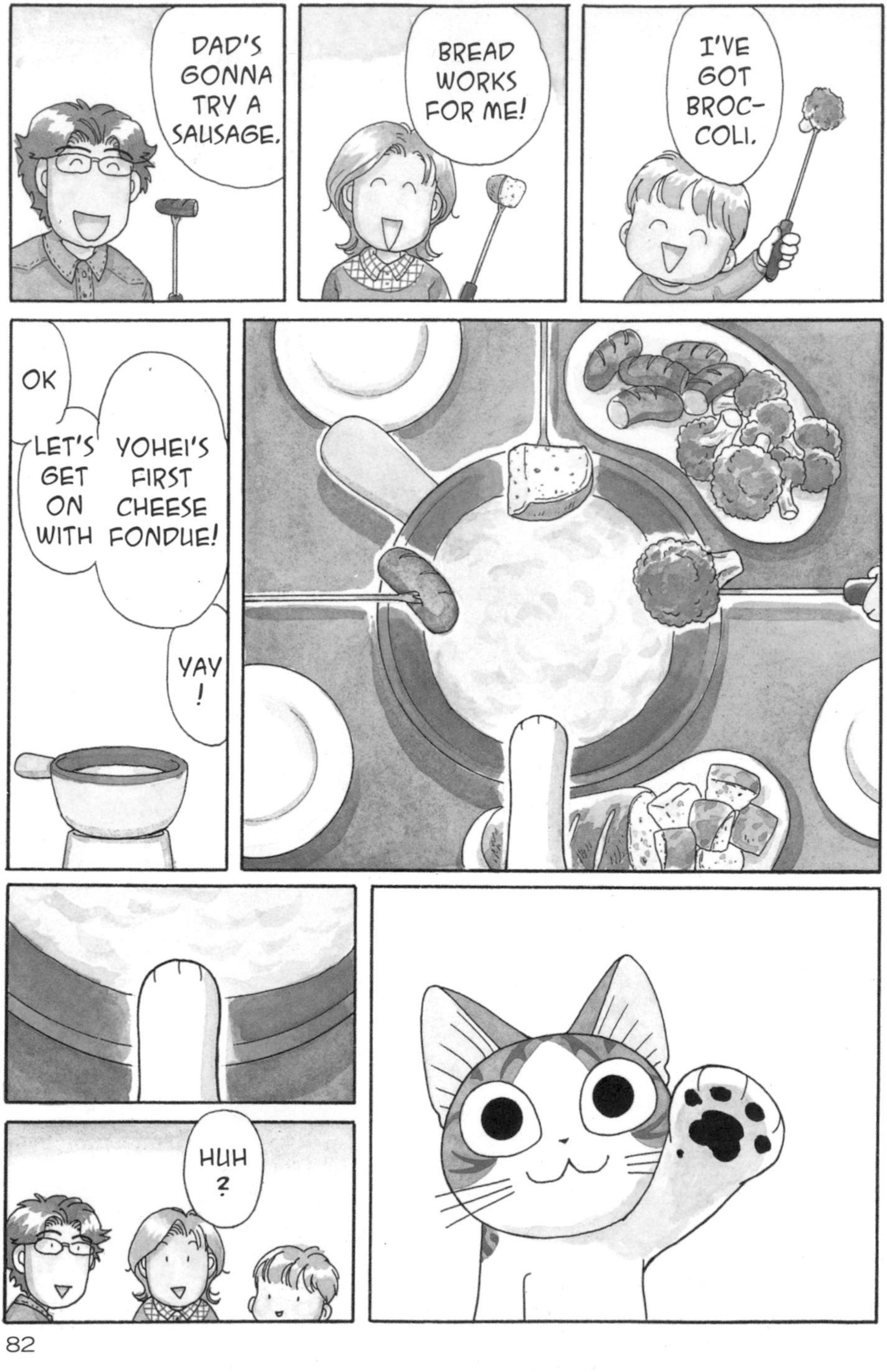
DAD'S GONNA TRY A SAUSAGE.
BREAD WORKS FOR ME!
I'VE GOT BROC-COLI.
OK
LET'S GET ON WITH
YOHEI'S FIRST CHEESE FONDUE!
YAY!
HUH?

REACH

CHI,
STOP!

WOAH, WHAT A FRIGHT!

WE DON'T WANT A CHI'S FONDUE!

SO SCAREWY.

FWIP

HEY?

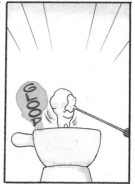

GLOOP

GLOOP

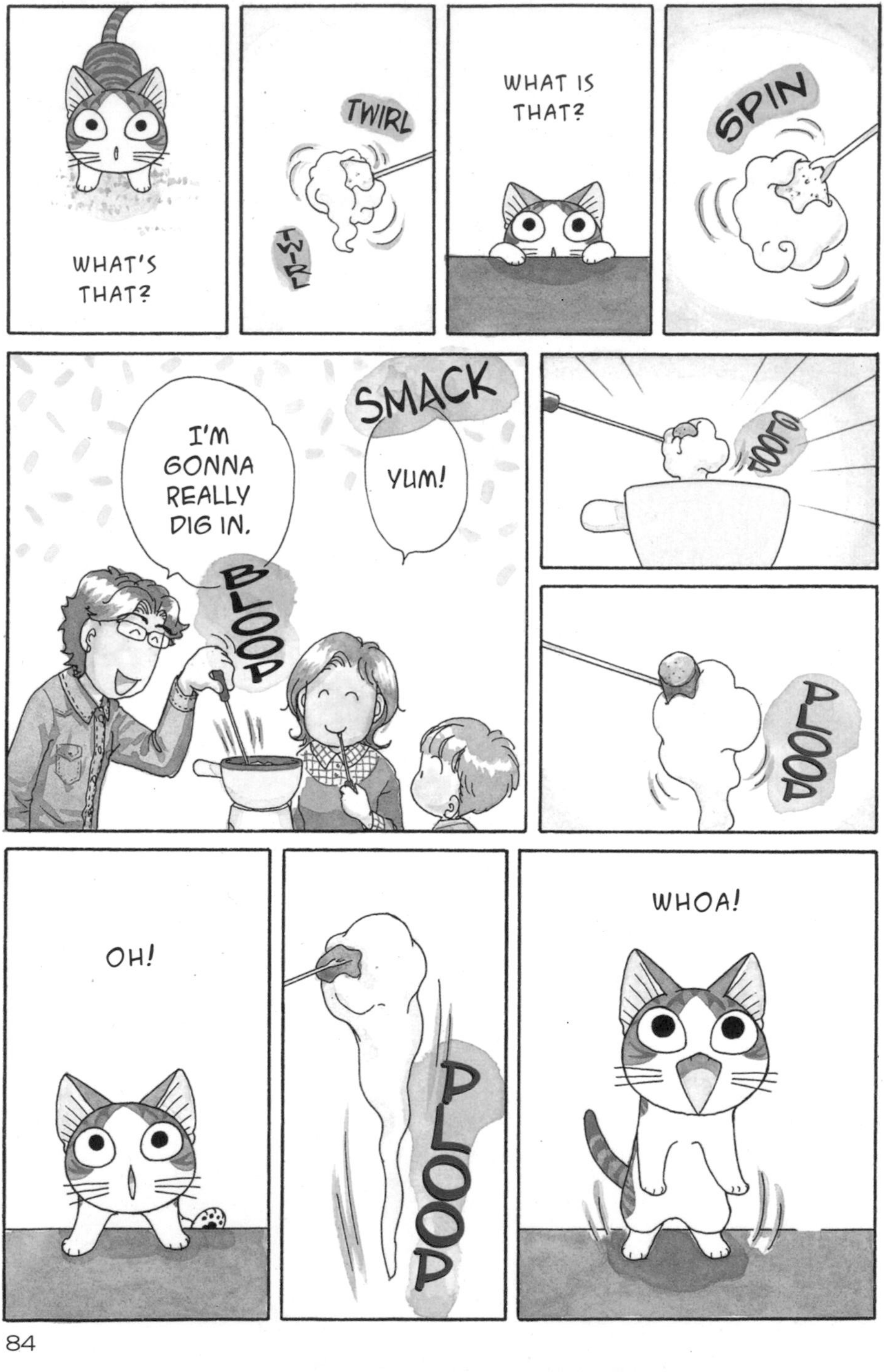
WHAT'S THAT?
TWIRL
TWIRL
WHAT IS THAT?
SPIN
SMACK
I'M GONNA REALLY DIG IN.
YUM!
BLOOP
PLOOP
PLOOP
OH!
PLOOP
WHOA!

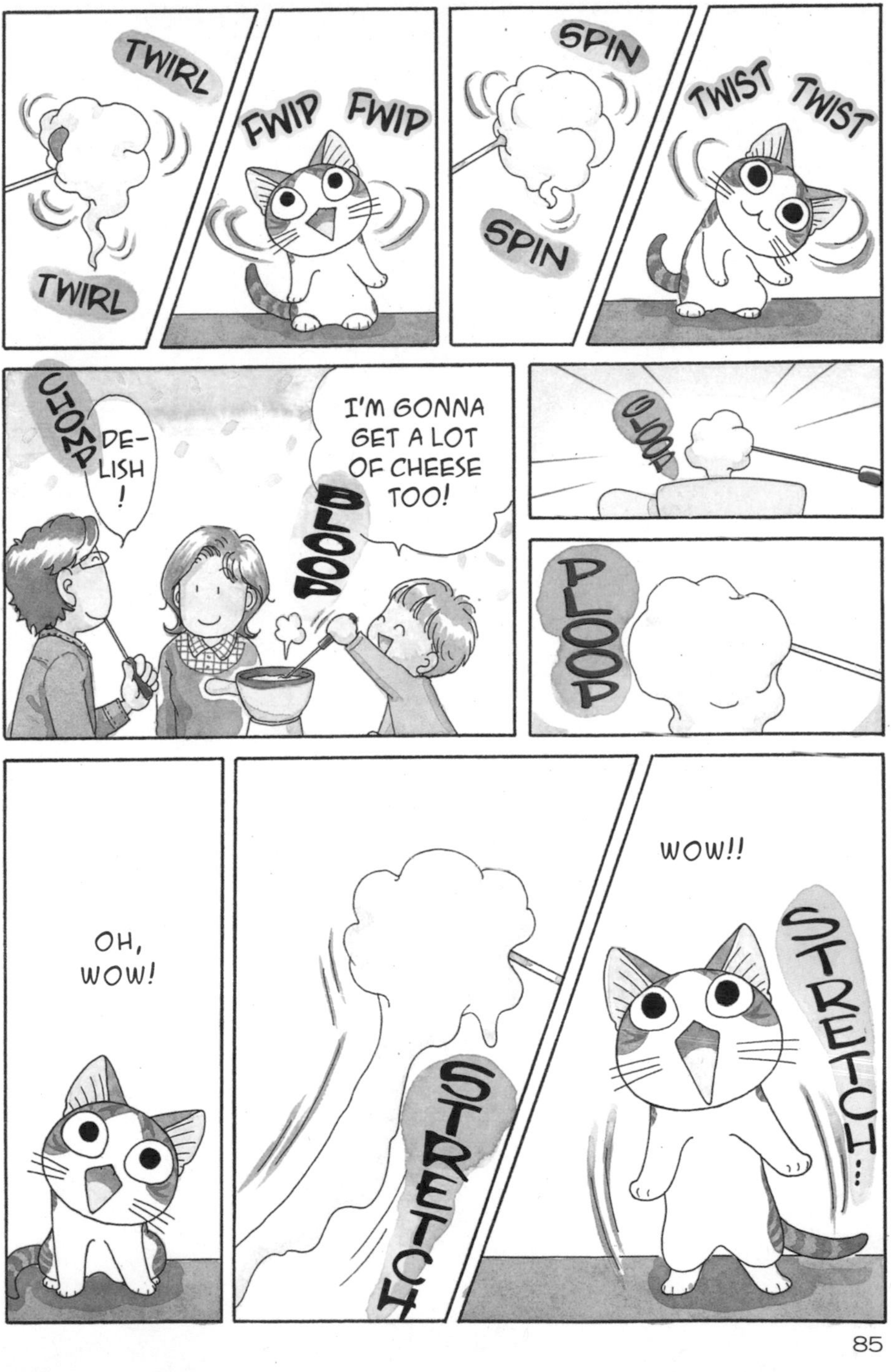
TWIRL
TWIRL
FWIP FWIP
SPIN
SPIN
TWIST TWIST
CHOMP
DE-
LISH
!
I'M GONNA
GET A LOT
OF CHEESE
TOO!
BLOOP
GLOOP
PLOOP
OH,
WOW!
STRETCH
WOW!!
STRETCH...

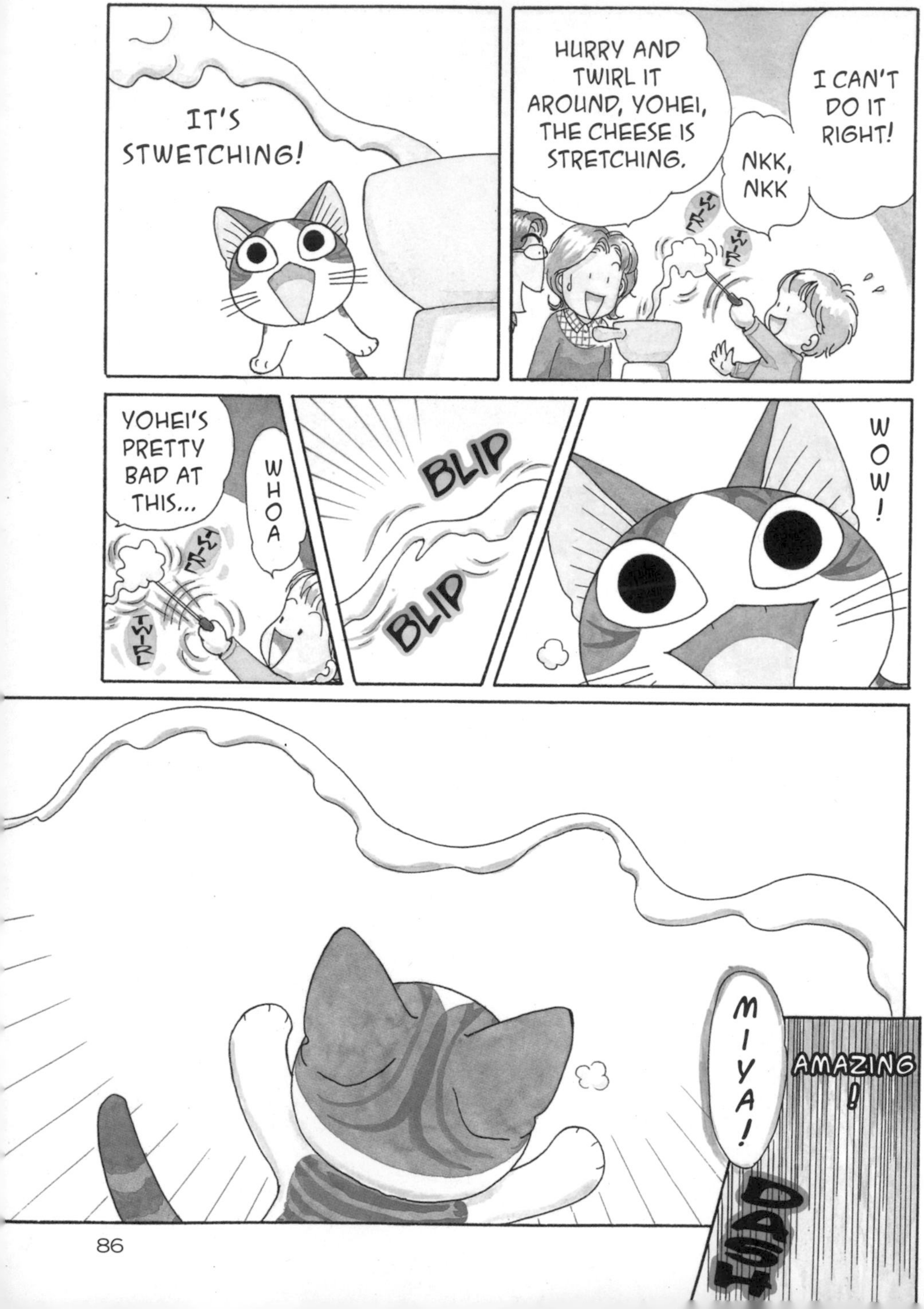
IT'S STWETCHING!
HURRY AND TWIRL IT AROUND, YOHEI, THE CHEESE IS STRETCHING.
NKK, NKK
I CAN'T DO IT RIGHT!
TWIRL
TWIRL
YOHEI'S PRETTY BAD AT THIS...
WHOA
TWIRL
TWIRL
BLIP
BLIP
WOW!
MIYA!
AMAZING!
DASH

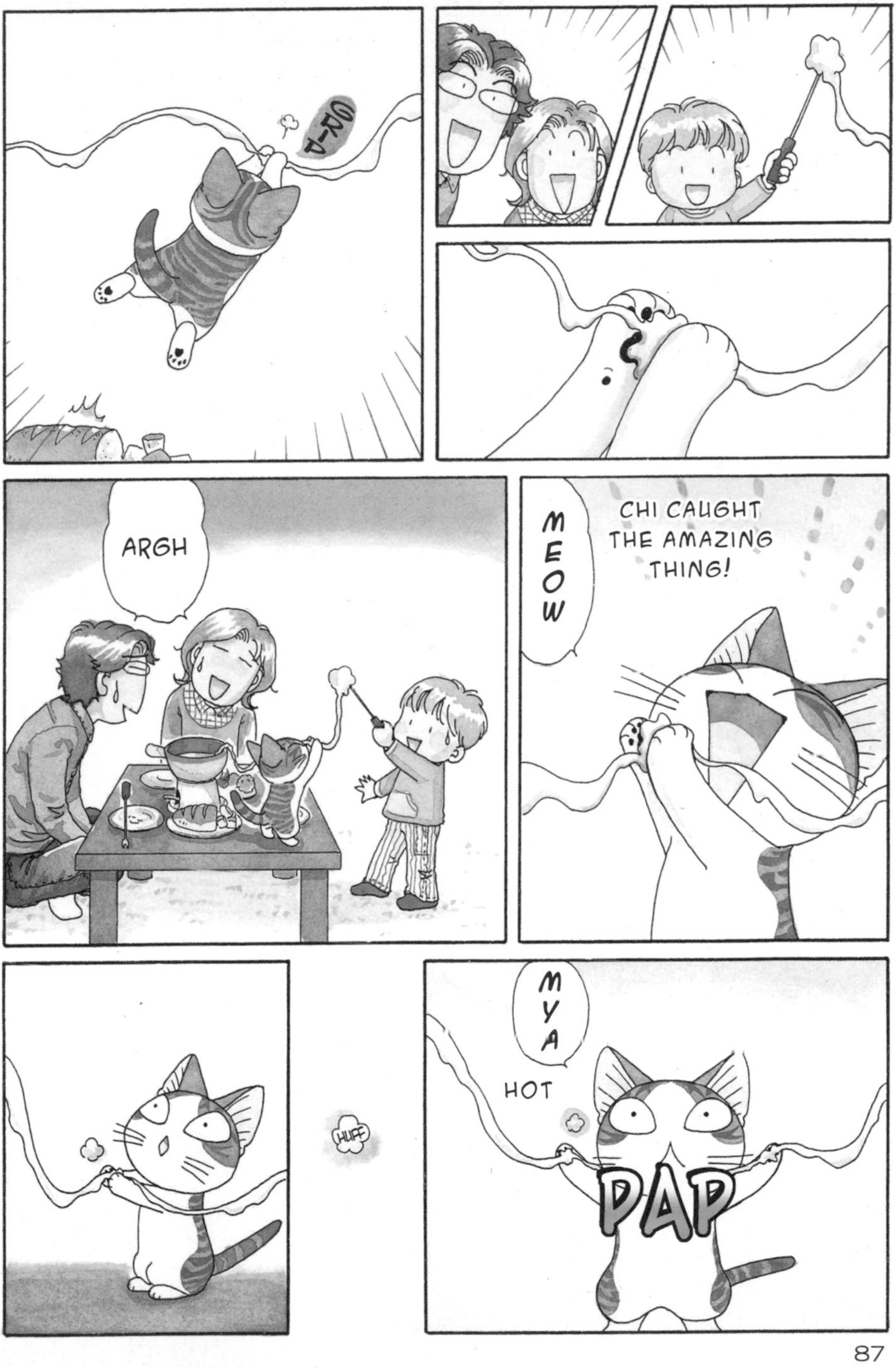
GRIP
ARGH
MEOW
CHI CAUGHT THE AMAZING THING!
HUFF
MYA
HOT
PAP

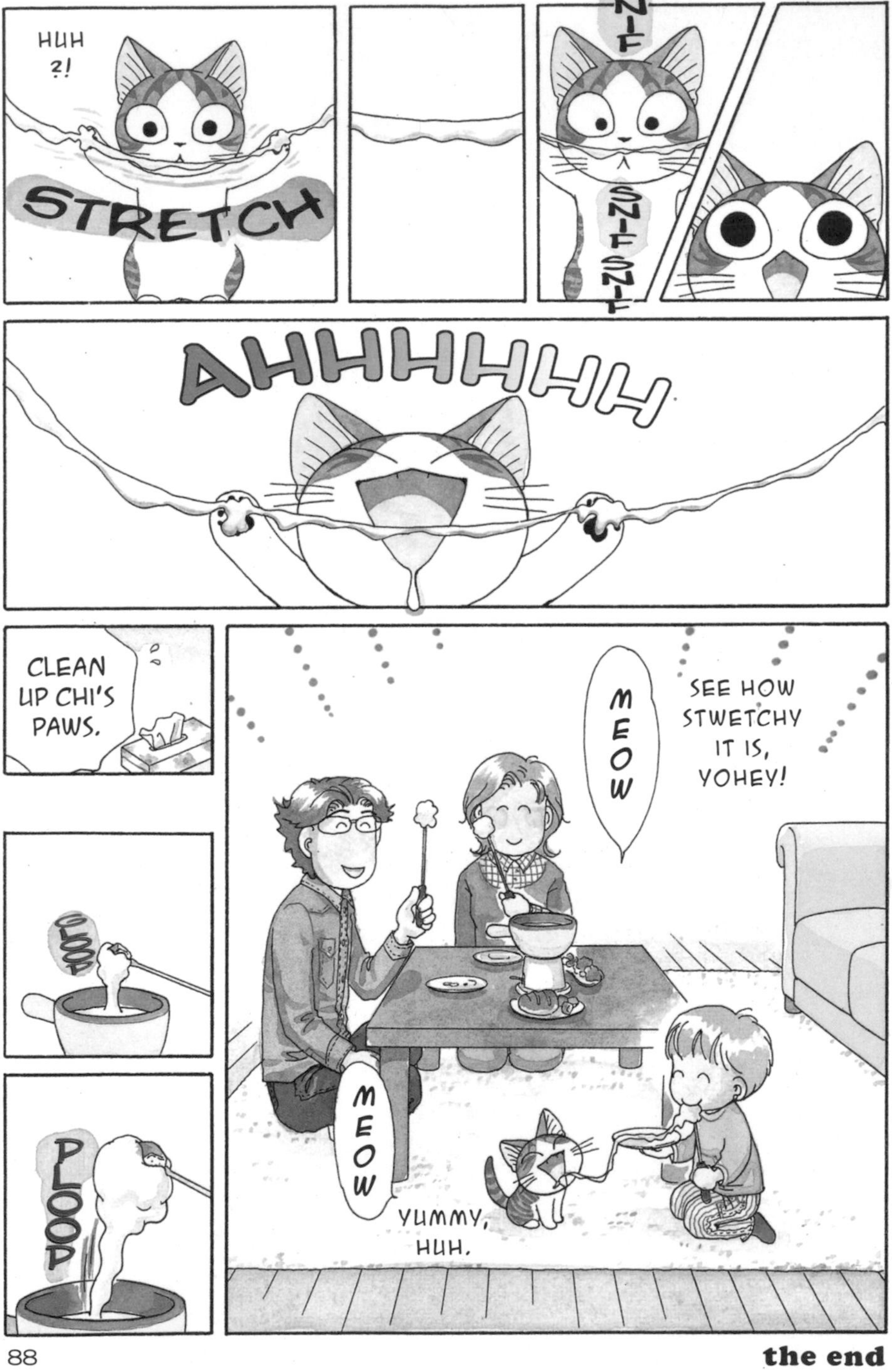
HUH ?!
STRETCH
SNIF
SNIF SNIF SNIF
AHHHHHH
CLEAN UP CHI'S PAWS.
GLOOP
PLOOP
MEOW
SEE HOW STWETCHY IT IS, YOHEY!
MEOW
YUMMY, HUH.



the end

## homemade 122: a cat feels a presence

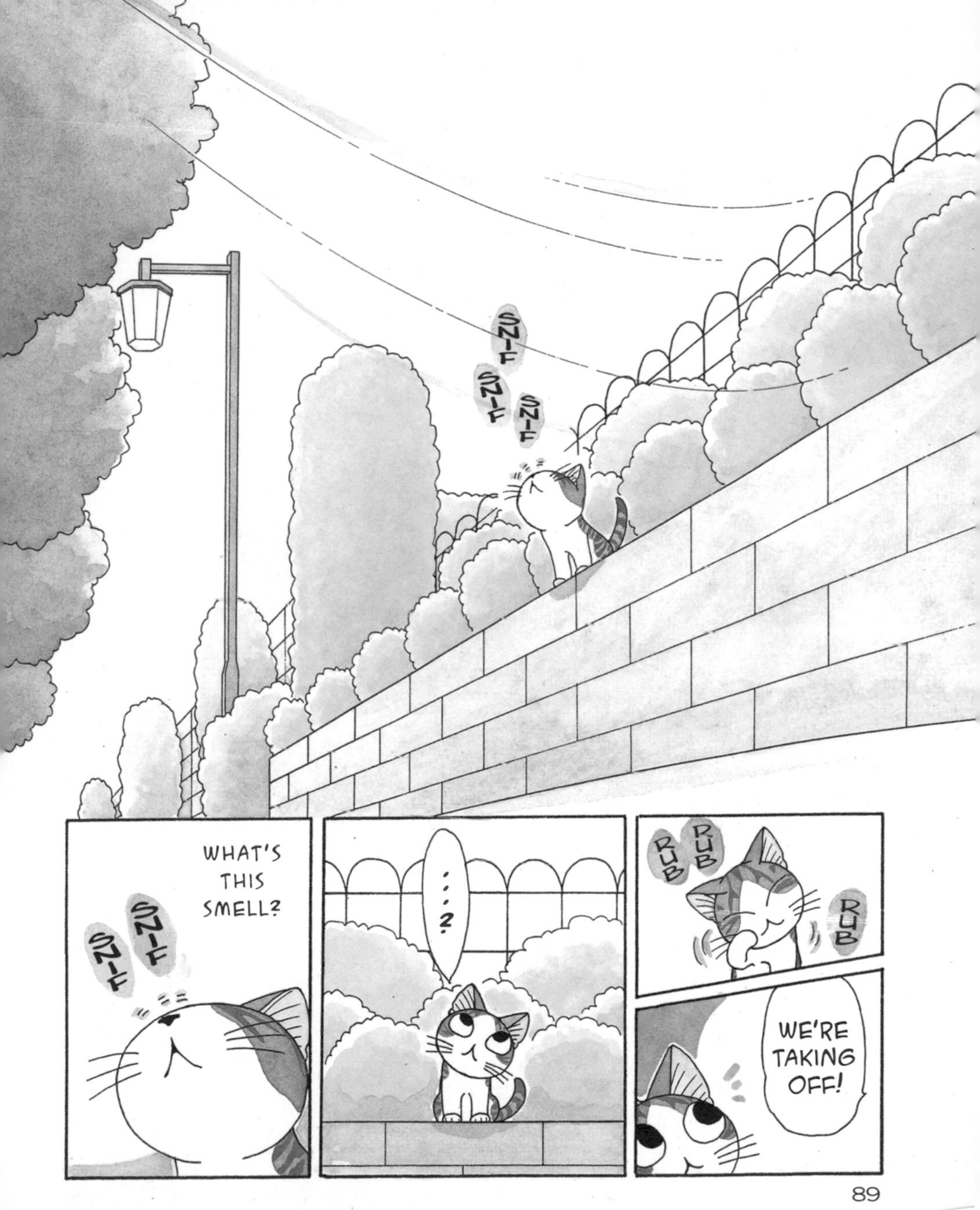
SNIF
SNIF
SNIF
SNIF
SNIF
WHAT'S THIS SMELL?
...?
RUB
RUB
RUB
WE'RE TAKING OFF!

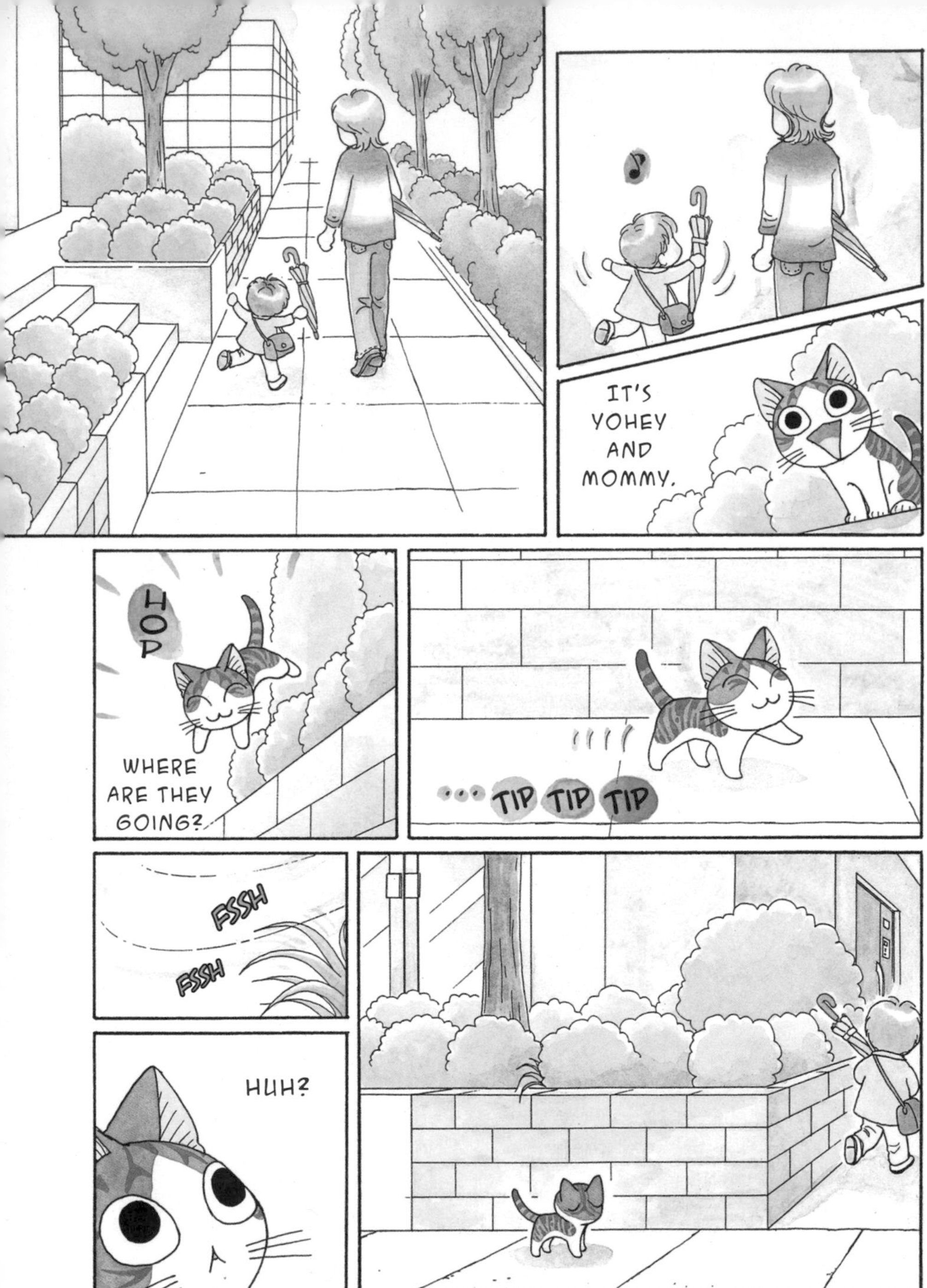
IT'S YOHEY AND MOMMY.
HOP
WHERE ARE THEY GOING?
...TIP TIP TIP
FSSH
FSSH
HUH?

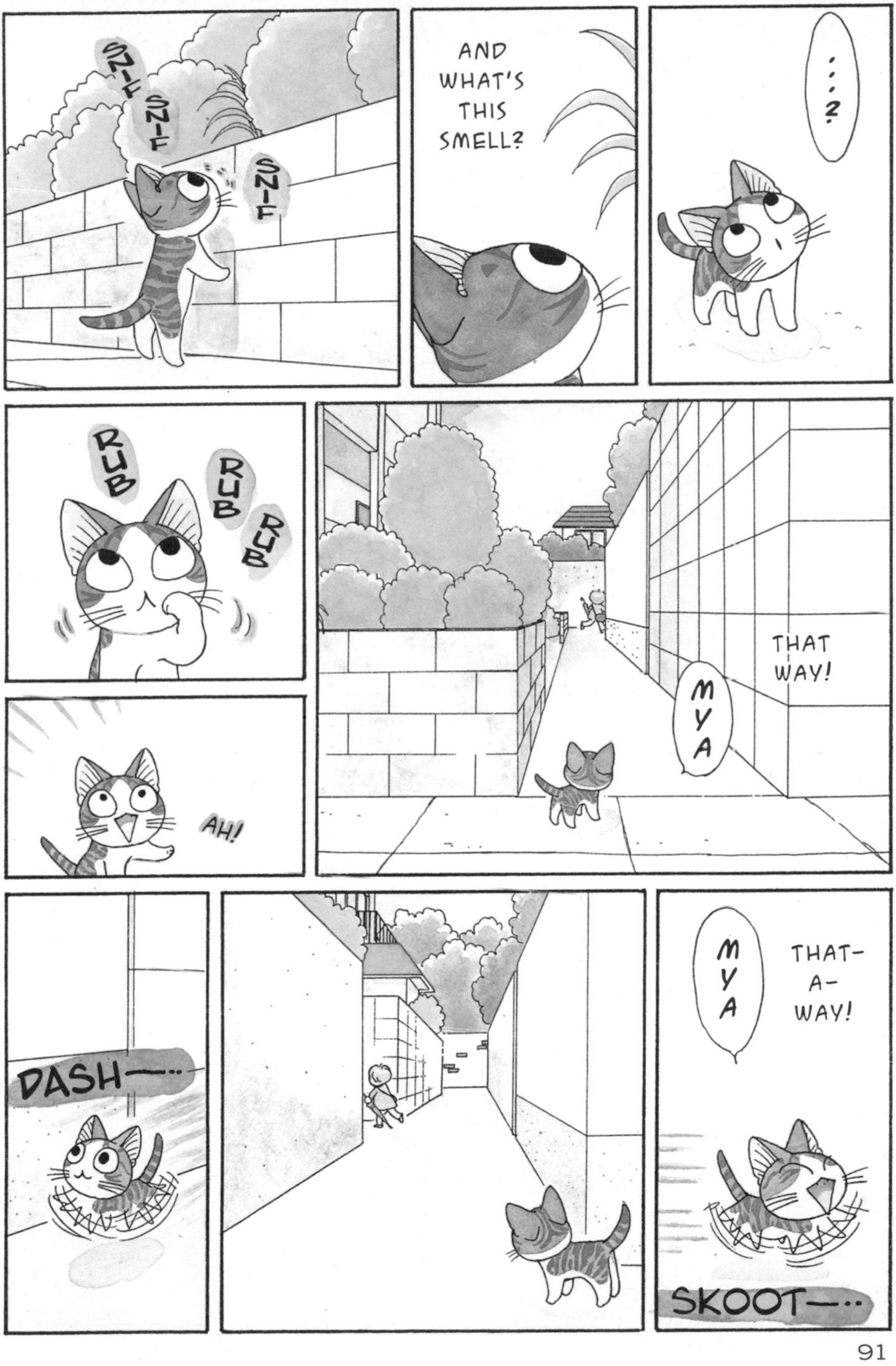
SNIF
SNIF
SNIF
AND WHAT'S THIS SMELL?
...?
RUB
RUB
RUB
AH!
THAT WAY!
MYA
DASH—..
MYA
THAT-A-WAY!
SKOOT—..

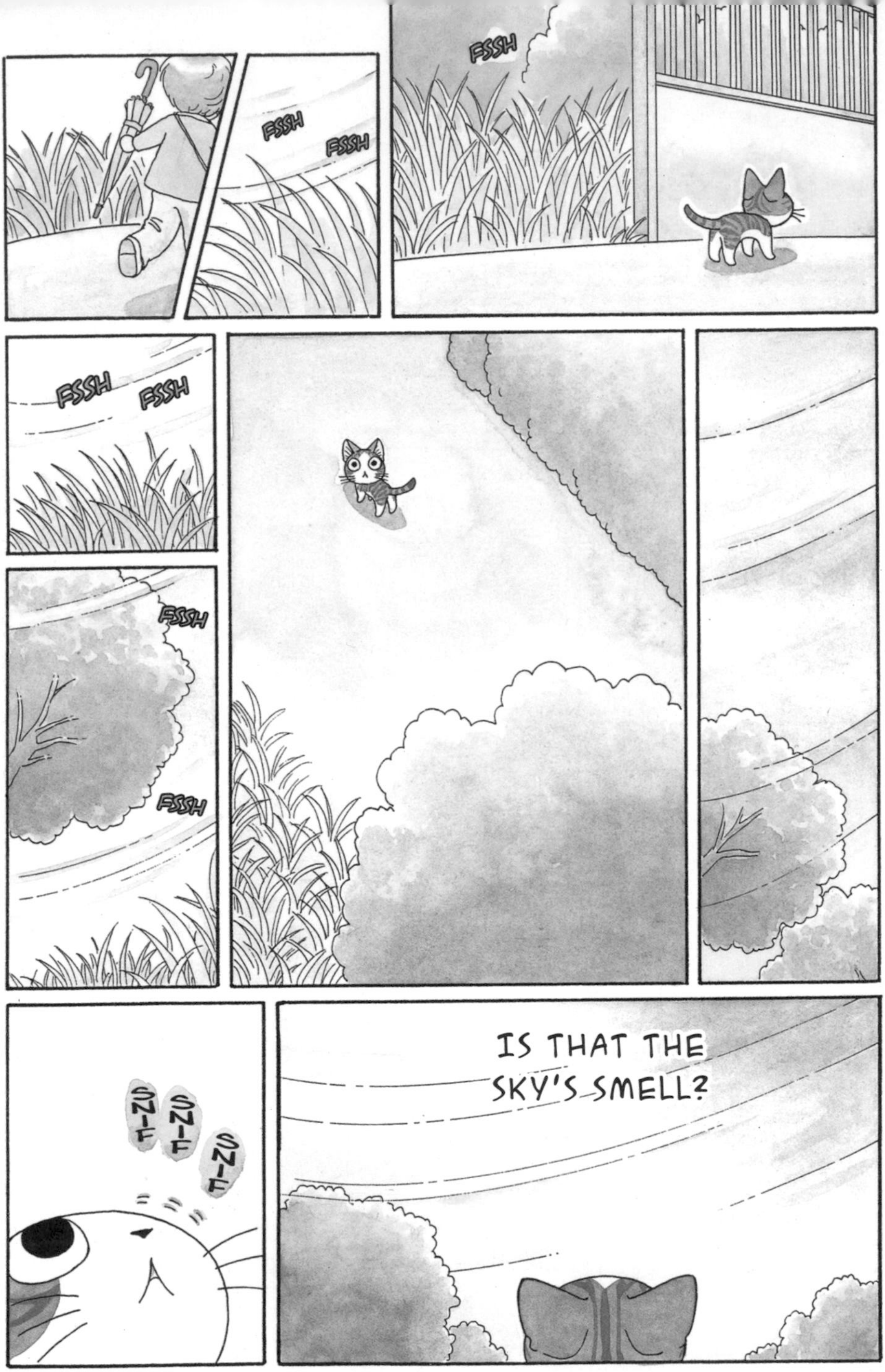
FSSH
FSSH
FSSH
FSSH
FSSH
FSSH
FSSH
SNIF
SNIF
SNIF
IS THAT THE SKY'S SMELL?

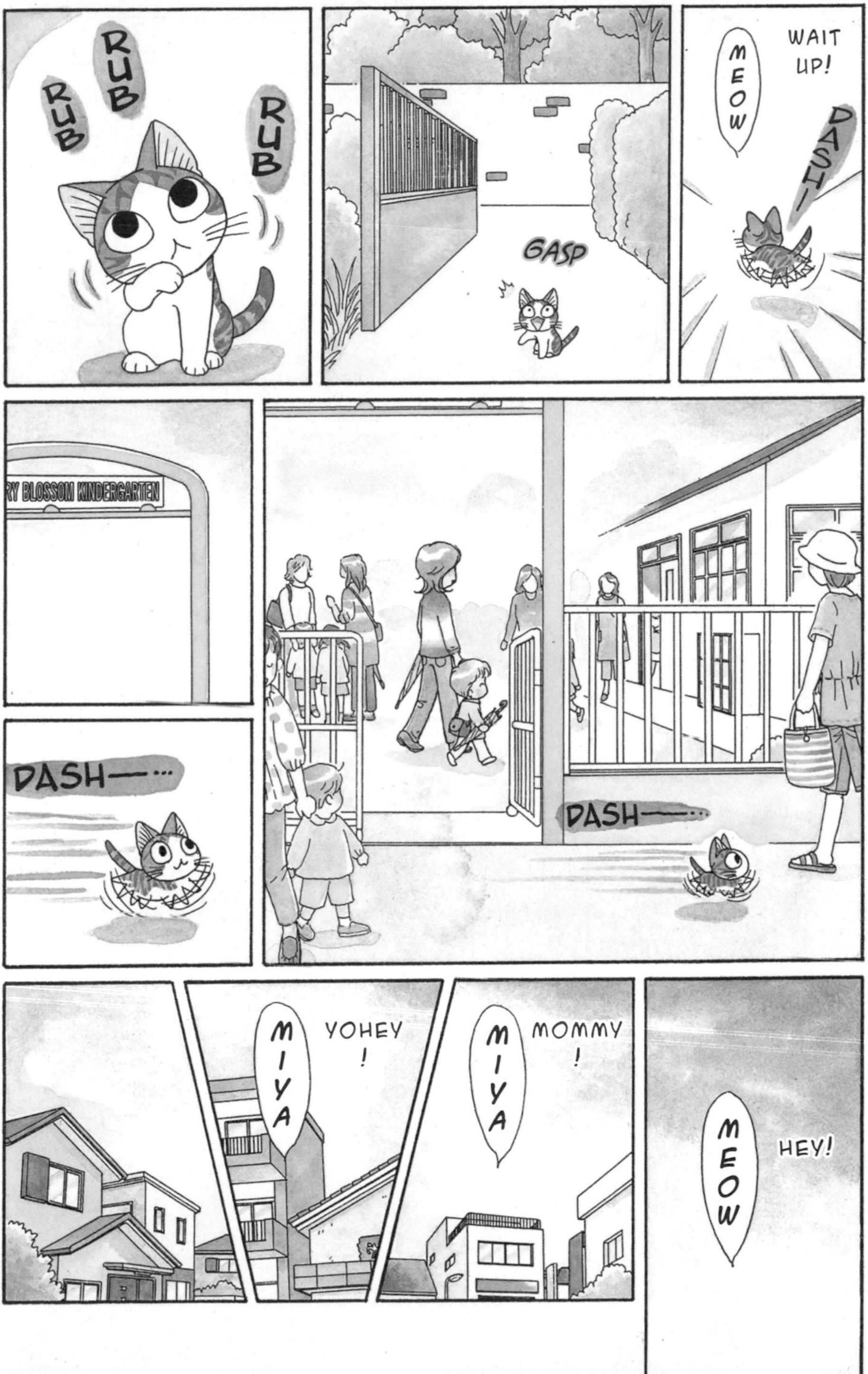
RUB
RUB
RUB
GASP
MEOW
WAIT UP!
DASH
RY BLOSSOM KINDERGARTEN
DASH—...
DASH—...
MIYA
YOHEY!
MIYA
MOMMY!
MEOW
HEY!

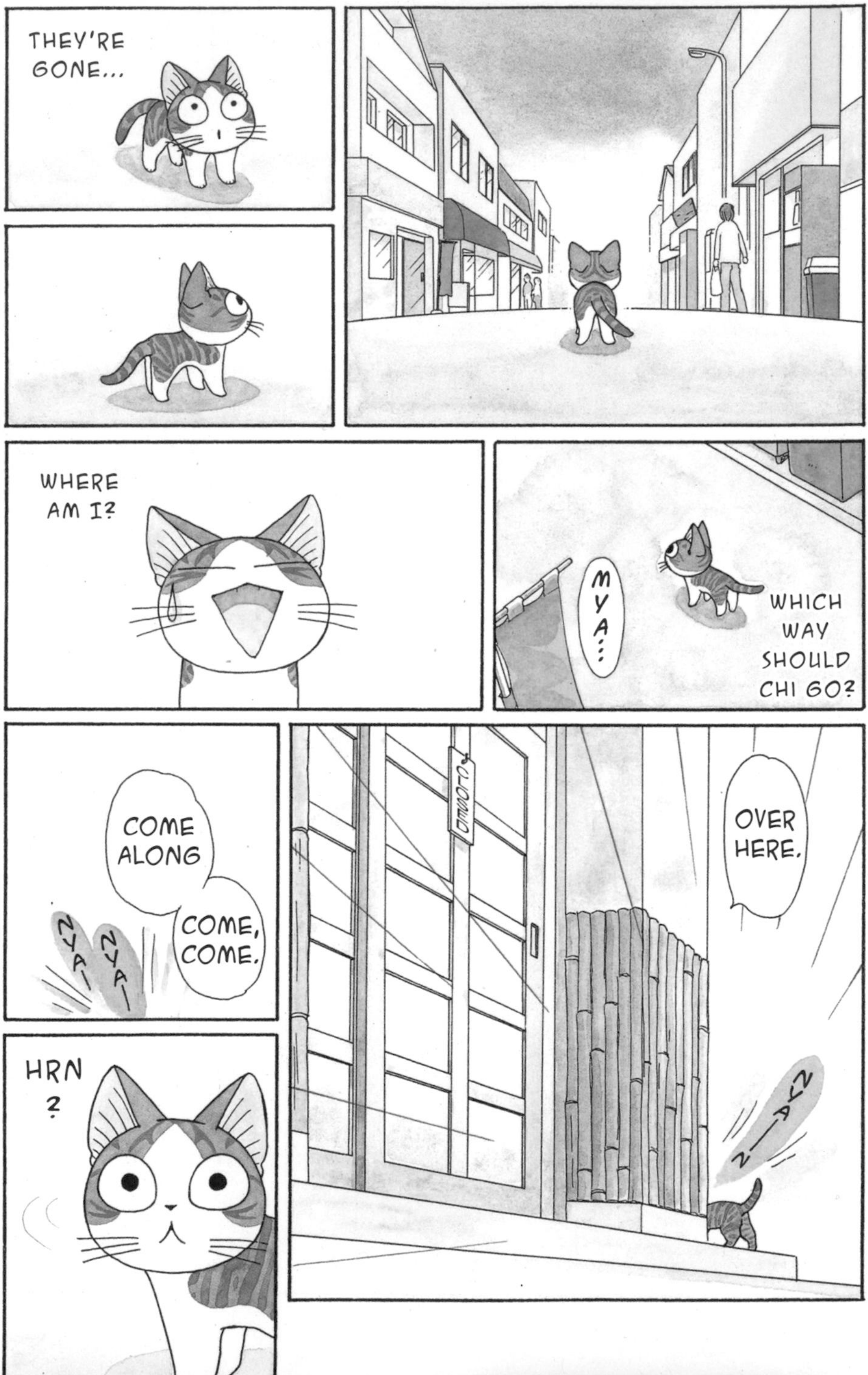

THEY'RE GONE...
WHERE AM I?
MYA...
WHICH WAY SHOULD CHI GO?
COME ALONG
COME, COME.
NYA NYA
CLOSED
OVER HERE.
NYA
HRN ?

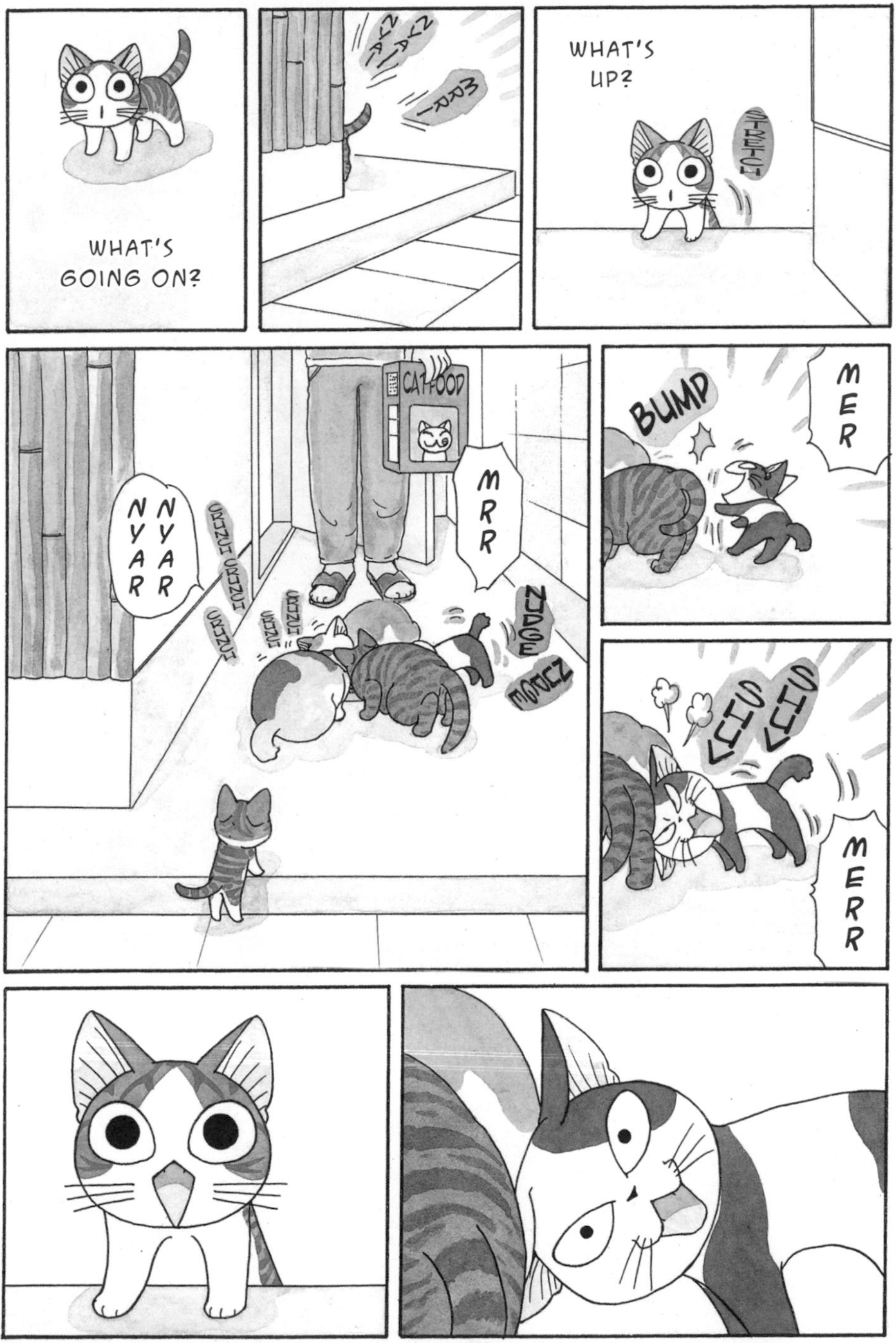
WHAT'S GOING ON?
NYA—
NYA—
MRR—
WHAT'S UP?
STRETCH
CATFOOD
NYAR NYAR
CRUNCH CRUNCH
CRUNCH
CRUNCH
CRUNCH
MRR
NUDGE
BUMP
MER
SHUV
SHUV
MERR

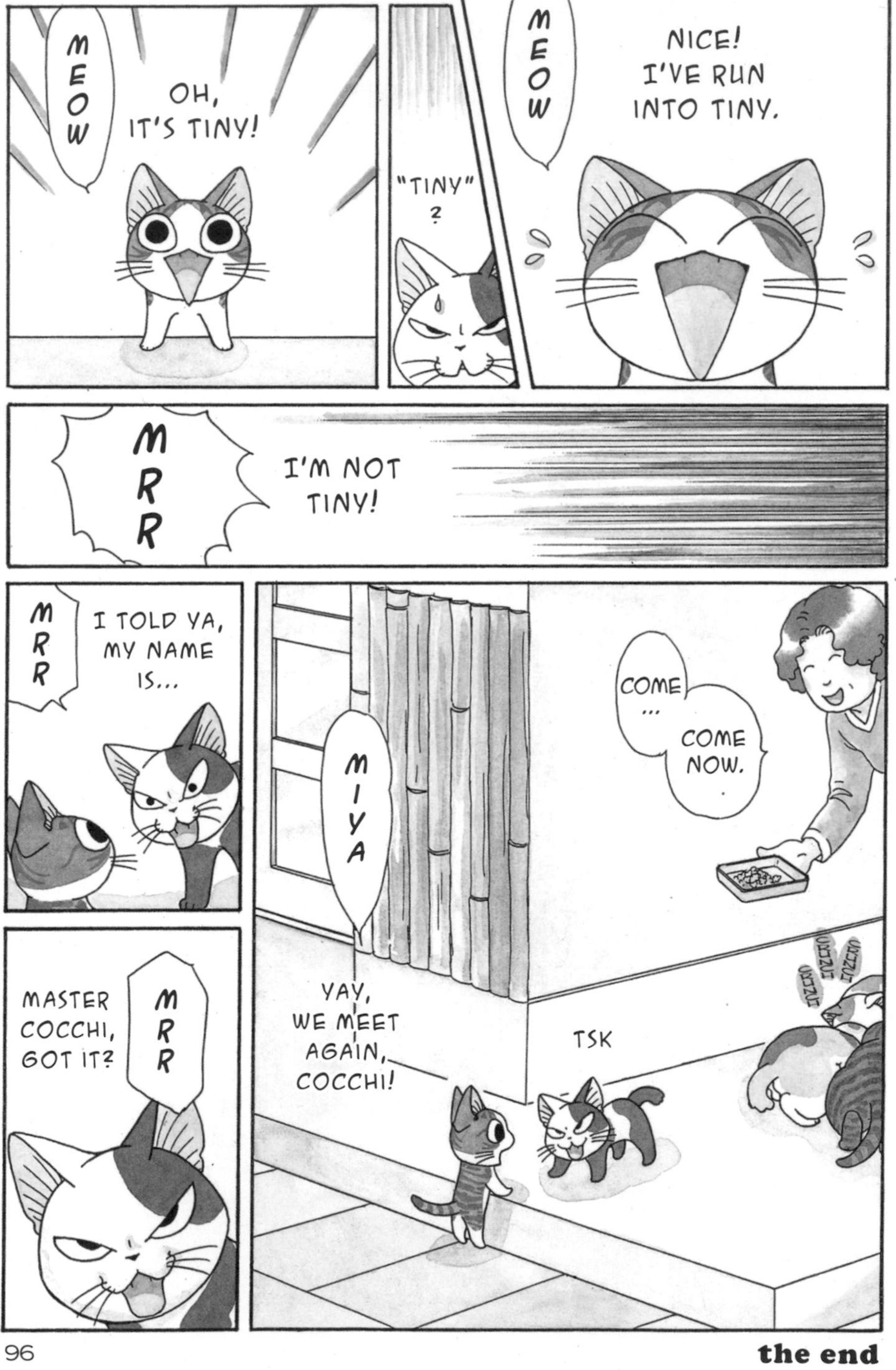
MEOW
OH, IT'S TINY!
"TINY"?
MEOW
NICE! I'VE RUN INTO TINY.
MRR
I'M NOT TINY!
MRR
I TOLD YA, MY NAME IS...
MASTER COCCHI, GOT IT?
MRR
COME... COME NOW.
MIYA
YAY, WE MEET AGAIN, COCCHI!
TSK

the end

# homemade 123: a cat senses an anomaly

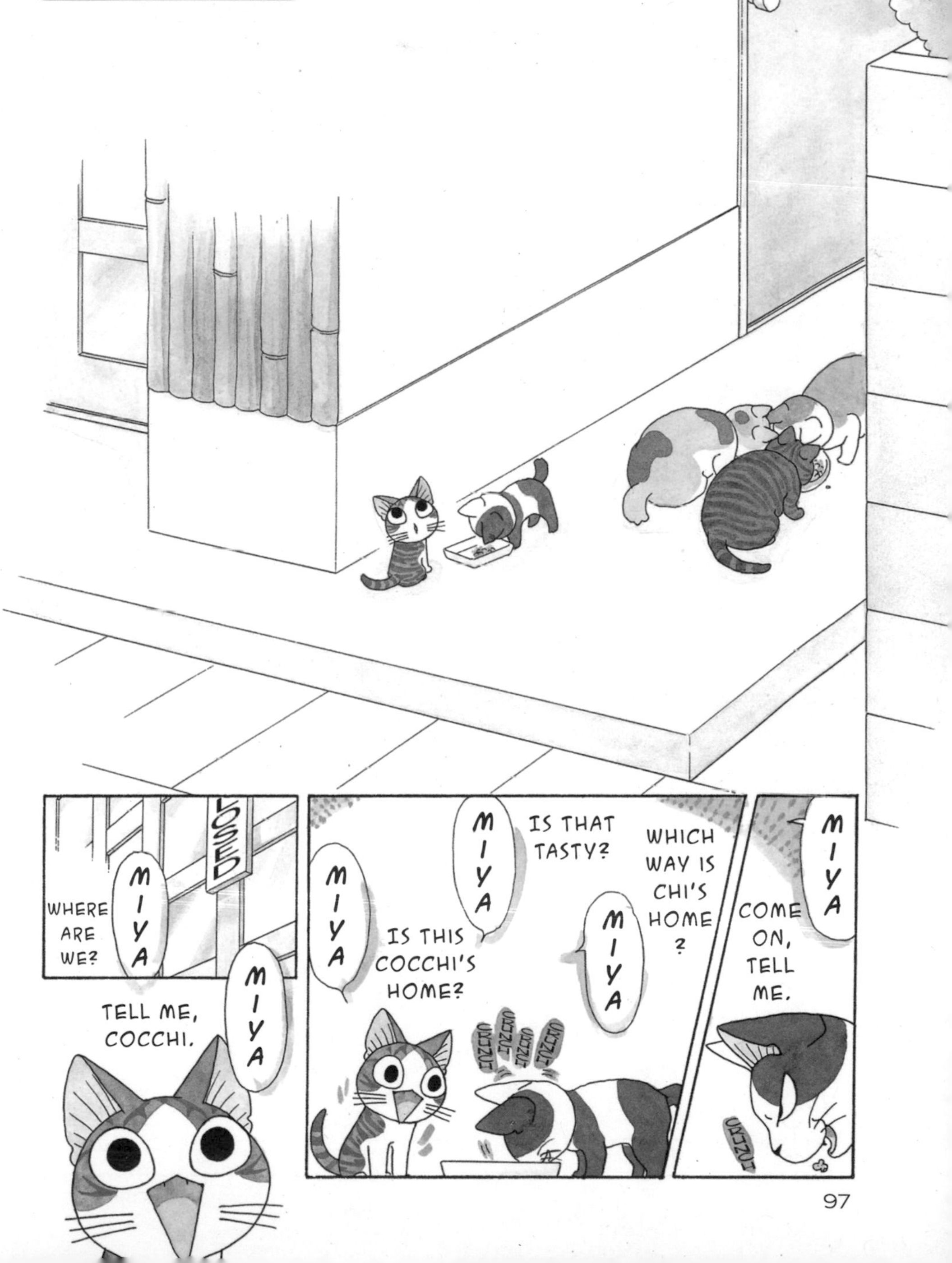
CLOSED
WHERE ARE WE?
MIYA
TELL ME, COCCHI.
MIYA
MIYA
IS THIS COCCHI'S HOME?
MIYA
IS THAT TASTY?
WHICH WAY IS CHI'S HOME?
MIYA
MIYA
COME ON, TELL ME.

MRR

QUIET!

LOPE

LOPE LOPE

SNIF SNIF SNIF SNIF SNIF SNIF SNIF SNIF SNIF

MEROWR MEROWR

MEROWR MEROWR

SLINK SLINK SLINK SLINK SLINK

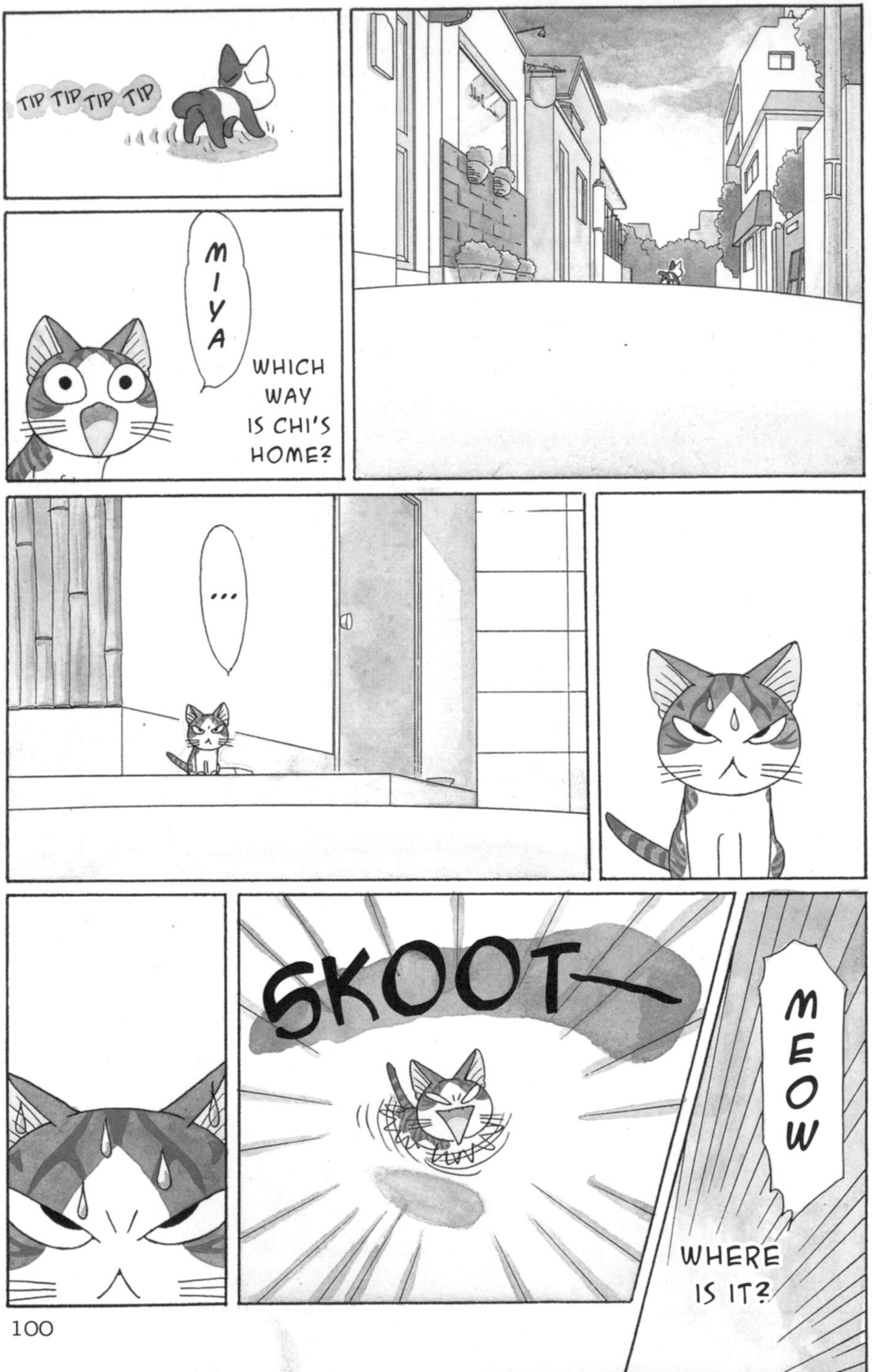
TIP TIP TIP TIP
MIYA
WHICH WAY IS CHI'S HOME?
...
SKOOT—
MEOW
WHERE IS IT?

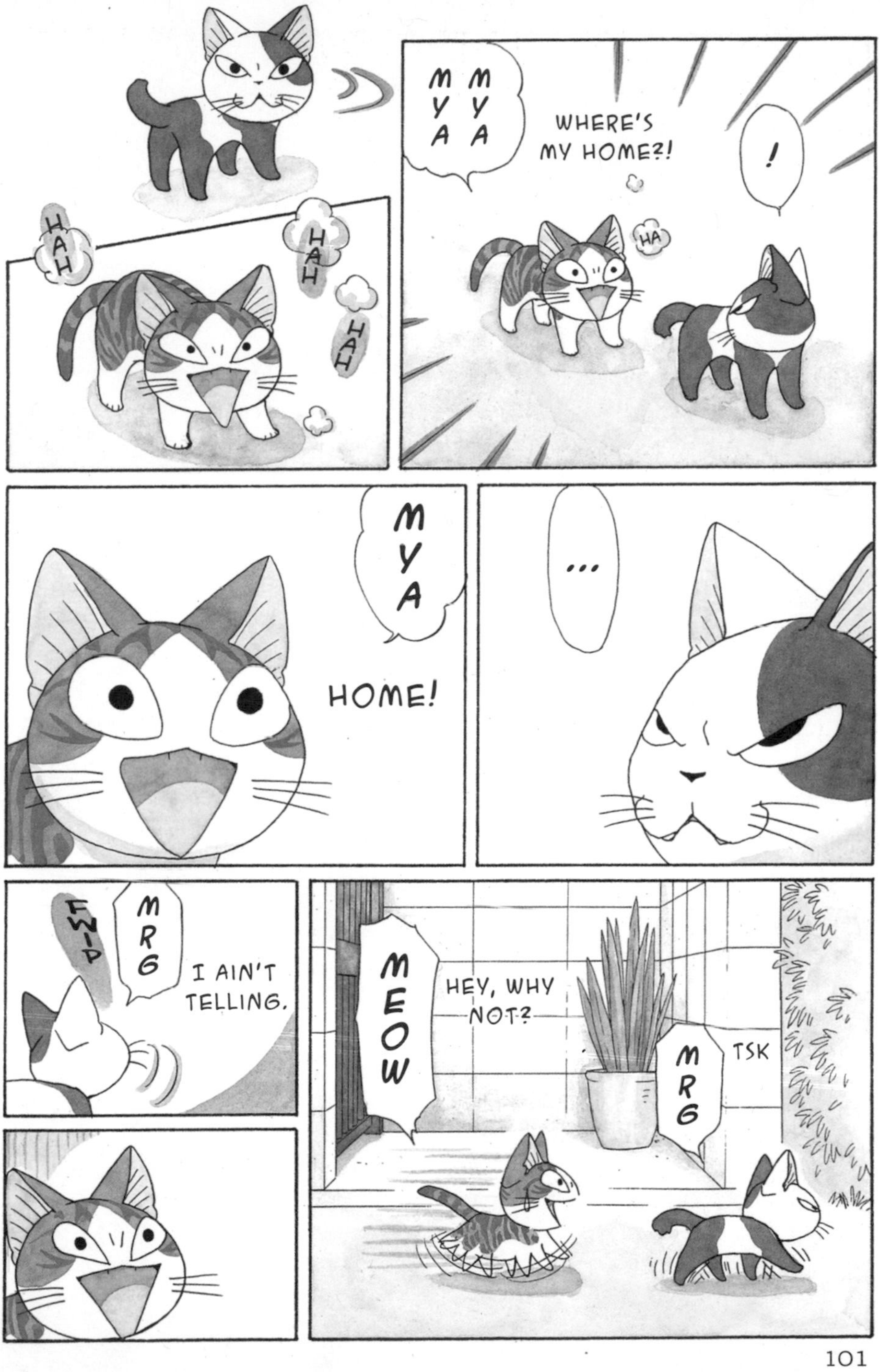
HAH
HAH
HAH
MYA MYA
WHERE'S MY HOME?!
HA
!
MYA
HOME!
...
FWIP
MRG
I AIN'T TELLING.
MEOW
HEY, WHY NOT?
MRG
TSK

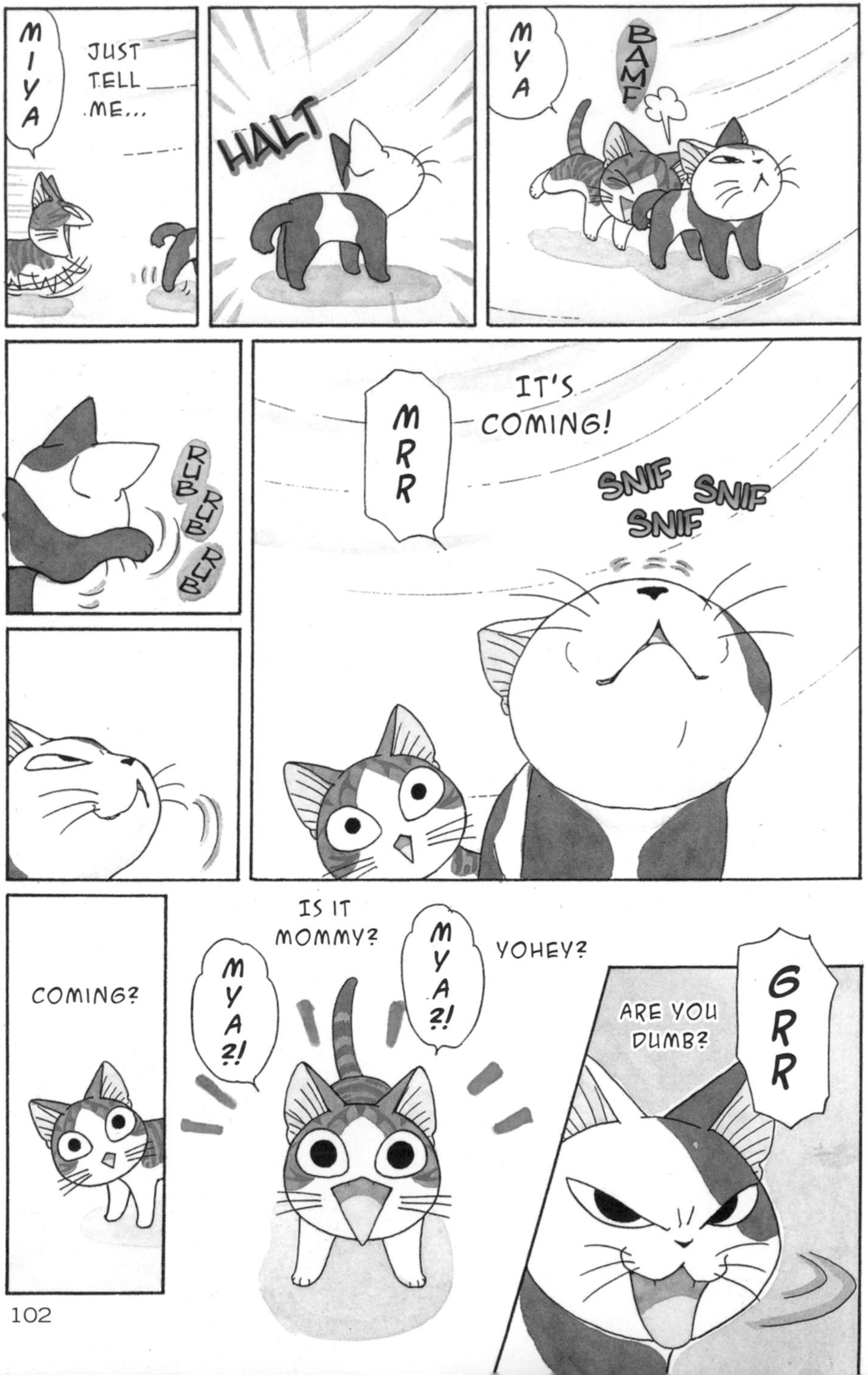
MIYA
JUST TELL ME...
HALT
MYA
BAMF
RUB RUB RUB
MRR
IT'S COMING!
SNIF SNIF SNIF
COMING?
IS IT MOMMY?
MYA?!
MYA?!
YOHEY?
ARE YOU DUMB?
GRR

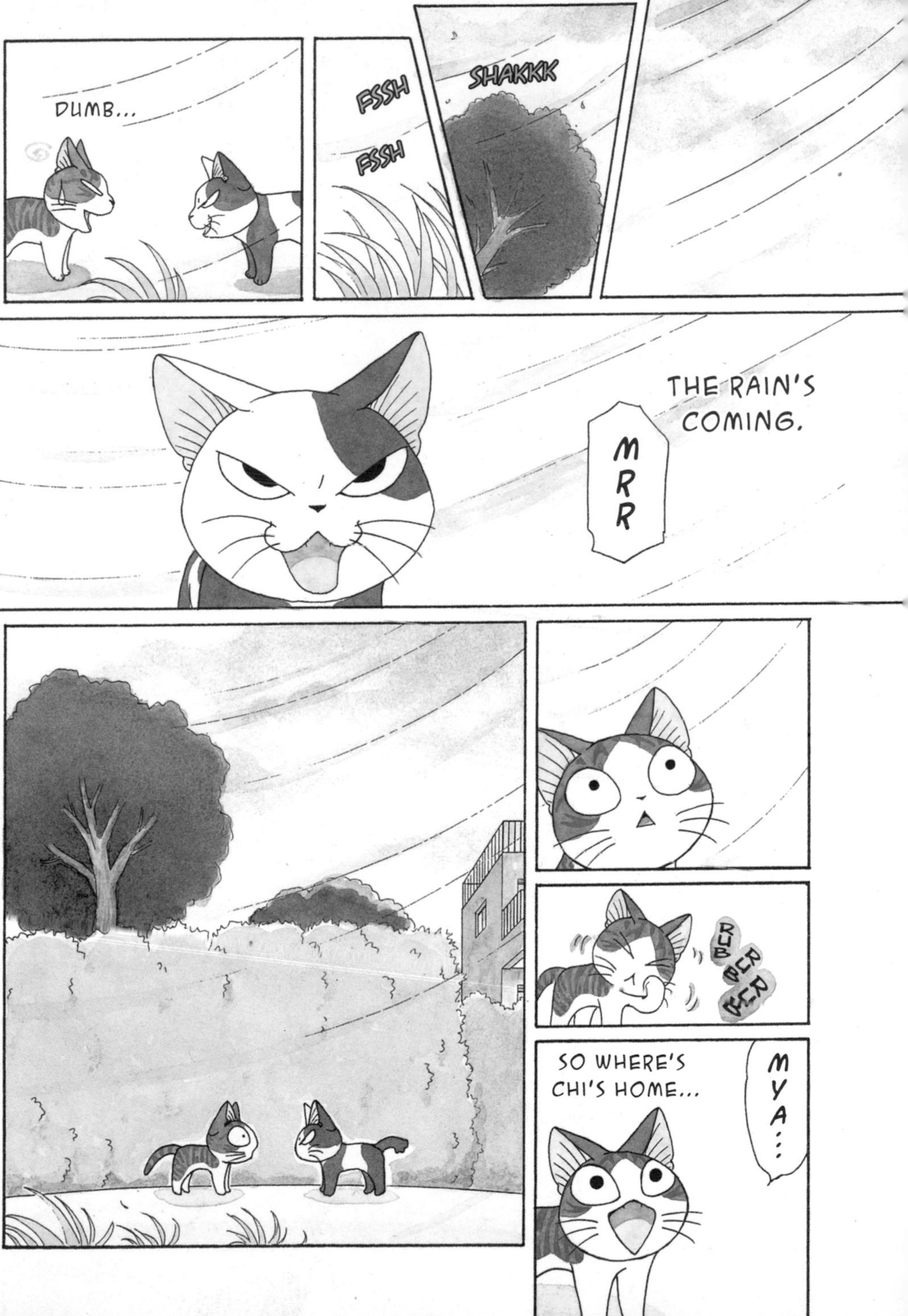

DUMB...
FSSH
FSSH
SHAKKK
MRR
THE RAIN'S COMING.
RUB RUB RUB
SO WHERE'S CHI'S HOME...
MYA...

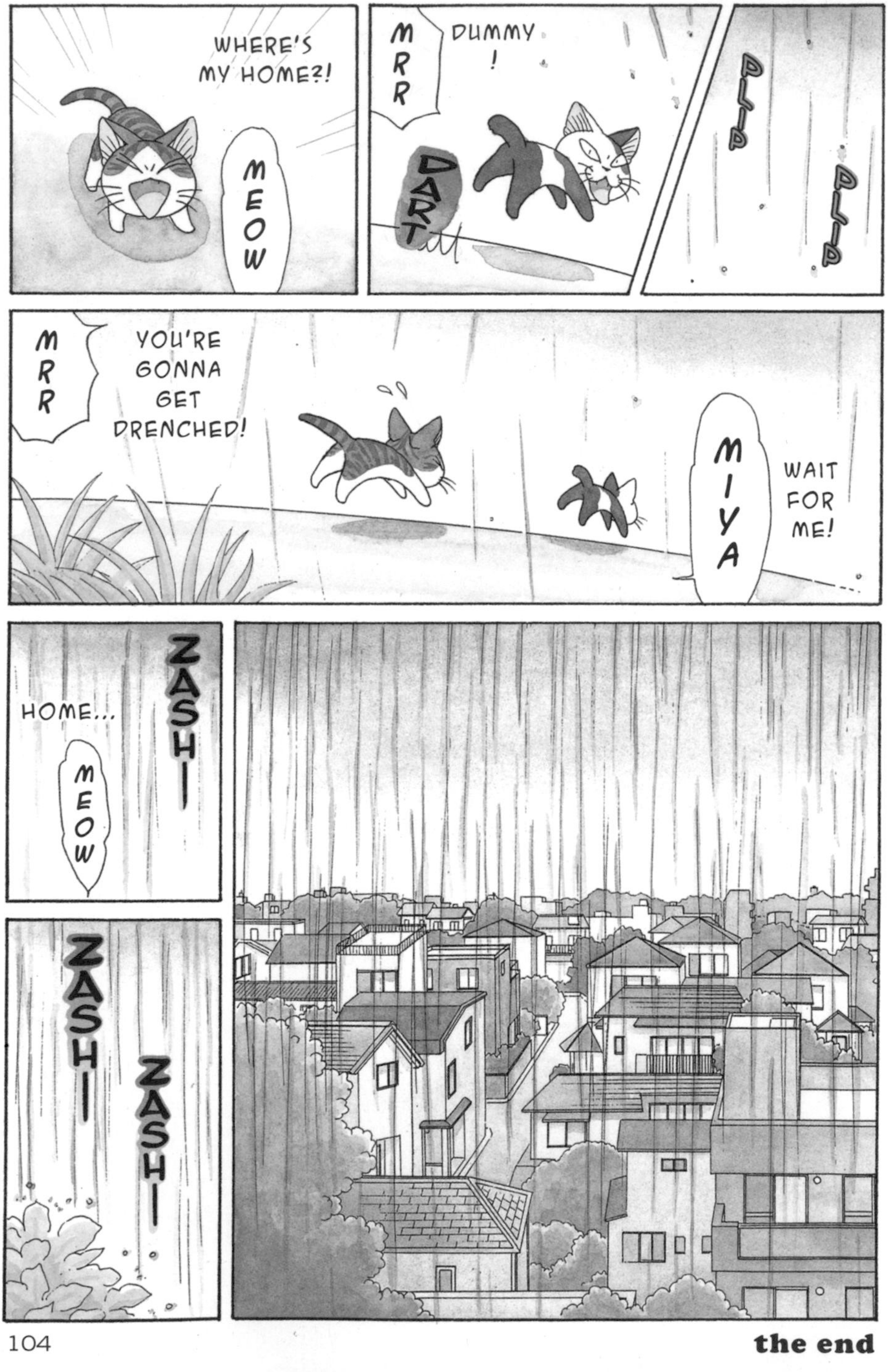
WHERE'S MY HOME?!
MEOW
MRR
DUMMY!
DART
PLIP
PLIP
MRR
YOU'RE GONNA GET DRENCHED!
MIYA
WAIT FOR ME!
HOME...
ZASHI
MEOW
ZASHI
ZASHI



the end

# homemade 124: a cat takes shelter from the rain

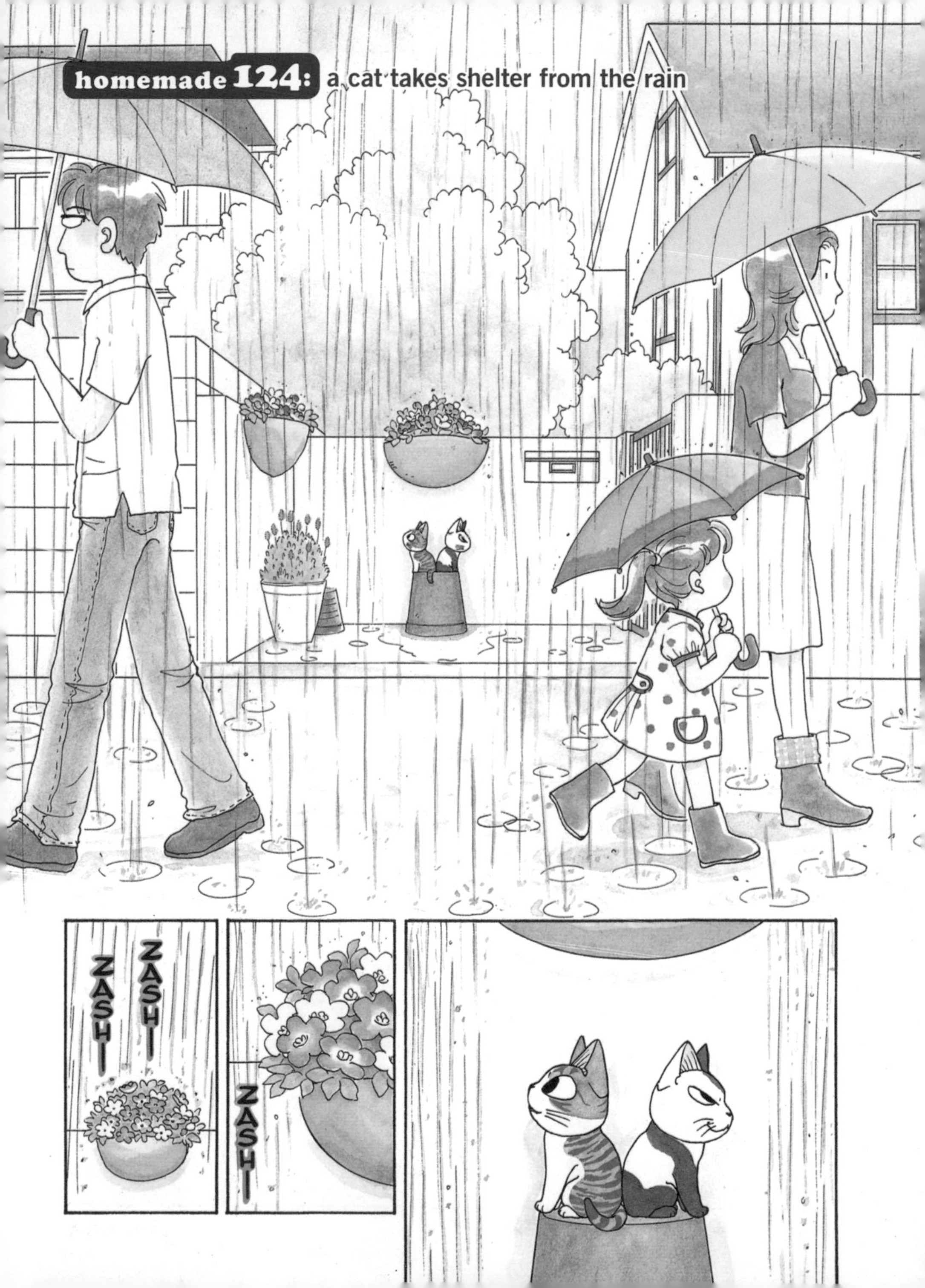
ZASHI
ZASHI
ZASHI

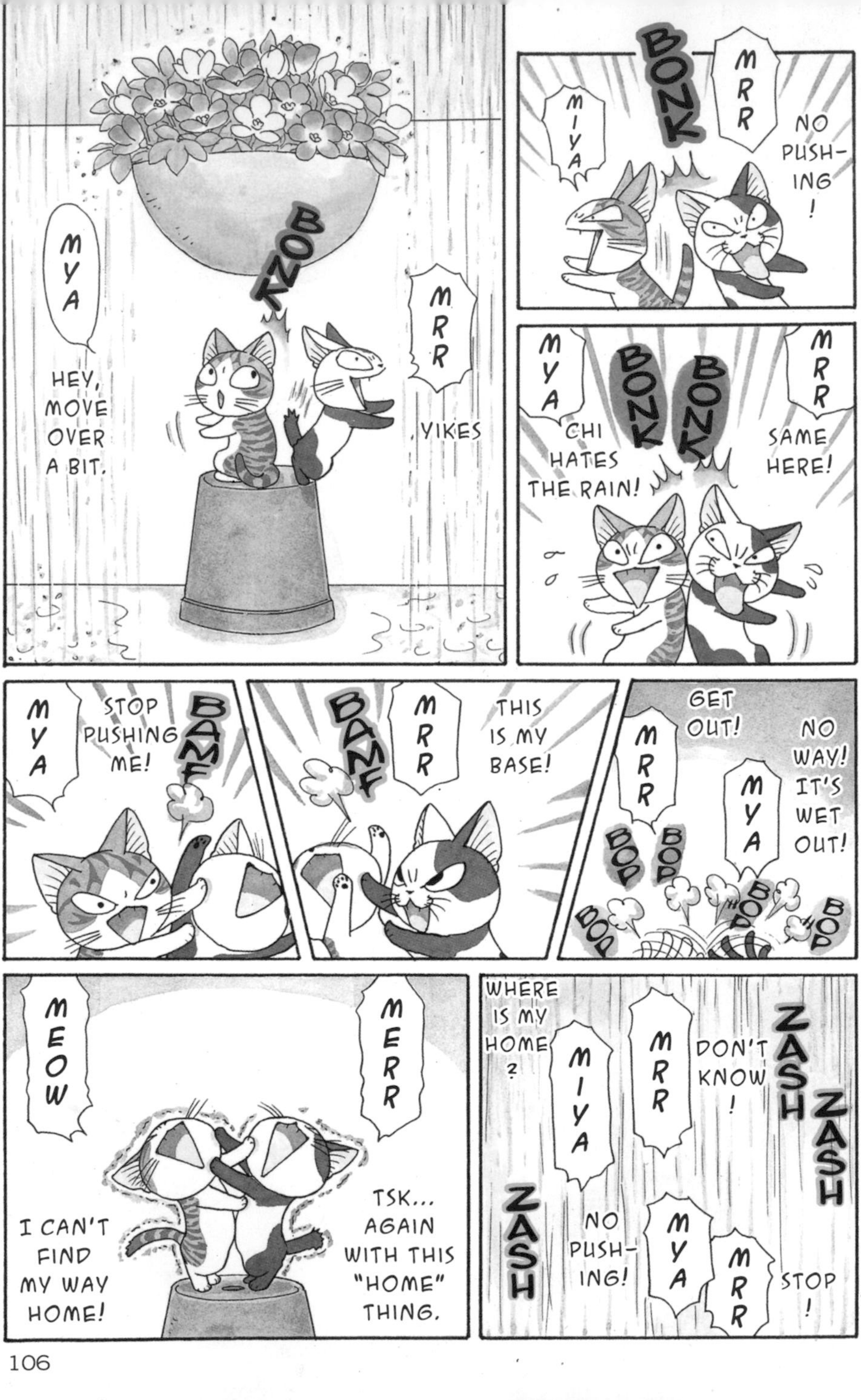
MYA
HEY, MOVE OVER A BIT.
BONK
MRR
YIKES
MIYA
BONK
MRR
NO PUSHING!
MYA
CHI HATES THE RAIN!
BONK
BONK
MRR
SAME HERE!
MYA
STOP PUSHING ME!
BAMF
BAMF
MRR
THIS IS MY BASE!
MRR
GET OUT!
MYA
NO WAY! IT'S WET OUT!
BOP
BOP
BOP
BOP
BOP
BOP
MEOW
I CAN'T FIND MY WAY HOME!
MERR
TSK... AGAIN WITH THIS "HOME" THING.
WHERE IS MY HOME?
MIYA
MRR
DON'T KNOW!
ZASH
ZASH
ZASH
NO PUSHING!
MYA
MRR
STOP!

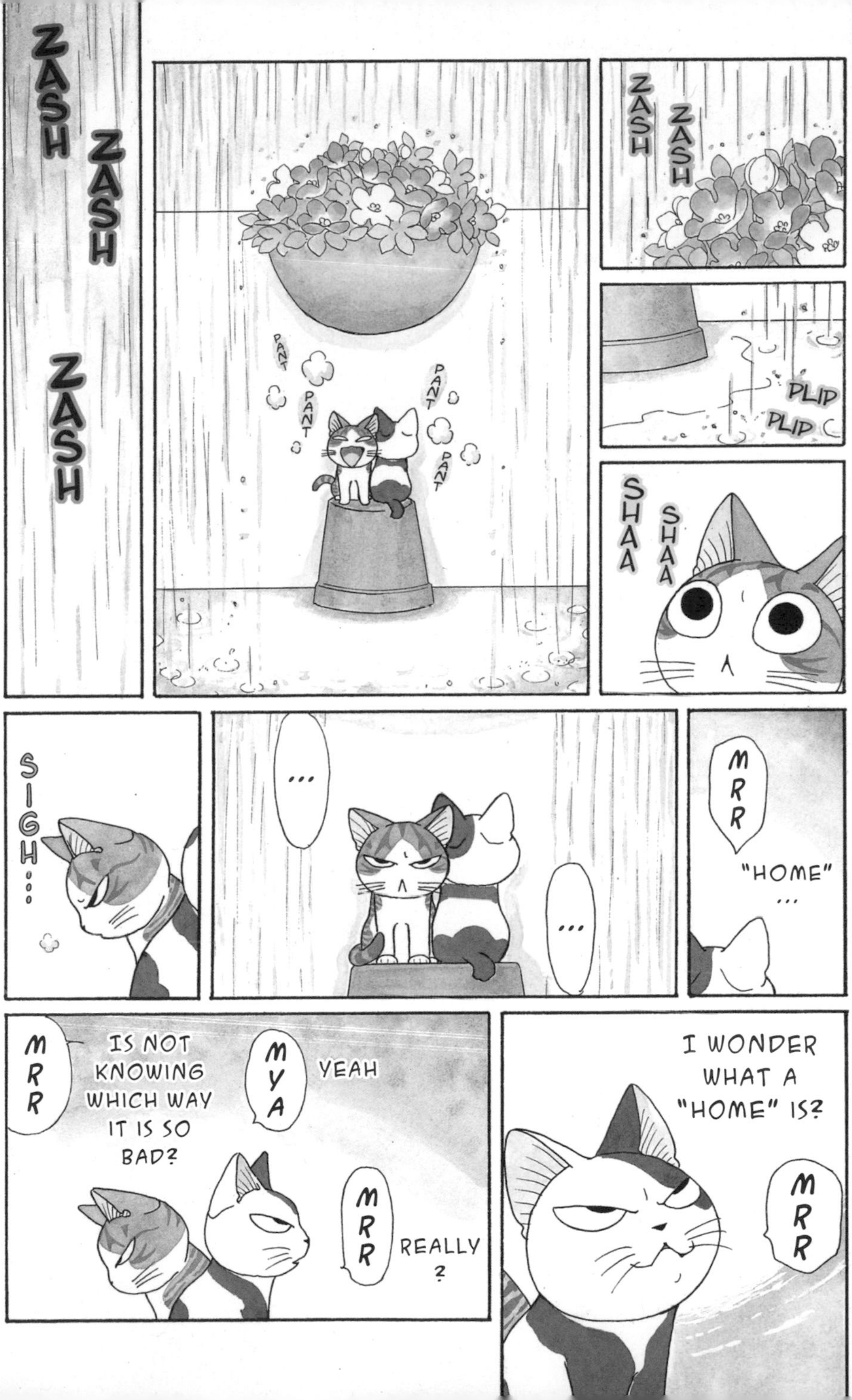
ZASH ZASH
ZASH
PANT
PANT
PANT
PANT
ZASH ZASH
PLIP
PLIP
SHAA SHAA
SIGH...
...
...
MRR
"HOME" ...
MRR
IS NOT KNOWING WHICH WAY IT IS SO BAD?
MYA
YEAH
MRR
REALLY?
I WONDER WHAT A "HOME" IS?
MRR

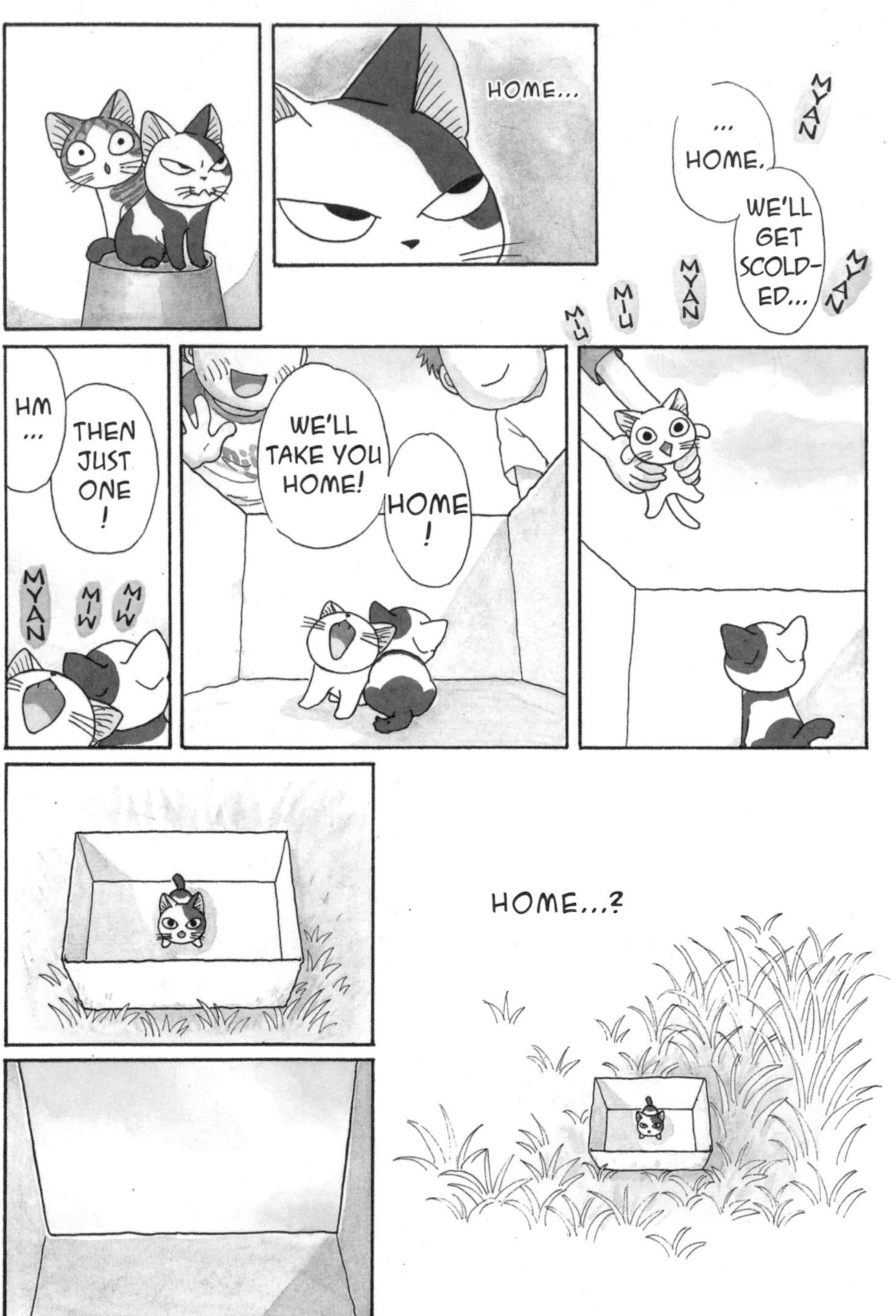
HOME...
... HOME.
WE'LL GET SCOLD-ED...
MYAN
MYAN
MIU
MIU
MYAN
HM ...
THEN JUST ONE!
MYAN
MIW
MIW
WE'LL TAKE YOU HOME!
HOME!
HOME...?

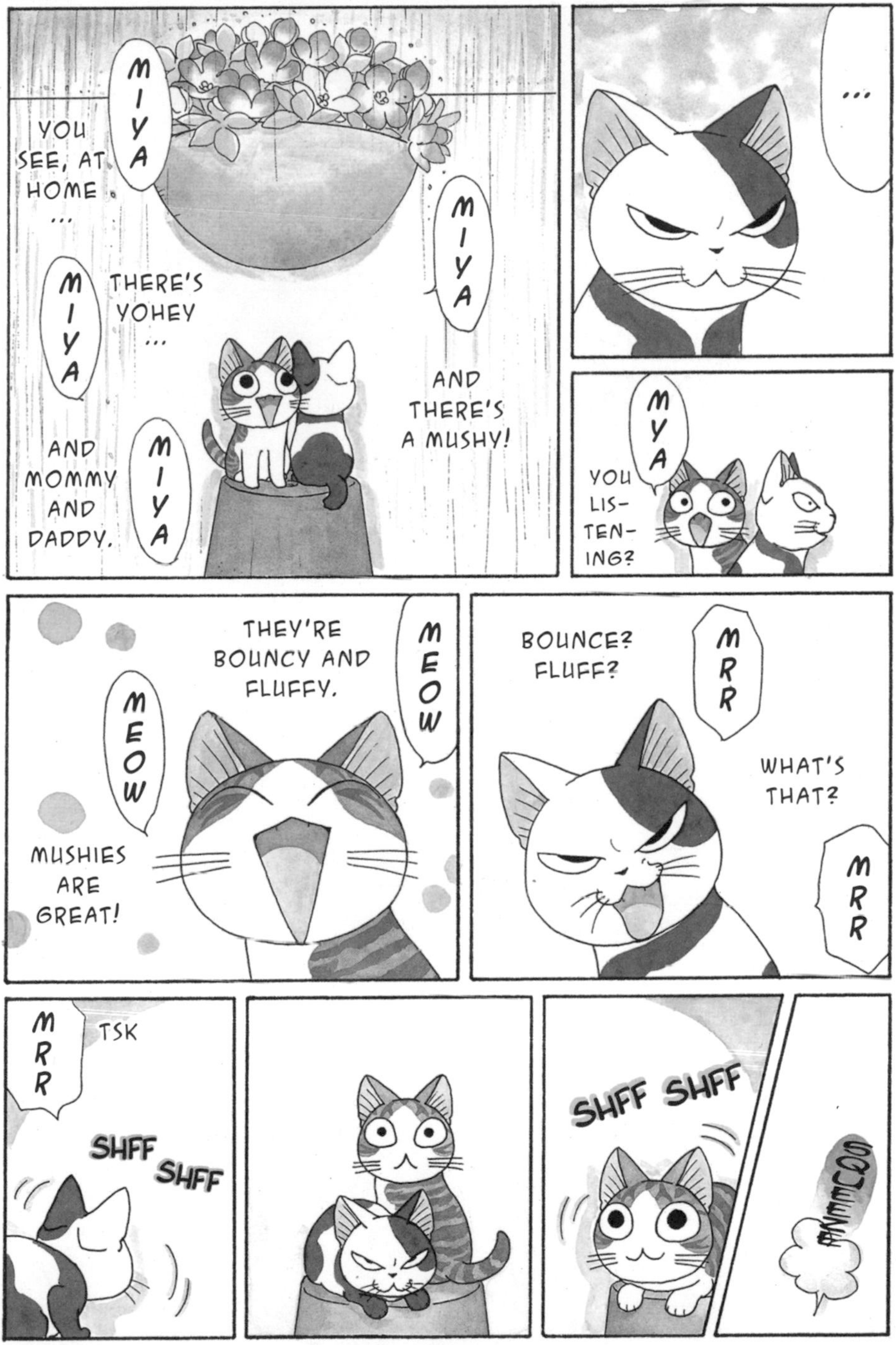
YOU SEE, AT HOME ...
MIYA
MIYA
THERE'S YOHEY ...
MIYA
AND MOMMY AND DADDY.
MIYA
AND THERE'S A MUSHY!
...
MYA
YOU LIS-TEN-ING?
THEY'RE BOUNCY AND FLUFFY.
MEOW
MEOW
MUSHIES ARE GREAT!
BOUNCE? FLUFF?
MRR
WHAT'S THAT?
MRR
MRR
TSK
SHFF SHFF
SHFF SHFF
SQUEEEE

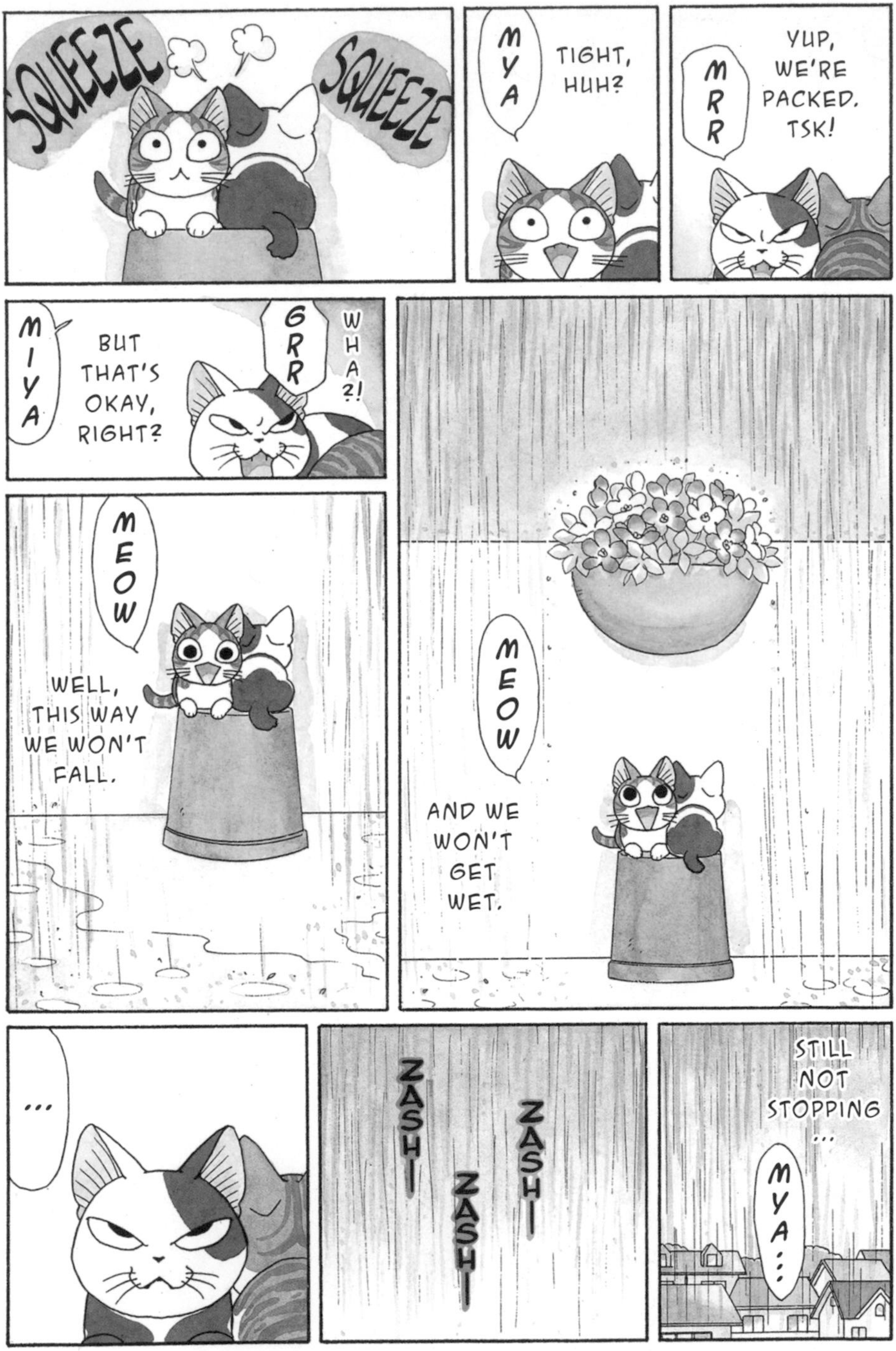
SQUEEZE
SQUEEZE
MYA
TIGHT, HUH?
MRR
YUP, WE'RE PACKED. TSK!
MIYA
BUT THAT'S OKAY, RIGHT?
GRR
WHA?!
MEOW
WELL, THIS WAY WE WON'T FALL.
MEOW
AND WE WON'T GET WET.
...
ZASHI
ZASHI
ZASHI
STILL NOT STOPPING...
MYA...

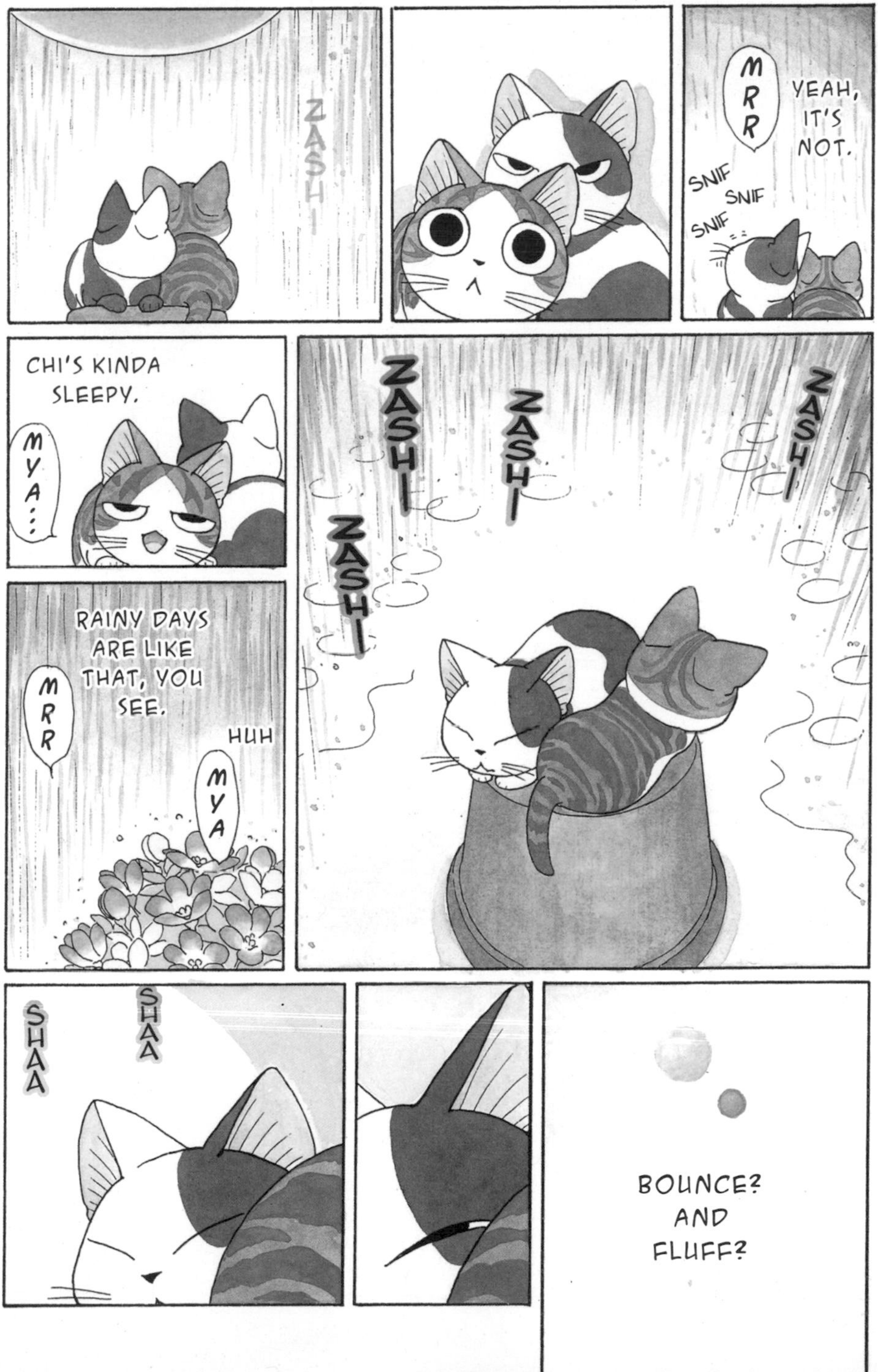
ZASHI
MRR
YEAH, IT'S NOT.
SNIF SNIF SNIF
CHI'S KINDA SLEEPY.
MYA...
ZASHI
ZASHI
ZASHI
ZASHI
RAINY DAYS ARE LIKE THAT, YOU SEE.
MRR
HUH
MYA
SHAA
SHAA
BOUNCE? AND FLUFF?

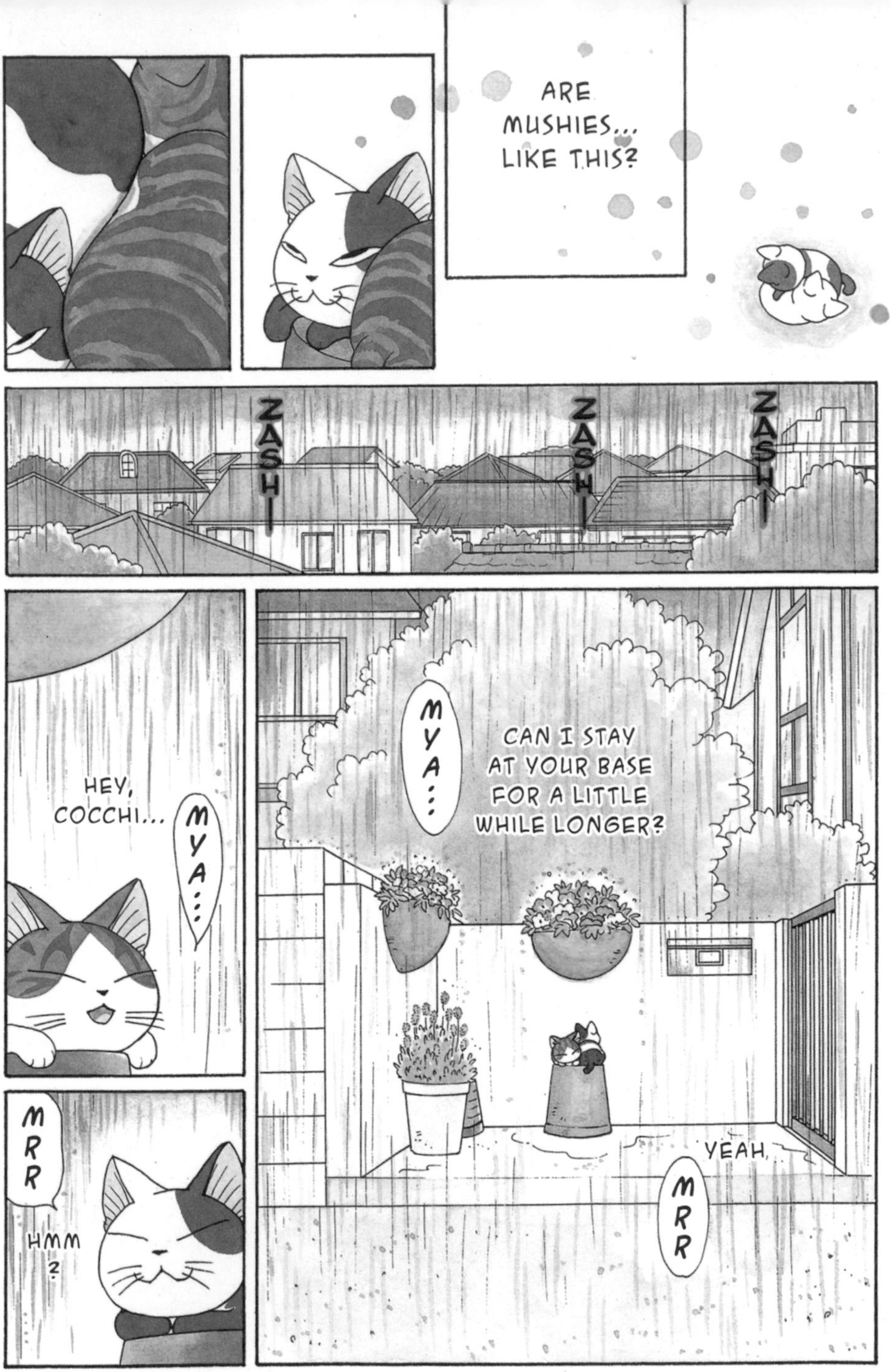
ARE MUSHIES... LIKE THIS?
ZASHI
ZASHI
ZASHI
HEY, COCCHI...
MYA...
MRR
HMM?
MYA...
CAN I STAY AT YOUR BASE FOR A LITTLE WHILE LONGER?
YEAH,
MRR



**the end**

# homemade 125: a cat goes halves

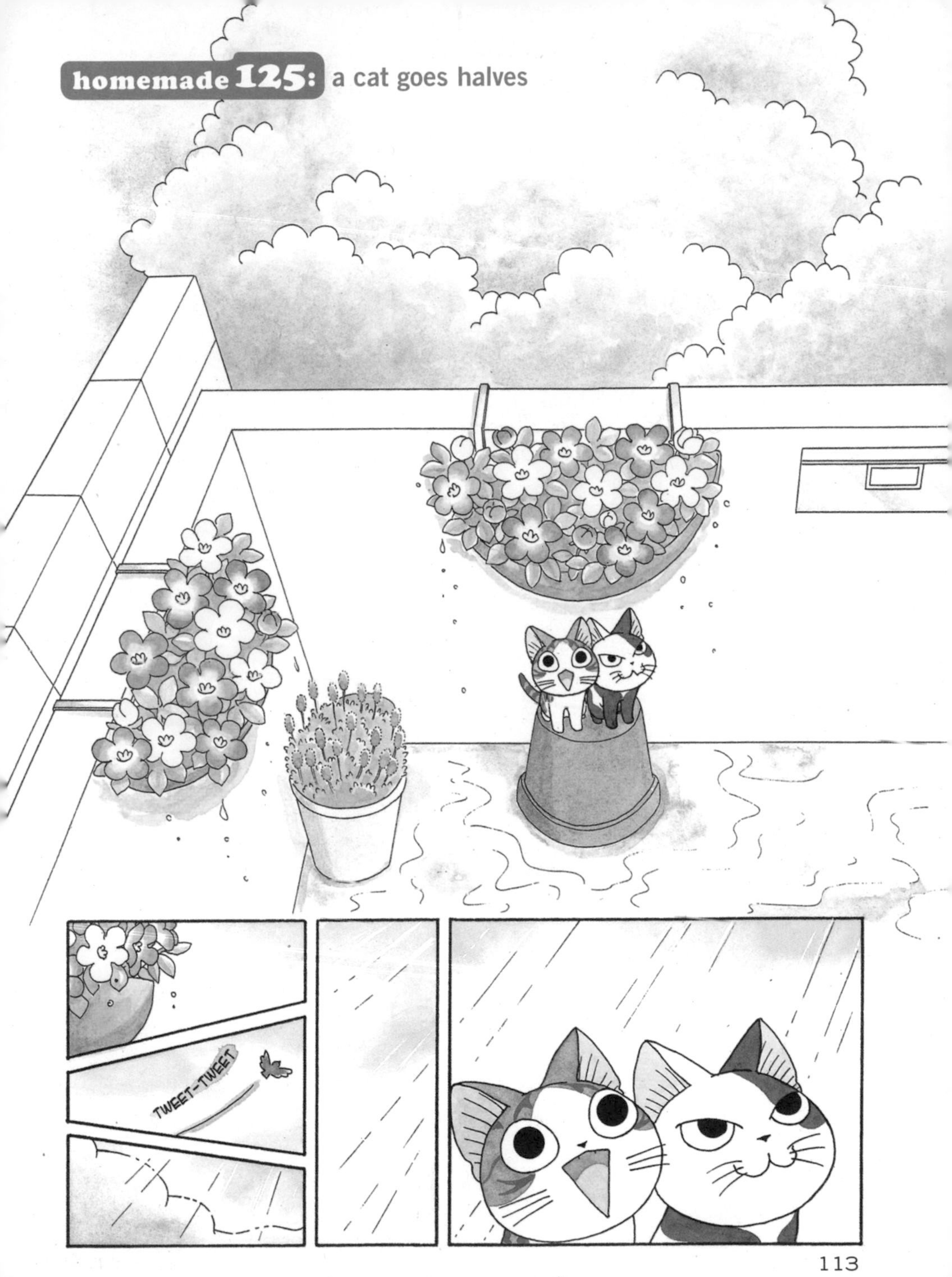
TWEET-TWEET

MRR LATER. I'M LEAV-ING.

MEOW WAIT UP, COC-CHI.

TMP TMP TMP

HOP

MEOW CHI'S COMING TOO!

TMP TMP TMP

SPLASH! !

MYA ARGH

MRR YOU ...!

114

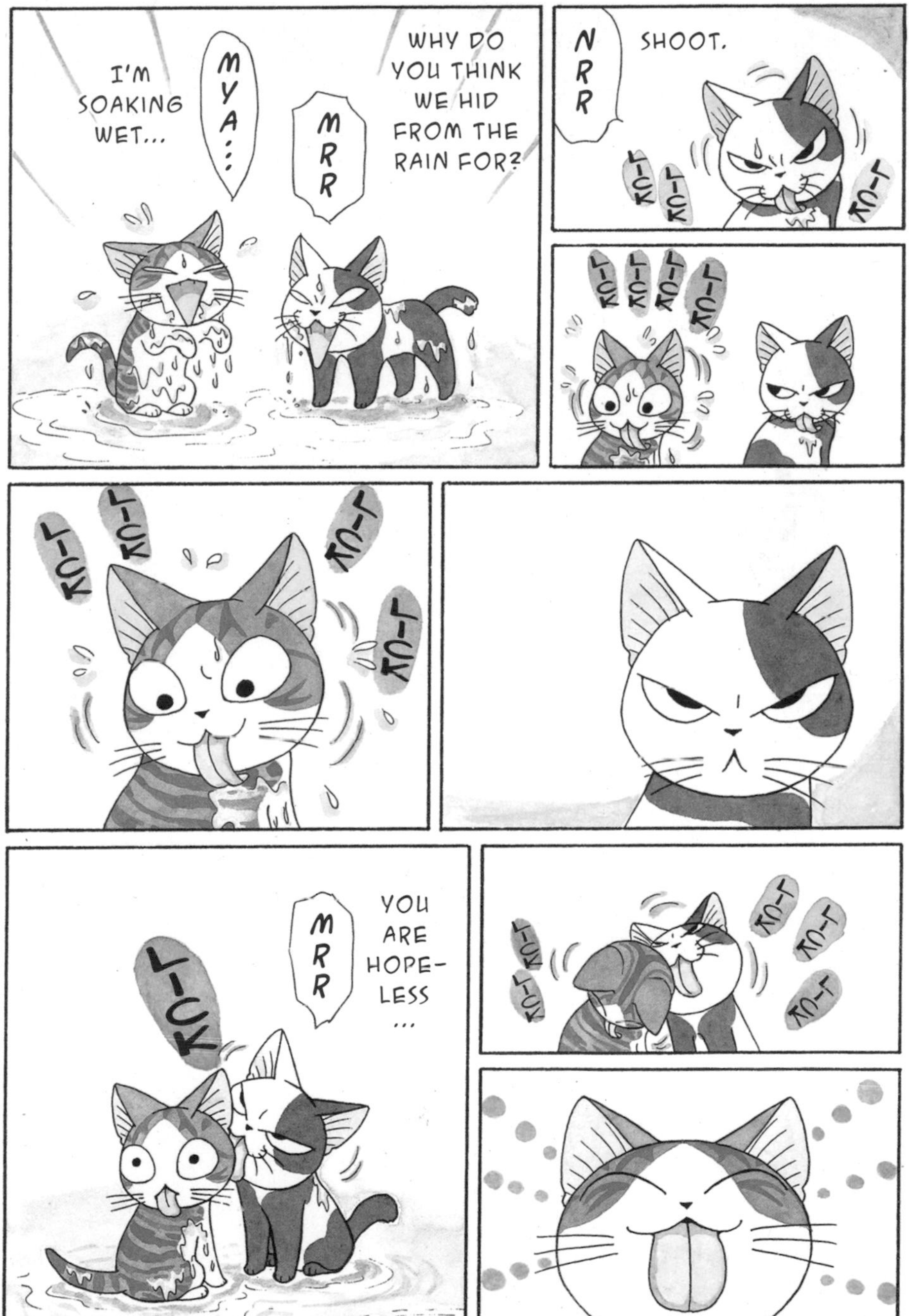
I'M SOAKING WET...
MYA...
MRR
WHY DO YOU THINK WE HID FROM THE RAIN FOR?
NRR
SHOOT.
LICK
LICK
LICK
LICK
LICK
LICK
LICK
LICK
LICK
LICK
LICK
LICK
MRR
YOU ARE HOPE-LESS...
LICK
LICK
LICK
LICK
LICK
LICK

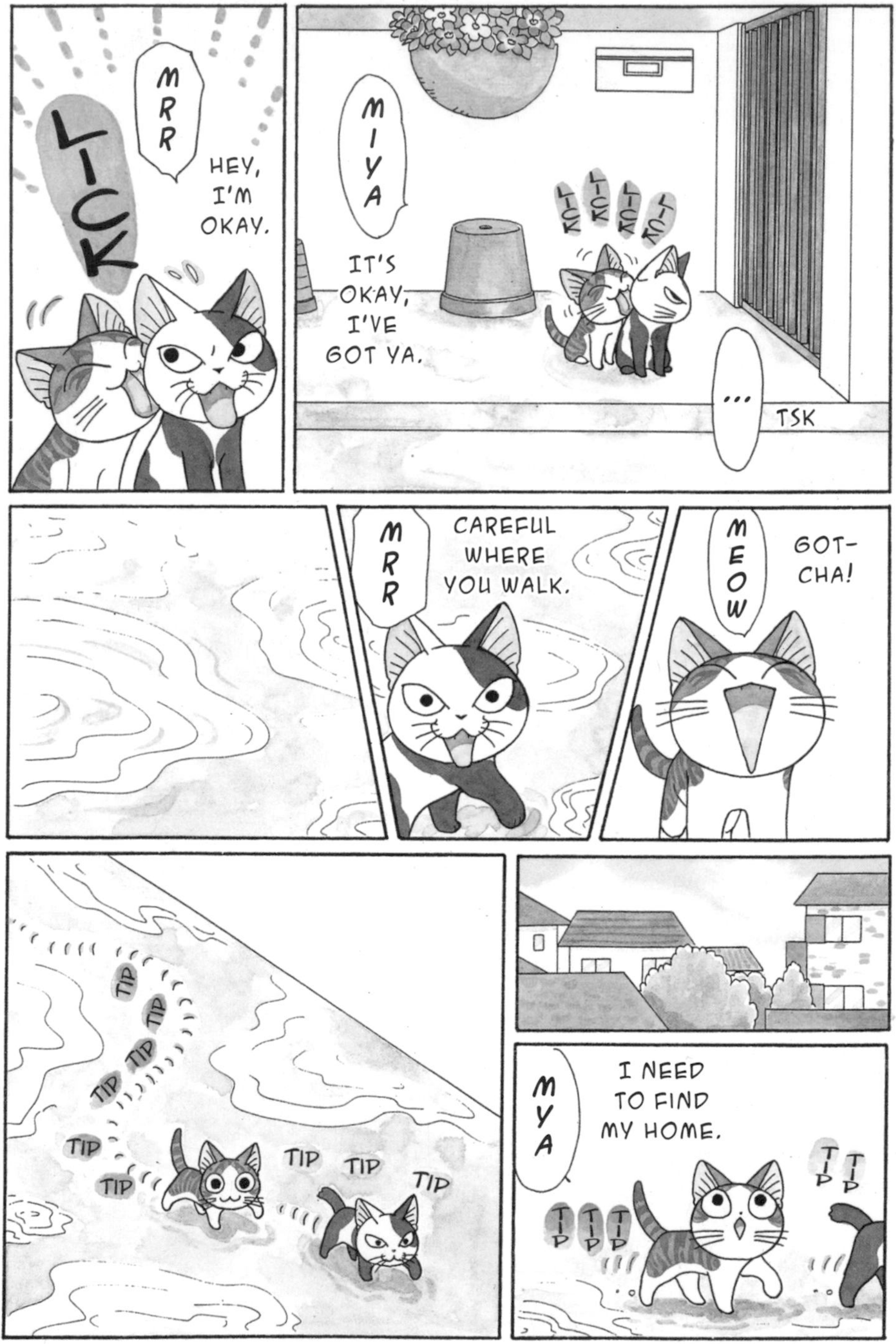
LICK
MRR
HEY, I'M OKAY.
MIYA
IT'S OKAY, I'VE GOT YA.
LICK LICK LICK LICK
...
TSK
MRR
CAREFUL WHERE YOU WALK.
MEOW
GOT-CHA!
TIP TIP TIP TIP TIP TIP TIP TIP TIP
MYA
I NEED TO FIND MY HOME.
TIP TIP TIP
TIP TIP

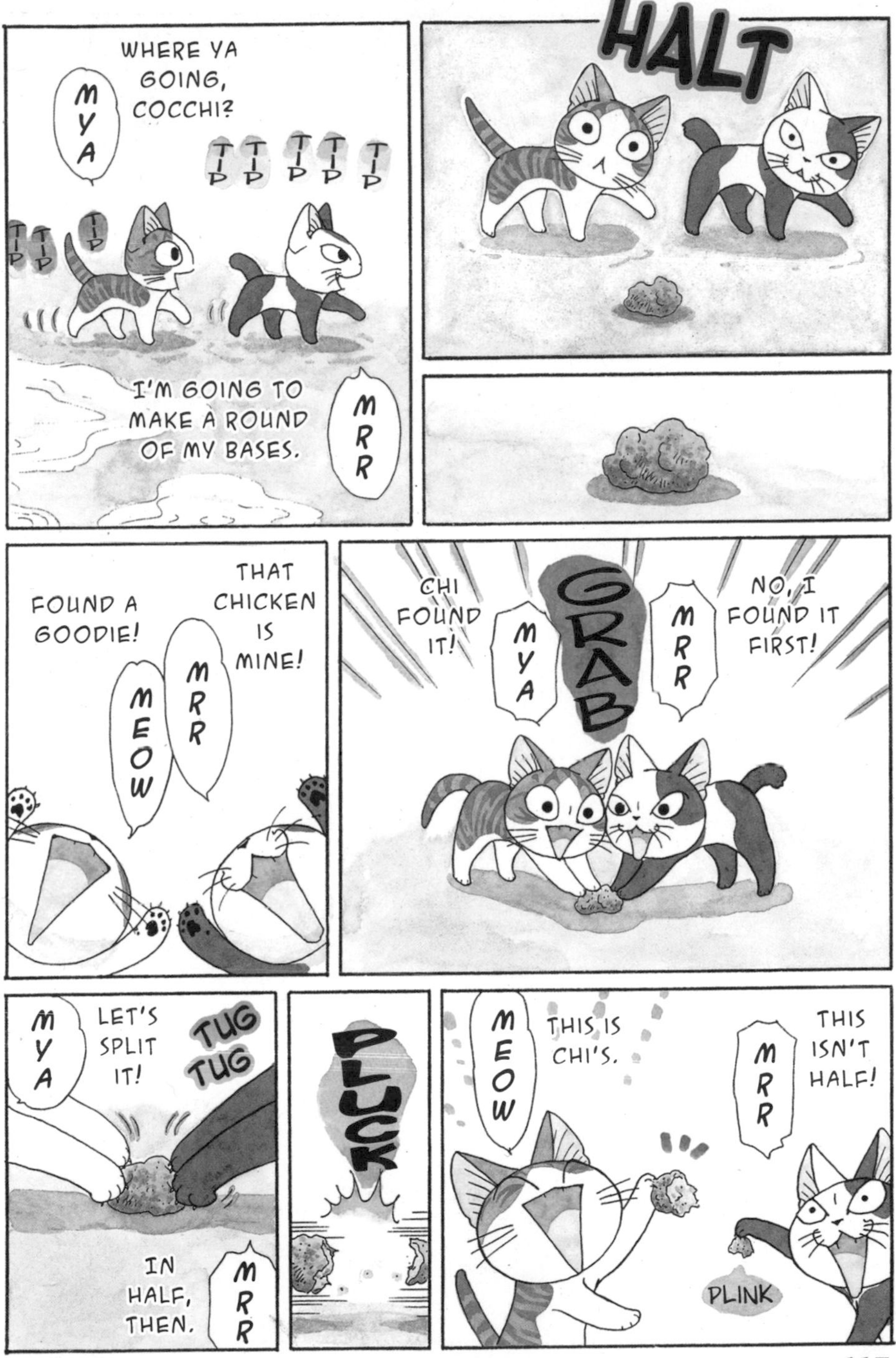
MYA
WHERE YA GOING, COCCHI?
TIP TIP TIP TIP TIP
TIP TIP TIP
I'M GOING TO MAKE A ROUND OF MY BASES.
MRR
HALT
FOUND A GOODIE!
THAT CHICKEN IS MINE!
MRR
MEOW
CHI FOUND IT!
MYA
GRAB
MRR
NO, I FOUND IT FIRST!
MYA
LET'S SPLIT IT!
TUG TUG
IN HALF, THEN.
MRR
PLUCK
MEOW
THIS IS CHI'S.
THIS ISN'T HALF!
MRR
PLINK

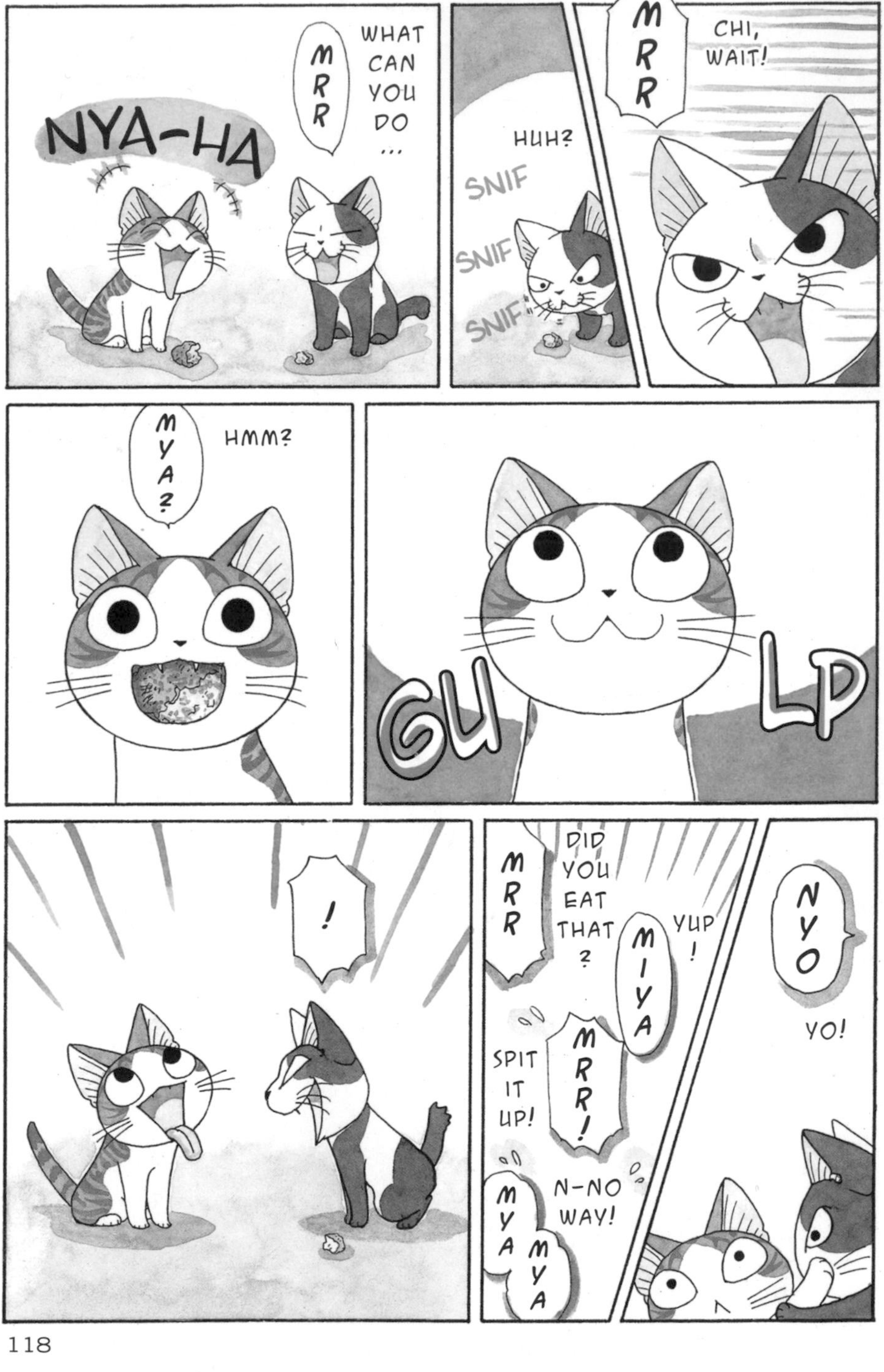
NYA-HA
MRR
WHAT CAN YOU DO ...
HUH?
SNIF
SNIF
SNIF
MRR
CHI, WAIT!
MYA?
HMM?
GU
LP
!
MRR
DID YOU EAT THAT?
MIYA
YUP!
MRR!
SPIT IT UP!
MYA MYA
N-NO WAY!
NYO
YO!

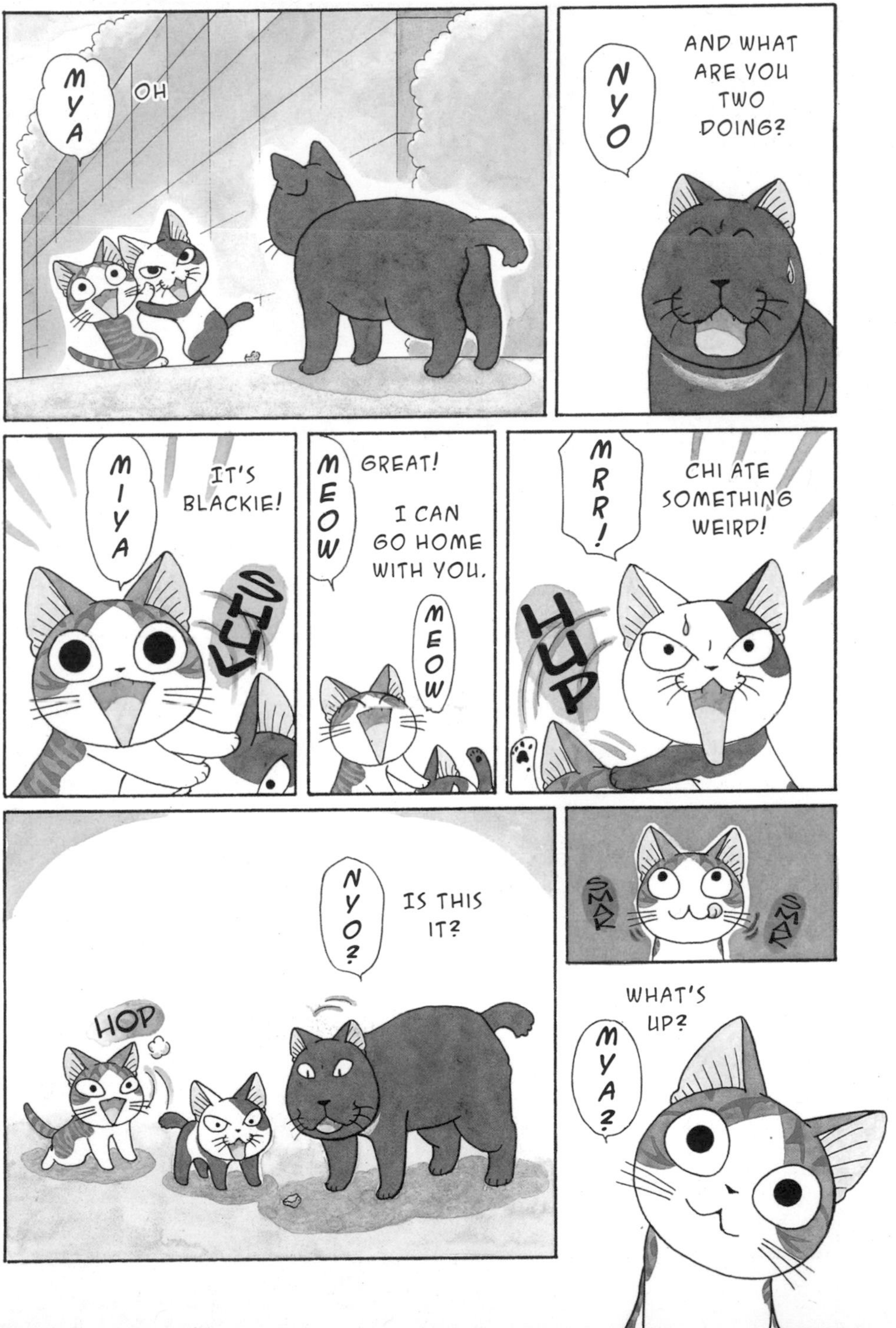
MYA
OH
NYO
AND WHAT ARE YOU TWO DOING?
MIYA
IT'S BLACKIE!
SHU
MEOW
GREAT!
I CAN GO HOME WITH YOU.
MEOW
MRR!
CHI ATE SOMETHING WEIRD!
HUP
NYO?
IS THIS IT?
HOP
SMAK
SMAK
WHAT'S UP?
MYA?

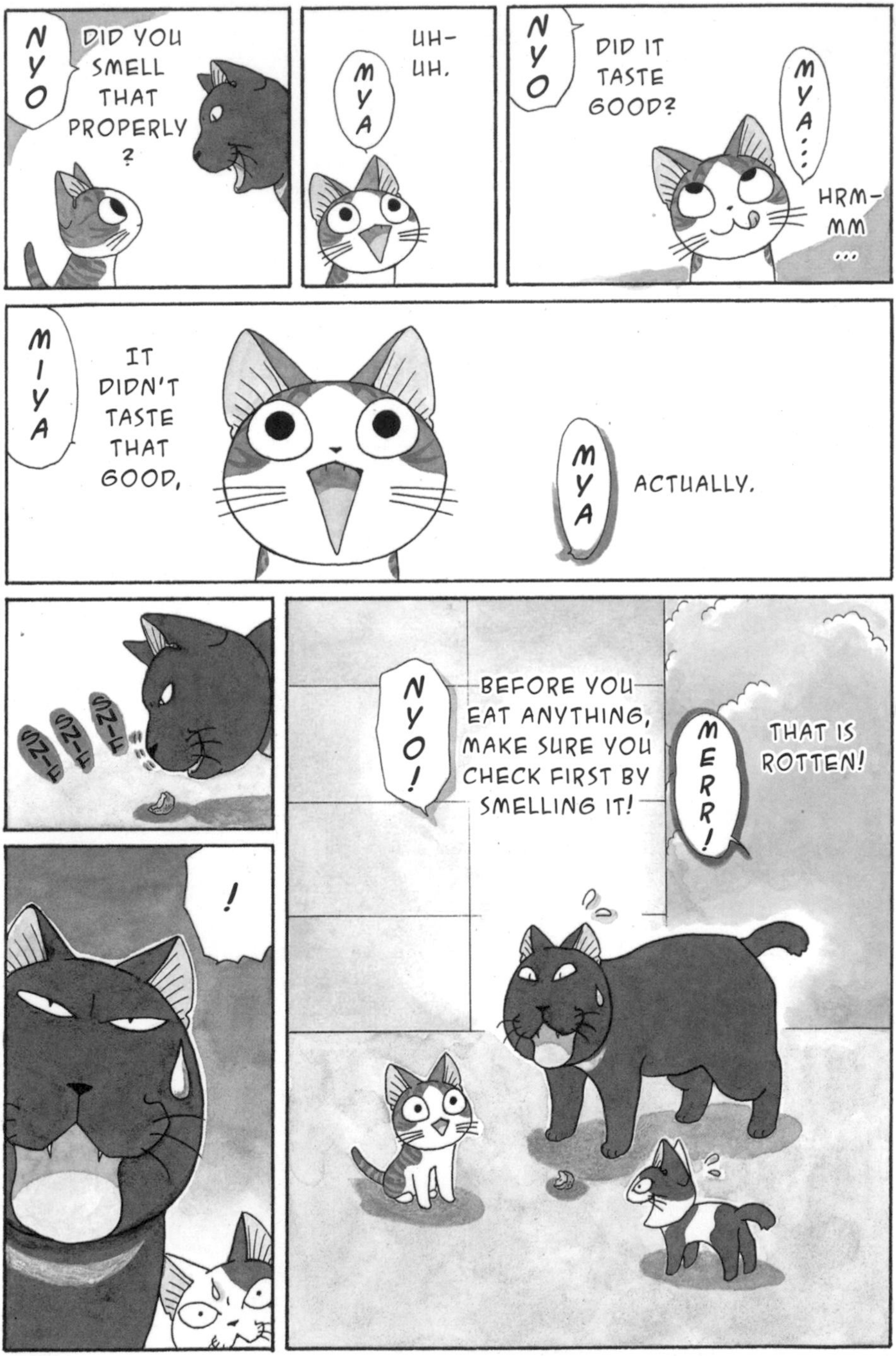
NYO
DID YOU SMELL THAT PROPERLY?
MYA
UH-UH.
NYO
DID IT TASTE GOOD?
MYA...
HRM-MM...
MIYA
IT DIDN'T TASTE THAT GOOD,
MYA
ACTUALLY.
SNIF SNIF SNIF
!
NYO!
BEFORE YOU EAT ANYTHING, MAKE SURE YOU CHECK FIRST BY SMELLING IT!
MERR!
THAT IS ROTTEN!

**the end**

# homemade 126: a cat has an emergency

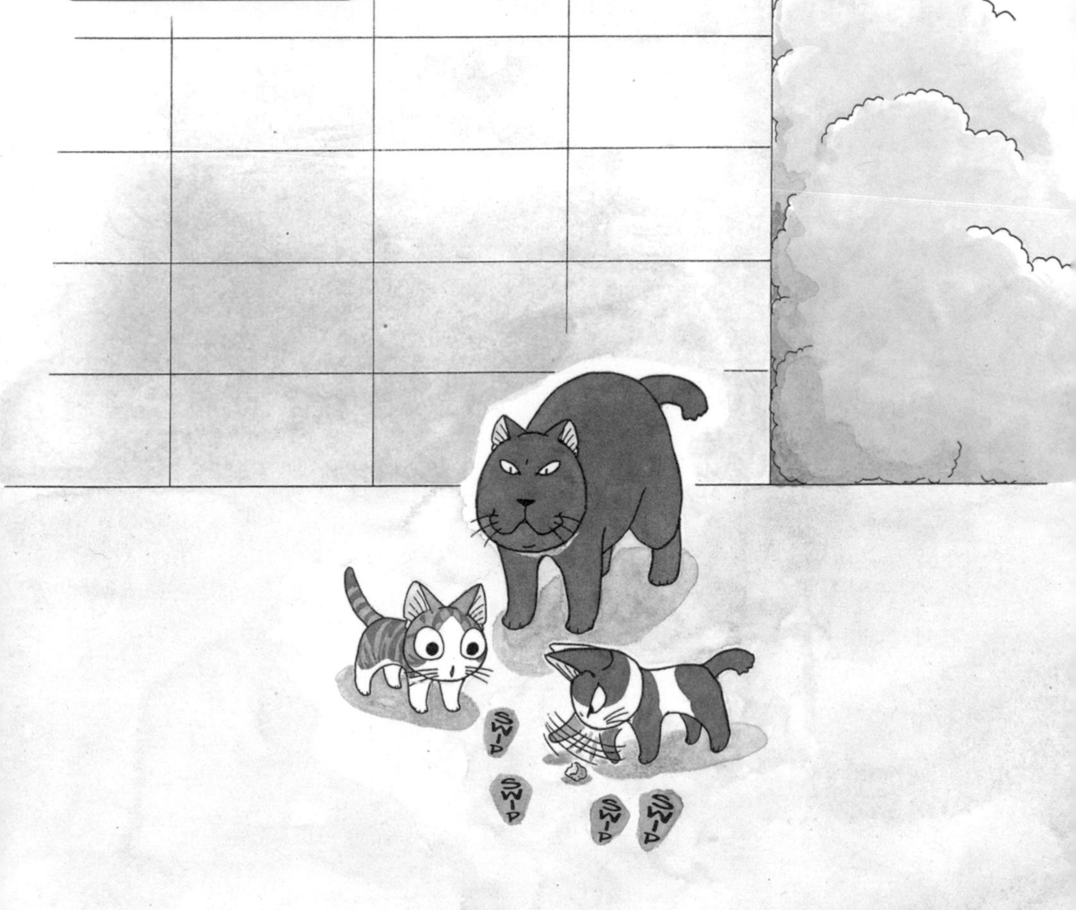
SWIP
SWIP
SWIP
SWIP

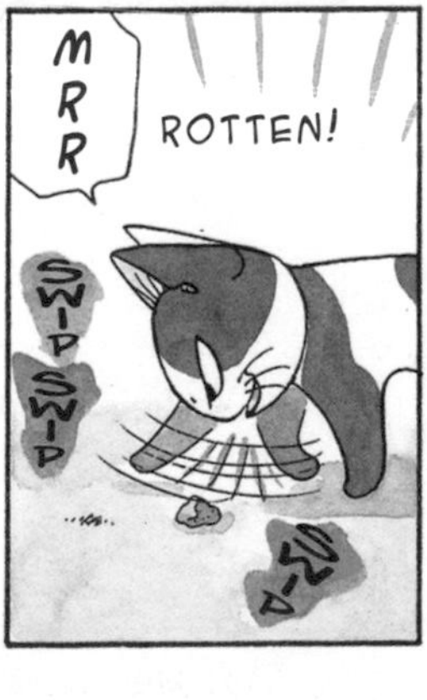
MRR
ROTTEN!
SWIP
SWIP
SWIP

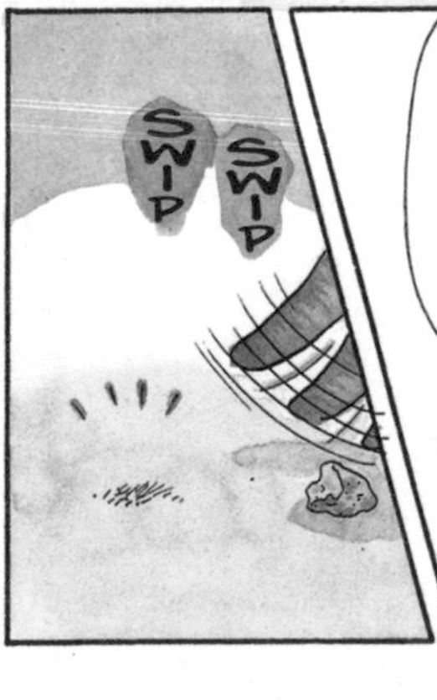
SWIP
SWIP

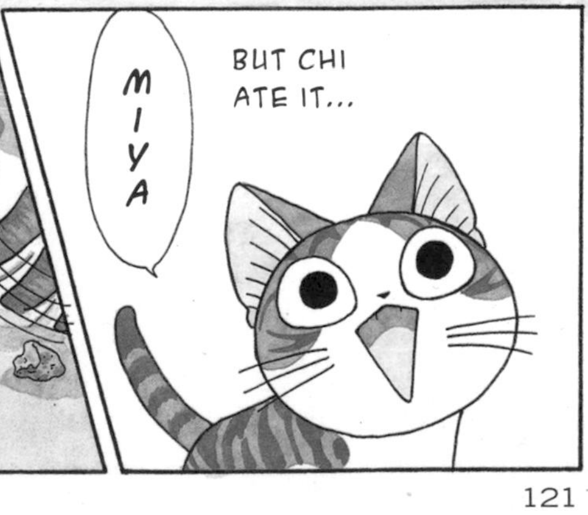
MIYA
BUT CHI ATE IT...

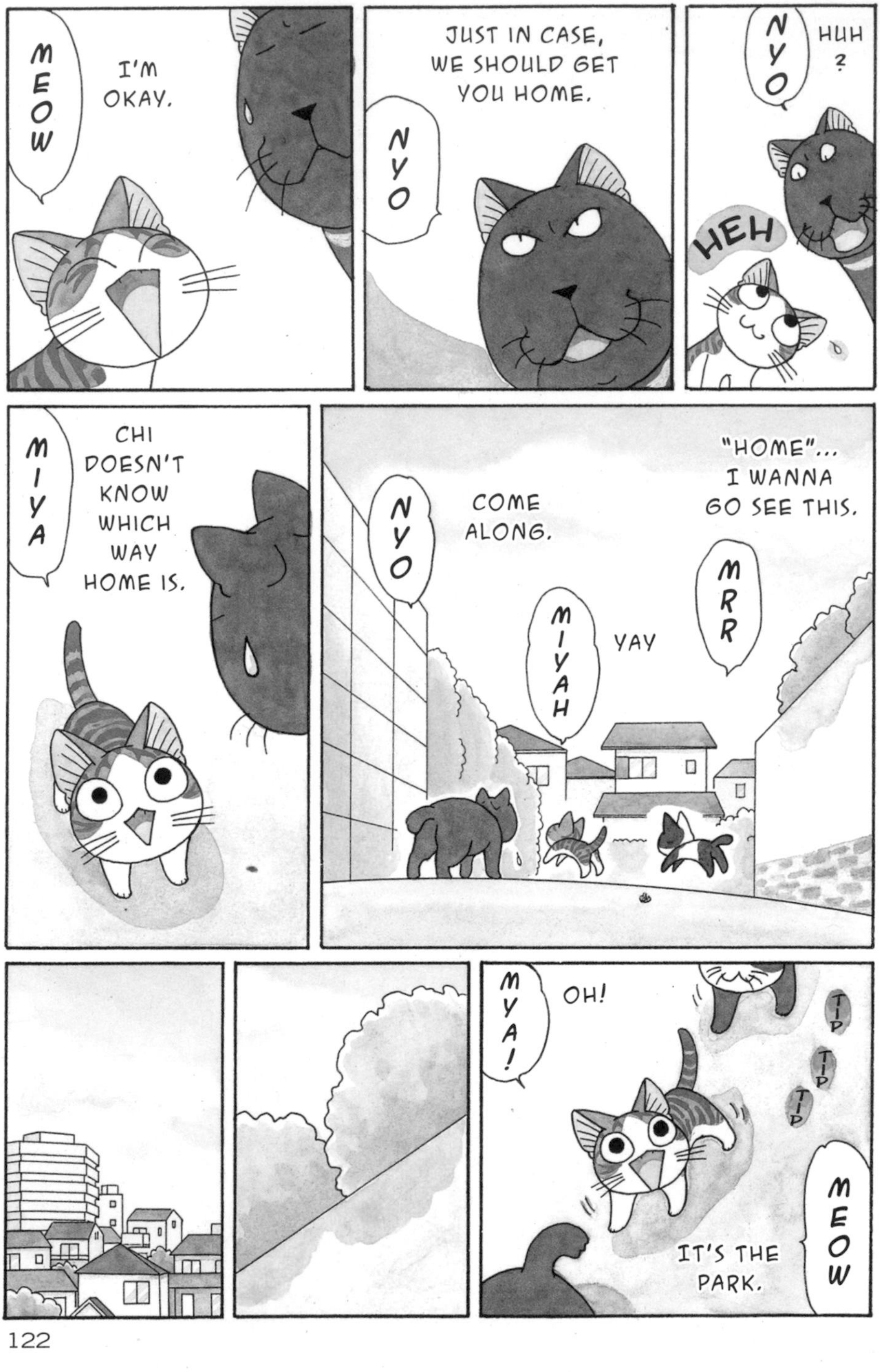
MEOW
I'M OKAY.
JUST IN CASE, WE SHOULD GET YOU HOME.
NYO
NYO
HUH?
HEH
MIYA
CHI DOESN'T KNOW WHICH WAY HOME IS.
NYO
COME ALONG.
"HOME"... I WANNA GO SEE THIS.
MIYAH
YAY
MRR
MYA!
OH!
TIP
TIP
TIP
MEOW
IT'S THE PARK.

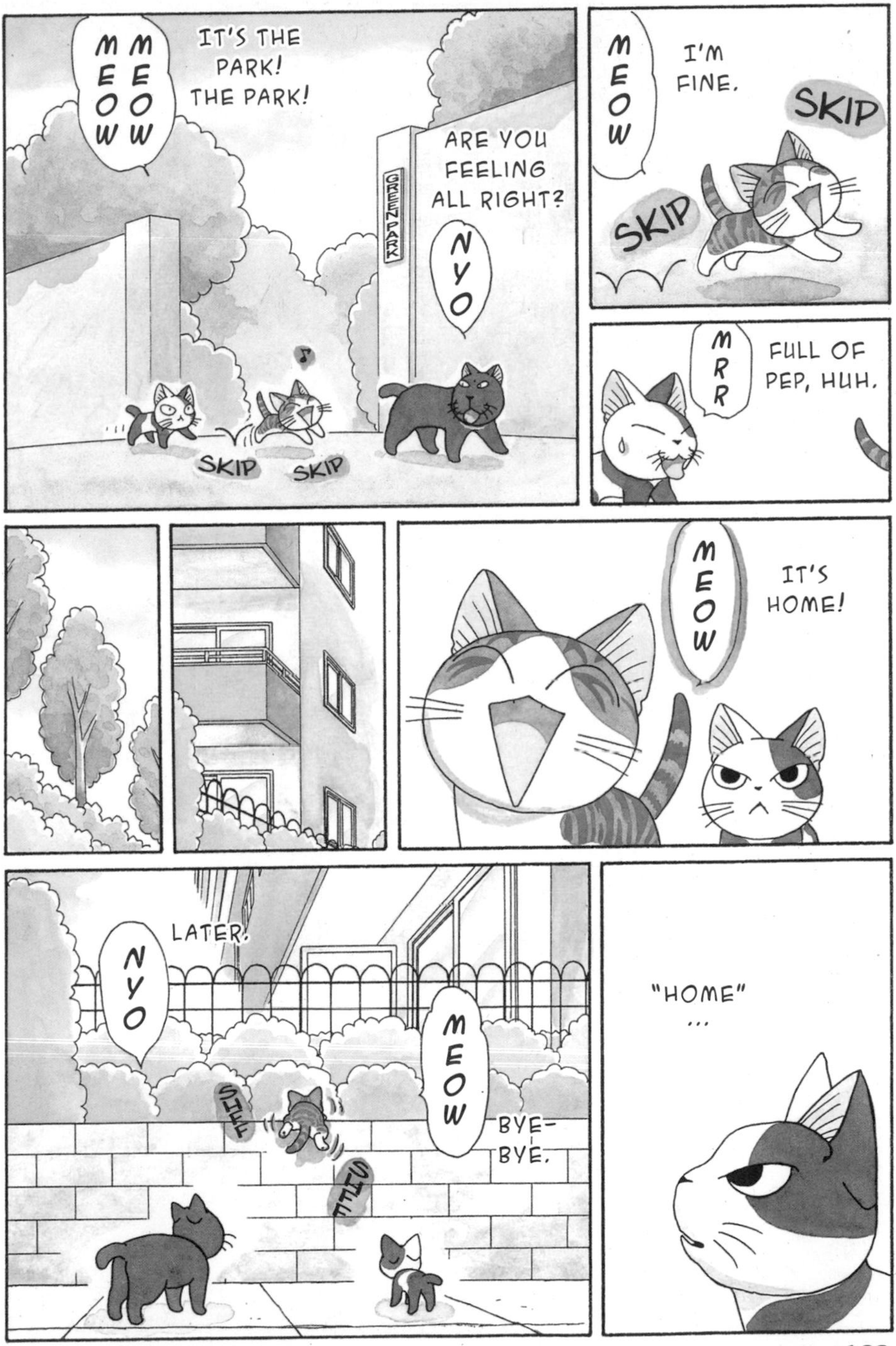
MEOW MEOW
IT'S THE PARK! THE PARK!
GREENPARK
ARE YOU FEELING ALL RIGHT?
NYO
SKIP
SKIP
MEOW
I'M FINE.
SKIP
SKIP
MRR
FULL OF PEP, HUH.
MEOW
IT'S HOME!
NYO
LATER.
SHFF
SHFF
MEOW
BYE-BYE.
"HOME" ...

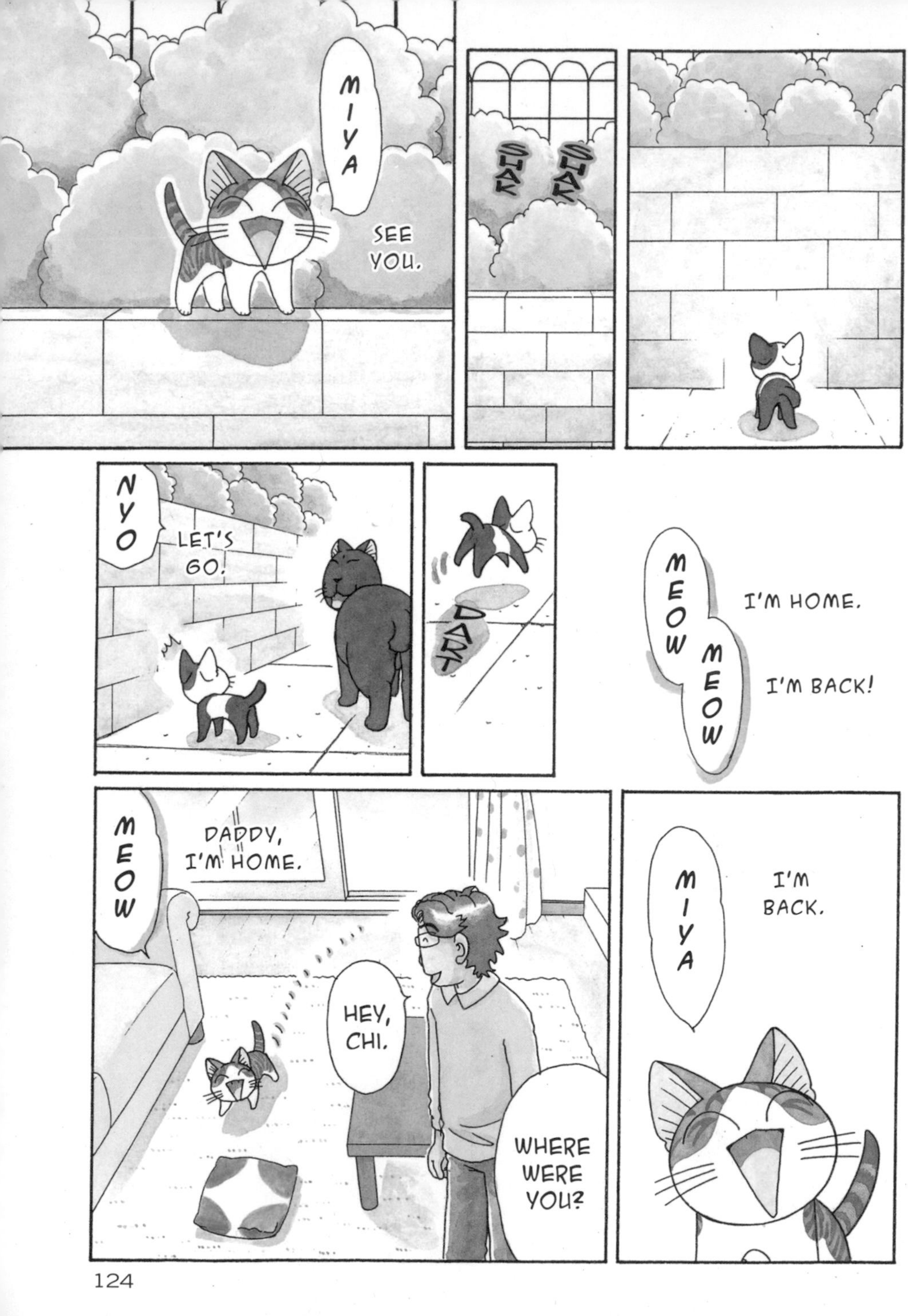

MIYA
SEE YOU.
SHAK
SHAK
NYO
LET'S GO.
DART
MEOW
I'M HOME.
MEOW
I'M BACK!
MEOW
DADDY, I'M HOME.
HEY, CHI.
WHERE WERE YOU?
MIYA
I'M BACK.

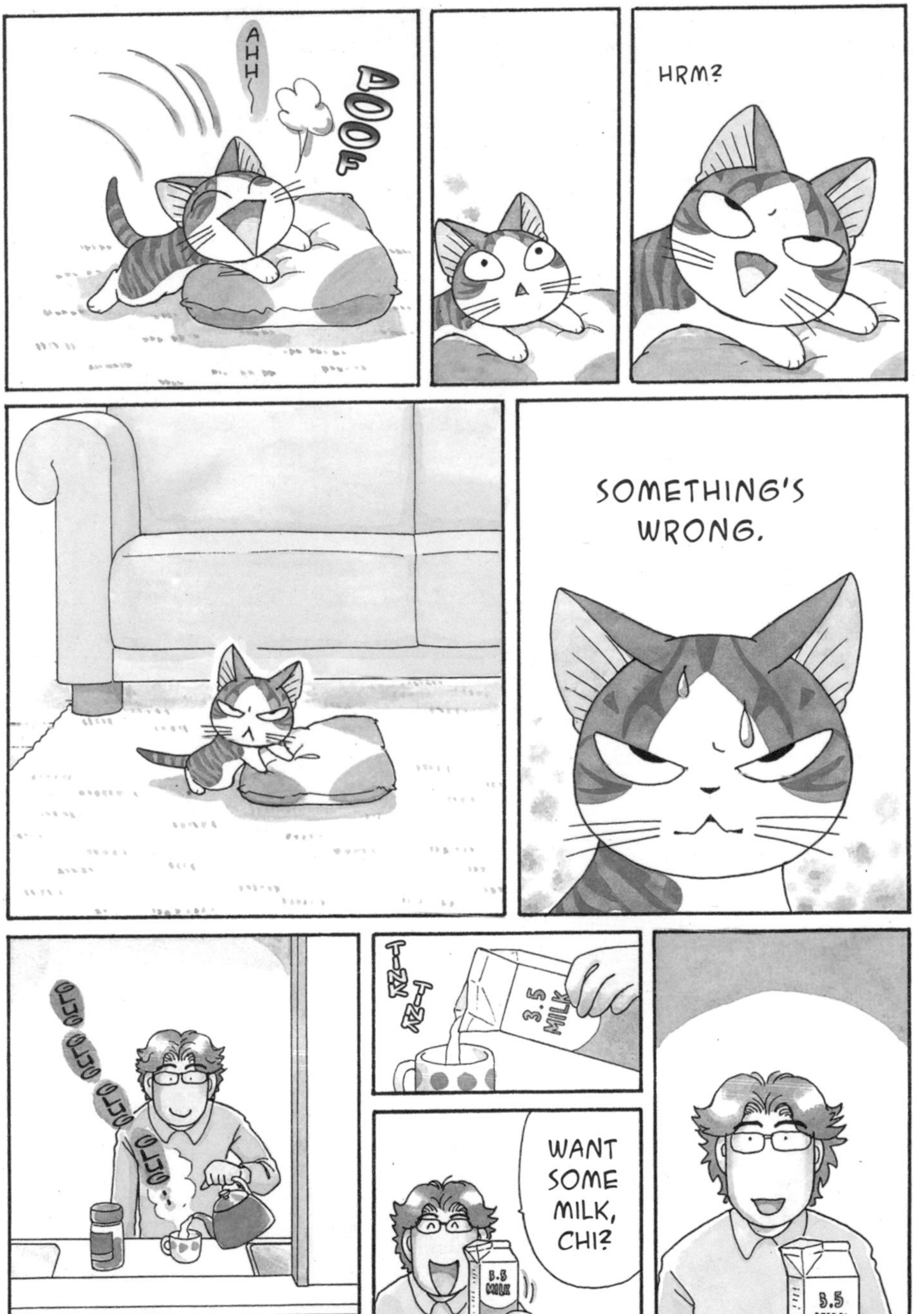
AHH~
POOF
HRM?
SOMETHING'S WRONG.
GLUG GLUG GLUG GLUG
TINK TINK
3.5 MILK
WANT SOME MILK, CHI?
3.5 MILK
3.5 MILK

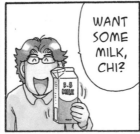

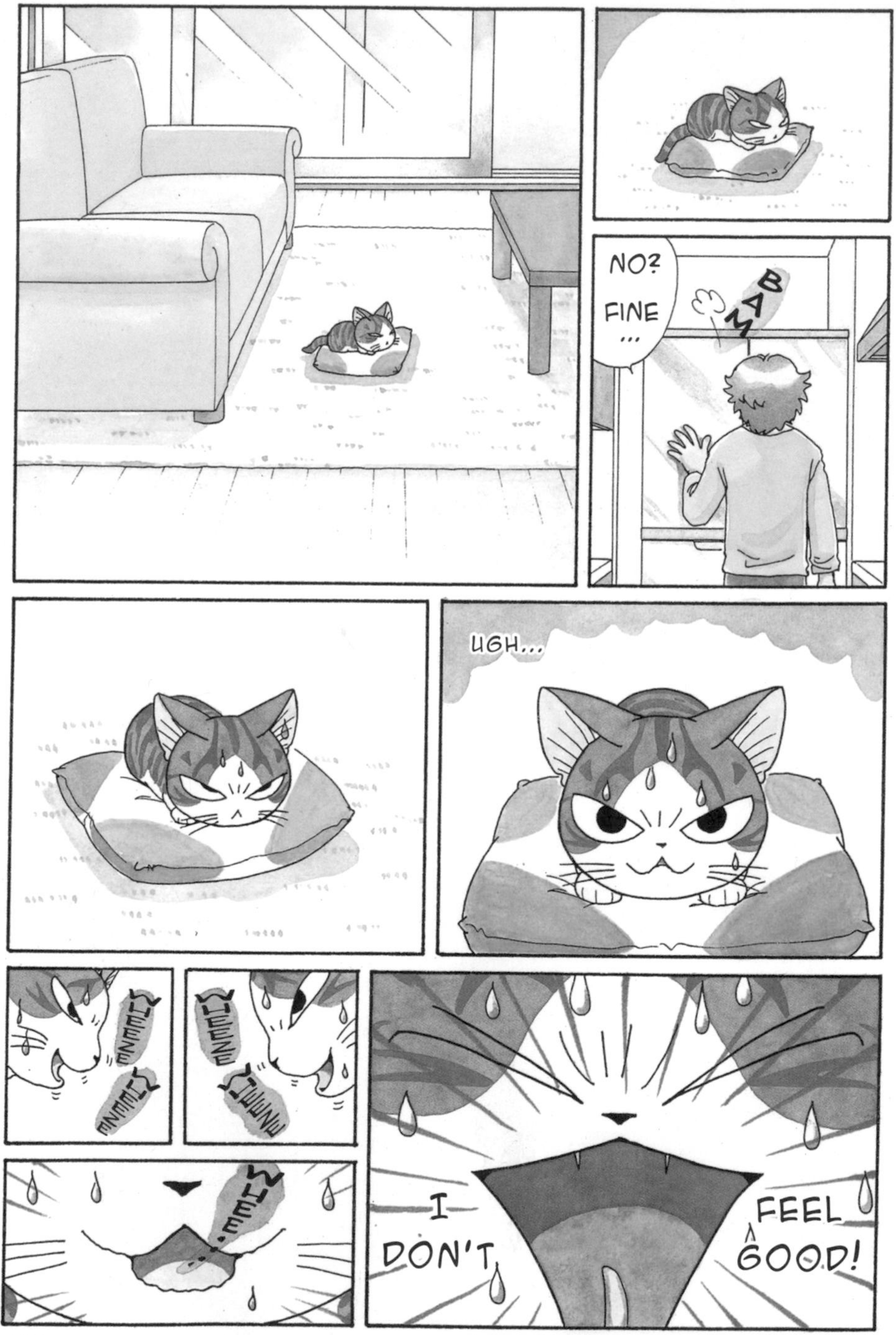
NO? FINE ...
BAM
UGH...
WHEENE
WHEEENE
WHEENE
WHEEENE
WHEE...
I DON'T FEEL GOOD!

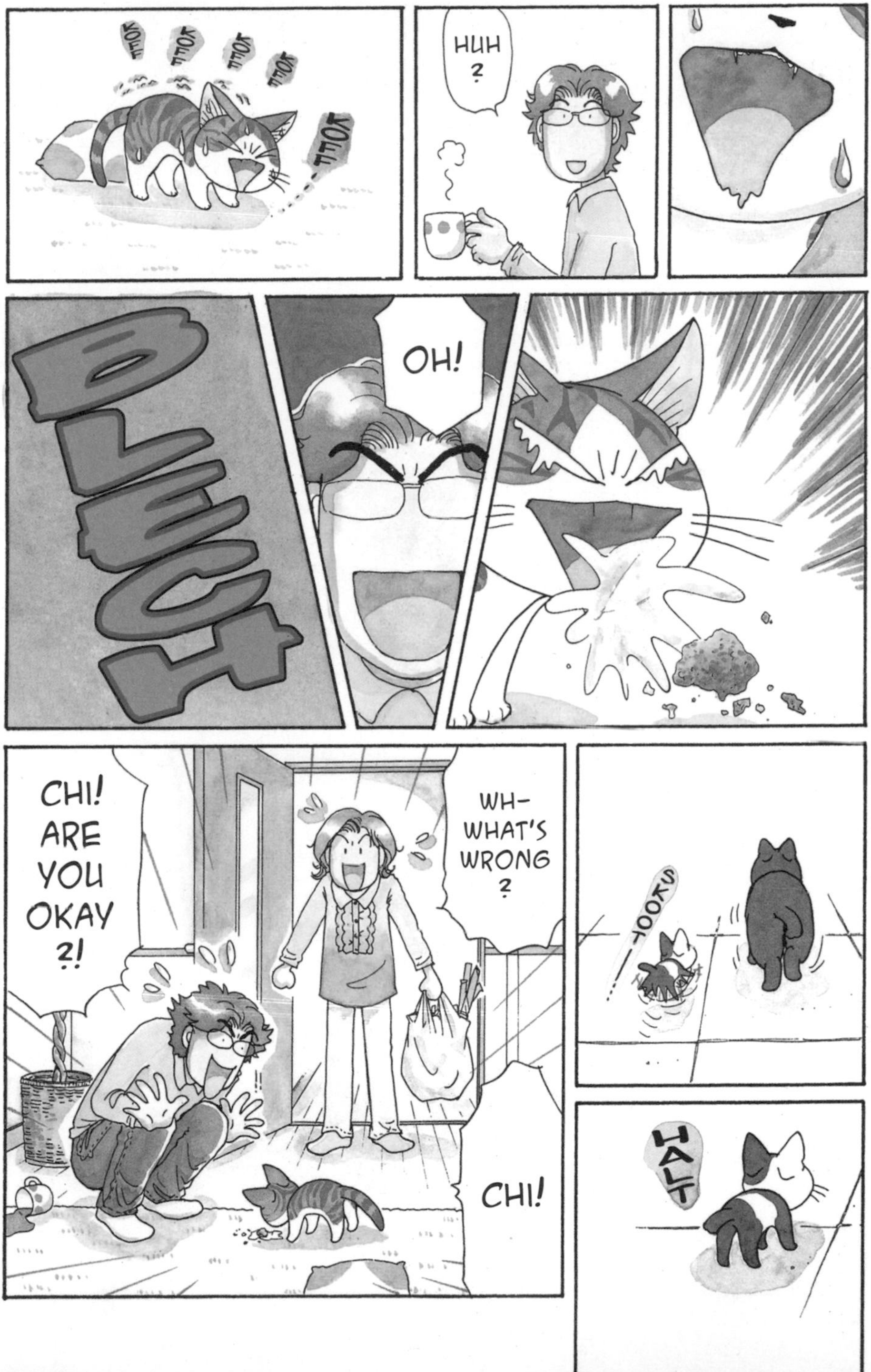
KOFF
KOFF
KOFF
KOFF
KOFF
HUH?
BLECH!
OH!
CHI! ARE YOU OKAY?!
WH-WHAT'S WRONG?
CHI!
SKOOT
HALT

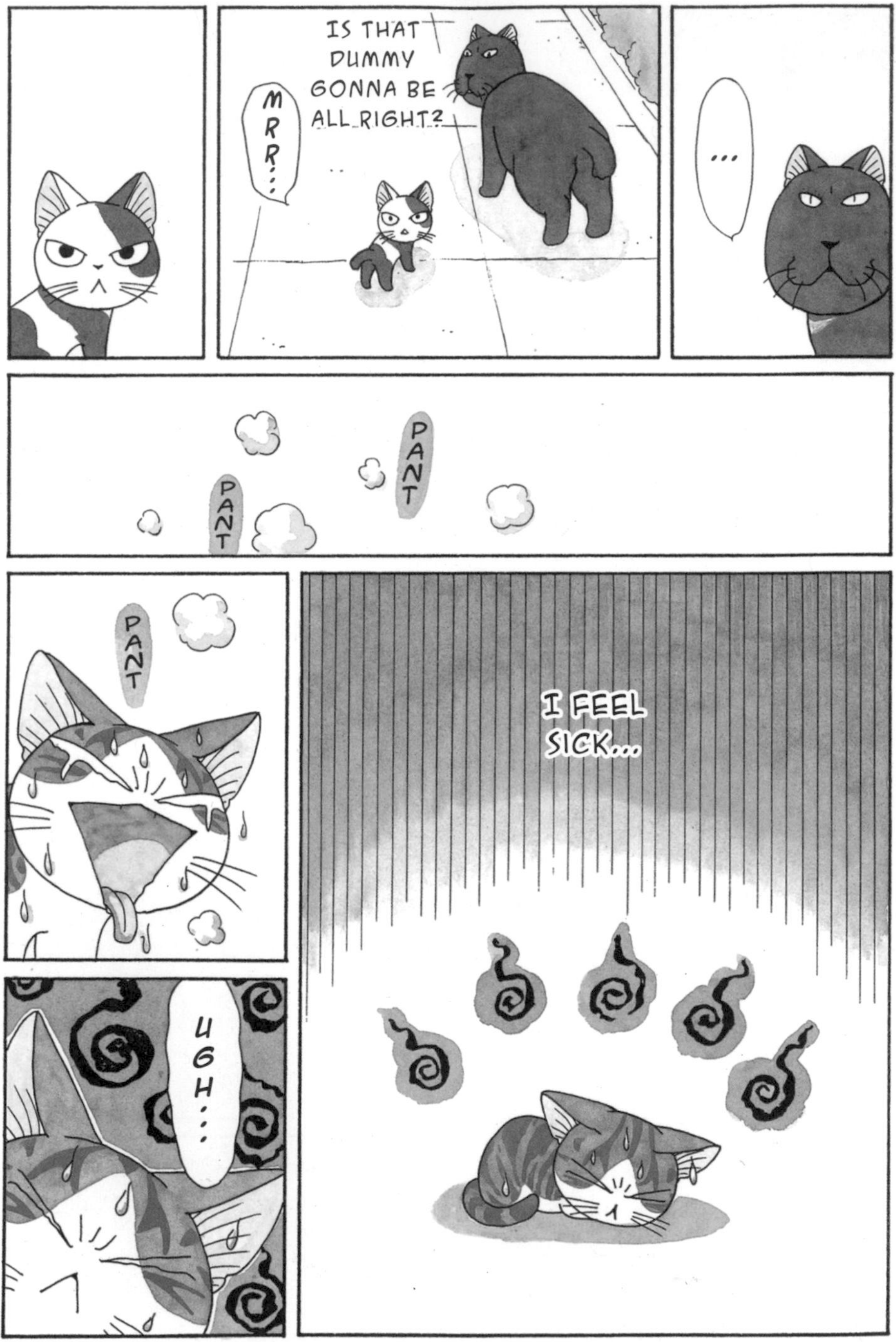

IS THAT DUMMY GONNA BE ALL RIGHT?
MRR...
...
PANT
PANT
PANT
I FEEL SICK...
UGH...




**the end**

## homemade 127: a cat vomits

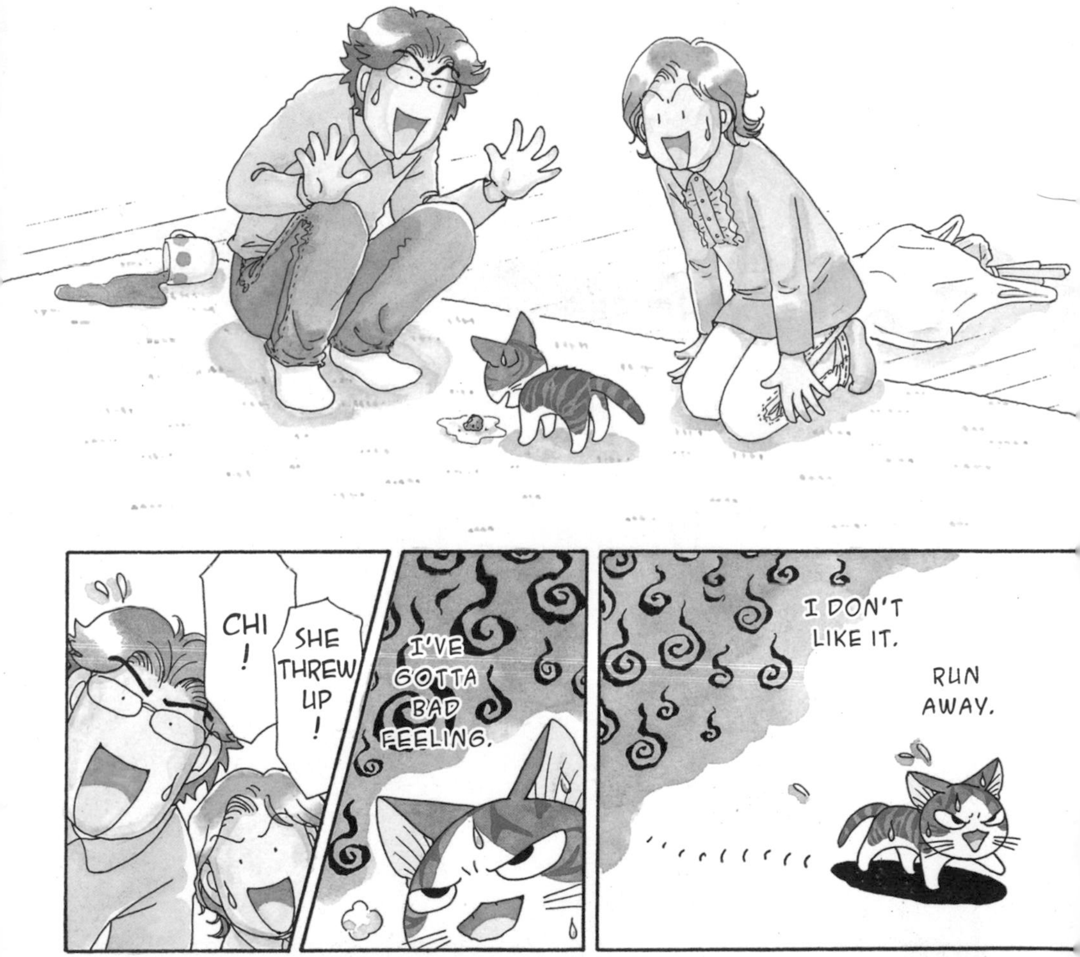
CHI!
SHE THREW UP!
I'VE GOTTA BAD FEELING.
I DON'T LIKE IT.
RUN AWAY.

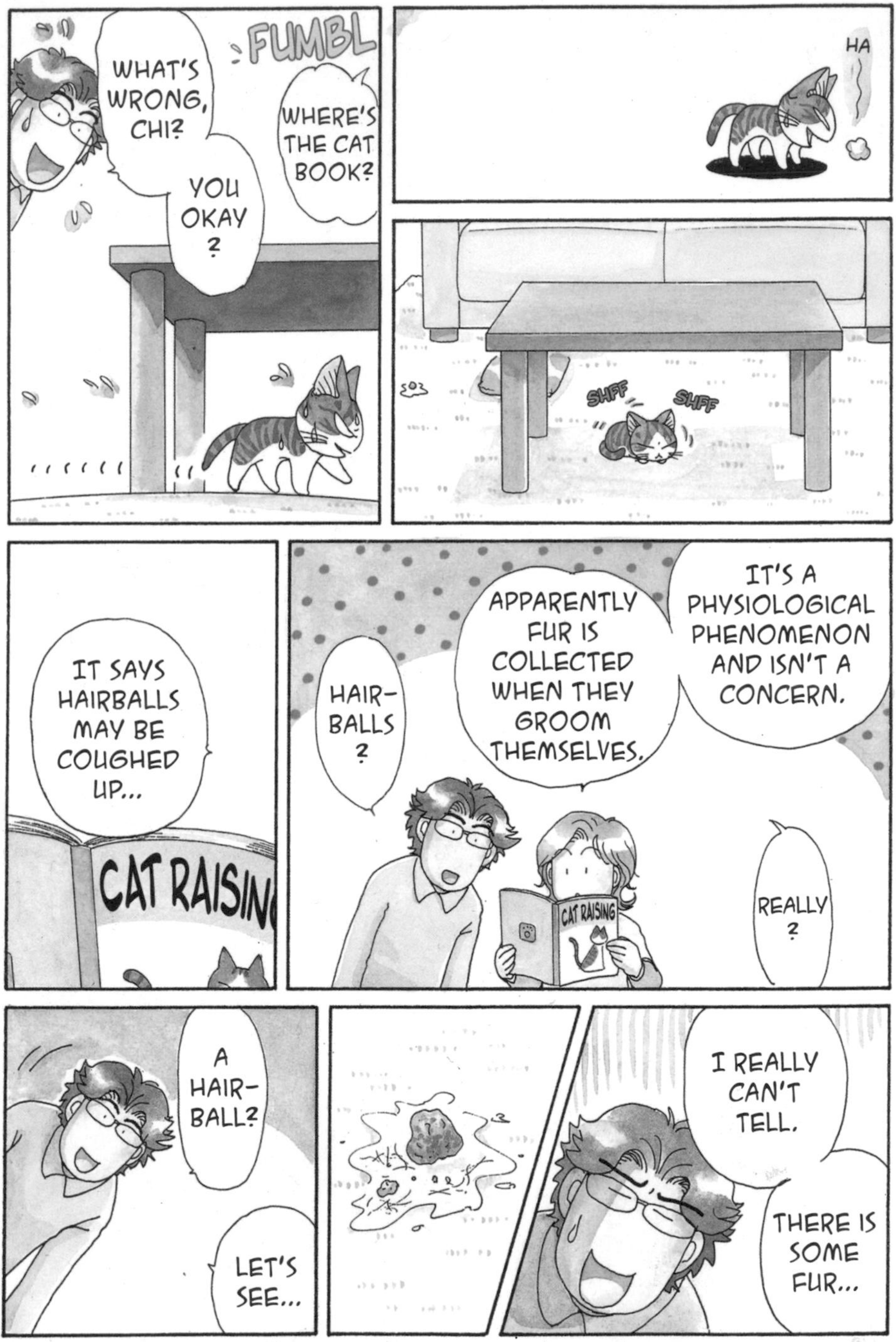

WHAT'S WRONG, CHI?
YOU OKAY?
FUMBL
WHERE'S THE CAT BOOK?
HA
SHFF
SHFF
IT SAYS HAIRBALLS MAY BE COUGHED UP...
CAT RAISING
HAIR-BALLS?
APPARENTLY FUR IS COLLECTED WHEN THEY GROOM THEMSELVES.
IT'S A PHYSIOLOGICAL PHENOMENON AND ISN'T A CONCERN.
CAT RAISING
REALLY?
A HAIR-BALL?
LET'S SEE...
I REALLY CAN'T TELL.
THERE IS SOME FUR...

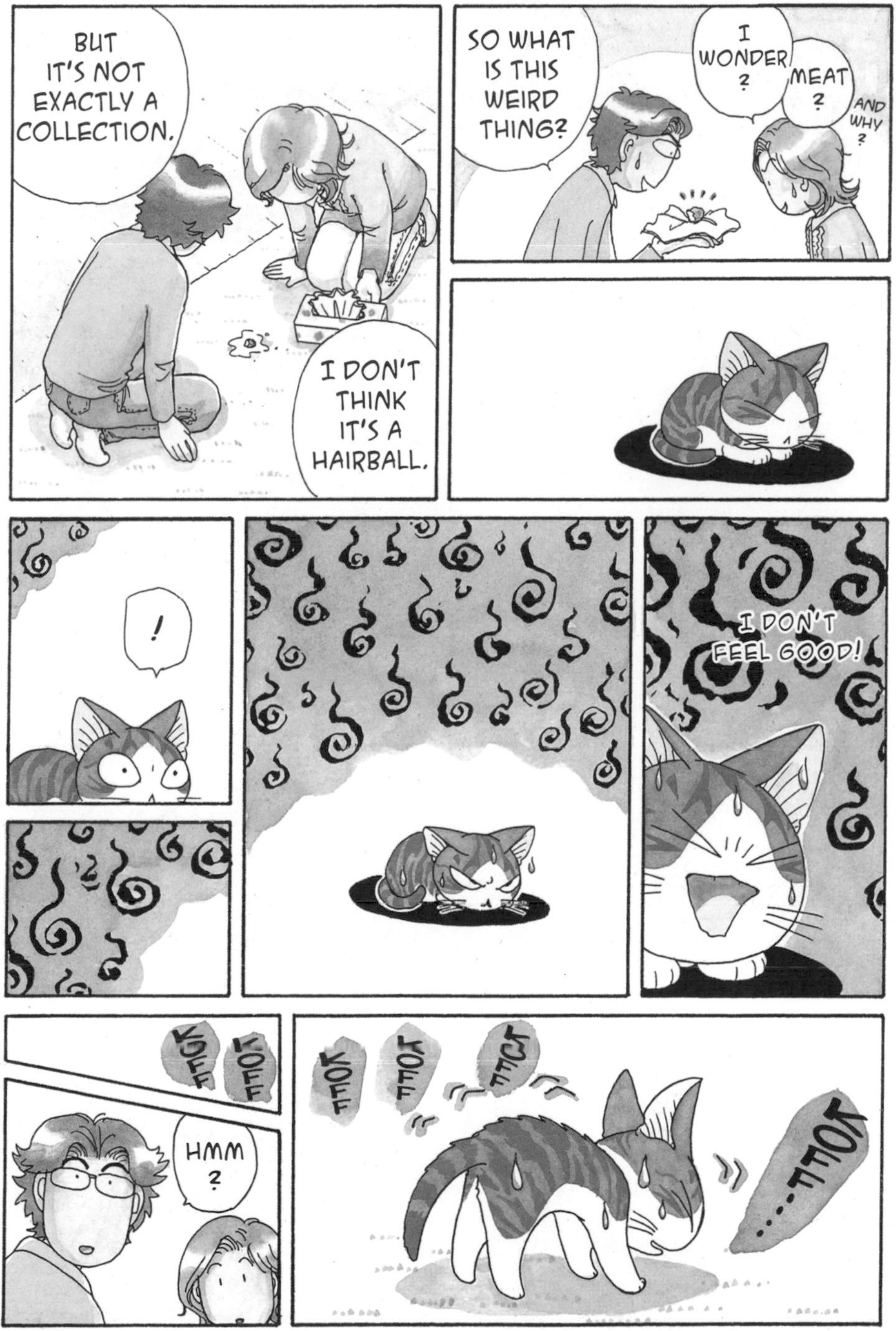
BUT IT'S NOT EXACTLY A COLLECTION.
I DON'T THINK IT'S A HAIRBALL.
SO WHAT IS THIS WEIRD THING?
I WONDER?
MEAT?
AND WHY?
!
I DON'T FEEL GOOD!
KOFF
KOFF
HMM?
KOFF
KOFF
KOFF
KOFF...

SHE VOMITED AGAIN!

THE BAD FEELING ...

GOTTA RUN AWAY.

AGGIT AGGIT

FWUMP

WHAT DID SHE SPIT UP THIS TIME?

A HAIR-BALL?

SOME-THING STRANGE?

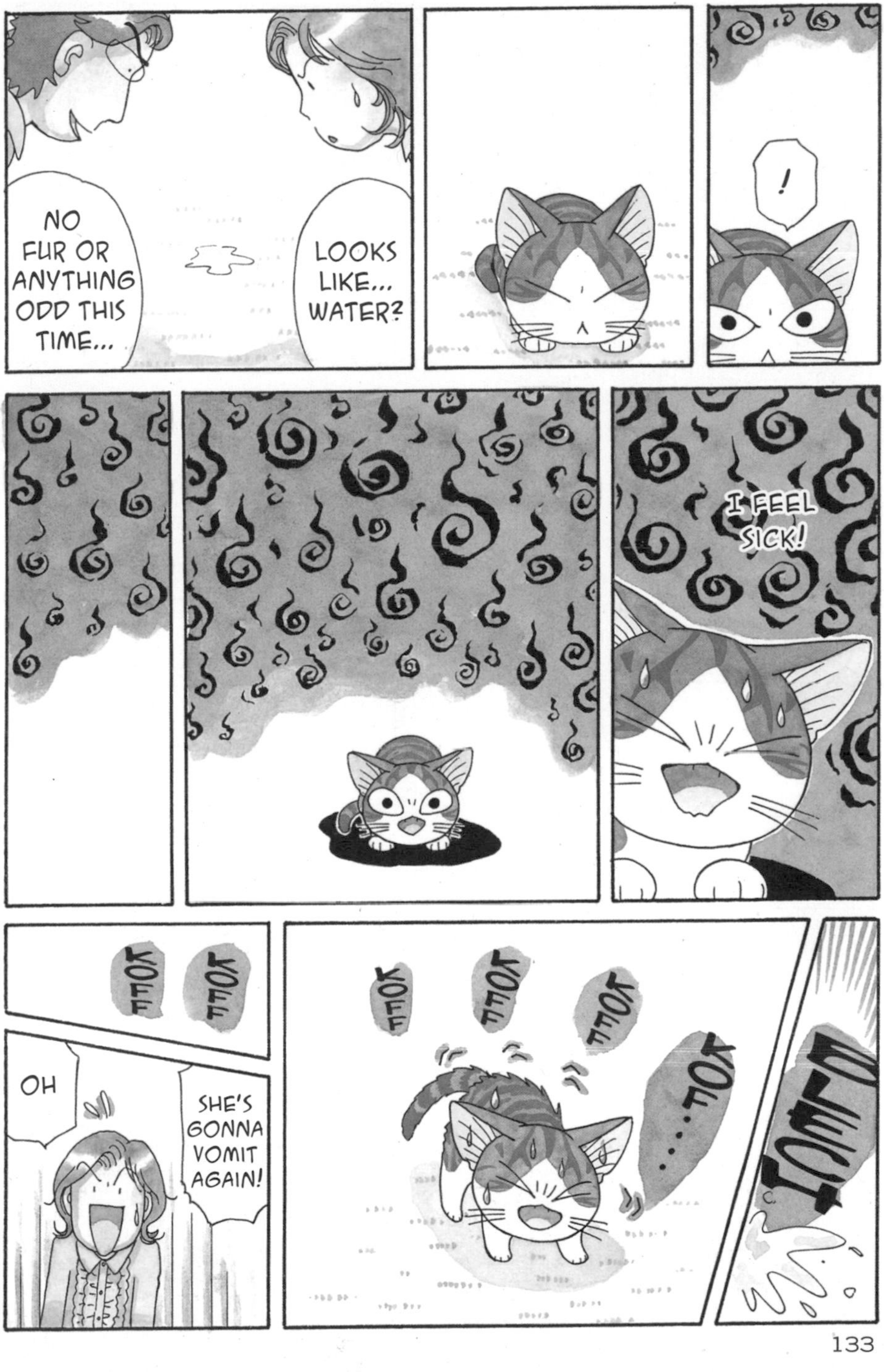
NO FUR OR ANYTHING ODD THIS TIME...
LOOKS LIKE... WATER?
!
I FEEL SICK!
KOFF
KOFF
OH
SHE'S GONNA VOMIT AGAIN!
KOFF
KOFF
KOFF
KOF...

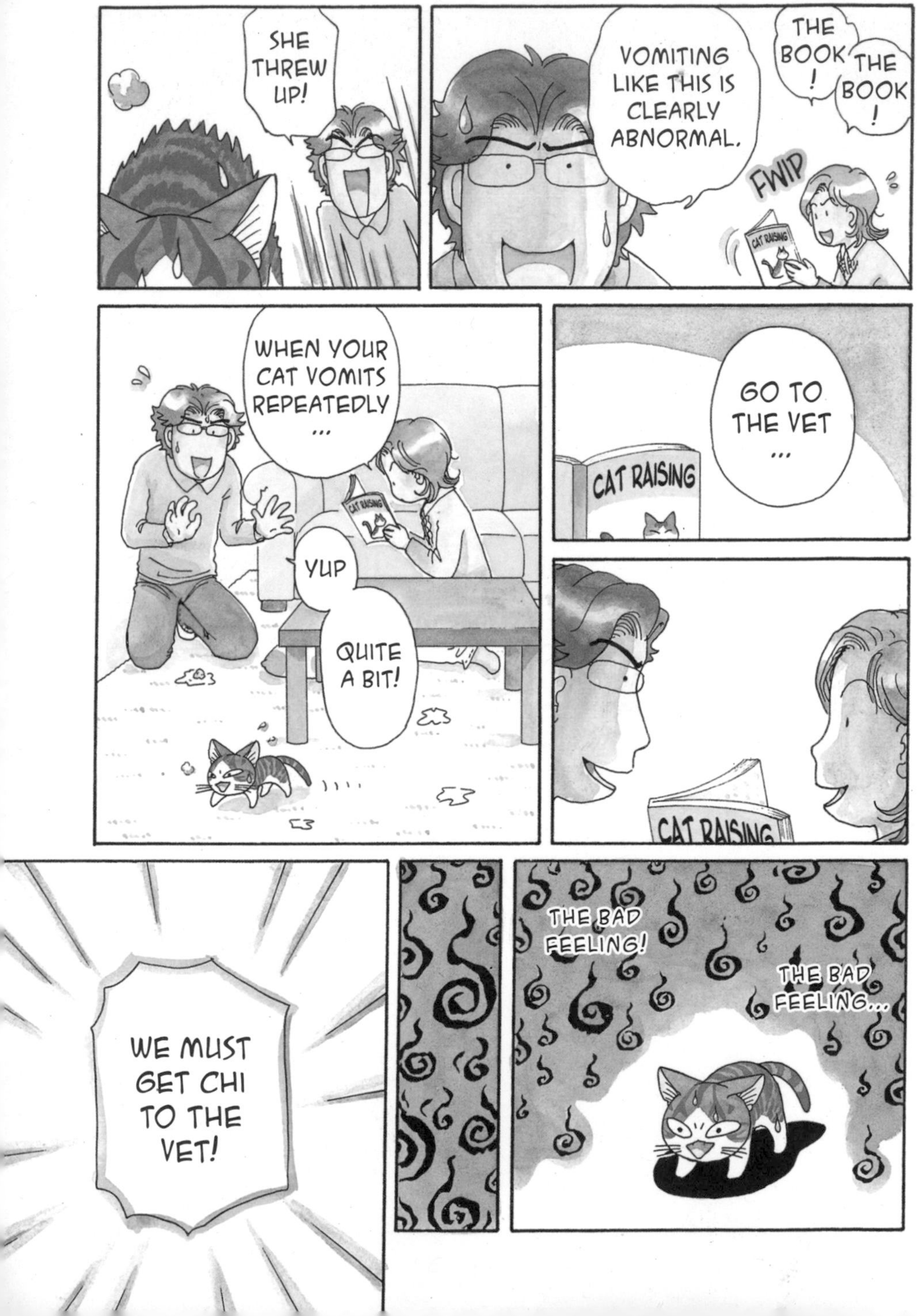
SHE THREW UP!
VOMITING LIKE THIS IS CLEARLY ABNORMAL.
THE BOOK!
THE BOOK!
FWIP
CAT RAISING
WHEN YOUR CAT VOMITS REPEATEDLY ...
CAT RAISING
YUP
QUITE A BIT!
GO TO THE VET ...
CAT RAISING
CAT RAISING
WE MUST GET CHI TO THE VET!
THE BAD FEELING!
THE BAD FEELING...

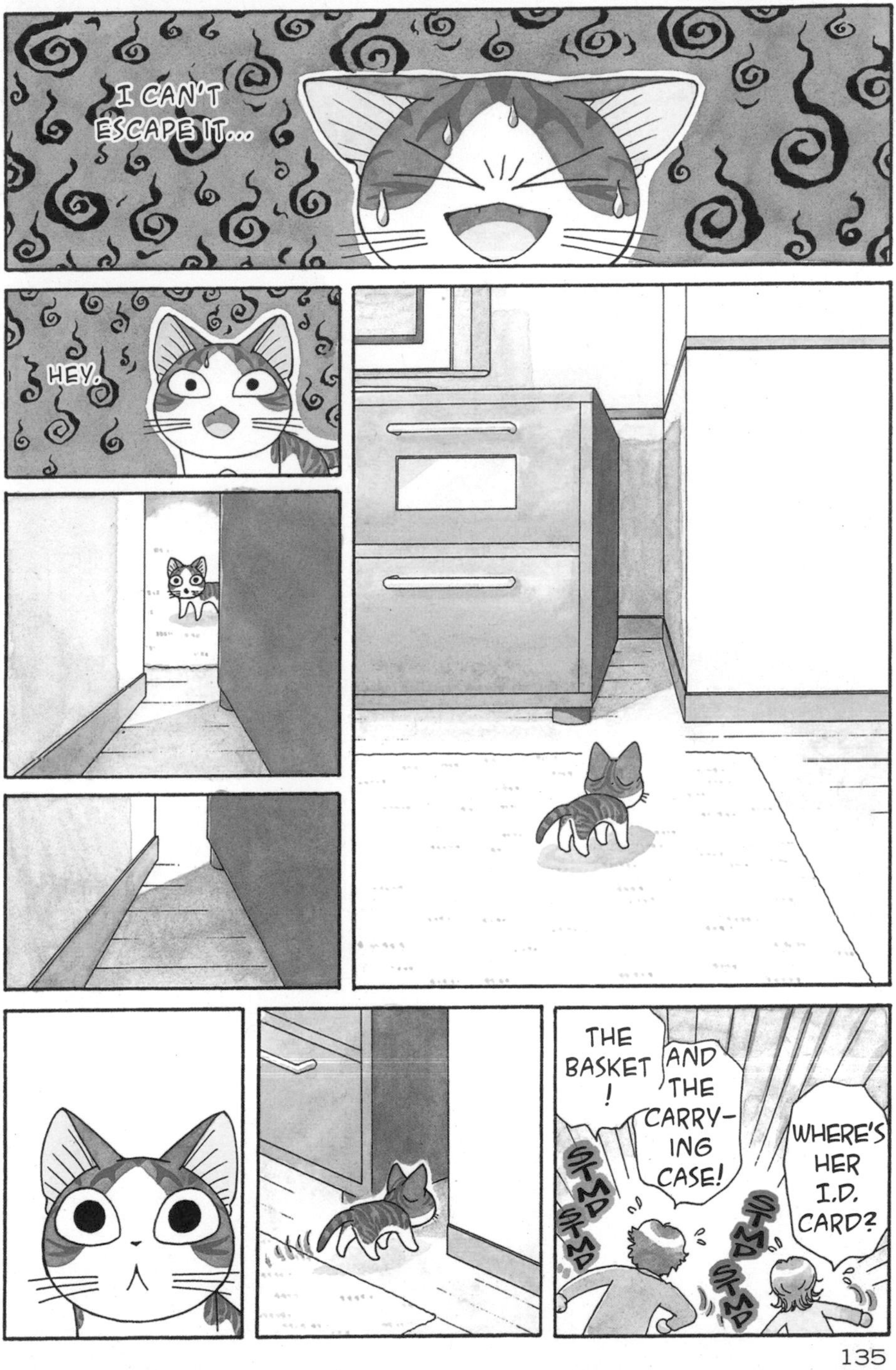
I CAN'T ESCAPE IT...
HEY.
THE BASKET!
AND THE CARRYING CASE!
STMP STMP
WHERE'S HER I.D. CARD?
STMP STMP

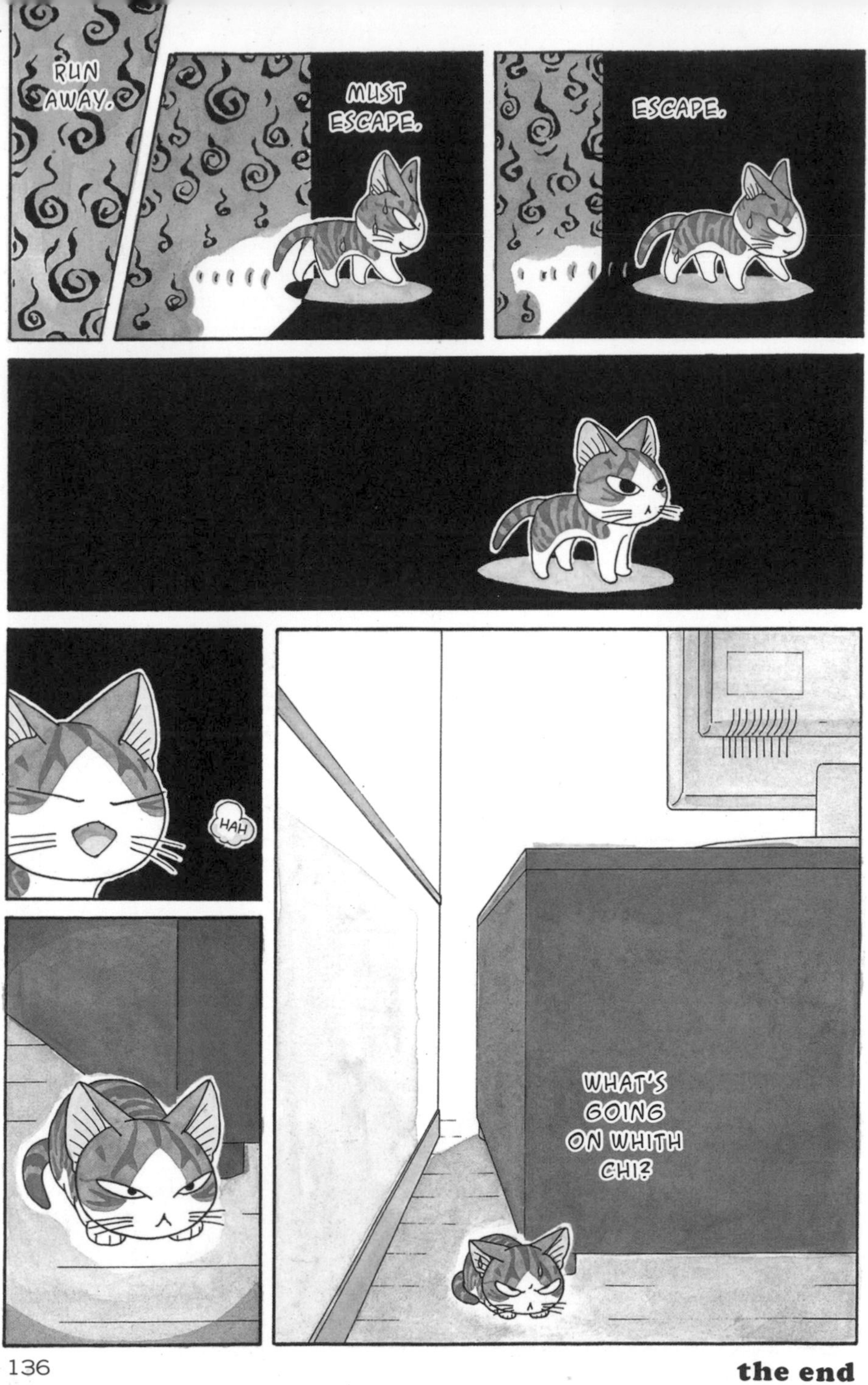
RUN AWAY.
MUST ESCAPE.
ESCAPE.
HAH
WHAT'S GOING ON WHITH CHI?



the end

# homemade 128: a cat hangs in there

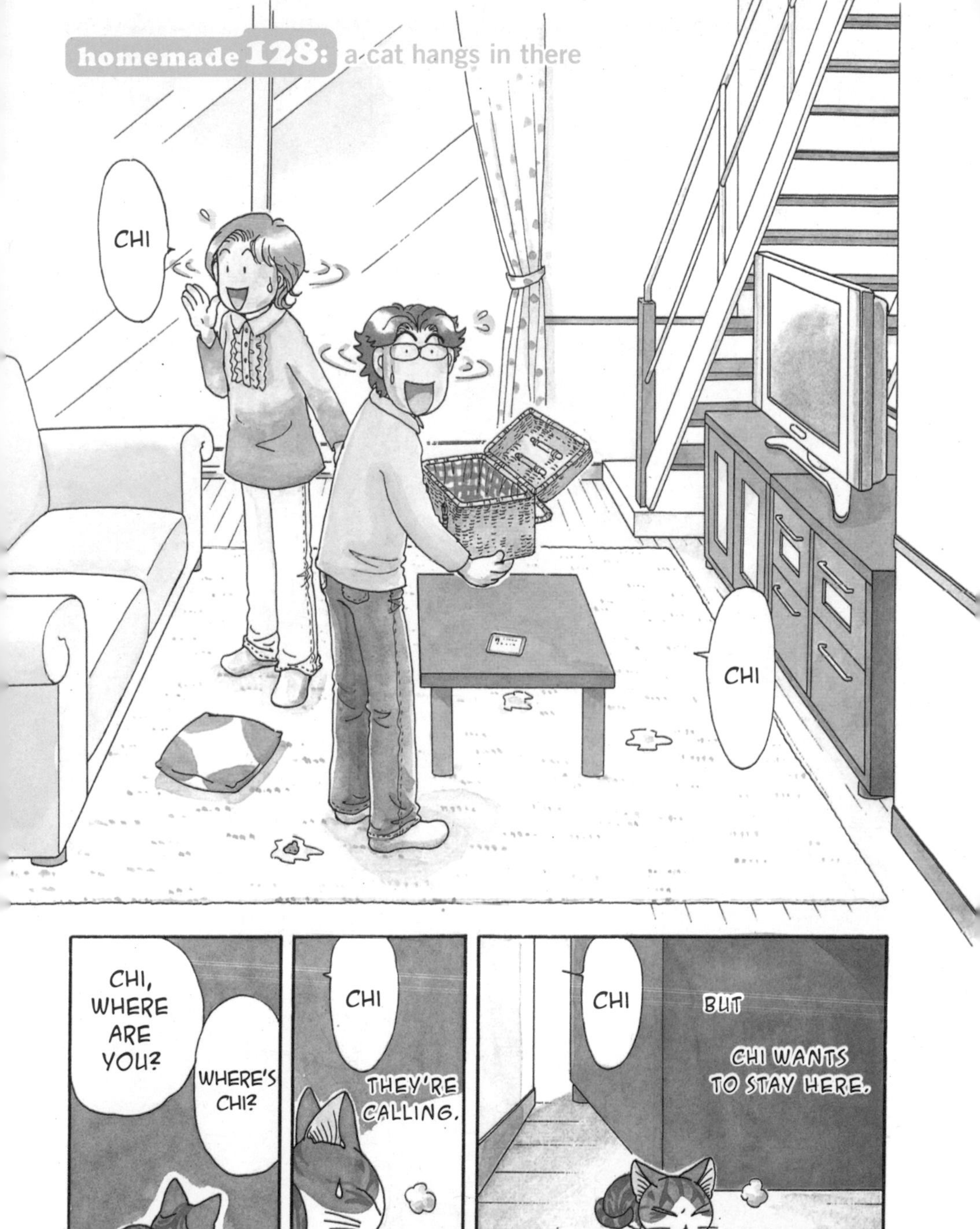
CHI
CHI
CHI, WHERE ARE YOU?
WHERE'S CHI?
CHI
THEY'RE CALLING.
CHI
BUT
CHI WANTS TO STAY HERE.

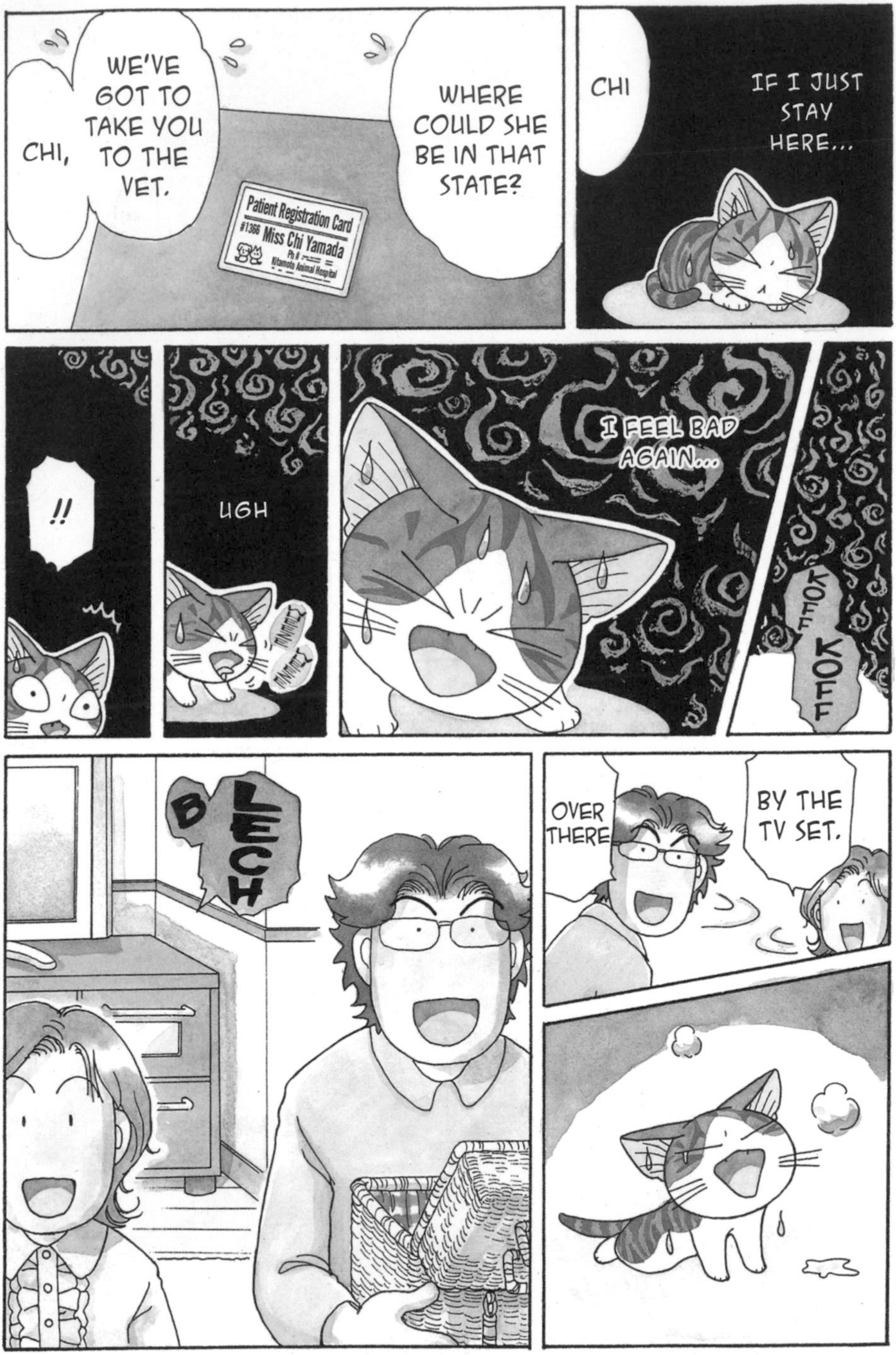
CHI,
WE'VE GOT TO TAKE YOU TO THE VET.
WHERE COULD SHE BE IN THAT STATE?
Patient Registration Card
#1366 Miss Chi Yamada
Kitamoto Animal Hospital
CHI
IF I JUST STAY HERE...
!!
UGH
I FEEL BAD AGAIN...
KOFF
KOFF
KOFF
BLECH
OVER THERE
BY THE TV SET.

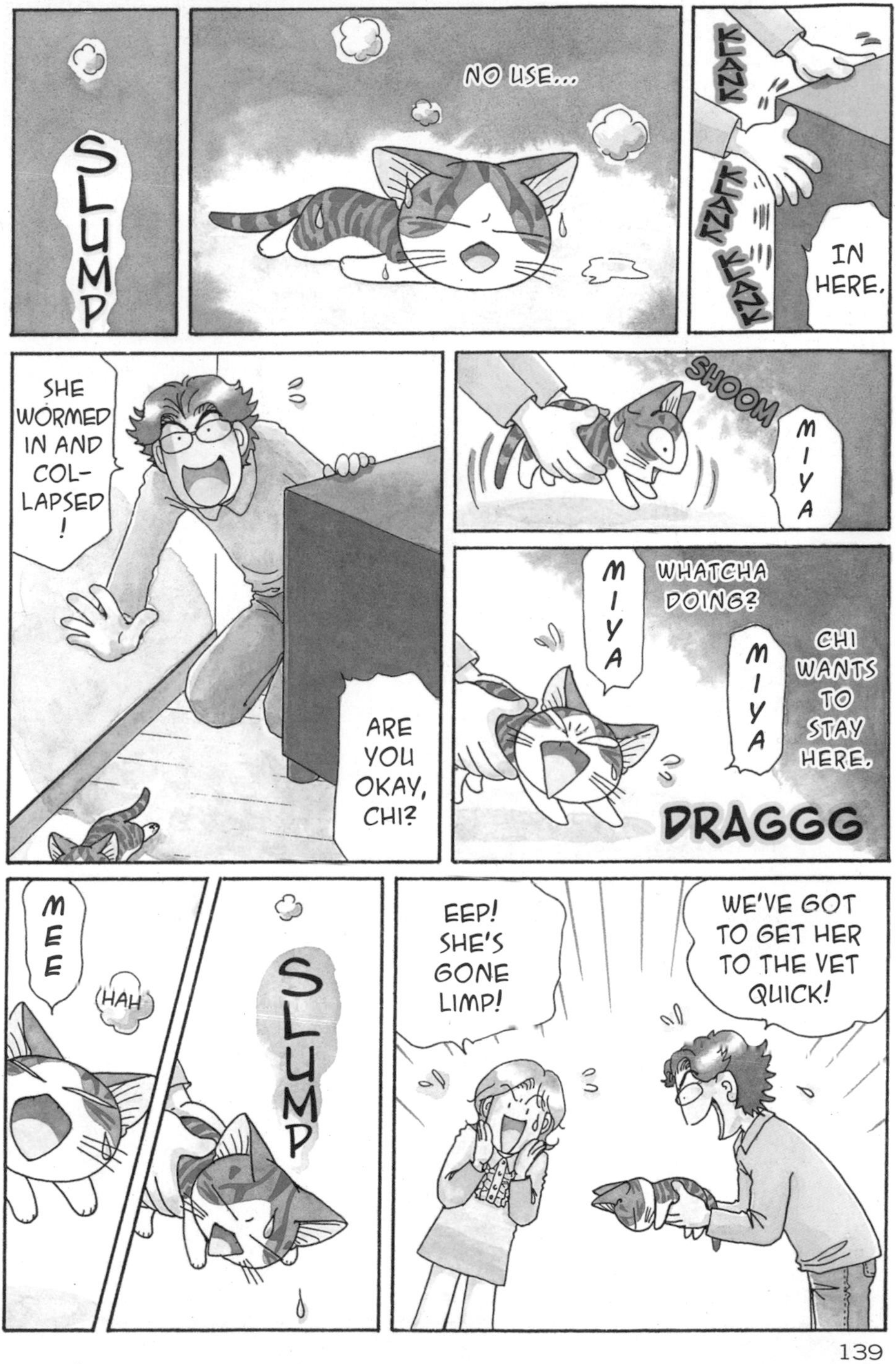
SLUMP
NO USE...
KLANK KLANK KLANK
IN HERE.
SHE WORMED IN AND COL-LAPSED!
ARE YOU OKAY, CHI?
SHOOM
MIYA
MIYA
WHATCHA DOING?
MIYA
CHI WANTS TO STAY HERE.
DRAGGG
MEE
HAH
SLUMP
EEP! SHE'S GONE LIMP!
WE'VE GOT TO GET HER TO THE VET QUICK!

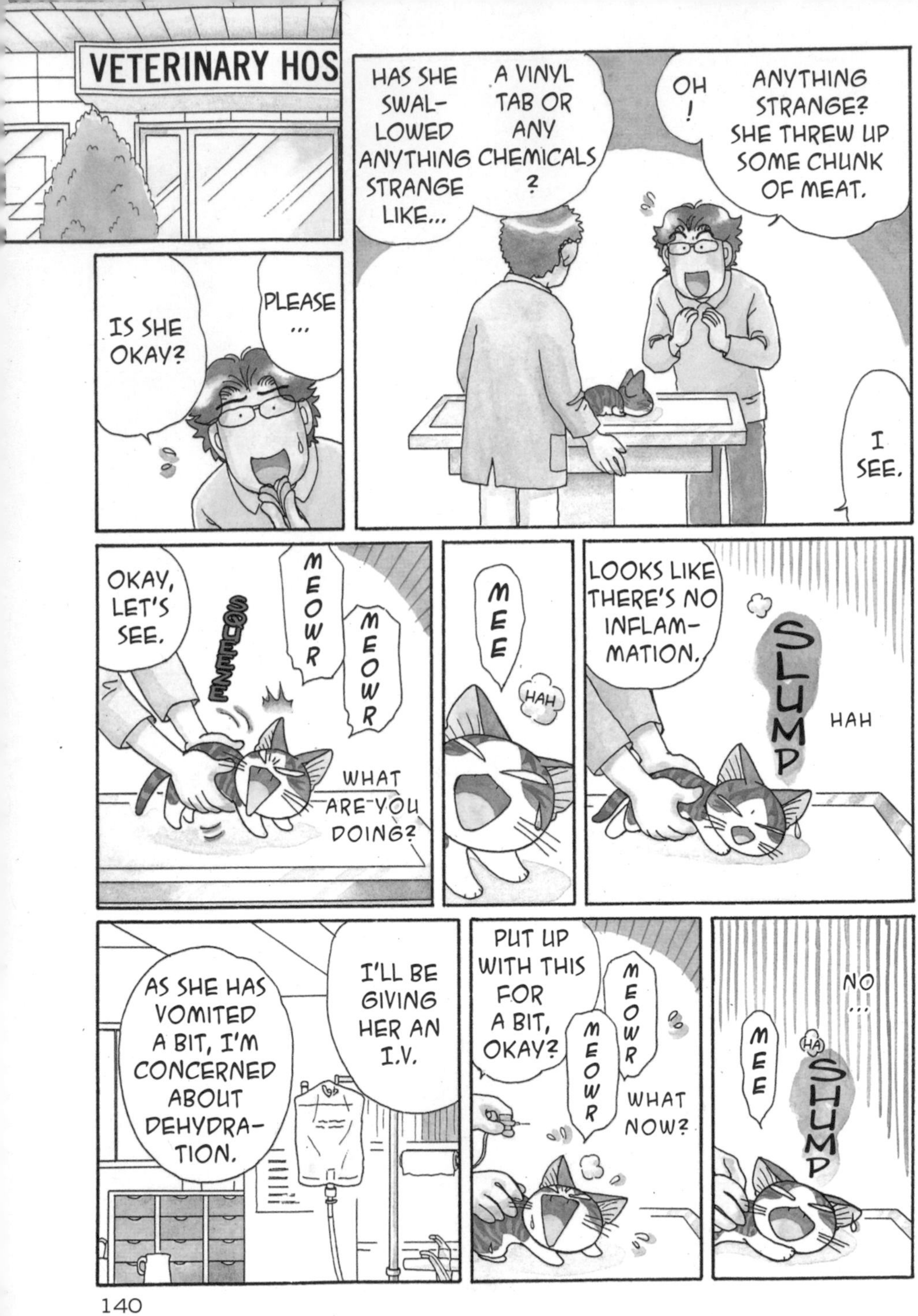
VETERINARY HOS
IS SHE OKAY?
PLEASE...
HAS SHE SWALLOWED ANYTHING STRANGE LIKE...
A VINYL TAB OR ANY CHEMICALS?
OH!
ANYTHING STRANGE? SHE THREW UP SOME CHUNK OF MEAT.
I SEE.
OKAY, LET'S SEE.
SQUEEZE
MEOWR
MEOWR
WHAT ARE YOU DOING?
MEE
HAH
LOOKS LIKE THERE'S NO INFLAMMATION.
SLUMP
HAH
AS SHE HAS VOMITED A BIT, I'M CONCERNED ABOUT DEHYDRATION.
I'LL BE GIVING HER AN I.V.
PUT UP WITH THIS FOR A BIT, OKAY?
MEOWR
MEOWR
WHAT NOW?
NO...
MEE
HA
SHUMP

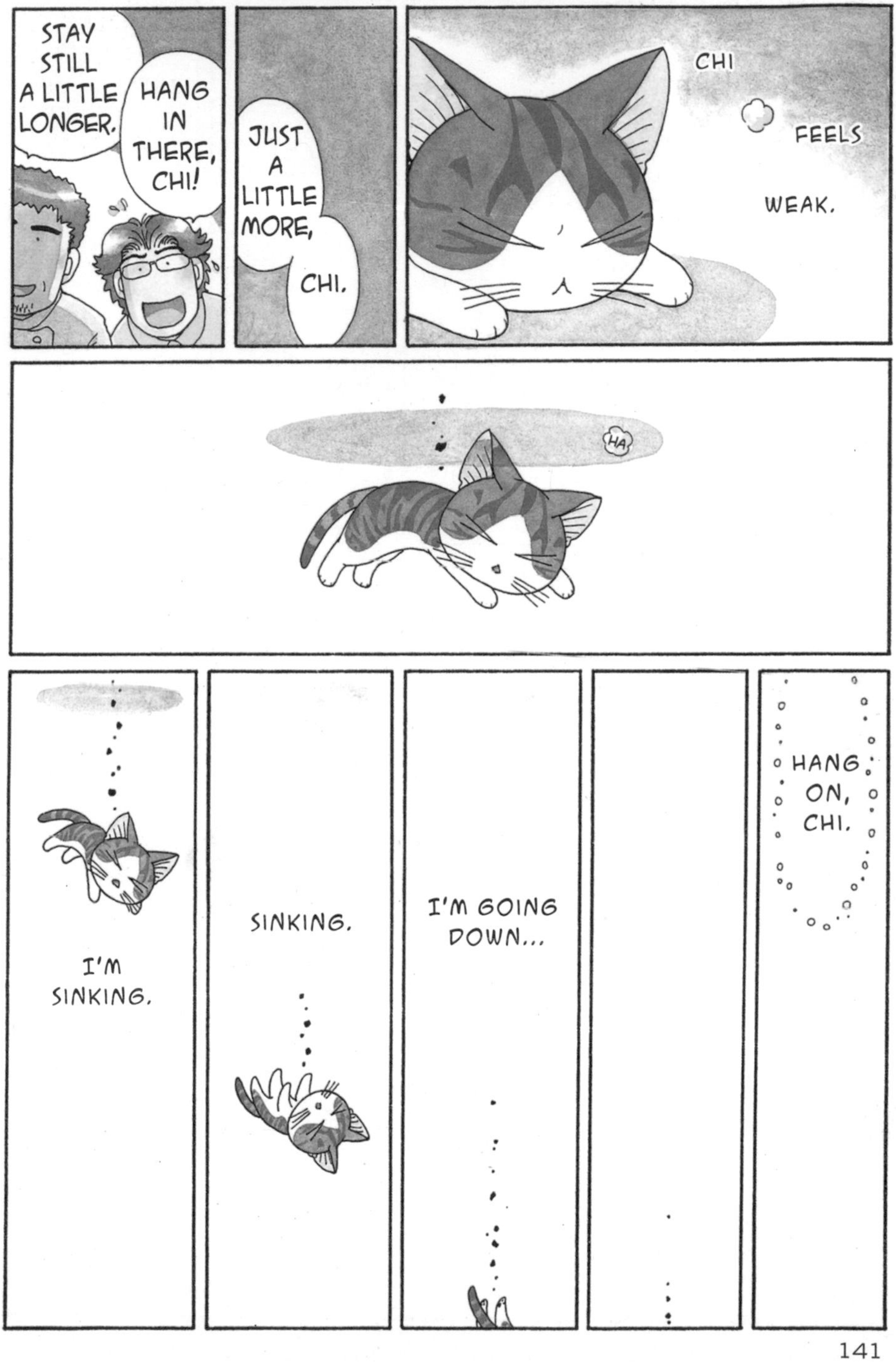
STAY STILL A LITTLE LONGER.
HANG IN THERE, CHI!
JUST A LITTLE MORE,
CHI.
CHI
FEELS
WEAK.
HA
I'M SINKING.
SINKING.
I'M GOING DOWN...
HANG ON, CHI.

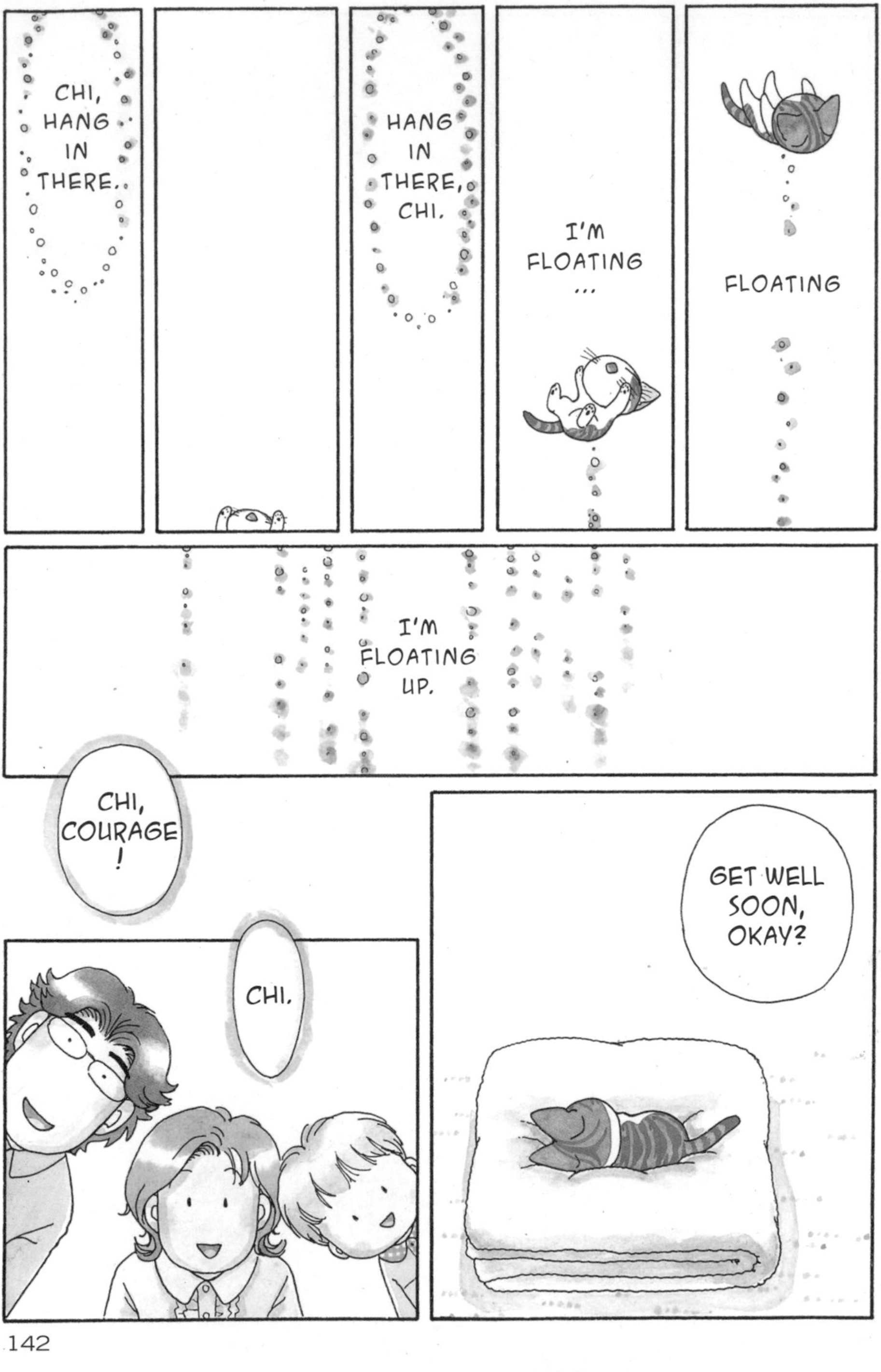
CHI, HANG IN THERE.
HANG IN THERE, CHI.
I'M FLOATING ...
FLOATING
I'M FLOATING UP.
CHI, COURAGE!
CHI.
GET WELL SOON, OKAY?

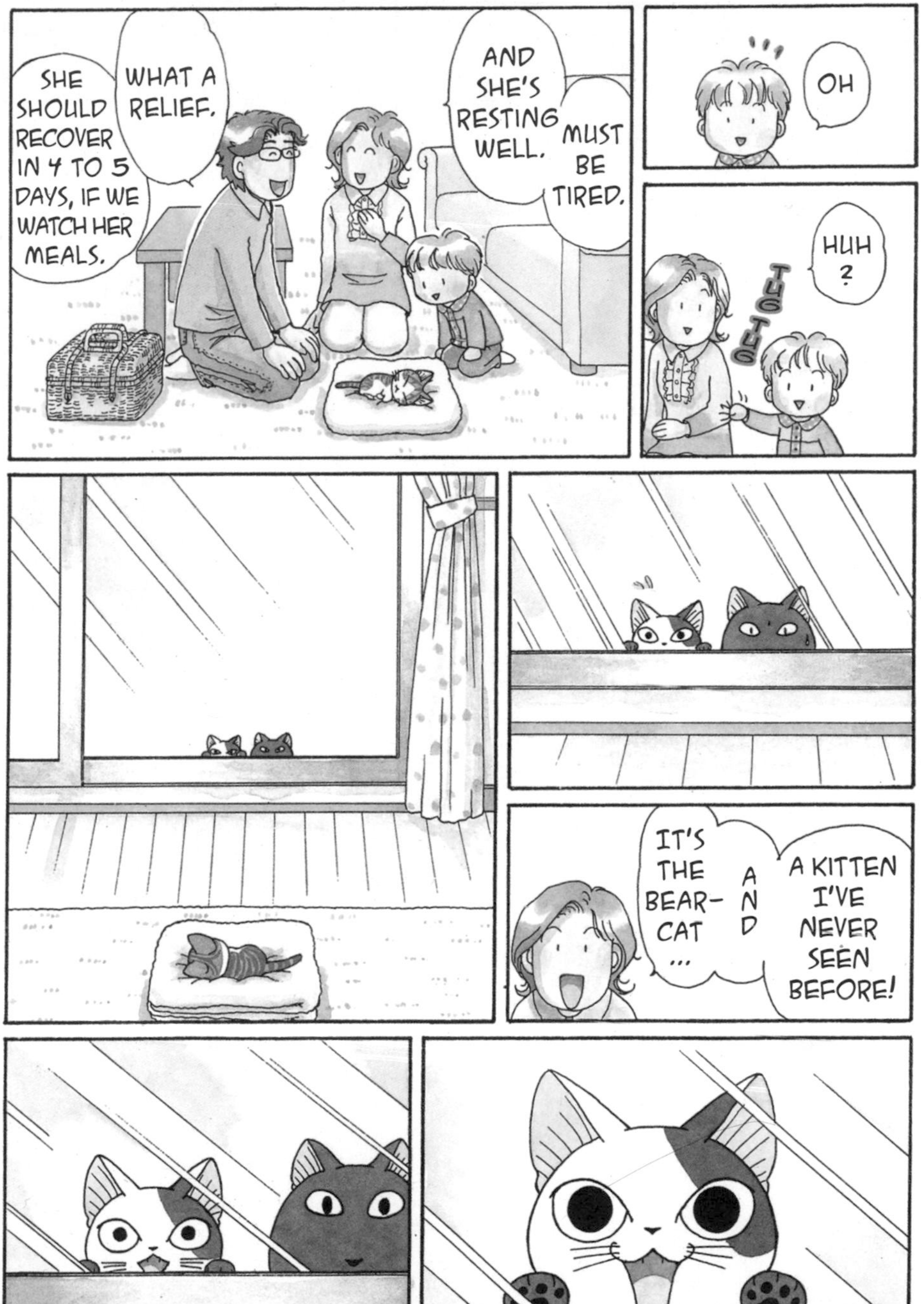
SHE SHOULD RECOVER IN 4 TO 5 DAYS, IF WE WATCH HER MEALS.
WHAT A RELIEF.
AND SHE'S RESTING WELL.
MUST BE TIRED.
OH
HUH?
TUG TUG
IT'S THE BEAR-CAT...
AND
A KITTEN I'VE NEVER SEEN BEFORE!

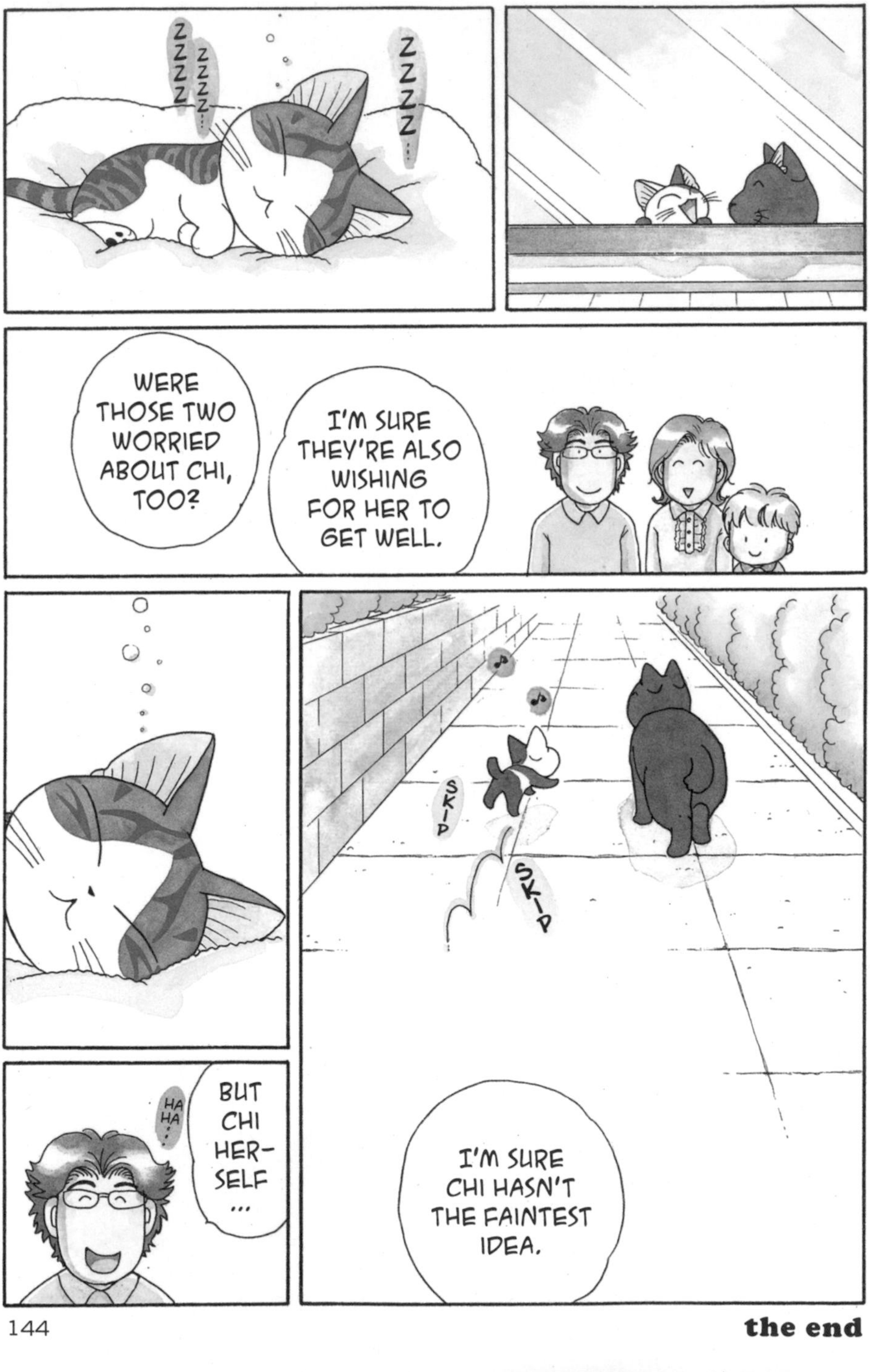
ZZZZ
ZZZZ...
ZZZZ...
WERE THOSE TWO WORRIED ABOUT CHI, TOO?
I'M SURE THEY'RE ALSO WISHING FOR HER TO GET WELL.
HA HA
BUT CHI HERSELF...
SKIP
SKIP
I'M SURE CHI HASN'T THE FAINTEST IDEA.

**the end**

# homemade 129: a cat manifests

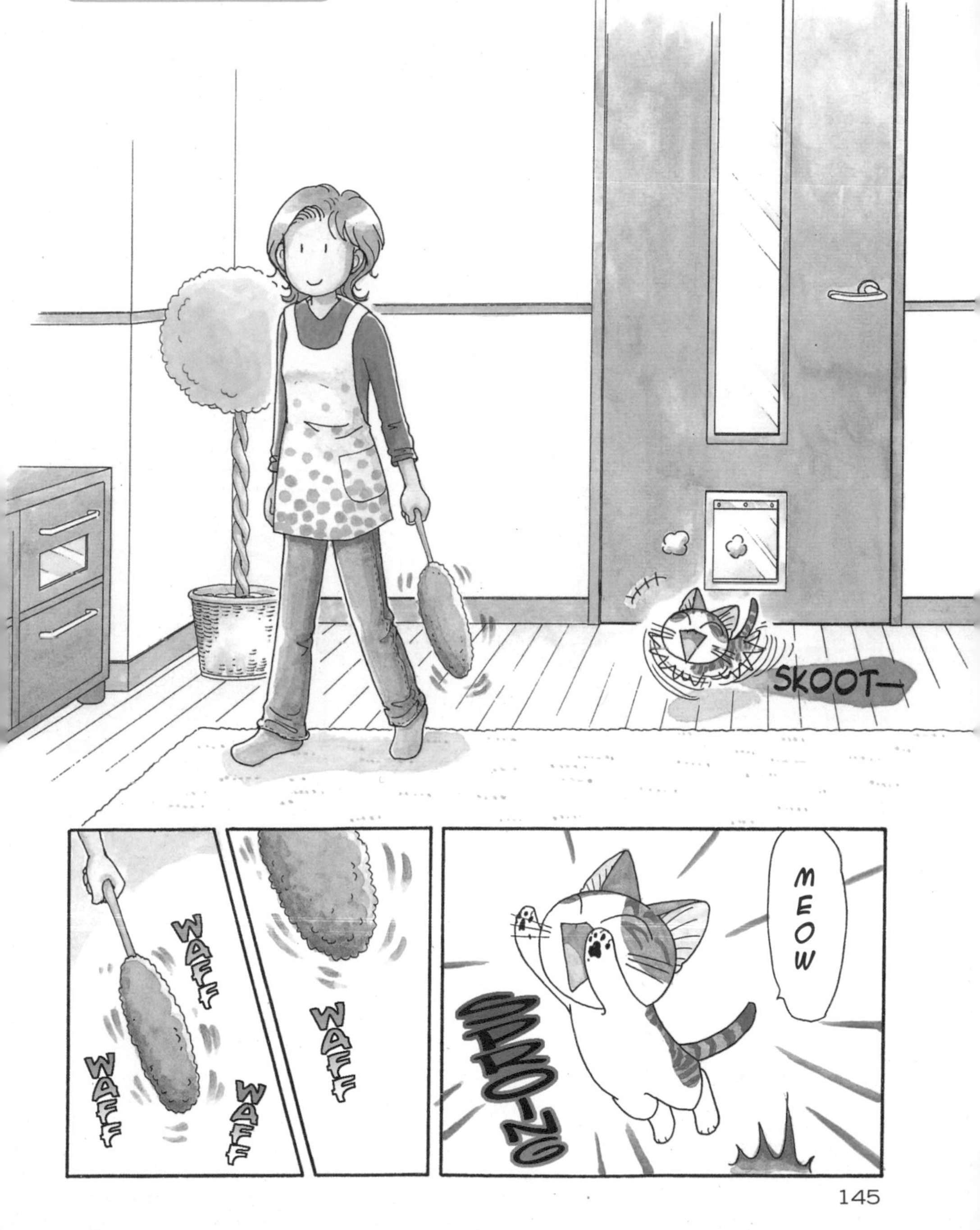
SKOOT—
WAFF
WAFF
WAFF
WAFF
MEOW
SPRO-NG

SWIFF

PLOP

RISE

SNIP
SNIP
SNIP

MEOW

SPROING

SWIFF

SMAK

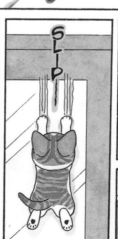

SLIP

SLUMP

WHUMP

146

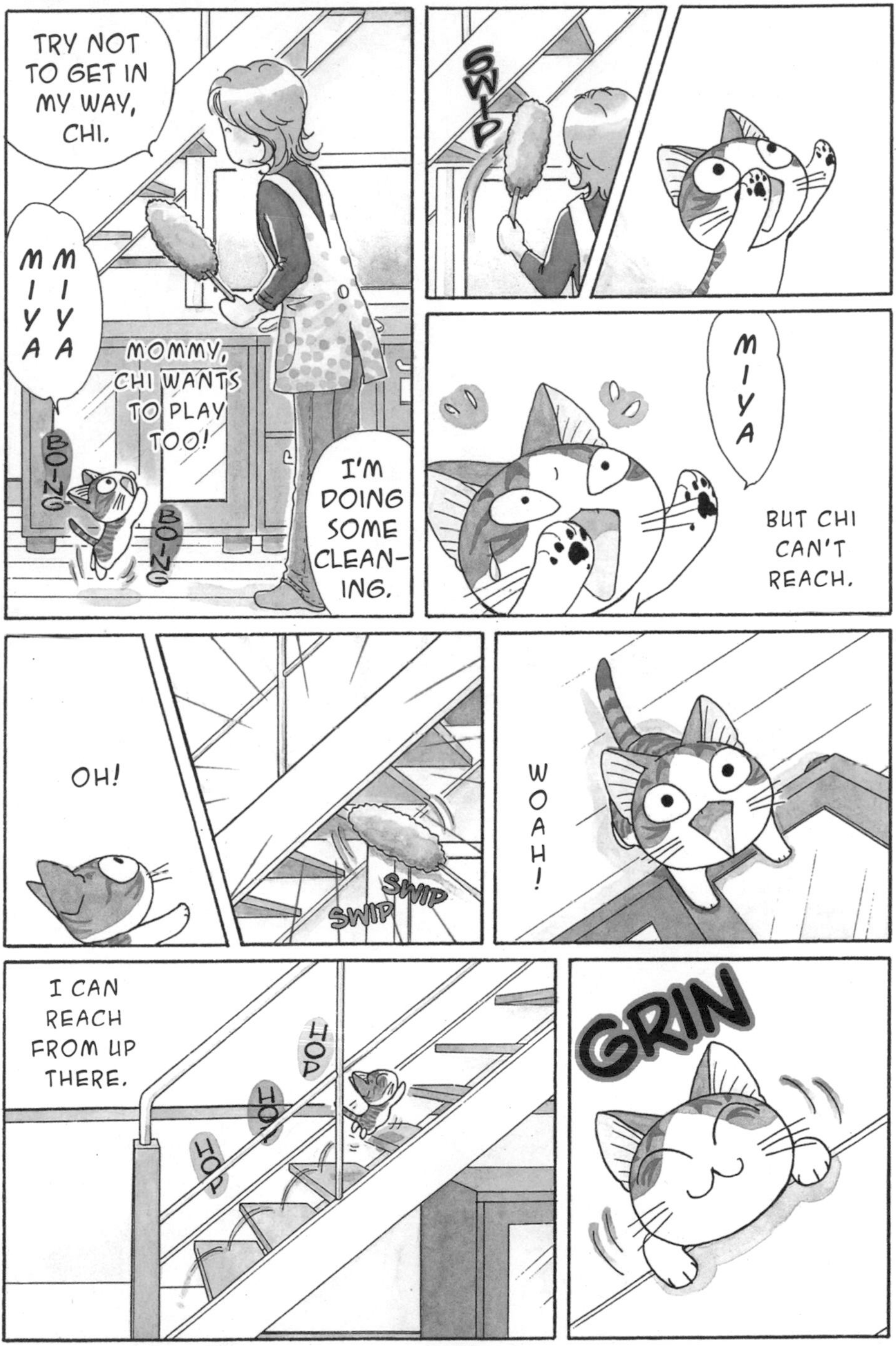
TRY NOT TO GET IN MY WAY, CHI.
MIYA MIYA
MOMMY, CHI WANTS TO PLAY TOO!
BOING BOING
I'M DOING SOME CLEAN-ING.
SWIP
MIYA
BUT CHI CAN'T REACH.
OH!
SWIP SWIP
WOAH!
I CAN REACH FROM UP THERE.
HOP HOP HOP
GRIN

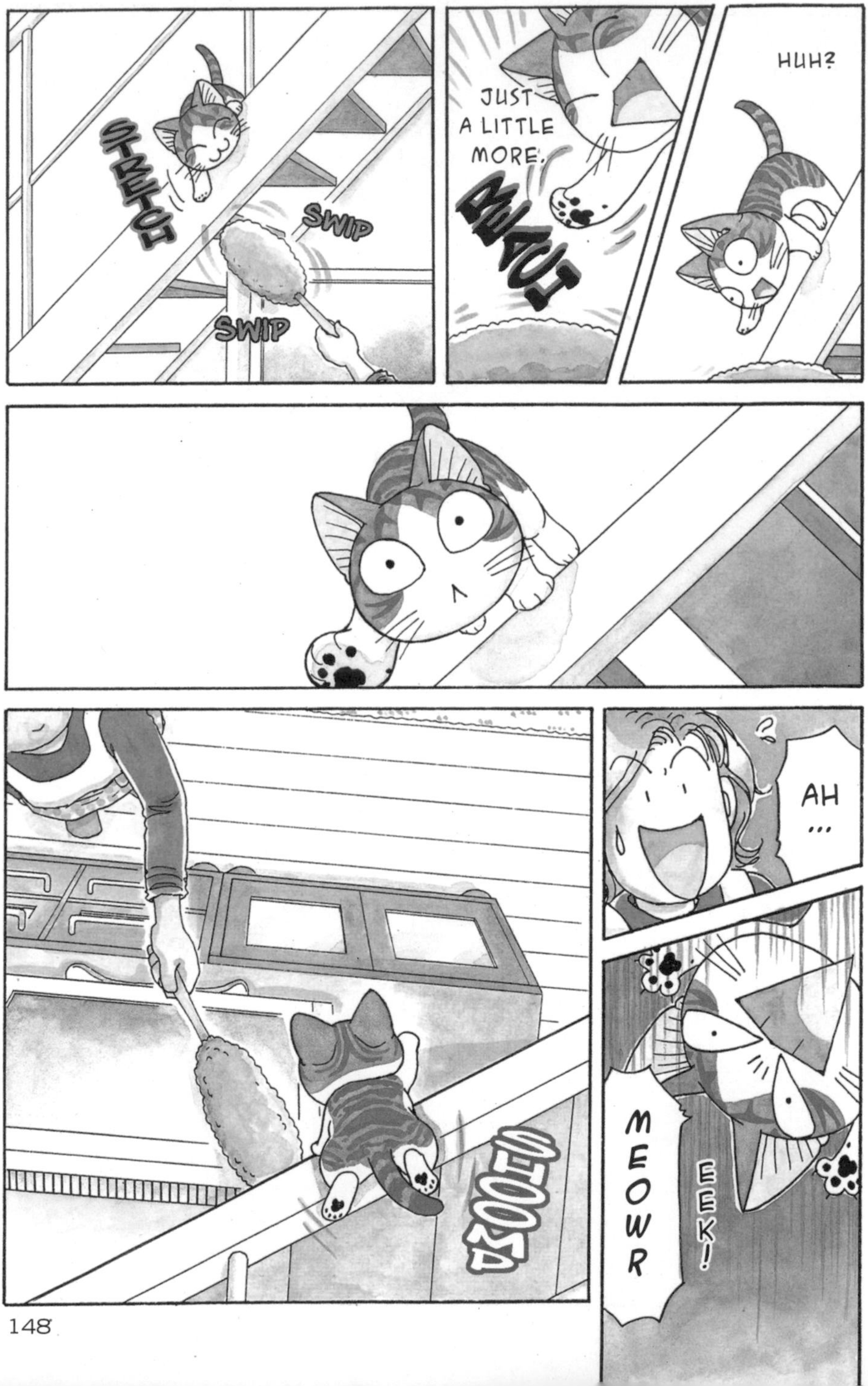
STRETCH
SWIP
SWIP
JUST A LITTLE MORE.
HUH?
SHOOMP
AH ...
MEOWR
EEEK!

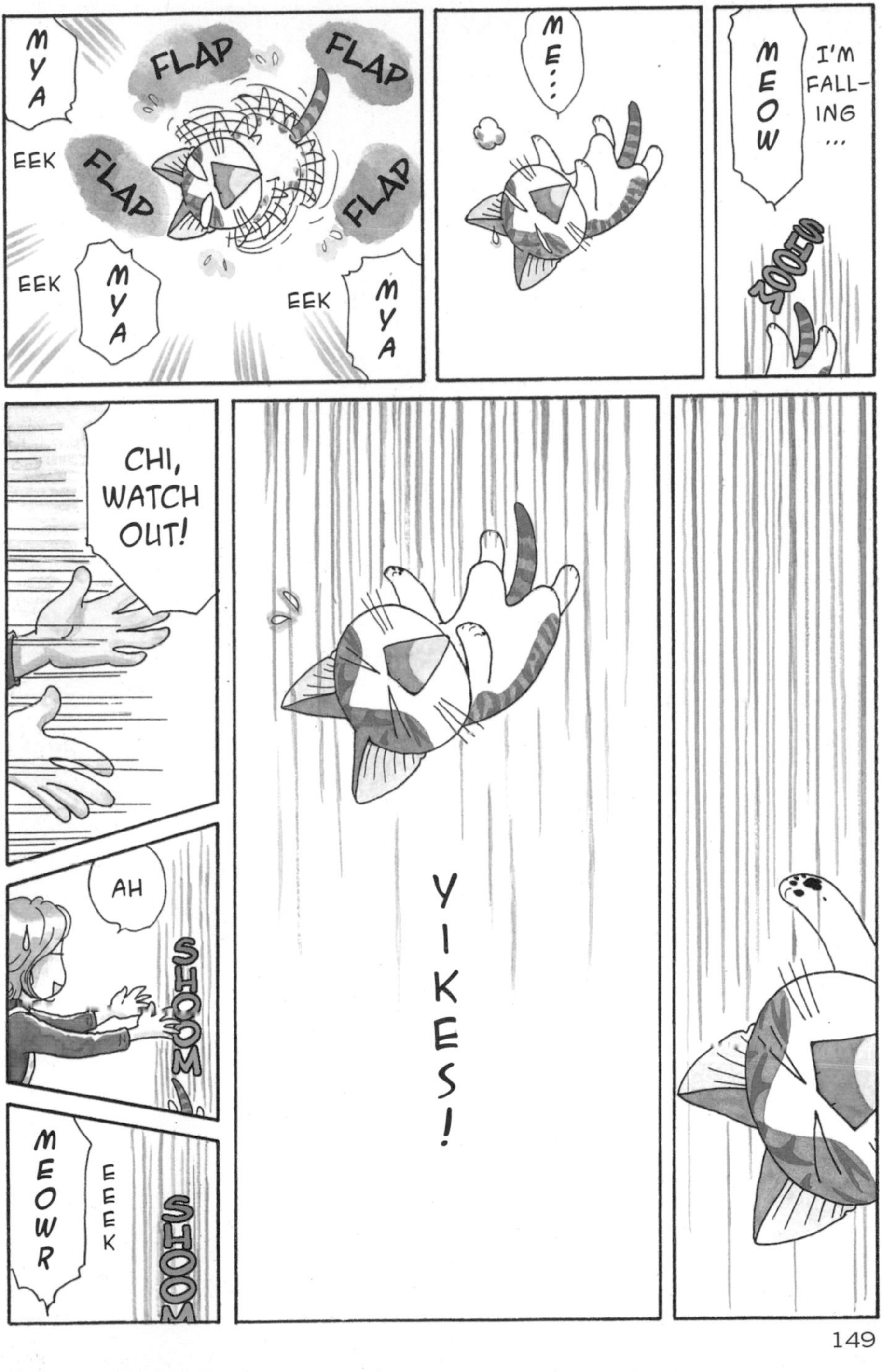
MYA
FLAP
FLAP
EEK
FLAP
FLAP
EEK
MYA
EEK
MYA
ME...
MEOW
I'M FALLING...
CHI, WATCH OUT!
AH
SHOOM
MEOWR
EEEEK
SHOOM
YIKES!

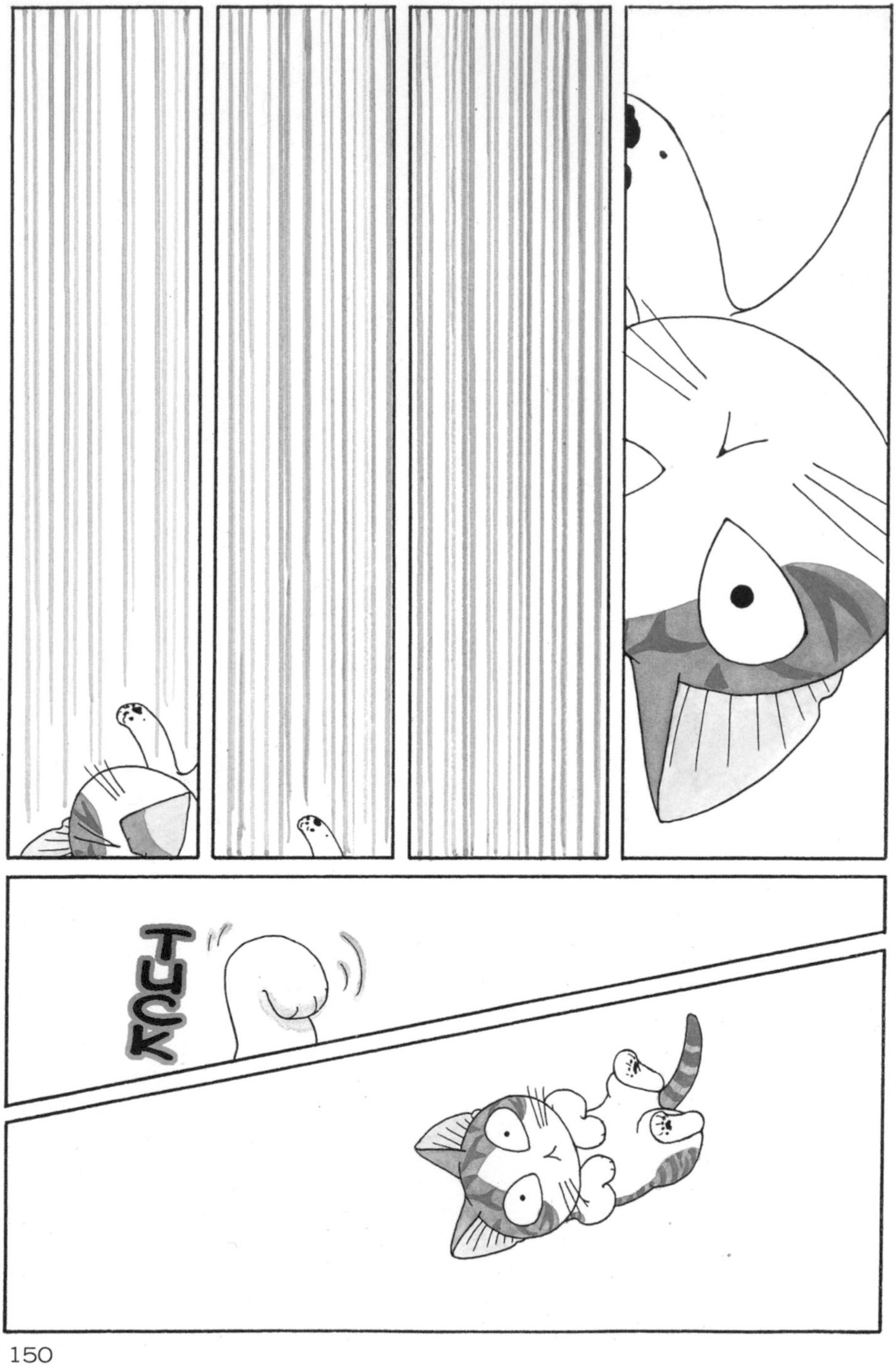
TUCK

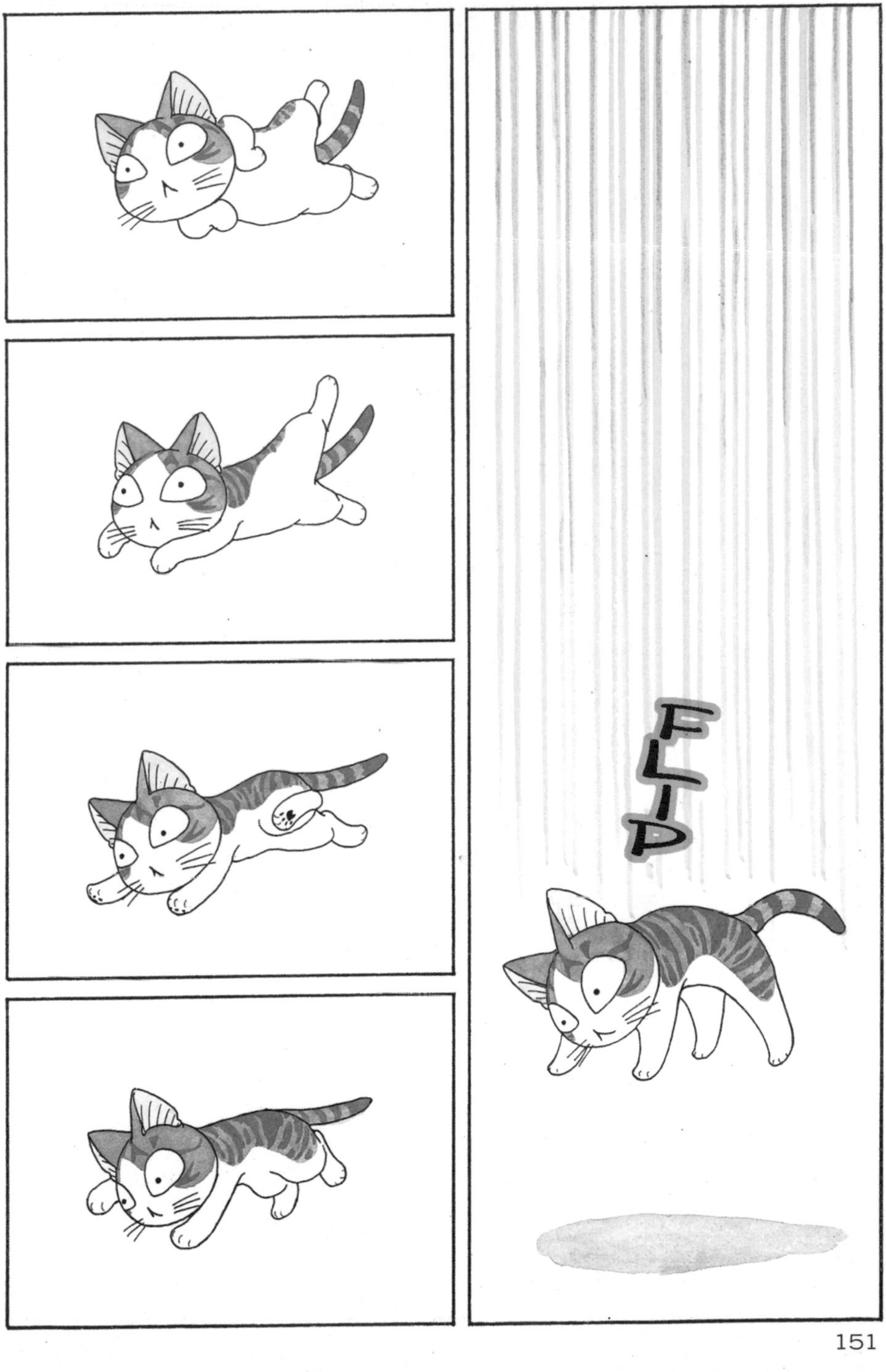
FLIP

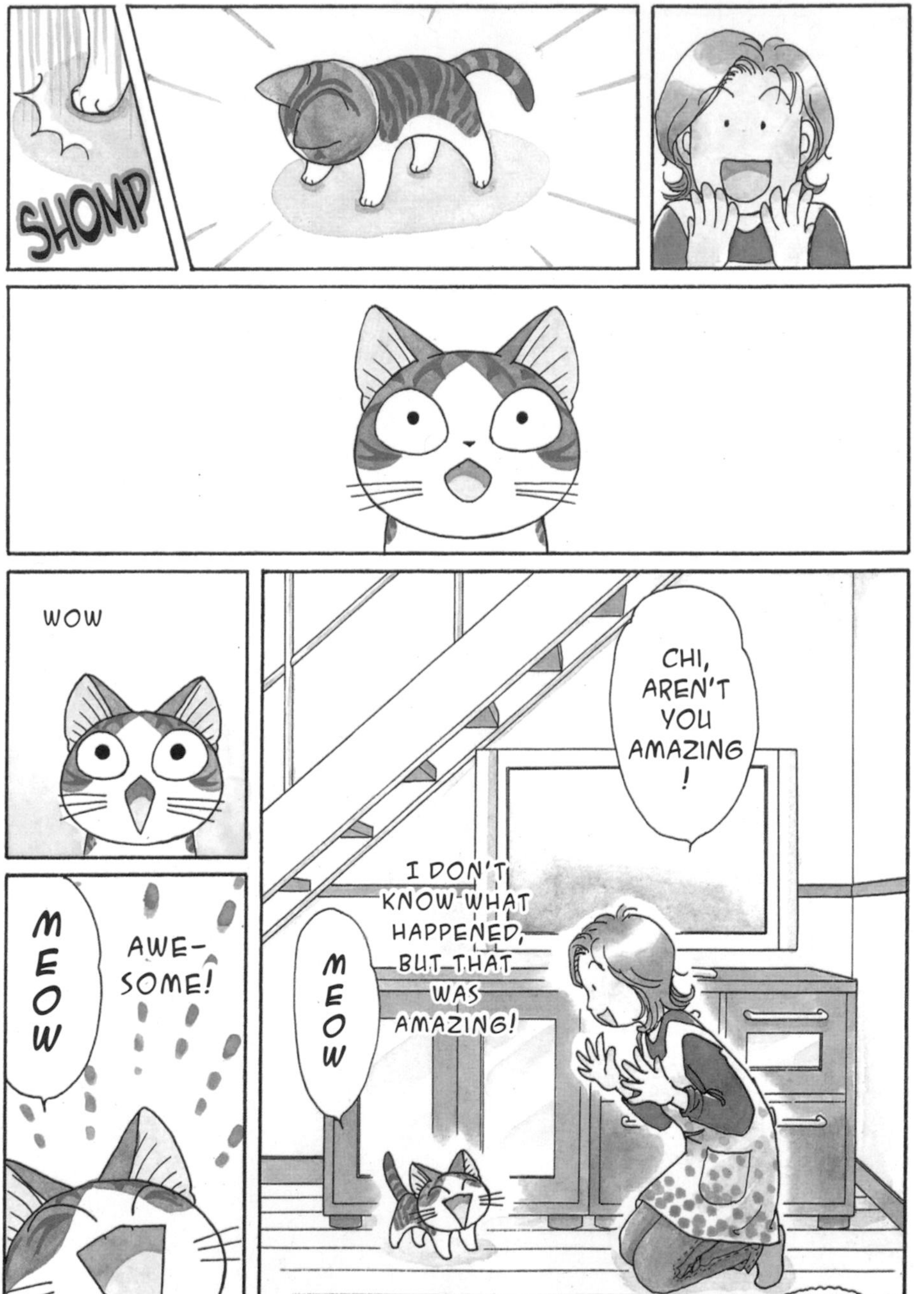
SHOMP
WOW
CHI, AREN'T YOU AMAZING!
MEOW
AWE-SOME!
MEOW
I DON'T KNOW WHAT HAPPENED, BUT THAT WAS AMAZING!



the end

## homemade 130: a cat anticipates

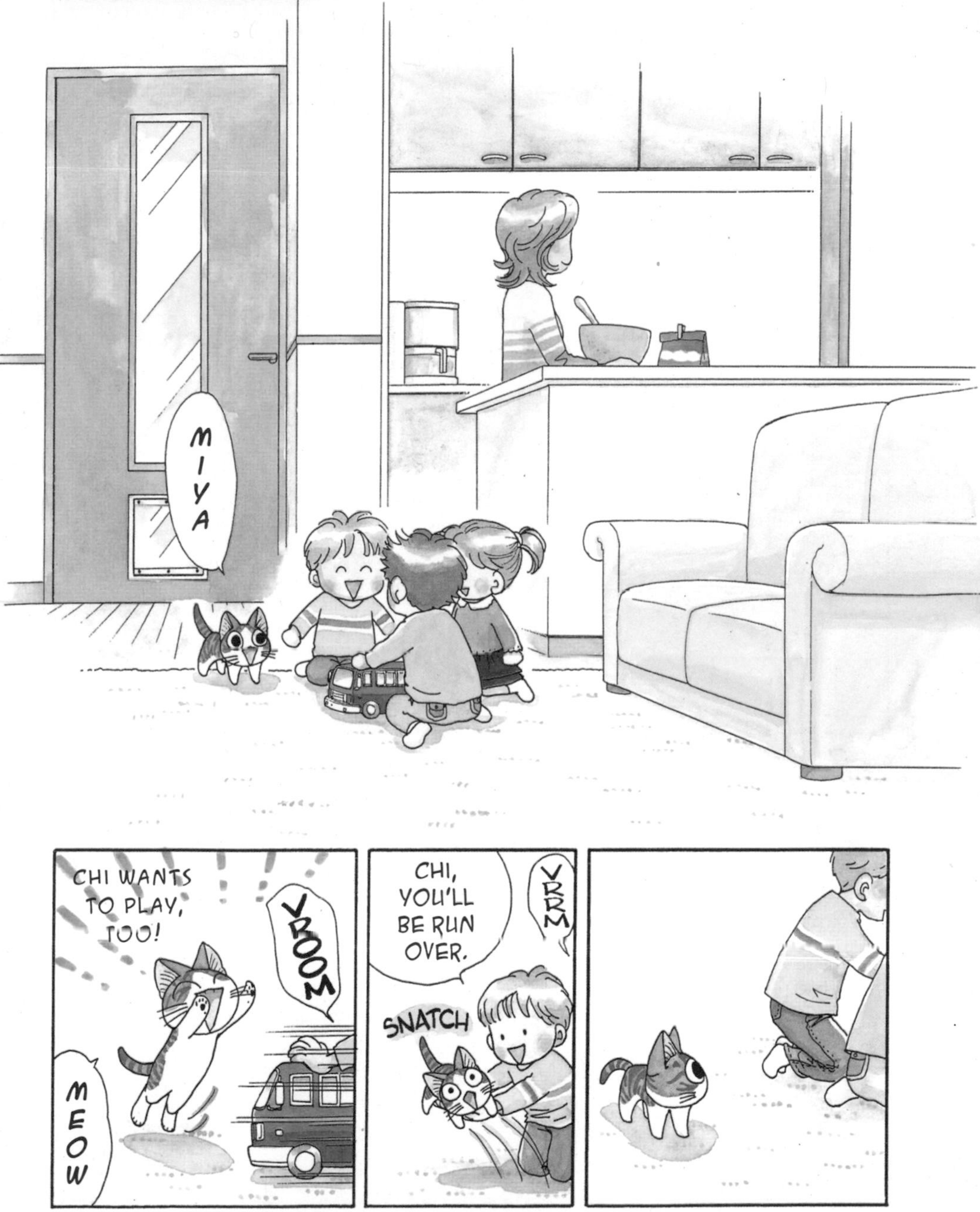
MIYA
CHI WANTS TO PLAY, TOO!
VROOM
MEOW
CHI, YOU'LL BE RUN OVER.
VRRM
SNATCH

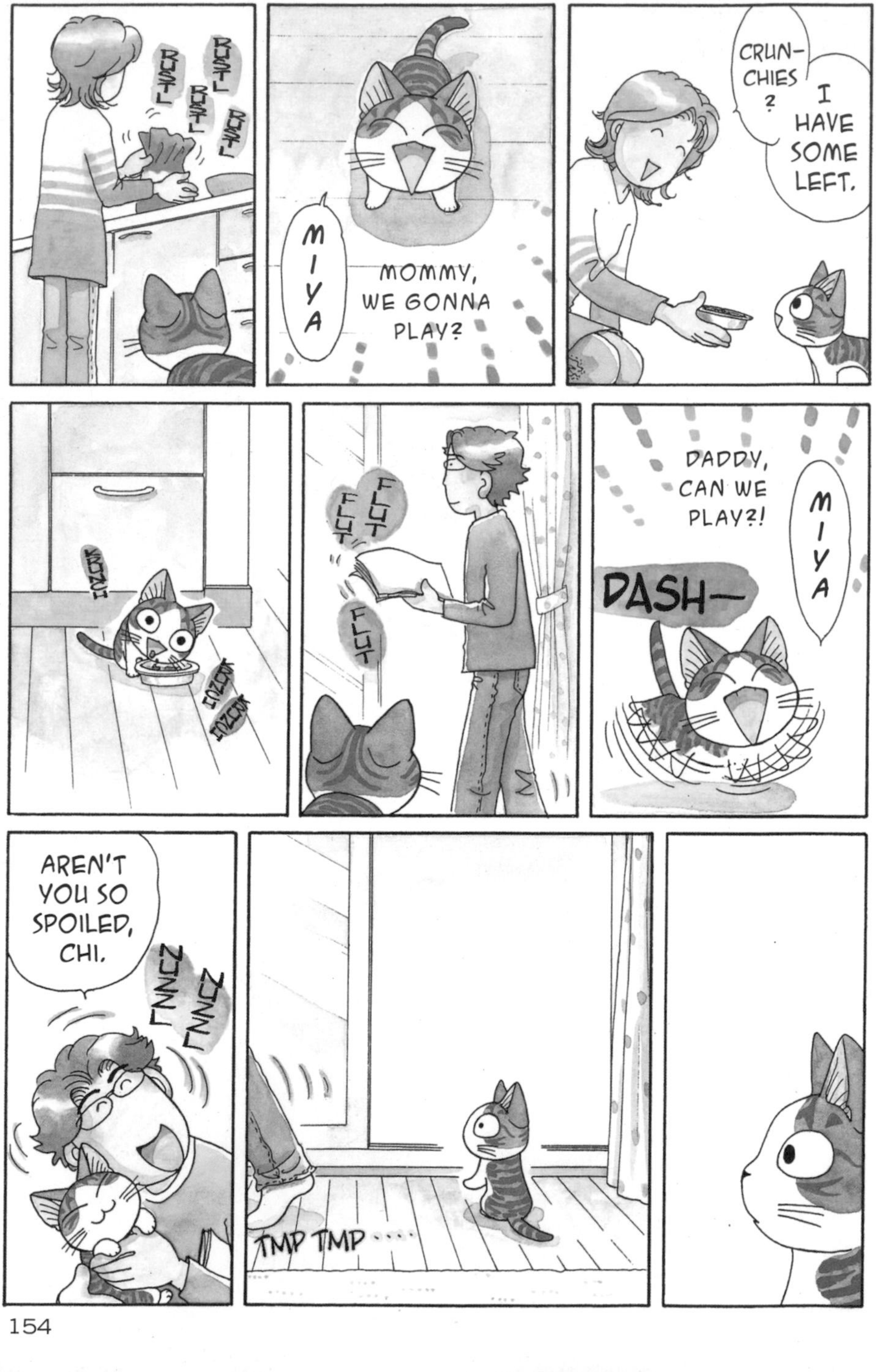
RUSTL
RUSTL
RUSTL
RUSTL
MIYA
MOMMY, WE GONNA PLAY?
CRUN- CHIES?
I HAVE SOME LEFT.
FLUT
FLUT
FLUT
DADDY, CAN WE PLAY?!
MIYA
DASH—
AREN'T YOU SO SPOILED, CHI.
NUZZL
NUZZL
TMP TMP ....

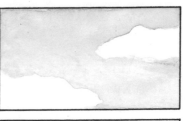

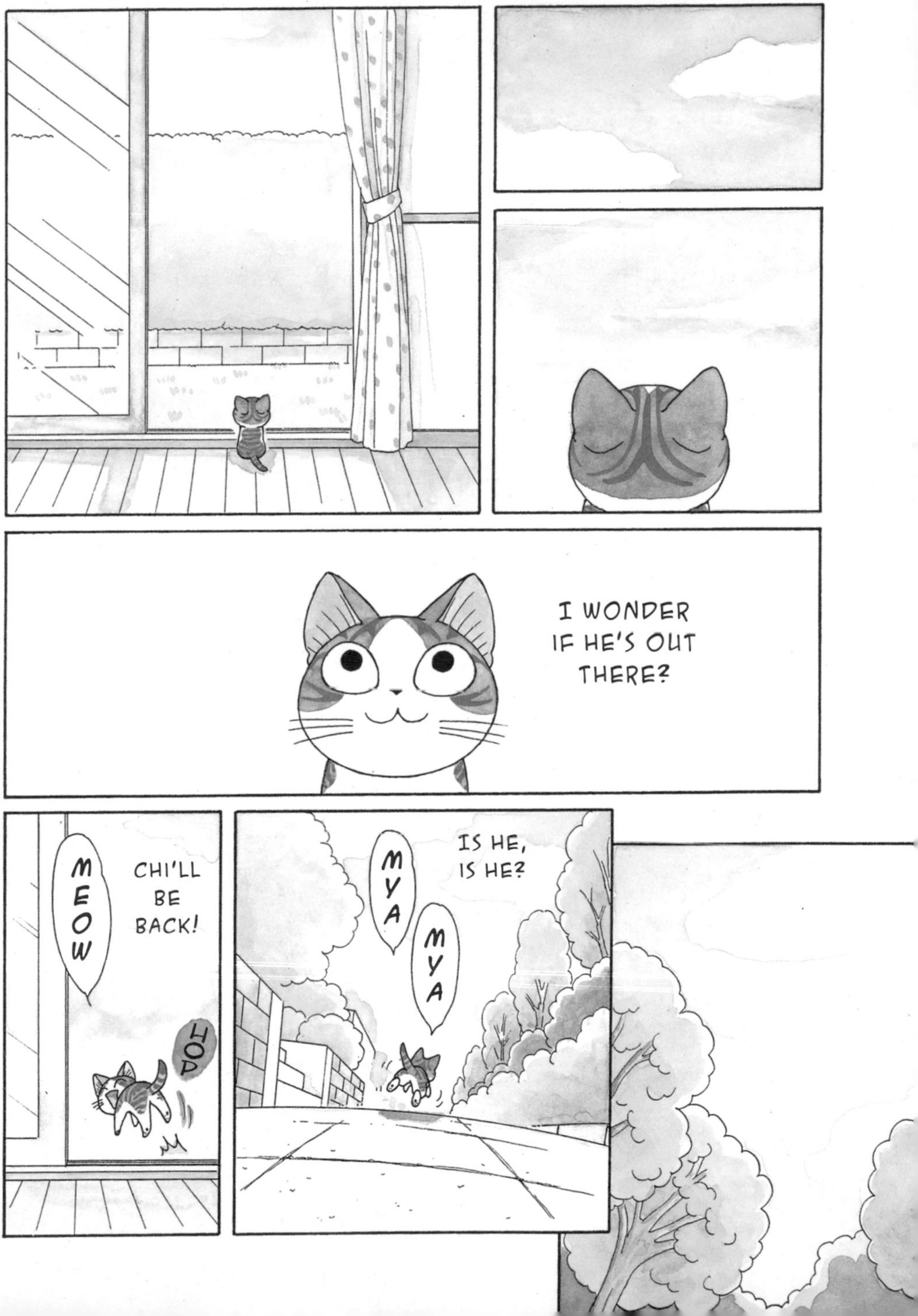
I WONDER IF HE'S OUT THERE?
MEOW
CHI'LL BE BACK!
HOP
MYA
IS HE, IS HE?
MYA

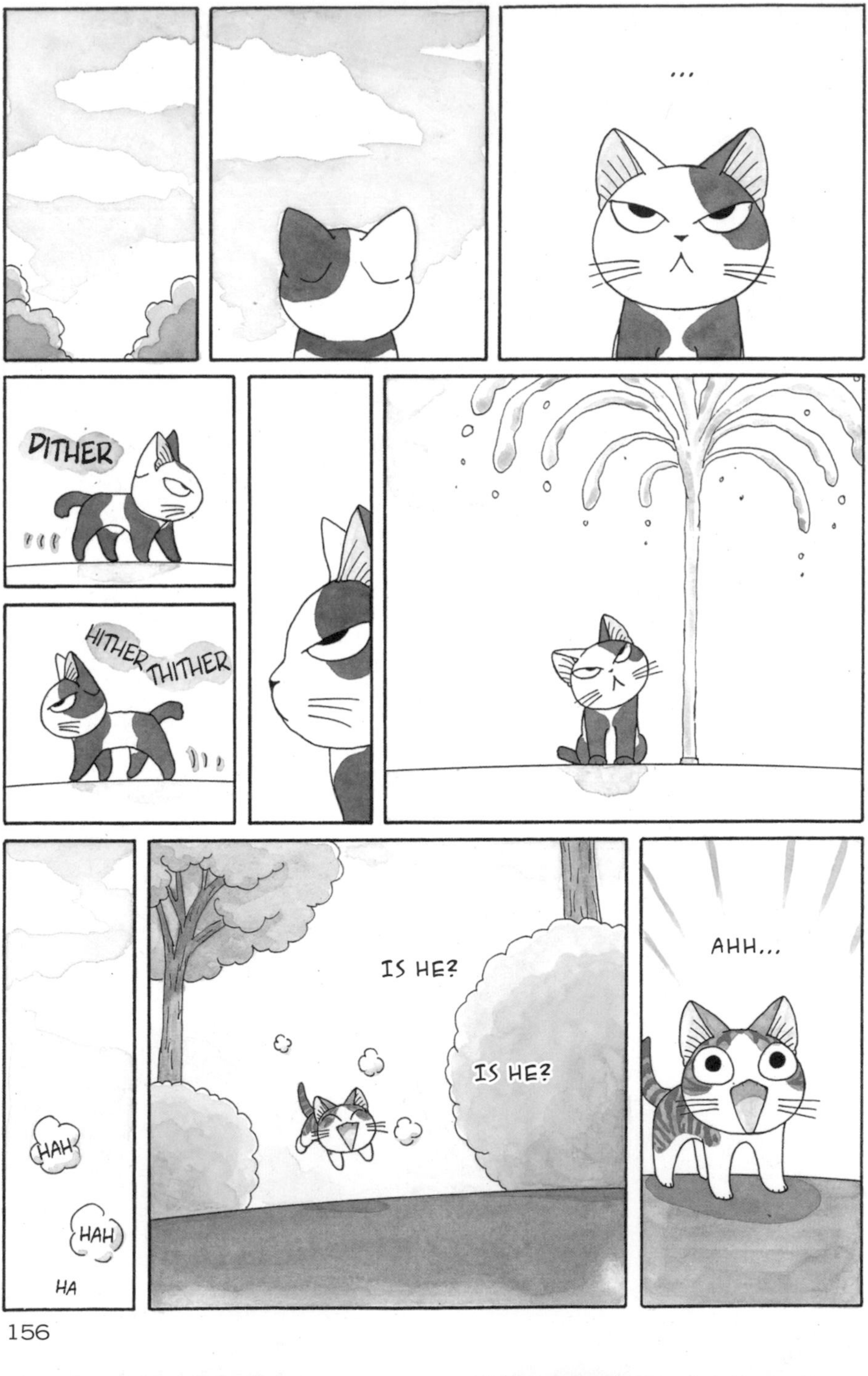
...
DITHER
HITHER
THITHER
HAH
HAH
HA
IS HE?
IS HE?
AHH...

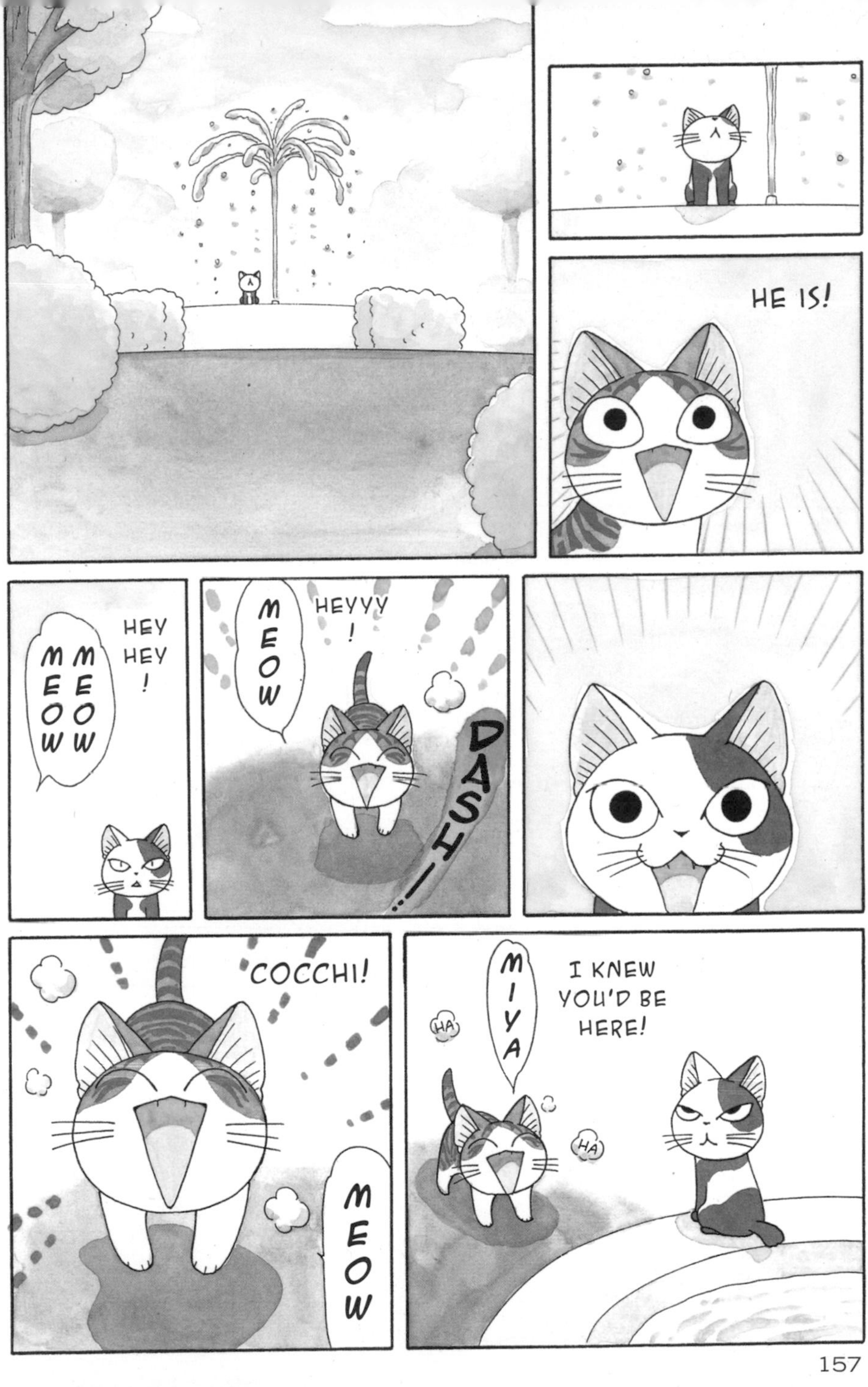
HE IS!
MEOW MEOW
HEY HEY!
MEOW
HEYYY!
DASH...!
COCCHI!
MEOW
MIYA
I KNEW YOU'D BE HERE!
HA
HA

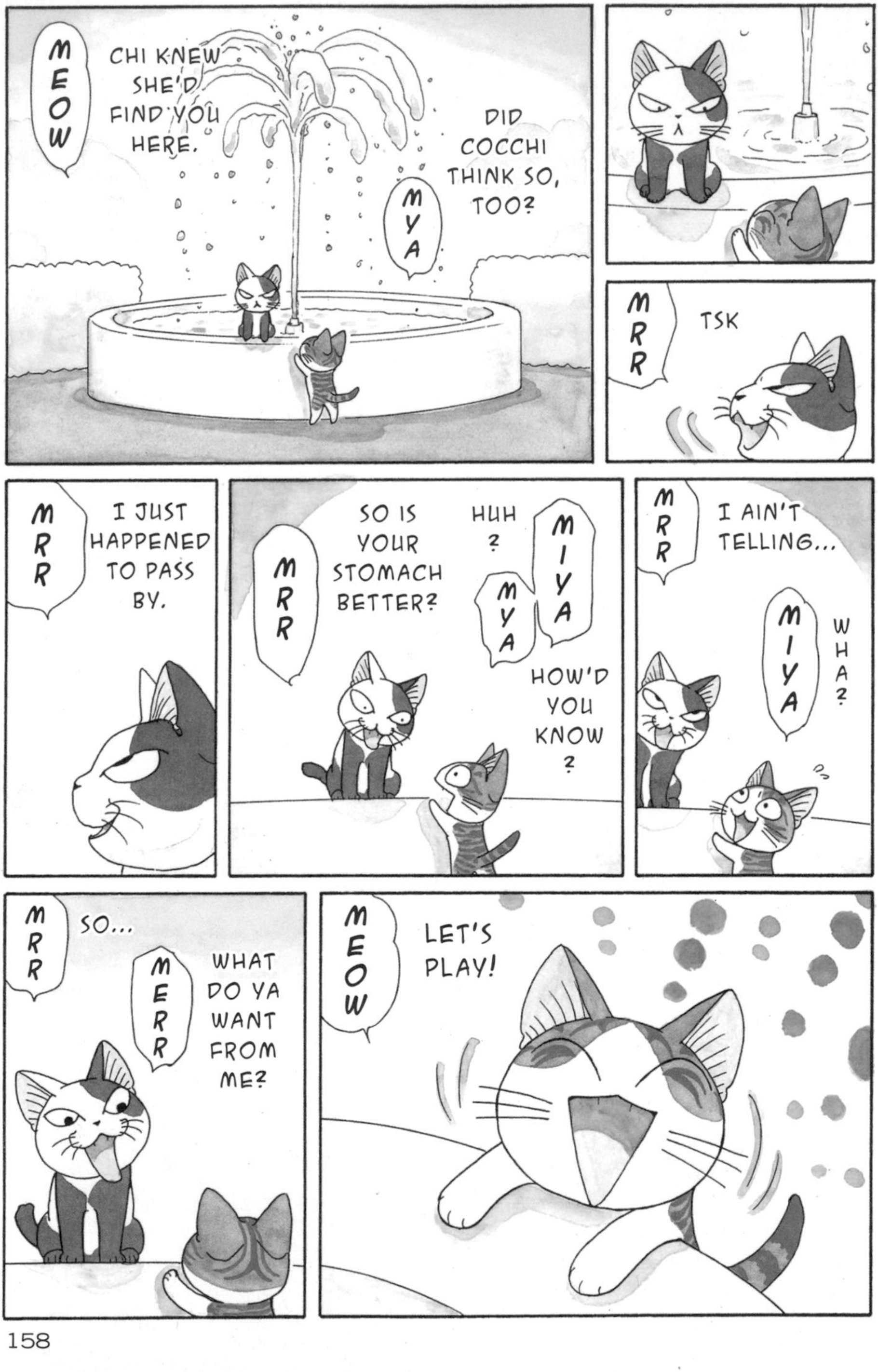
MEOW
CHI KNEW SHE'D FIND YOU HERE.
MYA
DID COCCHI THINK SO, TOO?
MRR
TSK
MRR
I JUST HAPPENED TO PASS BY.
MRR
SO IS YOUR STOMACH BETTER?
HUH?
MIYA
MYA
HOW'D YOU KNOW?
MRR
I AIN'T TELLING...
MIYA
WHA?
MRR
SO...
MERR
WHAT DO YA WANT FROM ME?
MEOW
LET'S PLAY!

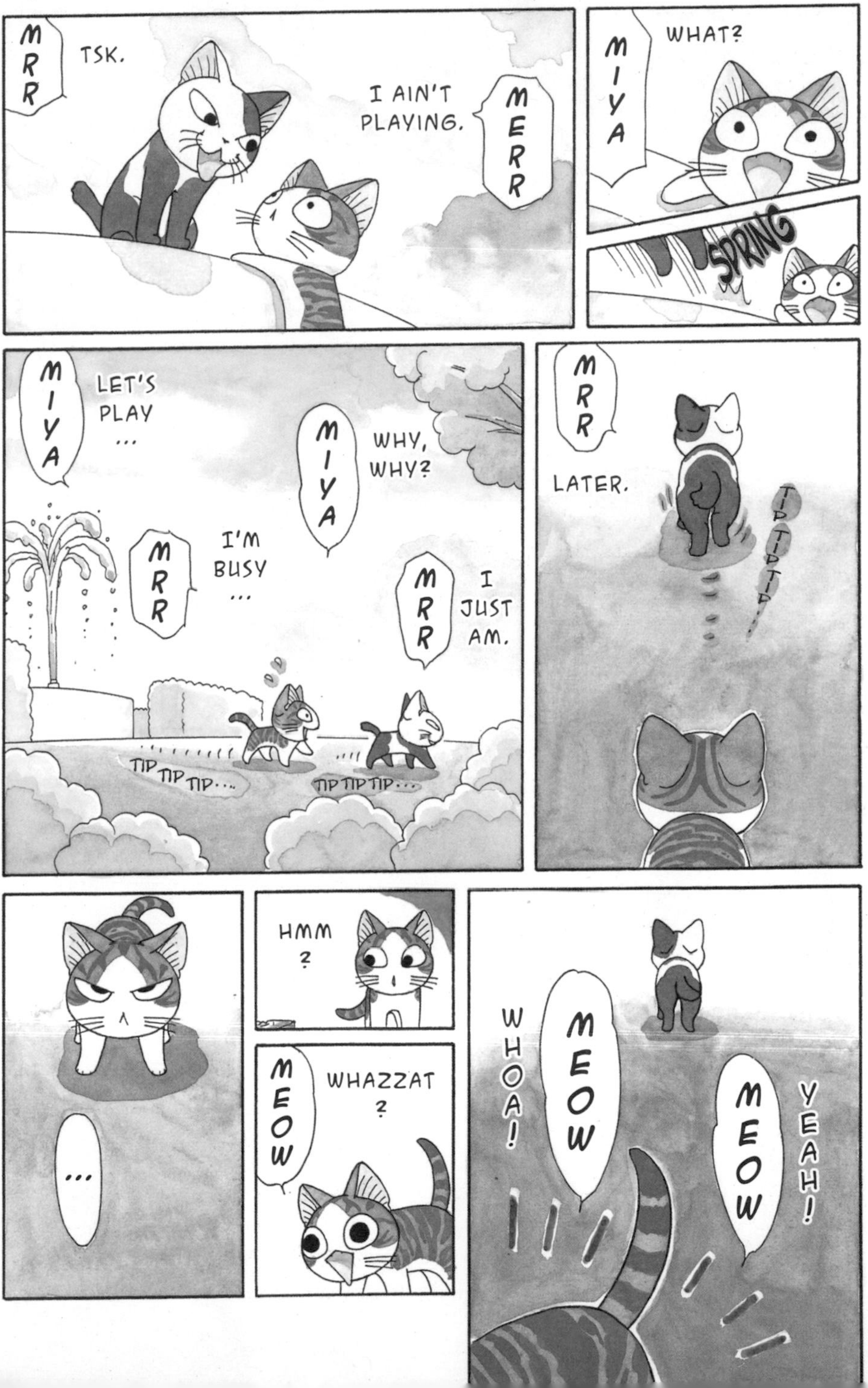
MRR
TSK.
I AIN'T PLAYING.
MERR
MIYA
WHAT?
SPRING
MIYA
LET'S PLAY ...
MIYA
WHY, WHY?
MRR
I'M BUSY ...
MRR
I JUST AM.
TIP TIP TIP...
TIP TIP TIP...
MRR
LATER.
TIP TIP TIP TIP...
...
HMM ?
MEOW
WHAZZAT ?
WHOA!
MEOW
MEOW
YEAH!

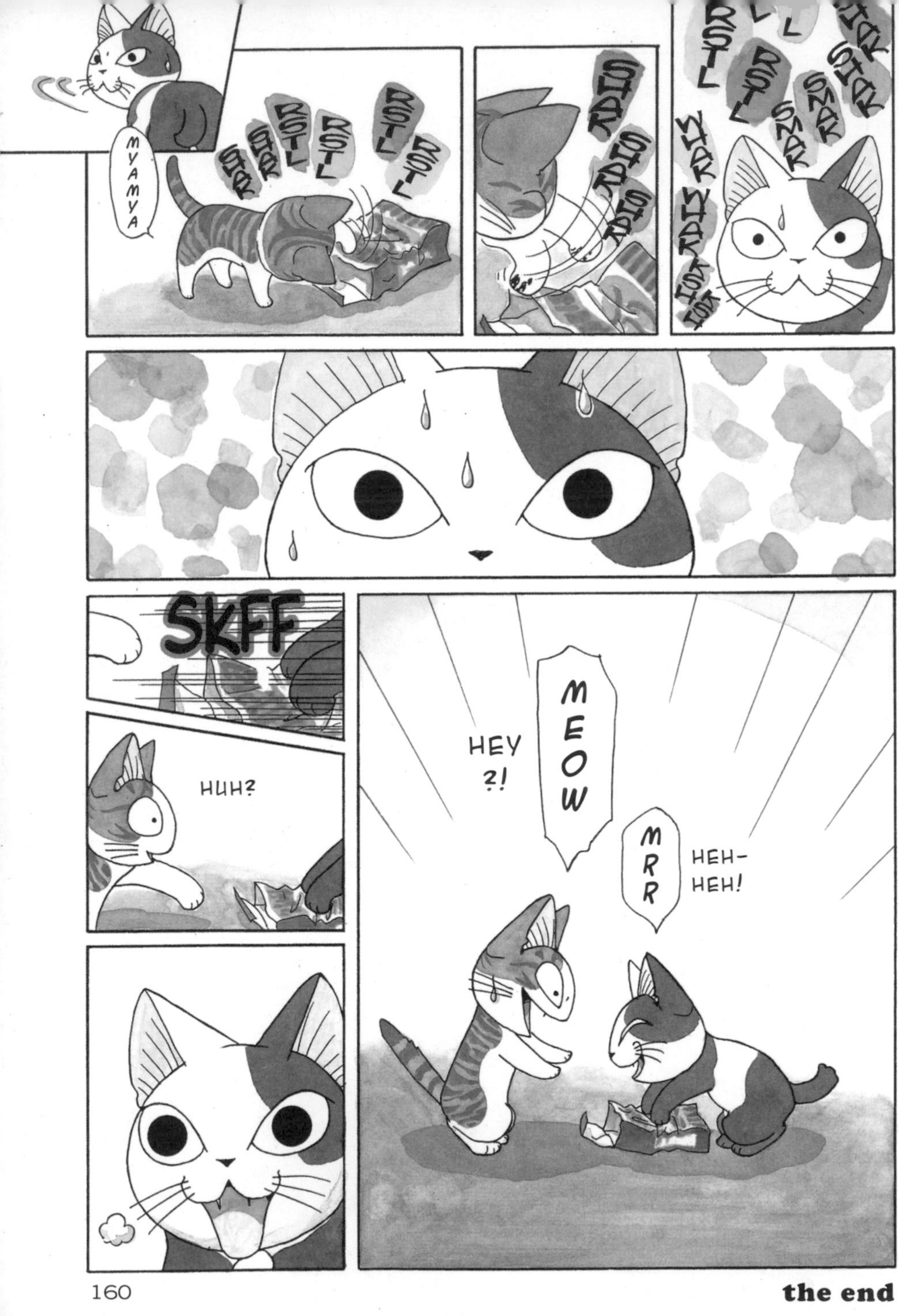
MYAMYA
SHAR SHAR RSTL RSTL RSTL RSTL
SHAR SHAR SHAR
RSTL RSTL SMAK SMAK STICK STICK
WHAK WHAK KSHHT
SKFF
HUH?
HEY ?!
MEOW
MRR
HEH-HEH!



**the end**

## homemade 131: a cat cases

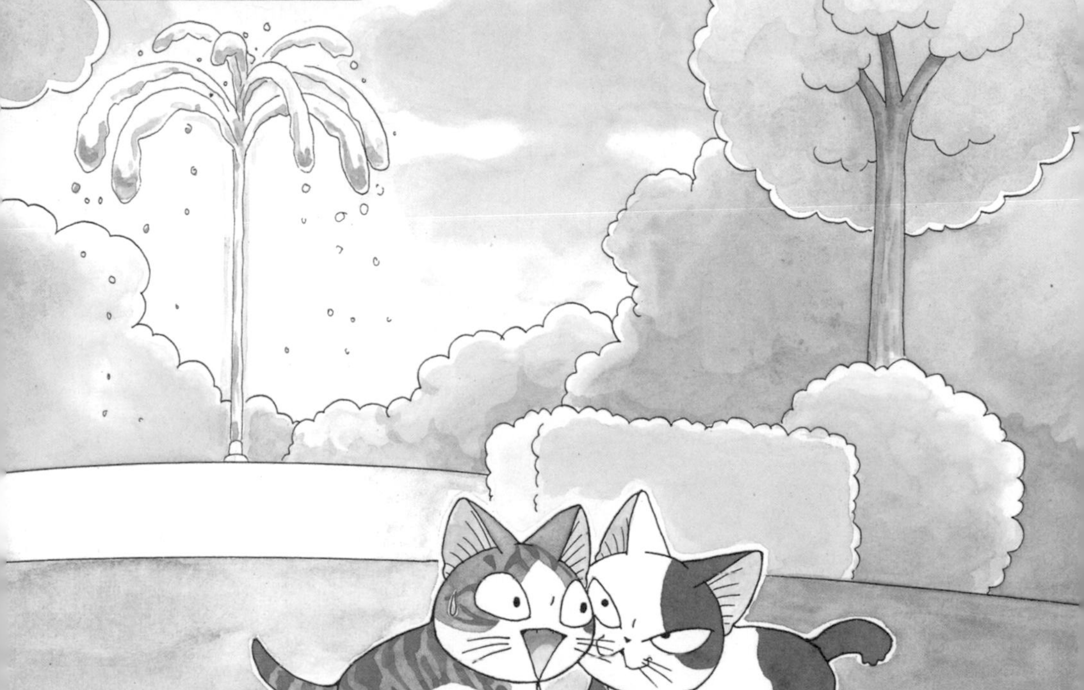

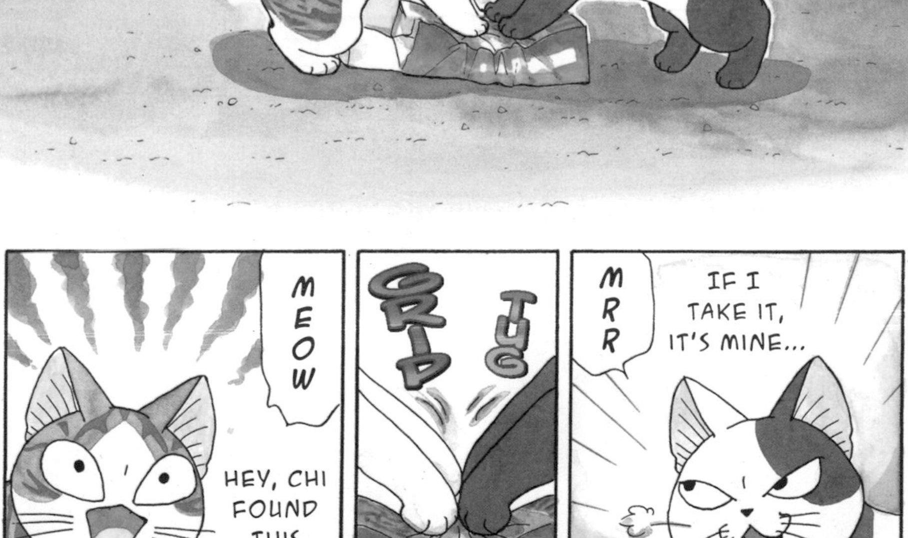
MEOW
HEY, CHI FOUND THIS FIRST.
GRIP
TUG
MRR
IF I TAKE IT, IT'S MINE...

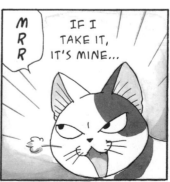

BUT CHI WAS PLAYING WITH IT.

MEOW

MRR

HOW NAIVE.

HUH?

MRR

YOU HAVEN'T CHECKED WHAT'S INSIDE?

MYA

MYA

C-CHI WAS THINKING TO.

MERR

REALLY?

!

MEOW

IT MIGHT BE SOMETHING AWESOME.

MEOW

MRR

AWESOME?

YEAH, SOMETHING AWESOME.

MRR

AWESOME... LIKE WHAT?

HUH?

MYA

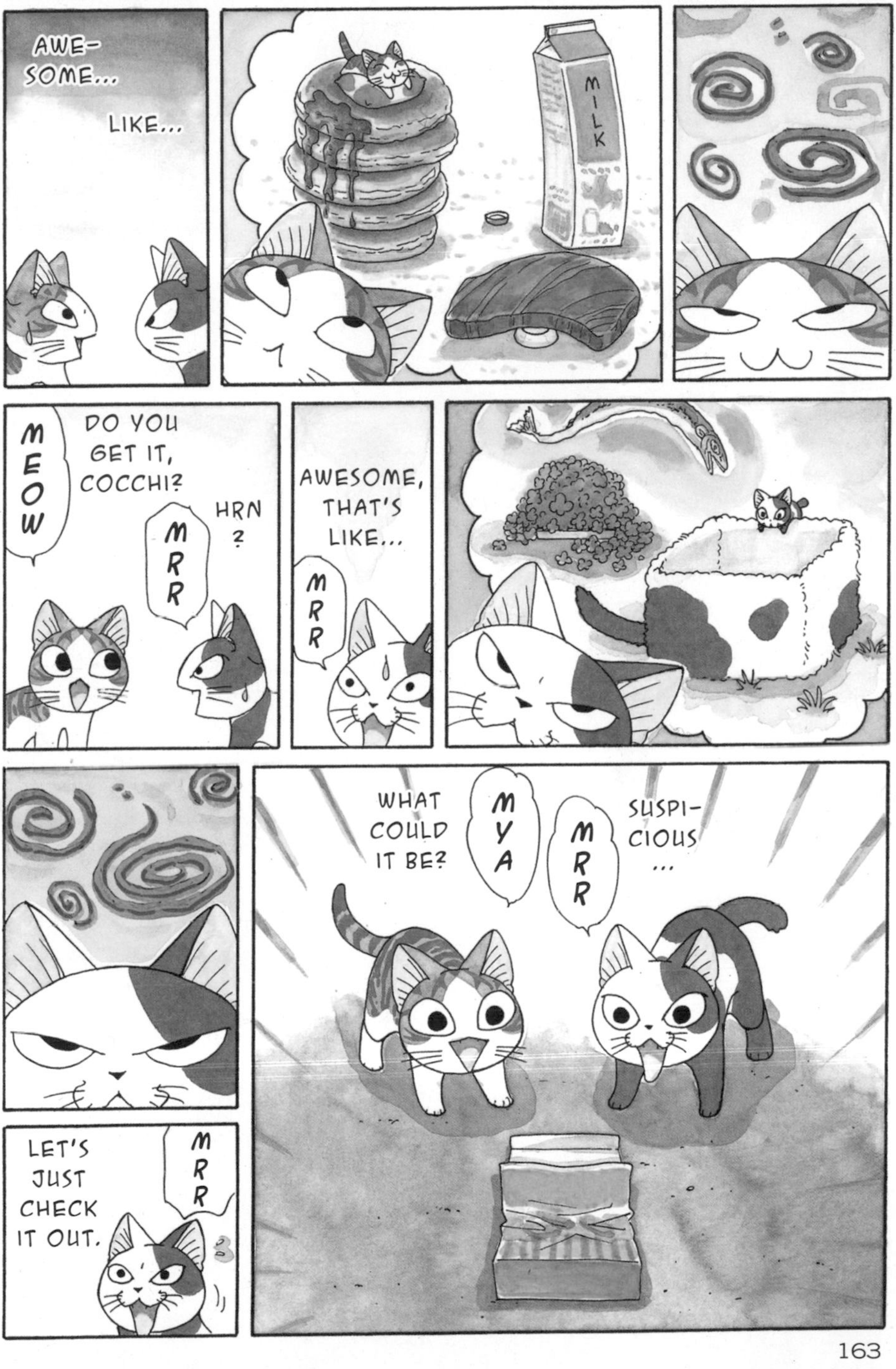
AWE-SOME...
LIKE...
MILK
MEOW
DO YOU GET IT, COCCHI?
MRR
HRN ?
AWESOME, THAT'S LIKE...
MRR
WHAT COULD IT BE?
MYA
MRR
SUSPI-CIOUS ...
LET'S JUST CHECK IT OUT.
MRR

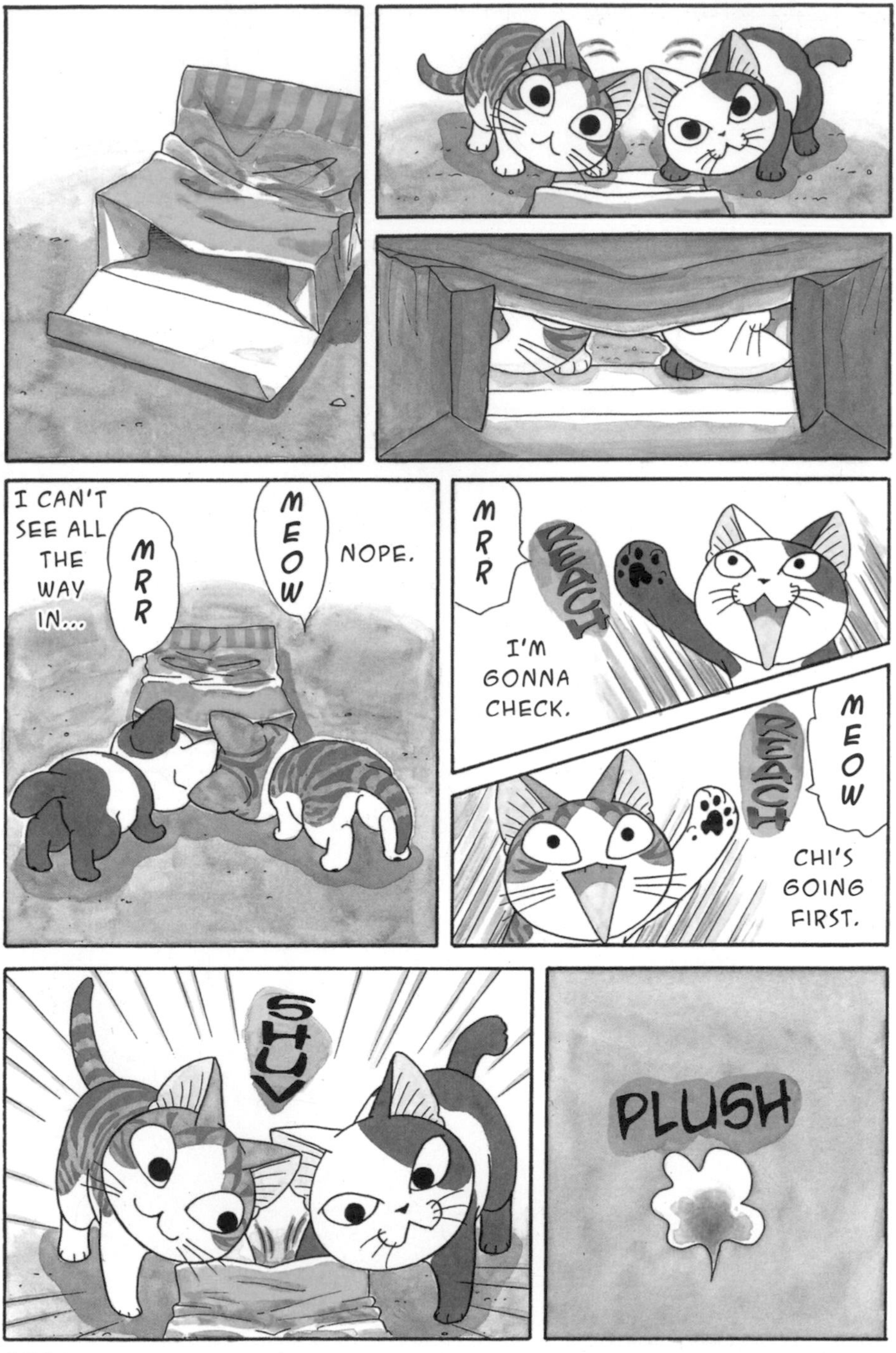
I CAN'T SEE ALL THE WAY IN...
MRR
MEOW
NOPE.
MRR
REACH
I'M GONNA CHECK.
REACH
MEOW
CHI'S GOING FIRST.
SHUV
PLUSH

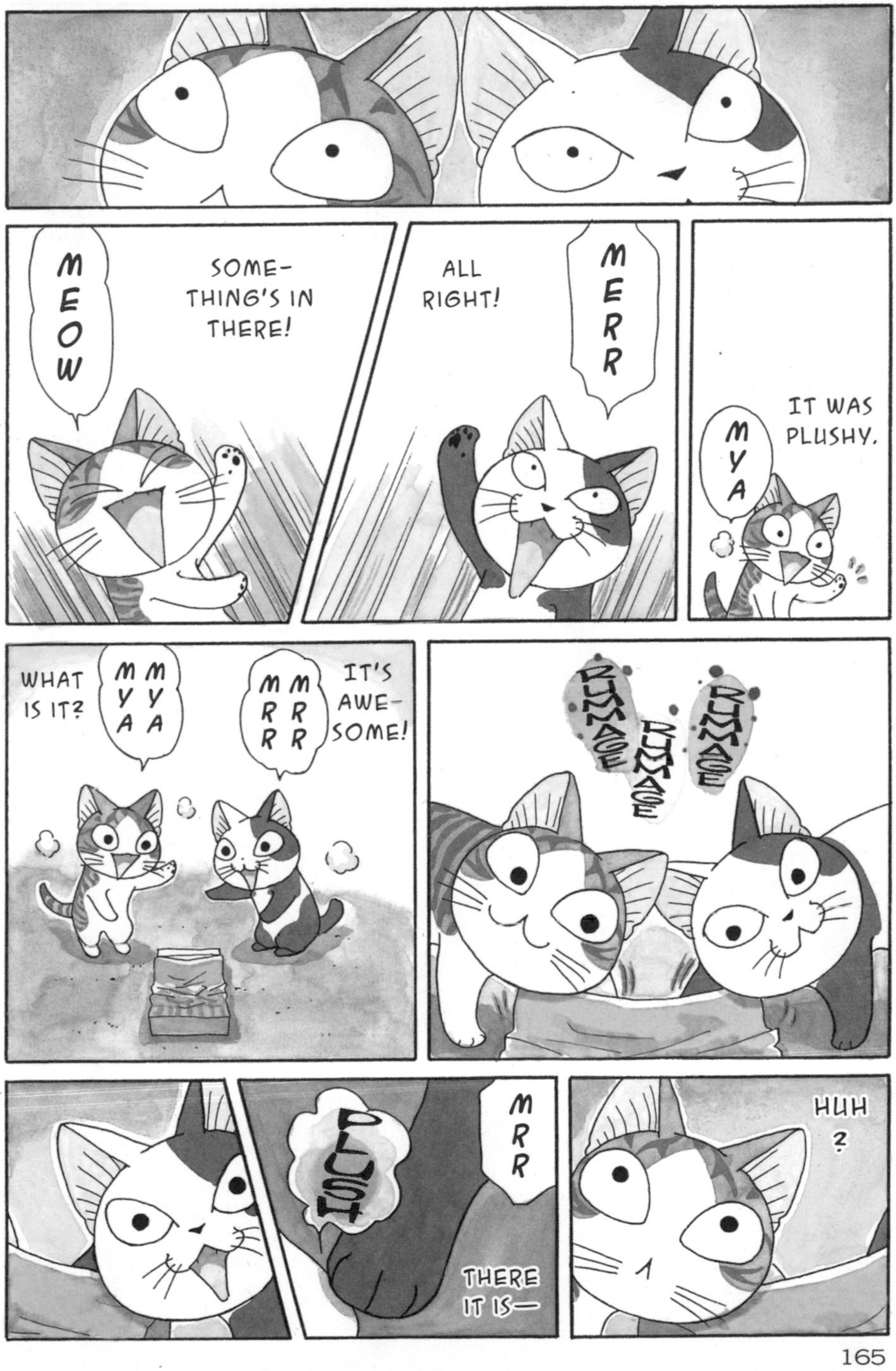

MEOW
SOME-THING'S IN THERE!
ALL RIGHT!
MERR
IT WAS PLUSHY.
MYA
WHAT IS IT?
MYA MYA
MRR MRR
IT'S AWE-SOME!
RUMMAGE RUMMAGE RUMMAGE
PLUSH
MRR
THERE IT IS—
HUH?

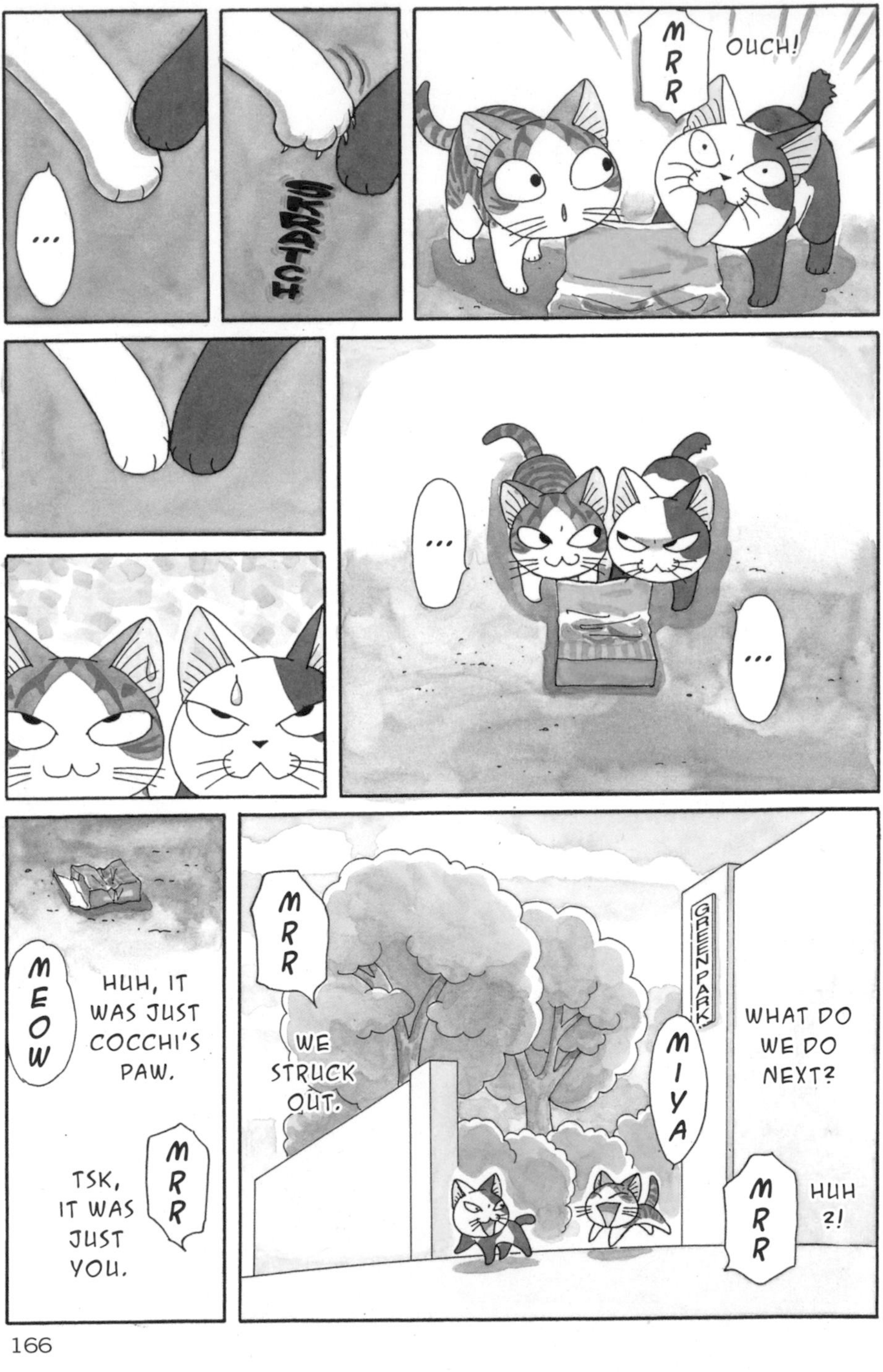
...
SKRATCH
MRR
OUCH!
...
...
MEOW
HUH, IT WAS JUST COCCHI'S PAW.
MRR
TSK, IT WAS JUST YOU.
MRR
WE STRUCK OUT.
GREENPARK
MIYA
WHAT DO WE DO NEXT?
MRR
HUH?!

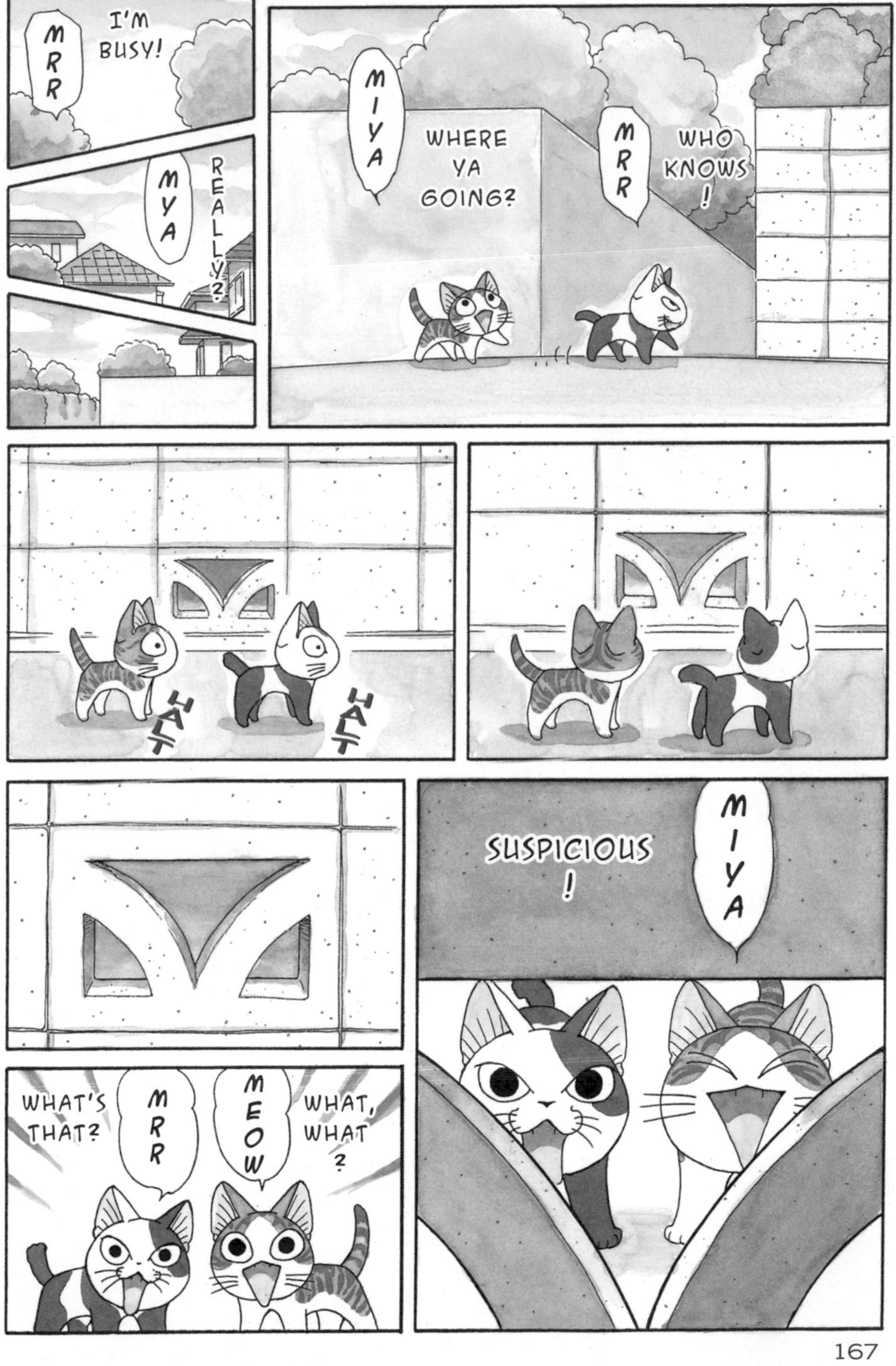
MRR
I'M BUSY!
MYA
REALLY?
MIYA
WHERE YA GOING?
MRR
WHO KNOWS!
HALT
HALT
SUSPICIOUS!
MIYA
WHAT'S THAT?
MRR
MEOW
WHAT, WHAT?

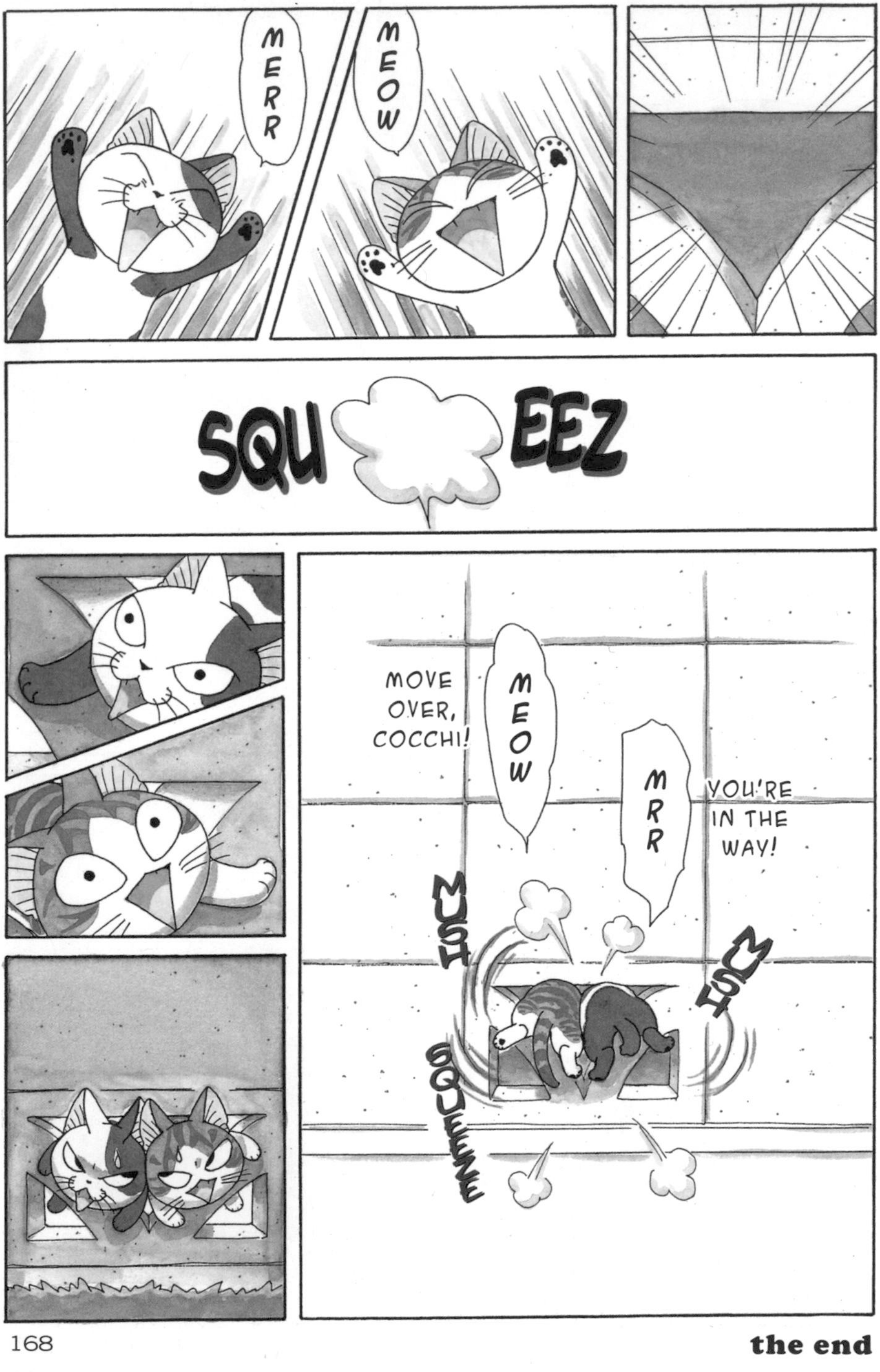
MERR
MEOW
SQU EEZ
MOVE OVER, COCCHI!
MEOW
MRR
YOU'RE IN THE WAY!
MUSH
MUSH
SQUEEZE

**the end**

## homemade 132: a cat is wowed

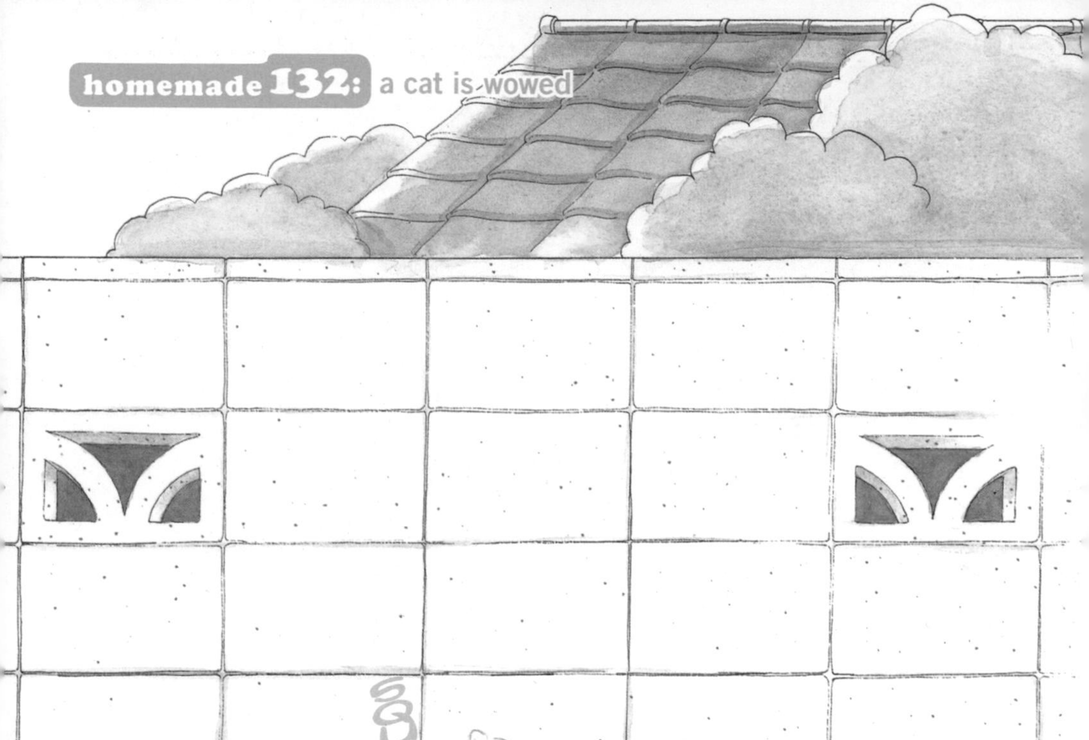
SQUEEEZE
SQUEEEZE

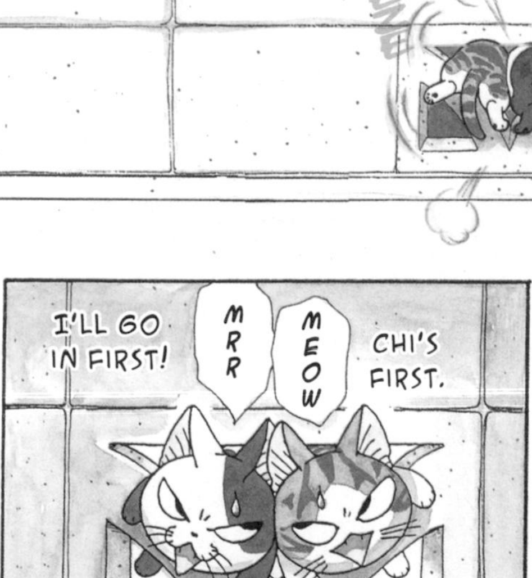
I'LL GO IN FIRST!
MRR
MEOW
CHI'S FIRST.

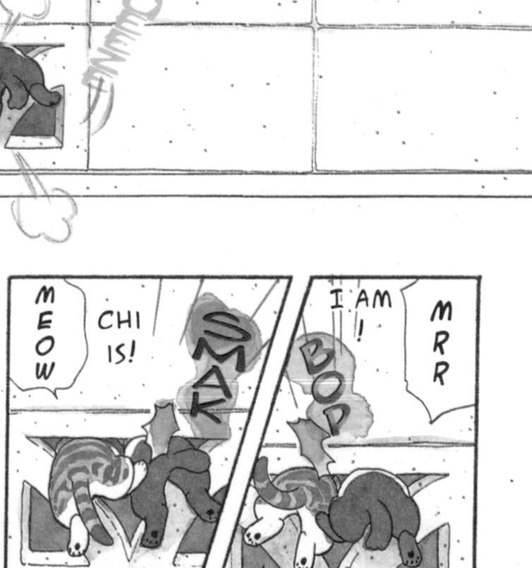
MEOW
CHI IS!
SMAK
OUCH!
MRR
I AM!
MRR
BOP
MYA
NOS!

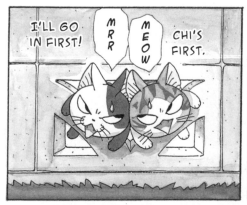

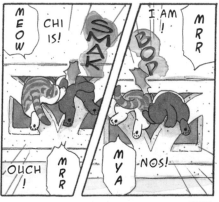

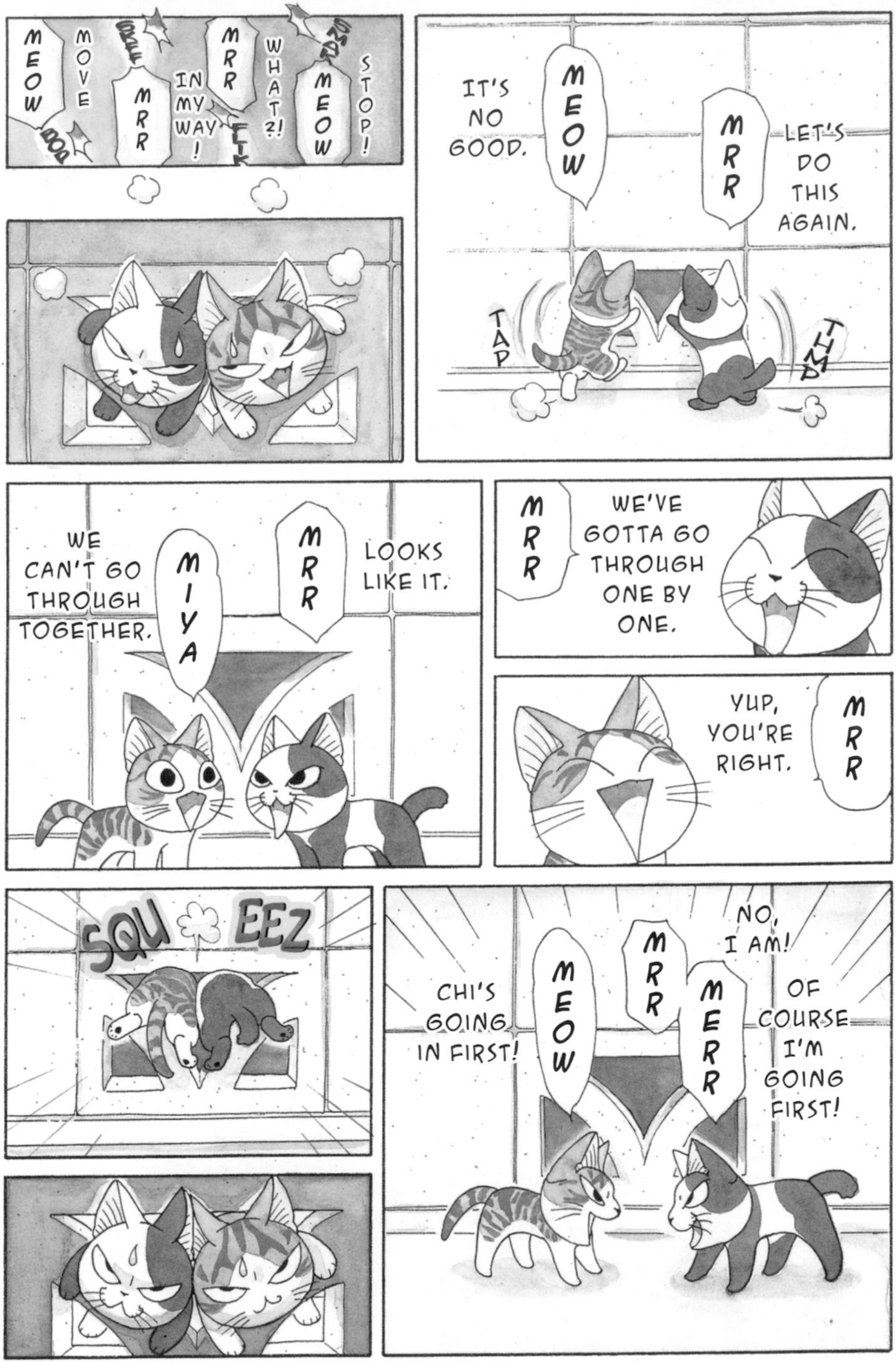
MEOW
MOVE
MRR
IN MY WAY!
MRR
WHAT?!
FLIK
MEOW
STOP!
BOP
IT'S NO GOOD.
MEOW
MRR
LET'S DO THIS AGAIN.
TAP
THMP
WE CAN'T GO THROUGH TOGETHER.
MIYA
MRR
LOOKS LIKE IT.
MRR
WE'VE GOTTA GO THROUGH ONE BY ONE.
YUP, YOU'RE RIGHT.
MRR
SQU EEZ
CHI'S GOING IN FIRST!
MEOW
MRR
NO, I AM!
MERR
OF COURSE I'M GOING FIRST!

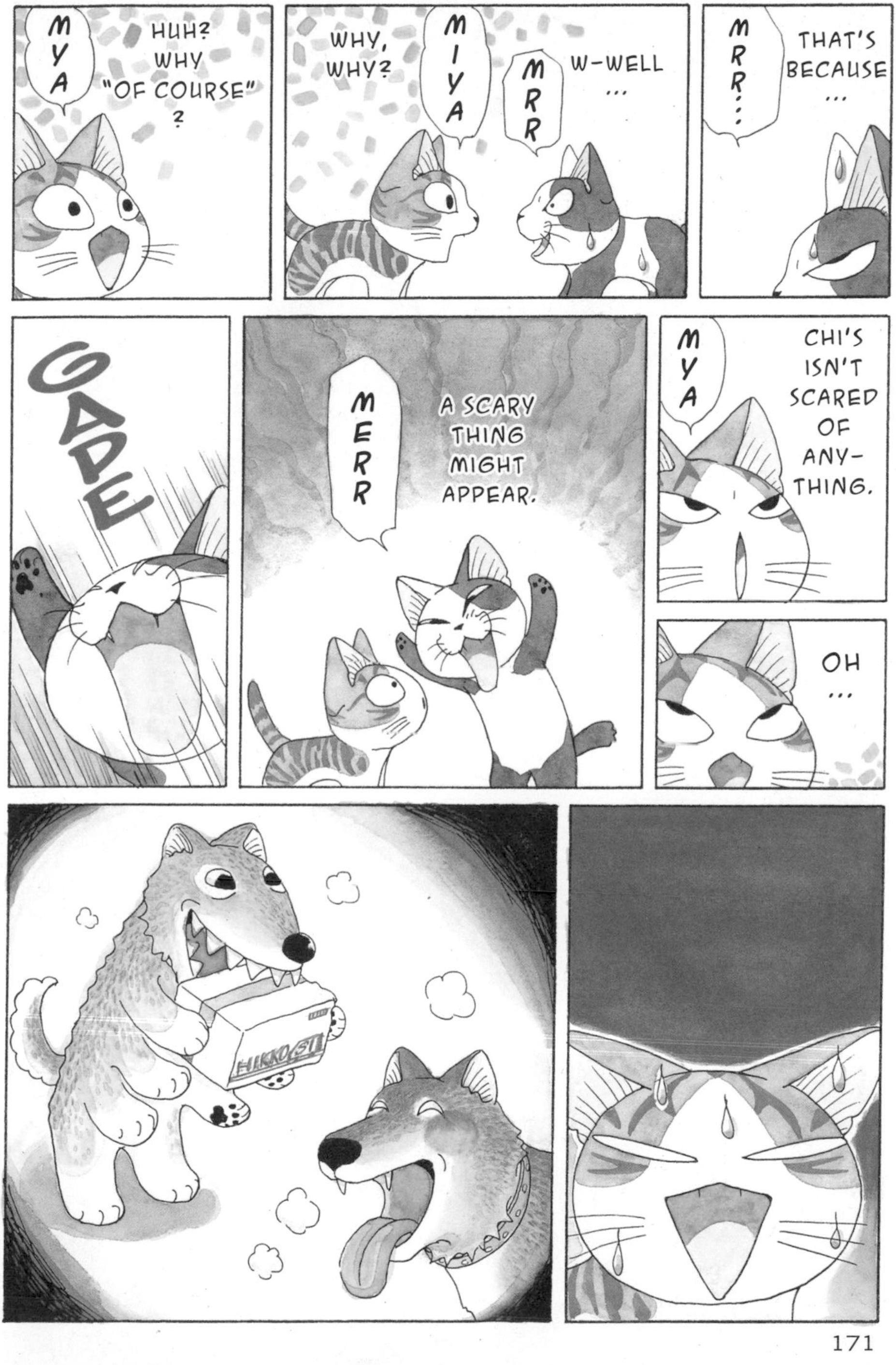

MYA
HUH? WHY "OF COURSE"?
WHY, WHY?
MIYA
MRR
W-WELL ...
MRR...
THAT'S BECAUSE ...
GAPE
MERR
A SCARY THING MIGHT APPEAR.
MYA
CHI'S ISN'T SCARED OF ANY-THING.
OH ...
HIKKOSHI

...

HEH
HEH

MRR

I'LL
GO ON
AHEAD
THEN.

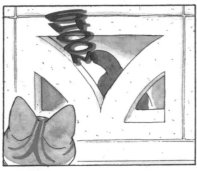

BOOM

MIYA

COCCHI,
ARE YOU
OKAY?

COME
ON
OVER.

MRR

DASH

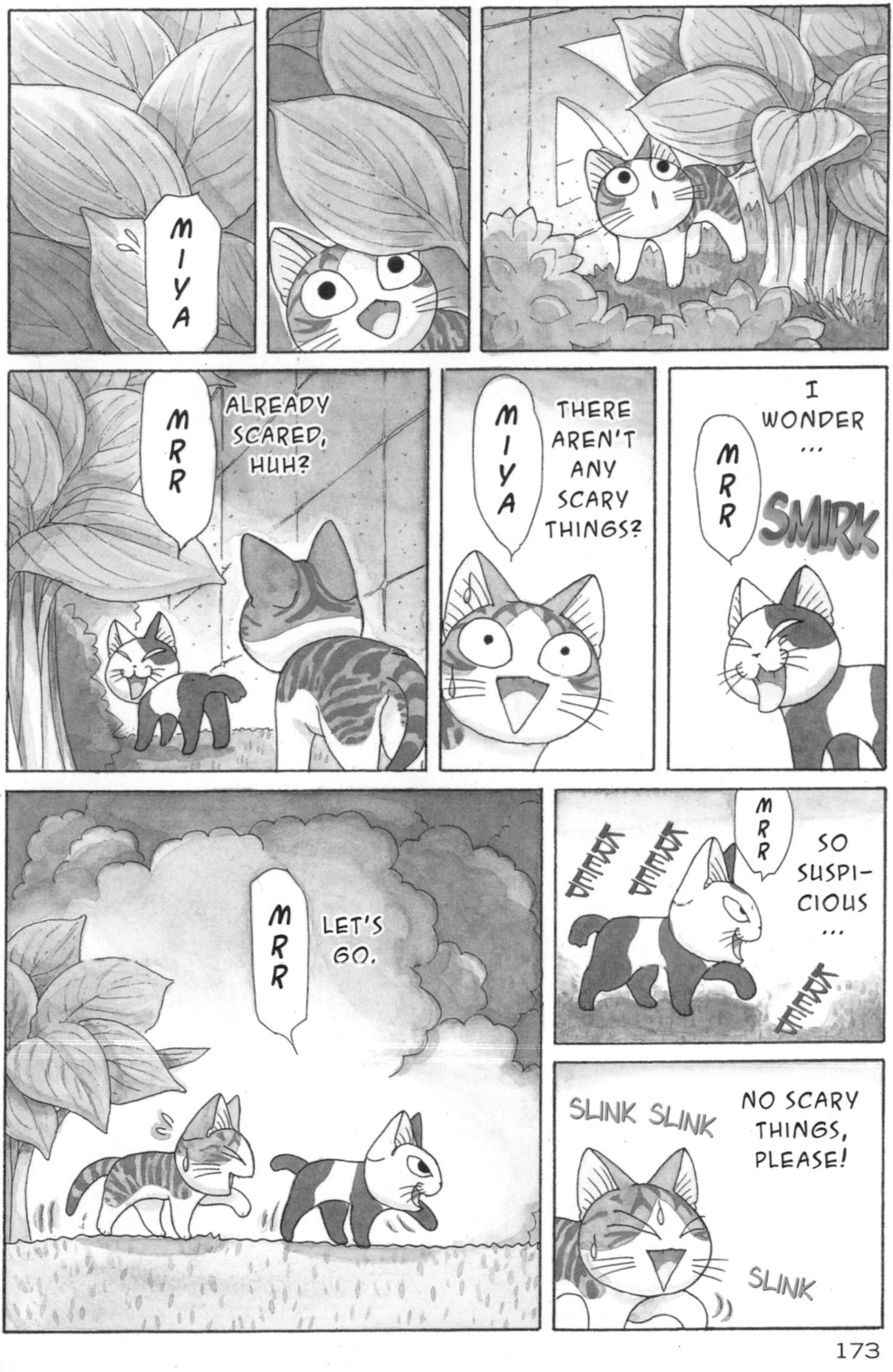

MIYA
MRR
ALREADY SCARED, HUH?
MIYA
THERE AREN'T ANY SCARY THINGS?
MRR
I WONDER ...
SMIRK
MRR
LET'S GO.
MRR
SO SUSPICIOUS ...
TREAD TREAD TREAD
SLINK SLINK
NO SCARY THINGS, PLEASE!
SLINK

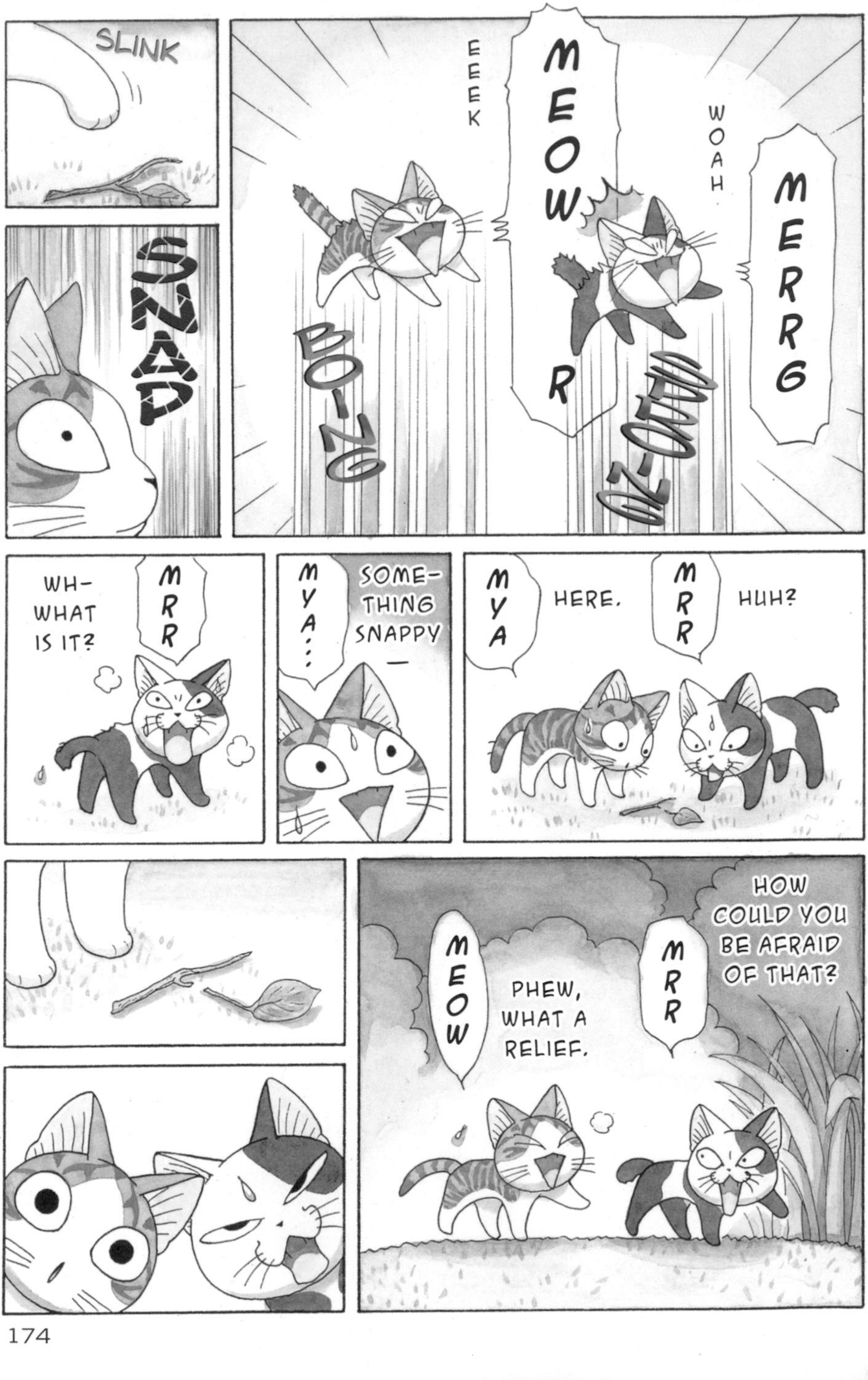
SLINK
SNAP
EEEK
MEOWR
BOING
WOAH
MERRG
BOING
WH- WHAT IS IT?
MRR
MYA...
SOME-THING SNAPPY—
MYA
HERE.
MRR
HUH?
MEOW
PHEW, WHAT A RELIEF.
MRR
HOW COULD YOU BE AFRAID OF THAT?

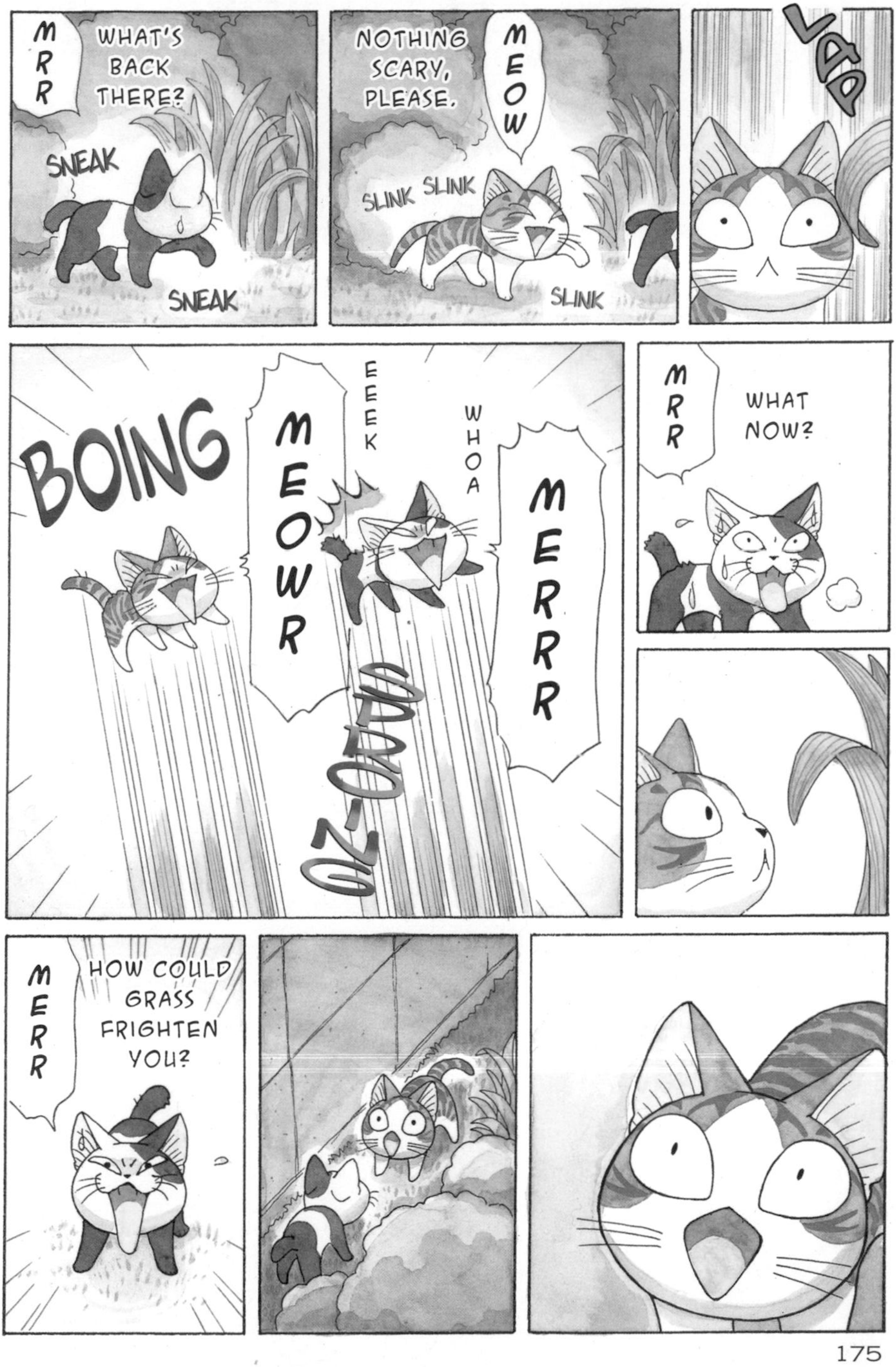
MRR
WHAT'S BACK THERE?
SNEAK
SNEAK
NOTHING SCARY, PLEASE.
MEOW
SLINK SLINK
SLINK
VAP
BOING
MEOWR
EEEK
WHOA
MERRRR
SPROING
MRR
WHAT NOW?
MERR
HOW COULD GRASS FRIGHTEN YOU?

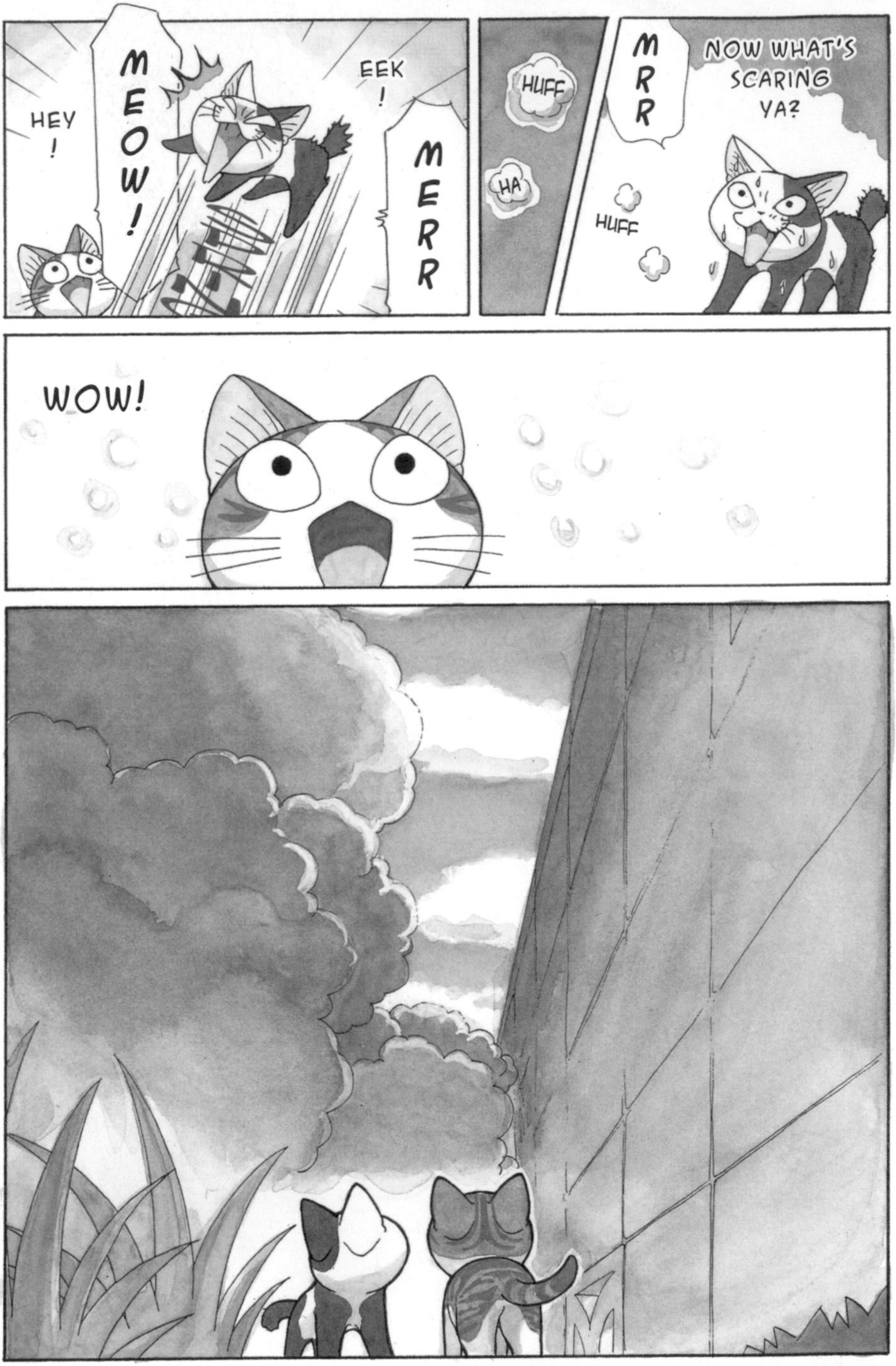
HEY!
MEOW!
EEK!
MERR
HUFF
HA
MRR
NOW WHAT'S SCARING YA?
HUFF
WOW!



**the end**

# homemade 133: a cat has a blast

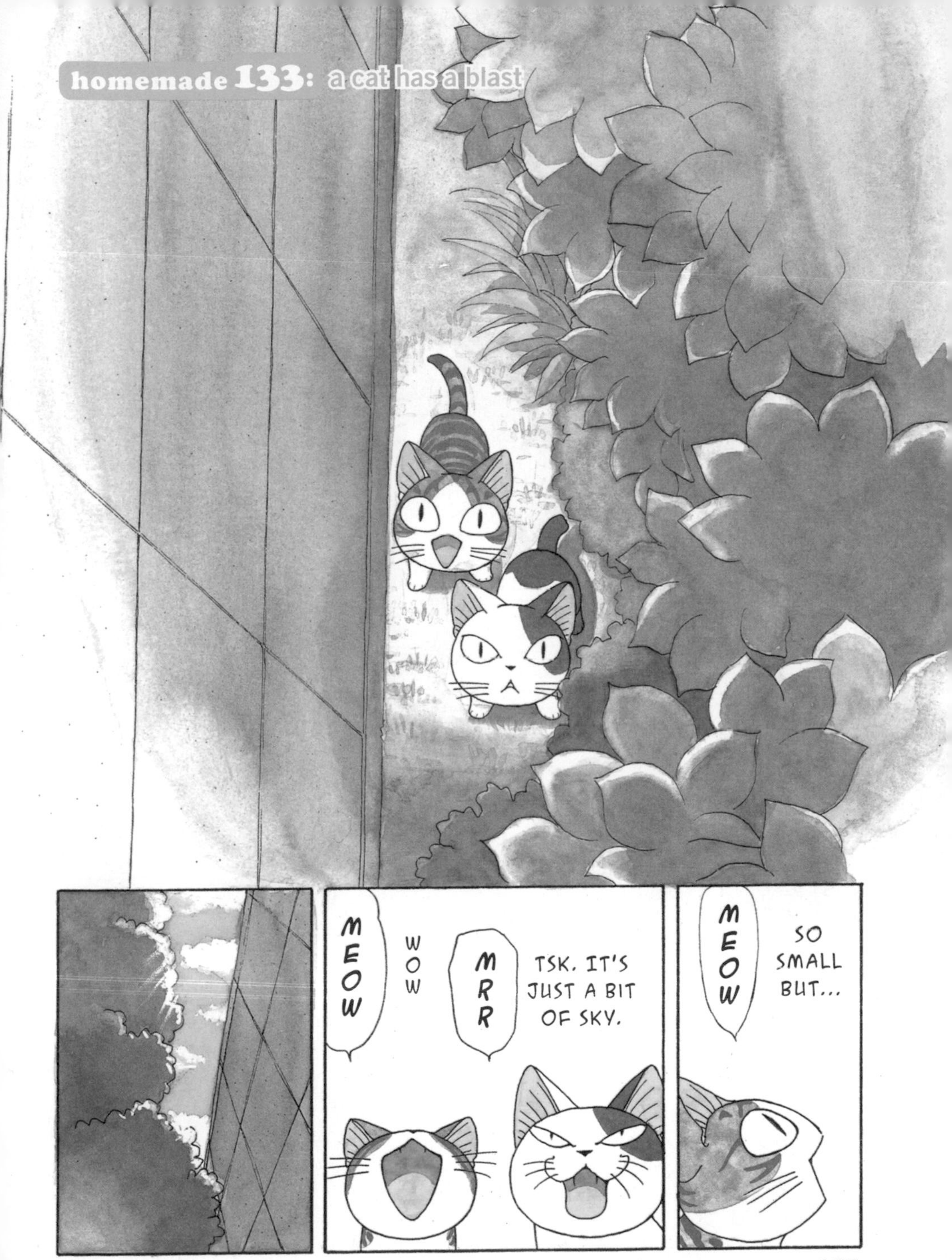
MEOW
WOW
MRR
TSK. IT'S JUST A BIT OF SKY.
MEOW
SO SMALL BUT...

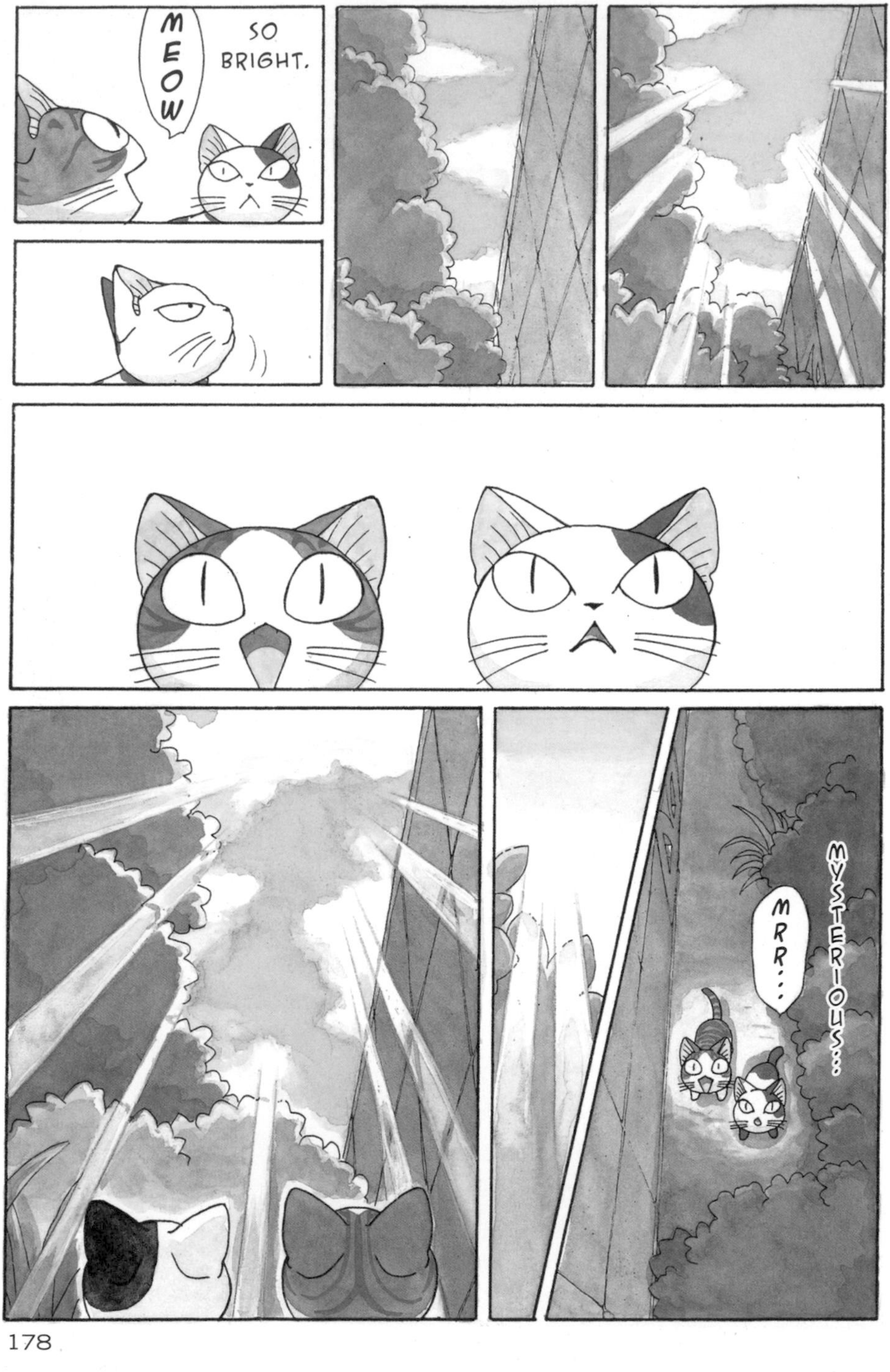
MEOW
SO BRIGHT.
MRR...
MYSTERIOUS...

MRR

THE LEAVES ARE RUSTLING.

MYA

IT'S DARK.

STARE

NASH

MRR

OY! THERE'S SOMETHING HERE!

MYA

REALLY? WHAT?

MRR

SHAK SHAK SHAK SHAK

COME ALONG, CHI.

MEOW

IS IT SAFE, COC- CHI?

NASH

179

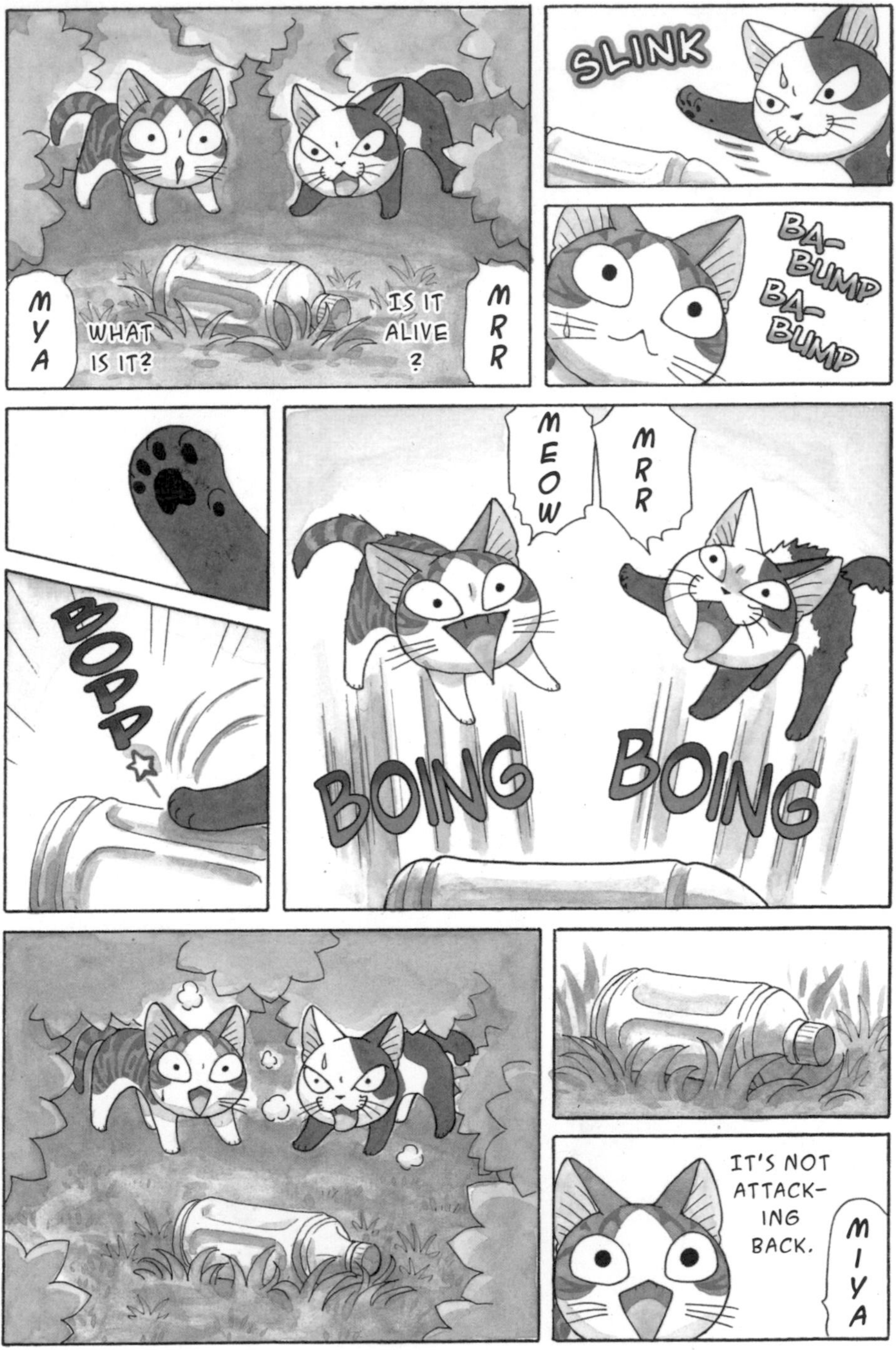
MYA
WHAT IS IT?
IS IT ALIVE?
MRR
SLINK
BA-BUMP BA-BUMP
BOPP
MEOW
MRR
BOING BOING
IT'S NOT ATTACKING BACK.
MIYA

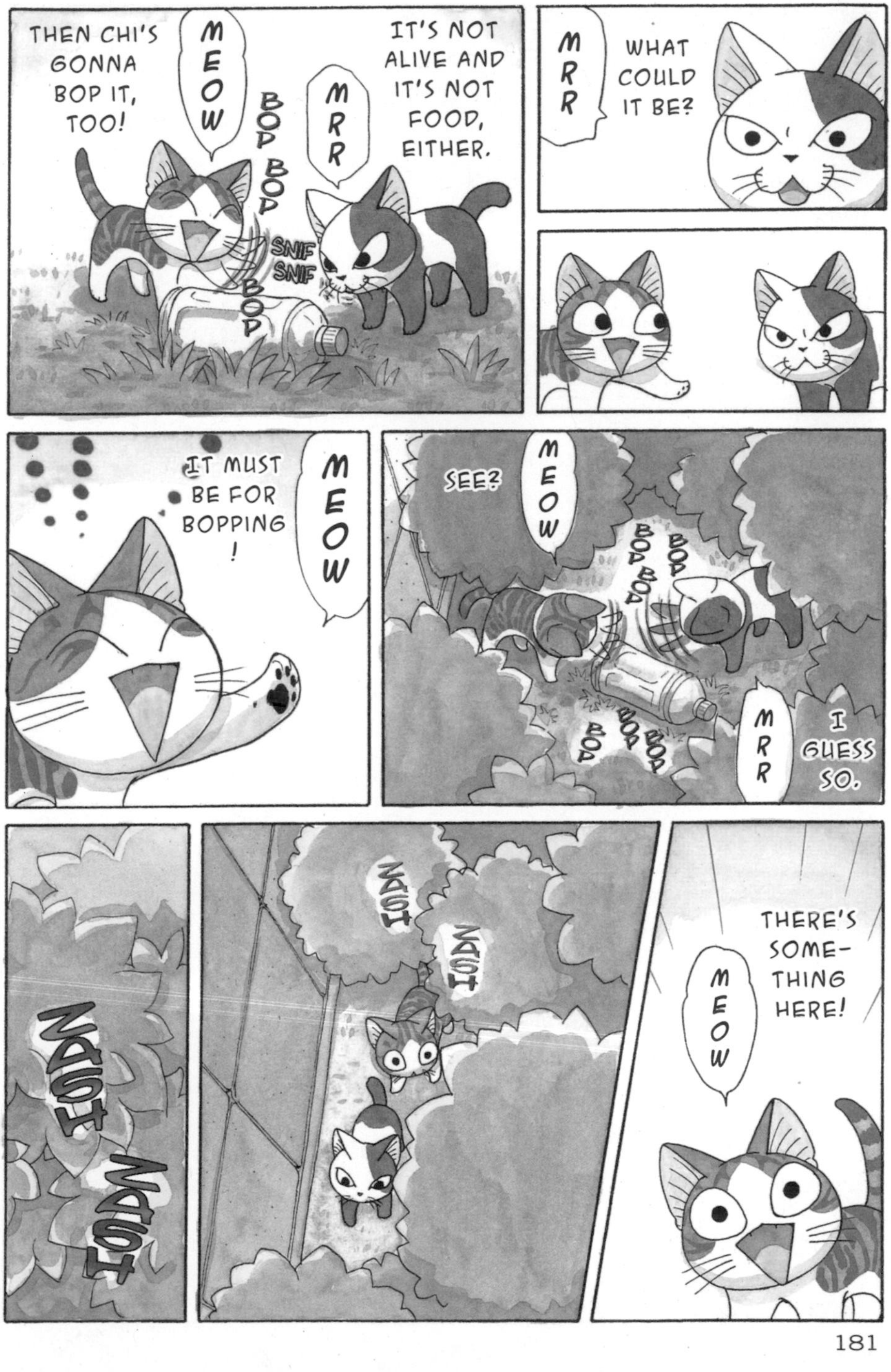
THEN CHI'S GONNA BOP IT, TOO!
MEOW
BOP BOP BOP
BOP BOP
MRR
IT'S NOT ALIVE AND IT'S NOT FOOD, EITHER.
SNIF SNIF
MRR
WHAT COULD IT BE?
IT MUST BE FOR BOPPING!
MEOW
SEE?
MEOW
BOP BOP BOP BOP
BOP BOP BOP
MRR
I GUESS SO.
ZASH ZASH
ZASH
ZASH
THERE'S SOME-THING HERE!
MEOW

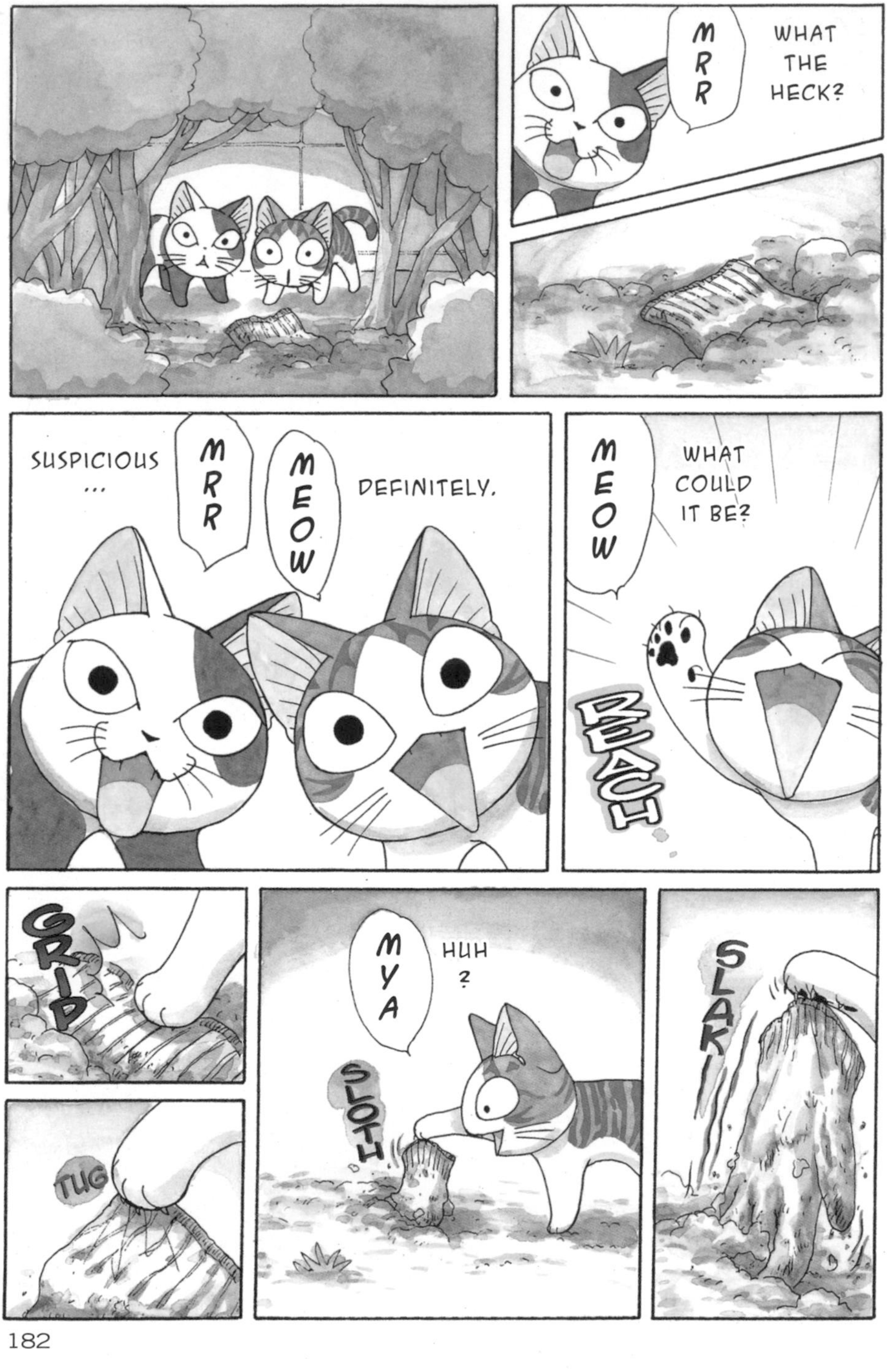
MRR
WHAT THE HECK?
SUSPICIOUS...
MRR
MEOW
DEFINITELY.
MEOW
WHAT COULD IT BE?
REACH
GRIP
TUG
MYA
HUH?
SLOTH
SLAK

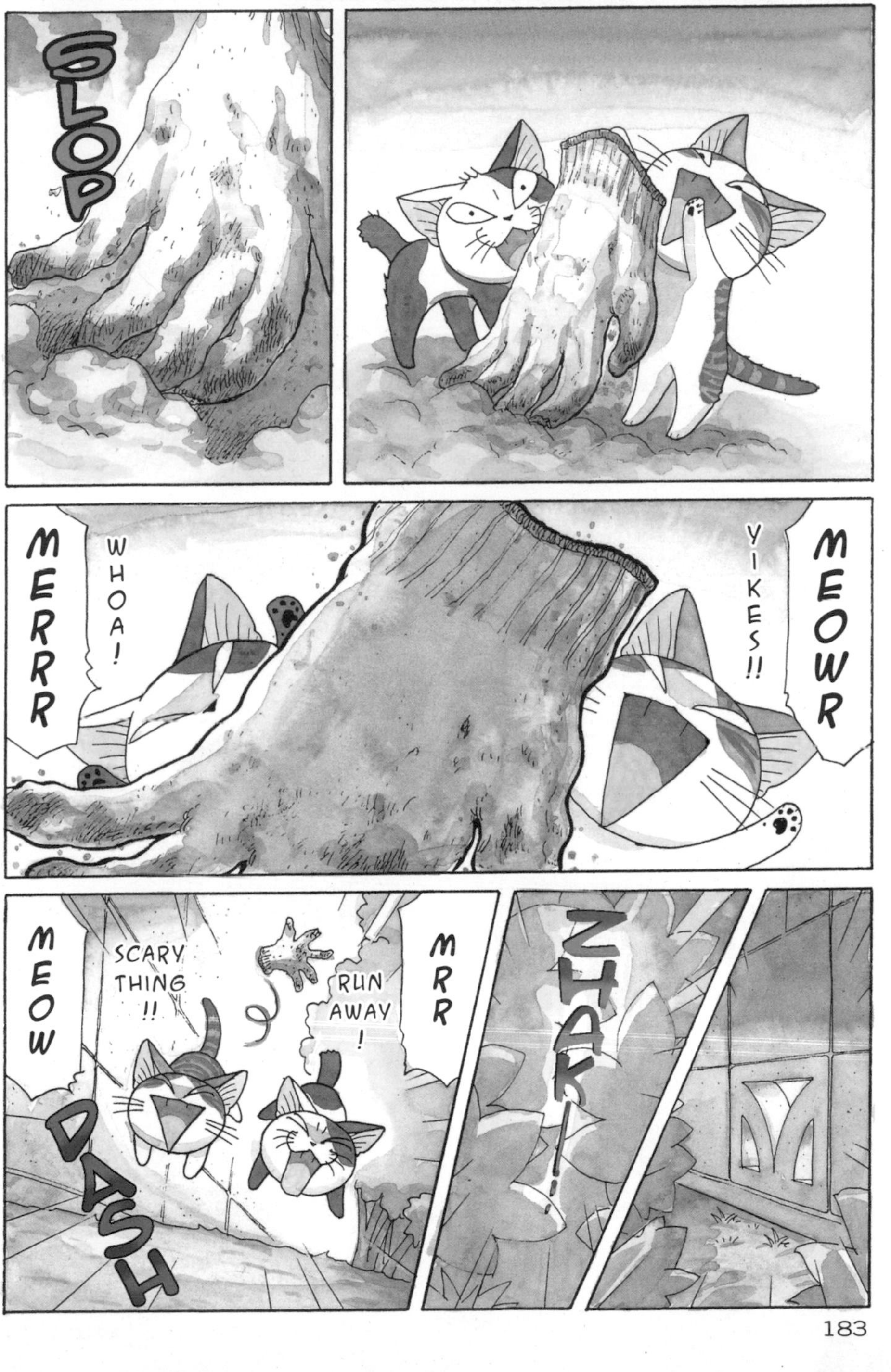
SLOP
MERRRR
WHOA!
YIKES!!
MEOWR
MEOW
SCARY THING!!
RUN AWAY!
MRR
DASH
ZHAK!!

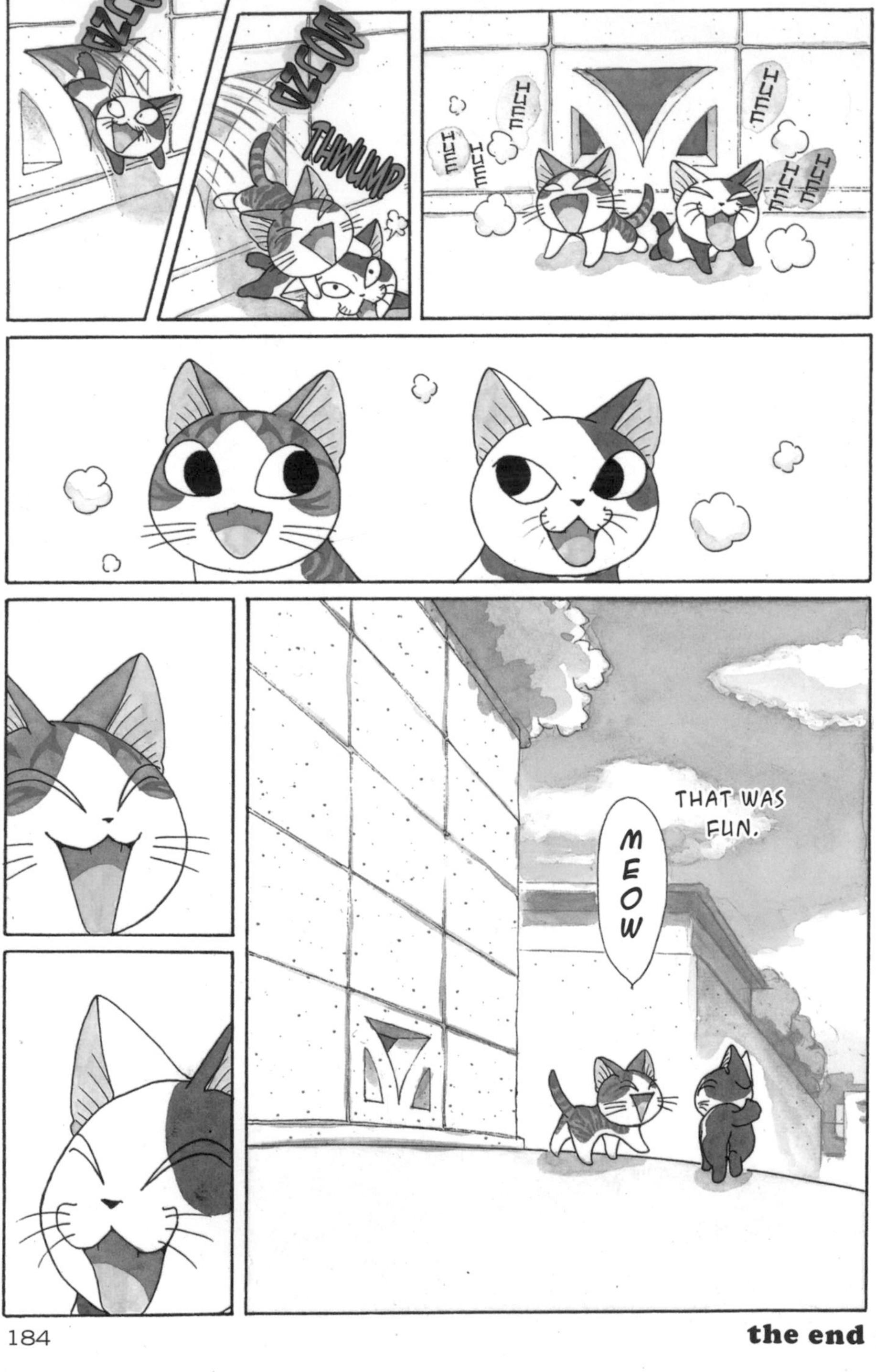
VZOOM
VZOOM
THWUMP
HUFF
HUFF
HUFF
HUFF
HUFF
HUFF
MEOW
THAT WAS FUN.



**the end**

# homemade 134: a cat is pursued

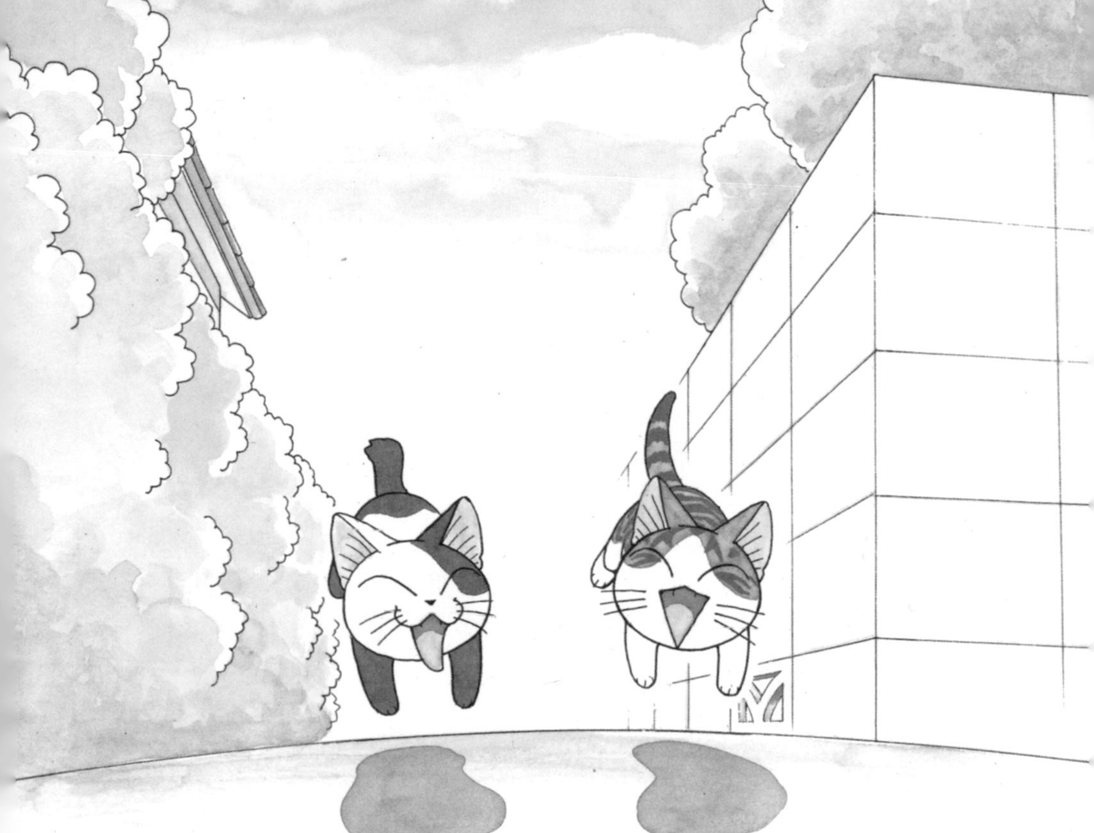

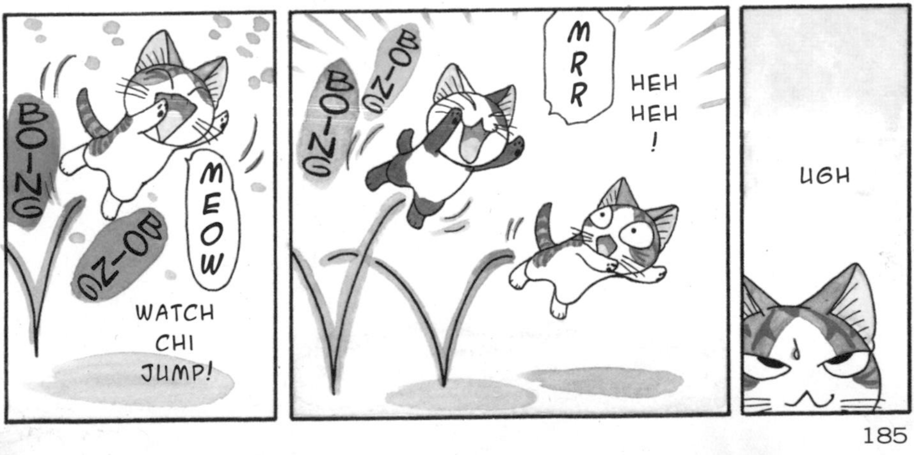
BOING
BO-ING
MEOW
WATCH CHI JUMP!
BOING
BO-ING
MRR
HEH HEH!
UGH

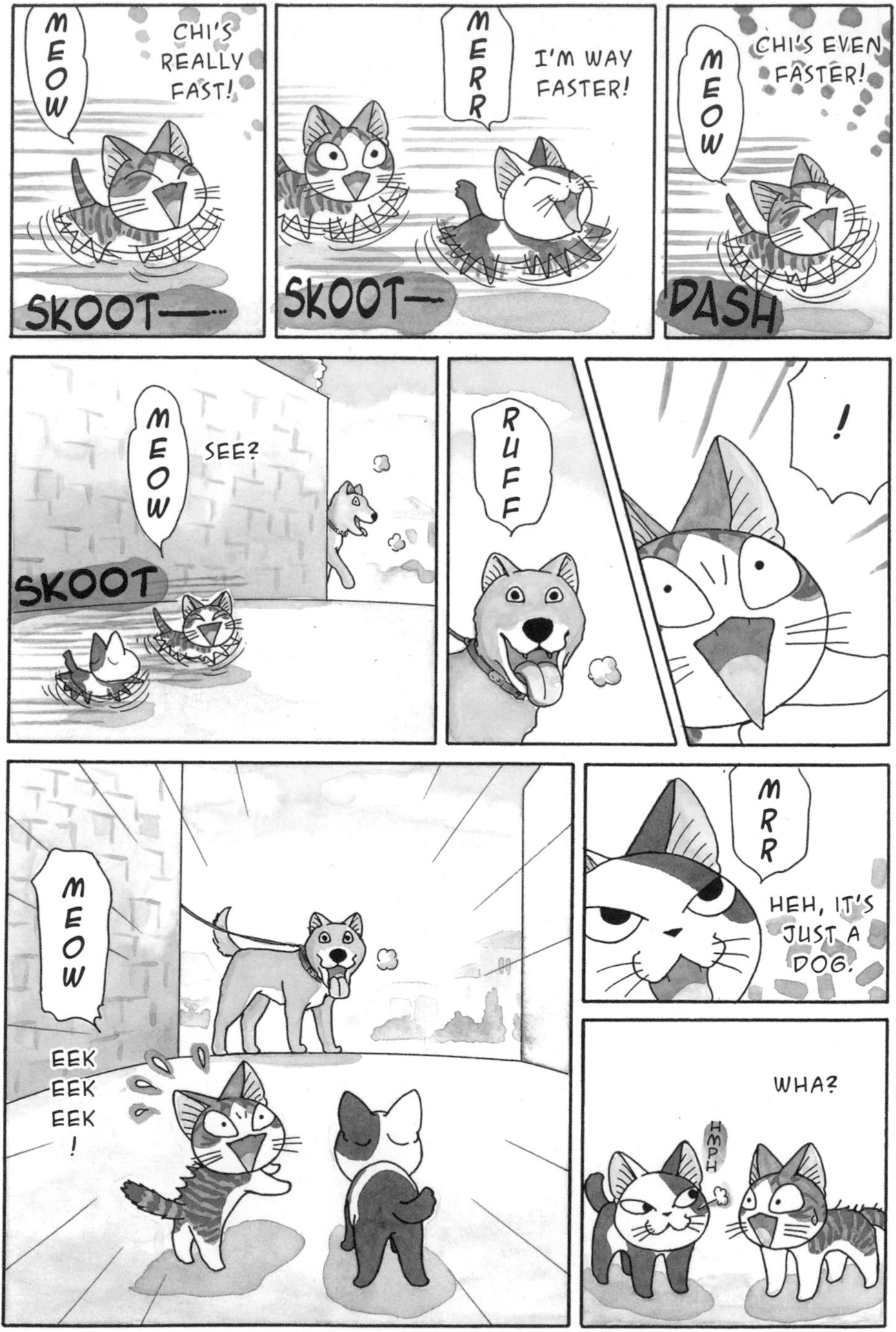
MEOW
CHI'S REALLY FAST!
SKOOT——
MERR
I'M WAY FASTER!
SKOOT—
MEOW
CHI'S EVEN FASTER!
DASH
MEOW
SEE?
SKOOT
RUFF
!
MEOW
EEK EEK EEK!
MRR
HEH, IT'S JUST A DOG.
WHA?
HMPH

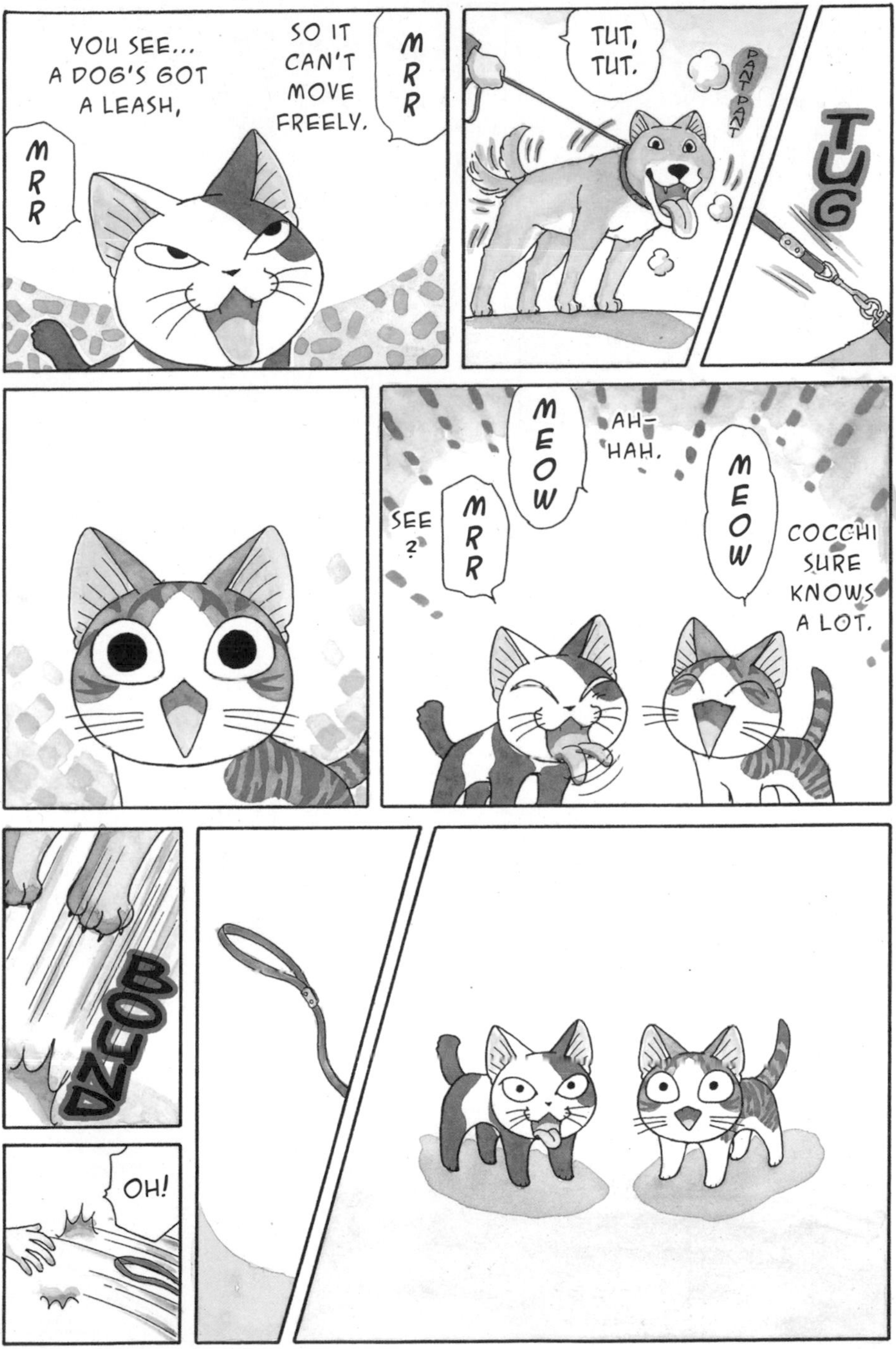
YOU SEE... A DOG'S GOT A LEASH,
MRR
SO IT CAN'T MOVE FREELY.
MRR
TUT, TUT.
PANT PANT
TUG
SEE?
MRR
MEOW
AH-HAH.
MEOW
COCCHI SURE KNOWS A LOT.
BOUND
OH!

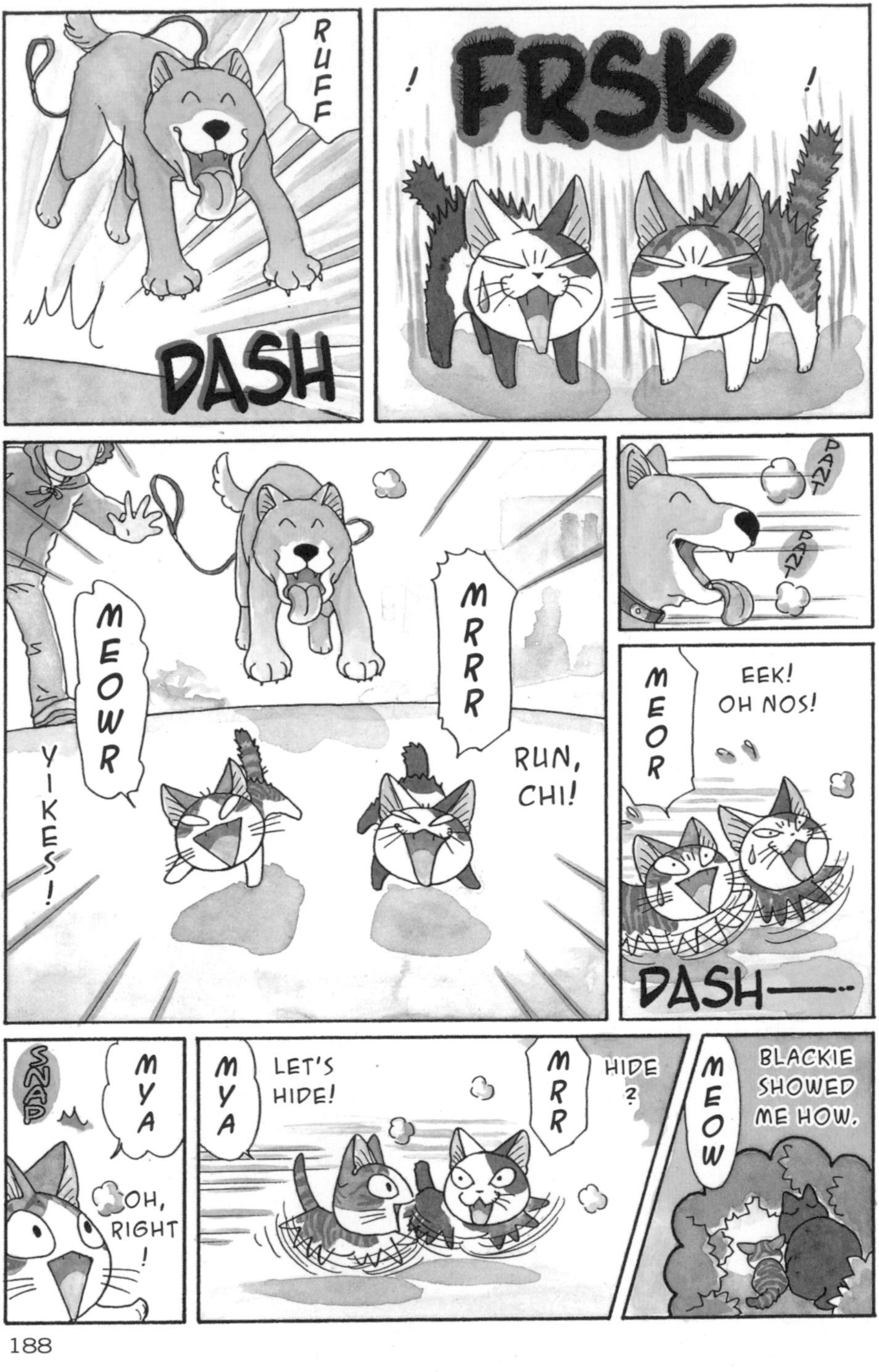
RUFF
DASH
!
FRSK
!
MEOWR
YIKES!
MRRR
RUN, CHI!
PANT
PANT
MEOR
EEK! OH NOS!
DASH
SNAP
MYA
OH, RIGHT!
MYA
LET'S HIDE!
MRR
HIDE?
MEOW
BLACKIE SHOWED ME HOW.

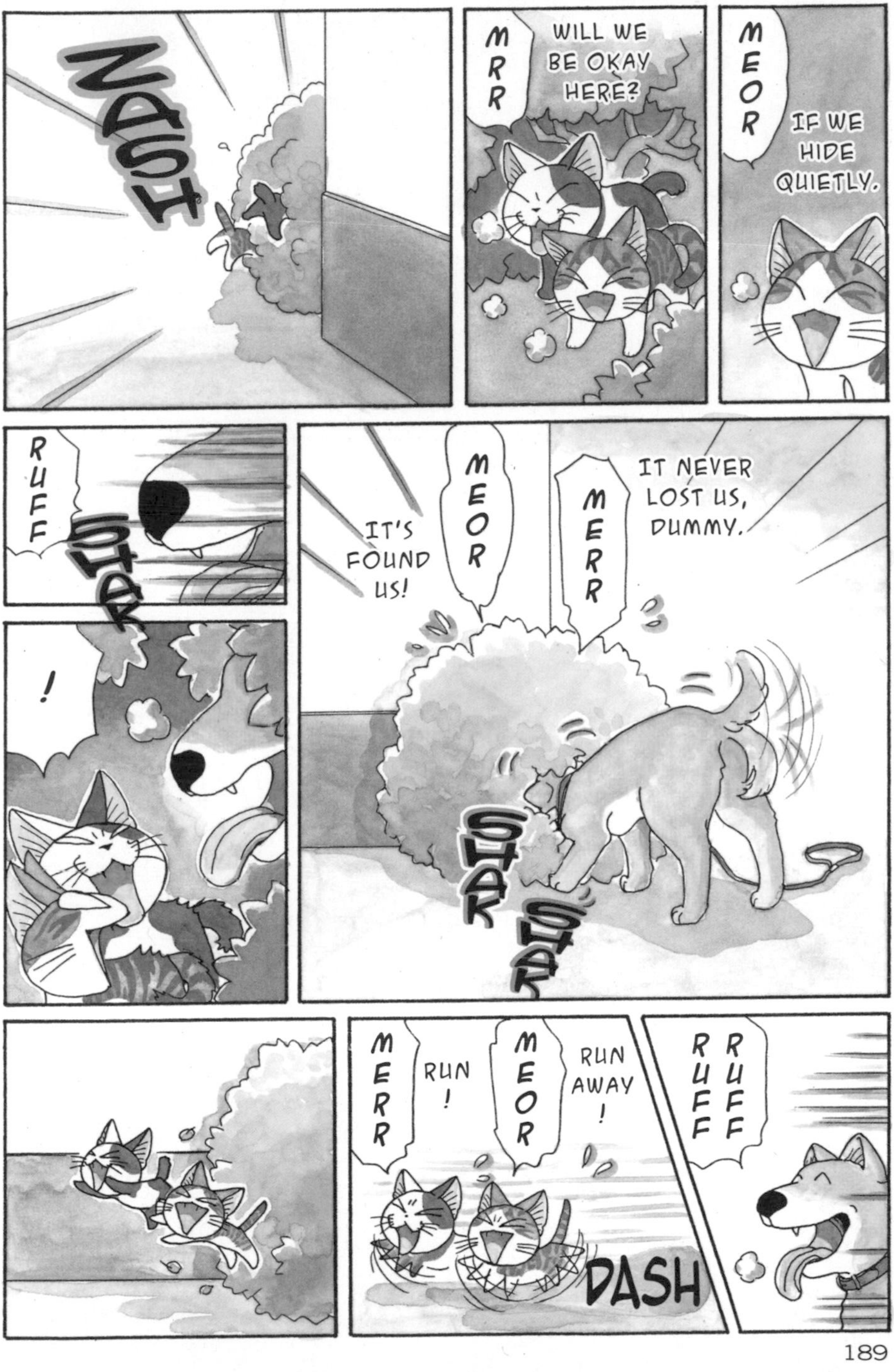
DASH
MRR
WILL WE BE OKAY HERE?
MEOR
IF WE HIDE QUIETLY.
RUFF
SHAR
!
MEOR
IT'S FOUND US!
MERR
IT NEVER LOST US, DUMMY.
SHAR
SHAR
MERR
RUN!
MEOR
RUN AWAY!
RUFF
RUFF
DASH

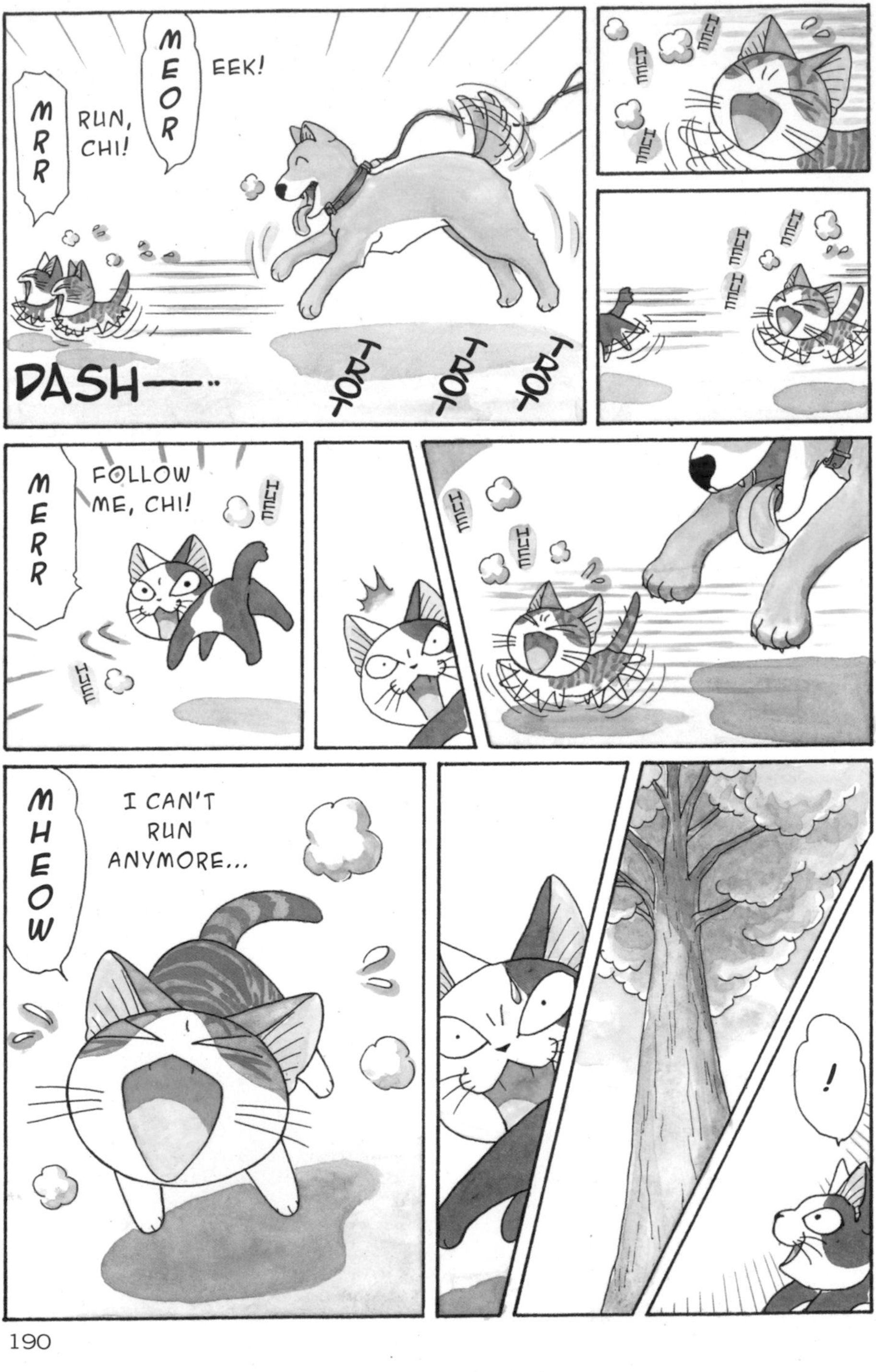
MEOR
EEK!
MRR
RUN, CHI!
DASH—..
TROT
TROT
TROT
HUFF
HUFF
HUFF
HUFF
HUFF
HUFF
HUFF
MERR
FOLLOW ME, CHI!
HUFF
HUFF
HUFF
HUFF
MHEOW
I CAN'T RUN ANYMORE...
!

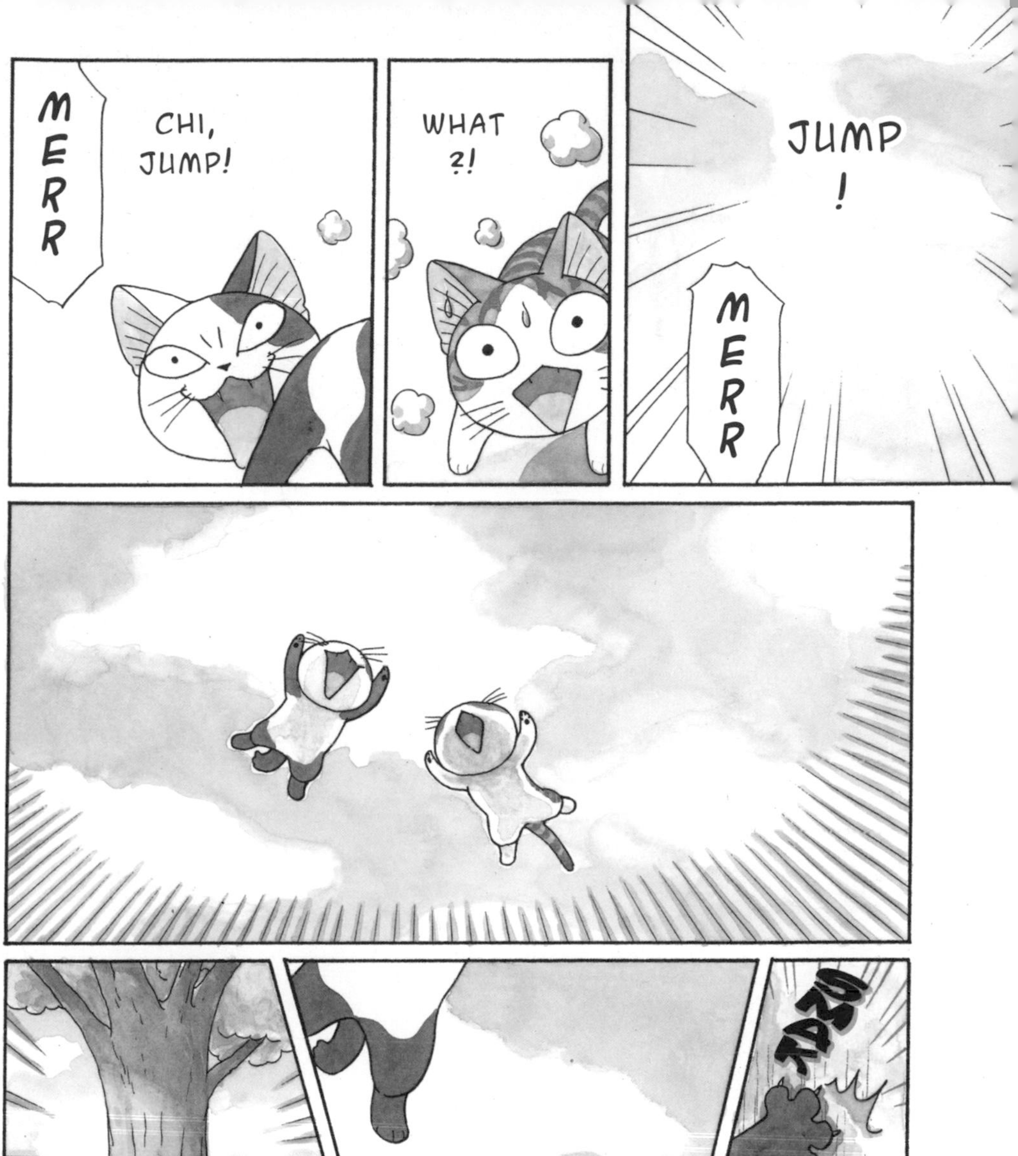
MERR
CHI, JUMP!
WHAT ?!
JUMP !
MERR
SWAT
GRIP

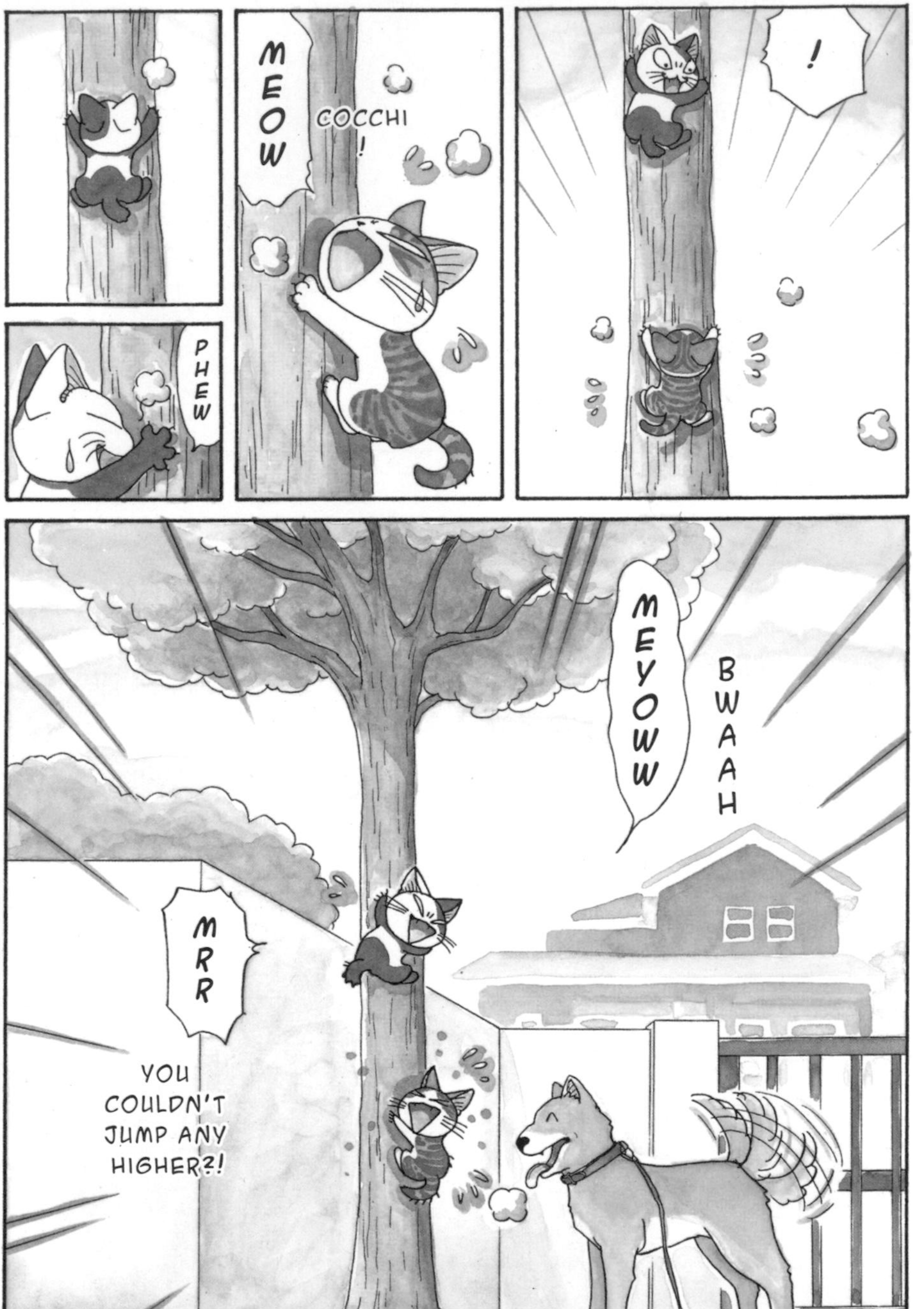
PHEW
MEOW
COCCHI!
!
MEYOWW
BWAAH
MRR
YOU COULDN'T JUMP ANY HIGHER?!

the end

# homemade 135: a cat is hemmed

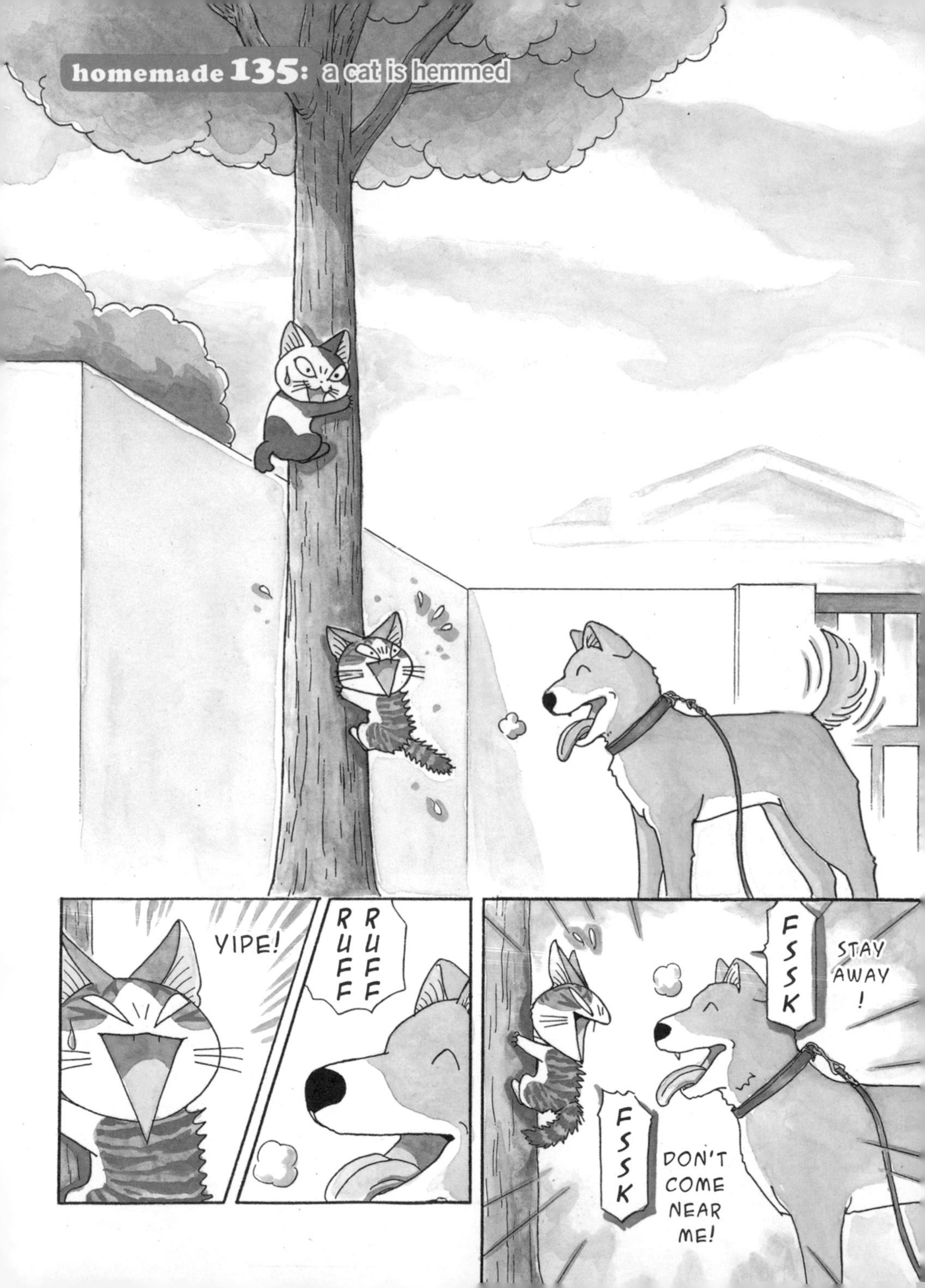

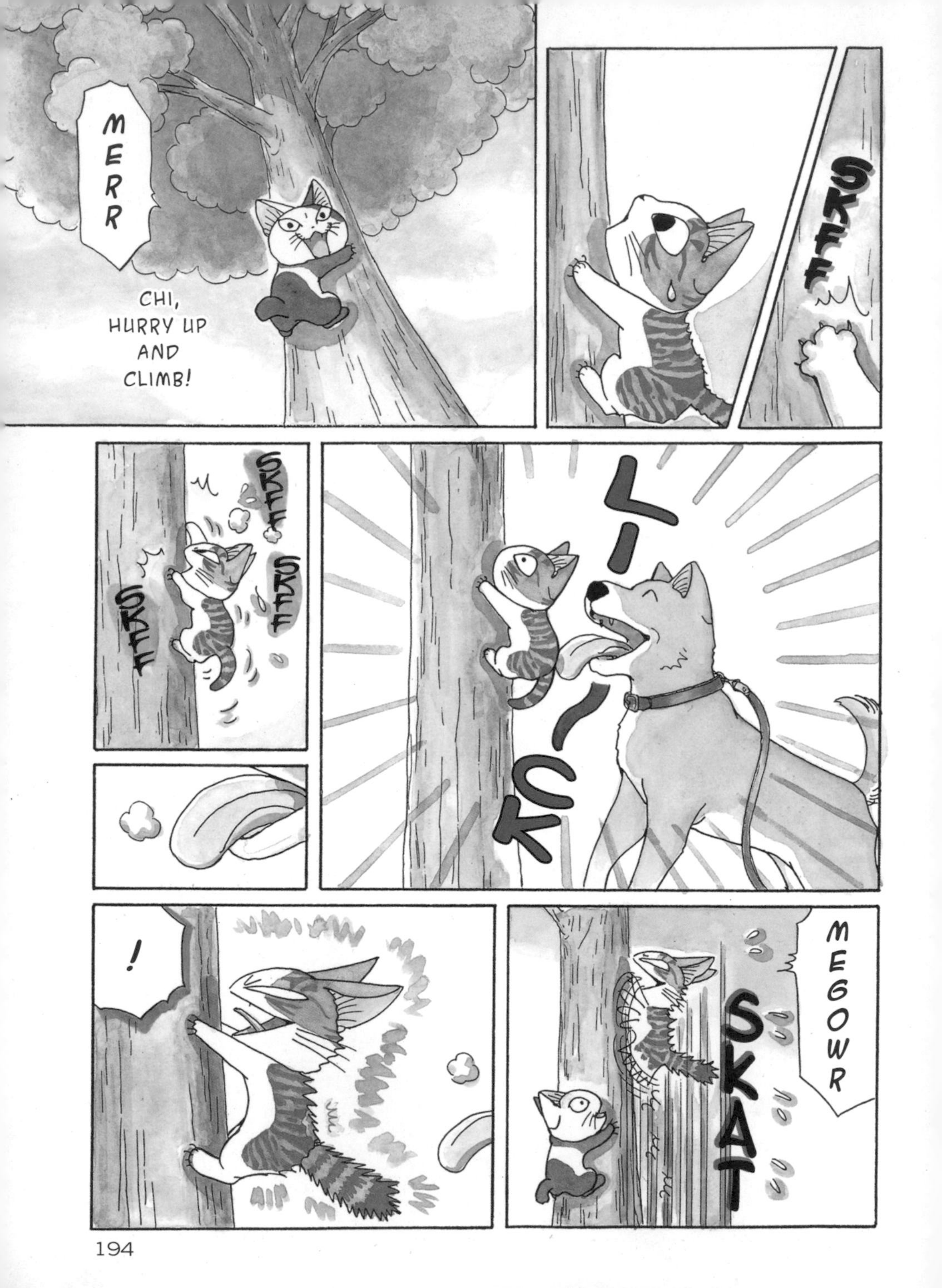

MERR
CHI, HURRY UP AND CLIMB!
SKFF
SKFF
SKFF
SKFF
LICK
!
MEGOWR
SKAT

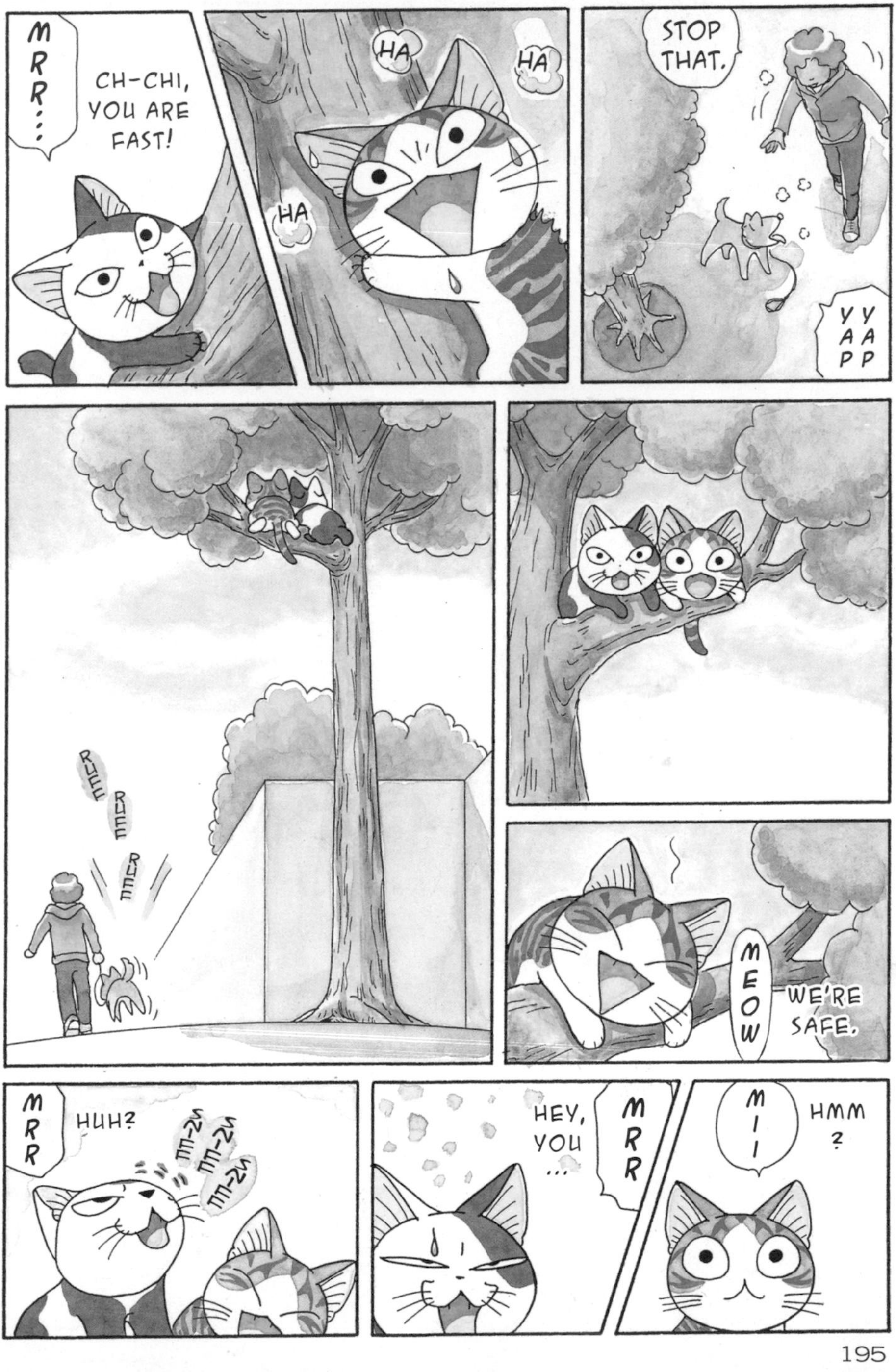
MRR...
CH-CHI, YOU ARE FAST!
HA
HA
HA
STOP THAT.
YAP YAP
RUFF
RUFF
RUFF
MEOW
WE'RE SAFE.
MRR
HUH?
HEY, YOU ...
MRR
MII
HMM ?

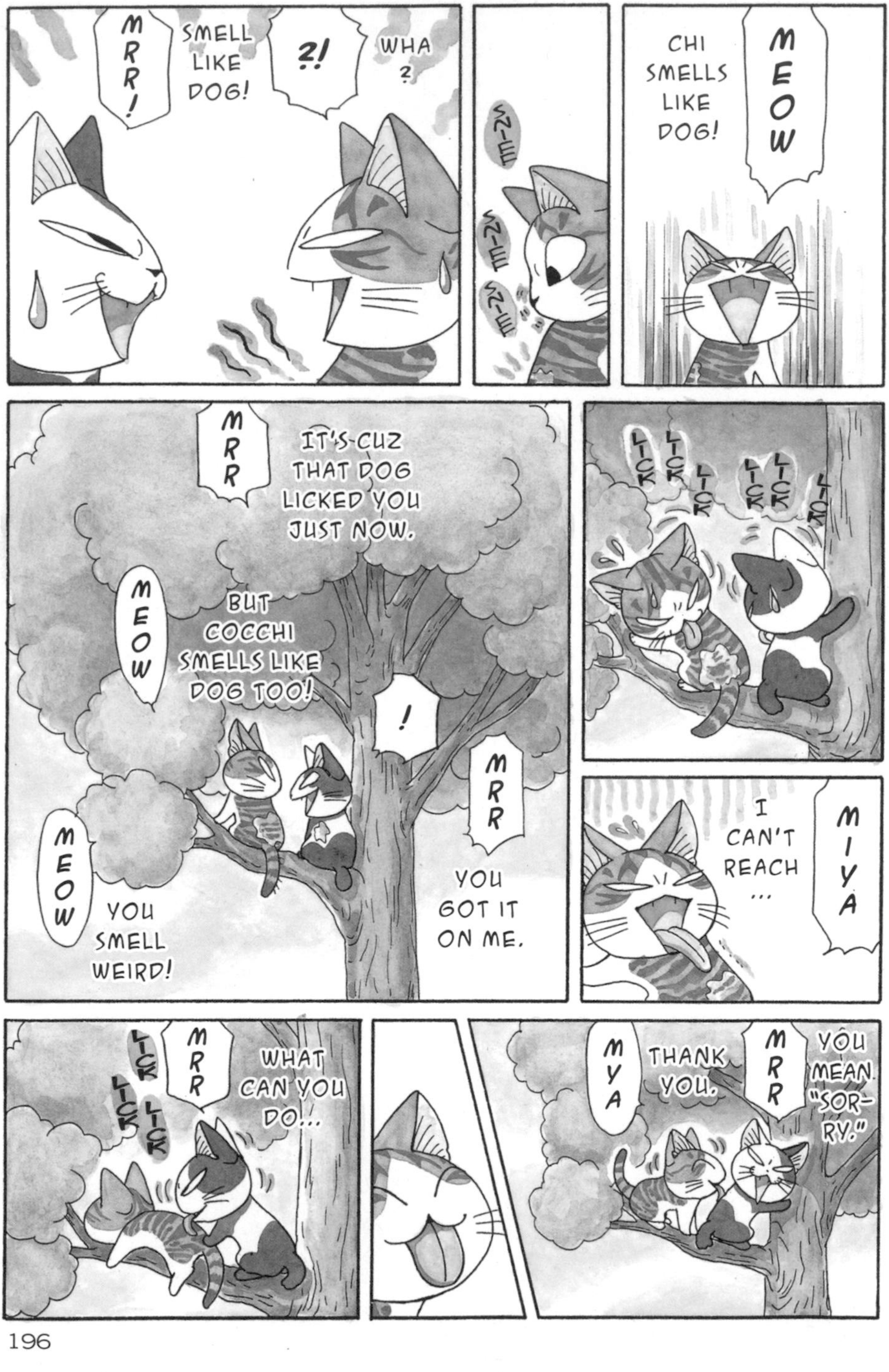
MRR!
SMELL LIKE DOG!
?!
WHA?
SNIFF
SNIFF
SNIFF
CHI SMELLS LIKE DOG!
MEOW
MRR
IT'S CUZ THAT DOG LICKED YOU JUST NOW.
MEOW
BUT COCCHI SMELLS LIKE DOG TOO!
!
MEOW
YOU SMELL WEIRD!
MRR
YOU GOT IT ON ME.
LICK
LICK
LICK
LICK
LICK
LICK
I CAN'T REACH...
MIYA
LICK
LICK
LICK
MRR
WHAT CAN YOU DO...
MYA
THANK YOU.
MRR
YOU MEAN "SORRY."

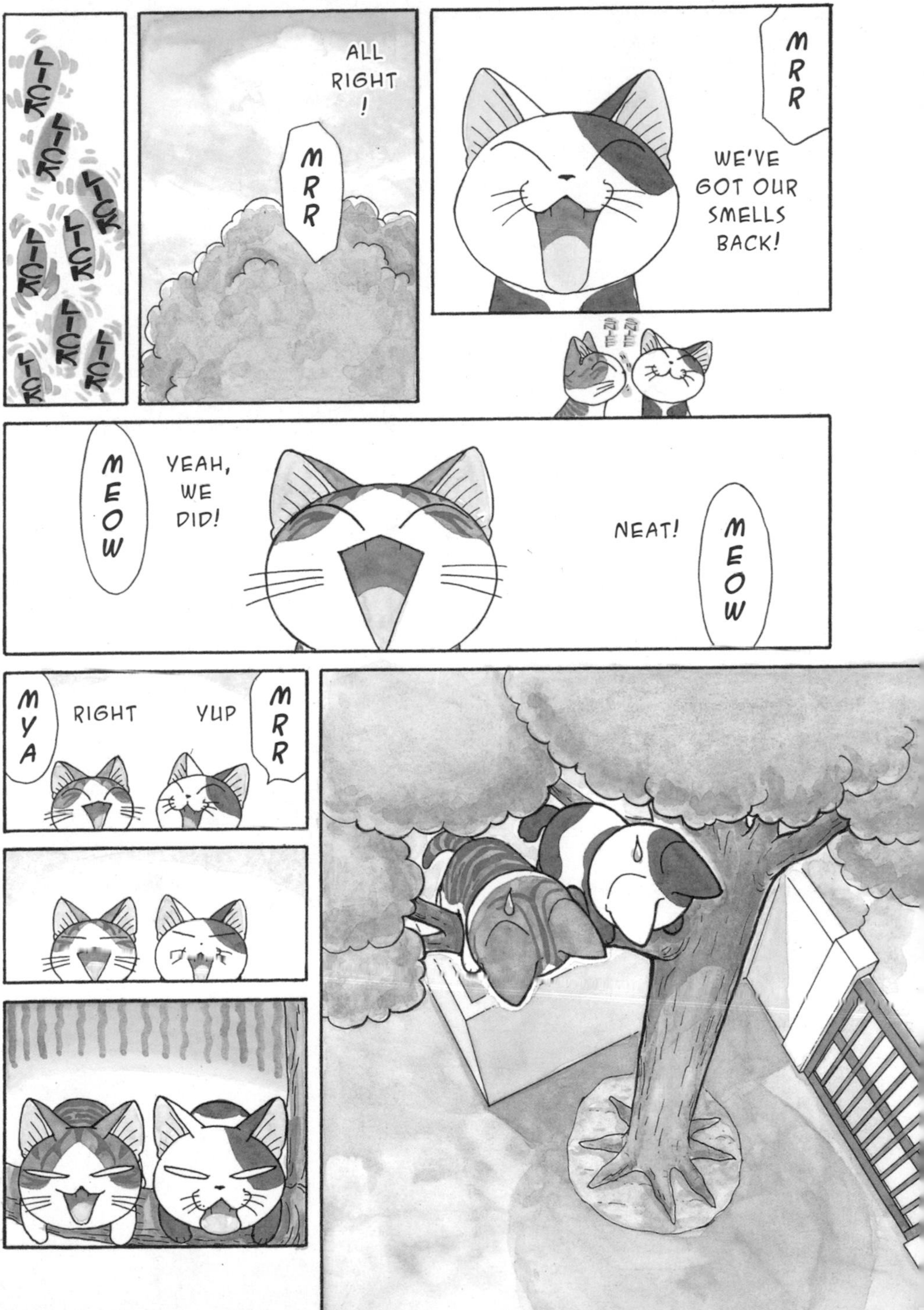
LICK
LICK
LICK
LICK
LICK
LICK
LICK
LICK
LICK
ALL RIGHT!
MRR
MRR
WE'VE GOT OUR SMELLS BACK!
MEOW
YEAH, WE DID!
NEAT!
MEOW
MYA
RIGHT
YUP
MRR

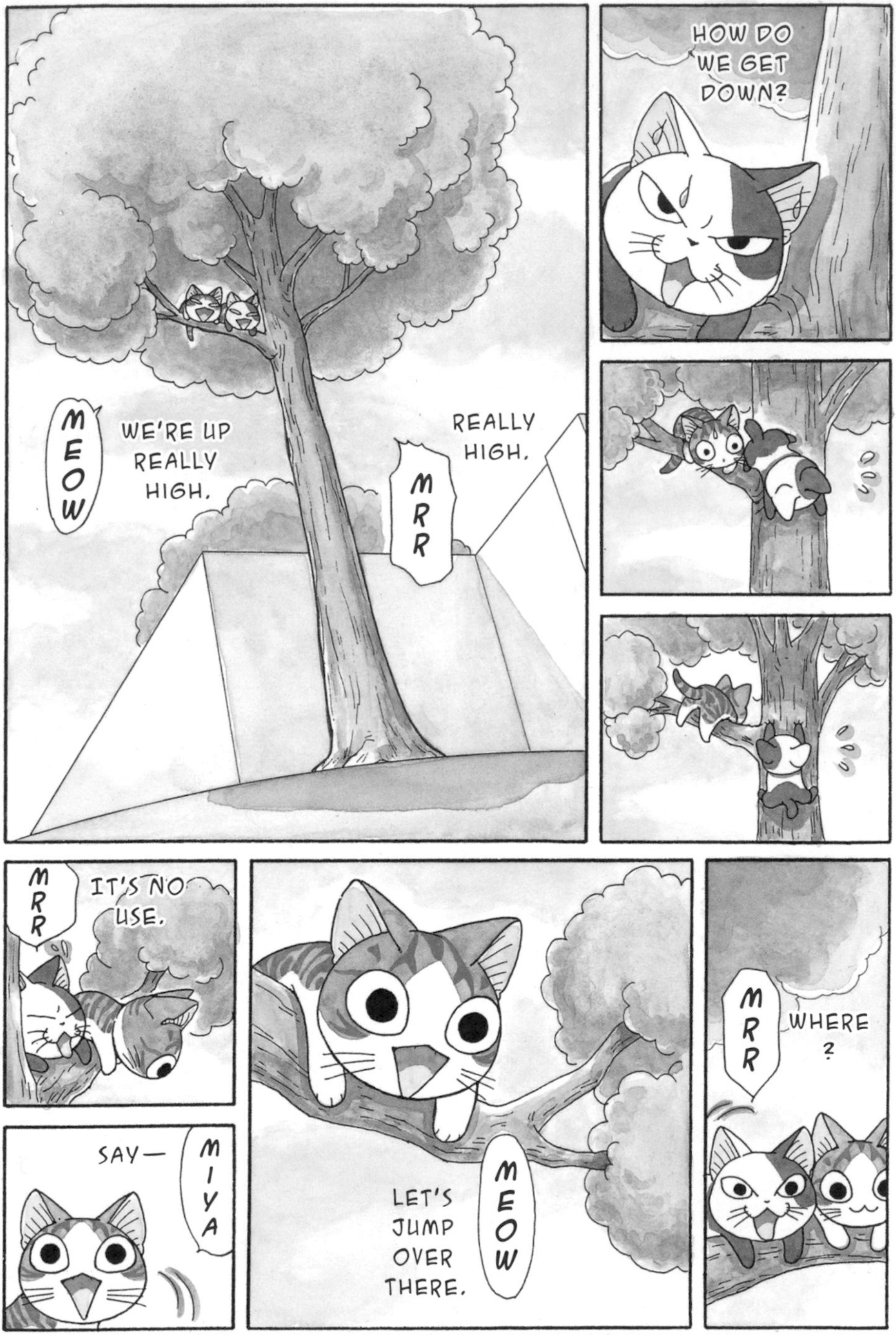
MEOW
WE'RE UP REALLY HIGH.
MRR
REALLY HIGH.
HOW DO WE GET DOWN?
MRR
IT'S NO USE.
SAY—
MIYA
MEOW
LET'S JUMP OVER THERE.
MRR
WHERE?

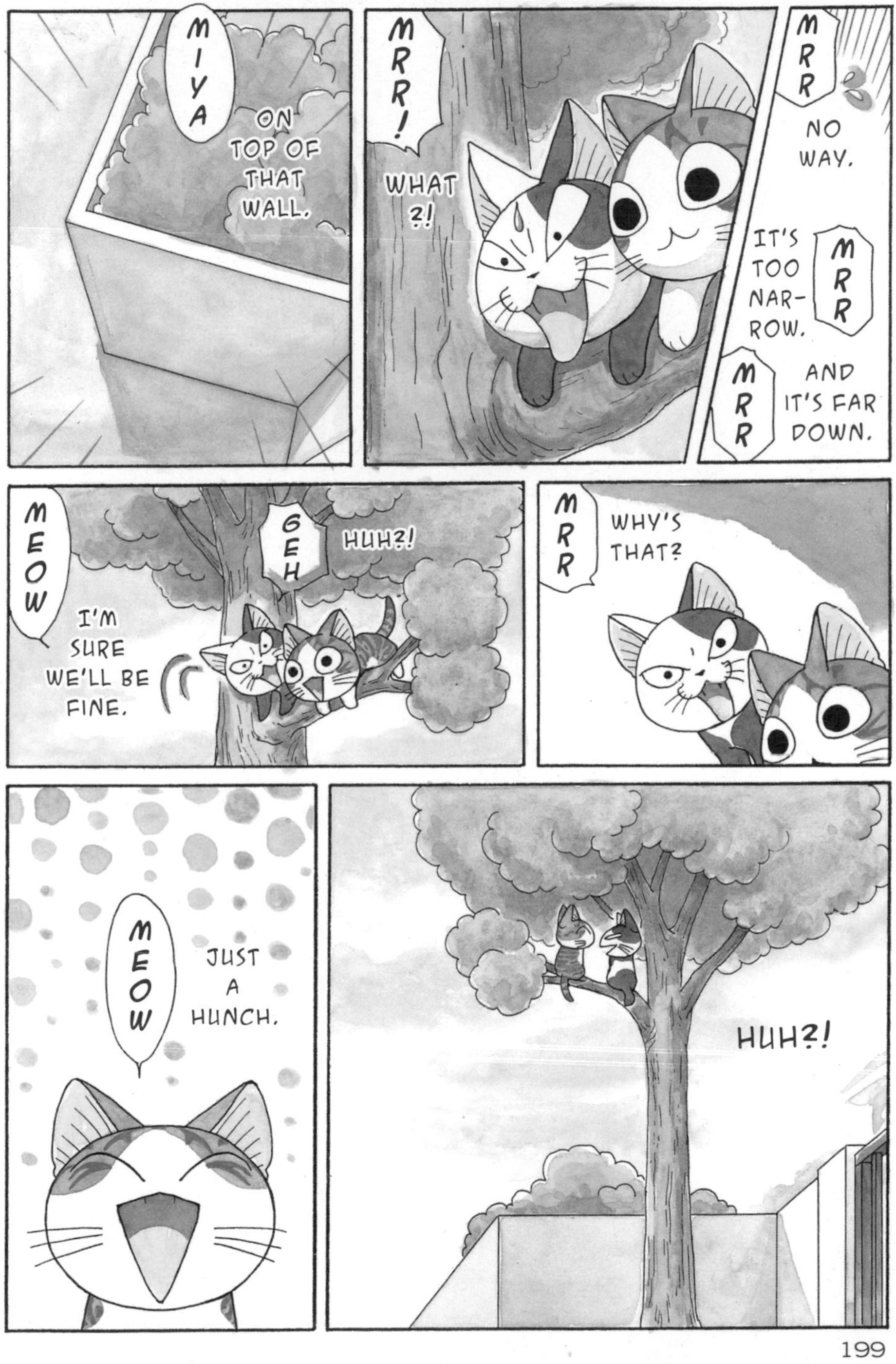
MIYA
ON TOP OF THAT WALL.
MRR!
WHAT?!
MRR
NO WAY.
IT'S TOO NAR-ROW.
MRR
MRR
AND IT'S FAR DOWN.
MEOW
I'M SURE WE'LL BE FINE.
GEH
HUH?!
MRR
WHY'S THAT?
MEOW
JUST A HUNCH.
HUH?!

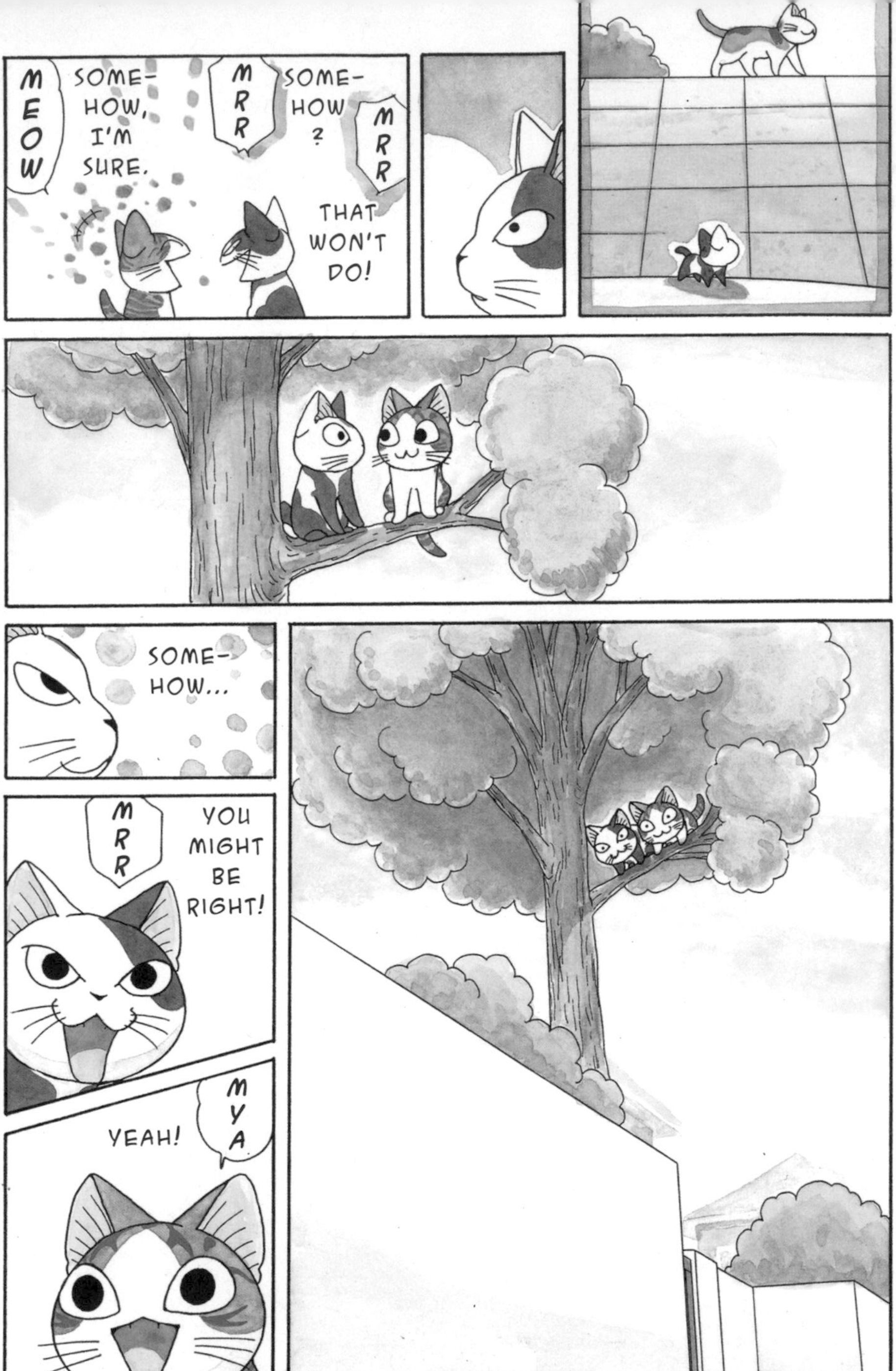
MEOW
SOME-HOW, I'M SURE.
MRR
SOME-HOW?
MRR
THAT WON'T DO!
SOME-HOW...
MRR
YOU MIGHT BE RIGHT!
YEAH!
MYA



**the end**

## homemade 136: a cat leaps

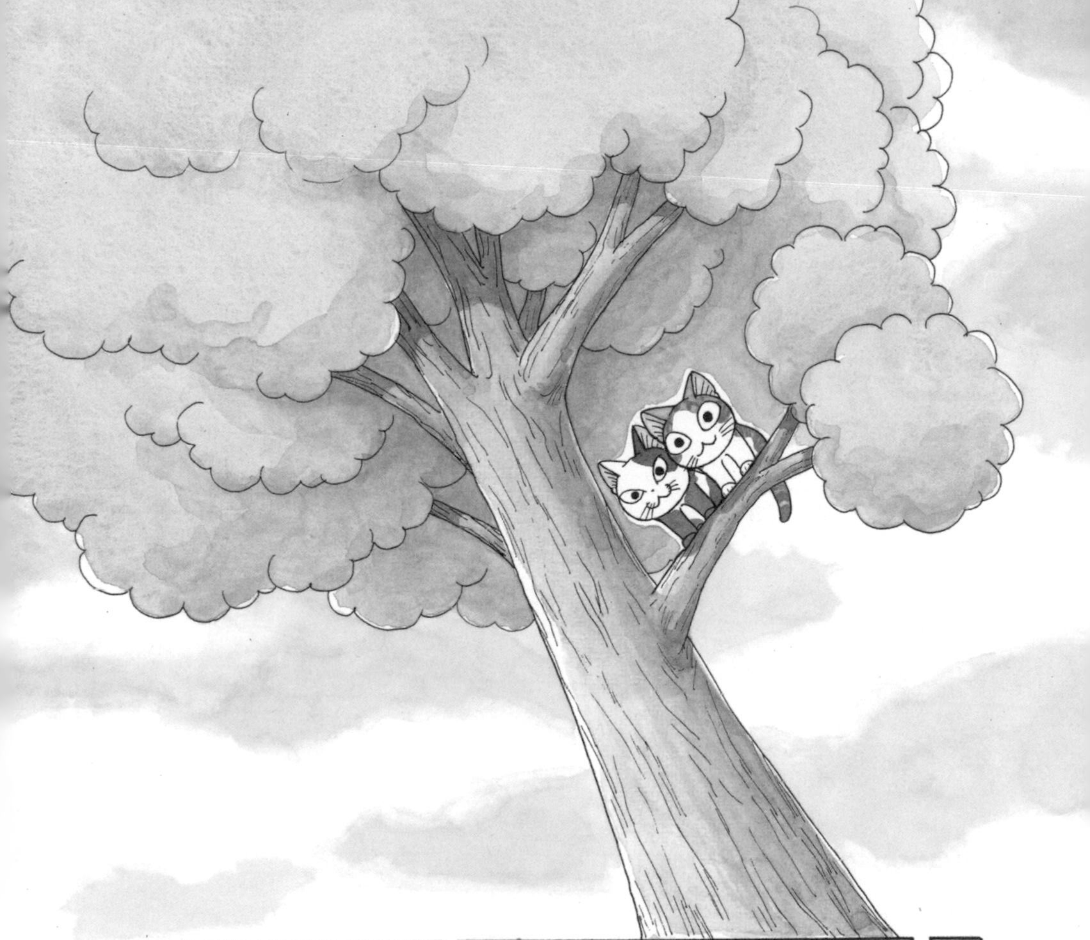

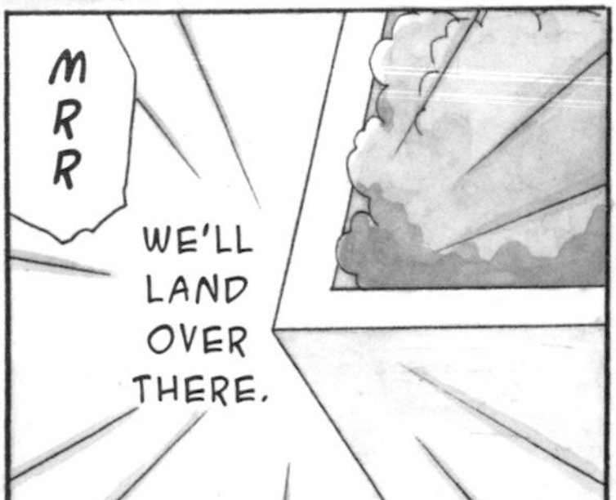
MRR
WE'LL LAND OVER THERE.

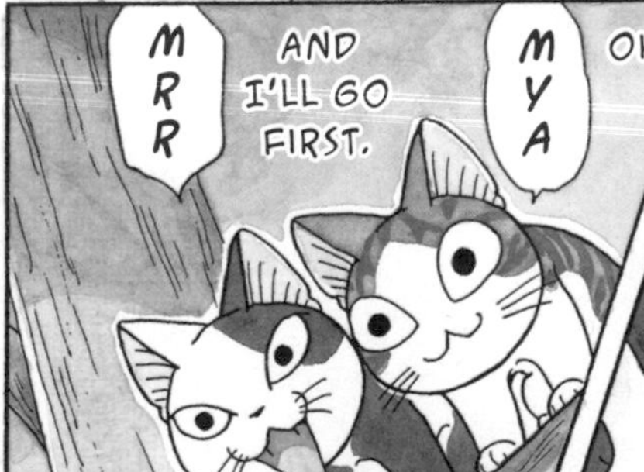
MRR
AND I'LL GO FIRST.
MYA
OK

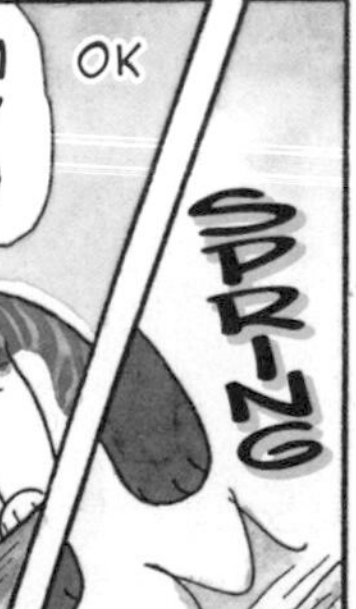
SPRING

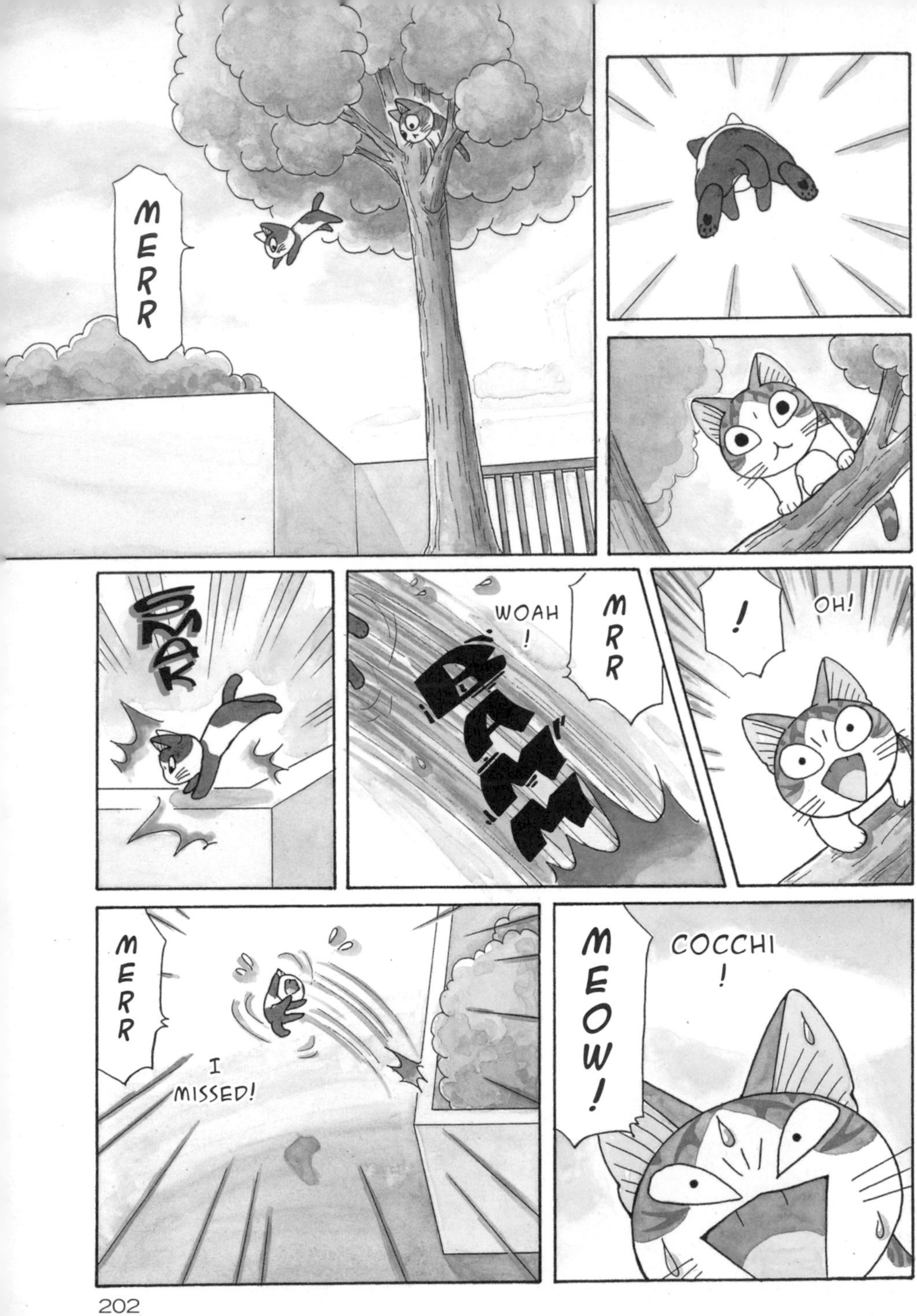
MERR
WOAH!
MRR
SMAK
BAMM
!
OH!
MERR
I MISSED!
COCCHI!
MEOW!

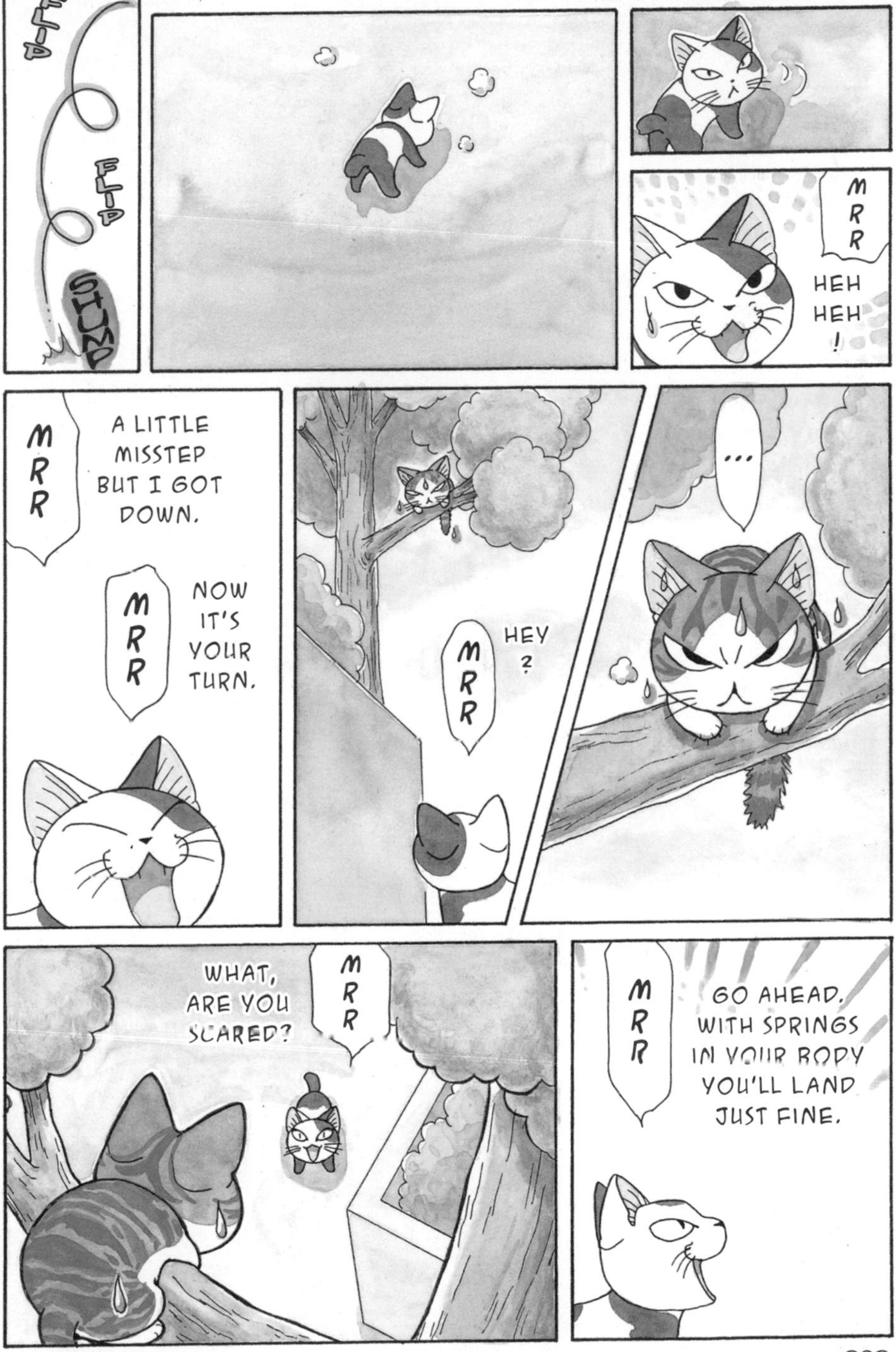
FLIP
FLIP
SHUMP
MRR
HEH HEH!
MRR
A LITTLE MISSTEP BUT I GOT DOWN.
MRR
NOW IT'S YOUR TURN.
MRR
HEY?
...
WHAT, ARE YOU SCARED?
MRR
MRR
GO AHEAD. WITH SPRINGS IN YOUR BODY YOU'LL LAND JUST FINE.

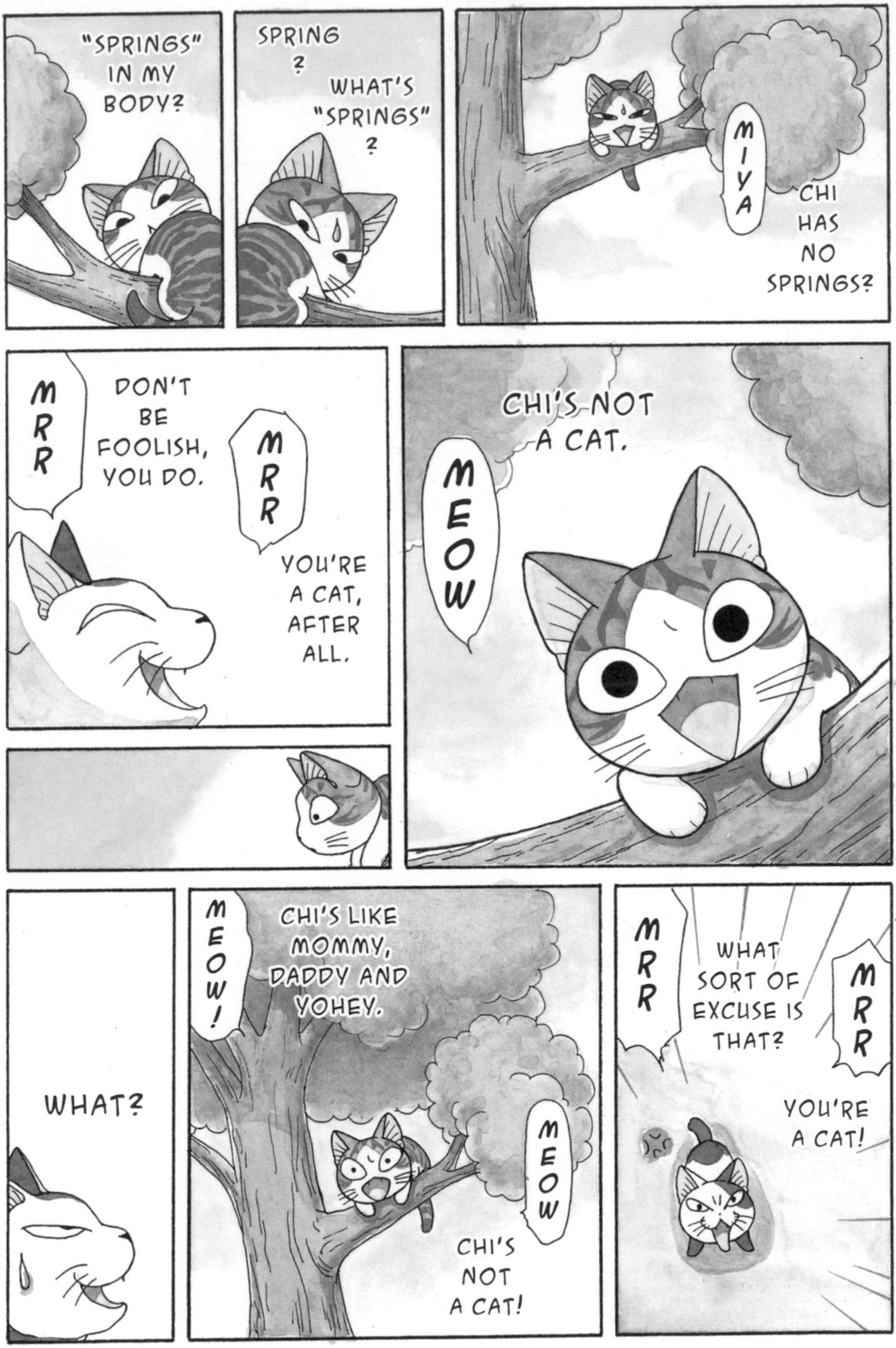
"SPRINGS" IN MY BODY?
SPRING?
WHAT'S "SPRINGS"?
MIYA
CHI HAS NO SPRINGS?
MRR
DON'T BE FOOLISH, YOU DO.
MRR
YOU'RE A CAT, AFTER ALL.
CHI'S NOT A CAT.
MEOW
WHAT?
MEOW!
CHI'S LIKE MOMMY, DADDY AND YOHEY.
MEOW
CHI'S NOT A CAT!
MRR
WHAT SORT OF EXCUSE IS THAT?
MRR
YOU'RE A CAT!

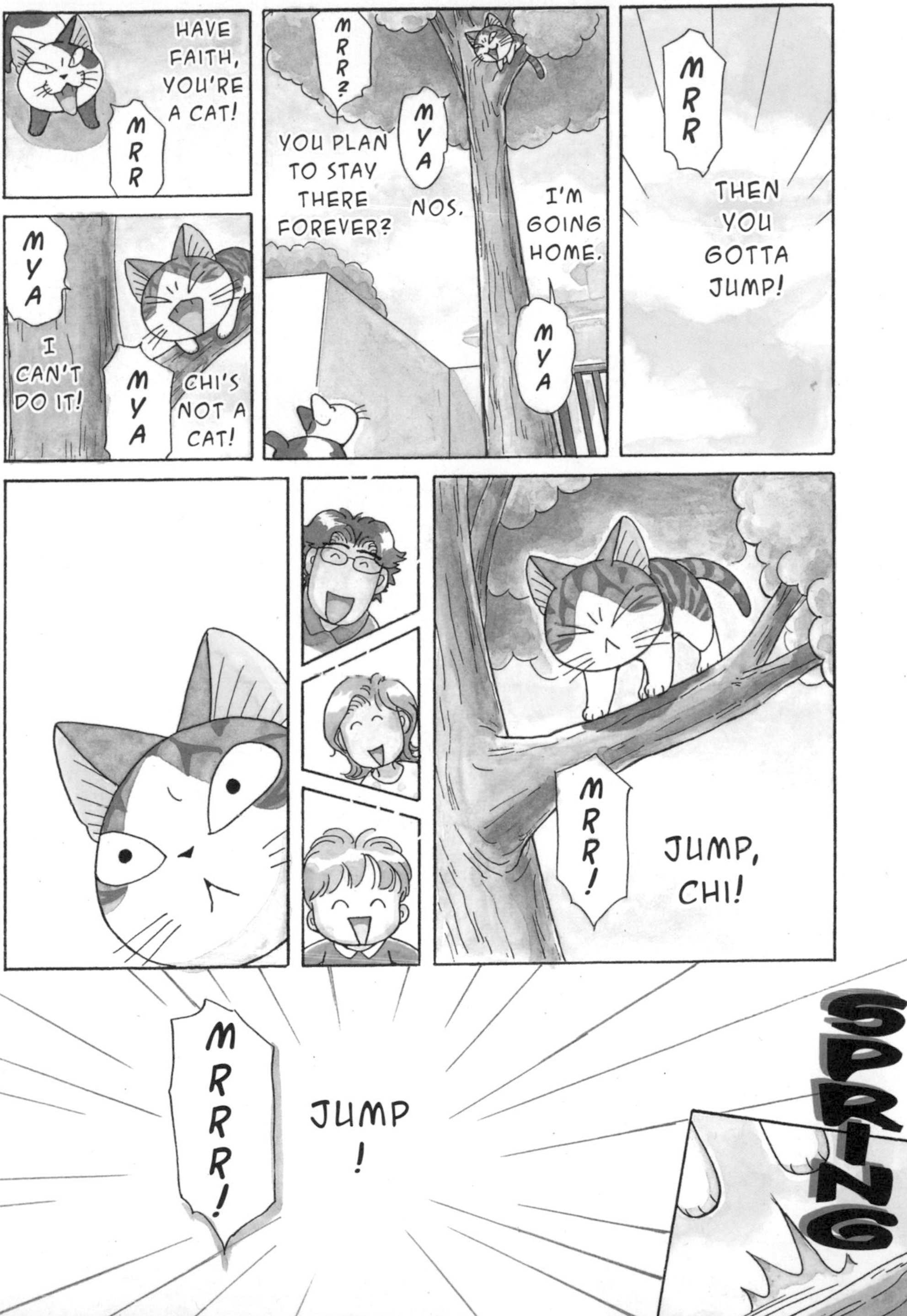
HAVE FAITH, YOU'RE A CAT!
MRR
MYA
I CAN'T DO IT!
MYA
CHI'S NOT A CAT!
MRR?
MYA
YOU PLAN TO STAY THERE FOREVER?
NOS.
I'M GOING HOME.
MYA
MRR
THEN YOU GOTTA JUMP!
MRR!
JUMP, CHI!
MRRRR!
JUMP!
SPRING

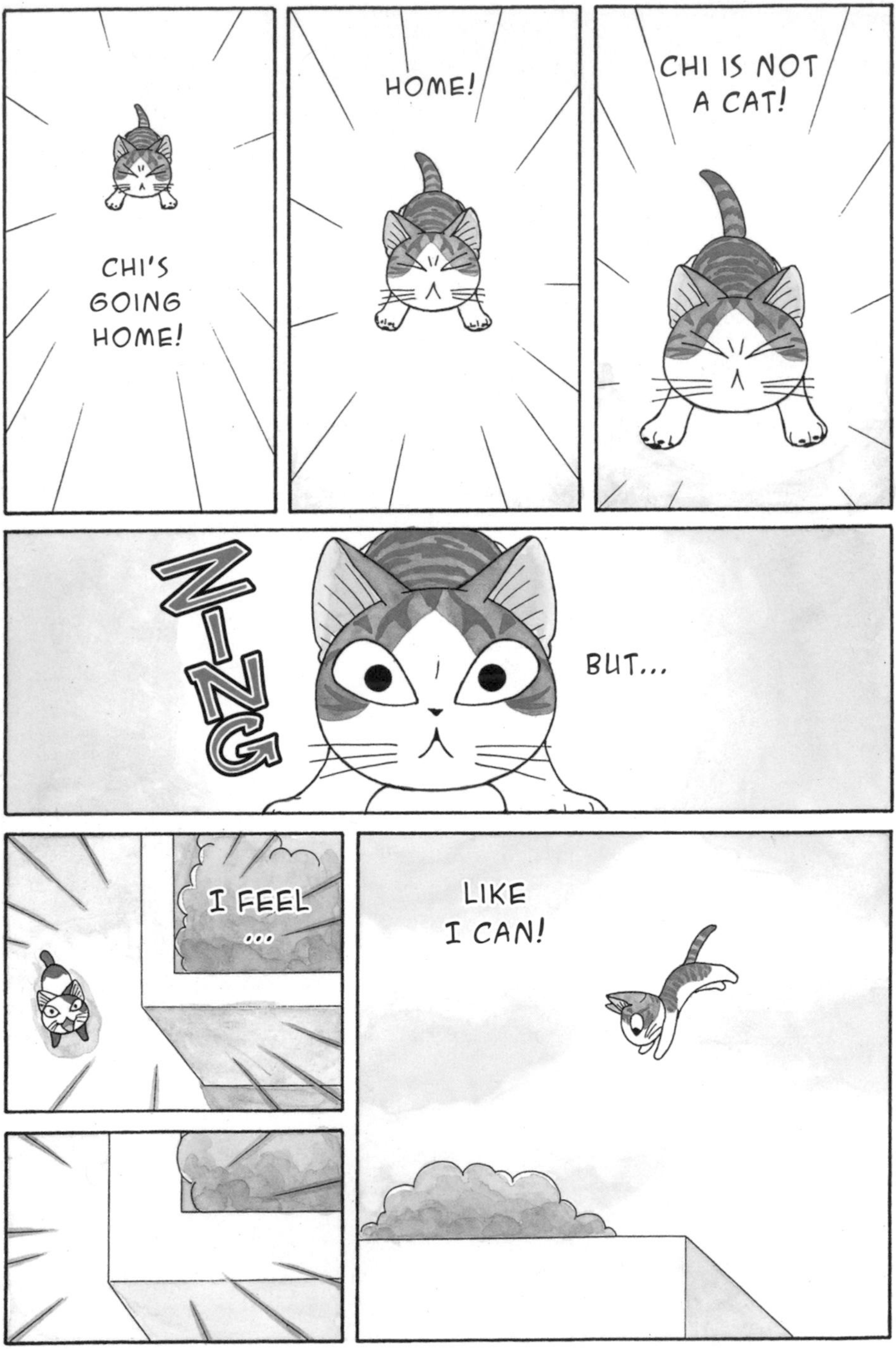
CHI'S GOING HOME!
HOME!
CHI IS NOT A CAT!
ZING
BUT...
I FEEL ...
LIKE I CAN!

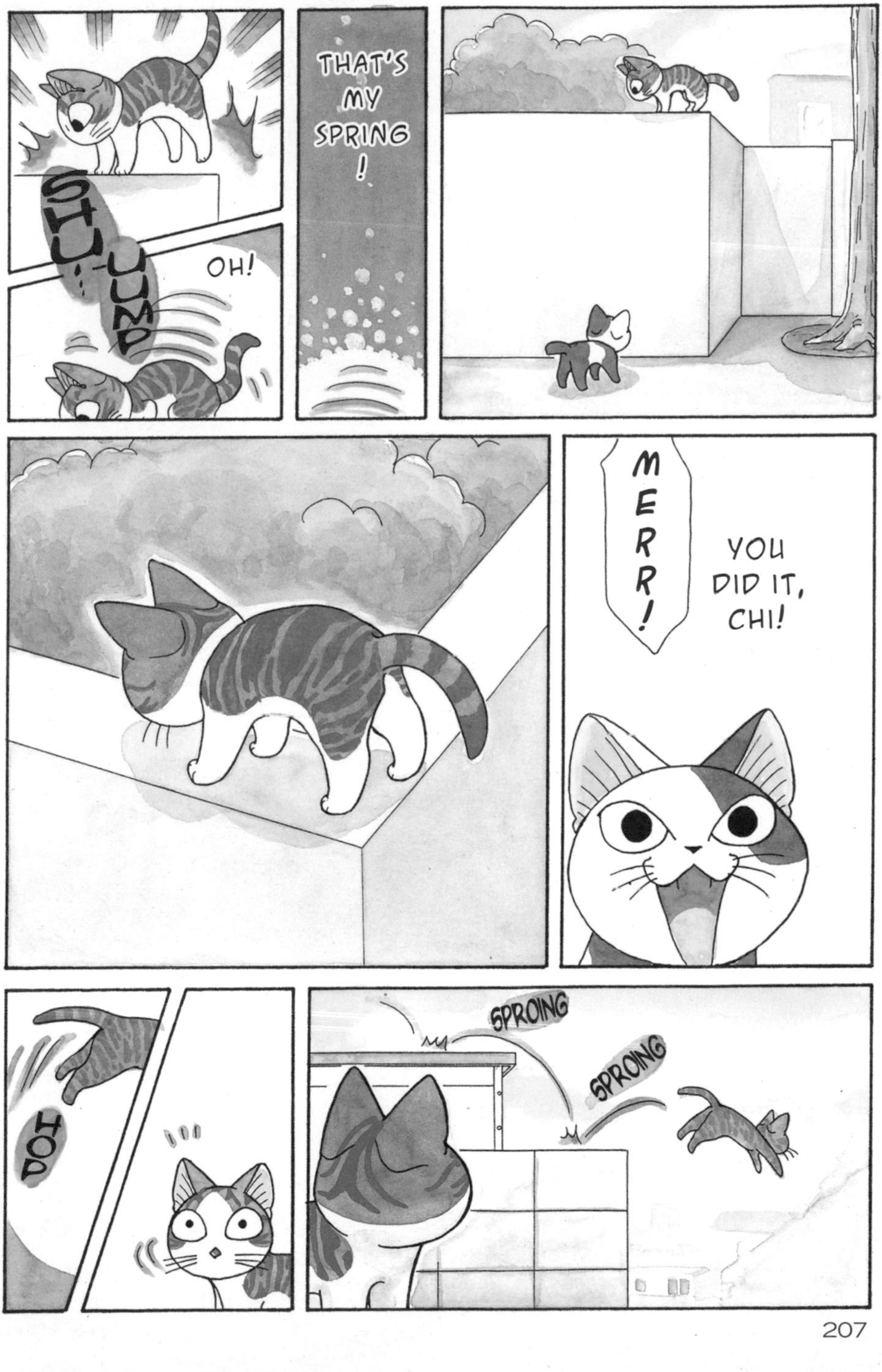
SHU-UUMP
OH!
THAT'S MY SPRING!
MERR!
YOU DID IT, CHI!
HOP
SPROING
SPROING

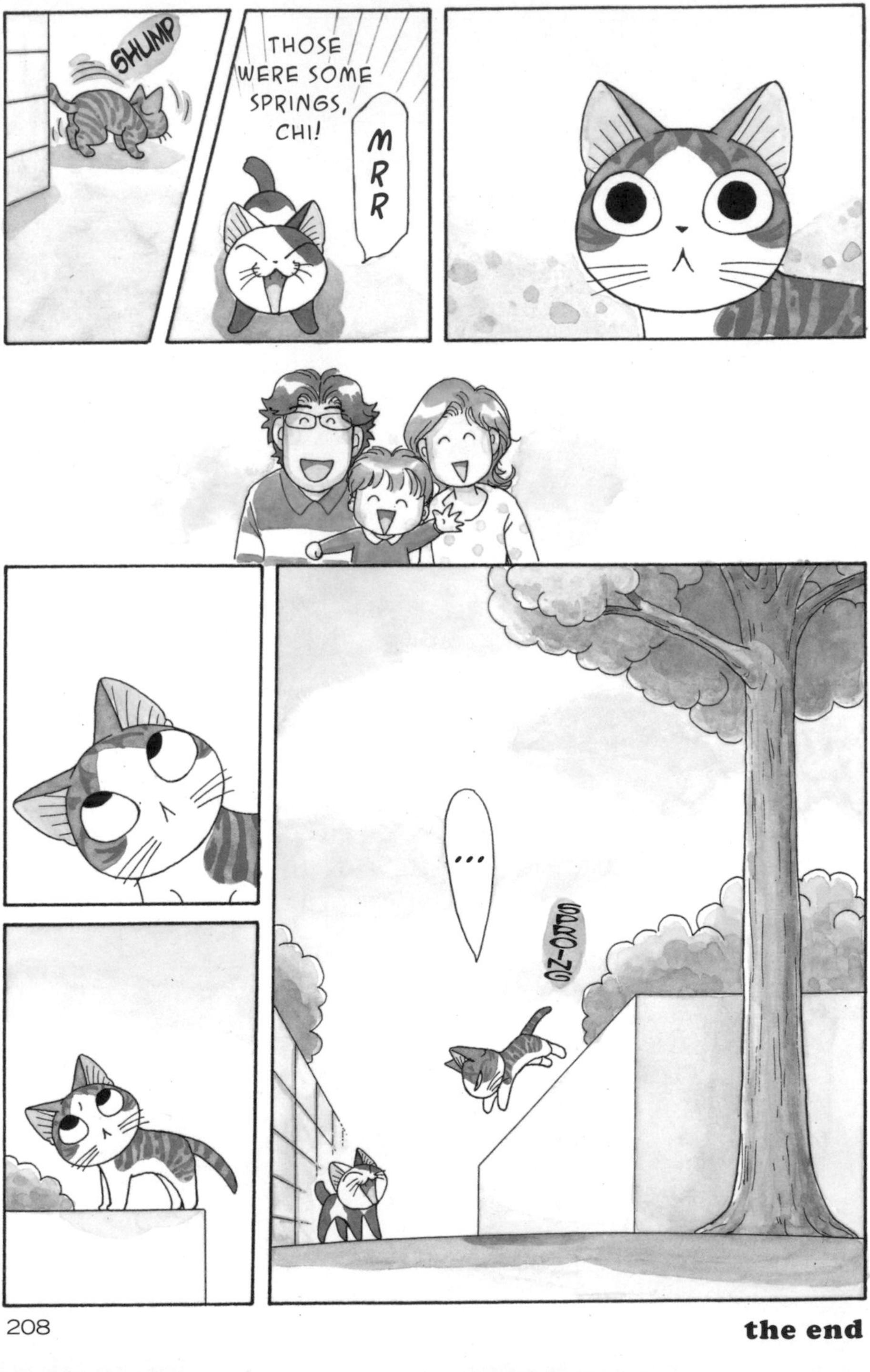
SHUMP
THOSE WERE SOME SPRINGS, CHI!
MRR
...
SPRO-ING

**the end**

# homemade 137: a cat returns

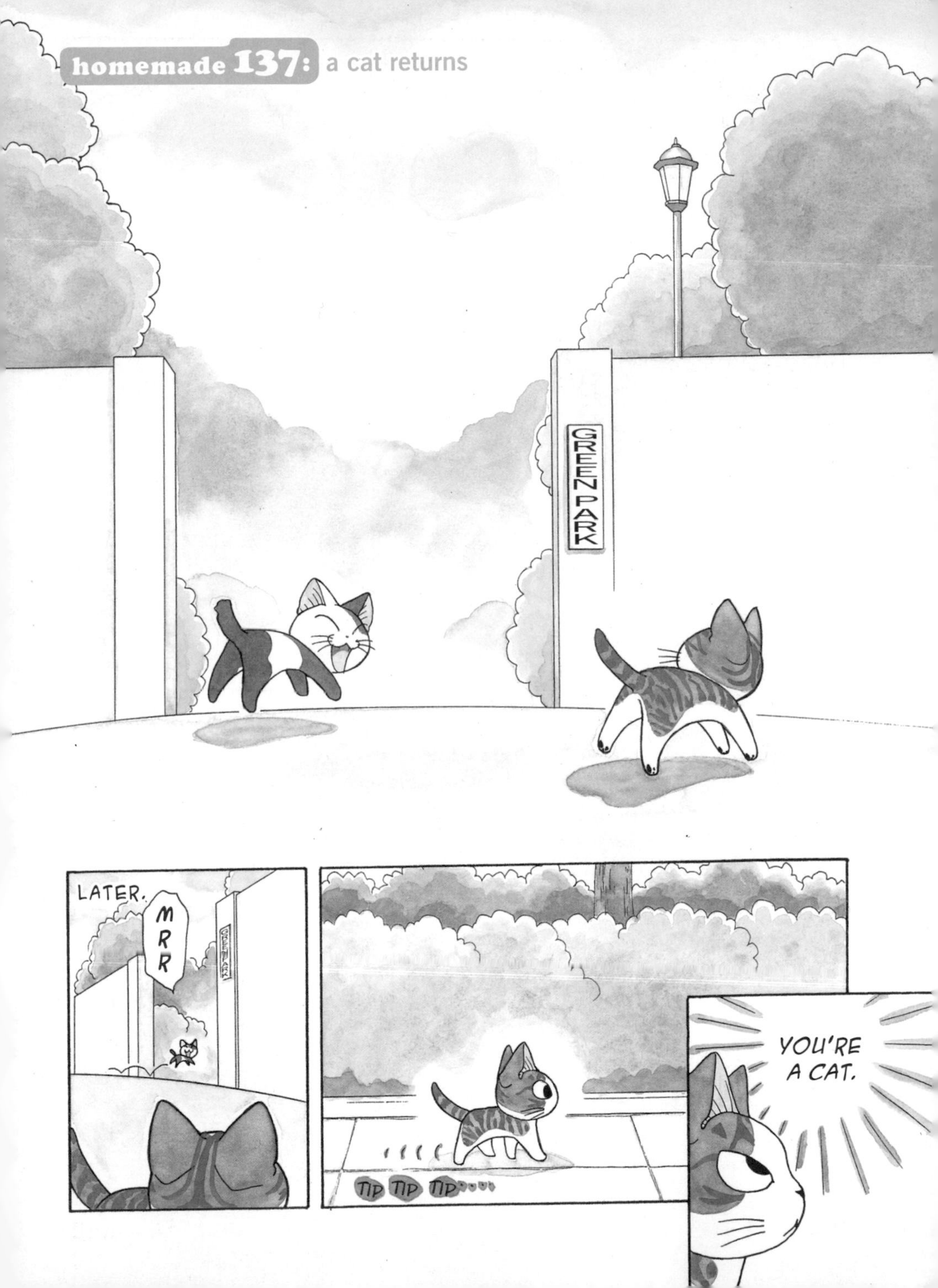
GREEN PARK
LATER.
MRR
GREEN PARK
TIP TIP TIP...
YOU'RE A CAT.

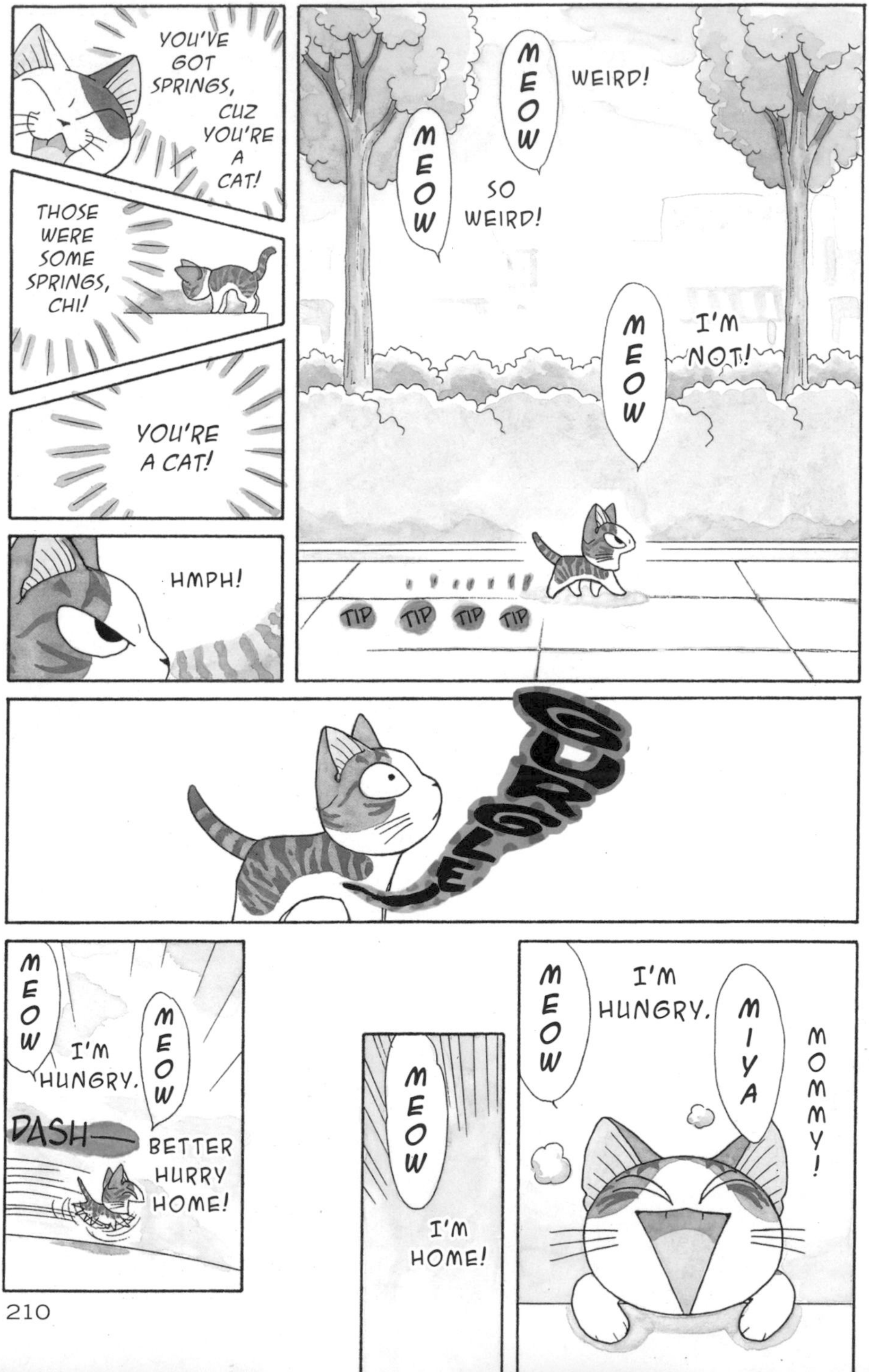
YOU'VE GOT SPRINGS, CUZ YOU'RE A CAT!
THOSE WERE SOME SPRINGS, CHI!
YOU'RE A CAT!
HMPH!
MEOW
WEIRD!
MEOW
SO WEIRD!
MEOW
I'M NOT!
TIP
TIP
TIP
TIP
GURGLE
MEOW
I'M HUNGRY.
MEOW
DASH—
BETTER HURRY HOME!
MEOW
I'M HOME!
MEOW
I'M HUNGRY.
MIYA
MOMMY!

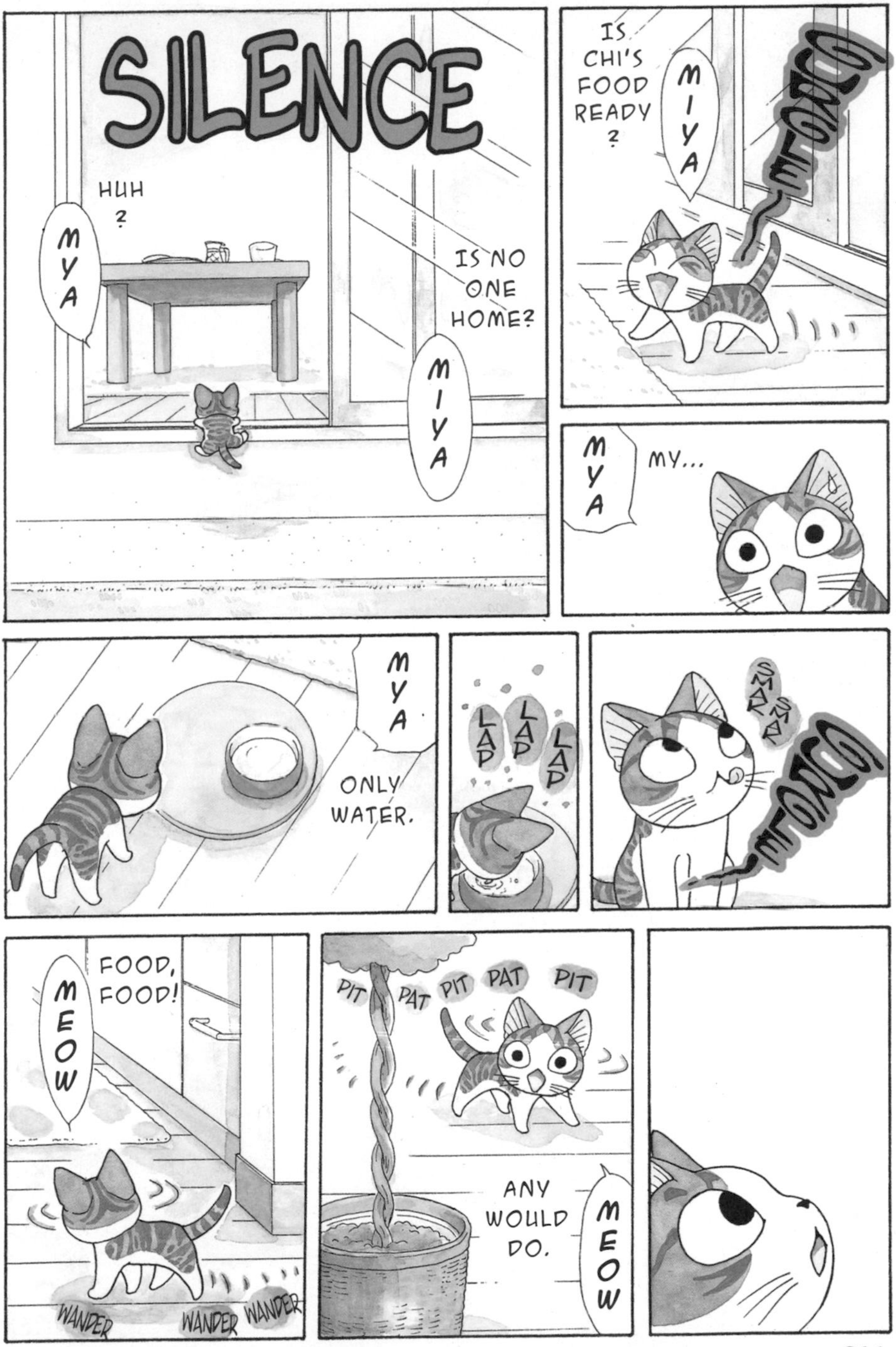
SILENCE
MYA
HUH?
IS NO ONE HOME?
MIYA
IS CHI'S FOOD READY?
MIYA
MYA
MY...
MYA
ONLY WATER.
LAP
LAP
LAP
MEOW
FOOD, FOOD!
WANDER
WANDER
WANDER
PIT
PAT
PIT
PAT
PIT
ANY WOULD DO.
MEOW

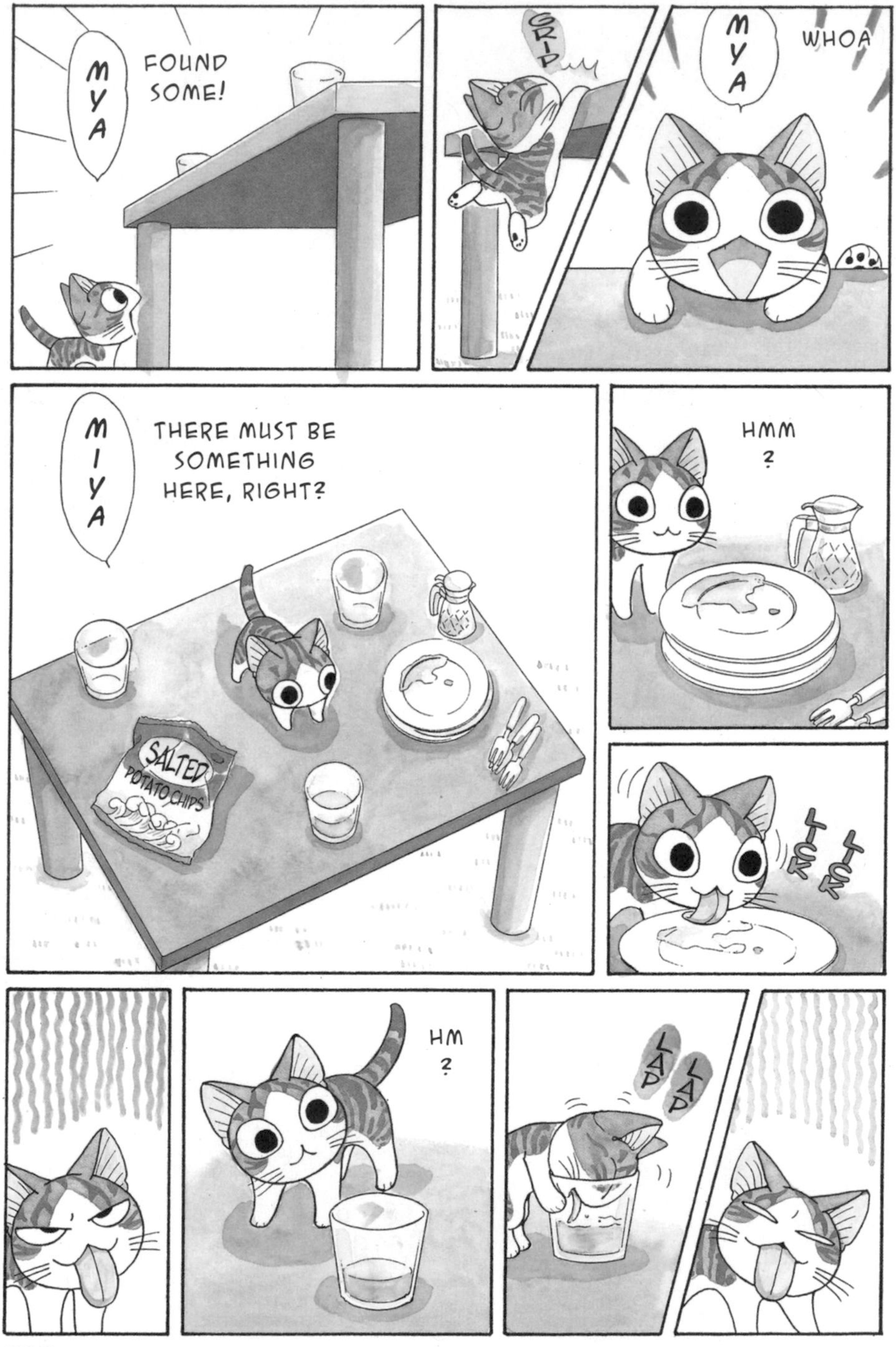
MYA
FOUND SOME!
GRIP
MYA
WHOA
MIYA
THERE MUST BE SOMETHING HERE, RIGHT?
SALTED POTATO CHIPS
HMM ?
LICK LICK
HM ?
LAP LAP

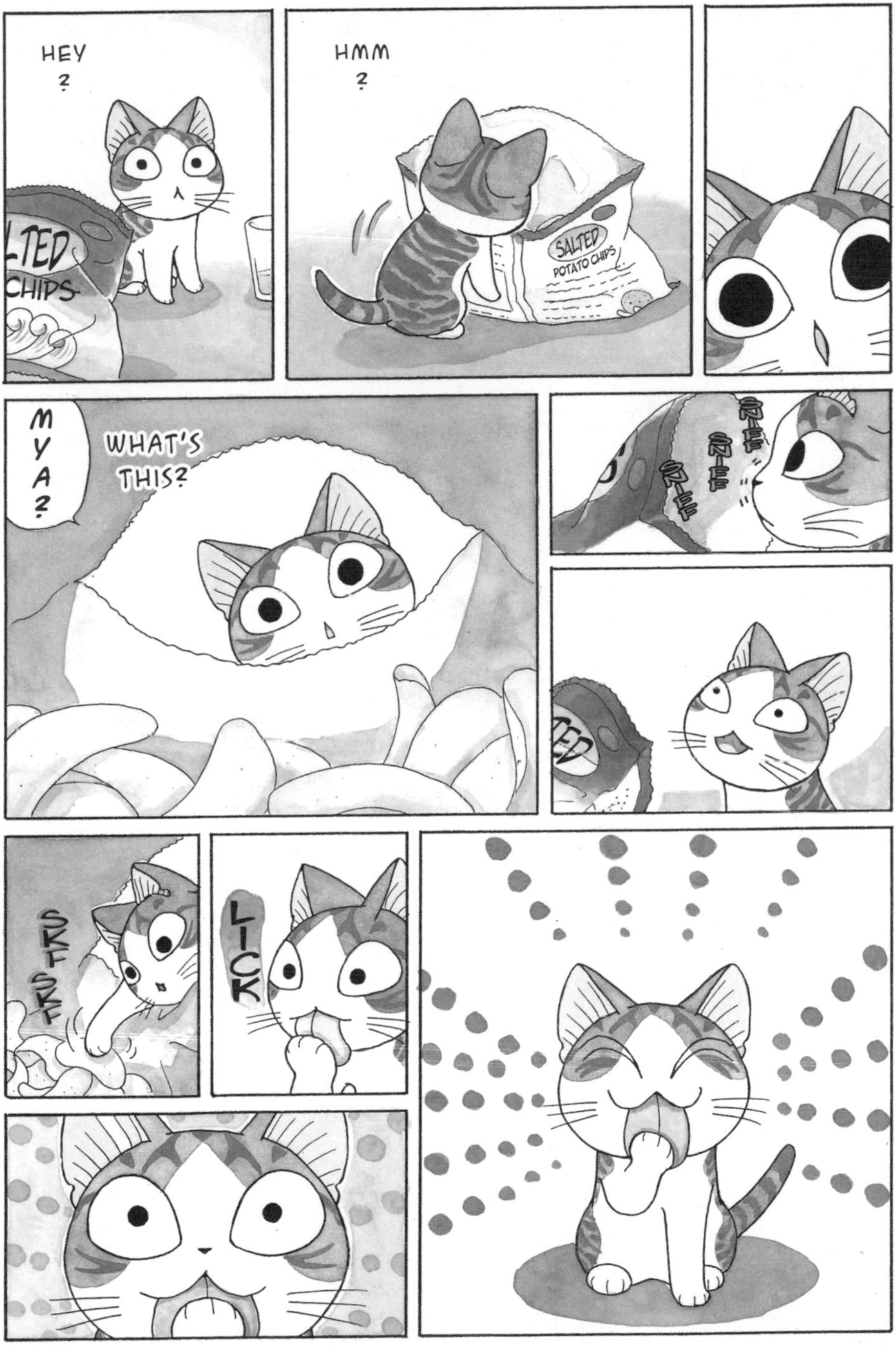
HEY
?
LTED
CHIPS
HMM
?
SALTED
POTATO CHIPS
MYA?
WHAT'S THIS?
SNIFF
SNIFF
SNIFF
TED
SKF SKF
LICK

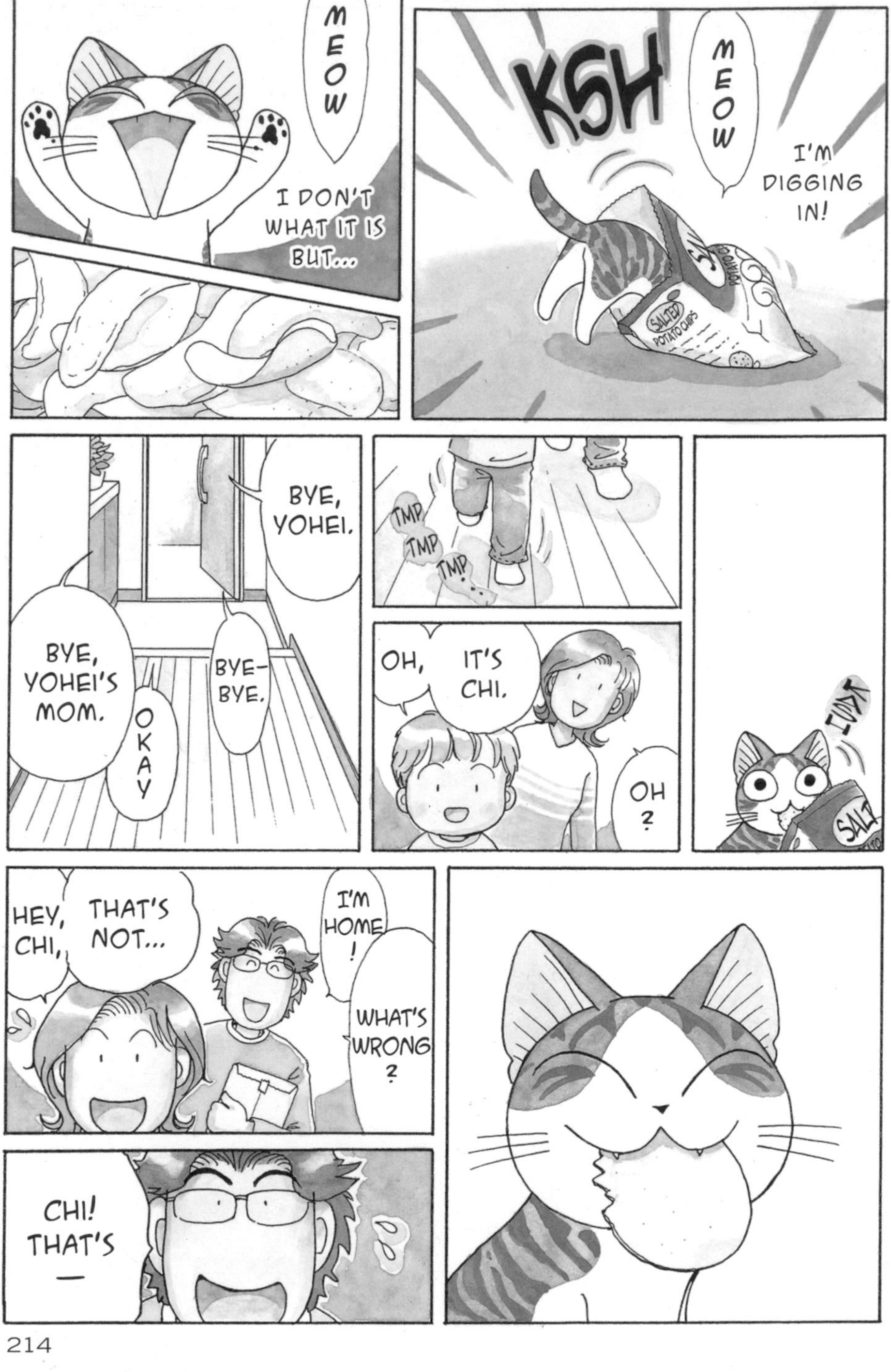
MEOW
I DON'T WHAT IT IS BUT...
KSH
MEOW
I'M DIGGING IN!
BYE, YOHEI.
BYE, YOHEI'S MOM.
BYE-BYE.
OKAY
TMP TMP TMP
OH,
IT'S CHI.
OH?
HEY, CHI,
THAT'S NOT...
I'M HOME!
WHAT'S WRONG?
CHI! THAT'S —

MEOW
WANNA HAVE SOME, TOO?!
MIYA
THEY'RE GOOD!

SALTED
POTATO

LET'S NOT, CHI.

SHOOP

HUH?

SALTED
POTATO CHIPS

WHAT?!

MIYA
HEY, WHY?

NOW HAVE SOMETHING GOOD.

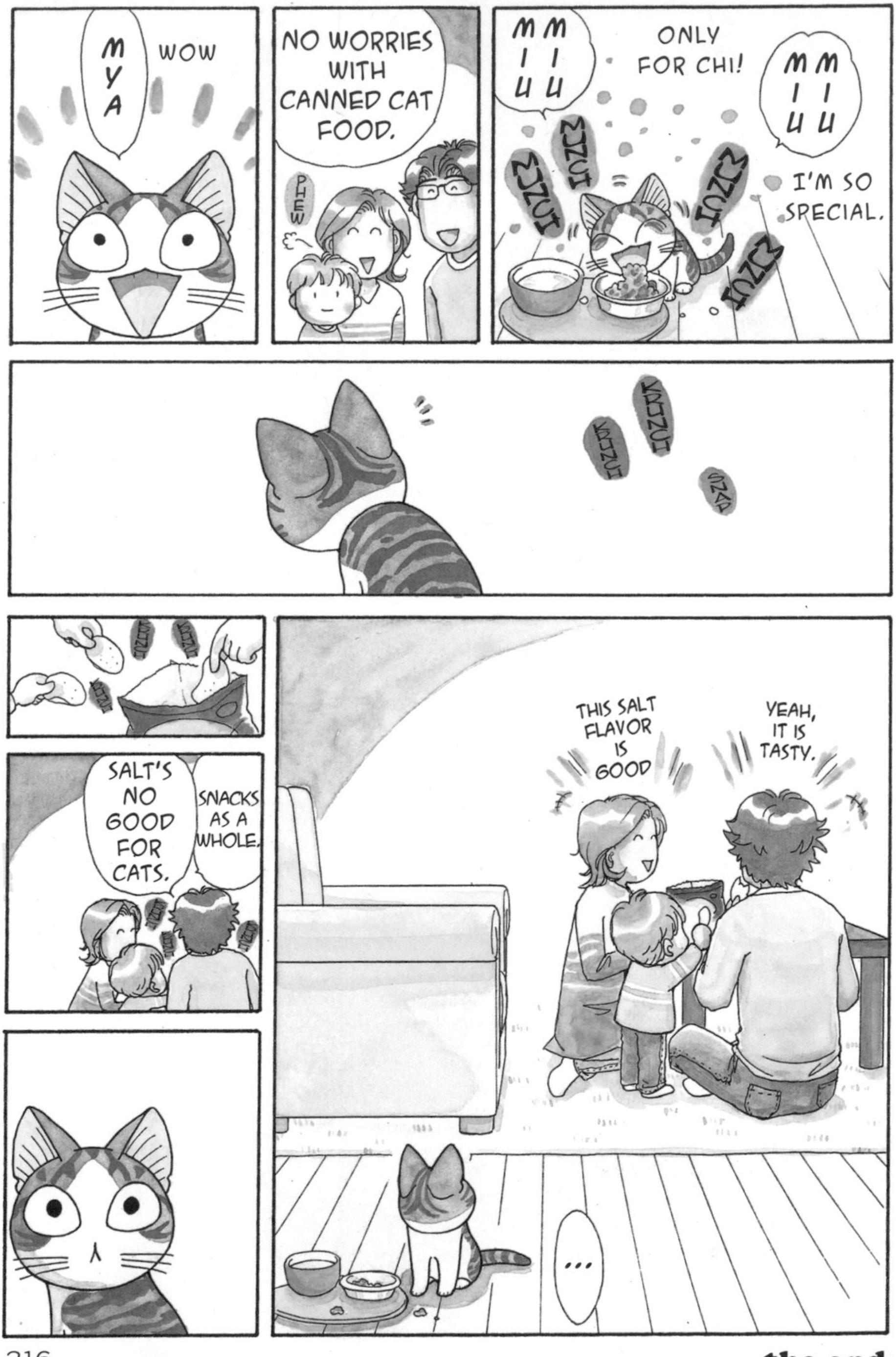

MYA
WOW
NO WORRIES WITH CANNED CAT FOOD.
PHEW
MM IIUU
ONLY FOR CHI!
MUNCH
MUNCH
MM IIUU
MUNCH
MUNCH
I'M SO SPECIAL.
KRUNCH
KRUNCH
SNAP
SALT'S NO GOOD FOR CATS.
SNACKS AS A WHOLE.
THIS SALT FLAVOR IS GOOD
YEAH, IT IS TASTY.
...




**the end**

## homemade 138: a cat relaxes

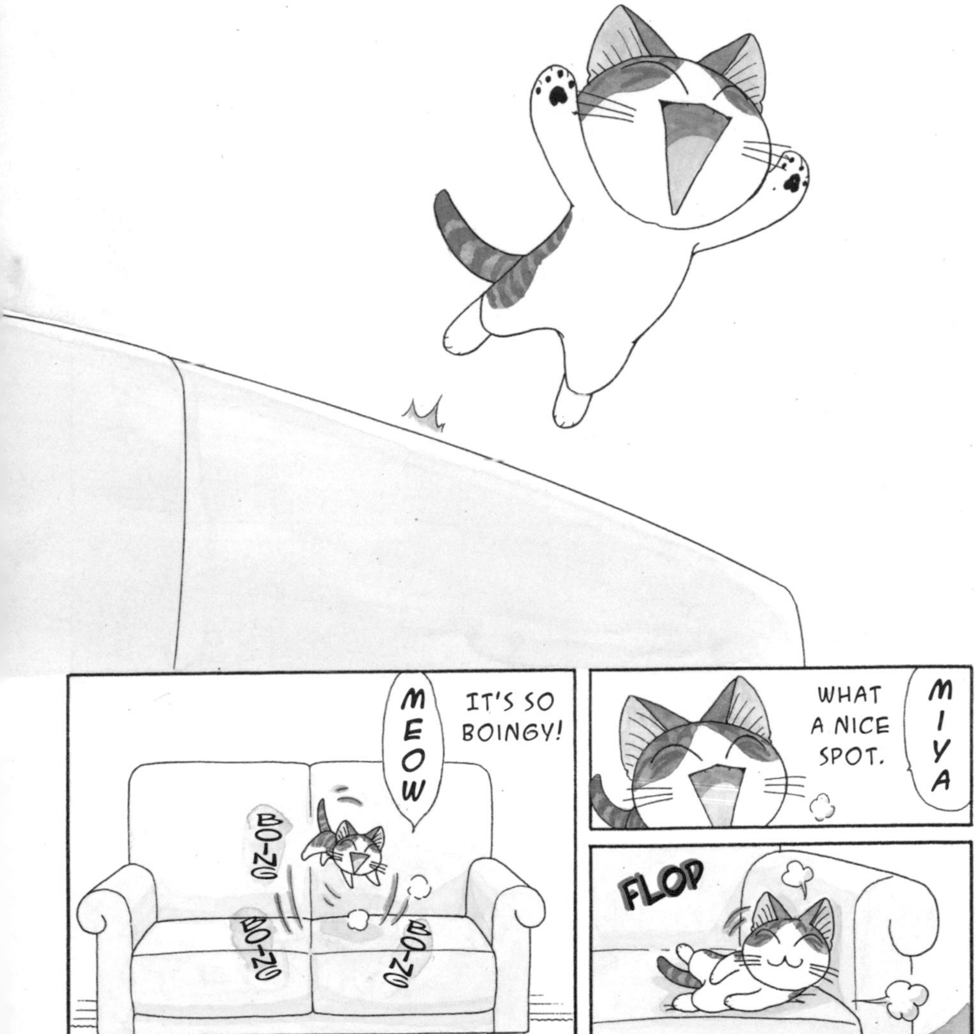
MEOW
IT'S SO BOINGY!
BOING
BOING
BOING
WHAT A NICE SPOT.
MIYA
FLOP

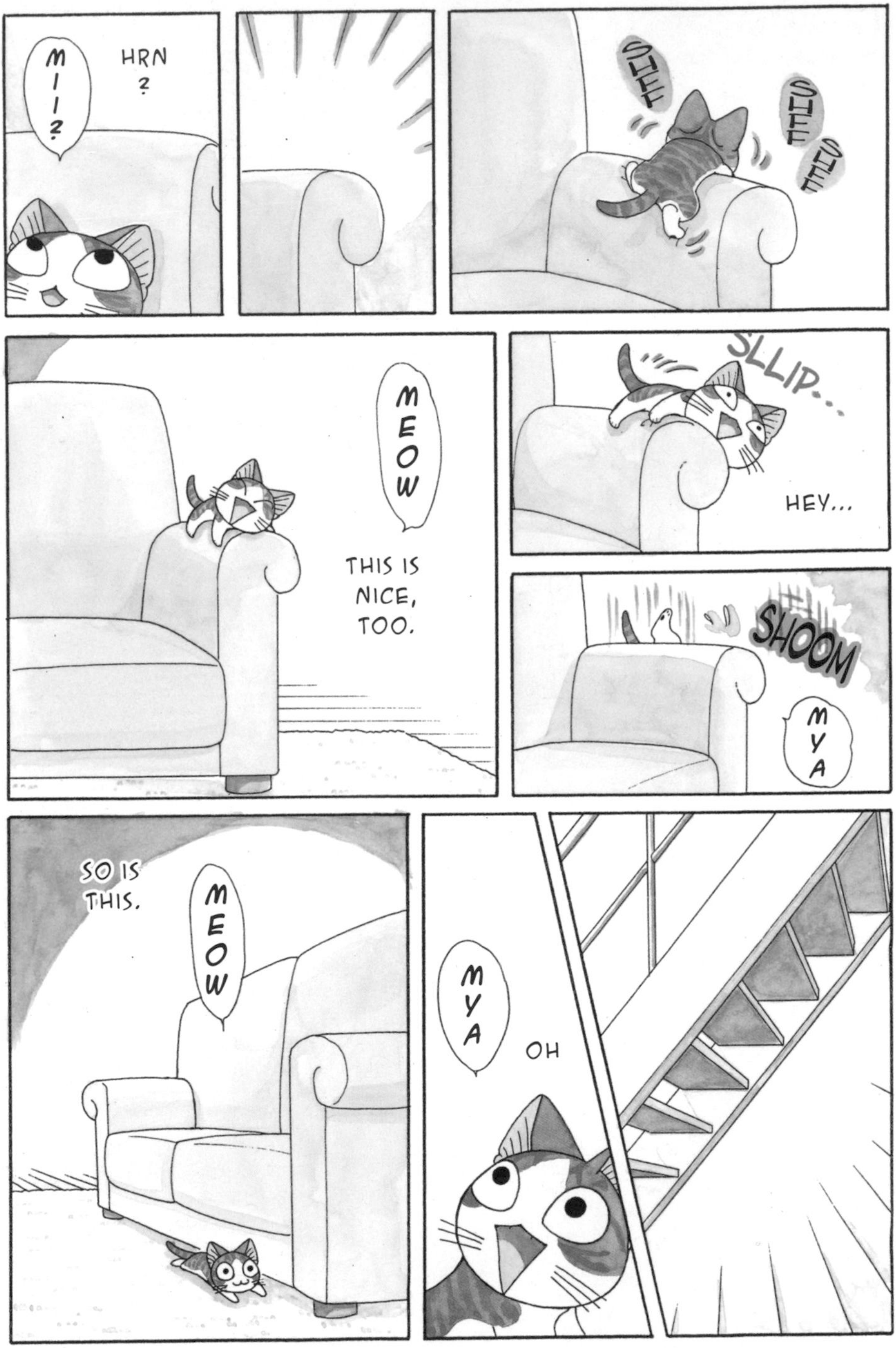
MII?
HRN?
SHEF SHEF SHEF
MEOW
THIS IS NICE, TOO.
SLLIP...
HEY...
SHOOM
MYA
SO IS THIS.
MEOW
MYA
OH

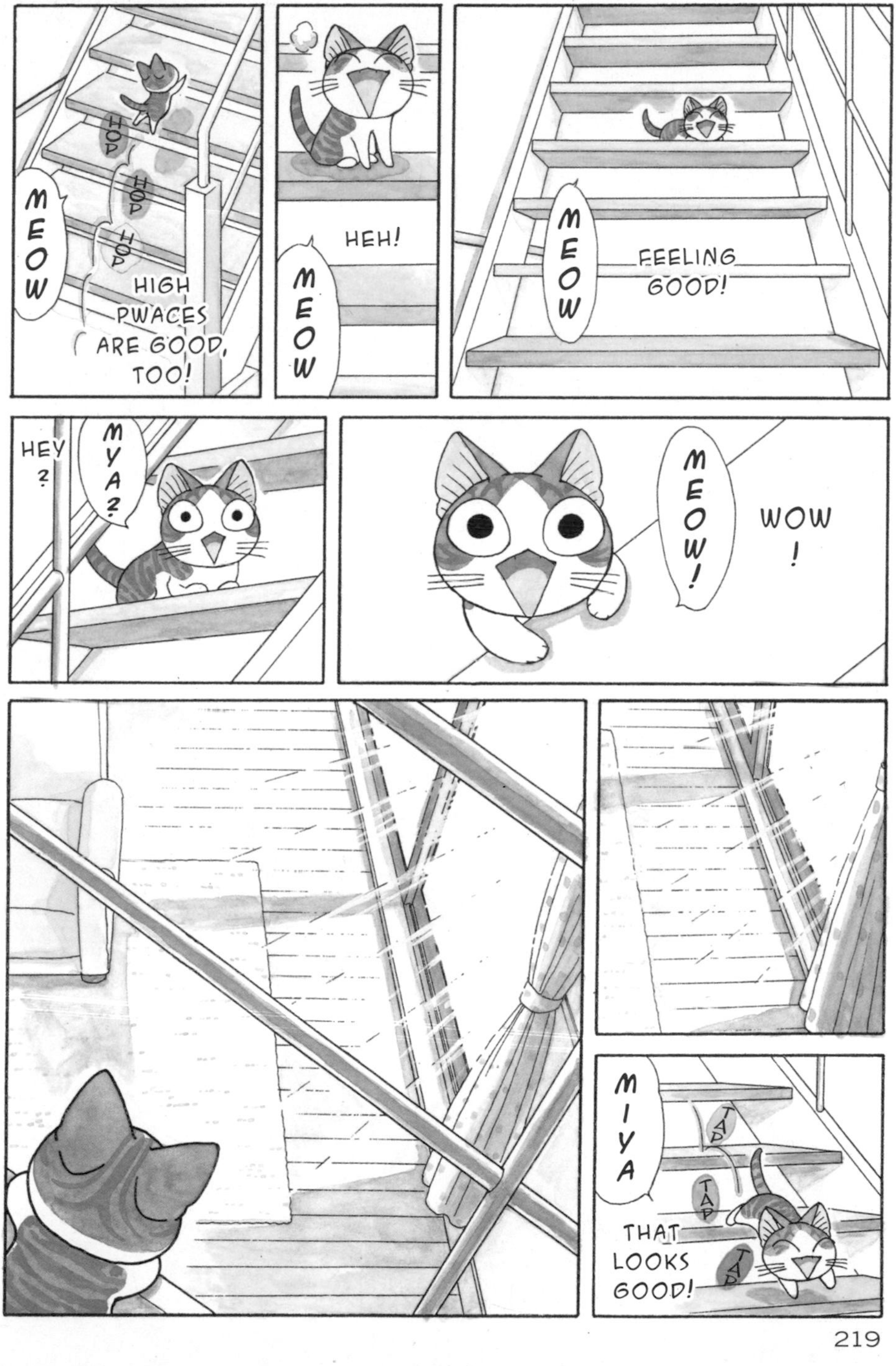
HOP
HOP
HOP
MEOW
HIGH PWACES ARE GOOD, TOO!
MEOW
HEH!
MEOW
FEELING GOOD!
MYA?
HEY?
MEOW!
WOW!
TAP
TAP
TAP
MIYA
THAT LOOKS GOOD!

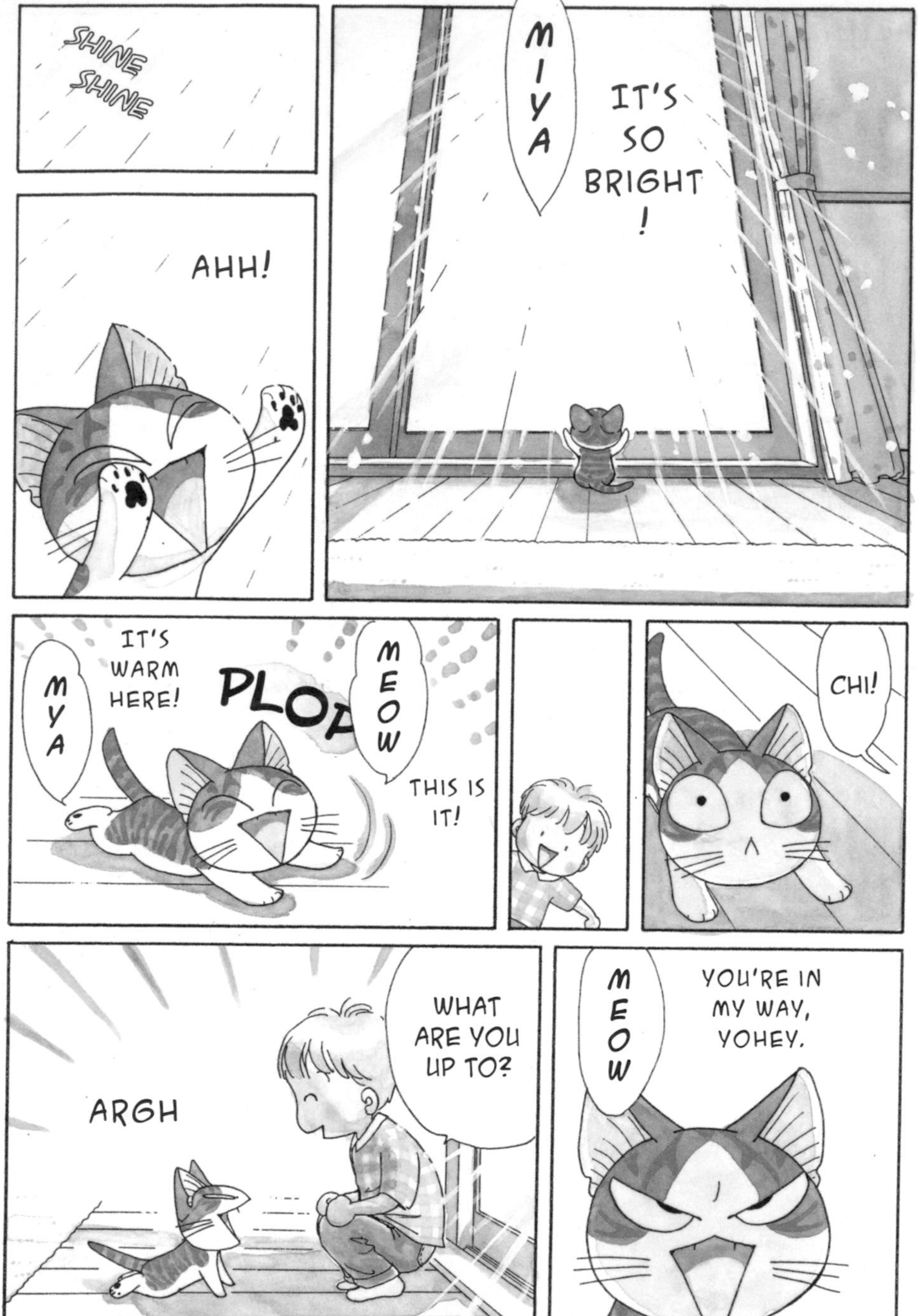
SHINE SHINE
AHH!
MIYA
IT'S SO BRIGHT!
MIYA
IT'S WARM HERE!
PLOP
MEOW
THIS IS IT!
CHI!
ARGH
WHAT ARE YOU UP TO?
MEOW
YOU'RE IN MY WAY, YOHEY.

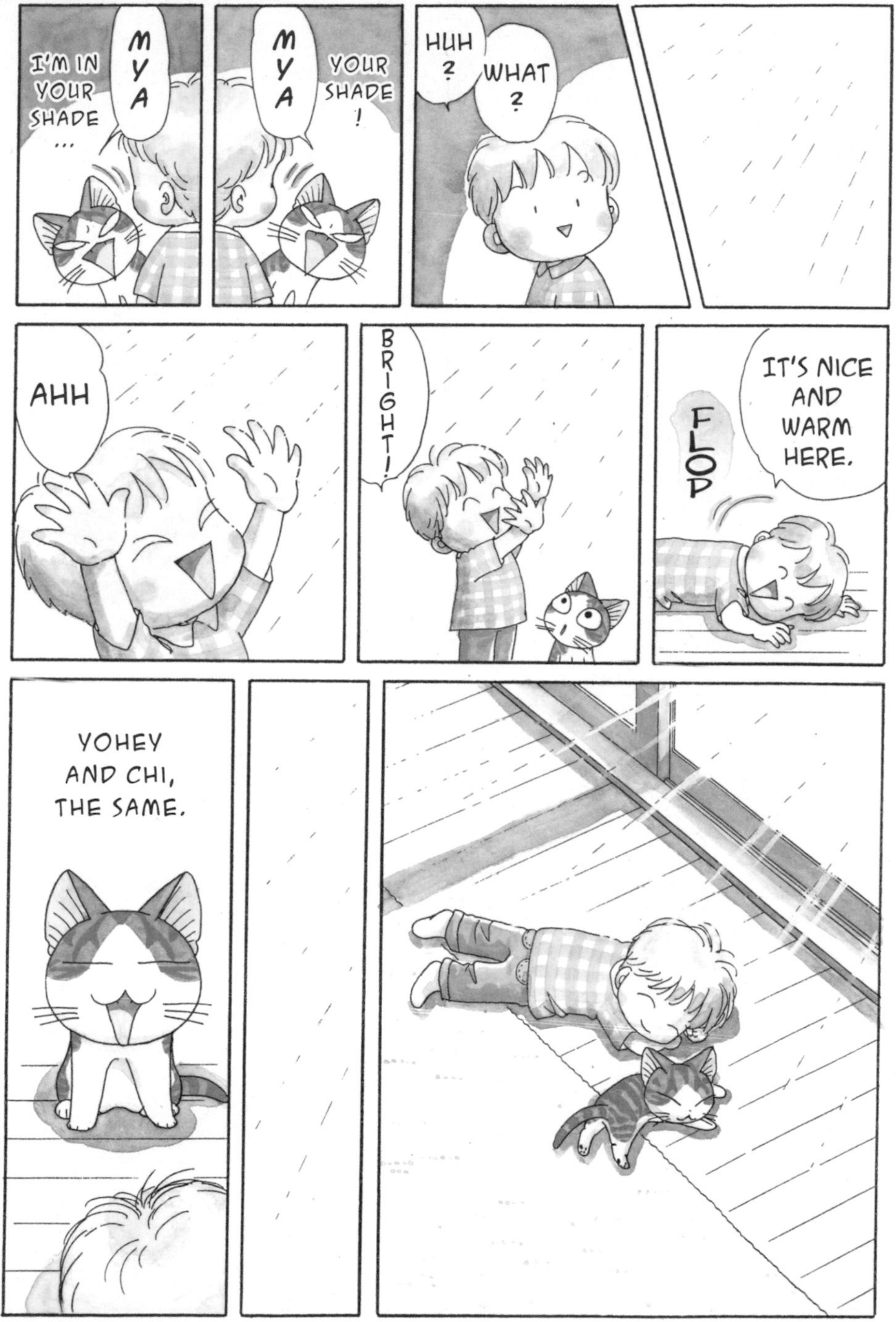
I'M IN YOUR SHADE ...
MYA
MYA
YOUR SHADE!
HUH?
WHAT?
AHH
BRIGHT!
FLOP
IT'S NICE AND WARM HERE.
YOHEY AND CHI, THE SAME.

HAH

IT'S
WARM

AND
SNUGGLY.

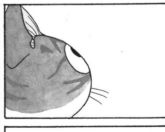

HAS
CHI
BEEN
ELSE-
WHERE
?

222

SOME-
WHERE
NOT
HERE?

SHFT

TIP

OH

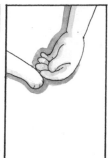

SQUEEZE

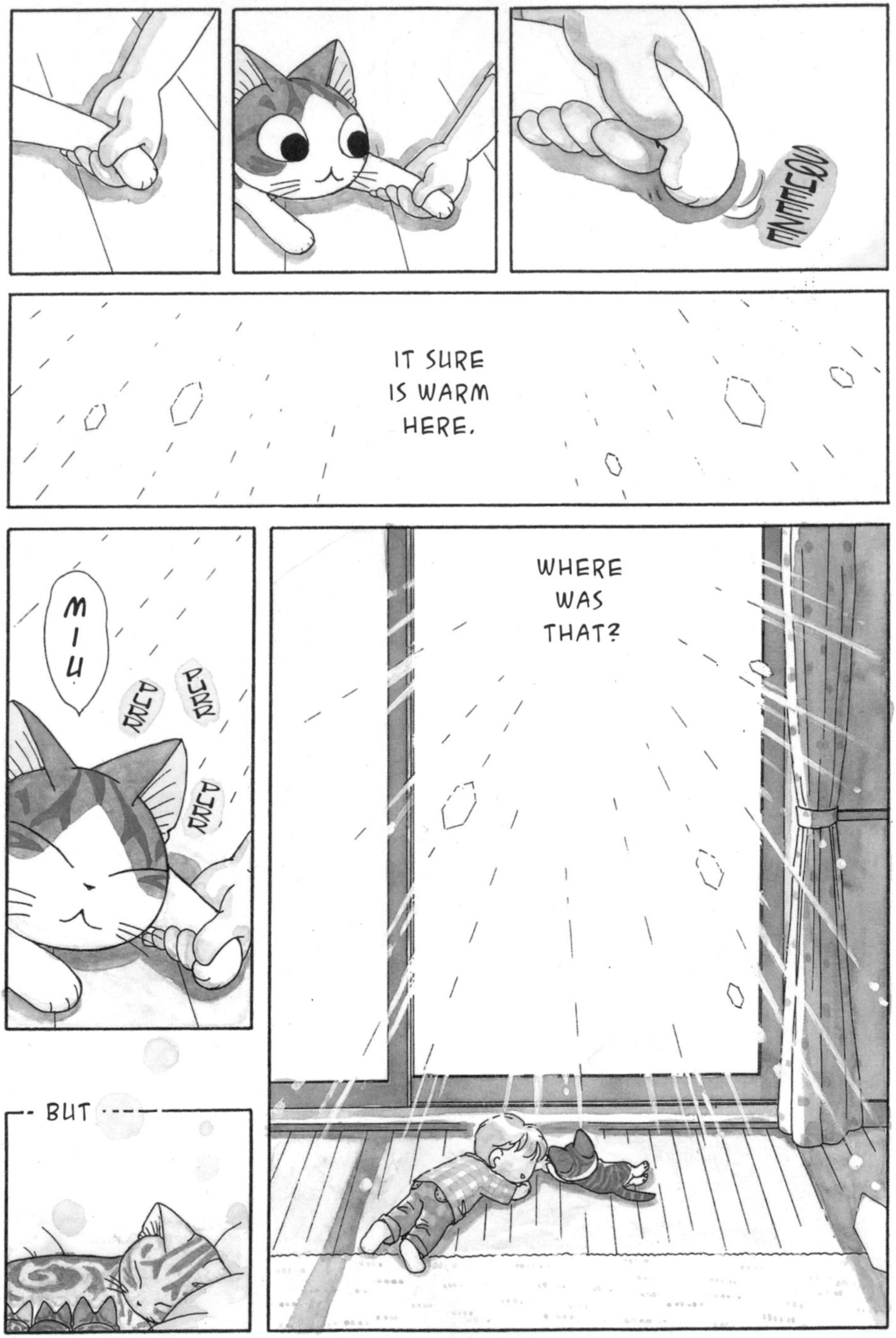

SQUEEZE
IT SURE IS WARM HERE.
MIU
PURR
PURR
PURR
BUT
WHERE WAS THAT?


**the end**

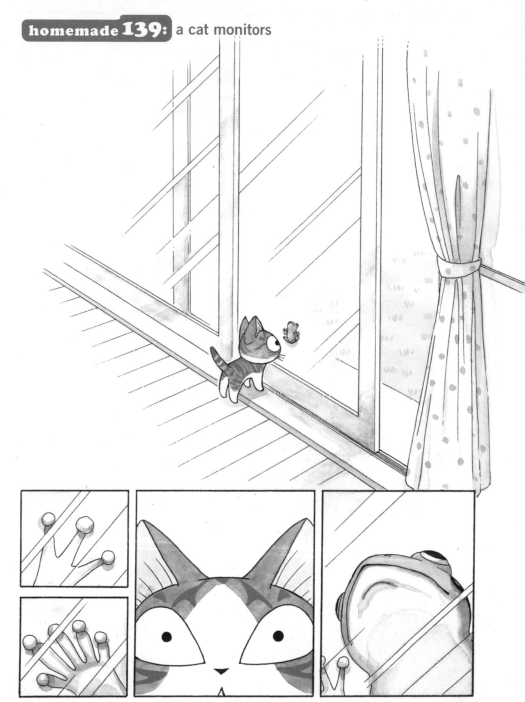

homemade **139:** a cat monitors

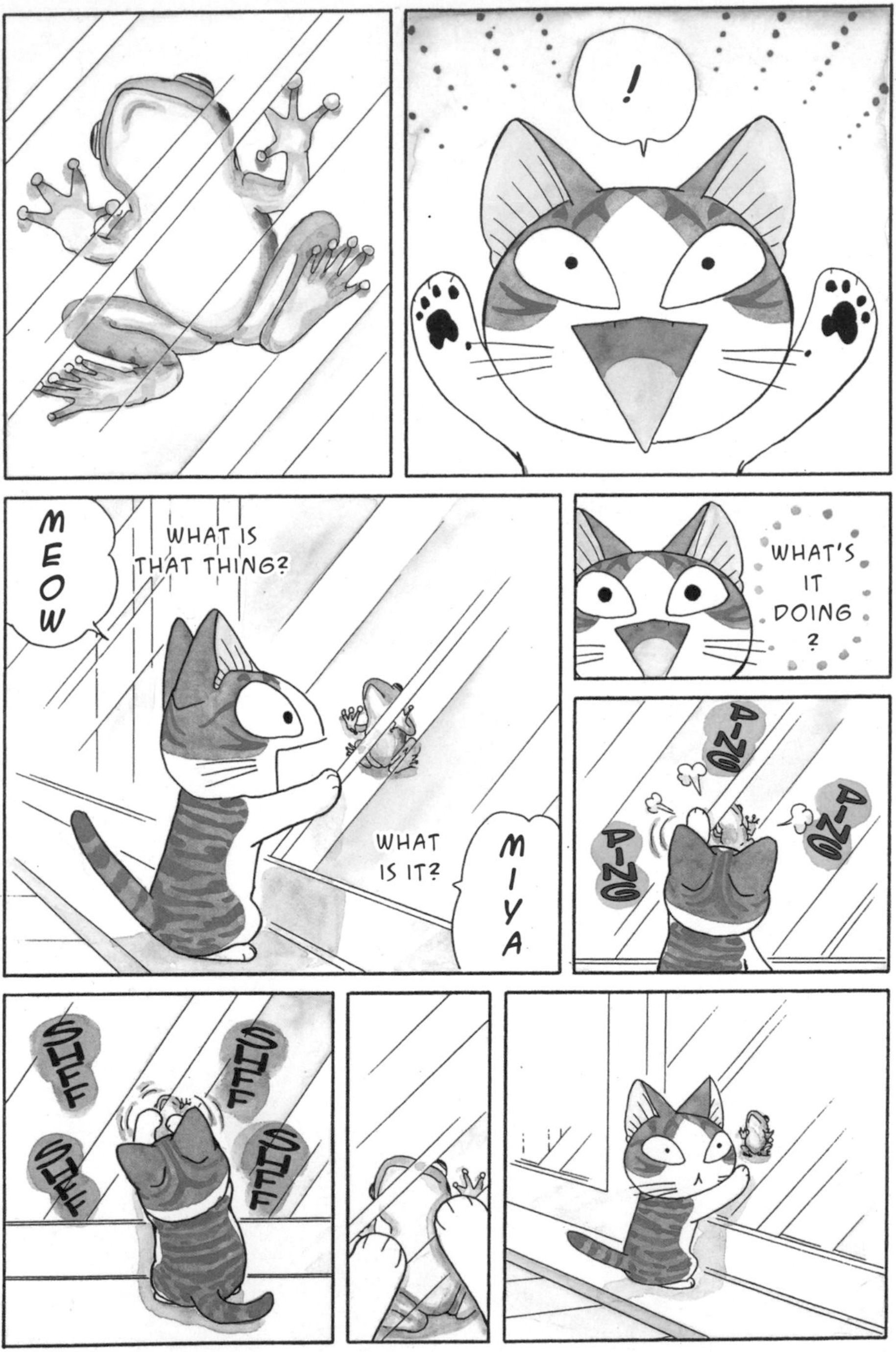
!
MEOW
WHAT IS THAT THING?
WHAT IS IT?
MIYA
WHAT'S IT DOING?
PING
PING
PING
SHFF
SHFF
SHFF
SHFF

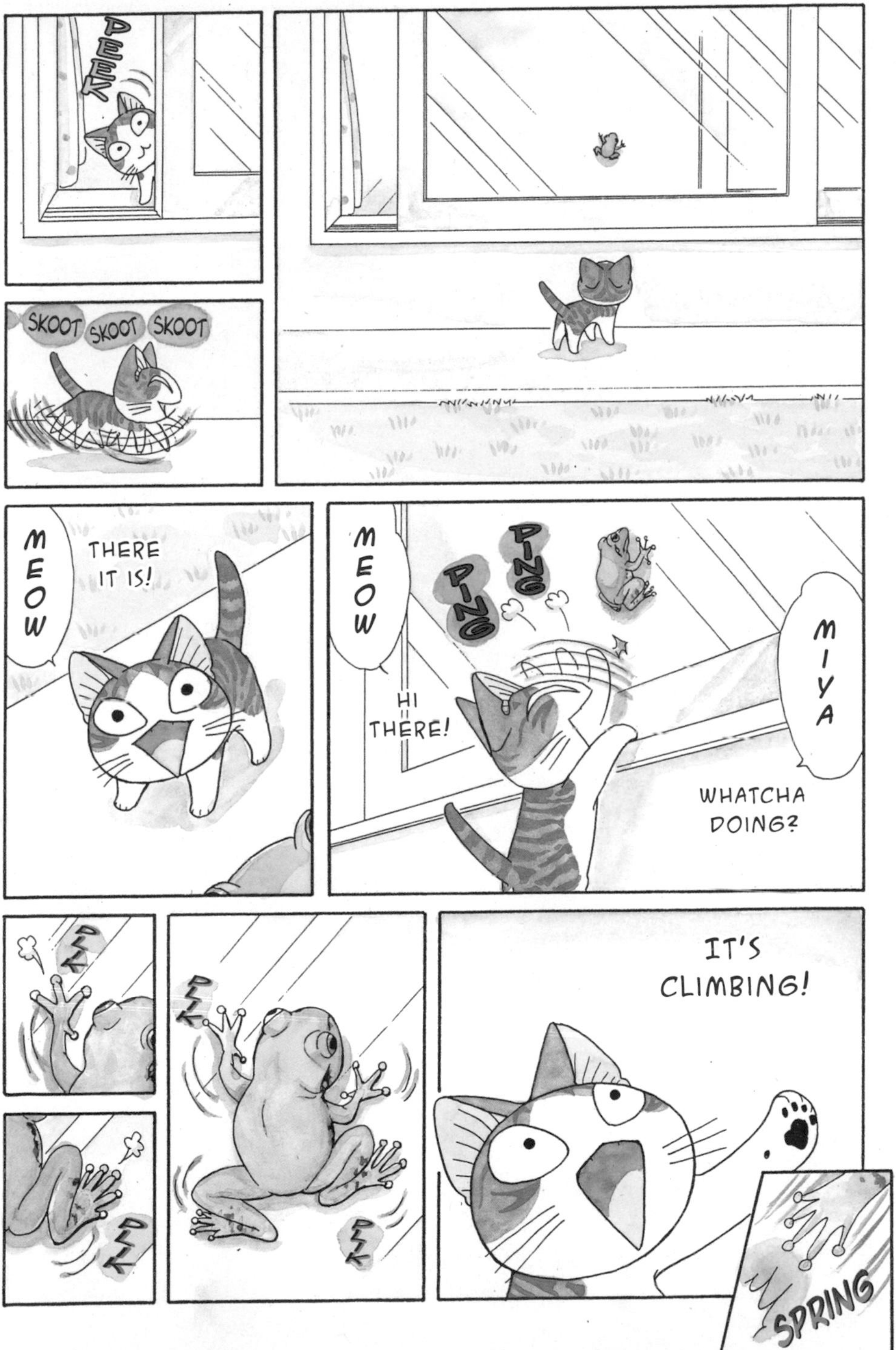
PEEK
SKOOT SKOOT SKOOT
MEOW
THERE IT IS!
MEOW
PING PING
HI THERE!
MIYA
WHATCHA DOING?
PLIK
PLIK
PLIK
PLIK
IT'S CLIMBING!
SPRING

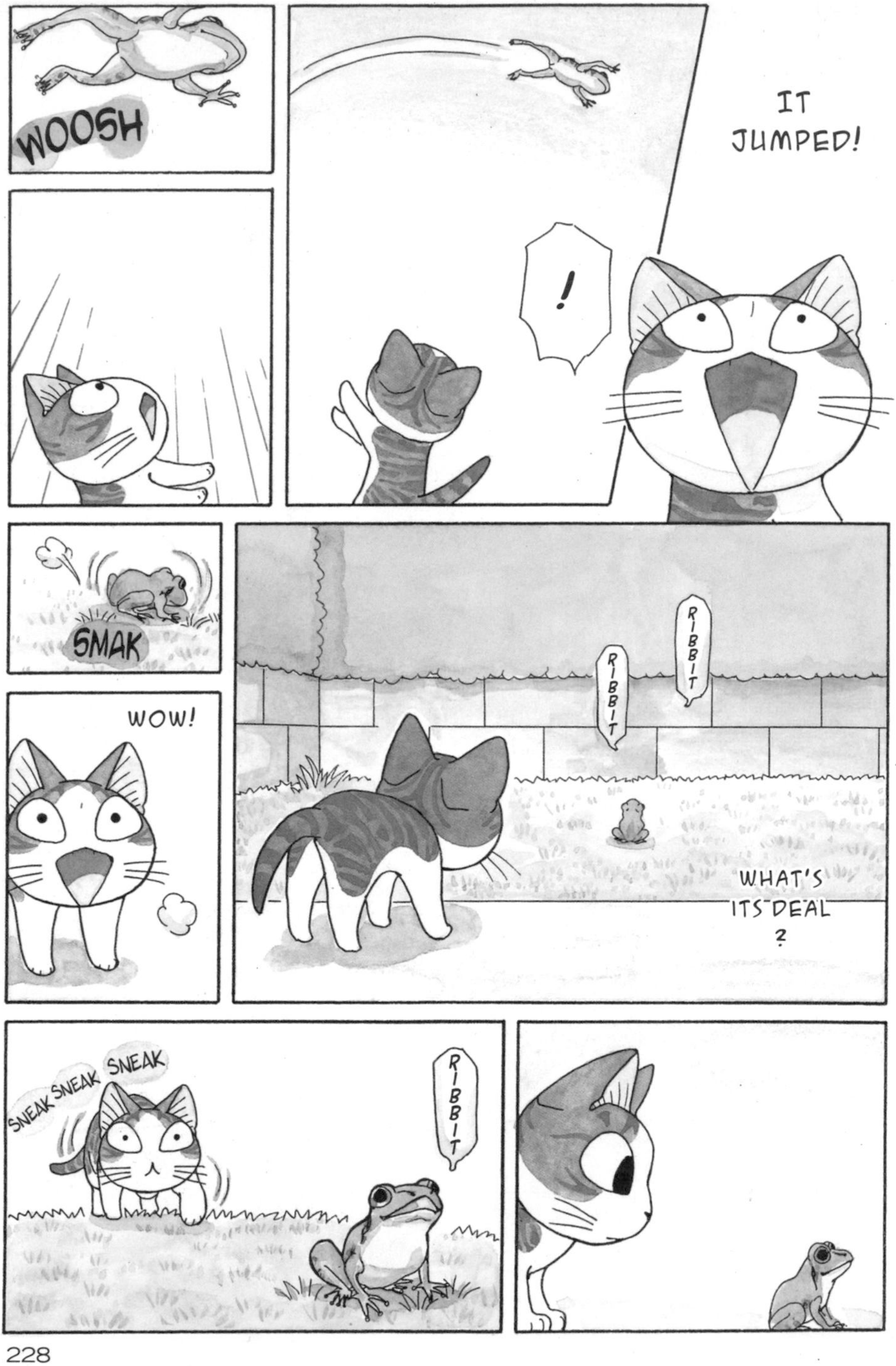
WOOSH
IT JUMPED!
!
SMAK
WOW!
RIBBIT
RIBBIT
WHAT'S ITS DEAL ?
SNEAK SNEAK SNEAK
RIBBIT

SLINK

OH MYA

HOP

SLIIINK

HEY MYA

HOP

SHFT

SUSPICIOUS!

TURN

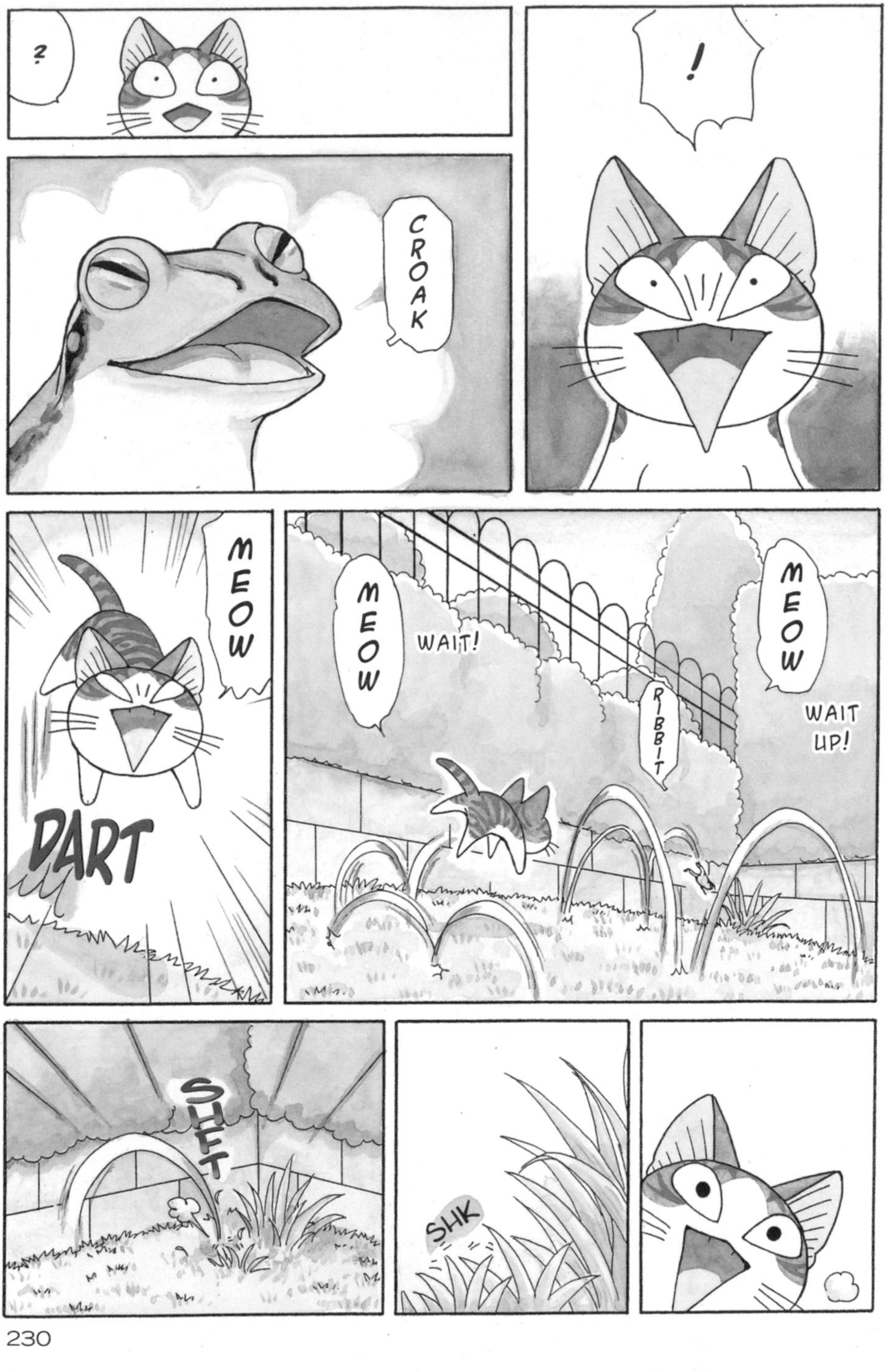
?
CROAK
!
MEOW
DART
MEOW
WAIT!
RIBBIT
MEOW
WAIT UP!
SHFT
SHK

NOWHERE TO RUN.
SHAK
SHAK
ZA
MEOWR
I'VE GOT YA!
WHUM
SH
RIBBIT
SMUSH
MYA?

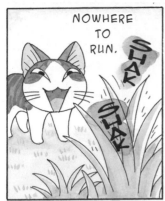

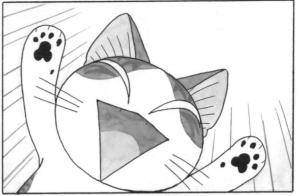

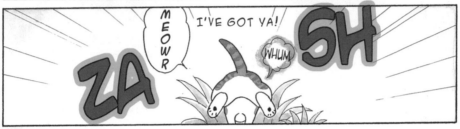

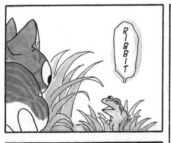

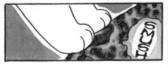

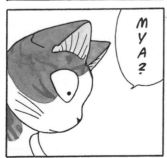

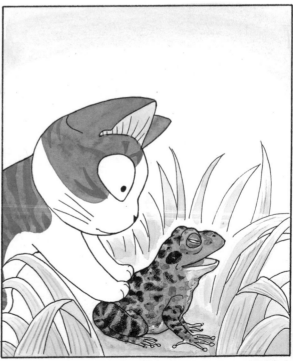

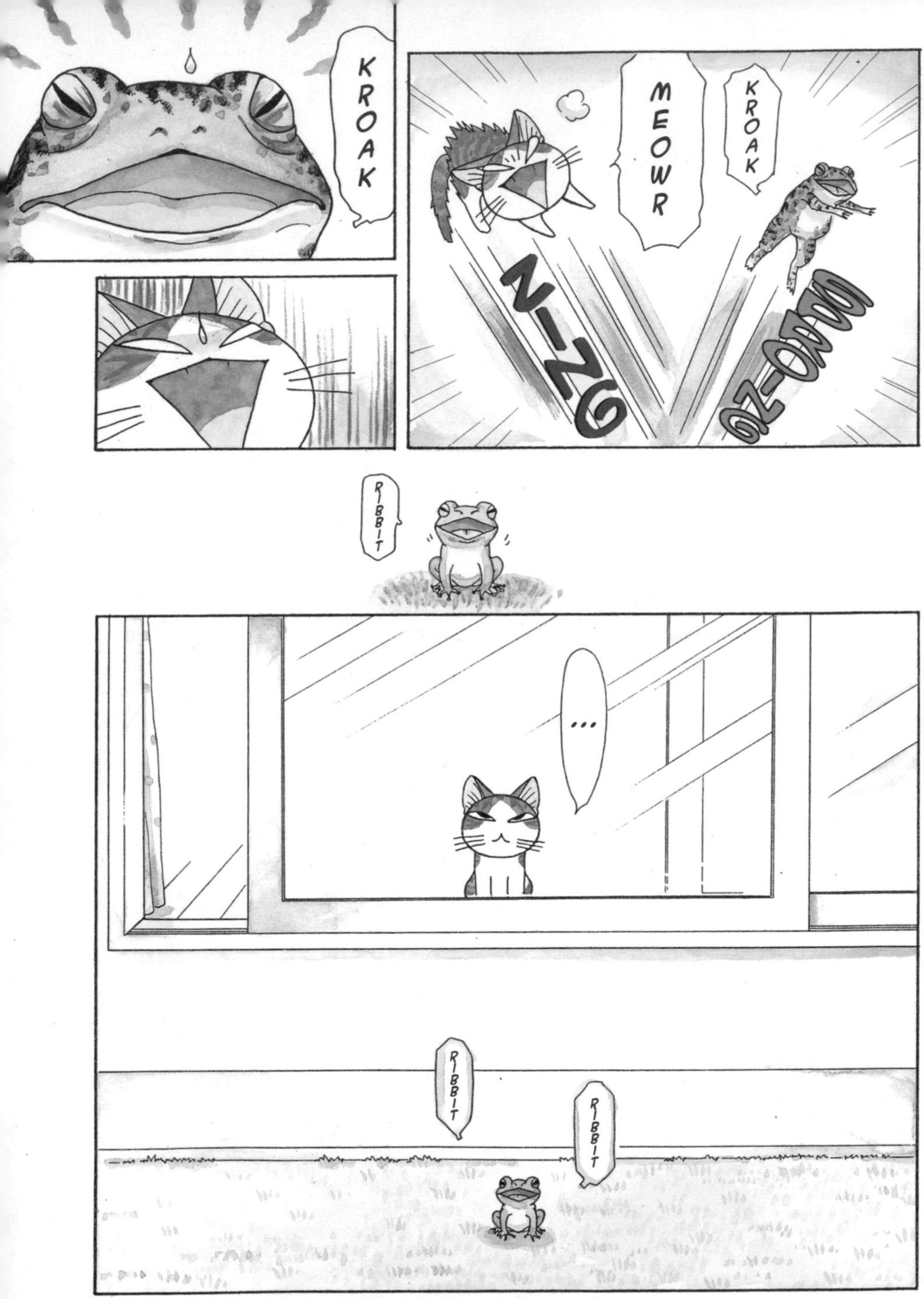
KROAK
MEOWR
KROAK
RIBBIT
...
RIBBIT
RIBBIT



the end

## homemade 140: a cat steps out

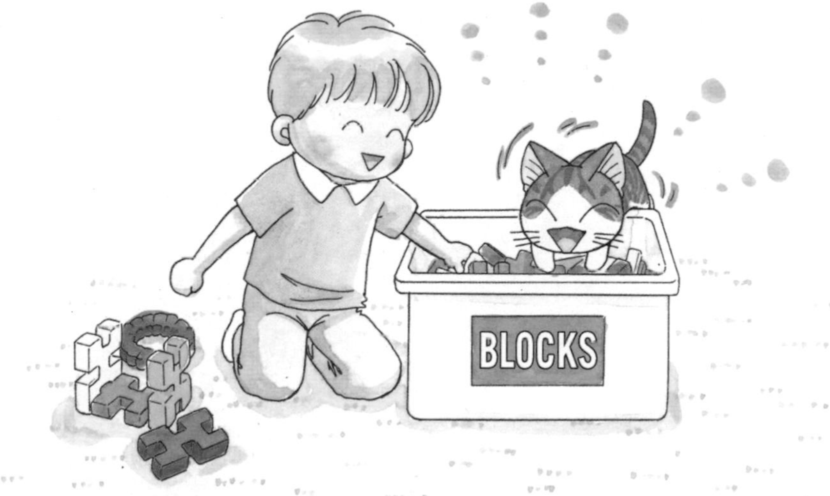
BLOCKS

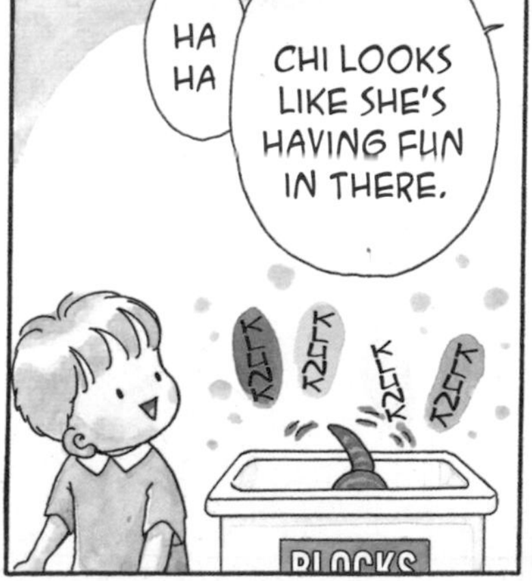
HA HA
CHI LOOKS LIKE SHE'S HAVING FUN IN THERE.
KLUNK
KLUNK
KLUNK
KLUNK

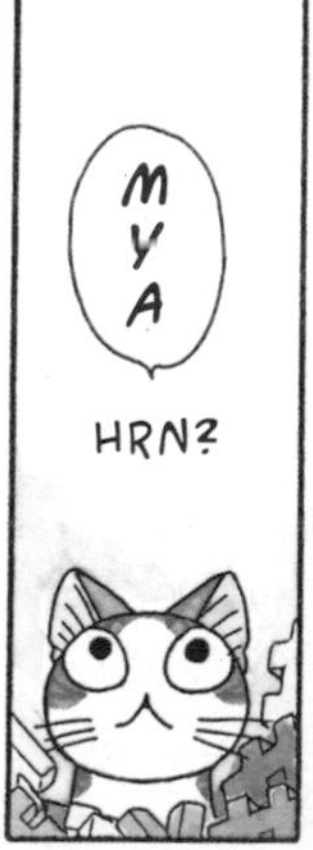
MYA
HRN?

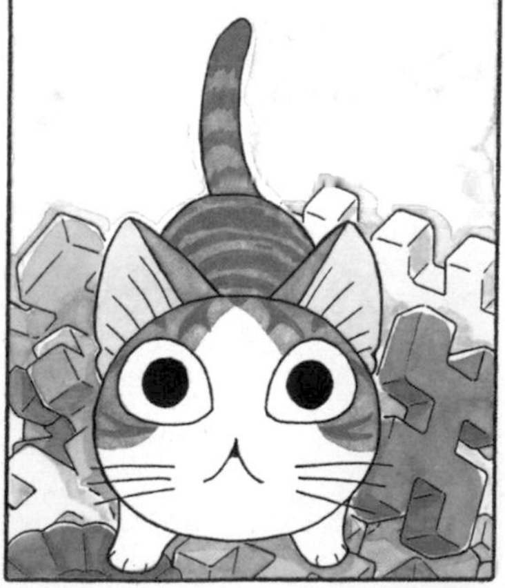

CHI LOVES TO PLAY WITH YOHEI.

SHE SURE DOES.

PAT

EVEN IF SHE'S PLAYING HER OWN GAMES.

RUB RUB RUB

BLOCKS

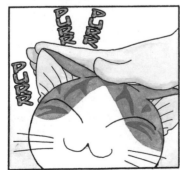

PURR PURR PURR

WANT SOME MILK, CHI?

MILK 3.5

!

RISE

234

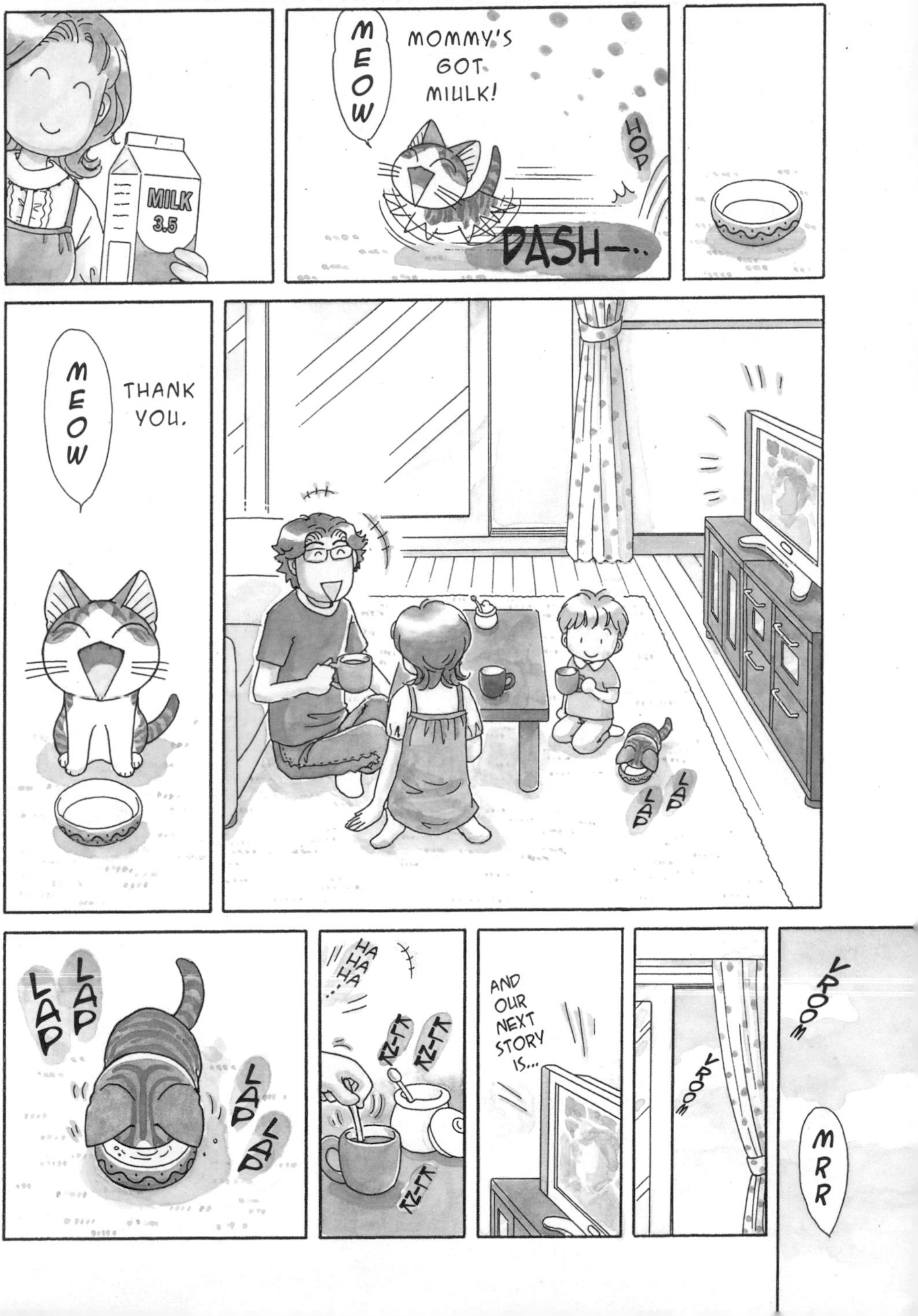
MILK 3.5
MEOW
MOMMY'S GOT MIULK!
HOP
DASH-..
MEOW
THANK YOU.
LAP LAP
LAP LAP
LAP LAP
HA HA HA...
TZ-TK TZ-TK
TZ-TK
AND OUR NEXT STORY IS...
VROOOM
VROOOM
MRR

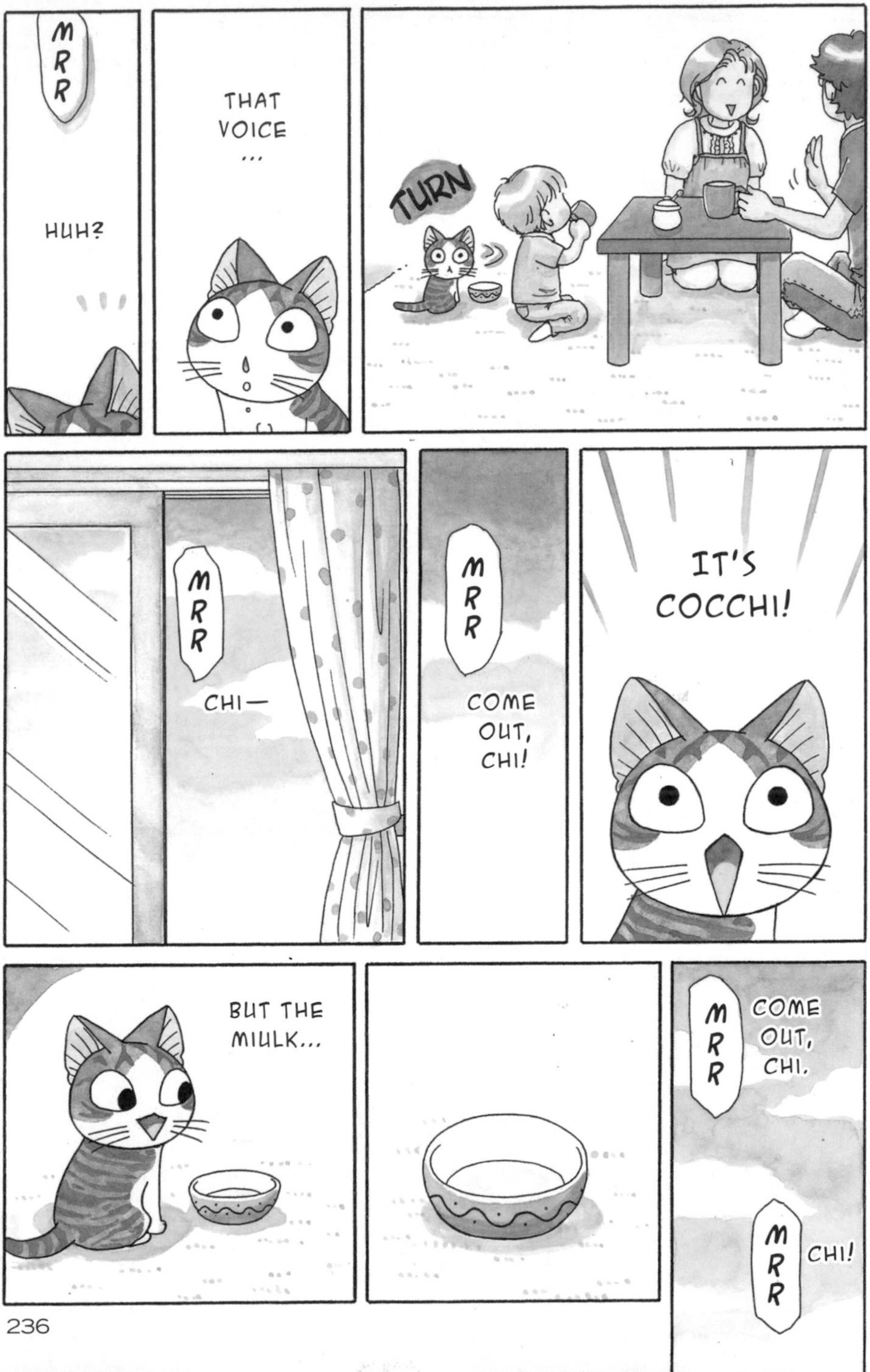
MRR
HUH?
THAT VOICE ...
TURN
MRR
CHI—
MRR
COME OUT, CHI!
IT'S COCCHI!
BUT THE MIULK...
MRR
COME OUT, CHI.
MRR
CHI!

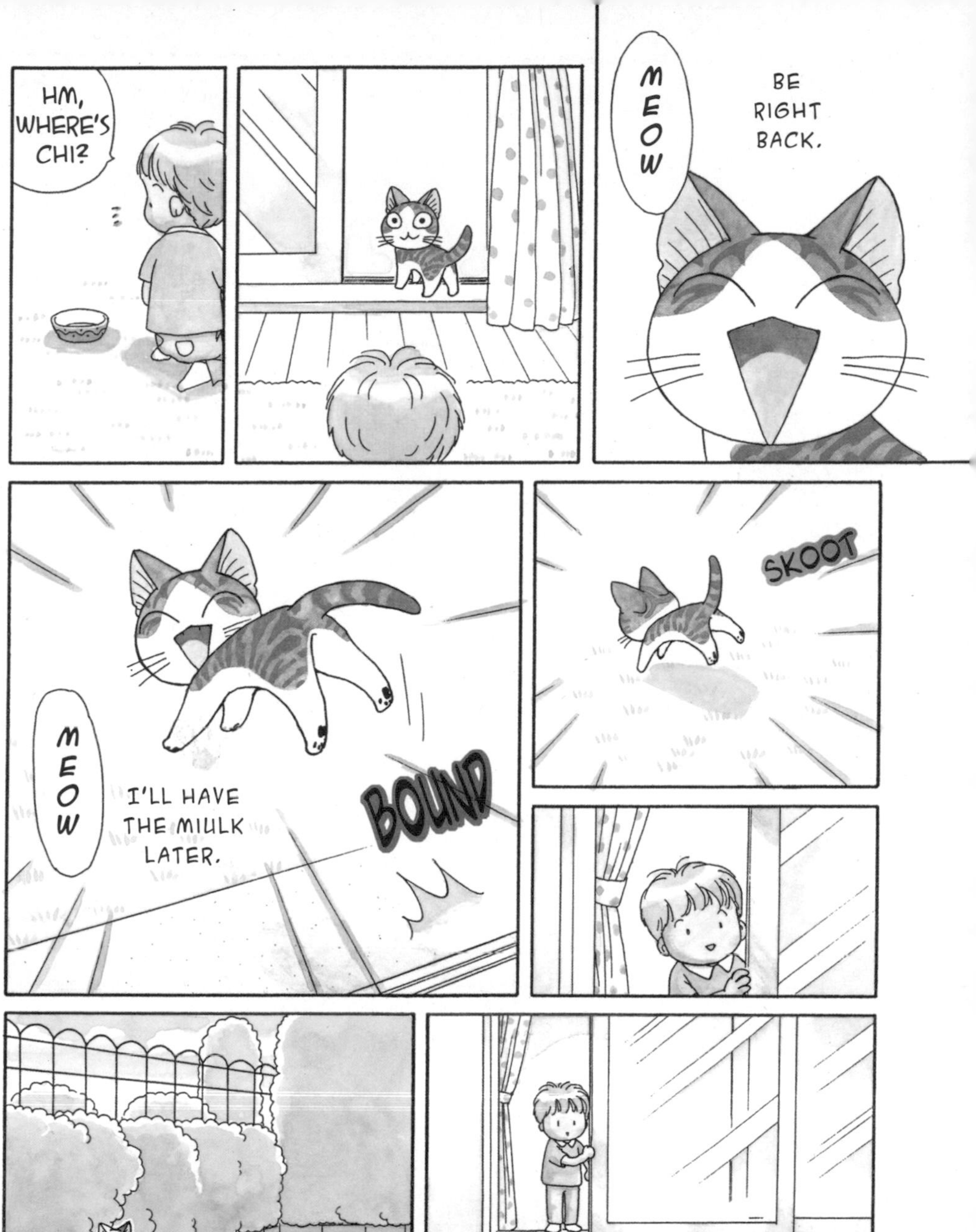
HM, WHERE'S CHI?
MEOW
BE RIGHT BACK.
MEOW
I'LL HAVE THE MIULK LATER.
BOUND
SKOOT

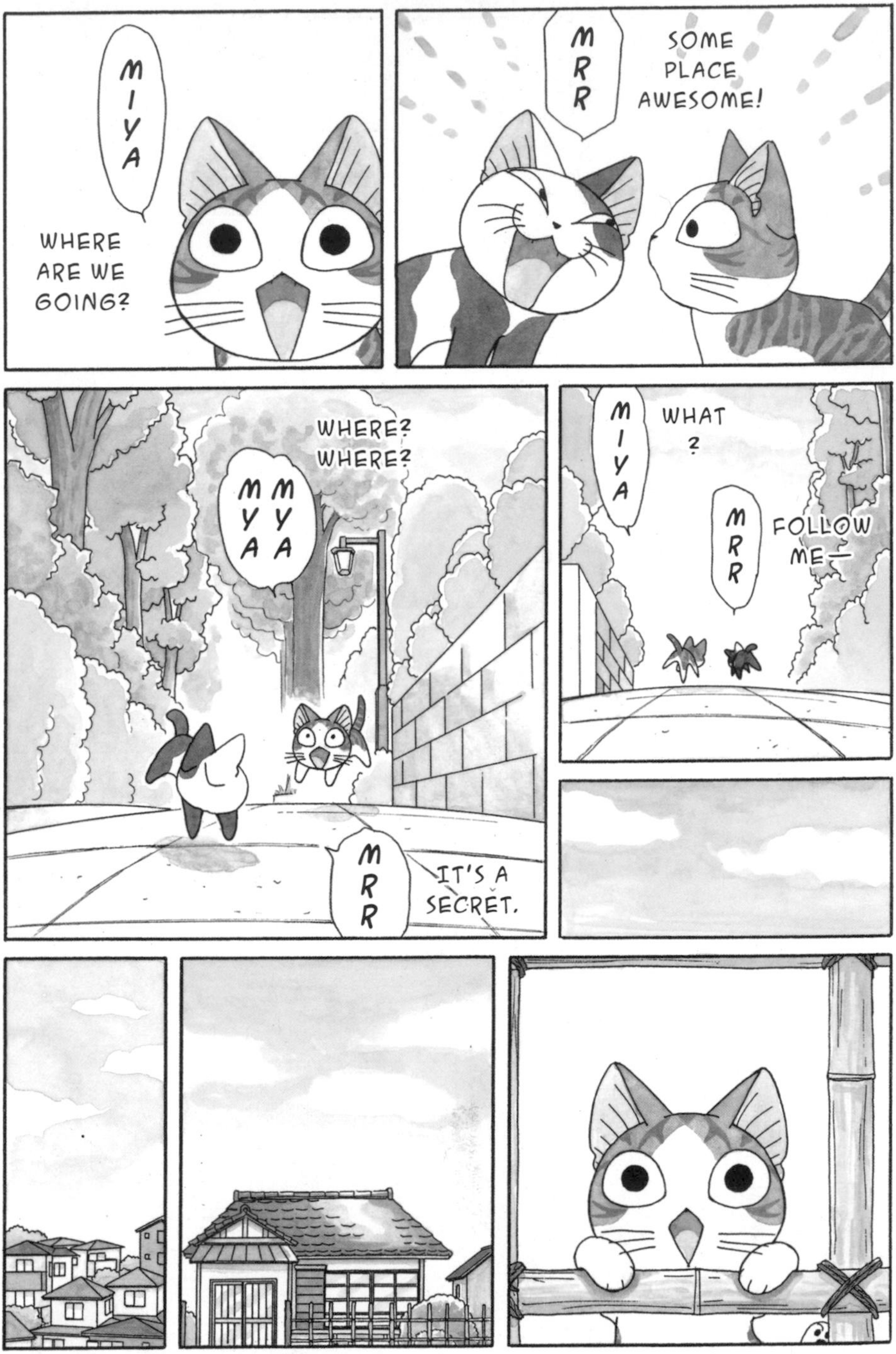
MIYA
WHERE ARE WE GOING?
MRR
SOME PLACE AWESOME!
MYA MYA
WHERE? WHERE?
MRR
IT'S A SECRET.
MIYA
WHAT?
MRR
FOLLOW ME—

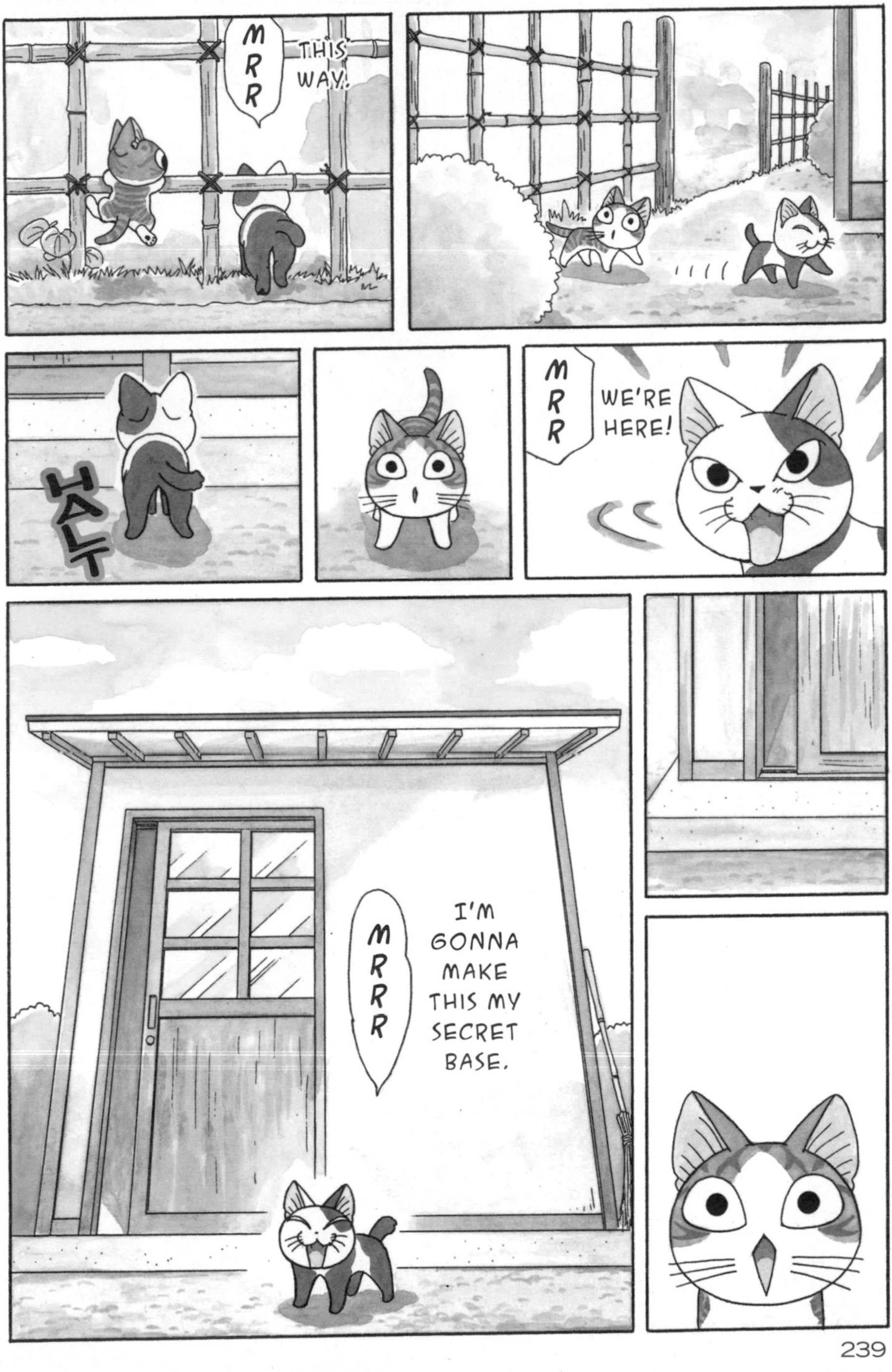
MRR
THIS WAY.
HALT
MRR
WE'RE HERE!
MRRR
I'M GONNA MAKE THIS MY SECRET BASE.

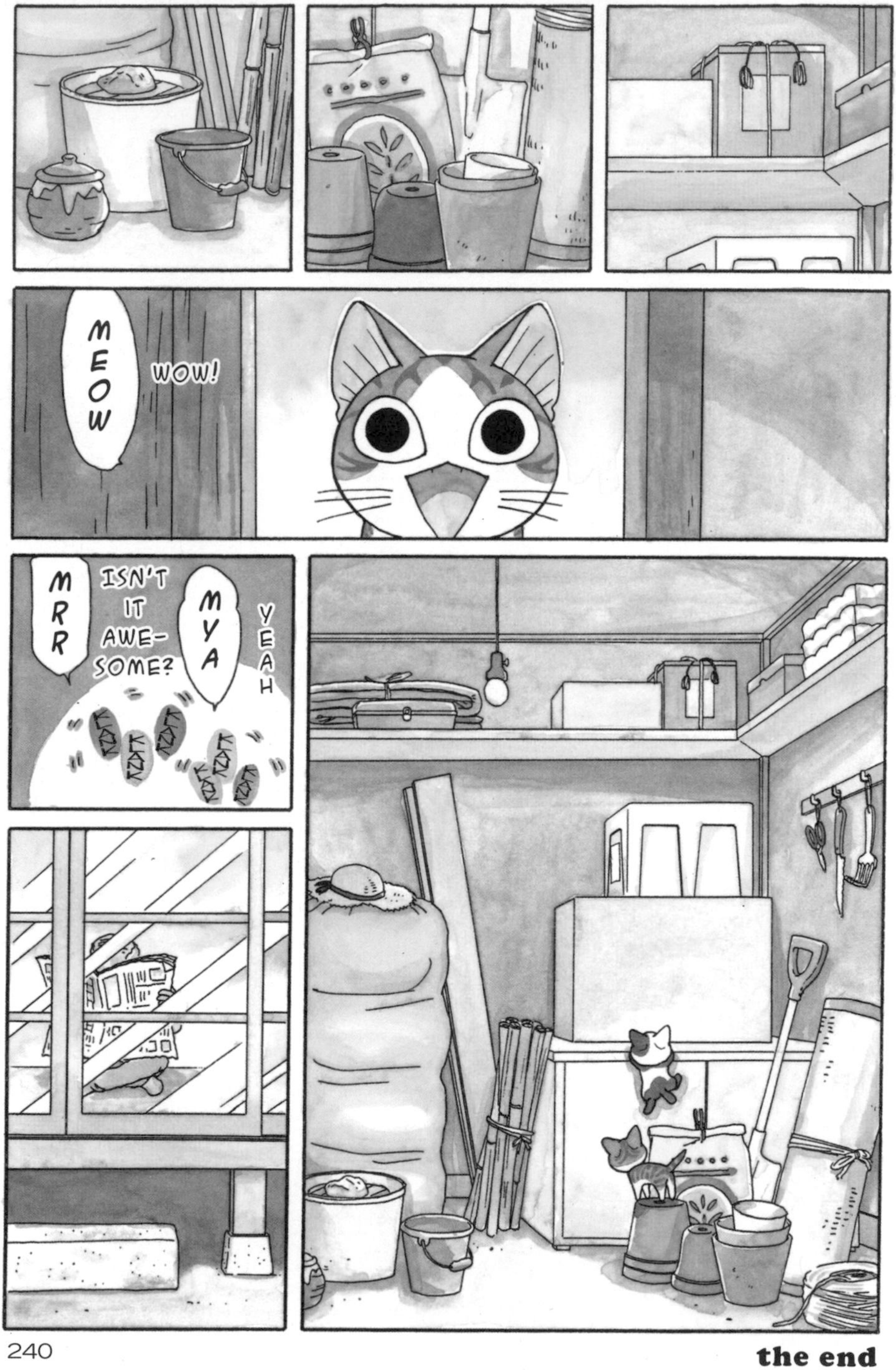
MEOW
WOW!
MRR
ISN'T IT AWE-SOME?
MYA
YEAH
KLANK
KLANK
KLANK
KLANK
KLANK
KLANK



**the end**

# homemade 141: a cat infiltrates

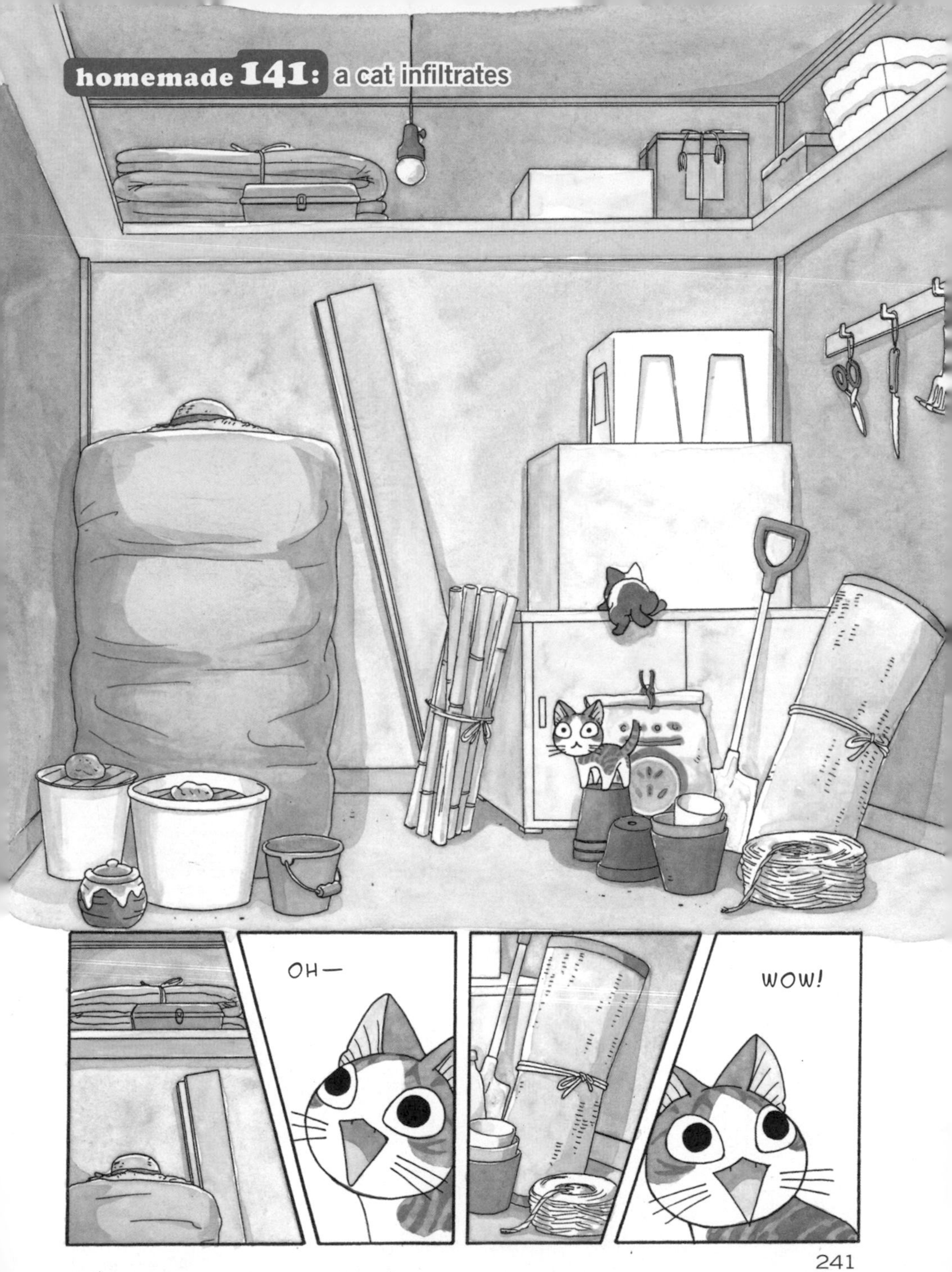
OH—
WOW!

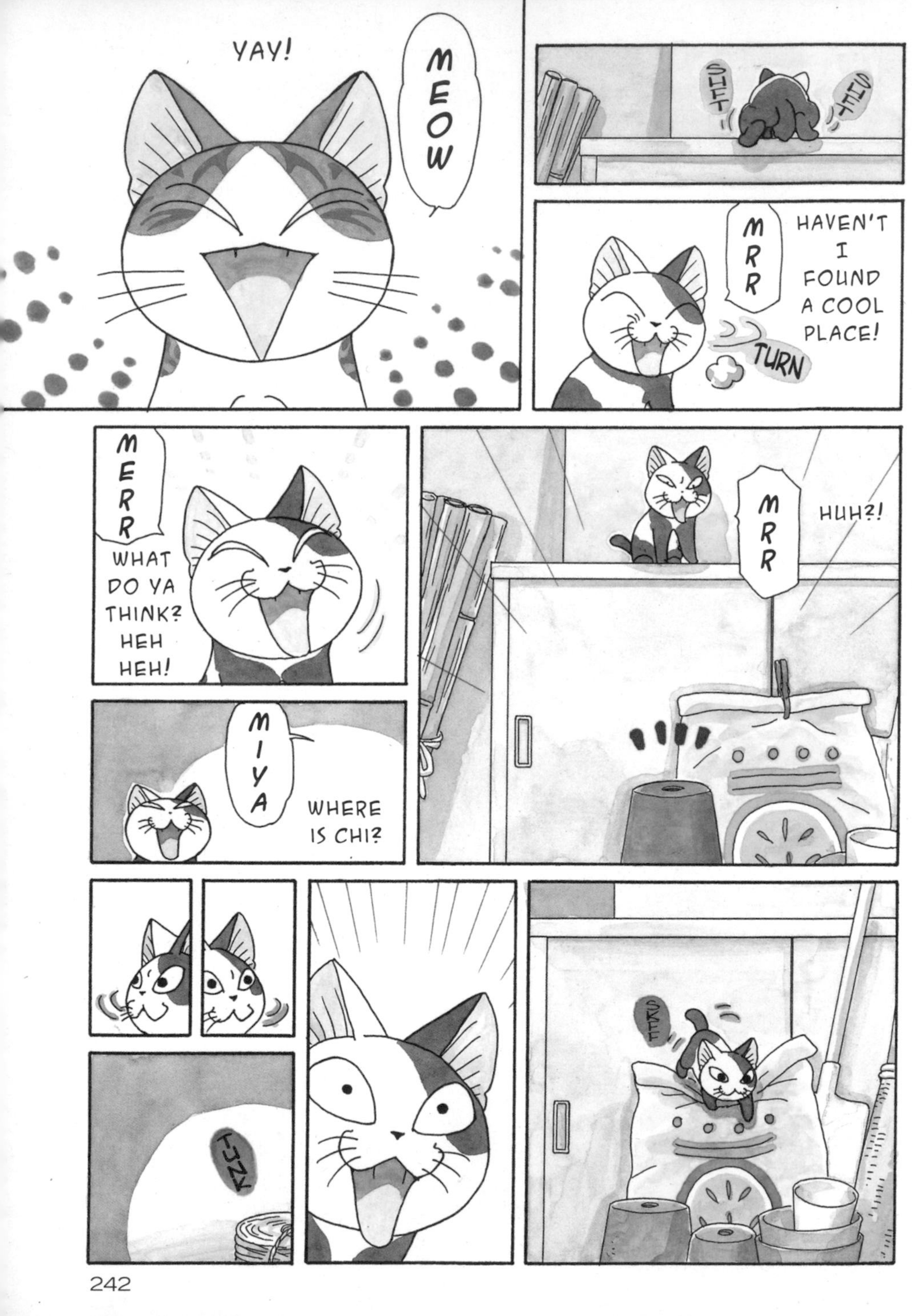
YAY!
MEOW
SHFT
SHFT
MRR
HAVEN'T I FOUND A COOL PLACE!
TURN
MERR
WHAT DO YA THINK? HEH HEH!
MIYA
WHERE IS CHI?
MRR
HUH?!
TUNK
SKFF

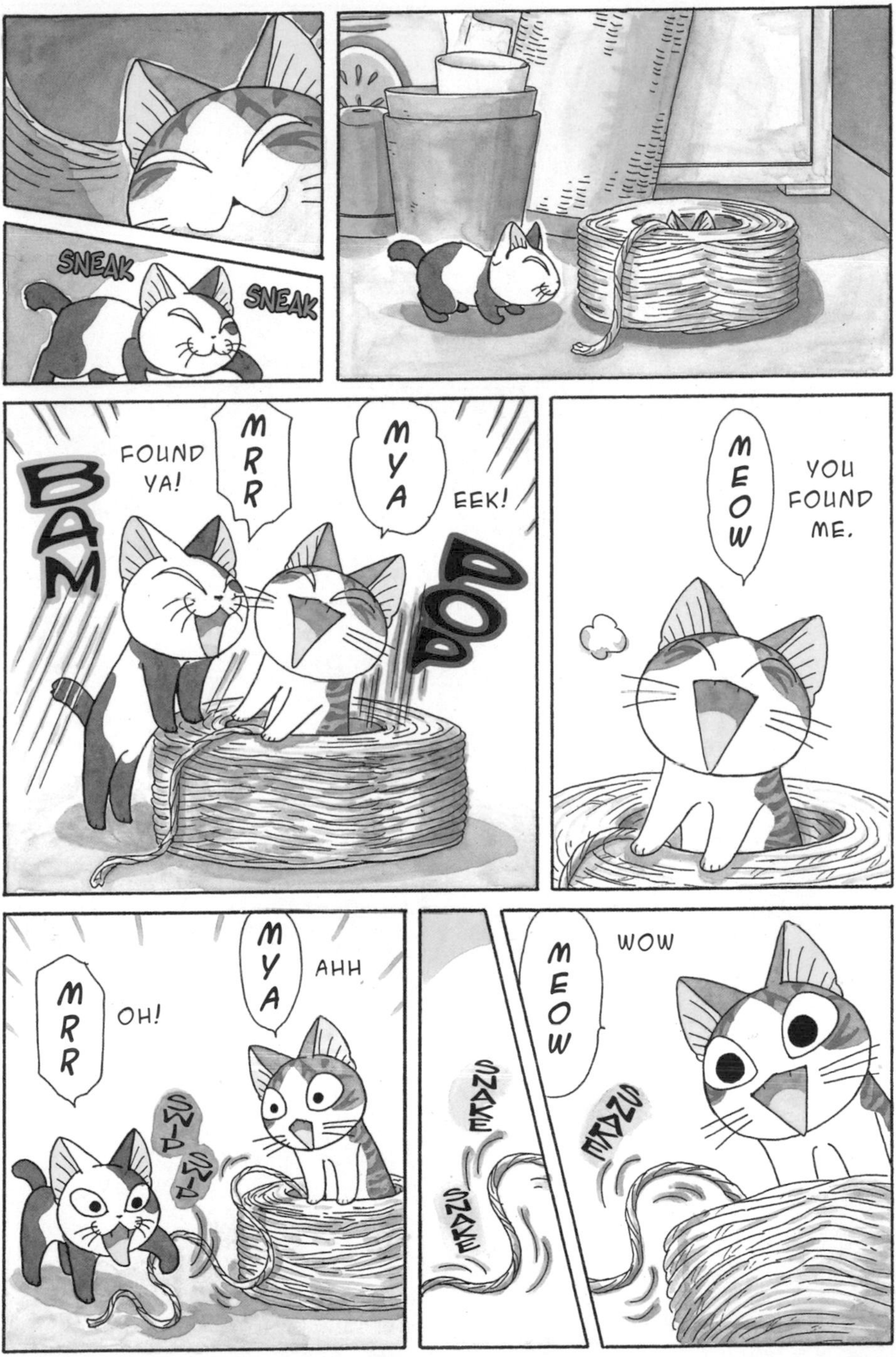
SNEAK
SNEAK
BAM
FOUND YA!
MRR
MYA
EEK!
POP
MEOW
YOU FOUND ME.
MRR
OH!
MYA
AHH
SWID
SWID
SNAKE
SNAKE
MEOW
WOW

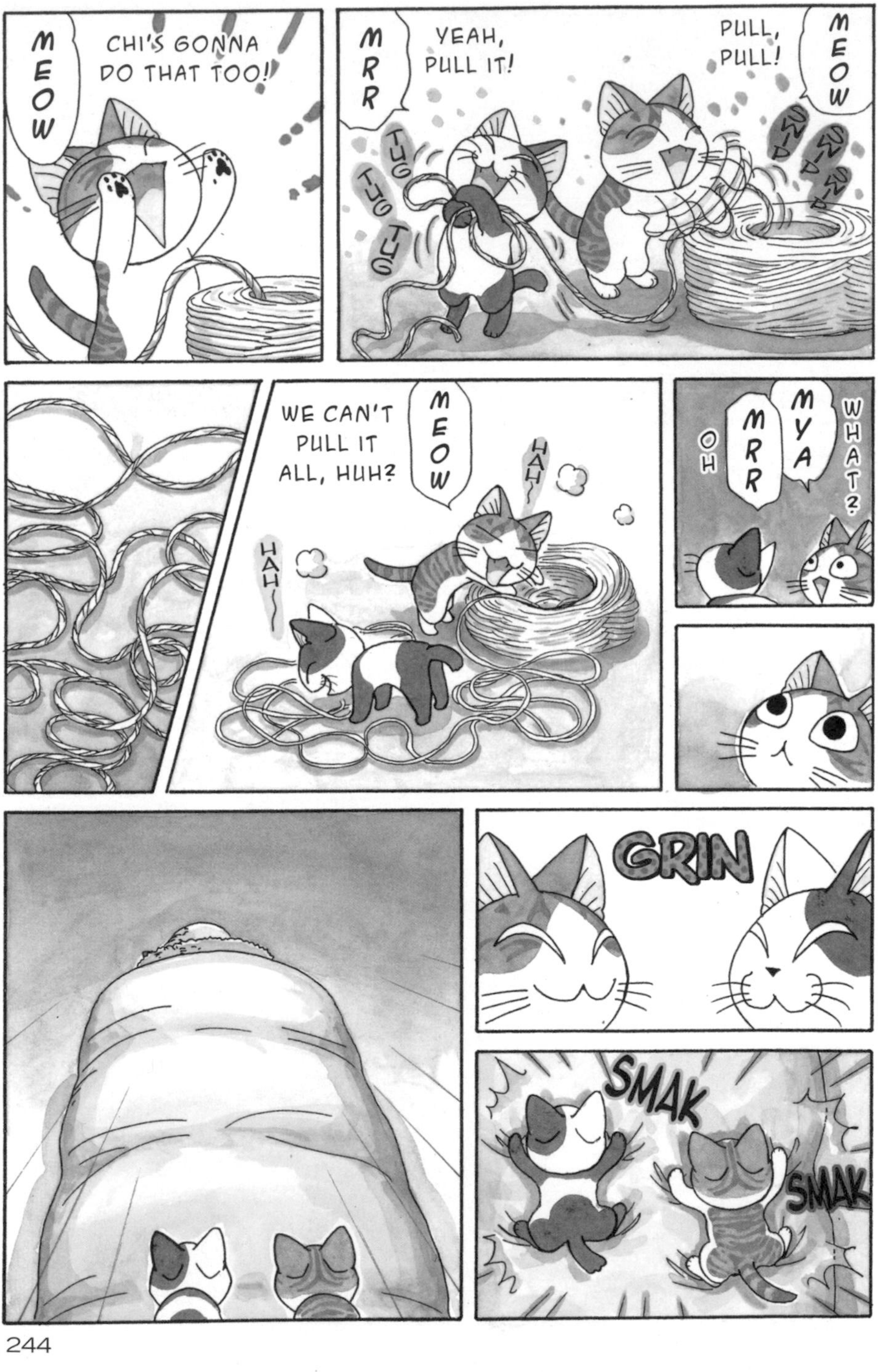
MEOW
CHI'S GONNA DO THAT TOO!
MRR
YEAH, PULL IT!
PULL, PULL!
MEOW
TUG TUG TUG TUG
SWIP SWIP SWIP SWIP
WE CAN'T PULL IT ALL, HUH?
MEOW
HAH~
HAH~
OH
MRR
MYA
WHAT?
GRIN
SMAK
SMAK

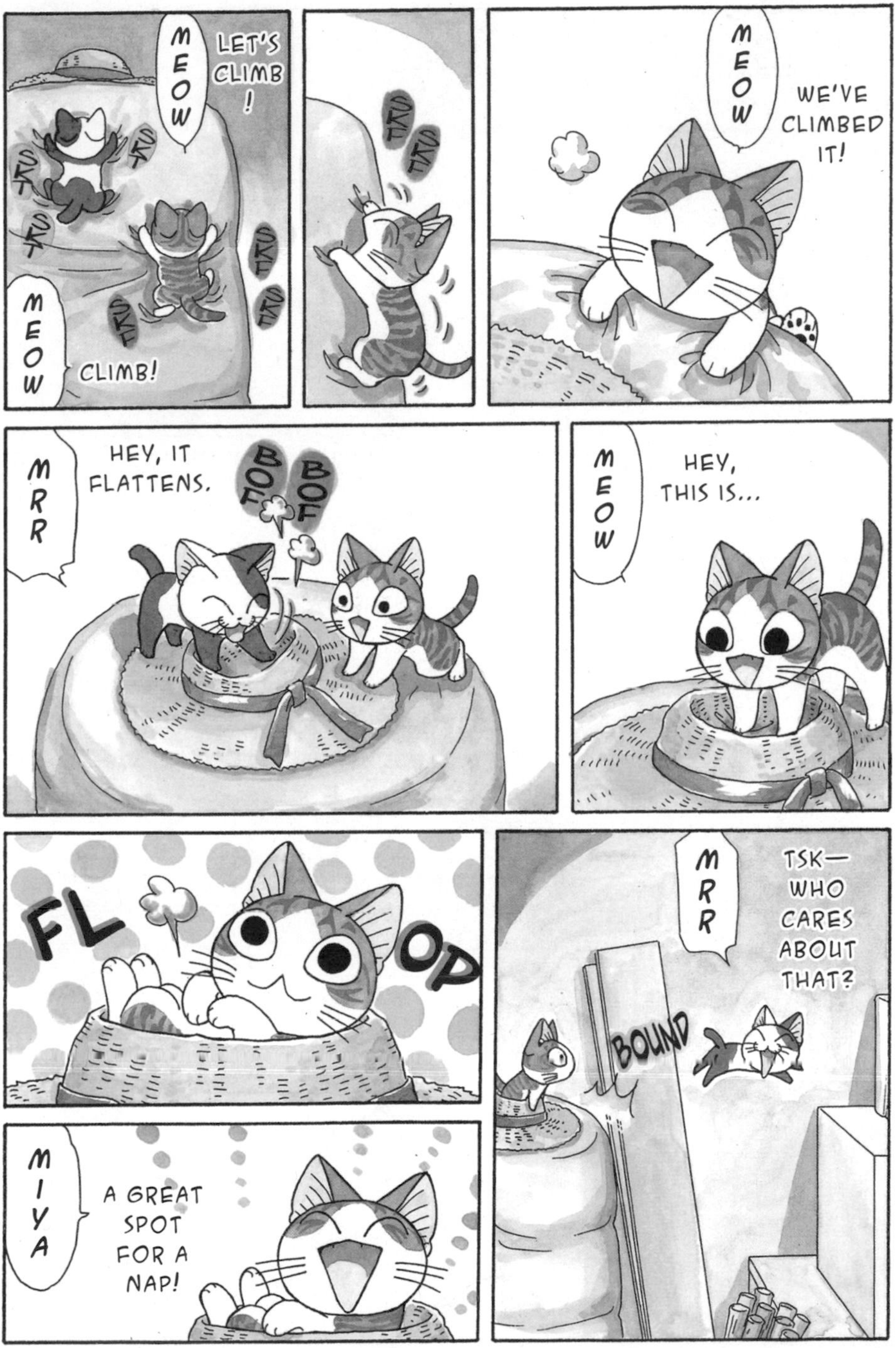
MEOW
LET'S CLIMB!
SKT SKT
SKT SKT
SKT SKT
MEOW
CLIMB!
SKT SKT
SKT SKT
MEOW
WE'VE CLIMBED IT!
MRR
HEY, IT FLATTENS.
BOF BOF
MEOW
HEY, THIS IS...
FLOP
MIYA
A GREAT SPOT FOR A NAP!
MRR
TSK—WHO CARES ABOUT THAT?
BOUND

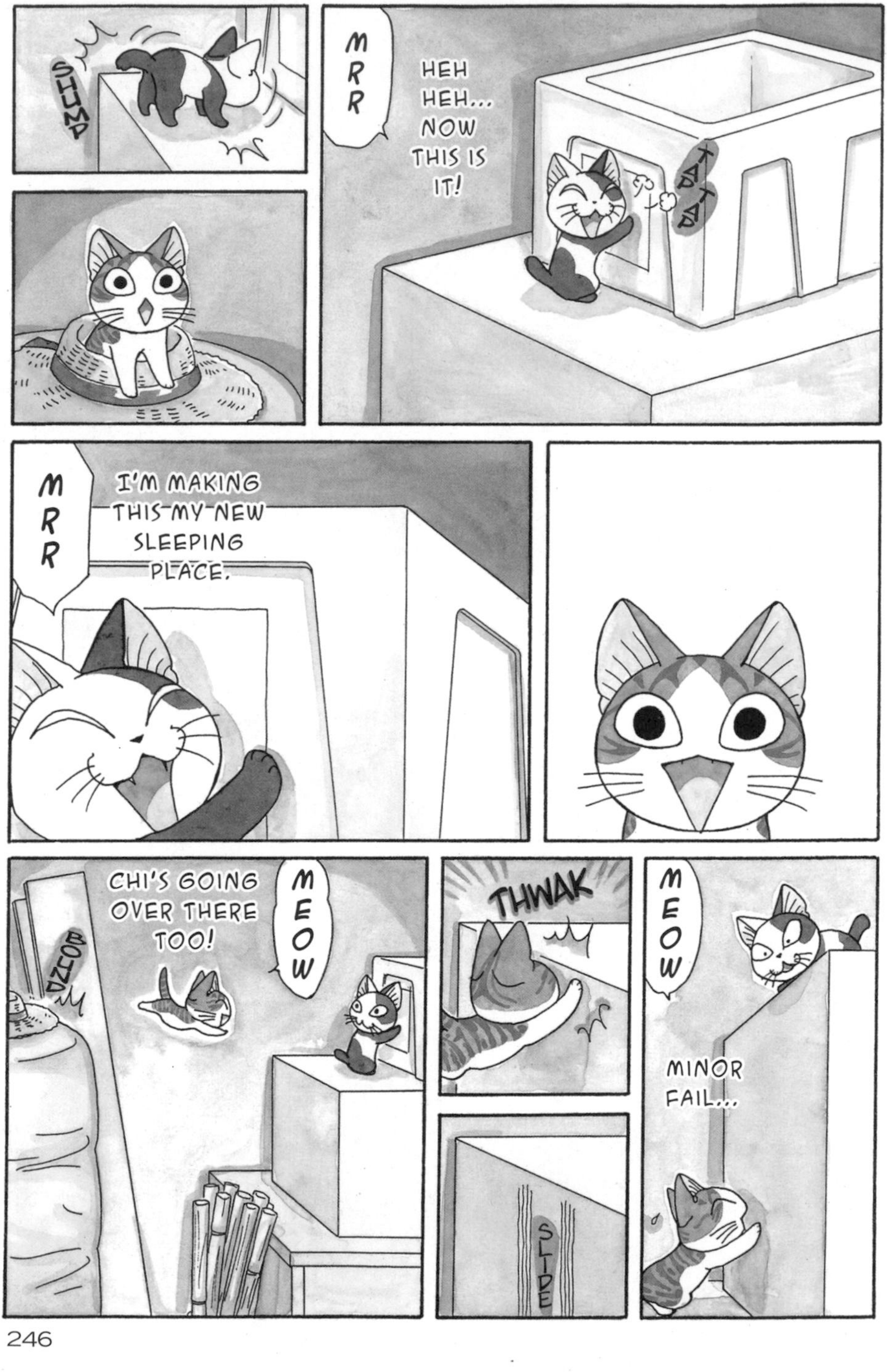
SHUMP
MRR
HEH HEH... NOW THIS IS IT!
TAP TAP
MRR
I'M MAKING THIS MY NEW SLEEPING PLACE.
BOUND
CHI'S GOING OVER THERE TOO!
MEOW
THWAK
MEOW
MINOR FAIL...
SLIDE

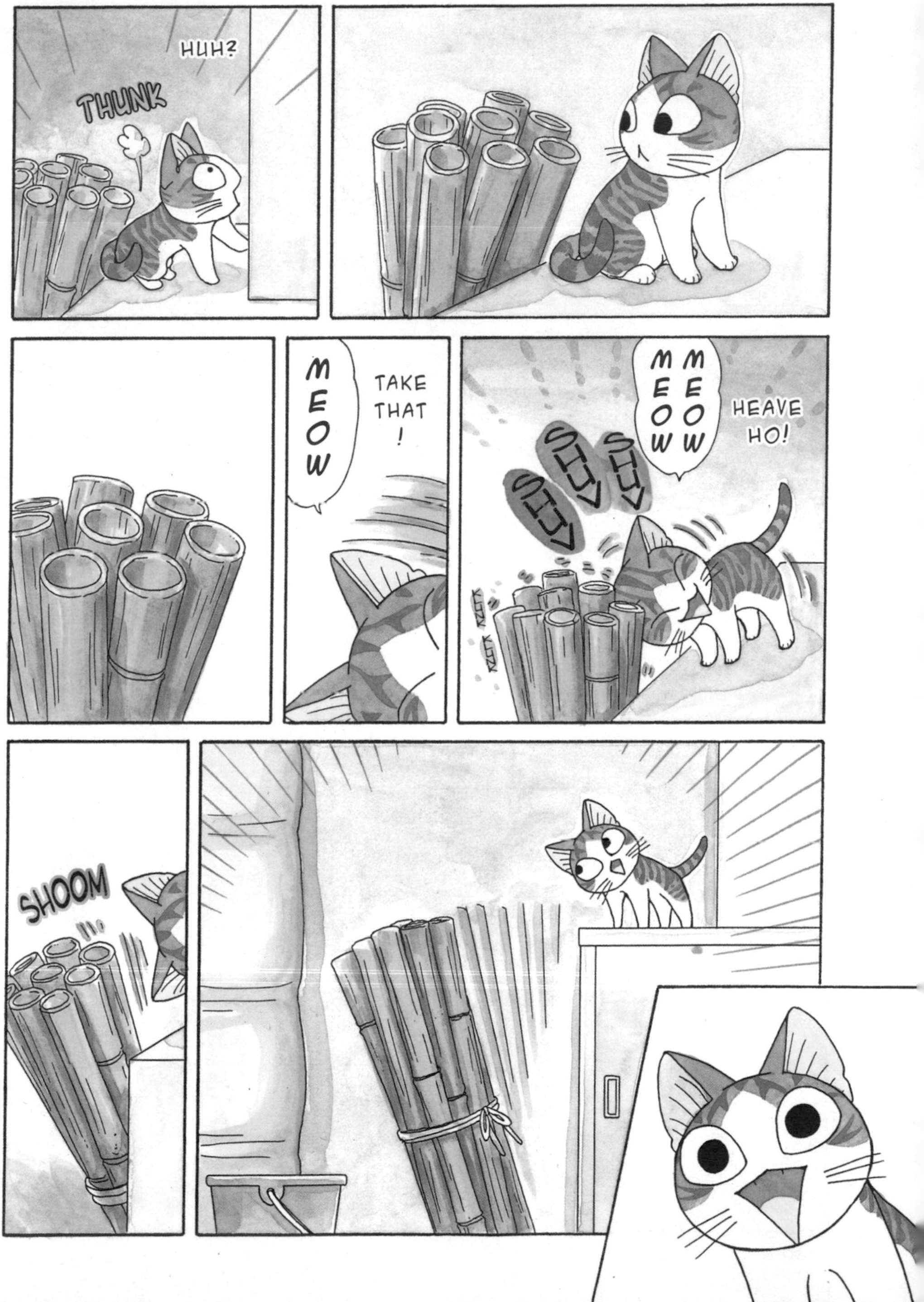
HUH?
THUNK
MEOW
TAKE THAT!
SHUV
SHUV
SHUV
MEOW
MEOW
HEAVE HO!
SHOOM

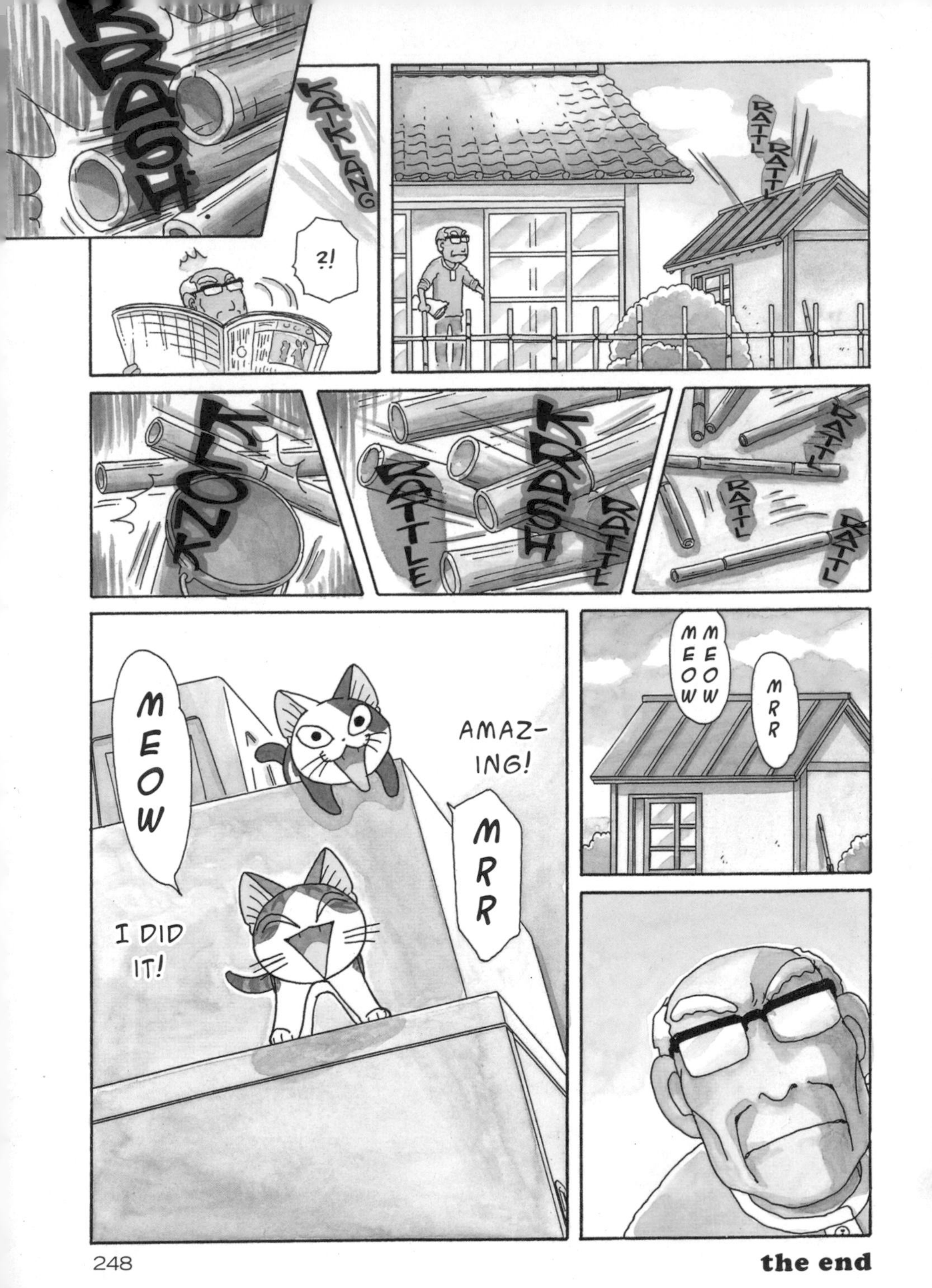
KRASH
KAKLANG
?!
RATTL RATTL
KLONK
RATTLE
KRASH
RATTL
RATTL
RATTL
RATTL
MEOW
AMAZING!
MRR
I DID IT!
MEOW MEOW
MRR



**the end**

## homemade 142: a cat judges

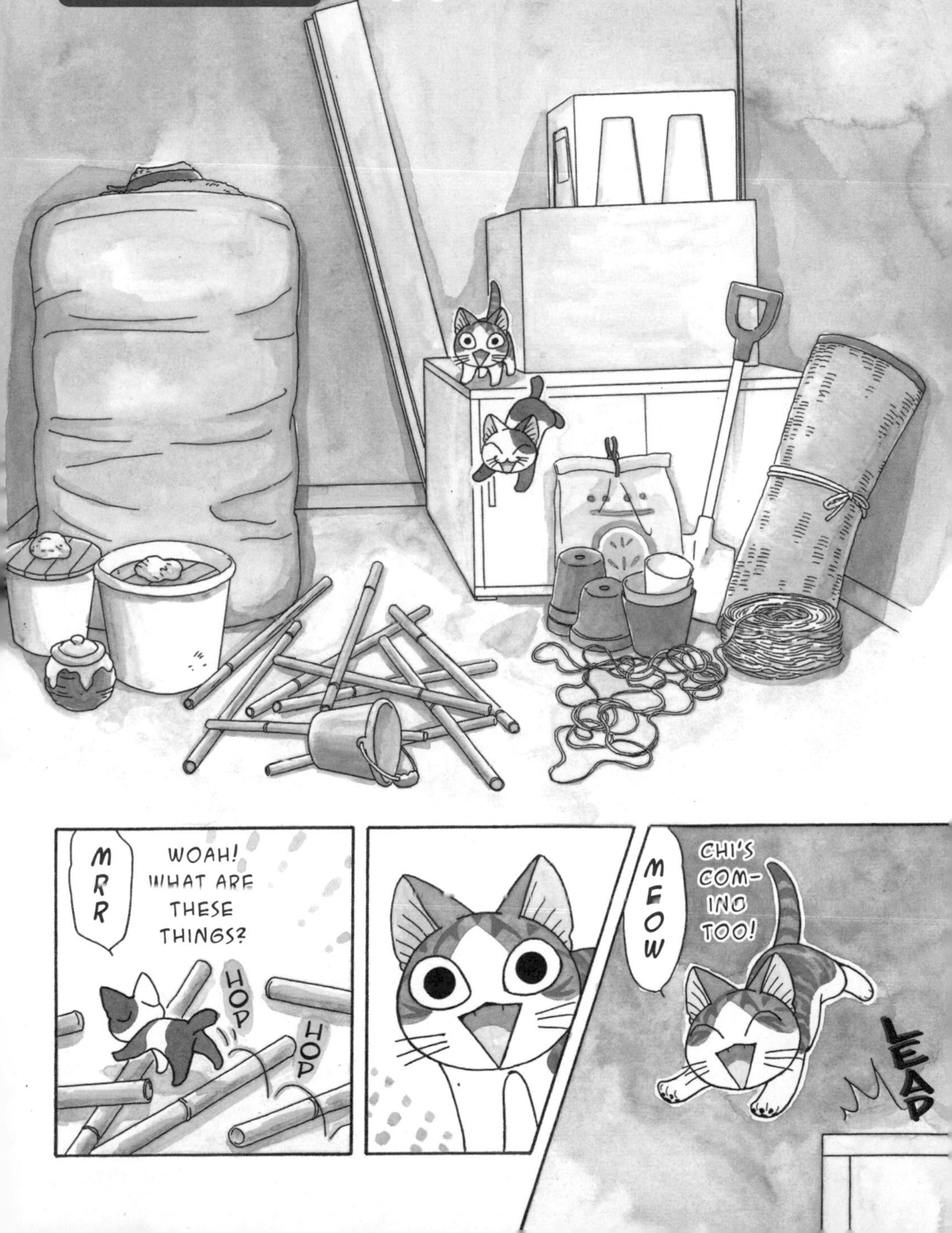
MRR
WOAH! WHAT ARE THESE THINGS?
HOP
HOP
MEOW
CHI'S COMING TOO!
LEAP

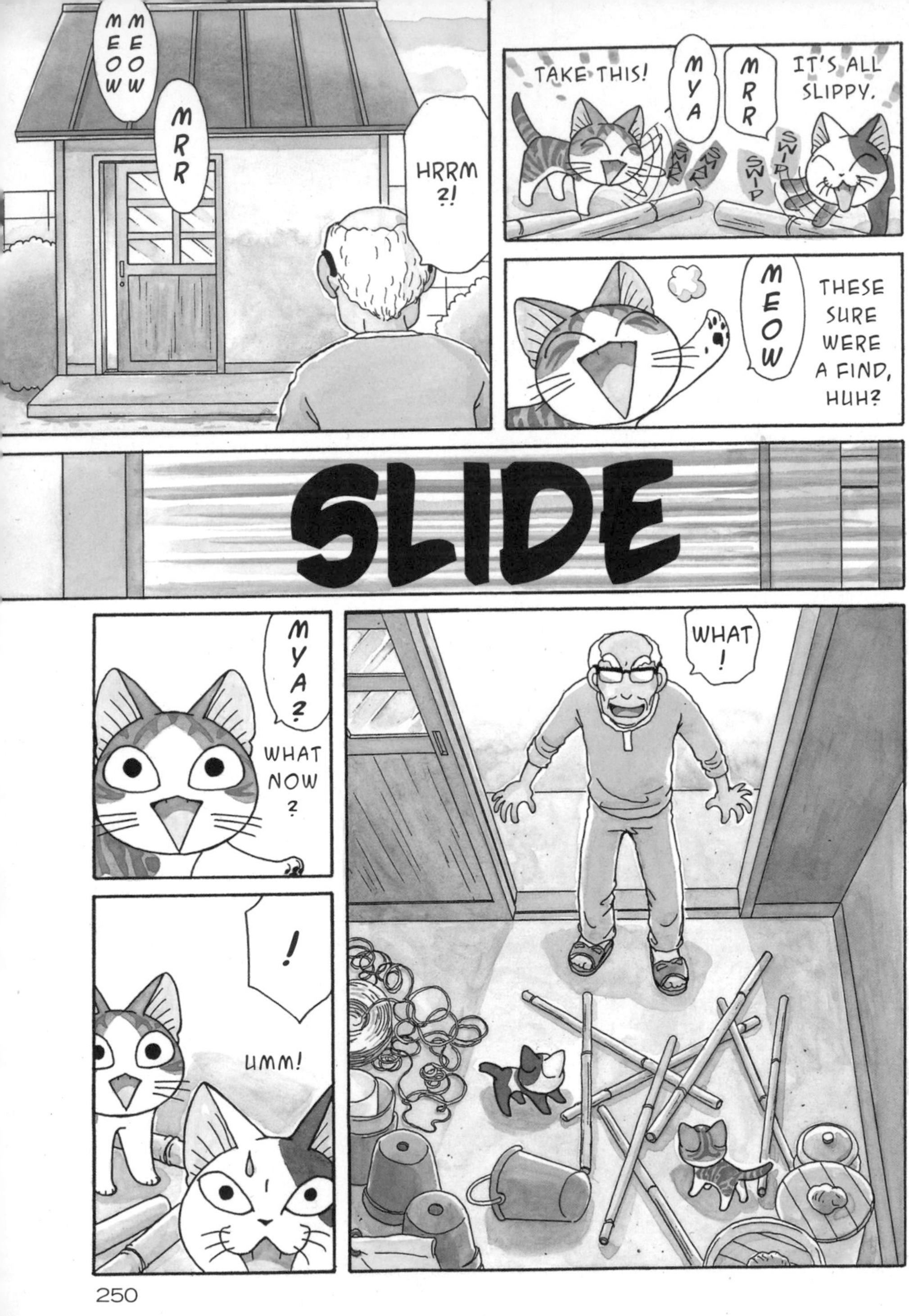
MEOW
MEOW
MRR
HRRM ?!
TAKE THIS!
MYA
SMAK
SMAK
MRR
SWIP
SWIP
IT'S ALL SLIPPY.
MEOW
THESE SURE WERE A FIND, HUH?
SLIDE
MYA?
WHAT NOW?
!
UMM!
WHAT!

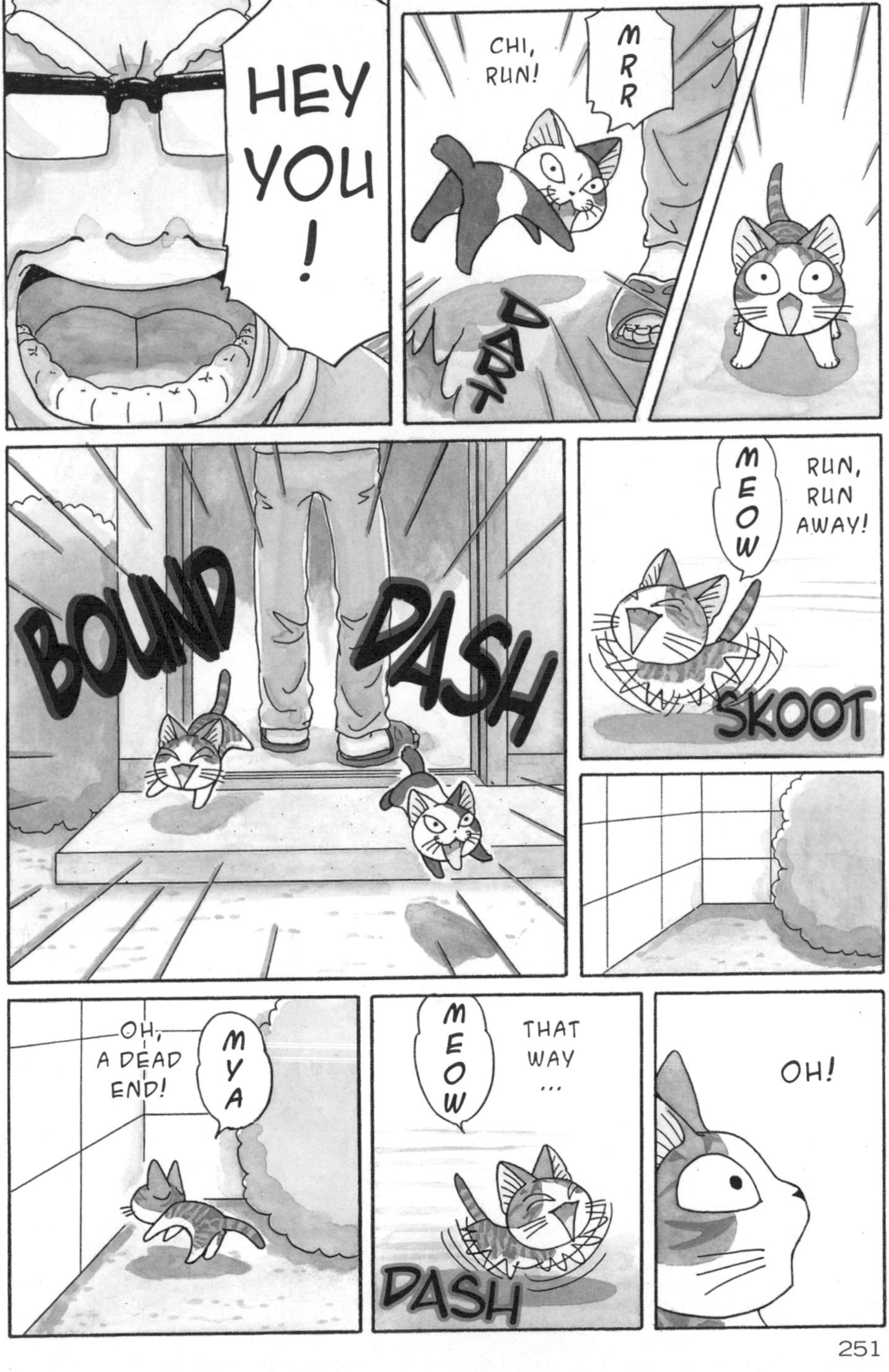
HEY YOU !
CHI, RUN!
MRR
DART
BOUND
DASH
MEOW
RUN, RUN AWAY!
SKOOT
OH, A DEAD END!
MYA
MEOW
THAT WAY ...
DASH
OH!

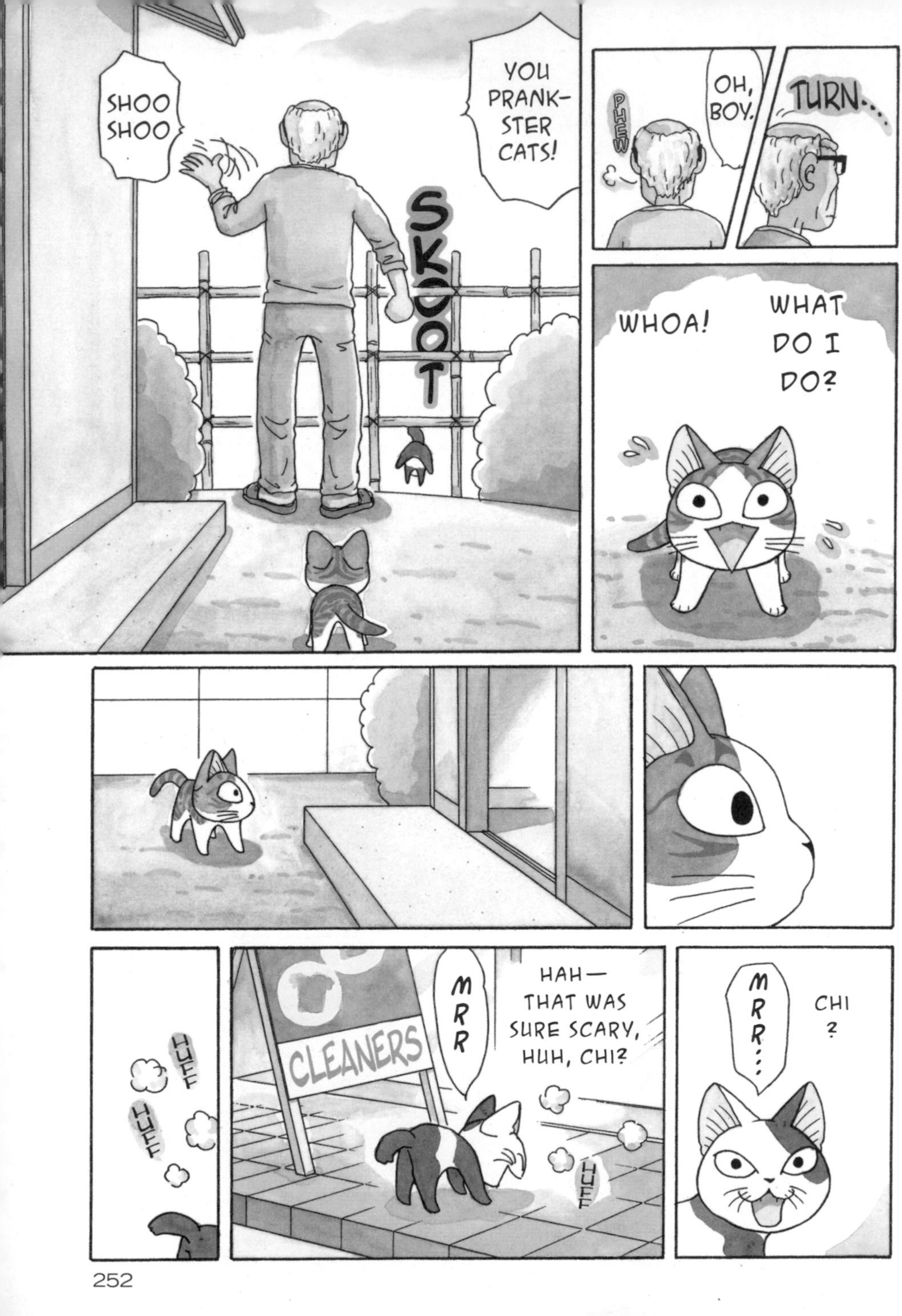
SHOO SHOO
YOU PRANK-STER CATS!
SKOOT
PHEW
OH, BOY.
TURN...
WHOA!
WHAT DO I DO?
HUFF
HUFF
MRR
HAH— THAT WAS SURE SCARY, HUH, CHI?
CLEANERS
HUFF
MRR...
CHI?

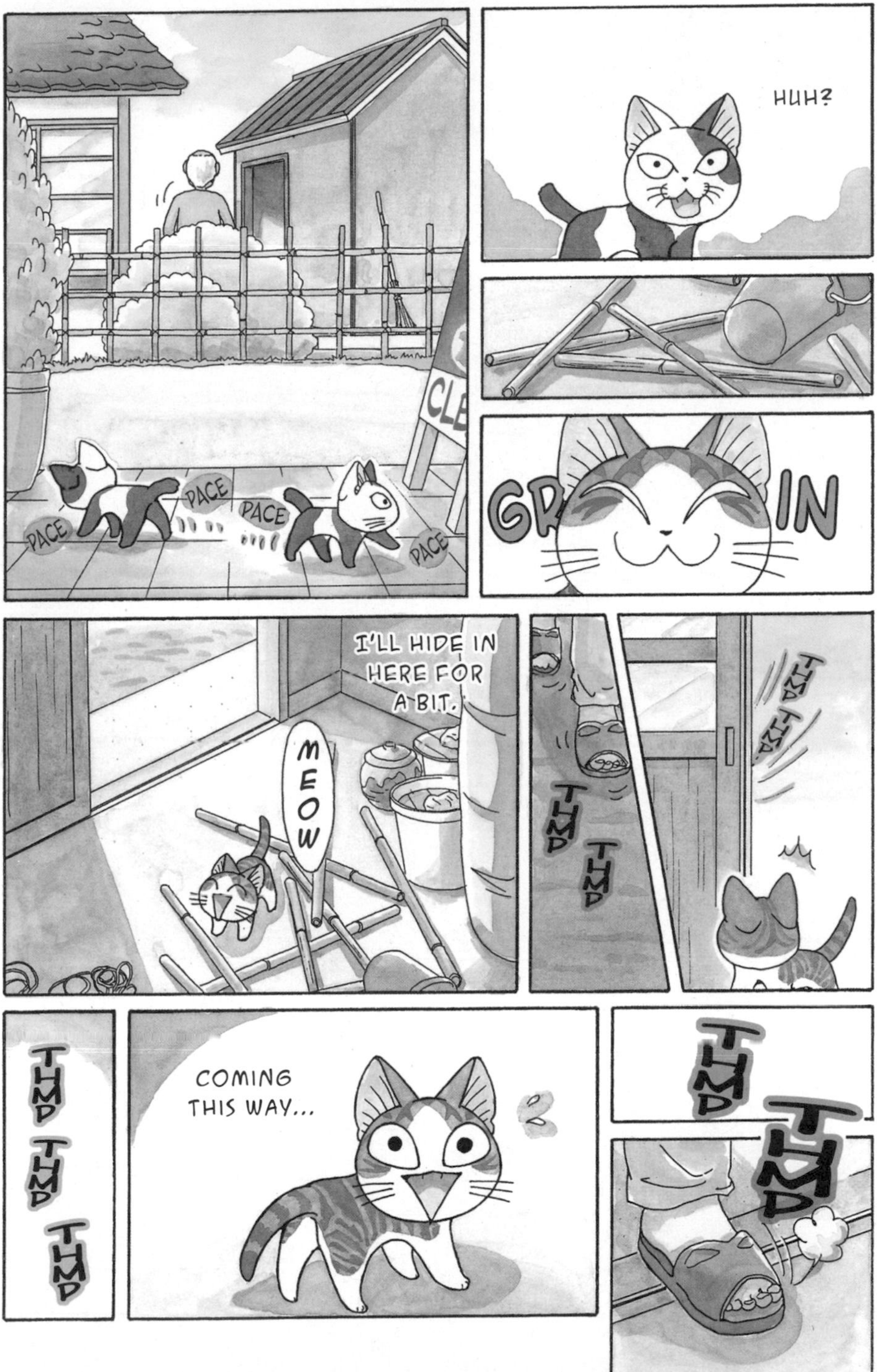

PACE
PACE
PACE
PACE
HUH?
GRIN
I'LL HIDE IN HERE FOR A BIT.
MEOW
THMP THMP
THMP THMP...
THMP THMP THMP
COMING THIS WAY...
THMP
THMP

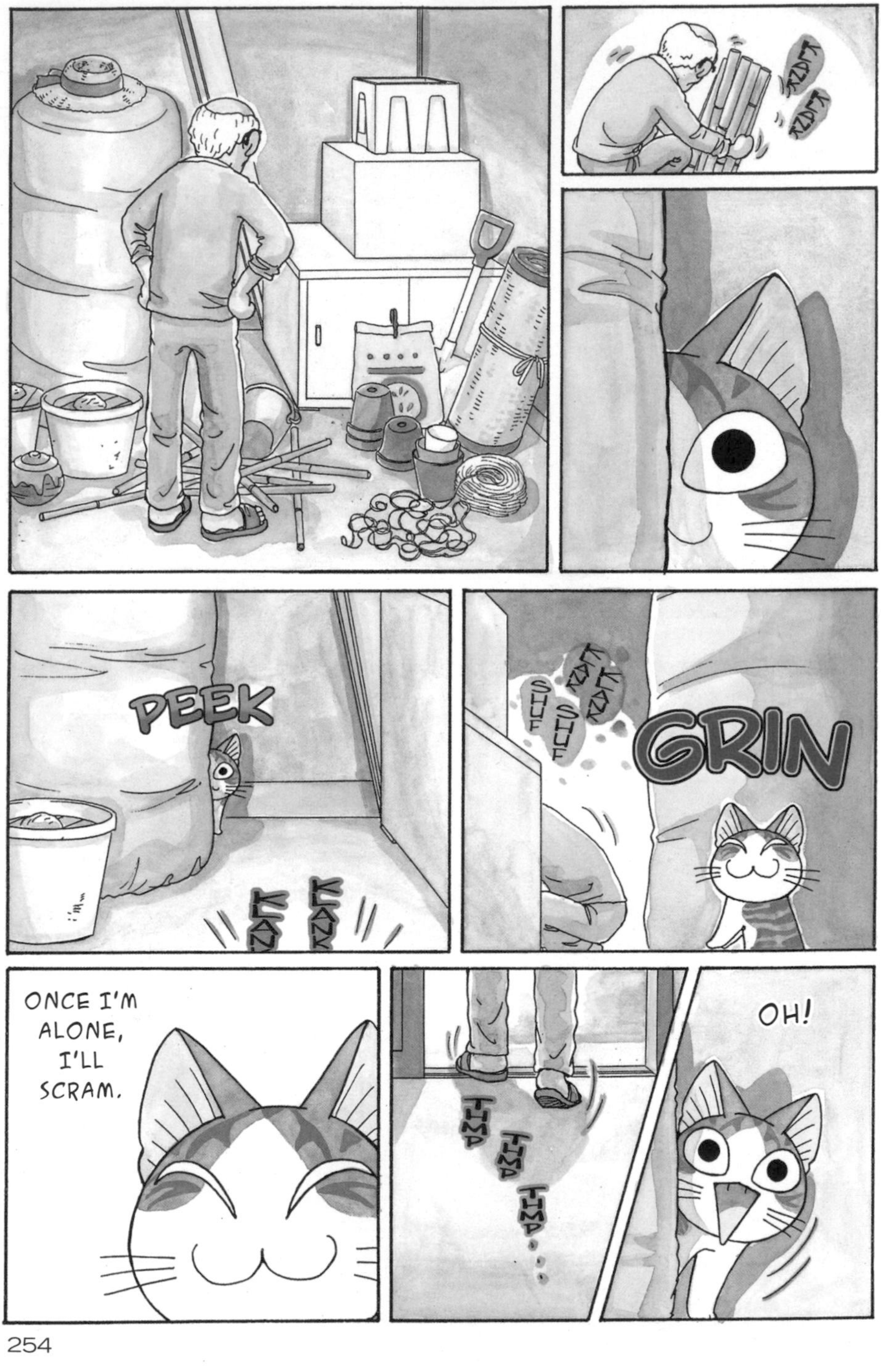
PEEK
KLANK
KLANK
SHUF
SHUF
GRIN
ONCE I'M ALONE, I'LL SCRAM.
THMP
THMP
THMP...
OH!

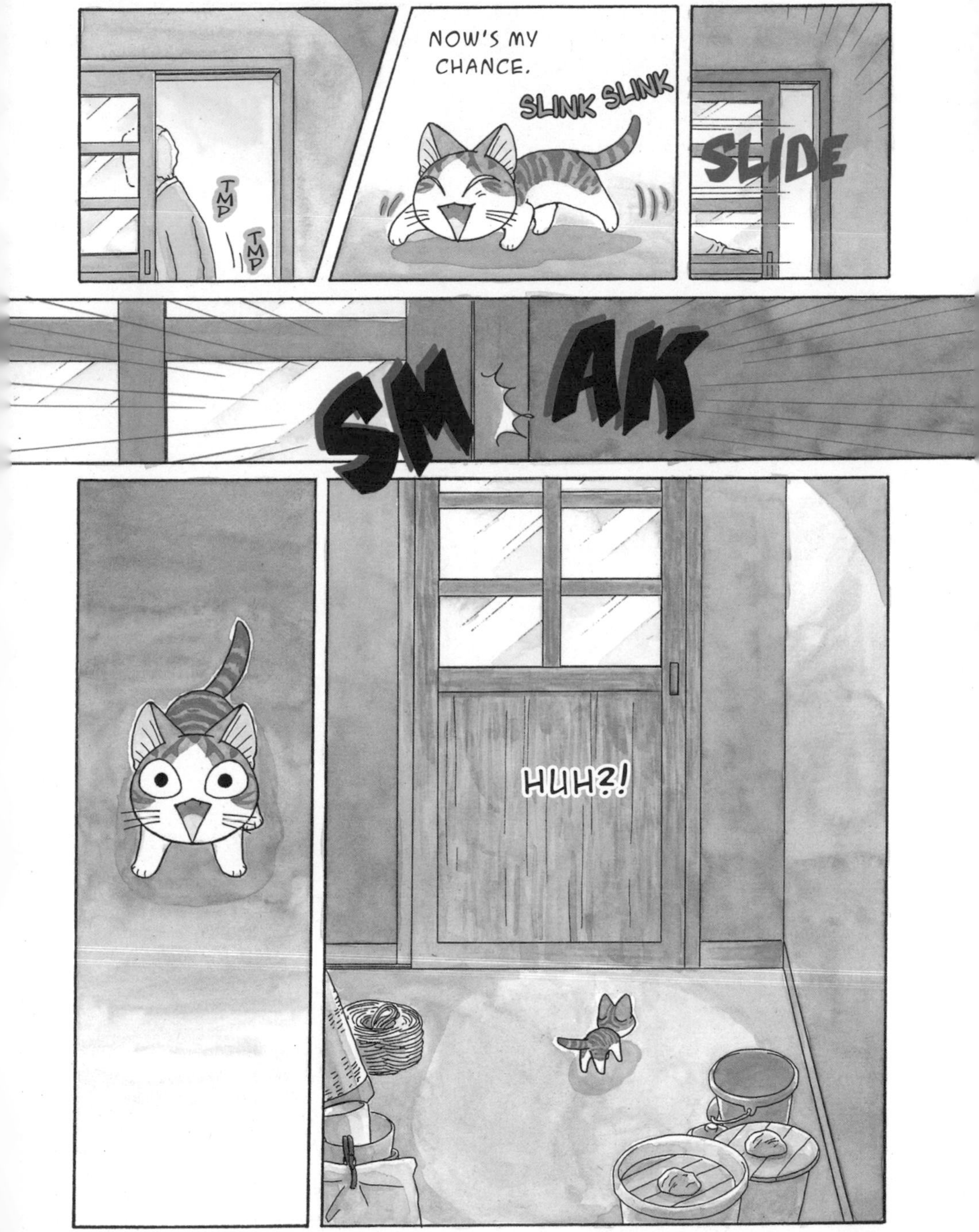
TMP
TMP
NOW'S MY CHANCE.
SLINK SLINK
SLIDE
SM AK
HUH?!

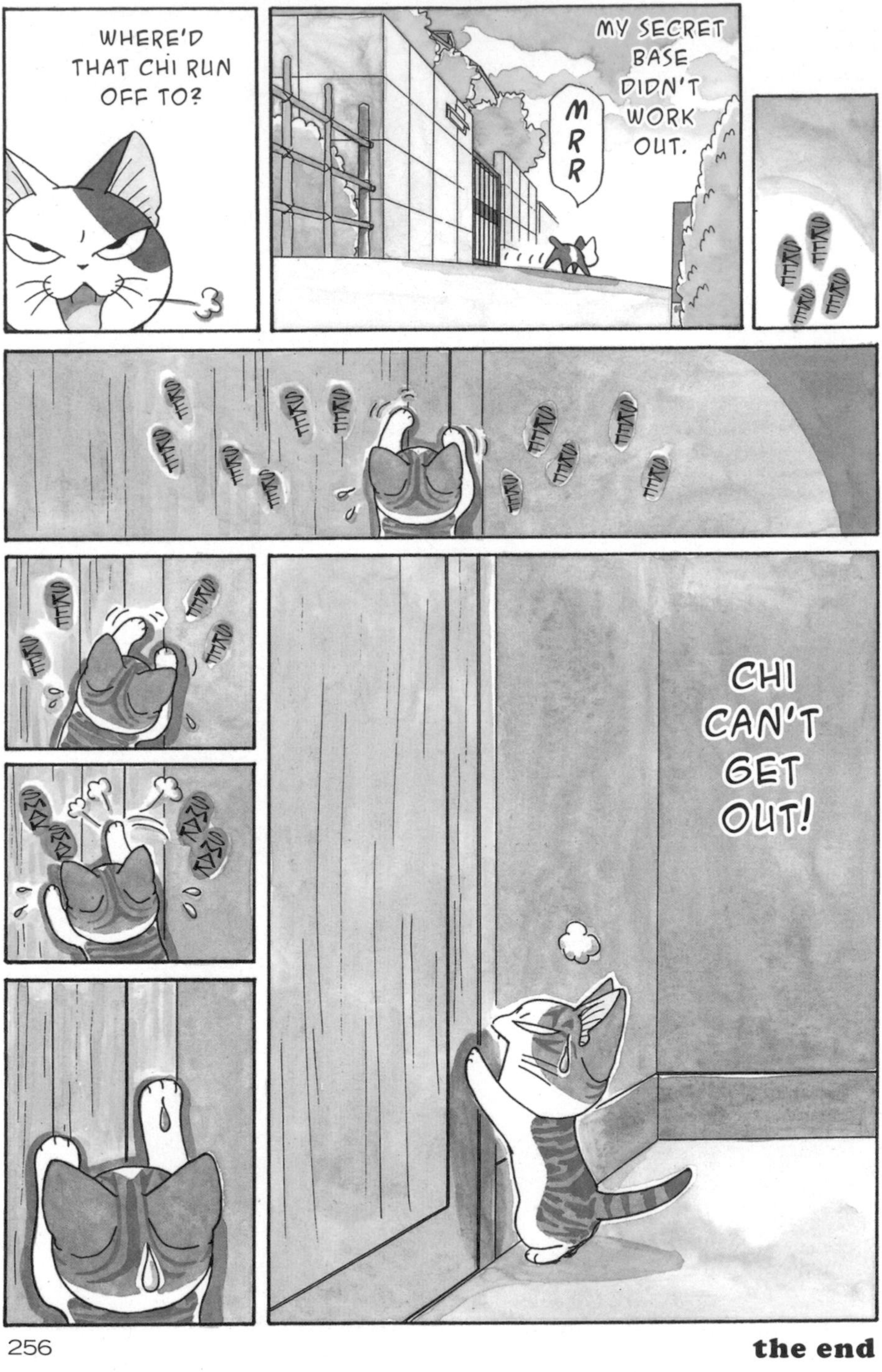
WHERE'D THAT CHI RUN OFF TO?
MY SECRET BASE DIDN'T WORK OUT.
MRR
SKREE
SKREE
SKREE
CHI CAN'T GET OUT!



the end

# homemade 143: a cat attempts

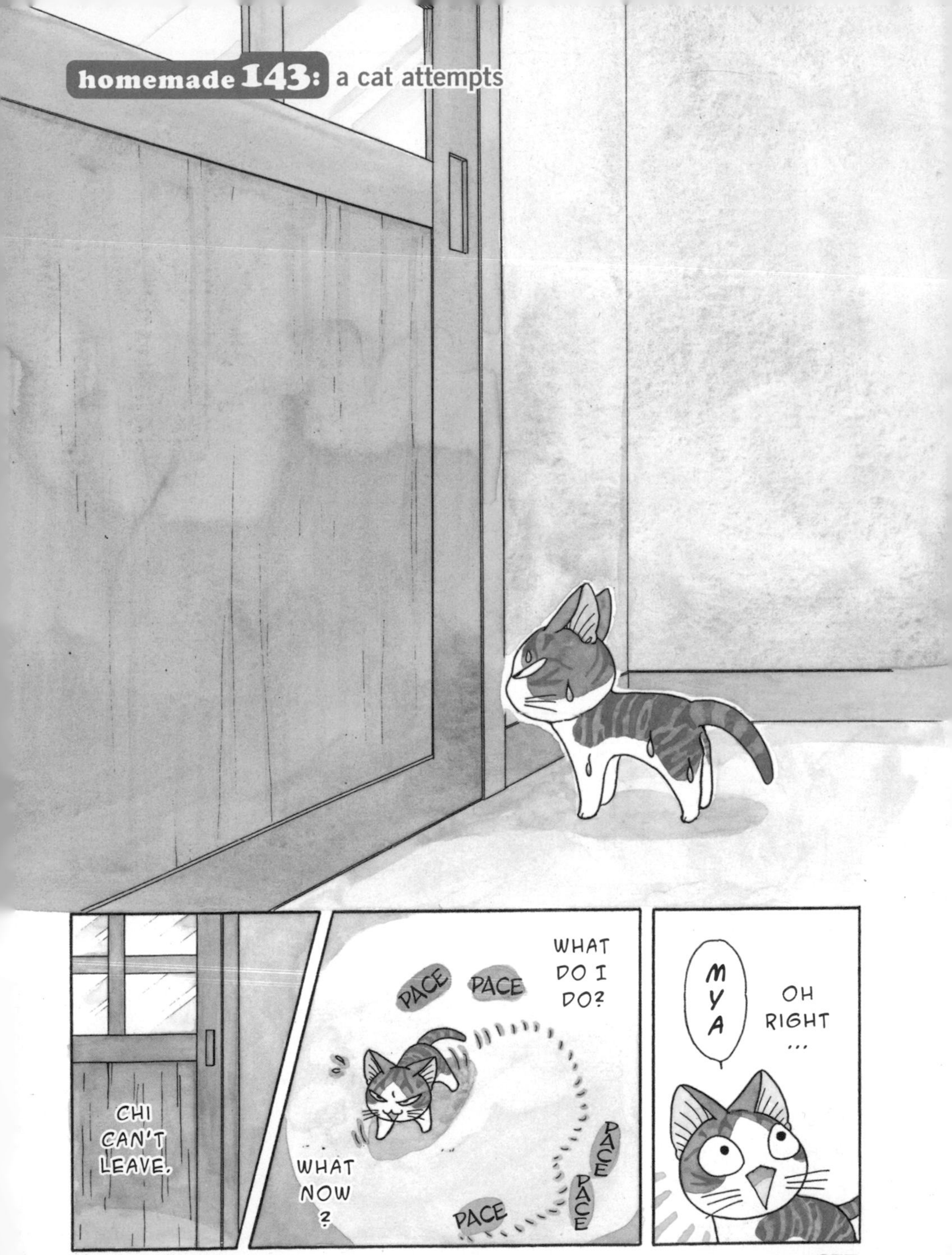
CHI CAN'T LEAVE.
PACE
PACE
WHAT DO I DO?
WHAT NOW?
PACE
PACE
PACE
MYA
OH RIGHT...

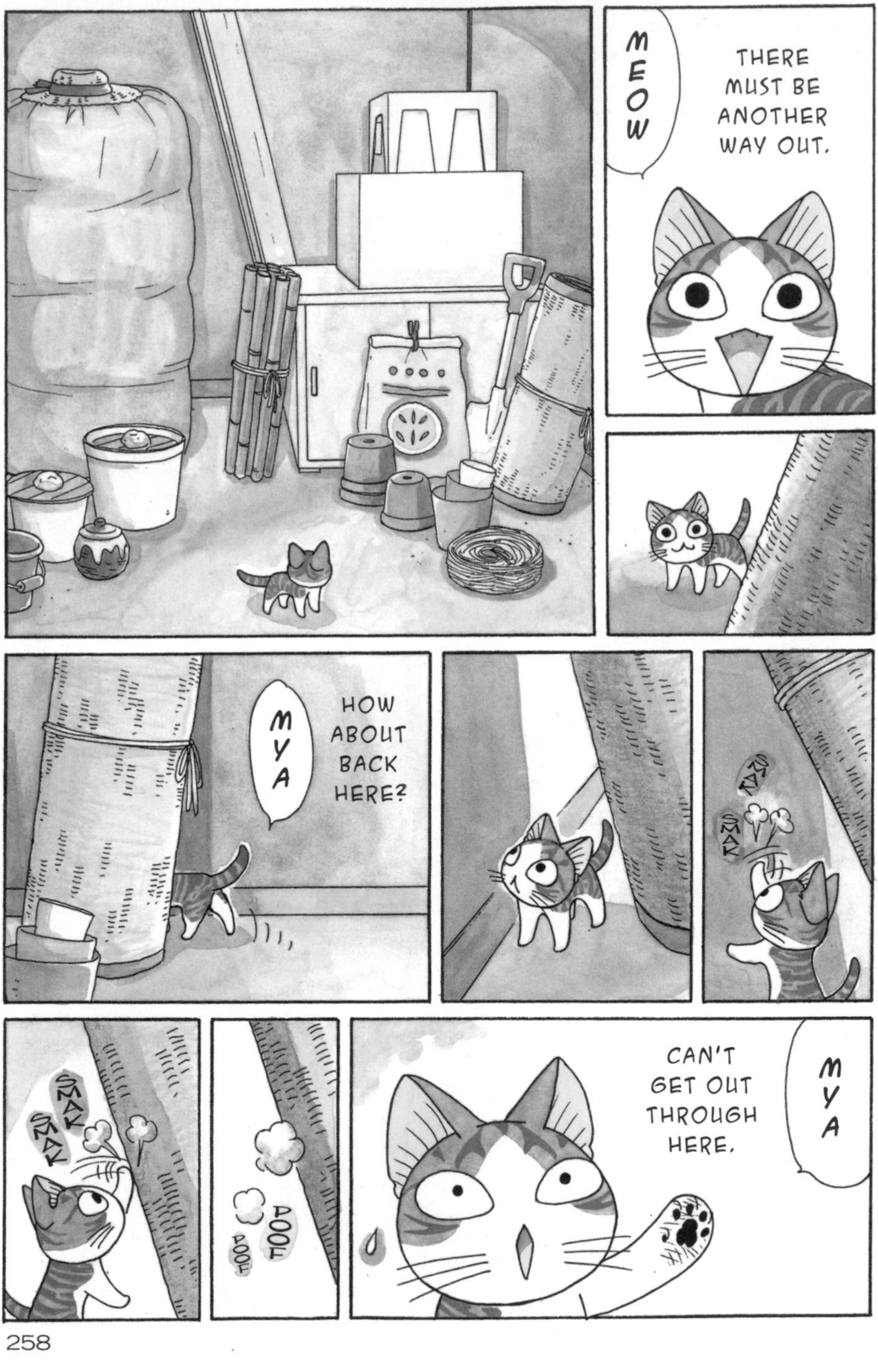
MEOW
THERE MUST BE ANOTHER WAY OUT.
MYA
HOW ABOUT BACK HERE?
SMAK
SMAK
SMAK
SMAK
POOF
POOF
CAN'T GET OUT THROUGH HERE.
MYA

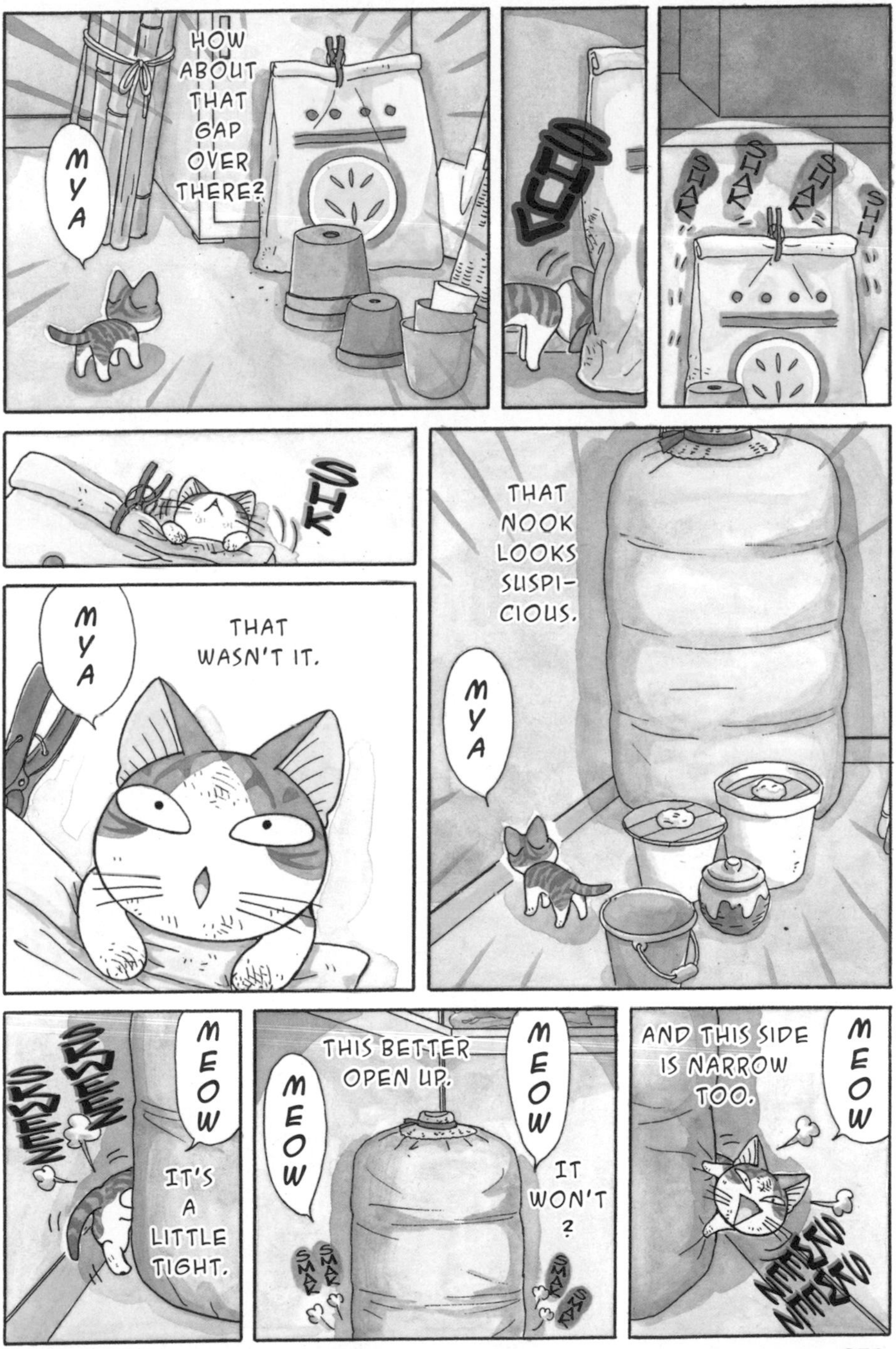
HOW ABOUT THAT GAP OVER THERE?
MYA
SHUF
SHAK SHAK SHAK SHH
SHK
MYA
THAT WASN'T IT.
THAT NOOK LOOKS SUSPI-CIOUS.
MYA
SWEEN SWEEN
MEOW
IT'S A LITTLE TIGHT.
THIS BETTER OPEN UP.
MEOW
MEOW
IT WON'T?
AND THIS SIDE IS NARROW TOO.
MEOW

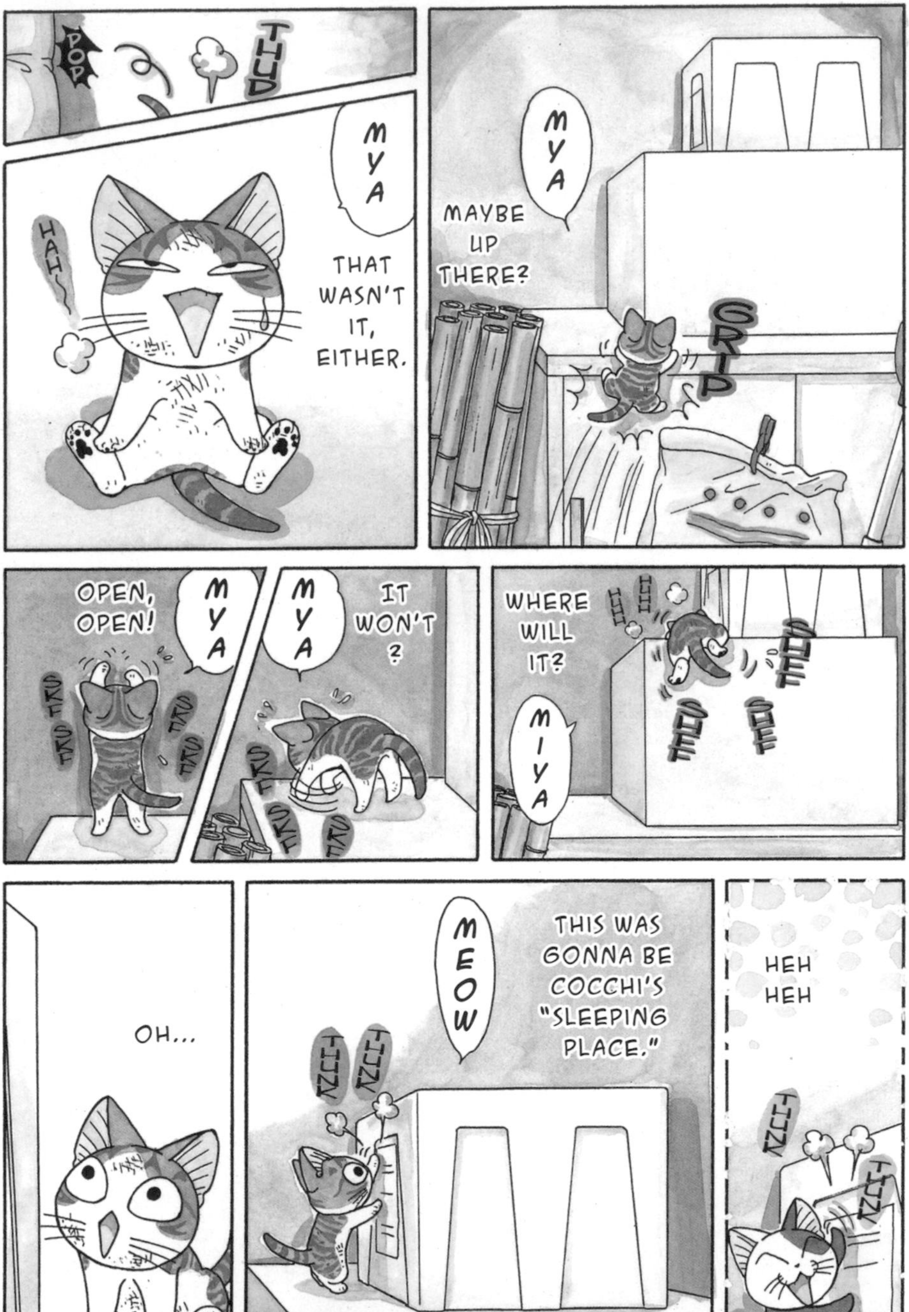
POP
THUD
HAH
MYA
THAT WASN'T IT, EITHER.
MYA
MAYBE UP THERE?
GRIP
OPEN, OPEN!
MYA
SKF SKF
SKF SKF
MYA
IT WON'T?
SKF SKF SKF
WHERE WILL IT?
MIYA
SHFF
SHFF
SHFF
OH...
MEOW
THIS WAS GONNA BE COCCHI'S "SLEEPING PLACE."
THUNK
THUNK
HEH HEH
THUNK
THUNK

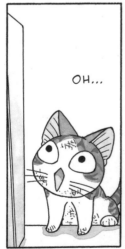

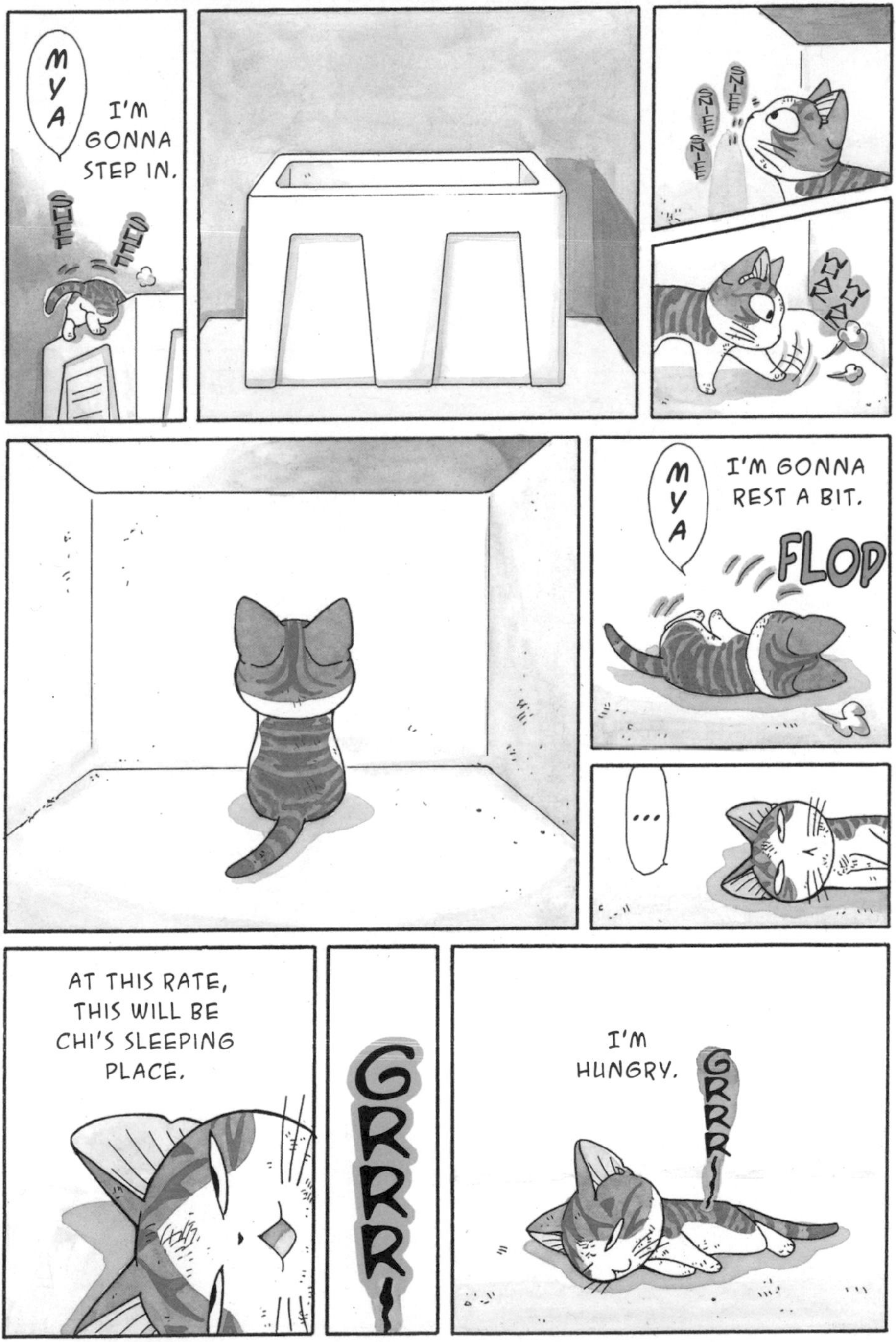
MYA
I'M GONNA STEP IN.
SHUFF
SHUFF
SNIFF
SNIFF
SNIFF
SNIFF
MYA
I'M GONNA REST A BIT.
FLOP
...
AT THIS RATE, THIS WILL BE CHI'S SLEEPING PLACE.
GRRRI
I'M HUNGRY.
GRRRI

MIULK
...

I SHOULD
HAVE
DRANK IT
ALL.

GRRRR

BLOCKS

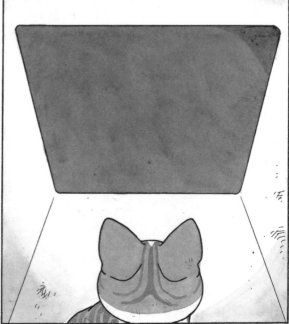

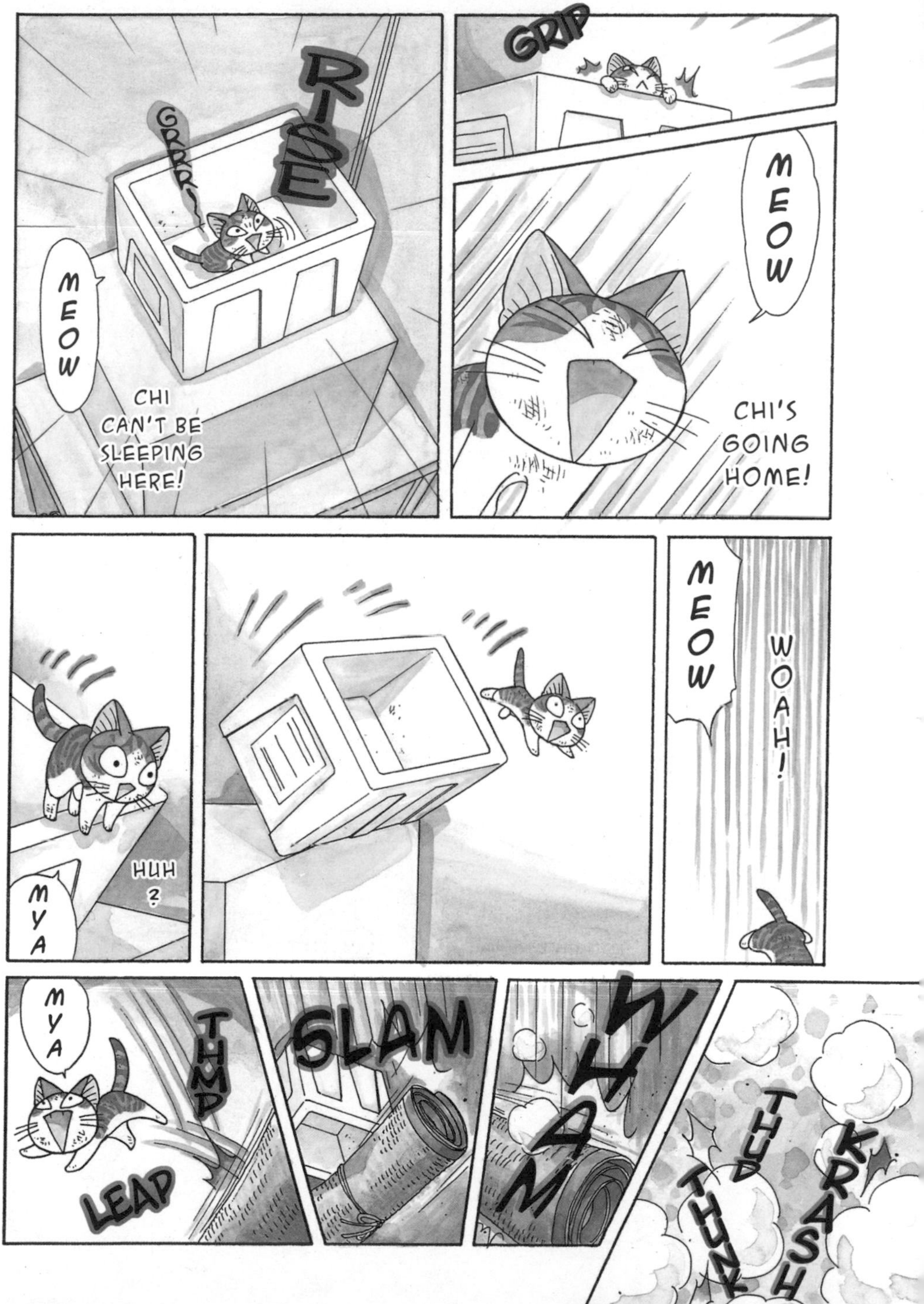
RISE
GRRRR
MEOW
CHI CAN'T BE SLEEPING HERE!
GRIP
MEOW
CHI'S GOING HOME!
MYA
HUH?
MEOW
WOAH!
MYA
THMP
LEAP
SLAM
WHAM
THUD
THUNK
KRASH

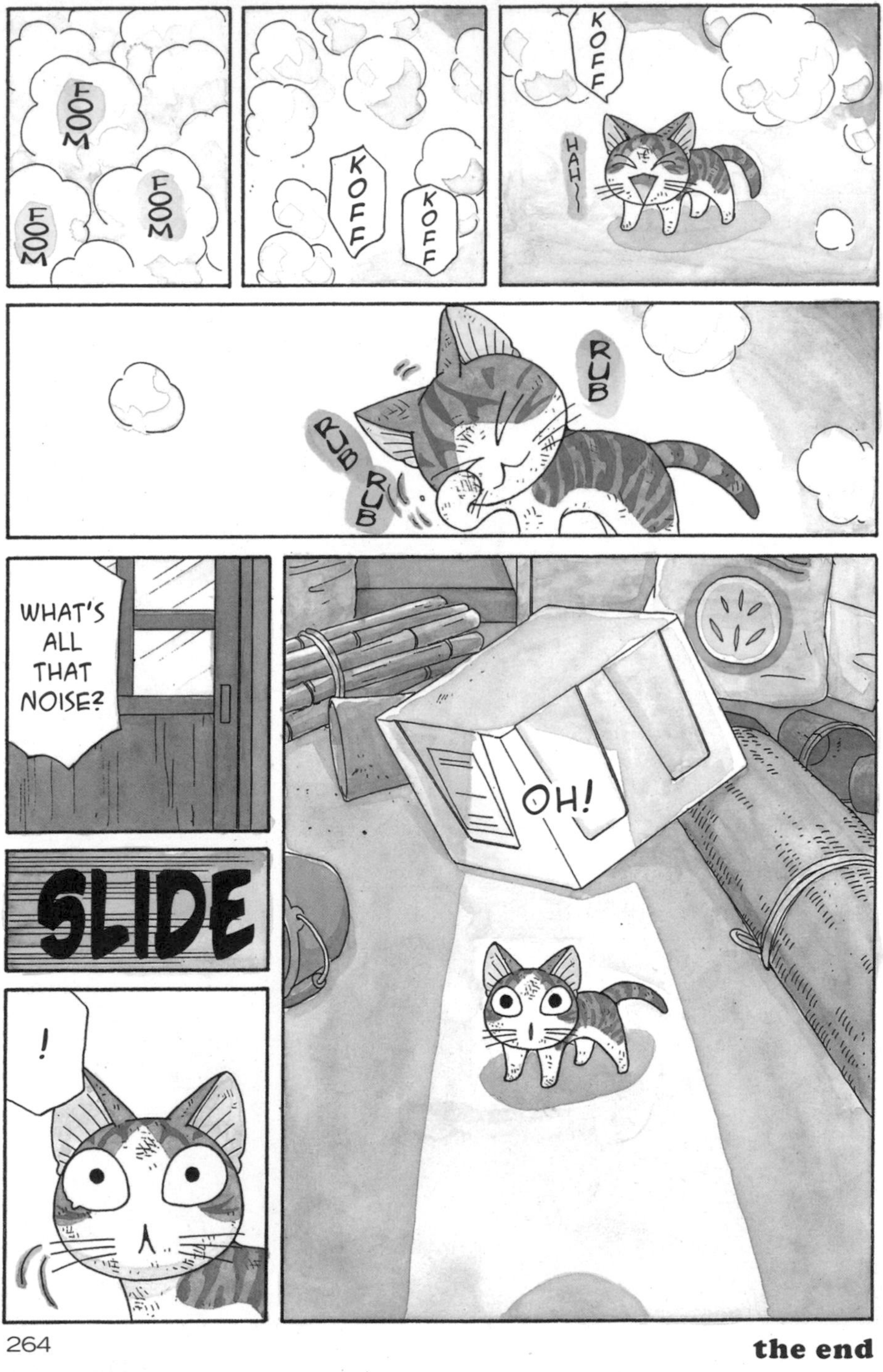
FOOM
FOOM
FOOM
KOFF
KOFF
KOFF
HAH~
RUB
RUB
RUB
WHAT'S ALL THAT NOISE?
SLIDE
!
OH!



the end

## homemade 144: a cat concerns

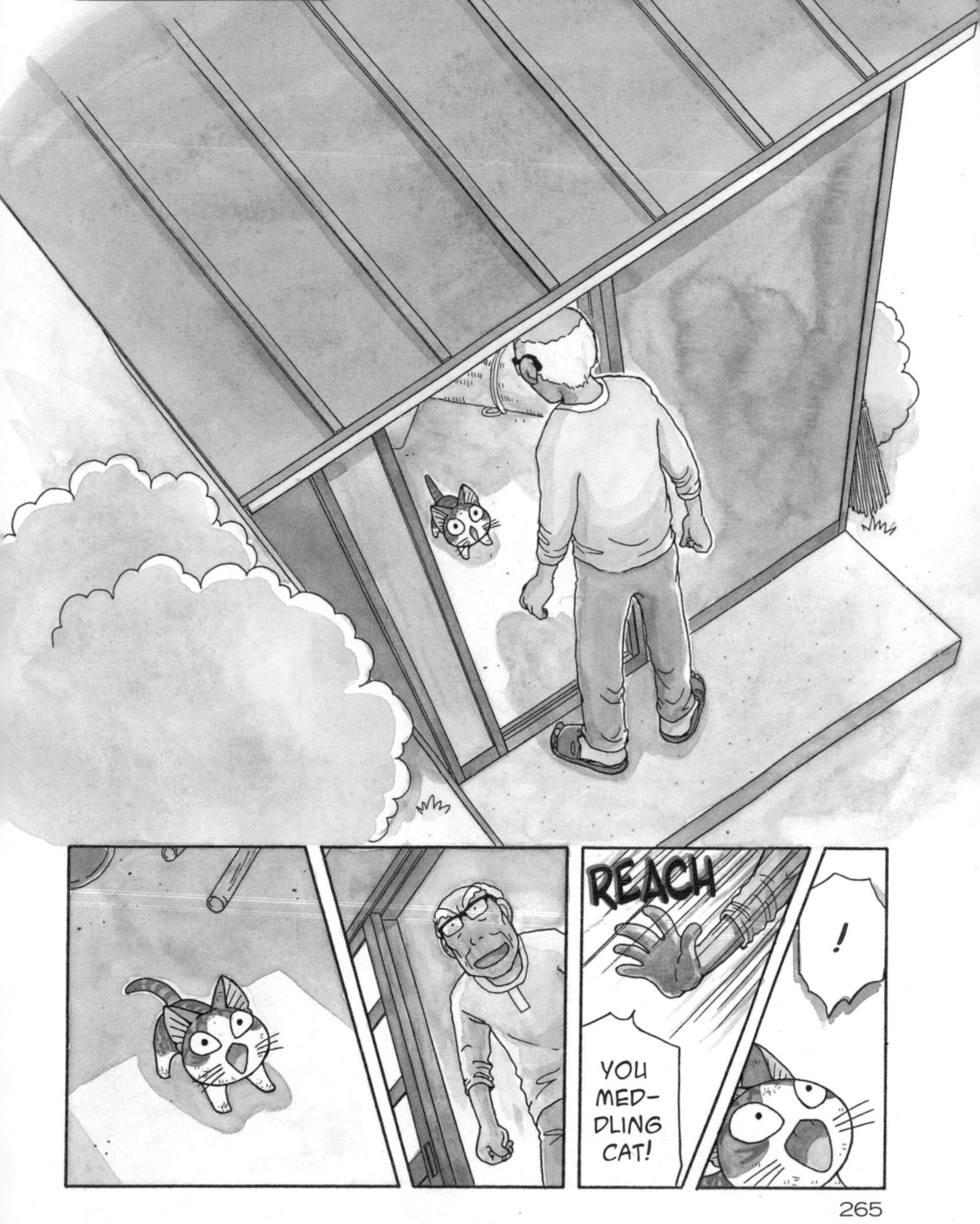

REACH
YOU MED-DLING CAT!
!

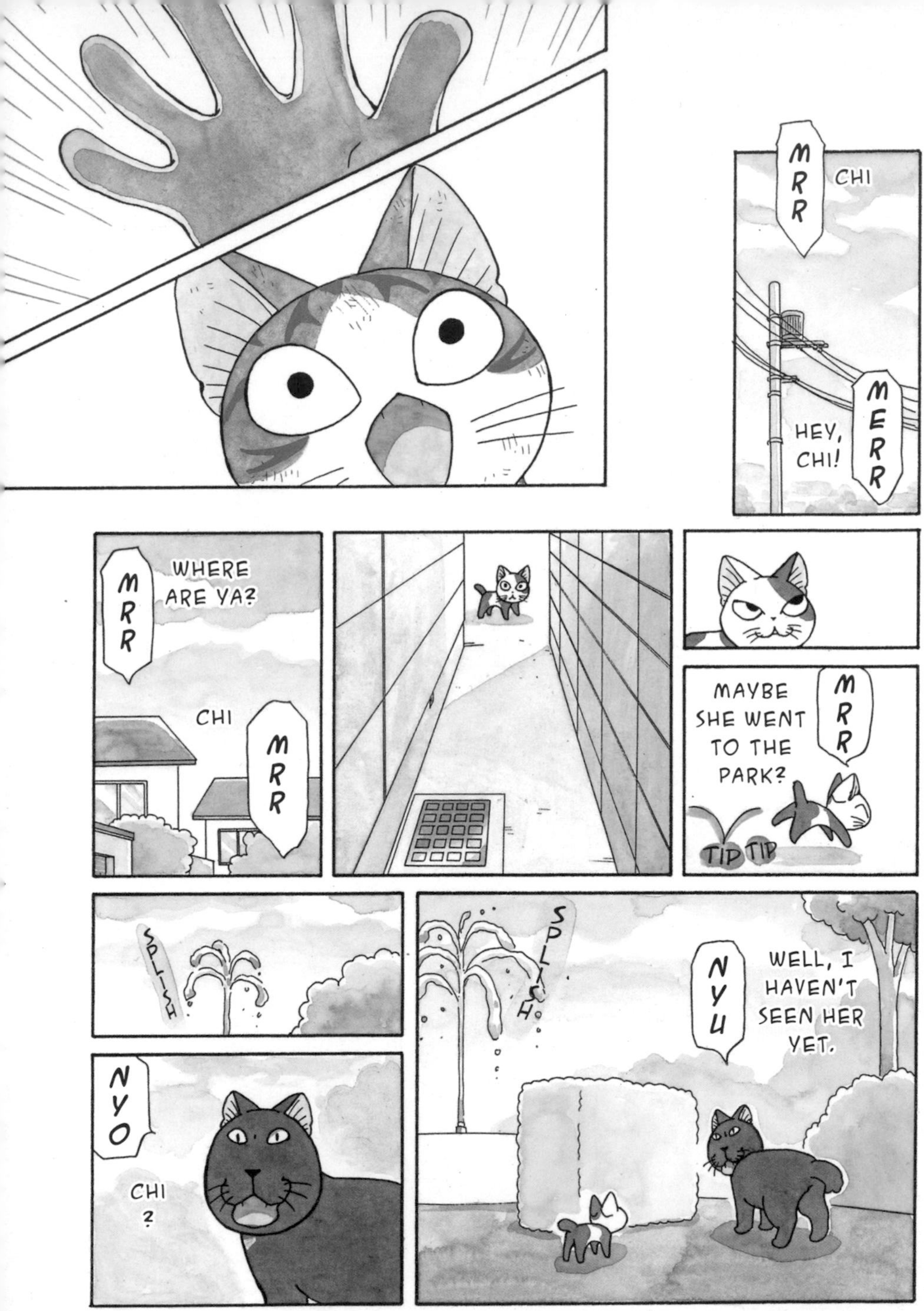
MRR
CHI
MERR
HEY, CHI!
MRR
WHERE ARE YA?
CHI
MRR
MAYBE SHE WENT TO THE PARK?
MRR
TIP TIP
SPLISH
NYO
CHI?
SPLISH
NYU
WELL, I HAVEN'T SEEN HER YET.

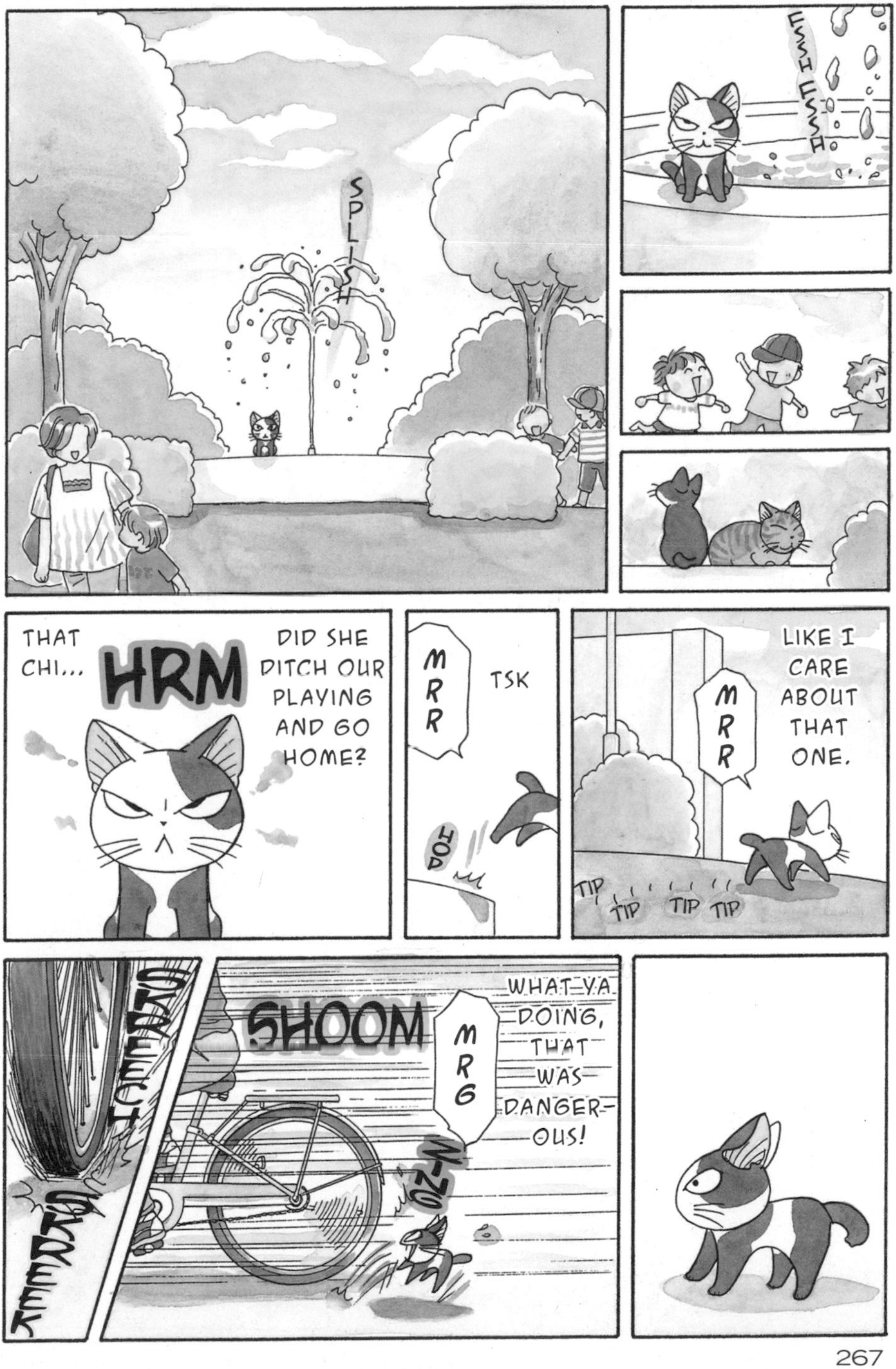
SPLISH
FSSH FSSH
THAT CHI...
HRM
DID SHE DITCH OUR PLAYING AND GO HOME?
MRR
TSK
HOP
MRR
LIKE I CARE ABOUT THAT ONE.
TIP TIP TIP TIP
SKREECH
SKREEEK
SHOOM
MRG
ZING
WHAT-YA DOING, THAT WAS DANGER-OUS!

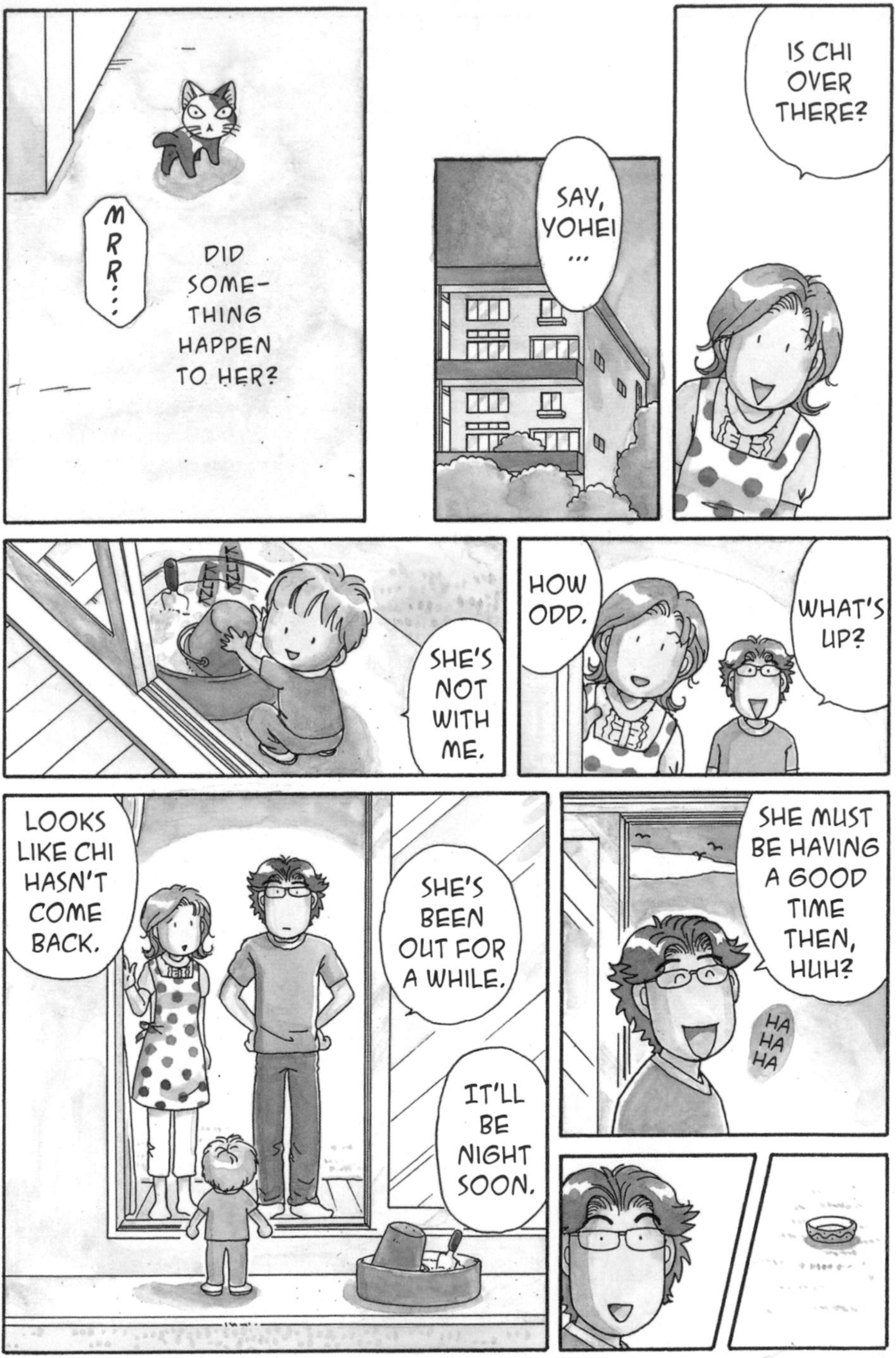
MRR...
DID SOMETHING HAPPEN TO HER?
SAY, YOHEI...
IS CHI OVER THERE?
KLUNK
KLUNK
SHE'S NOT WITH ME.
HOW ODD.
WHAT'S UP?
LOOKS LIKE CHI HASN'T COME BACK.
SHE'S BEEN OUT FOR A WHILE.
IT'LL BE NIGHT SOON.
SHE MUST BE HAVING A GOOD TIME THEN, HUH?
HA HA HA

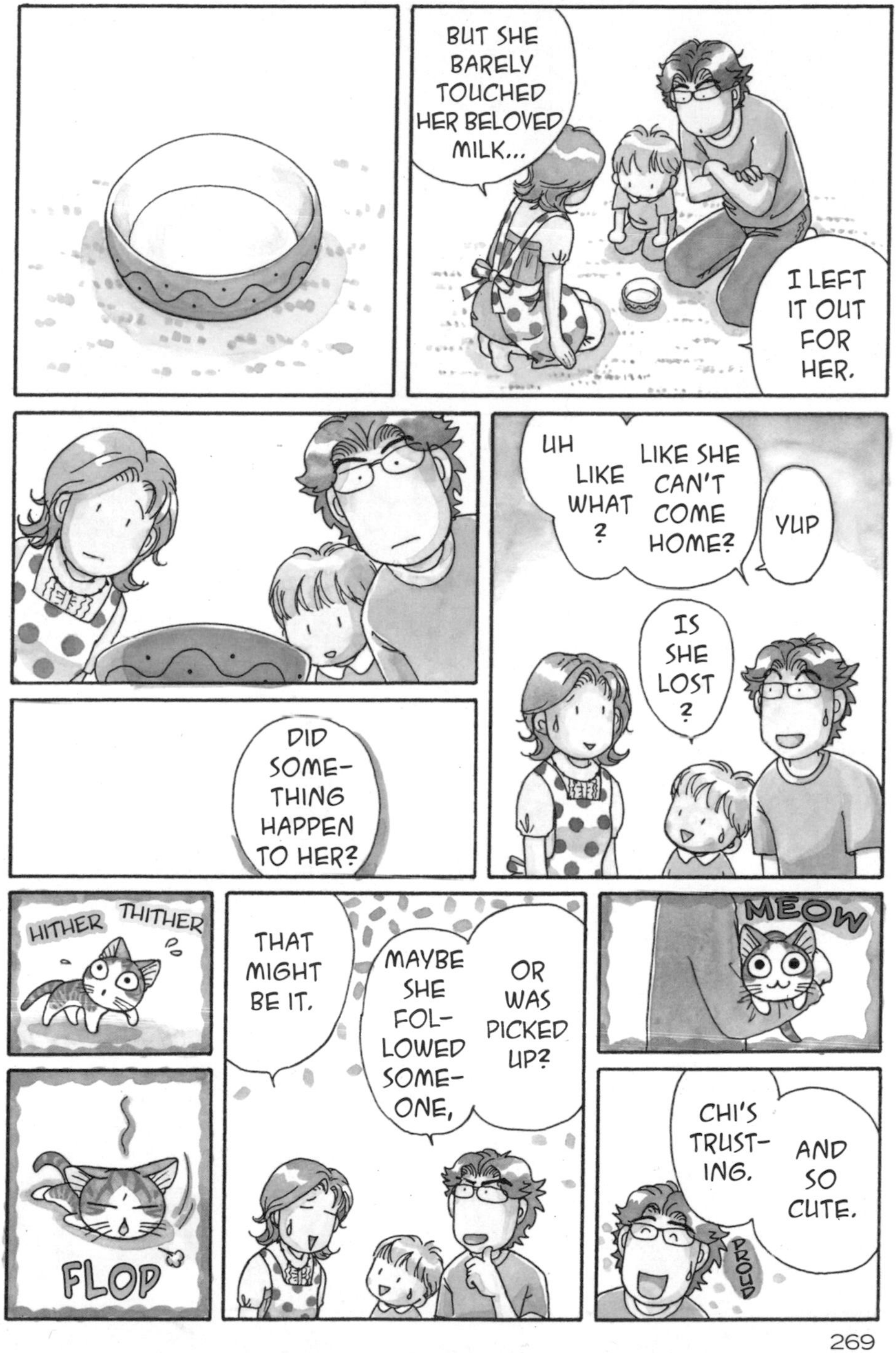

BUT SHE BARELY TOUCHED HER BELOVED MILK...
I LEFT IT OUT FOR HER.
UH LIKE WHAT?
LIKE SHE CAN'T COME HOME?
YUP
DID SOME-THING HAPPEN TO HER?
IS SHE LOST?
HITHER THITHER
FLOP
THAT MIGHT BE IT.
MAYBE SHE FOL-LOWED SOME-ONE,
OR WAS PICKED UP?
MEOW
CHI'S TRUST-ING.
AND SO CUTE.
PROUD

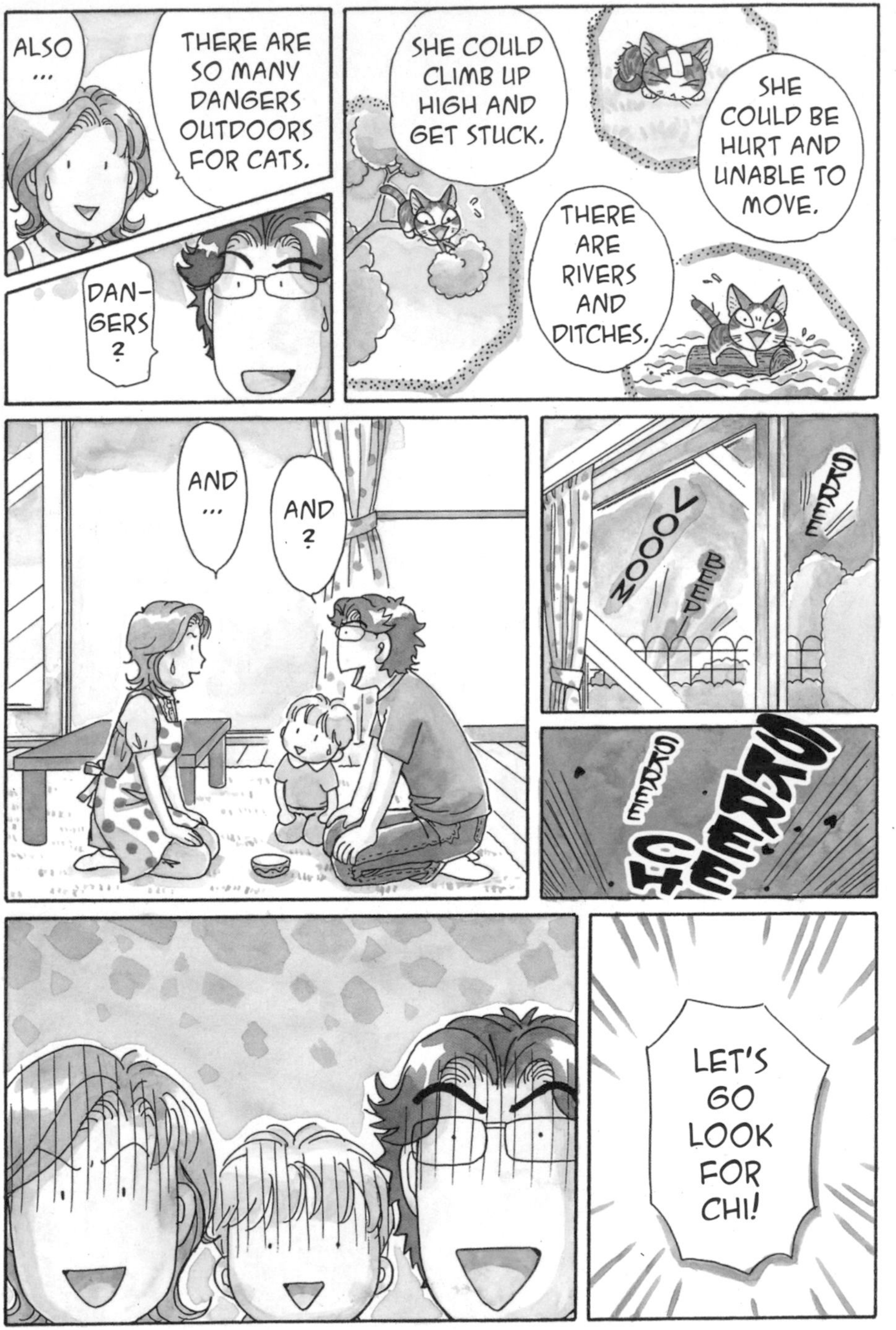
ALSO ...
THERE ARE SO MANY DANGERS OUTDOORS FOR CATS.
DAN-GERS?
SHE COULD CLIMB UP HIGH AND GET STUCK.
SHE COULD BE HURT AND UNABLE TO MOVE.
THERE ARE RIVERS AND DITCHES.
AND ...
AND?
VOOOOM
BEEP!
SKREE
SKREE
SKREEEECH
LET'S GO LOOK FOR CHI!

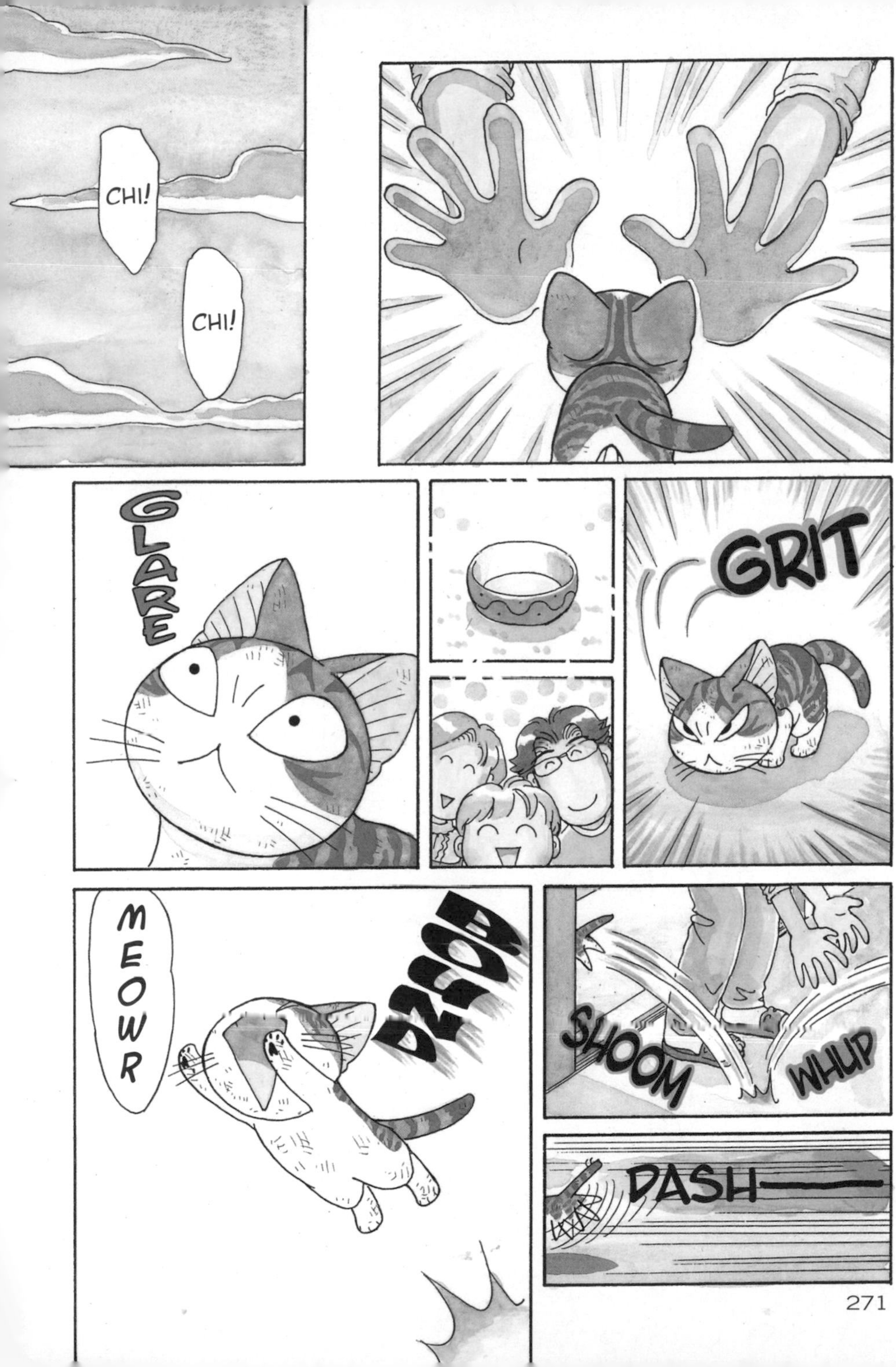

CHI!
CHI!
GLARE
GRIT
MEOWR
BOUND
SHOOM
WHUP
DASH

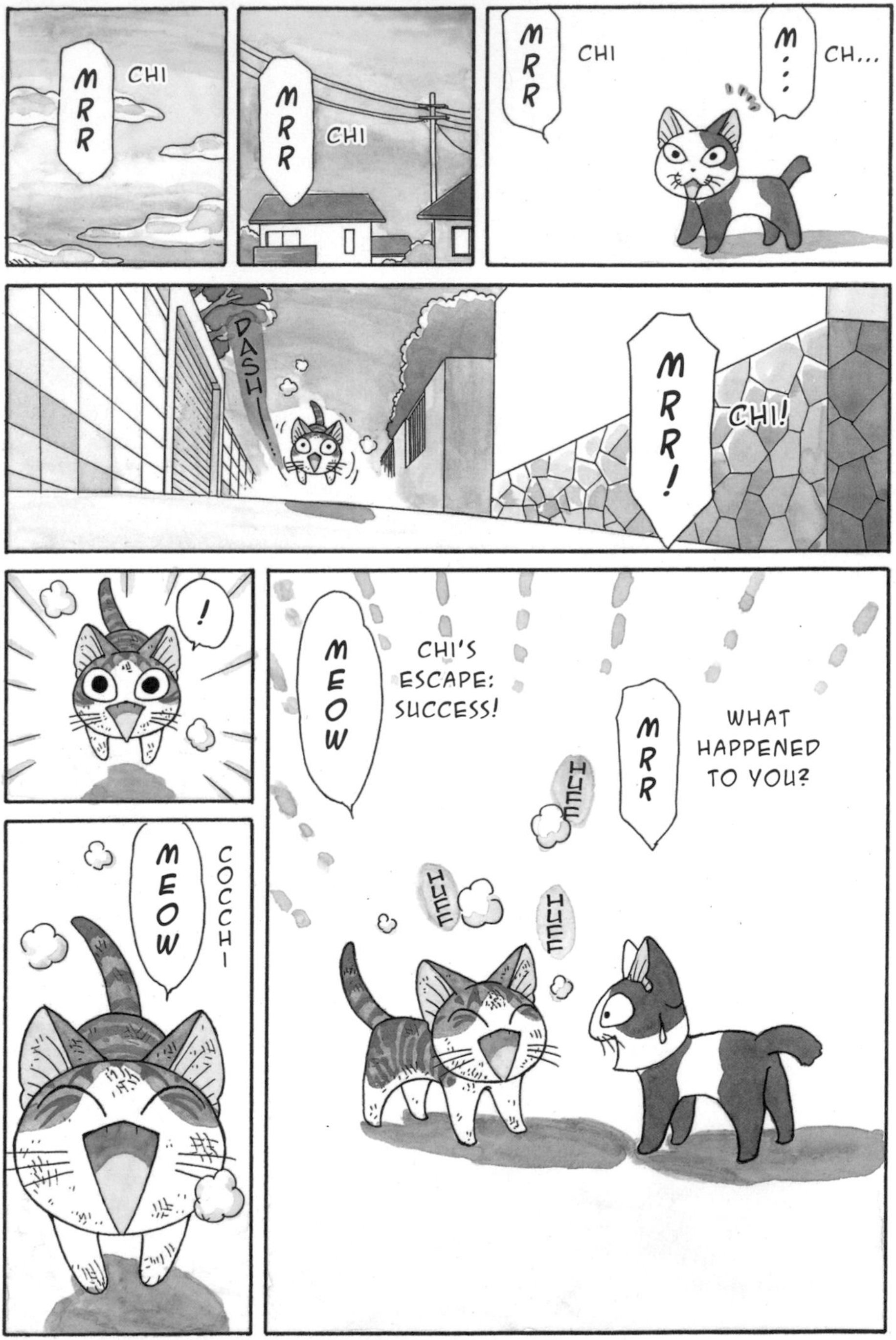
MRR
CHI
MRR
CHI
MRR
CHI
M...
CH...
DASH
MRR!
CHI!
!
MEOW
COCCHI
MEOW
CHI'S ESCAPE: SUCCESS!
HUFF
MRR
WHAT HAPPENED TO YOU?
HUFF
HUFF

the end

## homemade 145: a cat reconnects

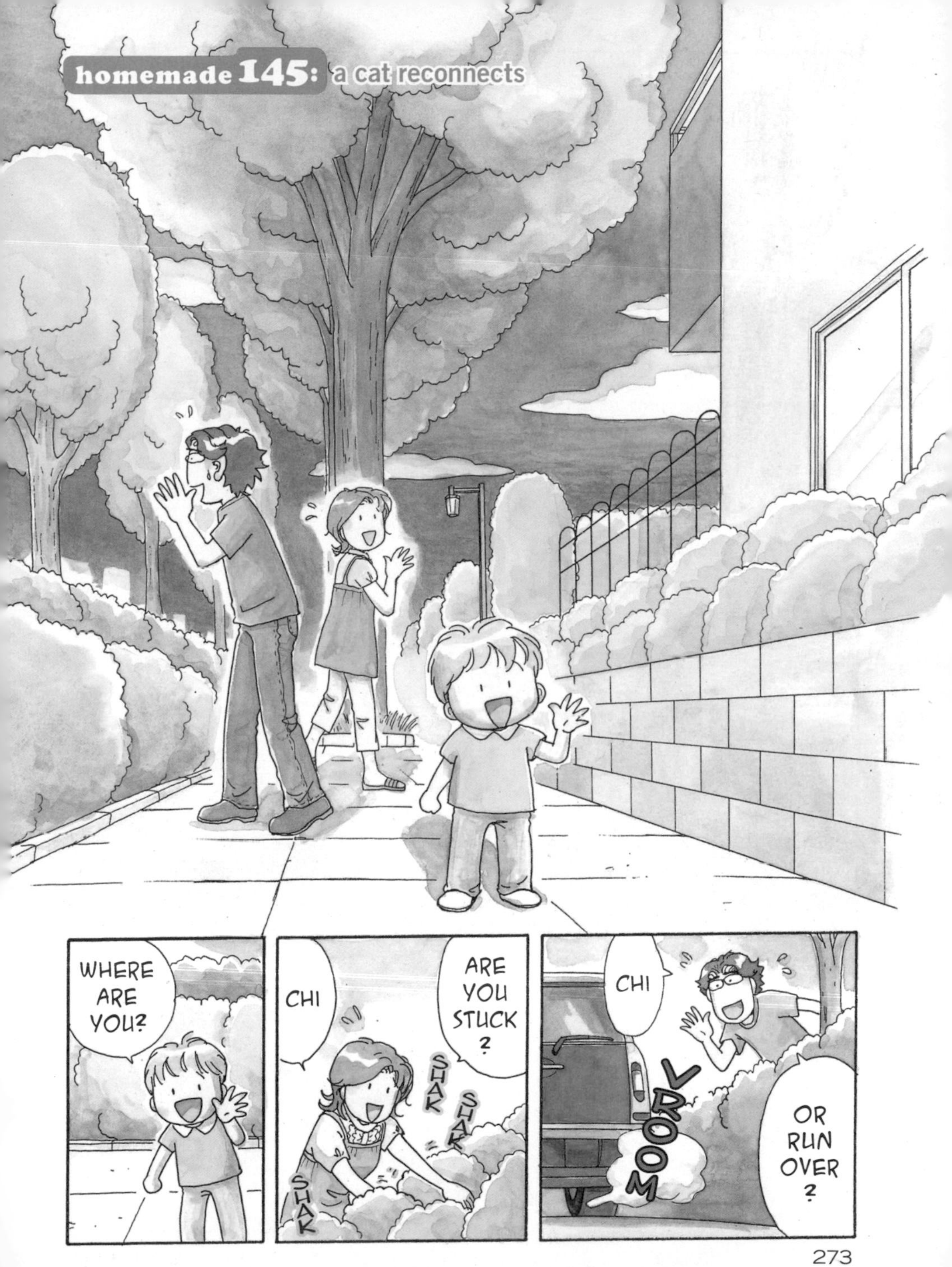
WHERE ARE YOU?
CHI
ARE YOU STUCK?
SHAK
SHAK
SHAK
CHI
VROOOOM
OR RUN OVER?

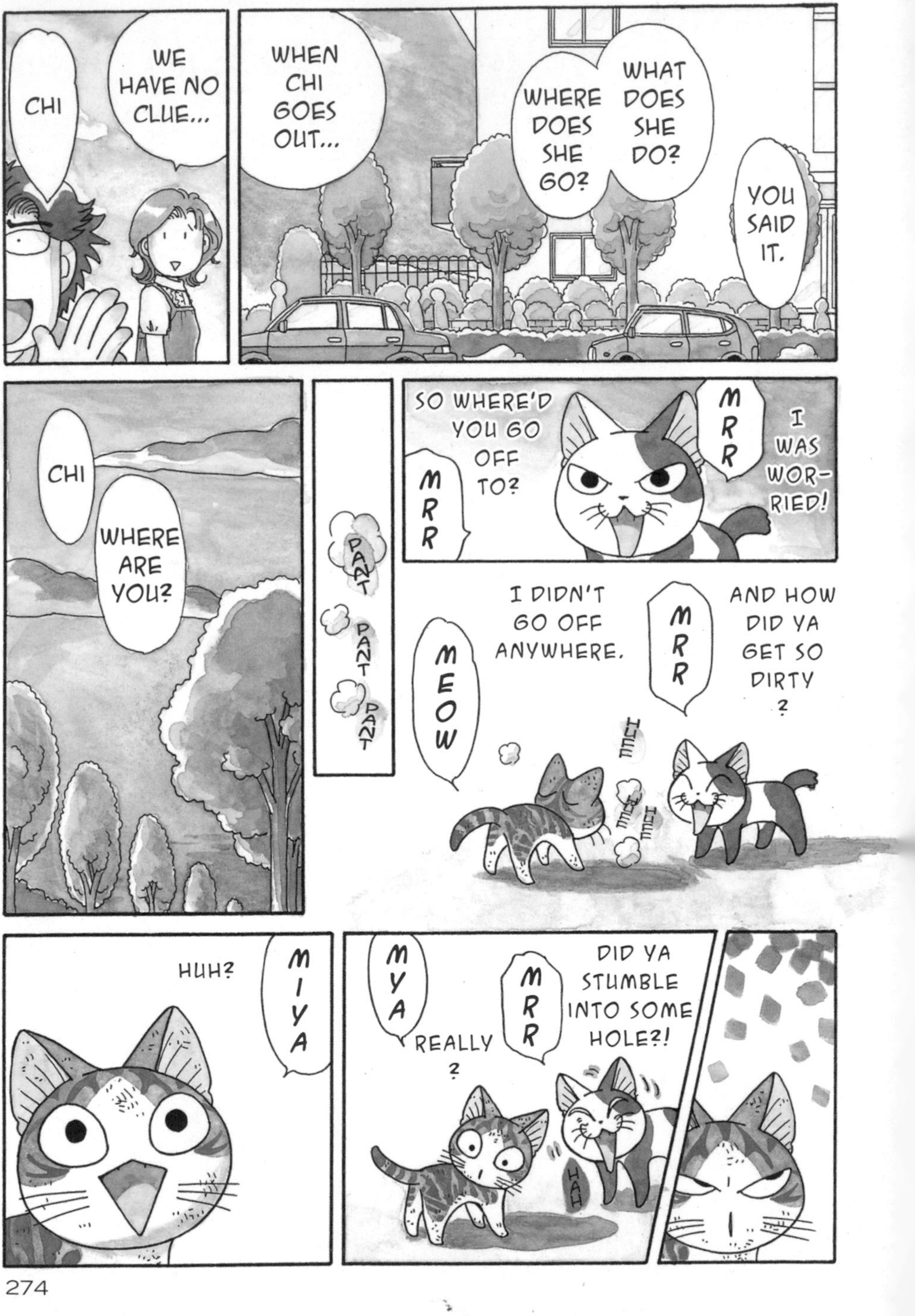
CHI
WE HAVE NO CLUE...
WHEN CHI GOES OUT...
WHERE DOES SHE GO?
WHAT DOES SHE DO?
YOU SAID IT.
CHI
WHERE ARE YOU?
PANT
PANT
PANT
SO WHERE'D YOU GO OFF TO?
MRR
MRR
I WAS WOR-RIED!
MEOW
I DIDN'T GO OFF ANYWHERE.
MRR
AND HOW DID YA GET SO DIRTY?
HUFF
HUFF
HUFF
HUH?
MIYA
MYA
REALLY?
MRR
DID YA STUMBLE INTO SOME HOLE?!
HAH

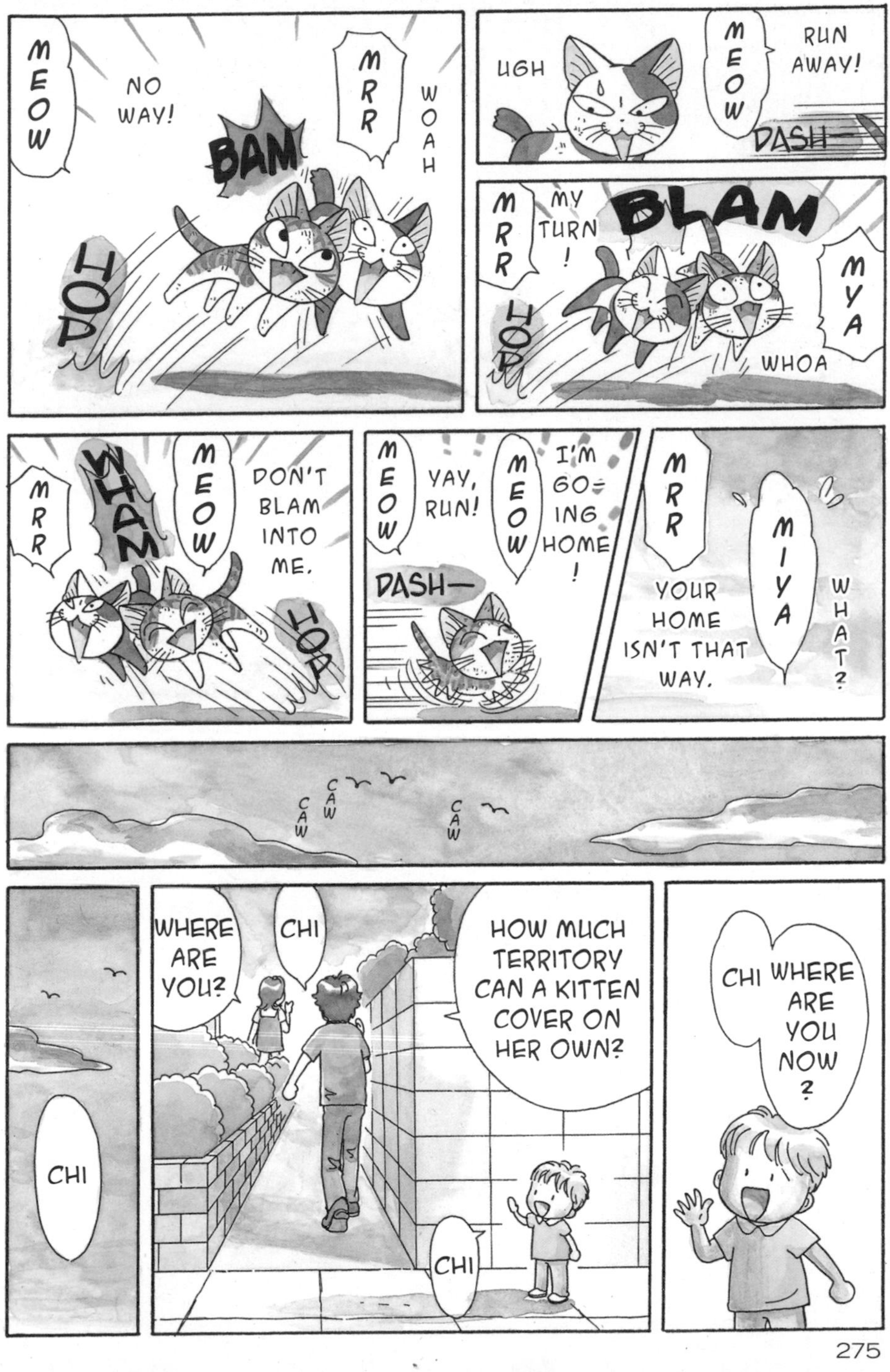
MEOW
NO WAY!
BAM
MRR
WOAH
HOP
UGH
MEOW
RUN AWAY!
DASH—
MRR
MY TURN!
BLAM
MYA
WHOA
HOP
MRR
WHAM
MEOW
DON'T BLAM INTO ME.
HOP
MEOW
YAY, RUN!
MEOW
I'M GO-ING HOME!
DASH—
MRR
MIYA
YOUR HOME ISN'T THAT WAY.
WHAT?
CAW CAW
CAW
CHI
WHERE ARE YOU?
CHI
HOW MUCH TERRITORY CAN A KITTEN COVER ON HER OWN?
CHI
CHI WHERE ARE YOU NOW?

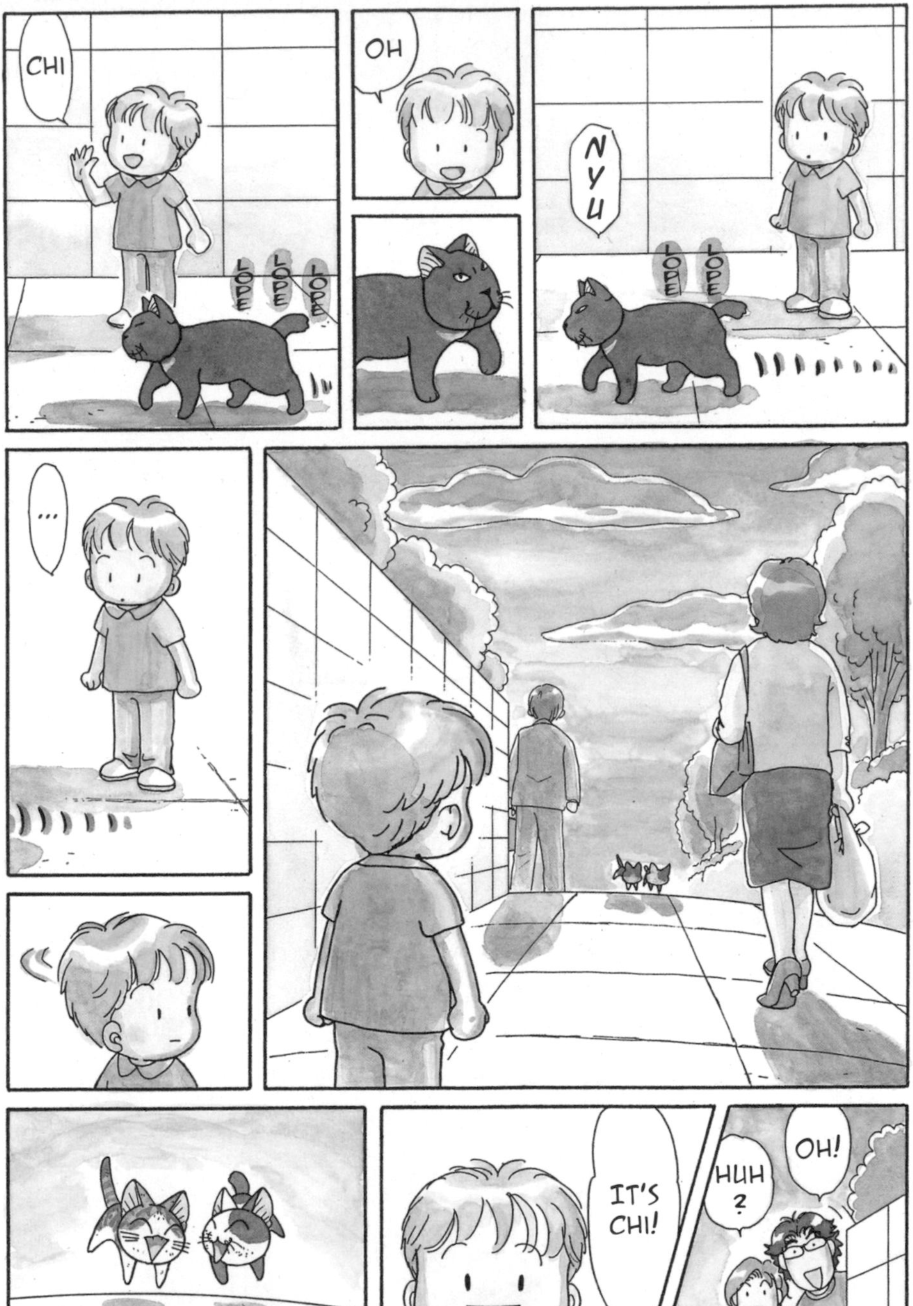
CHI
OH
LOPE LOPE LOPE
NYU
LOPE LOPE
...
IT'S CHI!
HUH?
OH!

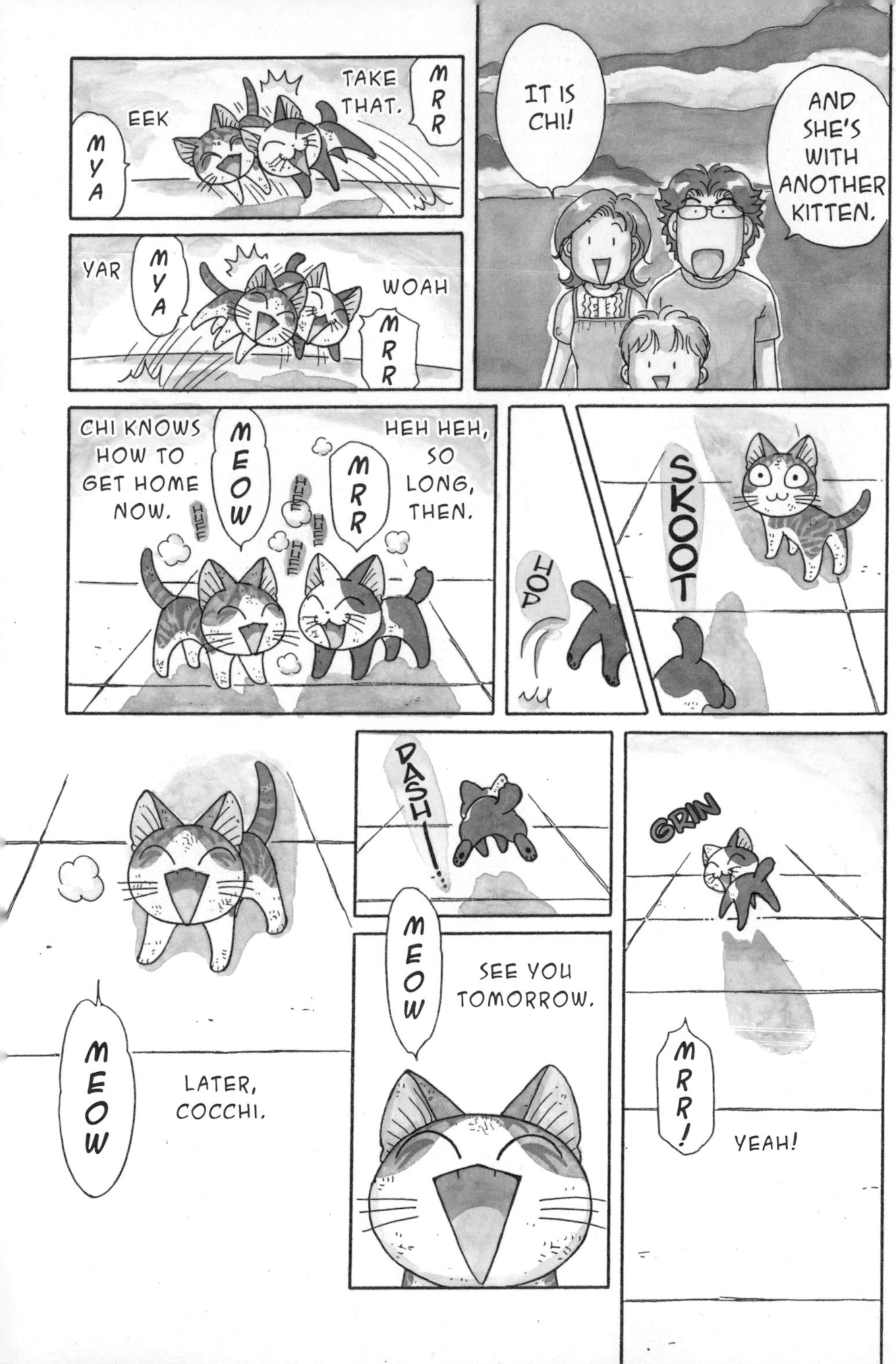
EEK
MYA
TAKE THAT.
MRR
YAR
MYA
WOAH
MRR
IT IS CHI!
AND SHE'S WITH ANOTHER KITTEN.
CHI KNOWS HOW TO GET HOME NOW.
MEOW
HUFF
HUFF
HUFF
HUFF
MRR
HEH HEH, SO LONG, THEN.
HOP
SKOOT
MEOW
LATER, COCCHI.
DASH!
MEOW
SEE YOU TOMORROW.
GRIN
MRR!
YEAH!

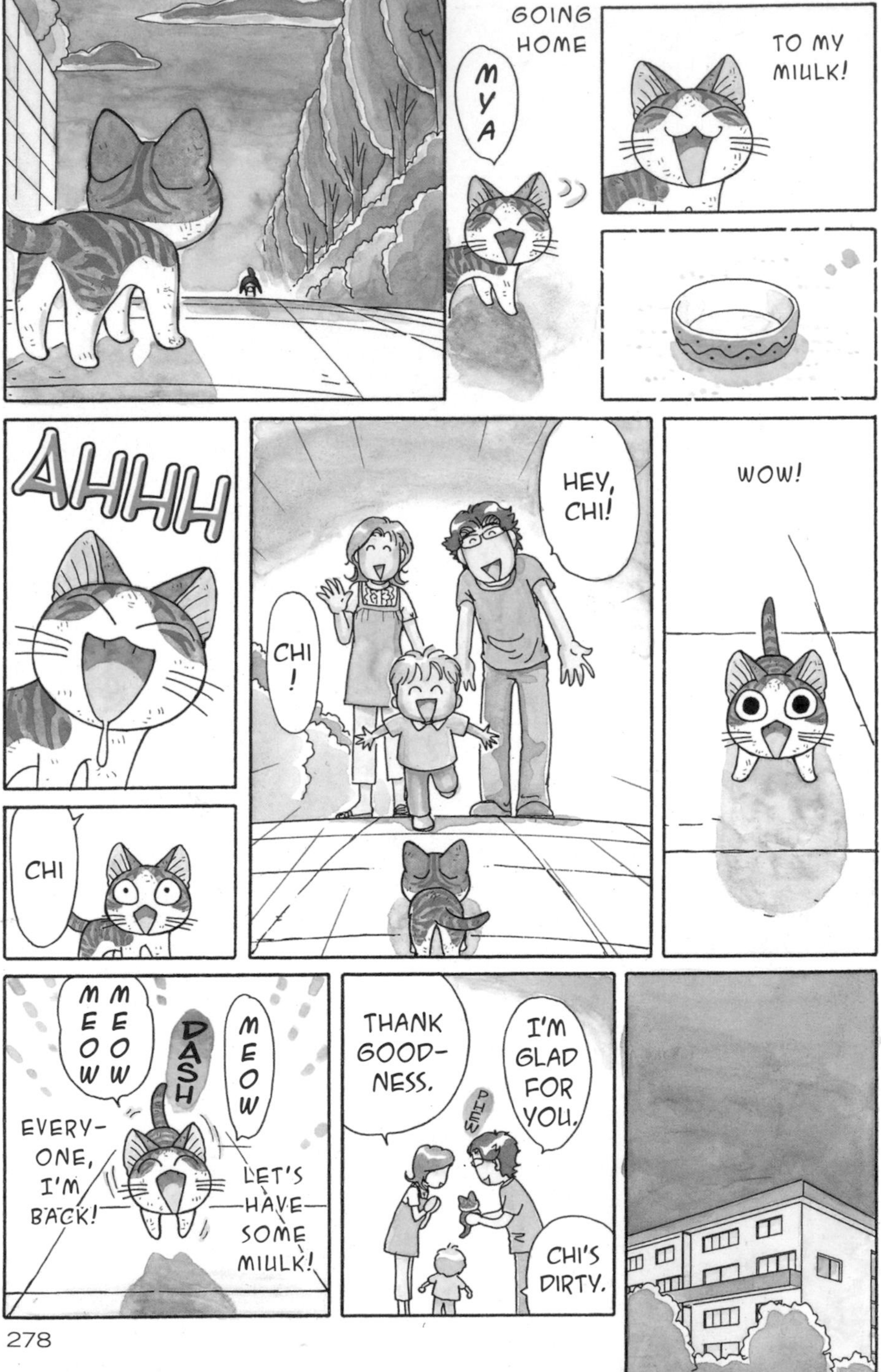
MYA
GOING HOME
TO MY MIULK!
AHHH
CHI
HEY, CHI!
CHI!
WOW!
MEOW MEOW
DASH
MEOW
EVERY-ONE, I'M BACK!
LET'S HAVE SOME MIULK!
THANK GOOD-NESS.
PHEW
I'M GLAD FOR YOU.
CHI'S DIRTY.

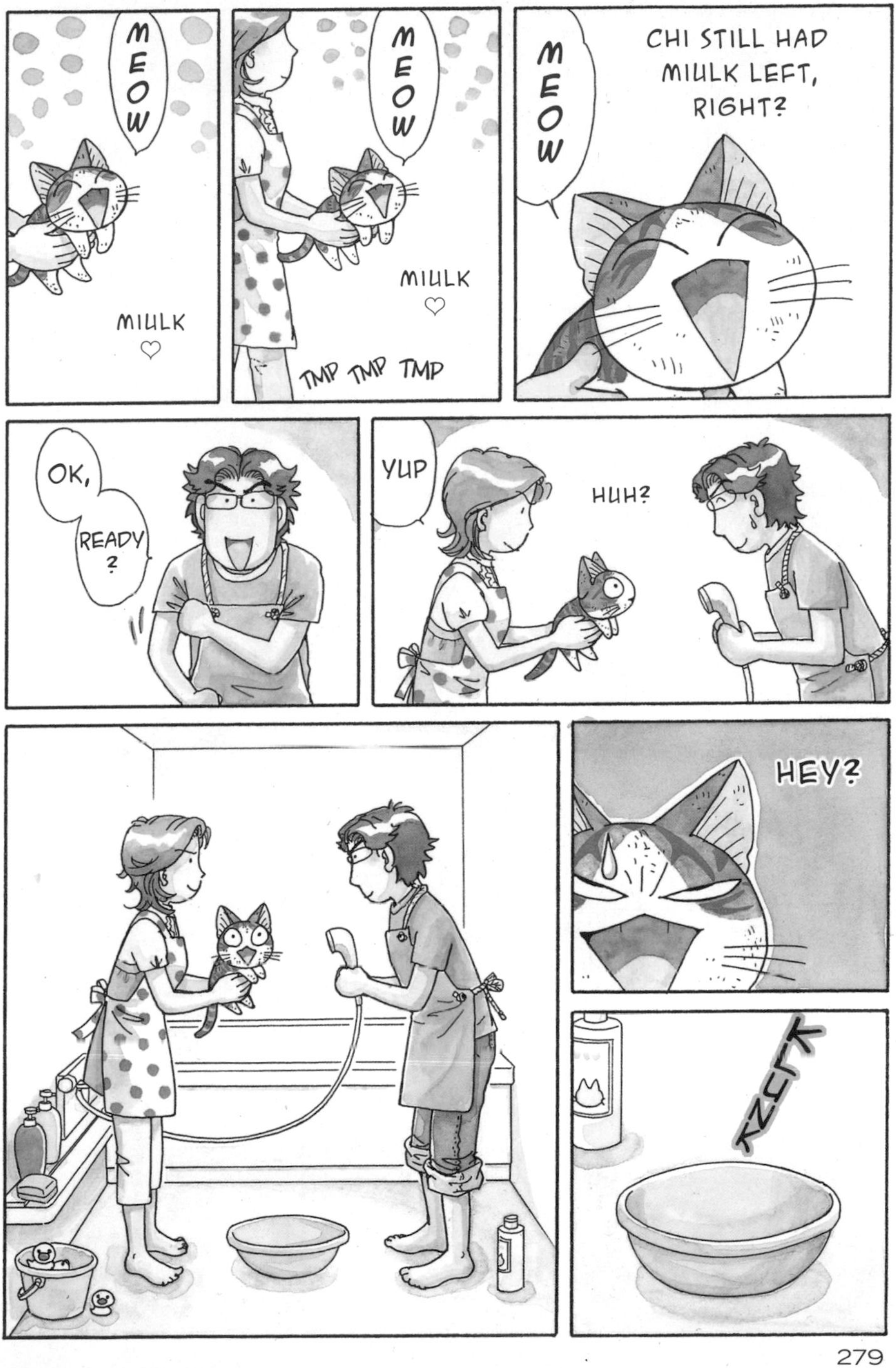
MEOW
MIULK ♡
MEOW
MIULK ♡
TMP TMP TMP
MEOW
CHI STILL HAD MIULK LEFT, RIGHT?
OK,
READY?
YUP
HUH?
HEY?

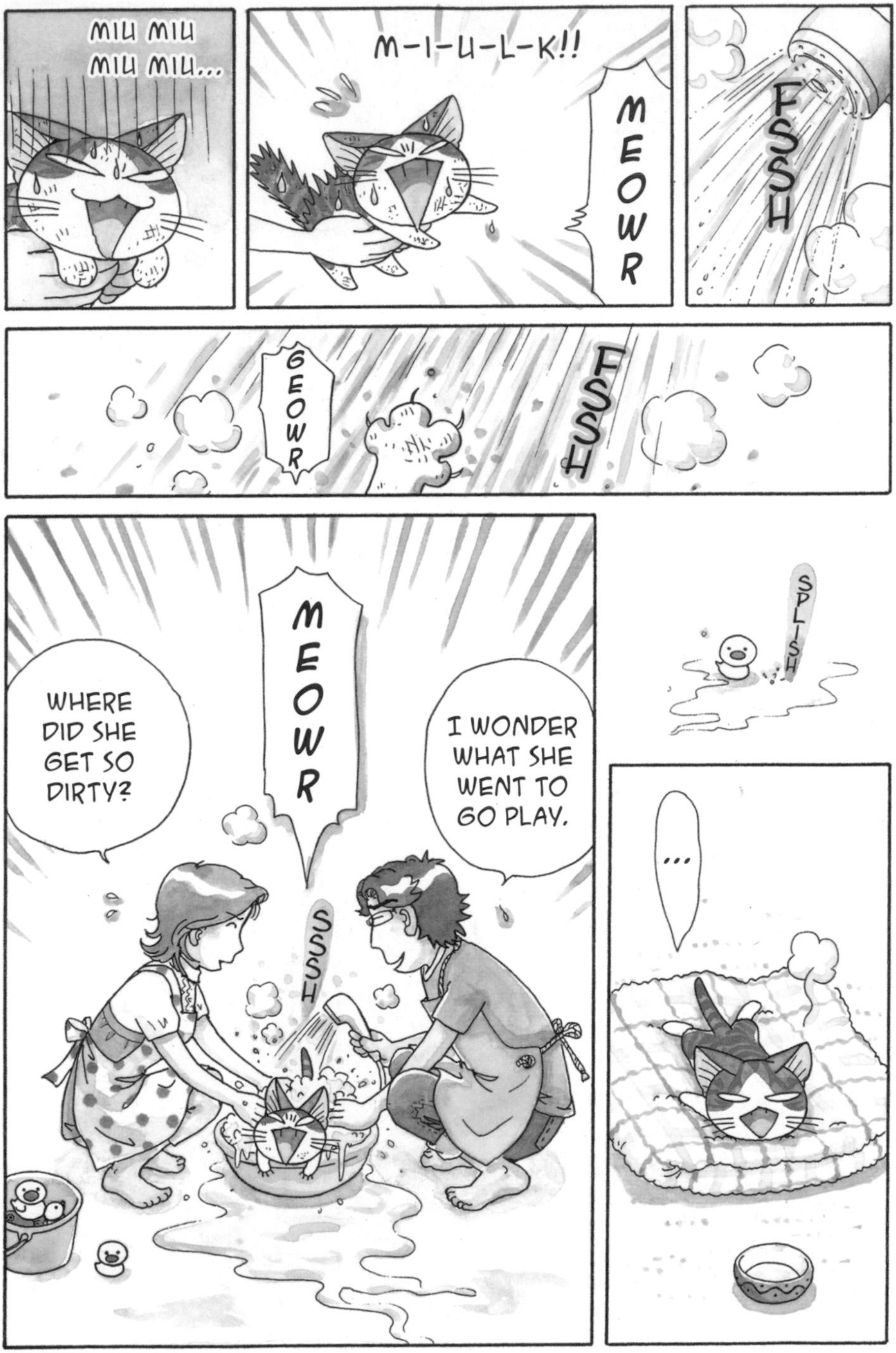
MIU MIU
MIU MIU...
M-I-U-L-K!!
MEOWR
FSSH
GEOWR
FSSH
MEOWR
WHERE DID SHE GET SO DIRTY?
I WONDER WHAT SHE WENT TO GO PLAY.
SSSH
SPLISH
...



**the end**

# homemade 146: a cat sheds tears

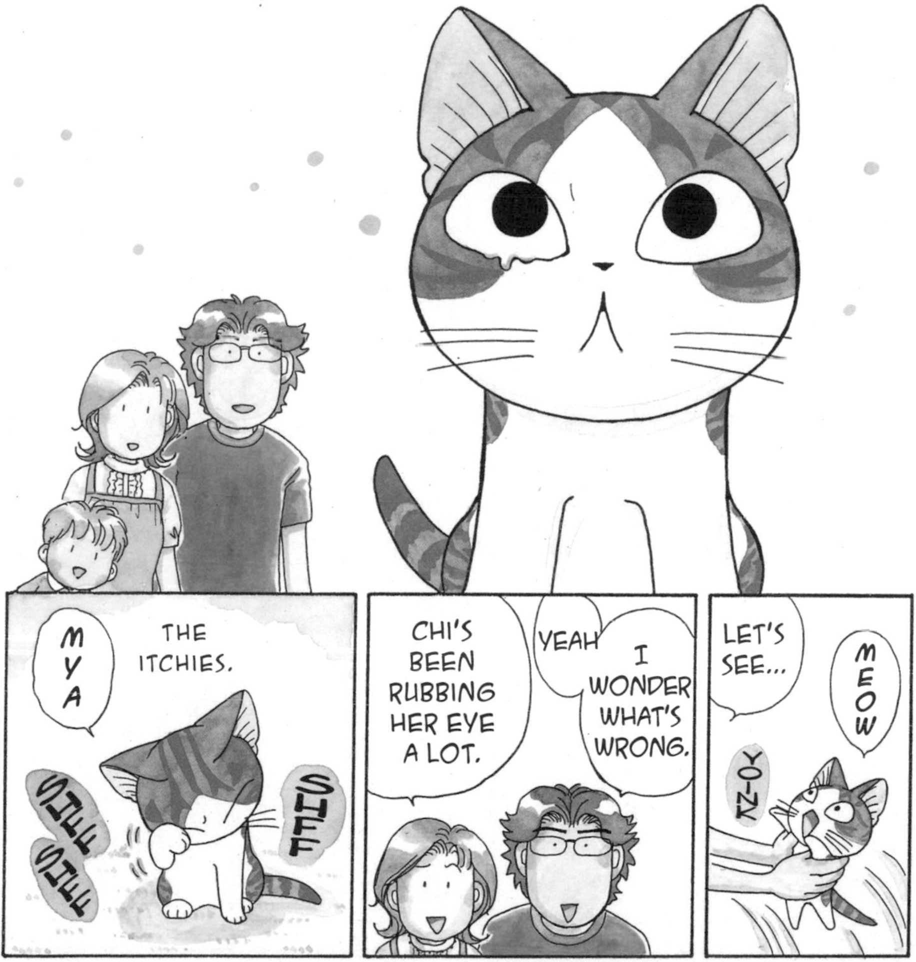
MYA
THE ITCHIES.
SHFF SHFF
SHFF
CHI'S BEEN RUBBING HER EYE A LOT.
YEAH
I WONDER WHAT'S WRONG.
LET'S SEE...
MEOW
YOINK

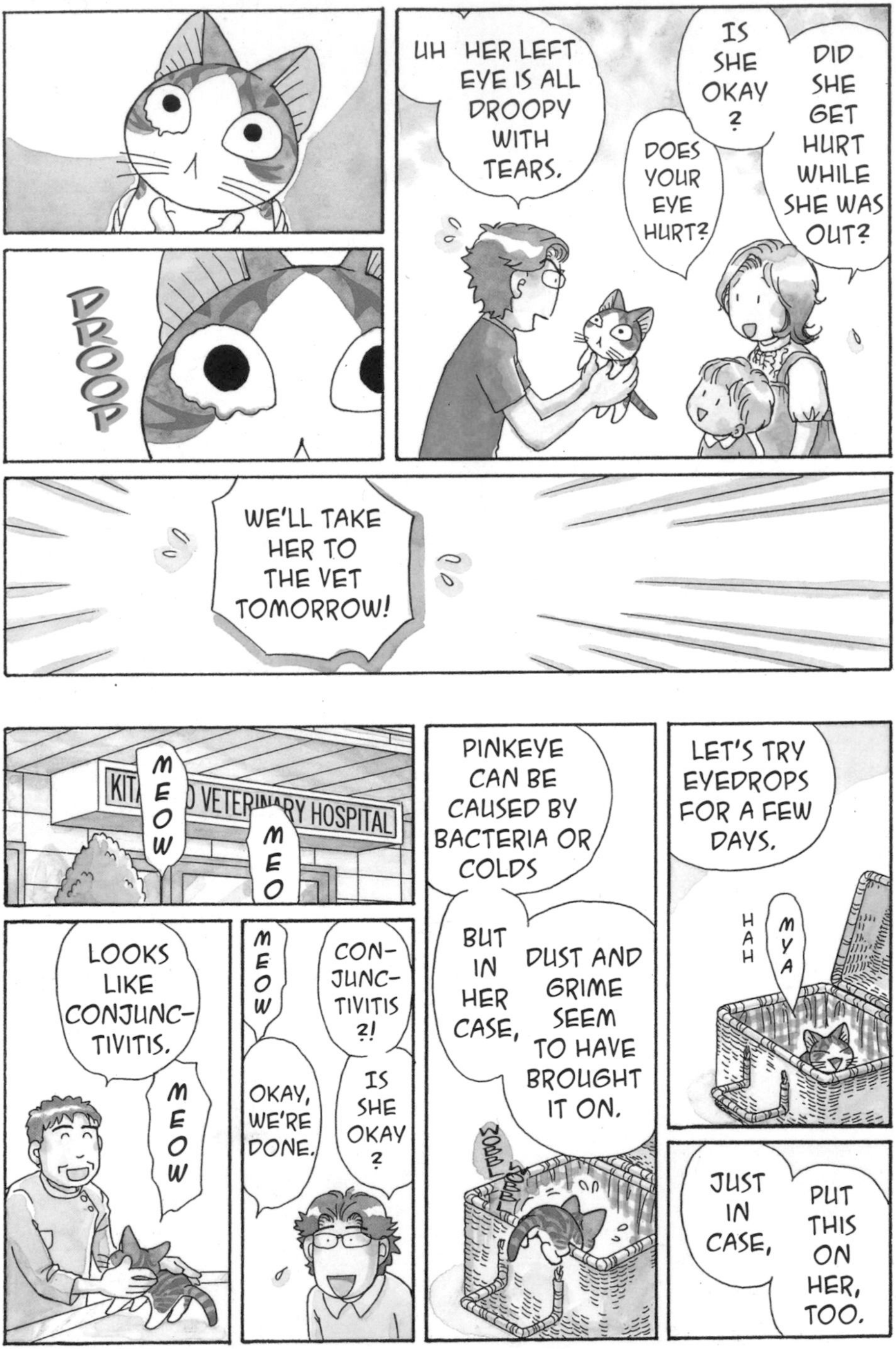
DROOP
UH HER LEFT EYE IS ALL DROOPY WITH TEARS.
IS SHE OKAY?
DID SHE GET HURT WHILE SHE WAS OUT?
DOES YOUR EYE HURT?
WE'LL TAKE HER TO THE VET TOMORROW!
KITA D VETERI RY HOSPITAL
MEOW
MEO
LOOKS LIKE CONJUNCTIVITIS.
MEOW
MEOW
CONJUNCTIVITIS?!
OKAY, WE'RE DONE.
IS SHE OKAY?
PINKEYE CAN BE CAUSED BY BACTERIA OR COLDS
BUT IN HER CASE,
DUST AND GRIME SEEM TO HAVE BROUGHT IT ON.
WOBBL WOBBL
LET'S TRY EYEDROPS FOR A FEW DAYS.
HAH
MYA
JUST IN CASE,
PUT THIS ON HER, TOO.

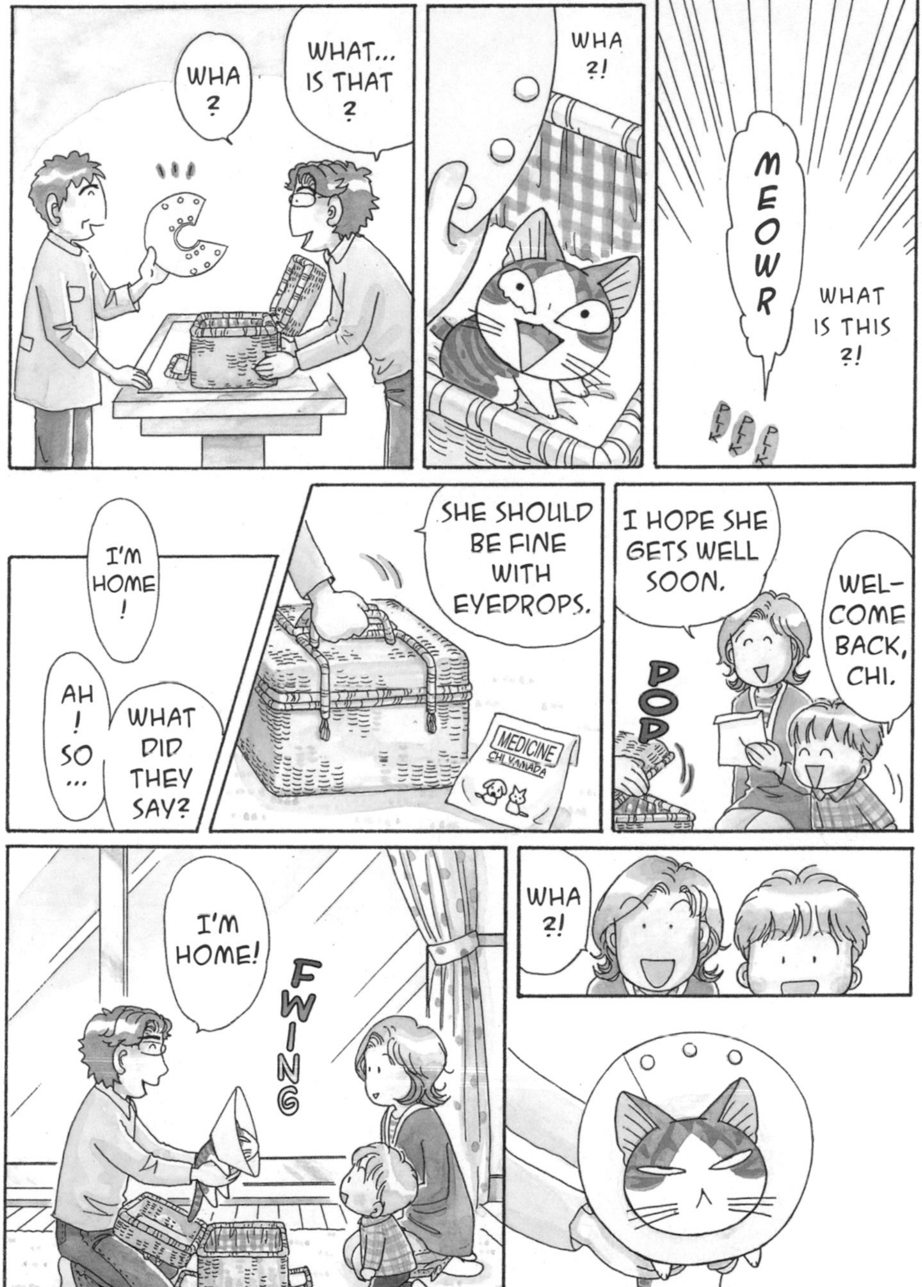
WHA?
WHAT... IS THAT?
WHA ?!
MEOWR
WHAT IS THIS ?!
PLIK PLIK PLIK
I'M HOME!
AH! SO...
WHAT DID THEY SAY?
SHE SHOULD BE FINE WITH EYEDROPS.
MEDICINE
CHI YAMADA
I HOPE SHE GETS WELL SOON.
WEL-COME BACK, CHI.
POP
I'M HOME!
FWING
WHA ?!

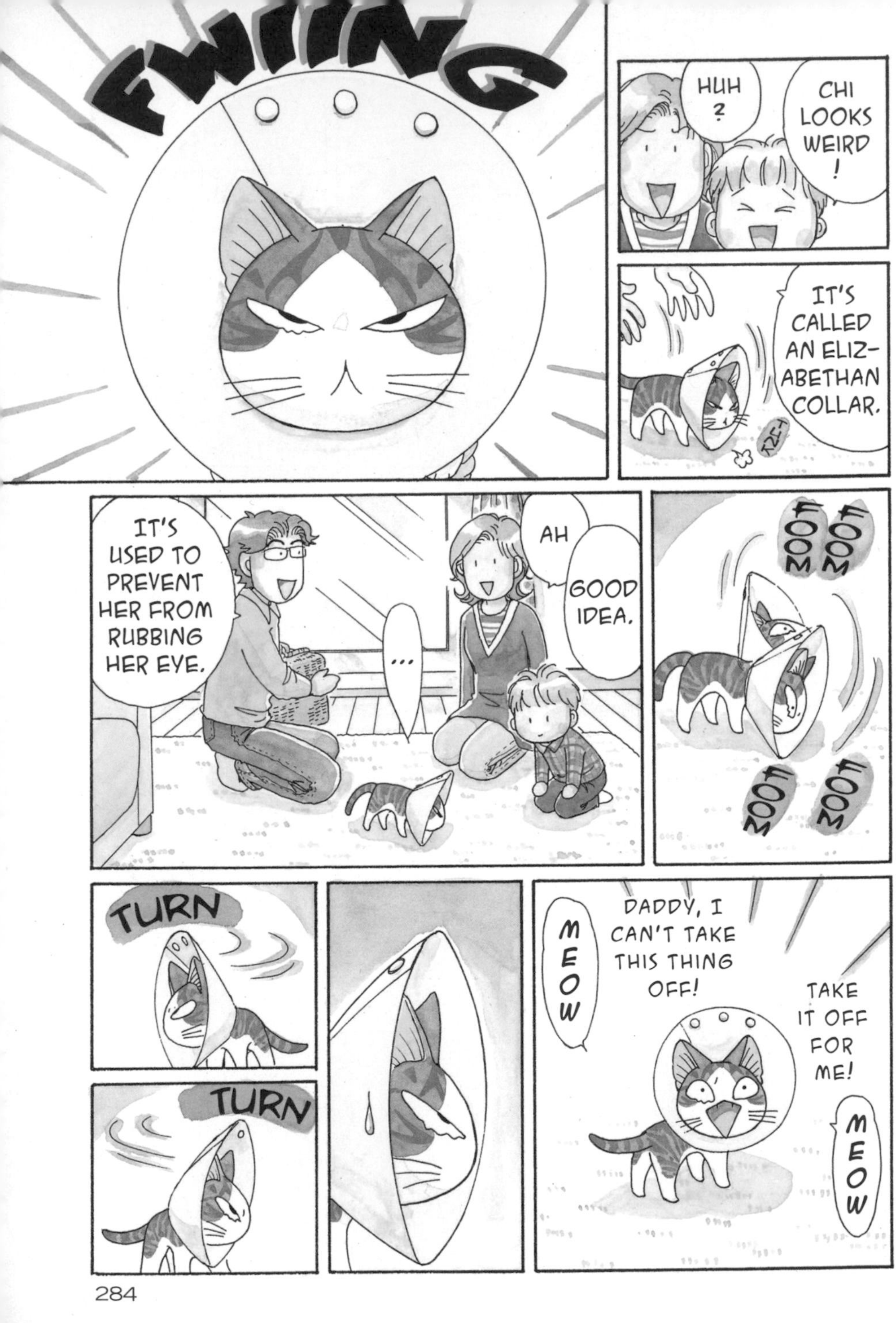
FWING
HUH?
CHI LOOKS WEIRD!
IT'S CALLED AN ELIZABETHAN COLLAR.
IT'S USED TO PREVENT HER FROM RUBBING HER EYE.
...
AH
GOOD IDEA.
FOOM FOOM
FOOM FOOM
TURN
TURN
MEOW
DADDY, I CAN'T TAKE THIS THING OFF!
TAKE IT OFF FOR ME!
MEOW

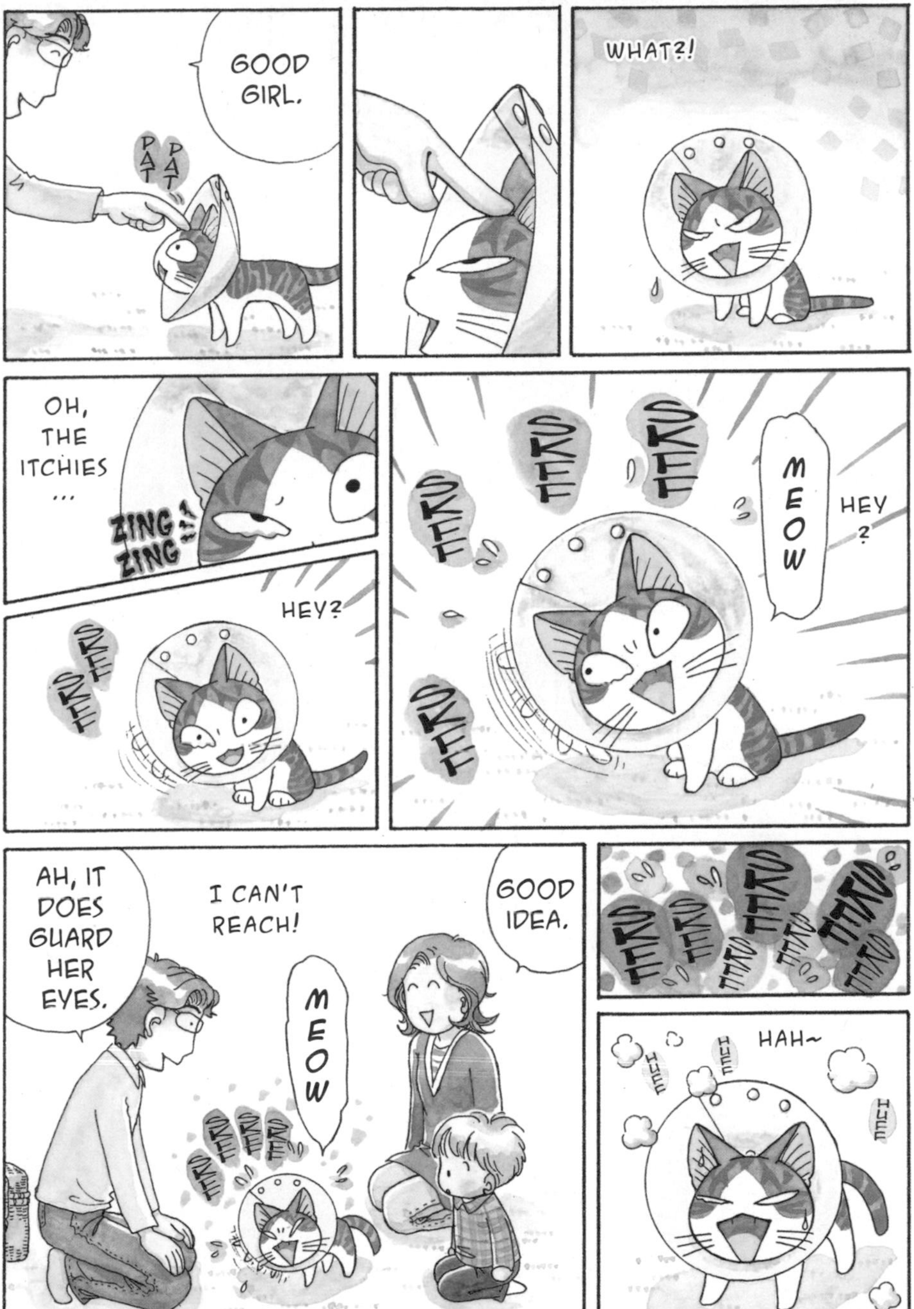
GOOD GIRL.
PAT PAT
WHAT?!
OH, THE ITCHIES...
ZING ZING
HEY?
SKFF SKFF
SKFF SKFF SKFF SKFF
MEOW
HEY?
AH, IT DOES GUARD HER EYES.
I CAN'T REACH!
GOOD IDEA.
MEOW
HAH~
HUFF HUFF HUFF

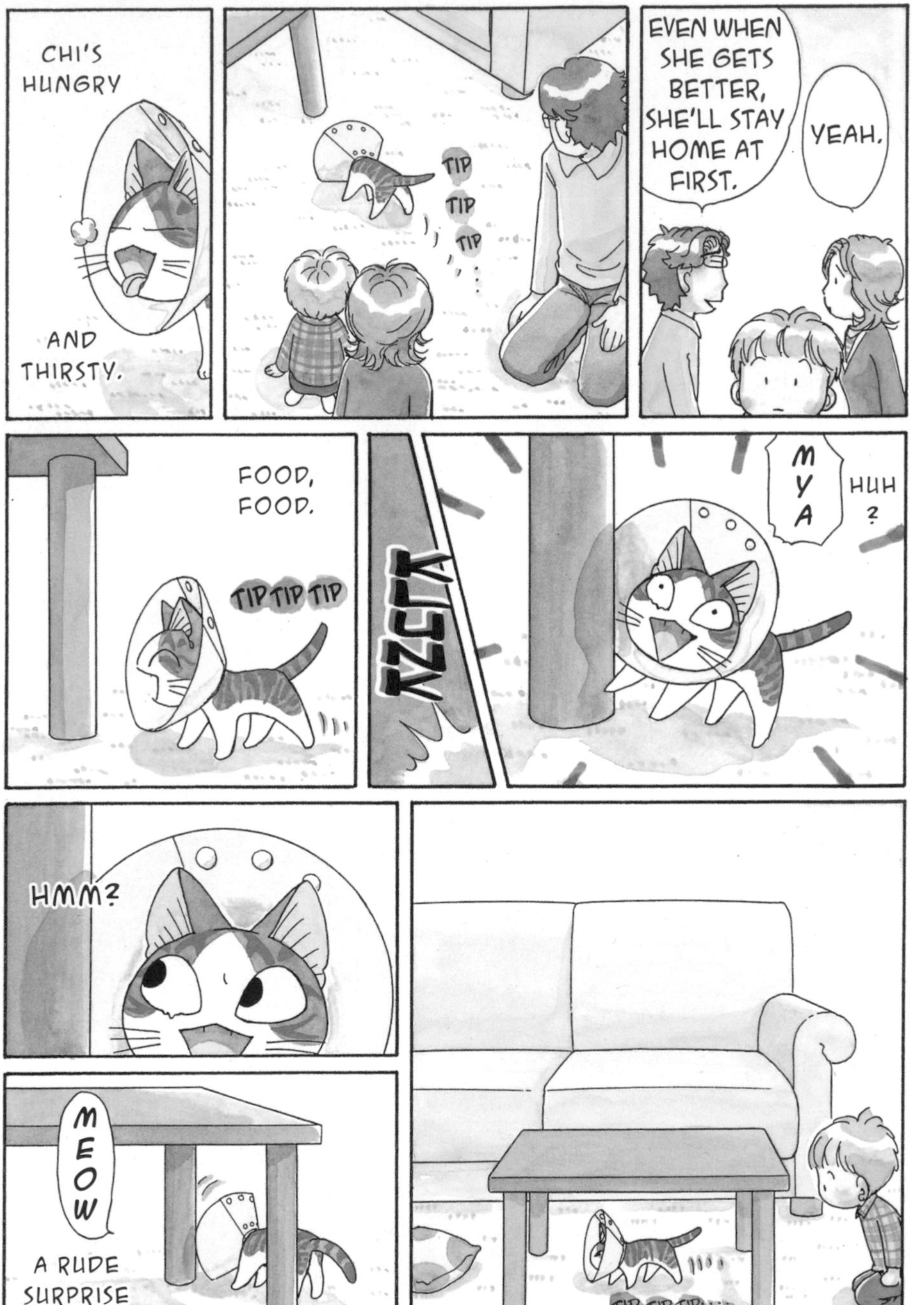
CHI'S HUNGRY
AND THIRSTY.
TIP
TIP
TIP
EVEN WHEN SHE GETS BETTER, SHE'LL STAY HOME AT FIRST.
YEAH.
FOOD, FOOD.
TIP TIP TIP
KLUNK
MYA
HUH?
HMM?
MEOW
A RUDE SURPRISE ...
TIP TIP TIP...

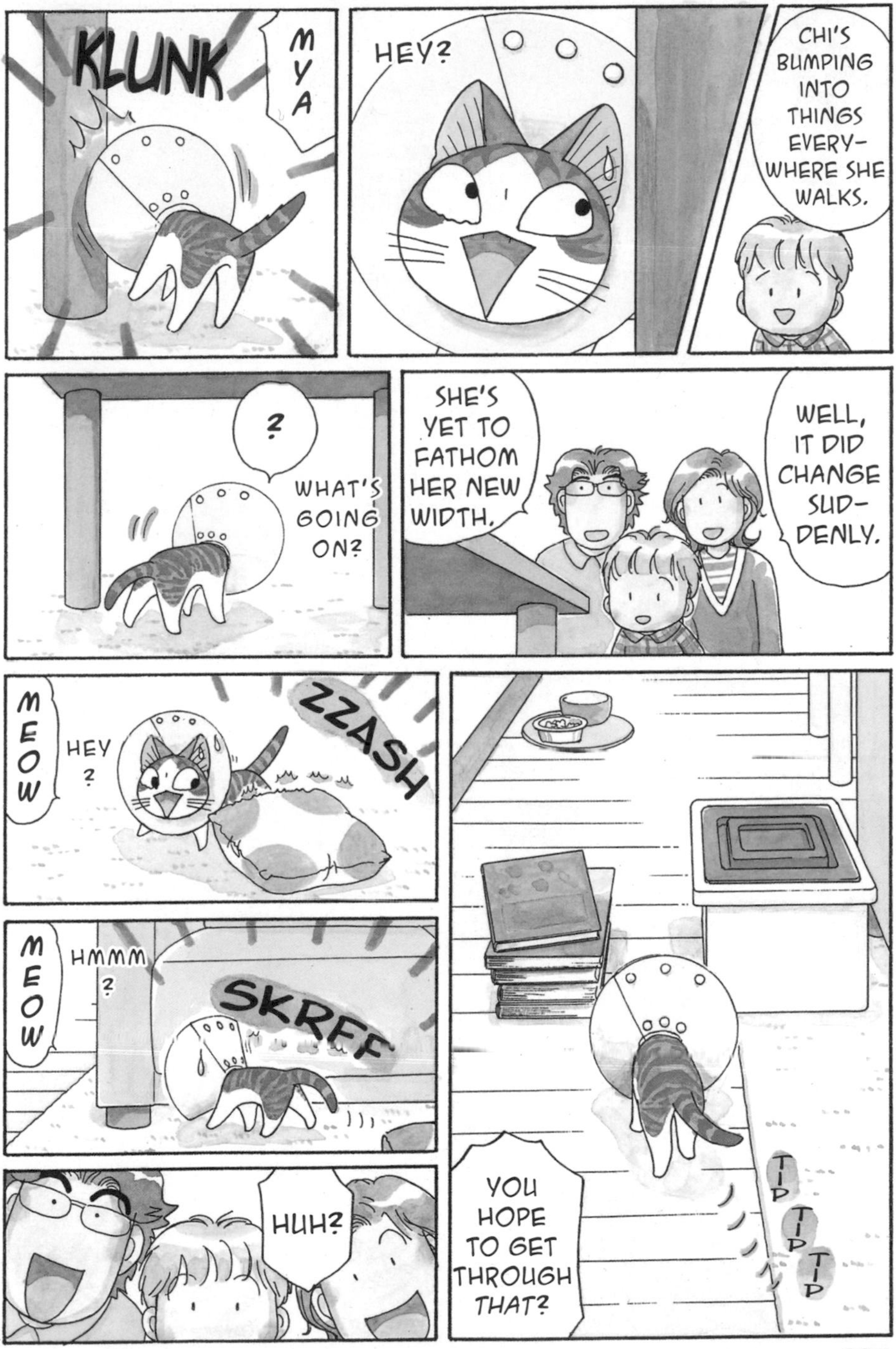
KLUNK
MYA
HEY?
CHI'S BUMPING INTO THINGS EVERY-WHERE SHE WALKS.
?
WHAT'S GOING ON?
SHE'S YET TO FATHOM HER NEW WIDTH.
WELL, IT DID CHANGE SUD-DENLY.
MEOW
HEY?
ZZASH
MEOW
HMMM?
SKRFF
HUH?
YOU HOPE TO GET THROUGH THAT?
TIP TIP TIP TIP

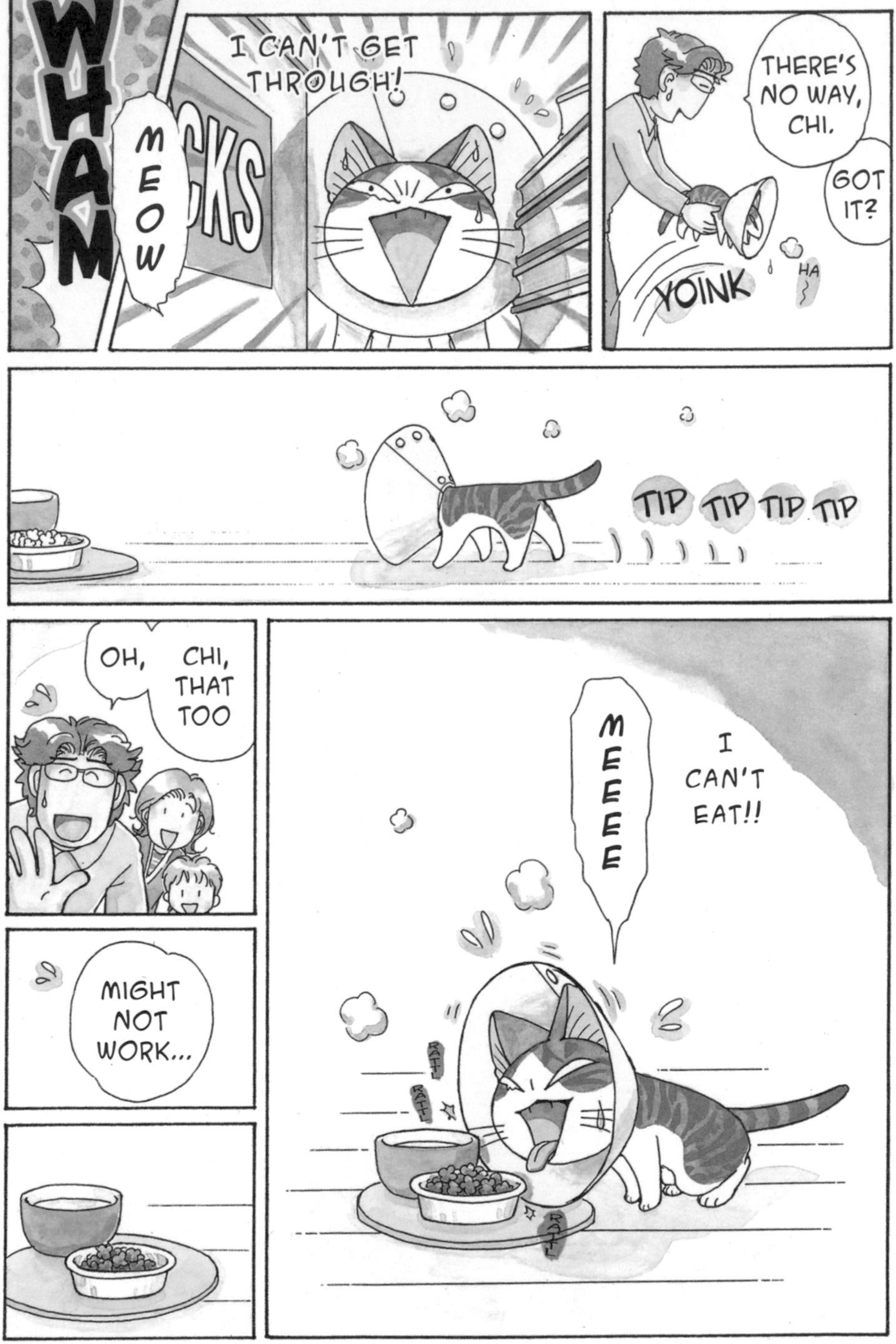
WHAM
MEOW
CKS
I CAN'T GET THROUGH!
THERE'S NO WAY, CHI.
GOT IT?
YOINK
HA
TIP TIP TIP TIP
OH, CHI, THAT TOO
MIGHT NOT WORK...
MEEEEE
I CAN'T EAT!!
RATT
RATT
RATT



the end

# homemade 147: a cat dislikes

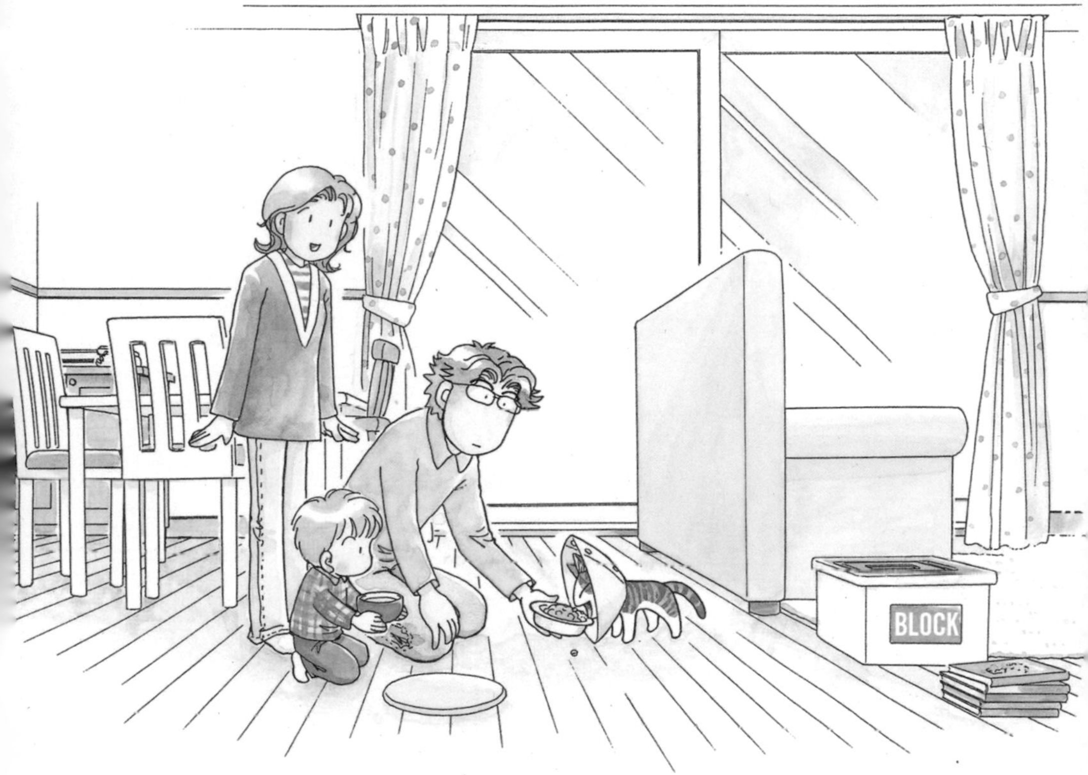
BLOCK

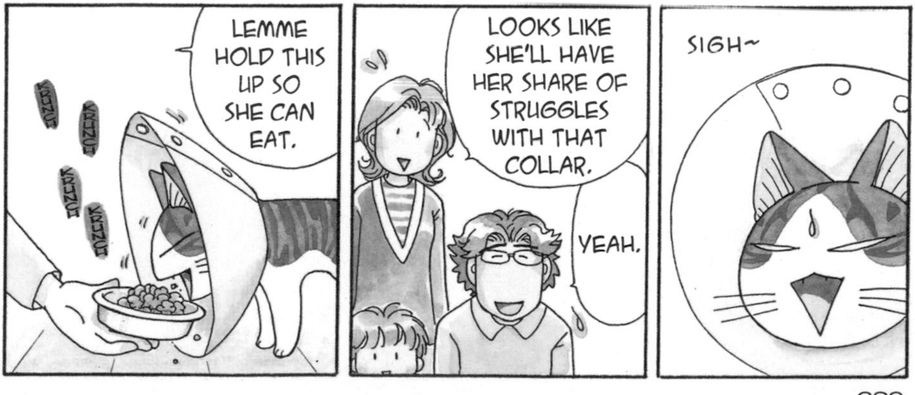
KRUNCH
KRUNCH
KRUNCH
KRUNCH
LEMME HOLD THIS UP SO SHE CAN EAT.
LOOKS LIKE SHE'LL HAVE HER SHARE OF STRUGGLES WITH THAT COLLAR.
YEAH.
SIGH~

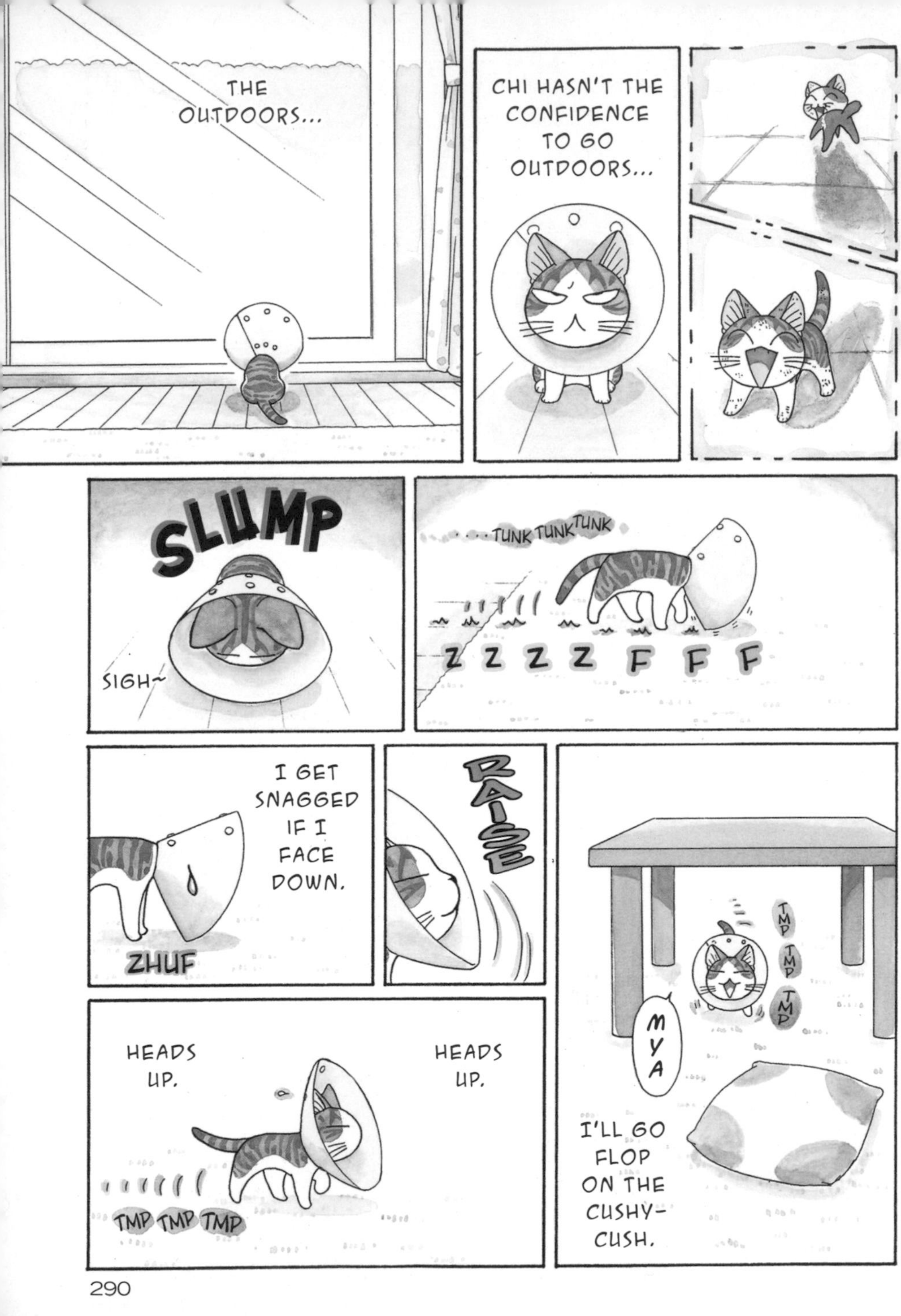
THE OUTDOORS...
CHI HASN'T THE CONFIDENCE TO GO OUTDOORS...
SLUMP
SIGH~
...TUNK TUNK TUNK
Z Z Z Z F F F
I GET SNAGGED IF I FACE DOWN.
ZHUF
RAISE
HEADS UP.
HEADS UP.
TMP TMP TMP
TMP TMP TMP
MYA
I'LL GO FLOP ON THE CUSHY-CUSH.

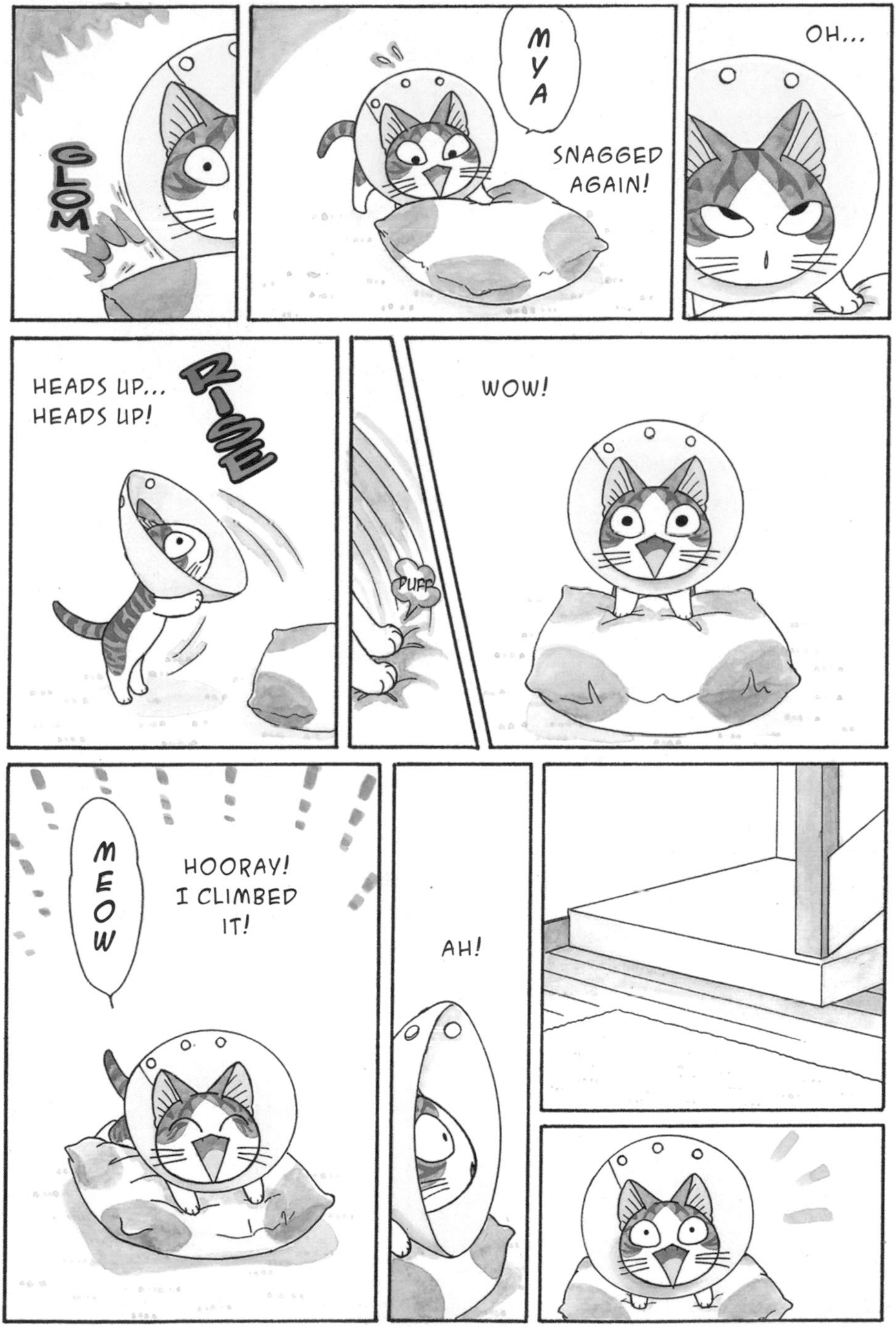
GLOM
MYA
SNAGGED AGAIN!
OH...
HEADS UP... HEADS UP!
RISE
PUFF
WOW!
MEOW
HOORAY! I CLIMBED IT!
AH!

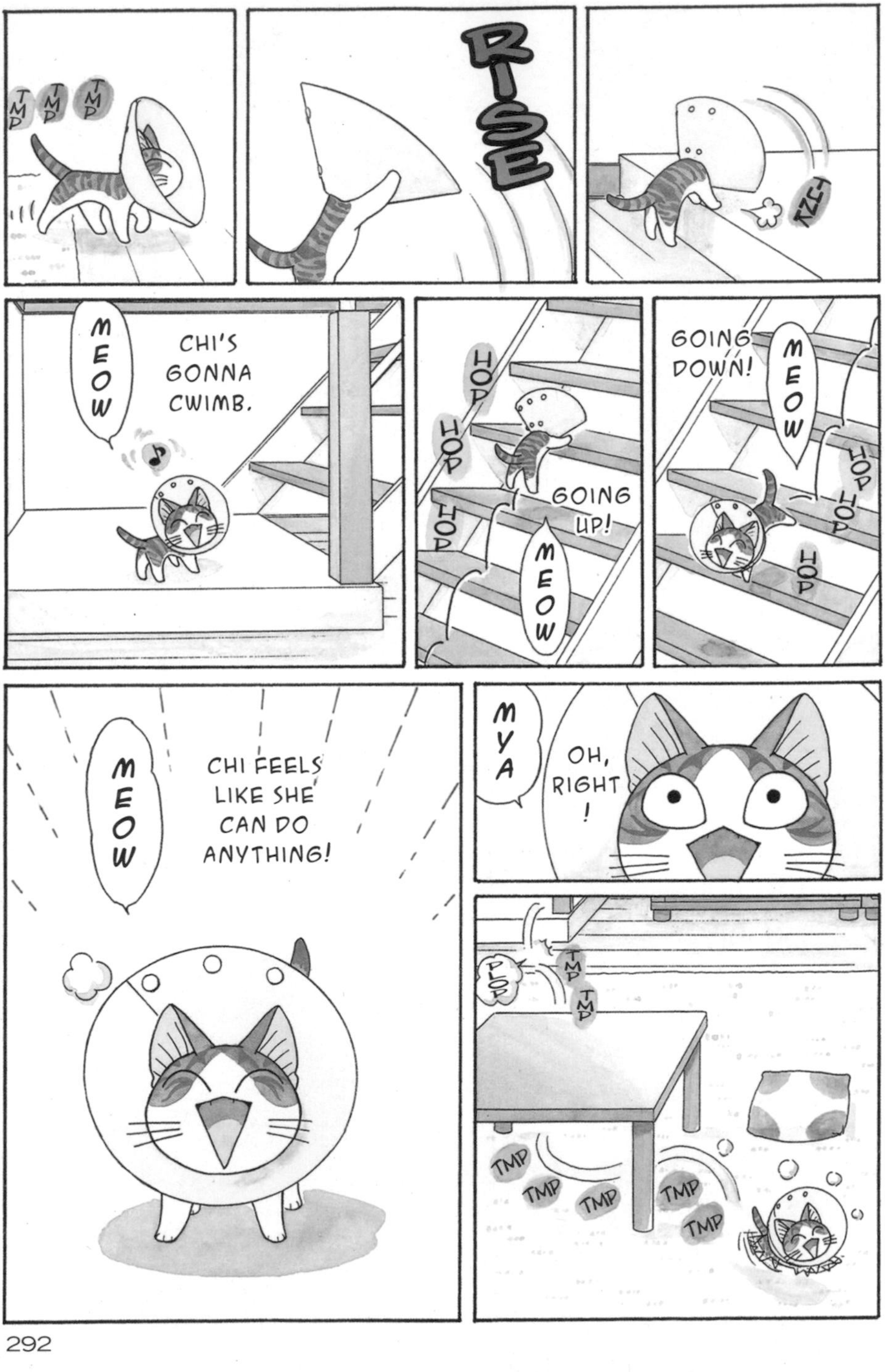
TMP TMP TMP
RISE
TUNK
MEOW
CHI'S GONNA CWIMB.
HOP HOP HOP
GOING UP!
MEOW
GOING DOWN!
MEOW
HOP HOP
HOP
MEOW
CHI FEELS LIKE SHE CAN DO ANYTHING!
MYA
OH, RIGHT!
PLOP
TMP TMP
TMP
TMP
TMP
TMP
TMP

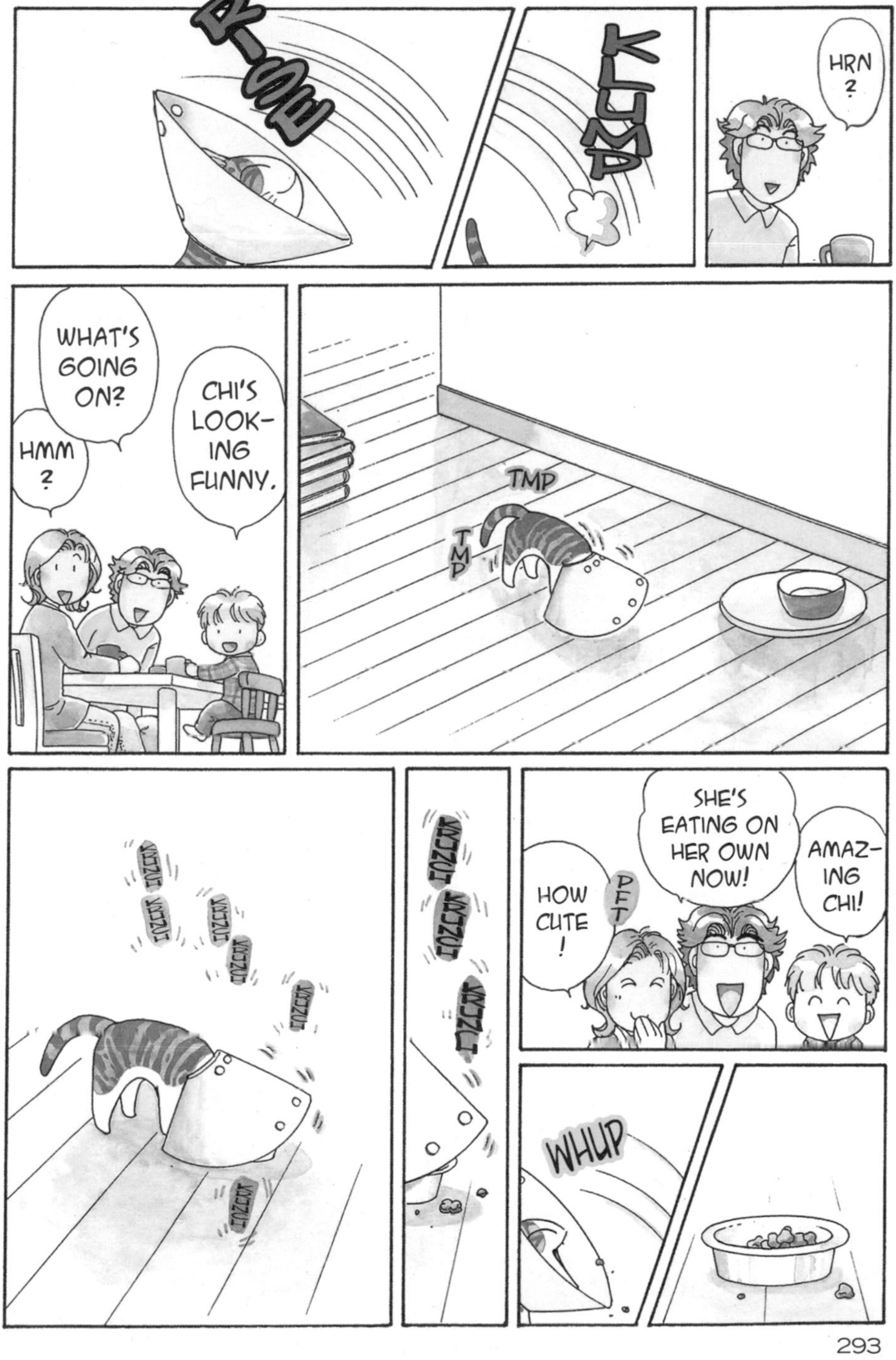
RISE
KLUMP
HRN?
WHAT'S GOING ON?
HMM?
CHI'S LOOKING FUNNY.
TMP
TMP
SHE'S EATING ON HER OWN NOW!
HOW CUTE!
PFT
AMAZING CHI!
WHUP

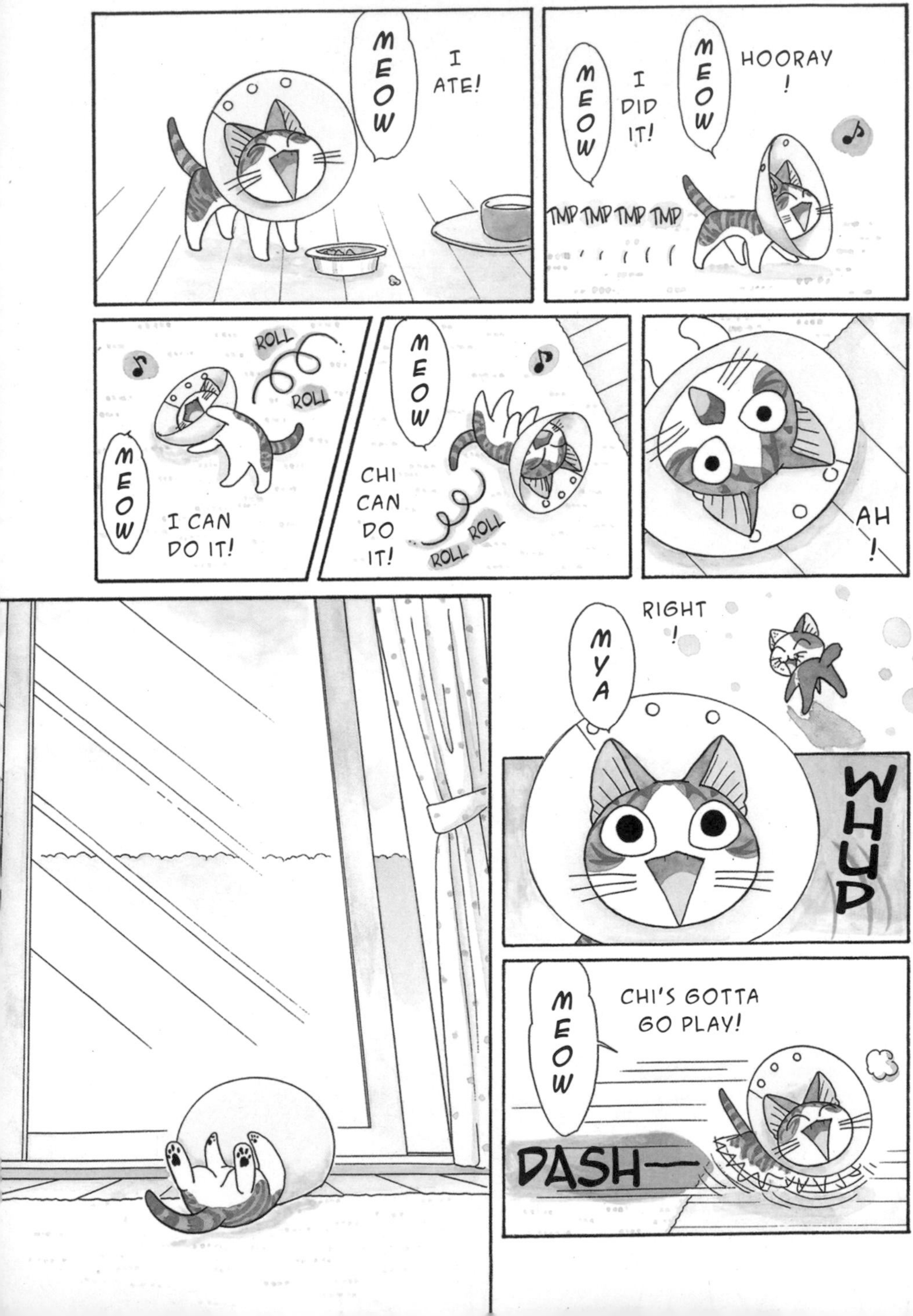
MEOW
I ATE!
MEOW
I DID IT!
MEOW
HOORAY!
TMP TMP TMP TMP
ROLL
ROLL
MEOW
I CAN DO IT!
MEOW
CHI CAN DO IT!
ROLL ROLL
ROLL
AH!
MYA
RIGHT!
WHUP
MEOW
CHI'S GOTTA GO PLAY!
DASH—

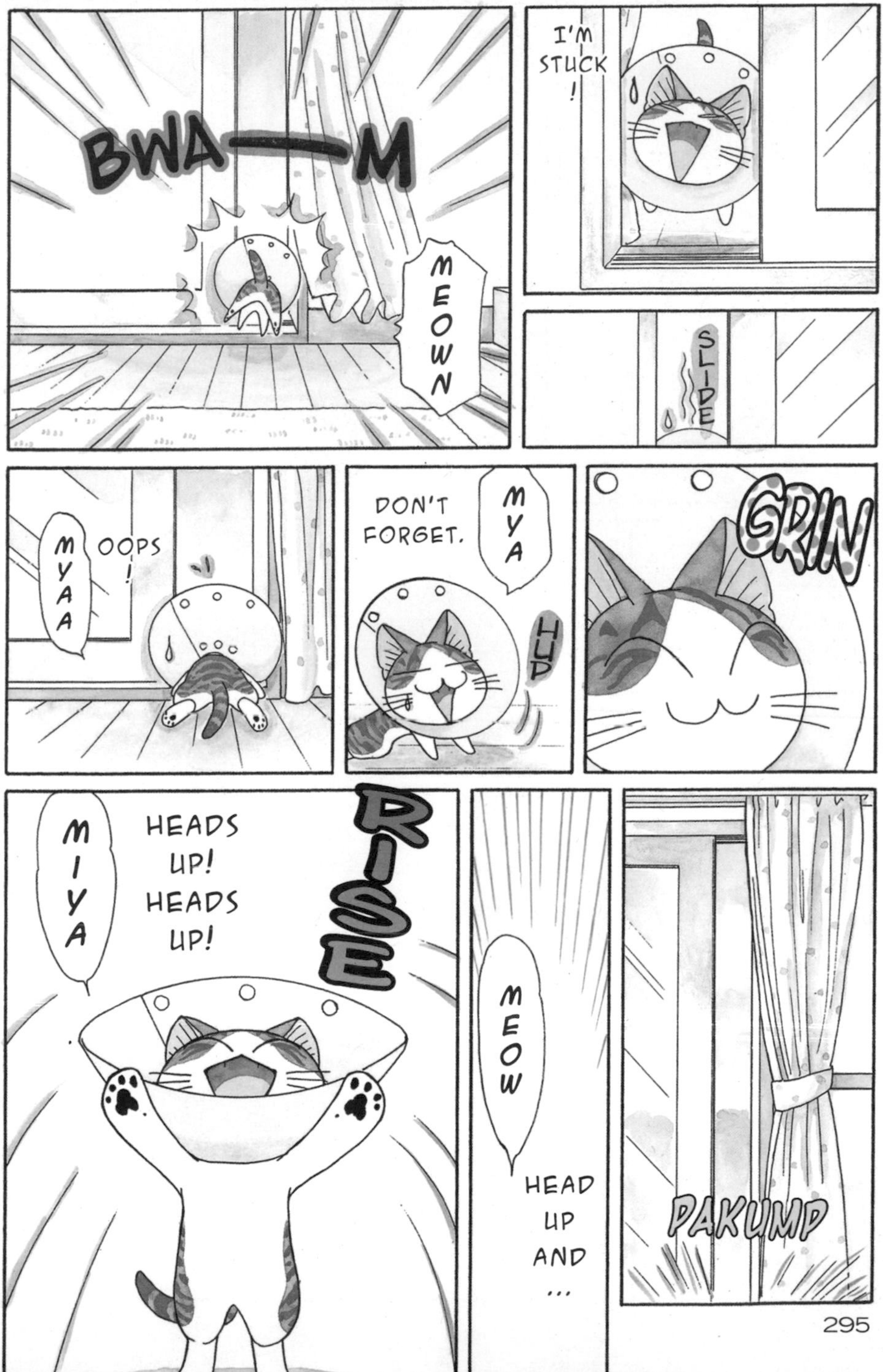
BWA—M
MEOWN
I'M STUCK!
SLIDE
MYAA
OOPS!
DON'T FORGET.
MYA
HUP
GRIN
MIYA
HEADS UP! HEADS UP!
RISE
MEOW
HEAD UP AND ...
PAKUMP

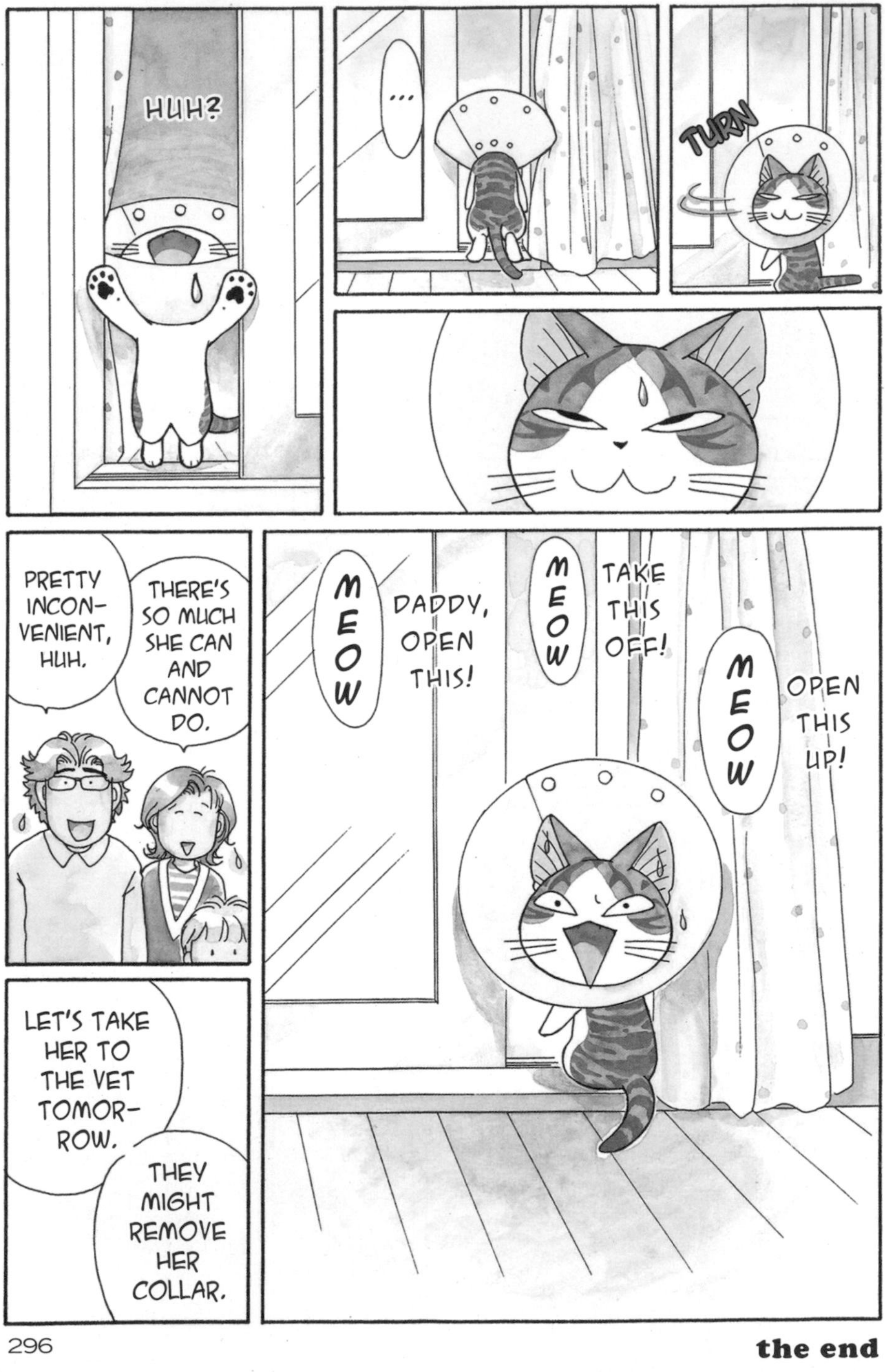
HUH?
...
TURN
PRETTY INCON-VENIENT, HUH.
THERE'S SO MUCH SHE CAN AND CANNOT DO.
MEOW
DADDY, OPEN THIS!
MEOW
TAKE THIS OFF!
MEOW
OPEN THIS UP!
LET'S TAKE HER TO THE VET TOMOR-ROW.
THEY MIGHT REMOVE HER COLLAR.



**the end**

## homemade 148: a cat begs

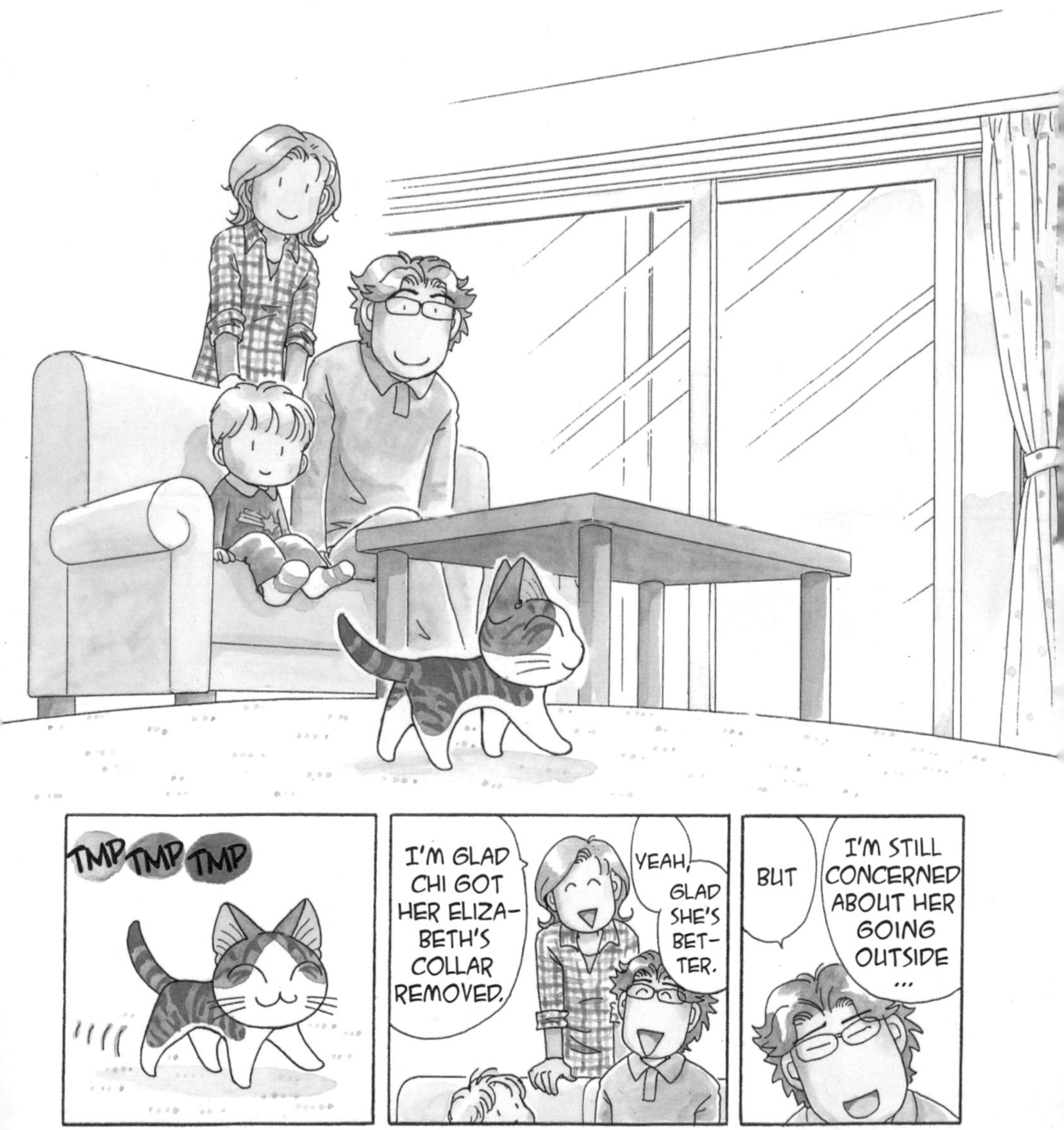

TMP TMP TMP
I'M GLAD CHI GOT HER ELIZA-BETH'S COLLAR REMOVED.
YEAH,
GLAD SHE'S BET-TER.
BUT
I'M STILL CONCERNED ABOUT HER GOING OUTSIDE ...

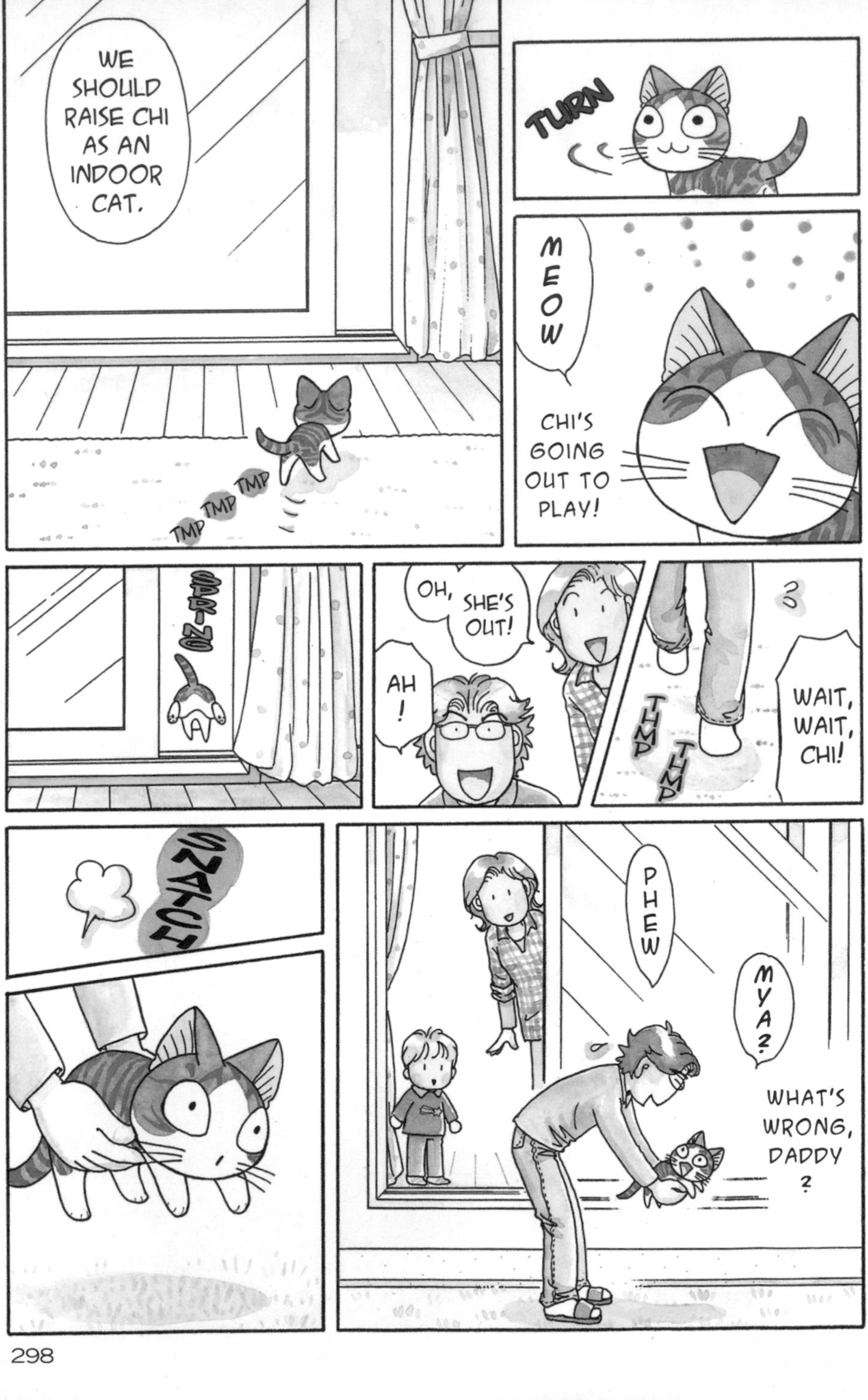
WE SHOULD RAISE CHI AS AN INDOOR CAT.
TMP TMP TMP TMP
TURN
MEOW
CHI'S GOING OUT TO PLAY!
SPRI-NG
OH, SHE'S OUT!
AH!
THMP THMP
WAIT, WAIT, CHI!
SNATCH
PHEW
MYA?
WHAT'S WRONG, DADDY?

HUH
?!

!

THMP
THMP

MEOW

CHI'S
HEADING
OUT!

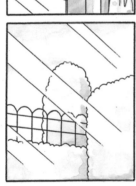

I DON'T
GET THIS,
DADDY.

BUT CHI'S
GOING OUT
STILL.

I KNOW
HOW TO
OPEN THIS.

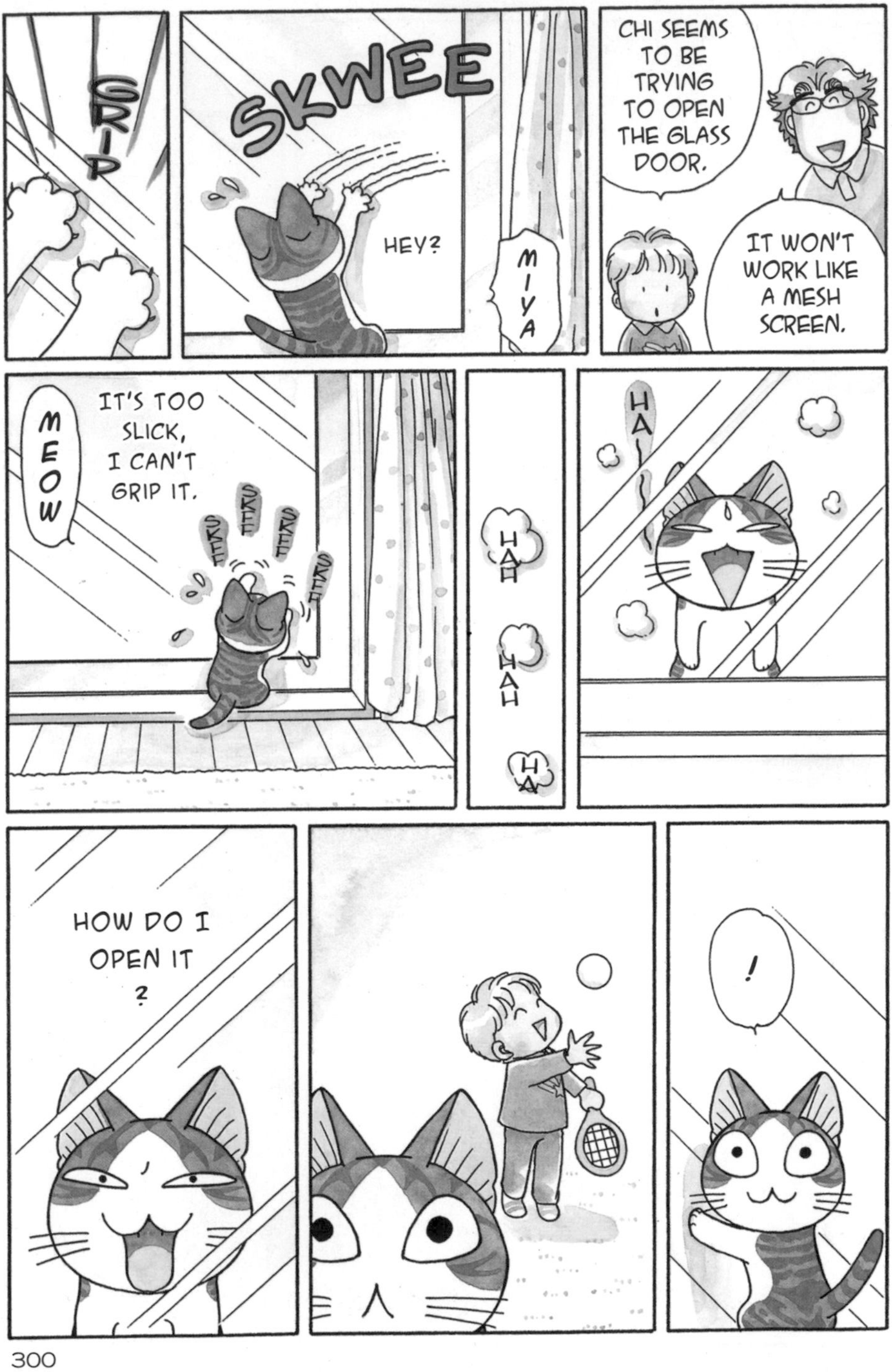
GRIP
SKWEE
HEY?
MIYA
CHI SEEMS TO BE TRYING TO OPEN THE GLASS DOOR.
IT WON'T WORK LIKE A MESH SCREEN.
MEOW
IT'S TOO SLICK, I CAN'T GRIP IT.
SKEE SKEE SKEE SKEE
HAH HAH HA
HA
HOW DO I OPEN IT ?
!

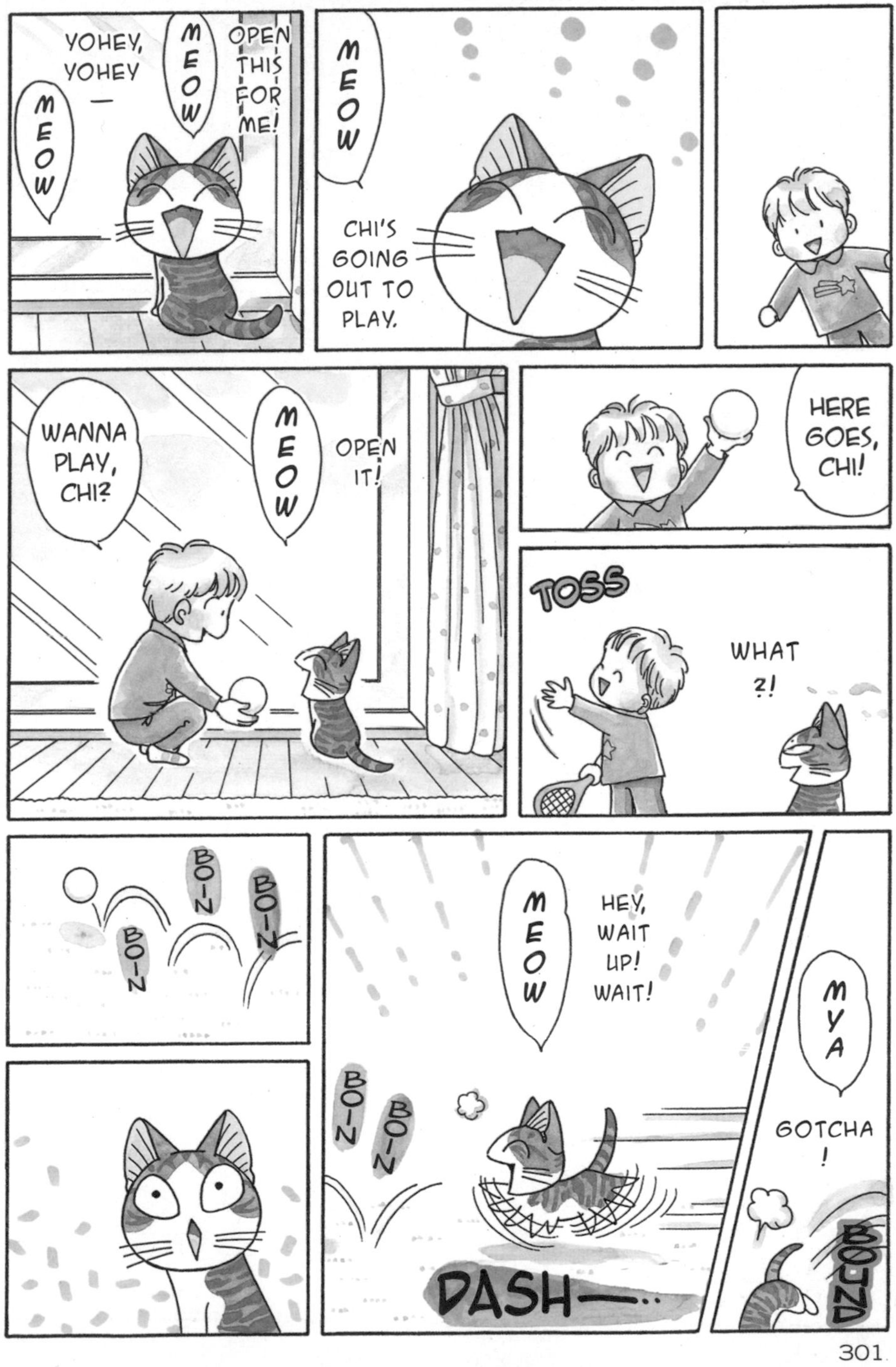
YOHEY, YOHEY —
MEOW
MEOW
OPEN THIS FOR ME!
MEOW
CHI'S GOING OUT TO PLAY.
WANNA PLAY, CHI?
MEOW
OPEN IT!
HERE GOES, CHI!
TOSS
WHAT ?!
BOIN
BOIN
BOIN
MEOW
HEY, WAIT UP! WAIT!
BOIN
BOIN
DASH—..
MYA
GOTCHA !
BOUND

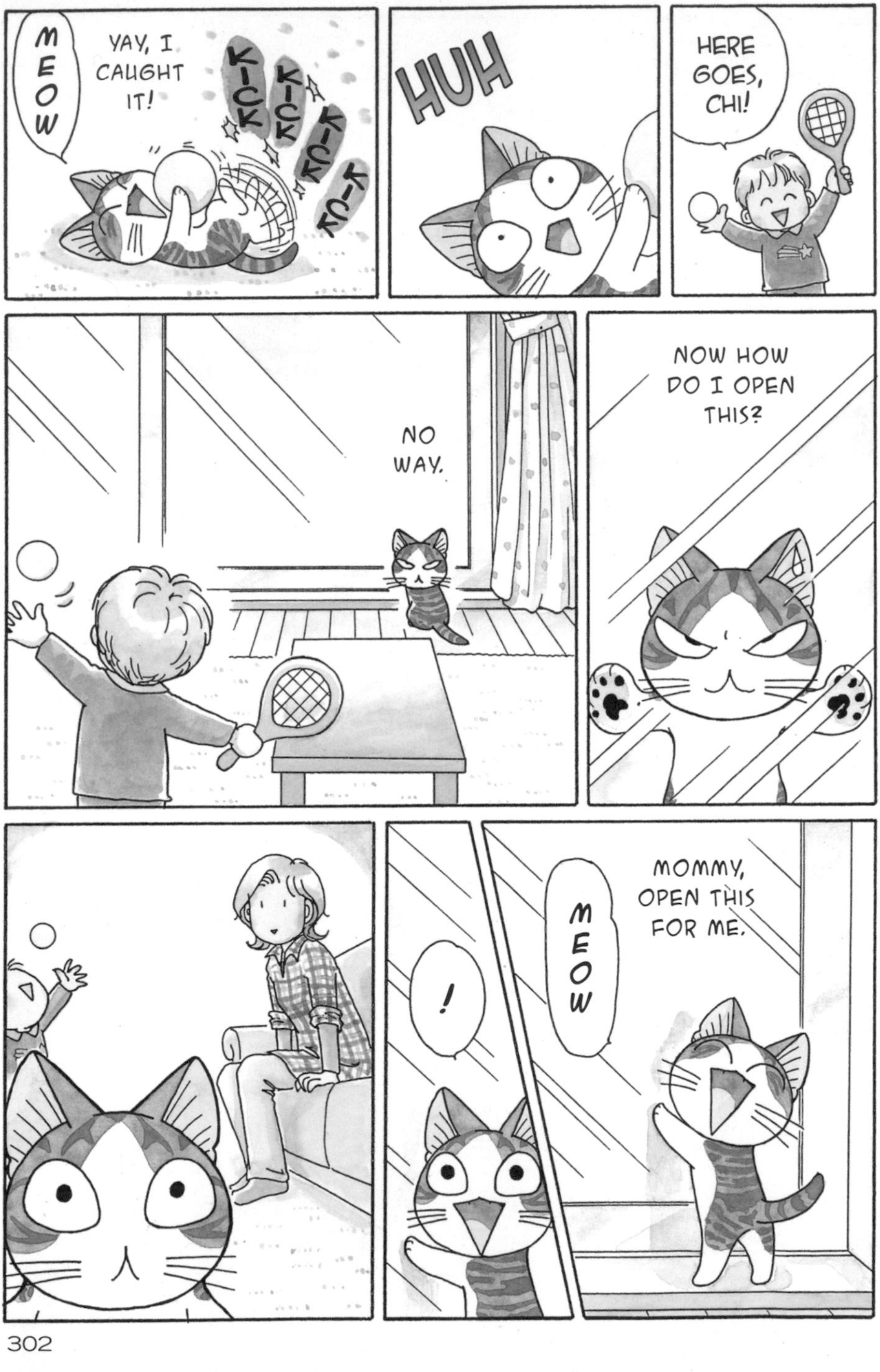
MEOW
YAY, I CAUGHT IT!
KICK KICK KICK KICK
HUH
HERE GOES, CHI!
NO WAY.
NOW HOW DO I OPEN THIS?
!
MEOW
MOMMY, OPEN THIS FOR ME.

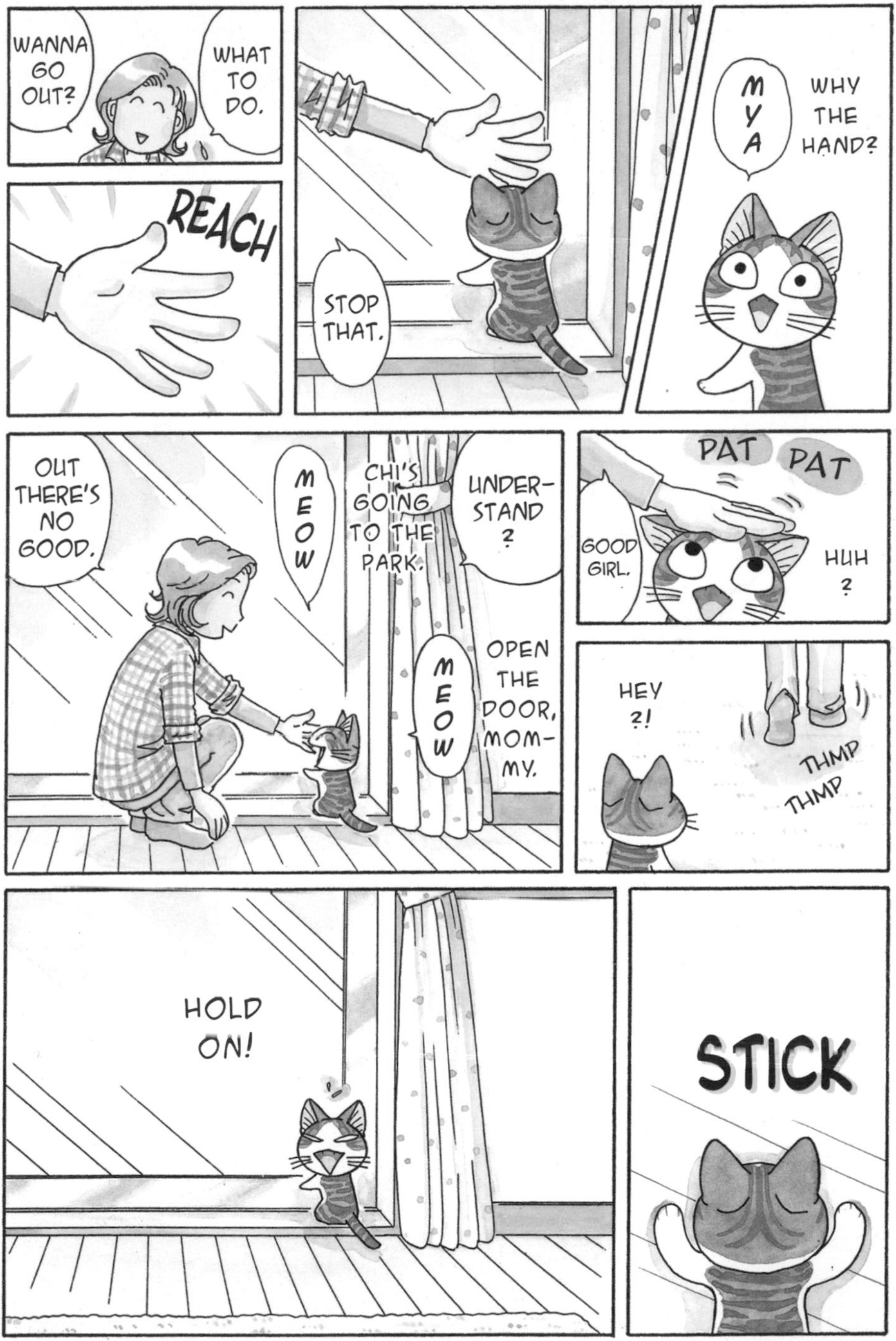
WANNA GO OUT?
WHAT TO DO.
REACH
STOP THAT.
MYA
WHY THE HAND?
OUT THERE'S NO GOOD.
MEOW
CHI'S GOING TO THE PARK.
UNDER-STAND?
MEOW
OPEN THE DOOR, MOM-MY.
PAT PAT
GOOD GIRL.
HUH?
HEY?!
THMP THMP
HOLD ON!
STICK

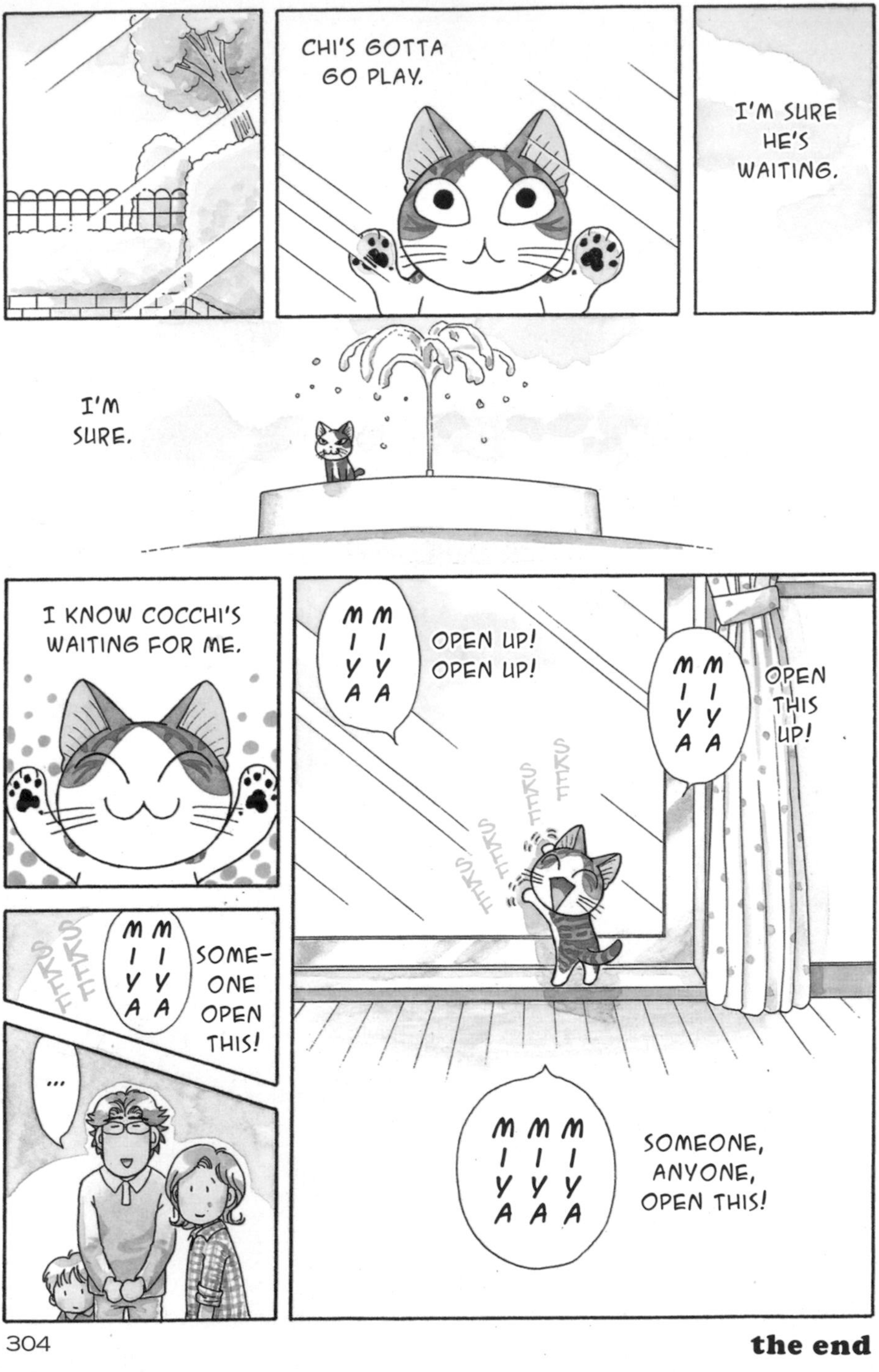
CHI'S GOTTA GO PLAY.
I'M SURE HE'S WAITING.
I'M SURE.
I KNOW COCCHI'S WAITING FOR ME.
SKFF SKFF
MIYA MIYA
SOME-ONE OPEN THIS!
...
MIYA MIYA
OPEN UP! OPEN UP!
MIYA MIYA
OPEN THIS UP!
SKFF SKFF SKFF SKFF
MIYA MIYA MIYA
SOMEONE, ANYONE, OPEN THIS!

**the end**

## homemade 149: a cat is impatient

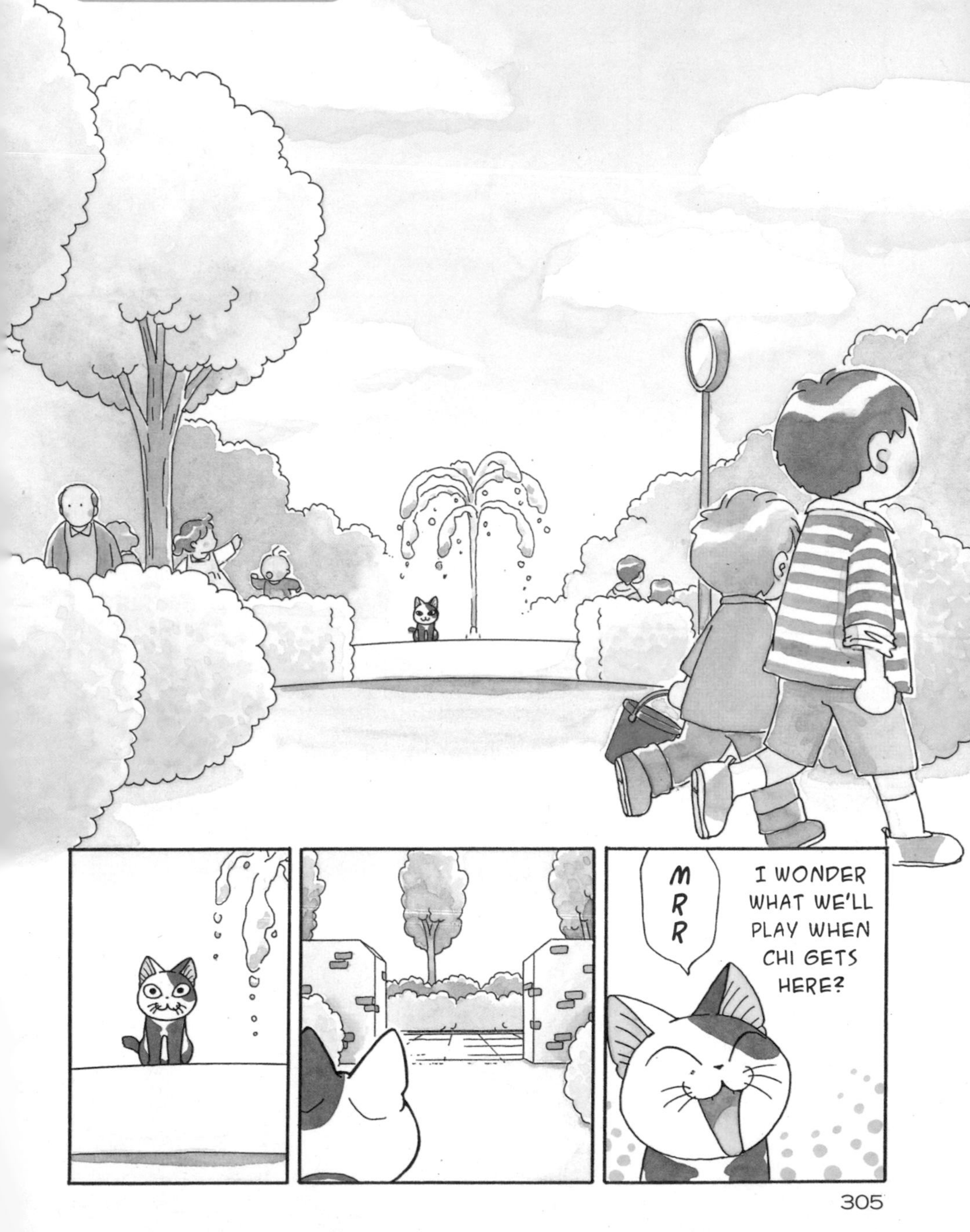
MRR
I WONDER WHAT WE'LL PLAY WHEN CHI GETS HERE?

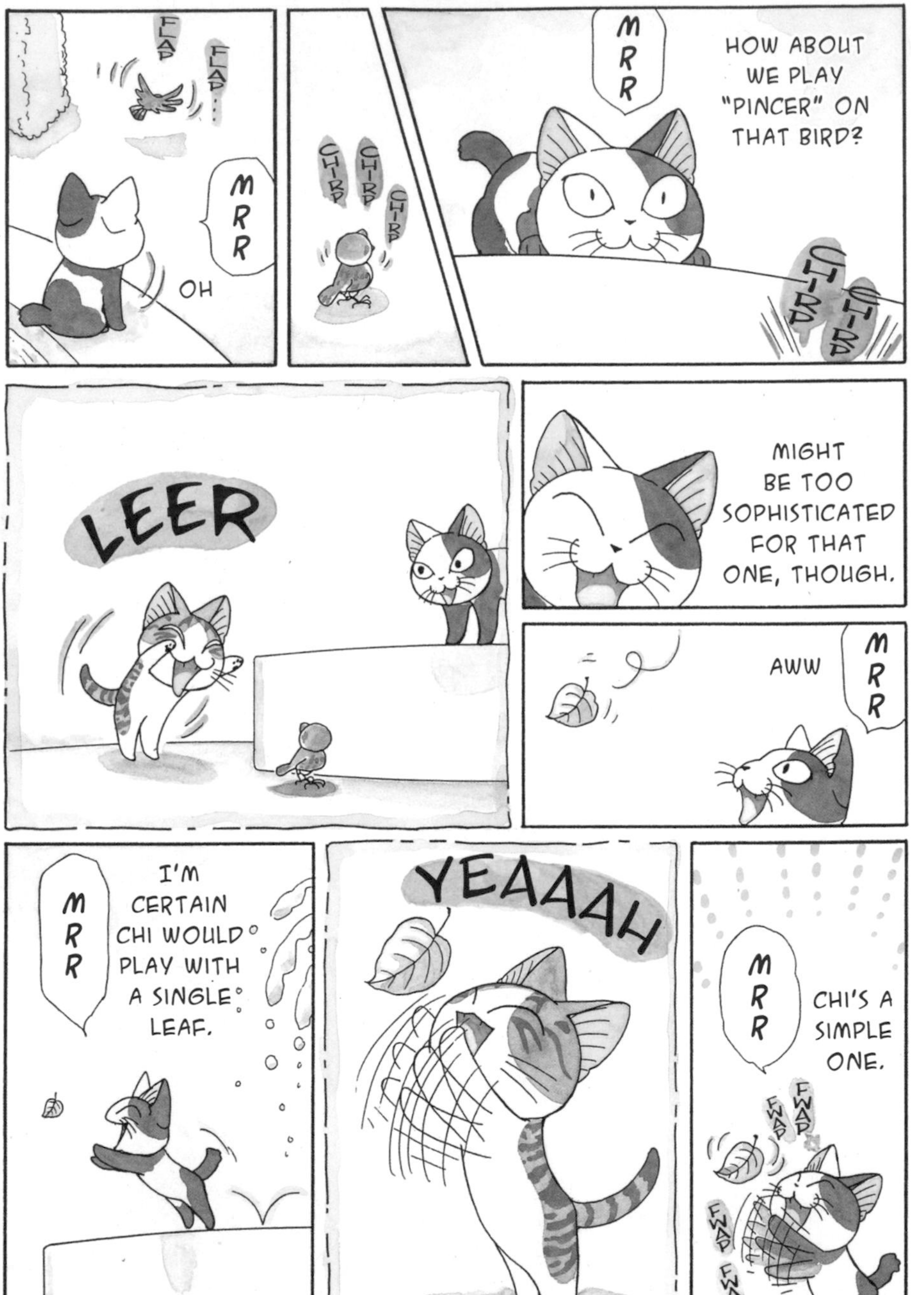
FLAP
FLAP...
MRR
OH
CHIRP
CHIRP
CHIRP
MRR
HOW ABOUT WE PLAY "PINCER" ON THAT BIRD?
CHIRP
CHIRP
LEER
MIGHT BE TOO SOPHISTICATED FOR THAT ONE, THOUGH.
AWW
MRR
MRR
I'M CERTAIN CHI WOULD PLAY WITH A SINGLE LEAF.
YEAAAH
MRR
CHI'S A SIMPLE ONE.
FWAP
FWAP
FWAP
FWAP

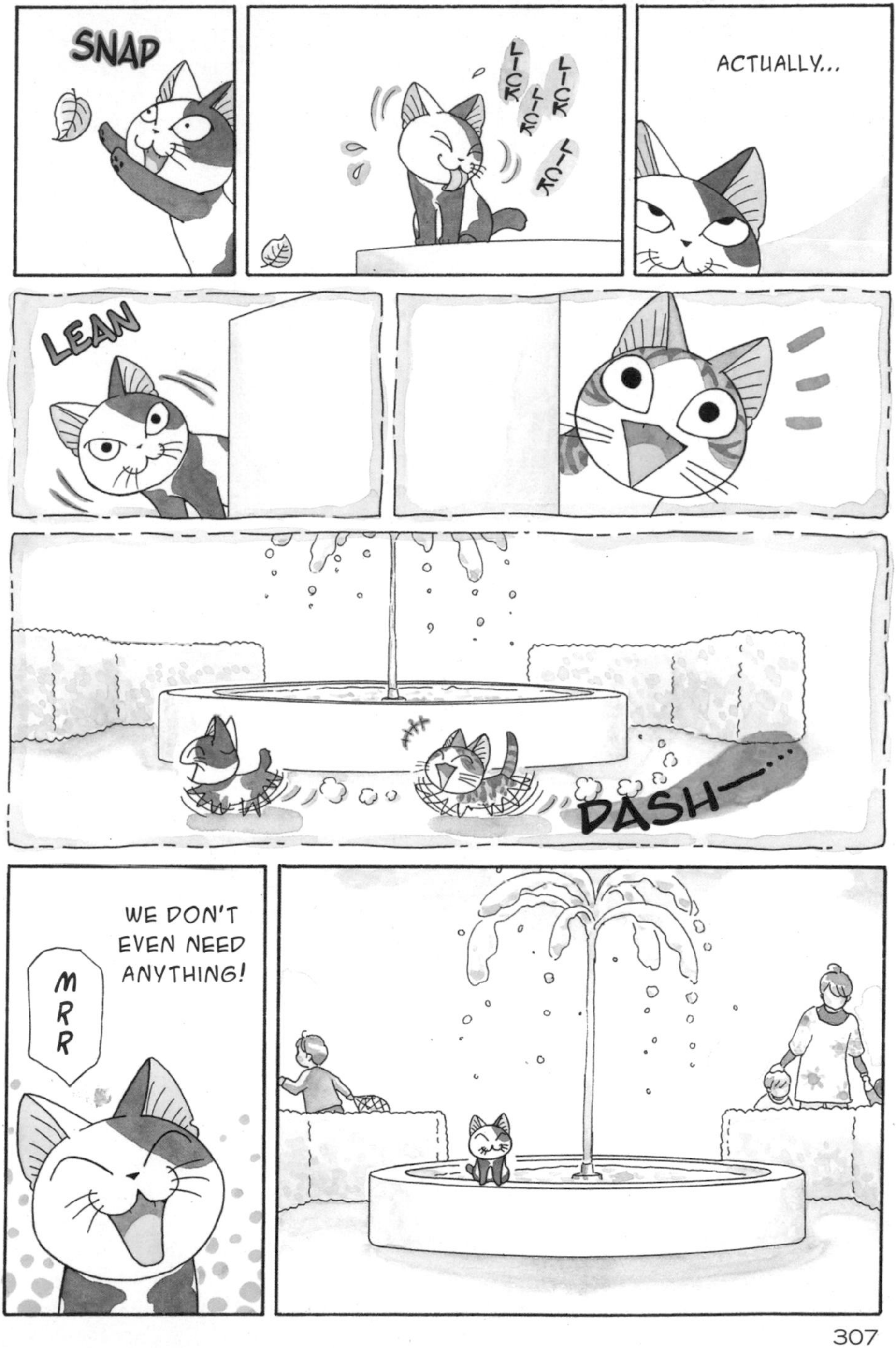
SNAP
LICK LICK LICK LICK
ACTUALLY...
LEAN
DASH—...
WE DON'T EVEN NEED ANYTHING!
MRR

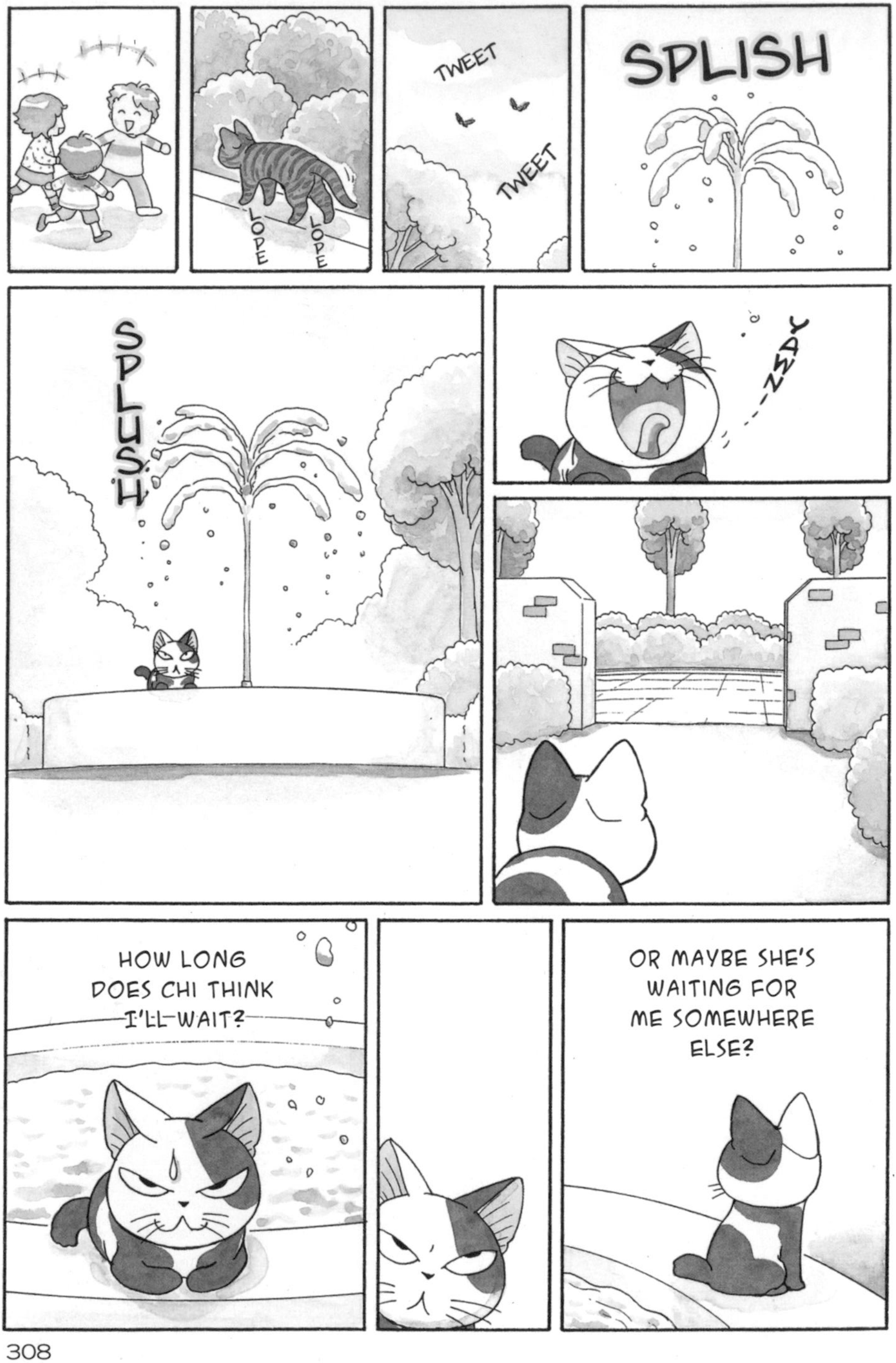
LOPE
LOPE
TWEET
TWEET
SPLISH
SPLUSH
YAWN
HOW LONG DOES CHI THINK I'LL WAIT?
OR MAYBE SHE'S WAITING FOR ME SOMEWHERE ELSE?

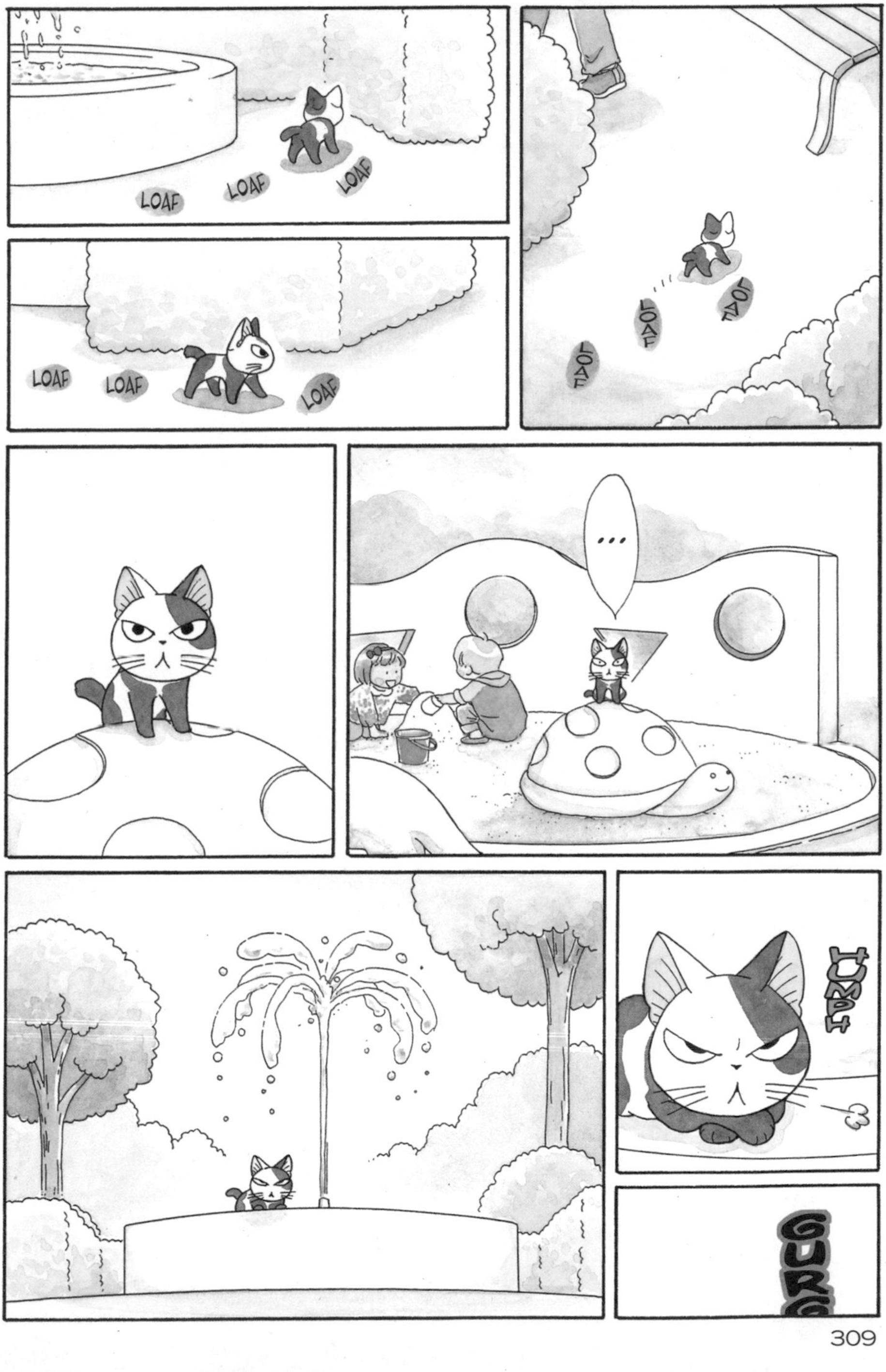
LOAF
LOAF
LOAF
LOAF
LOAF
LOAF
LOAF
LOAF
LOAF
...
HUMPH
GURG

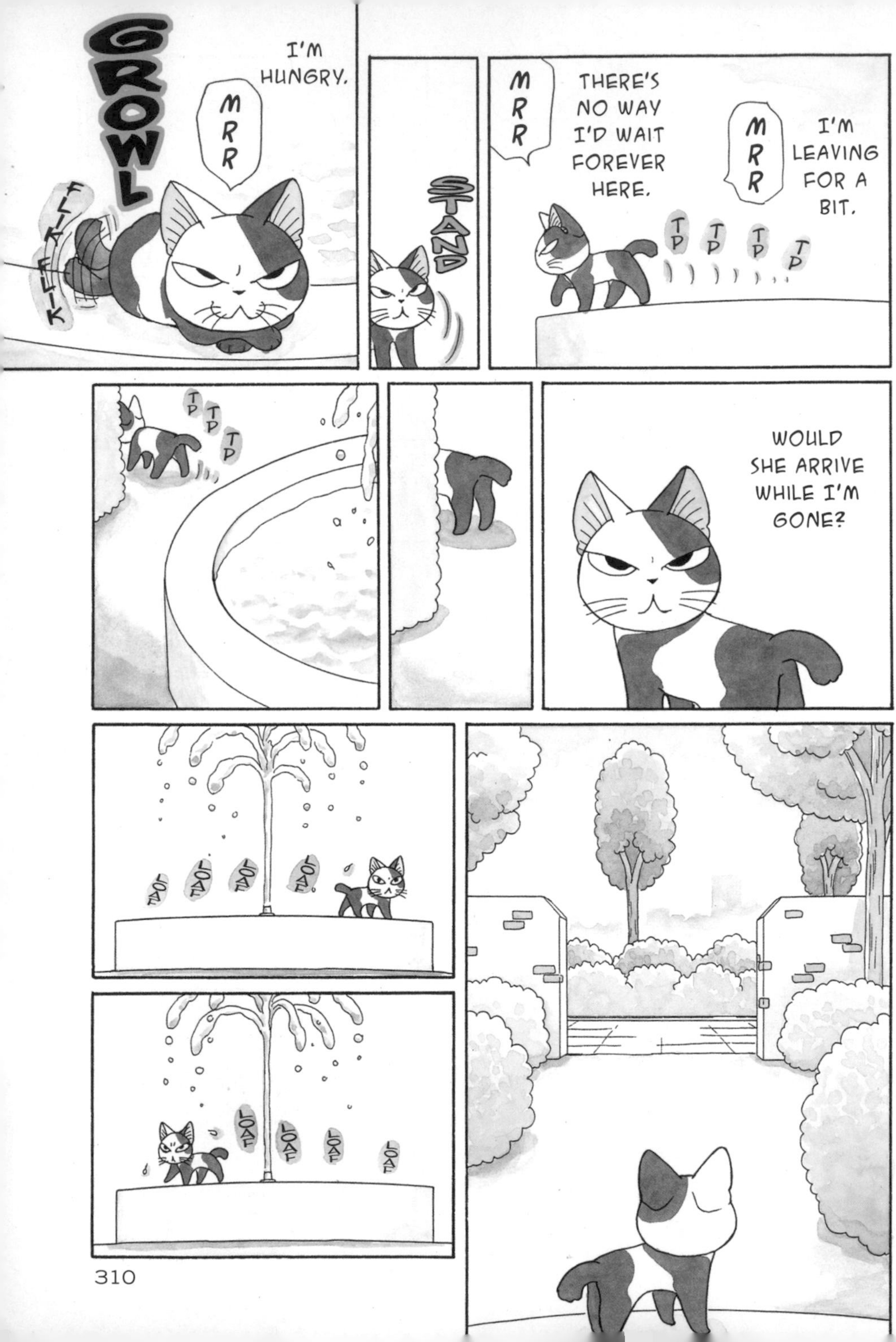
GROWL
FLIK FLIK
MRR
I'M HUNGRY.
STAND
MRR
THERE'S NO WAY I'D WAIT FOREVER HERE.
MRR
I'M LEAVING FOR A BIT.
TP TP TP TP
TP TP TP
WOULD SHE ARRIVE WHILE I'M GONE?
LOAF LOAF LOAF LOAF
LOAF LOAF LOAF LOAF

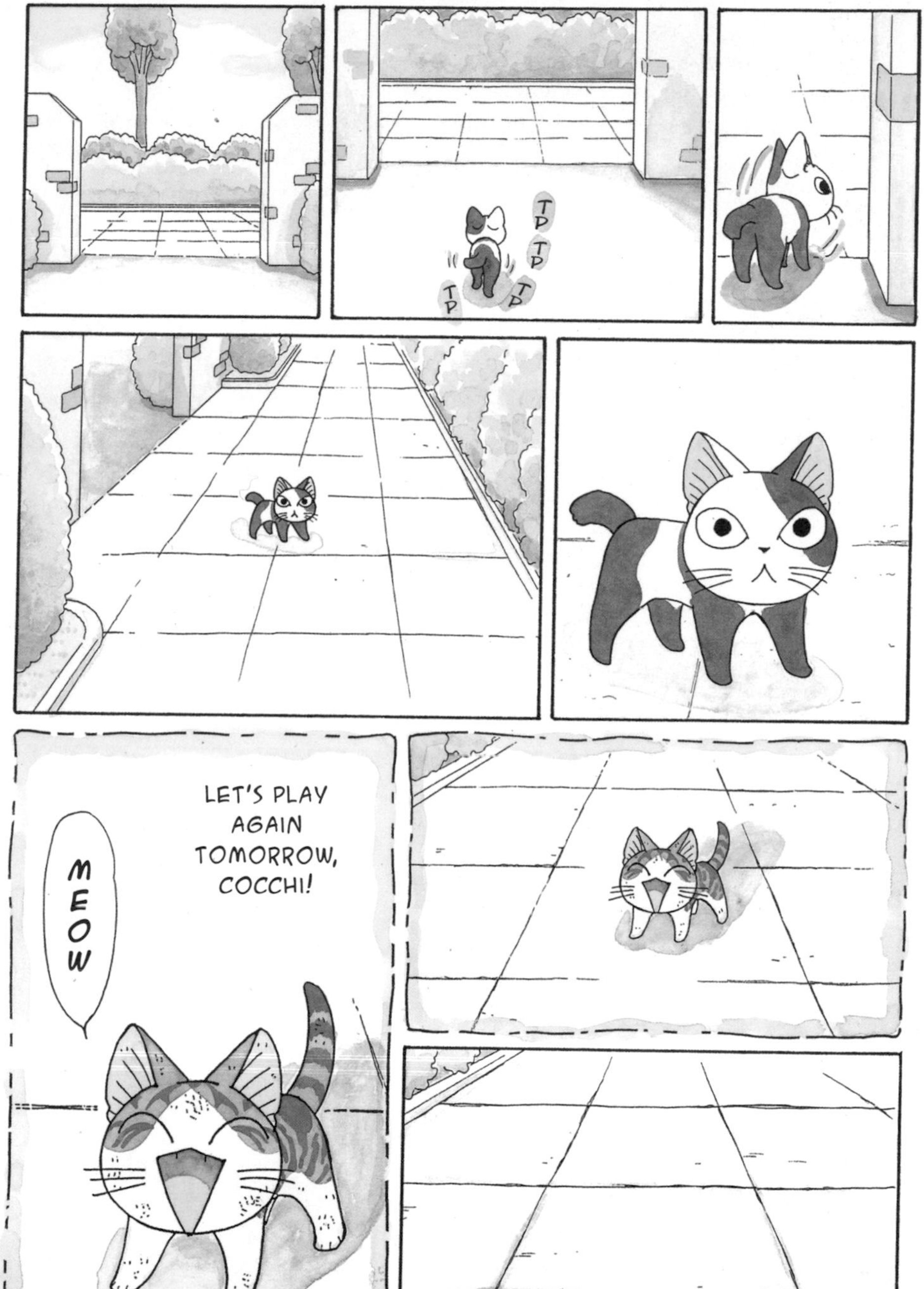
TP
TP
TP
TP
TP
LET'S PLAY AGAIN TOMORROW, COCCHI!
MEOW

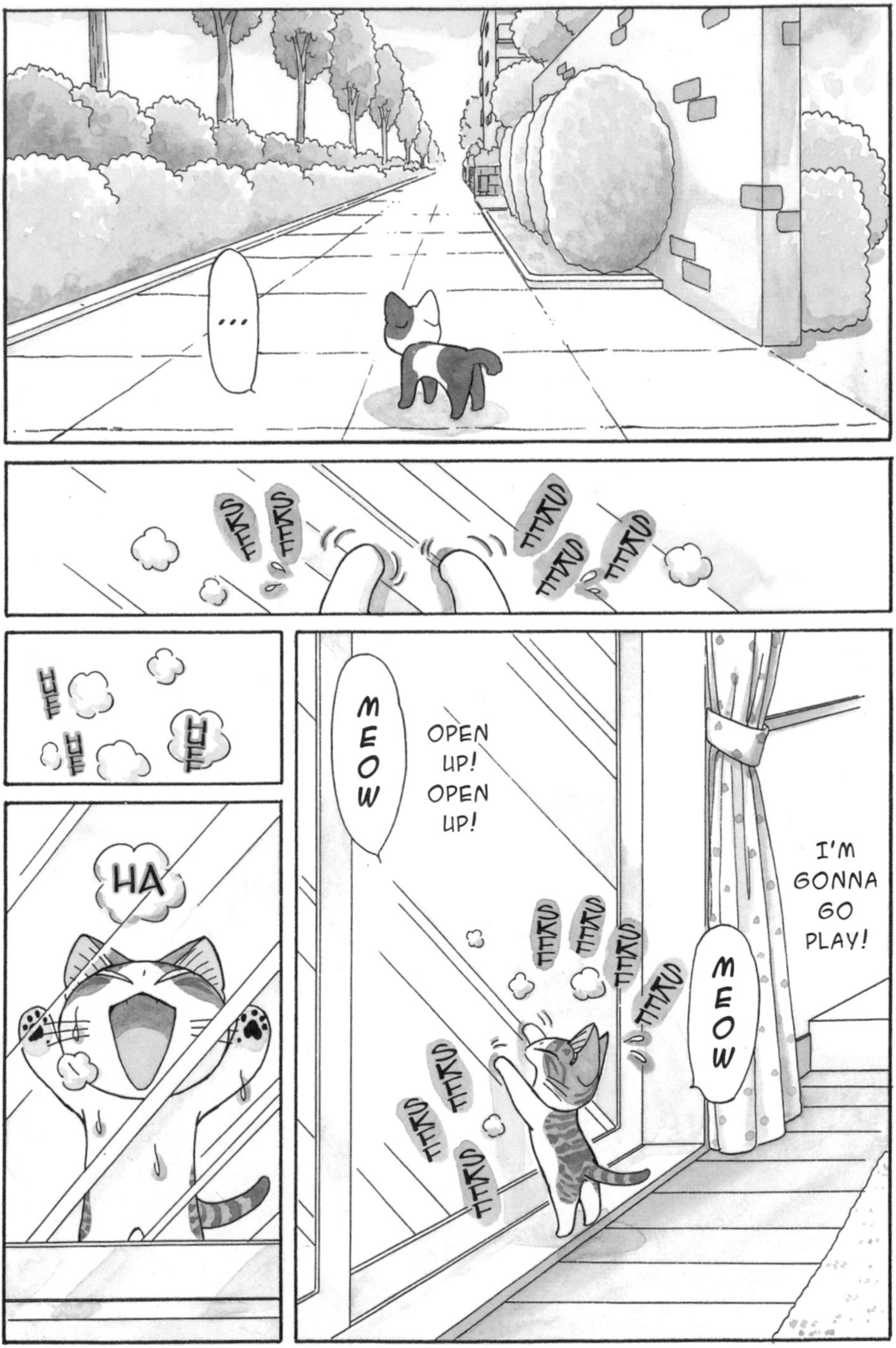
...
SKEE
SKEE
HUFF
HUFF
HUFF
HA
MEOW
OPEN UP! OPEN UP!
SKEE
SKEE
MEOW
I'M GONNA GO PLAY!



**the end**

# homemade 150: a cat is crossed

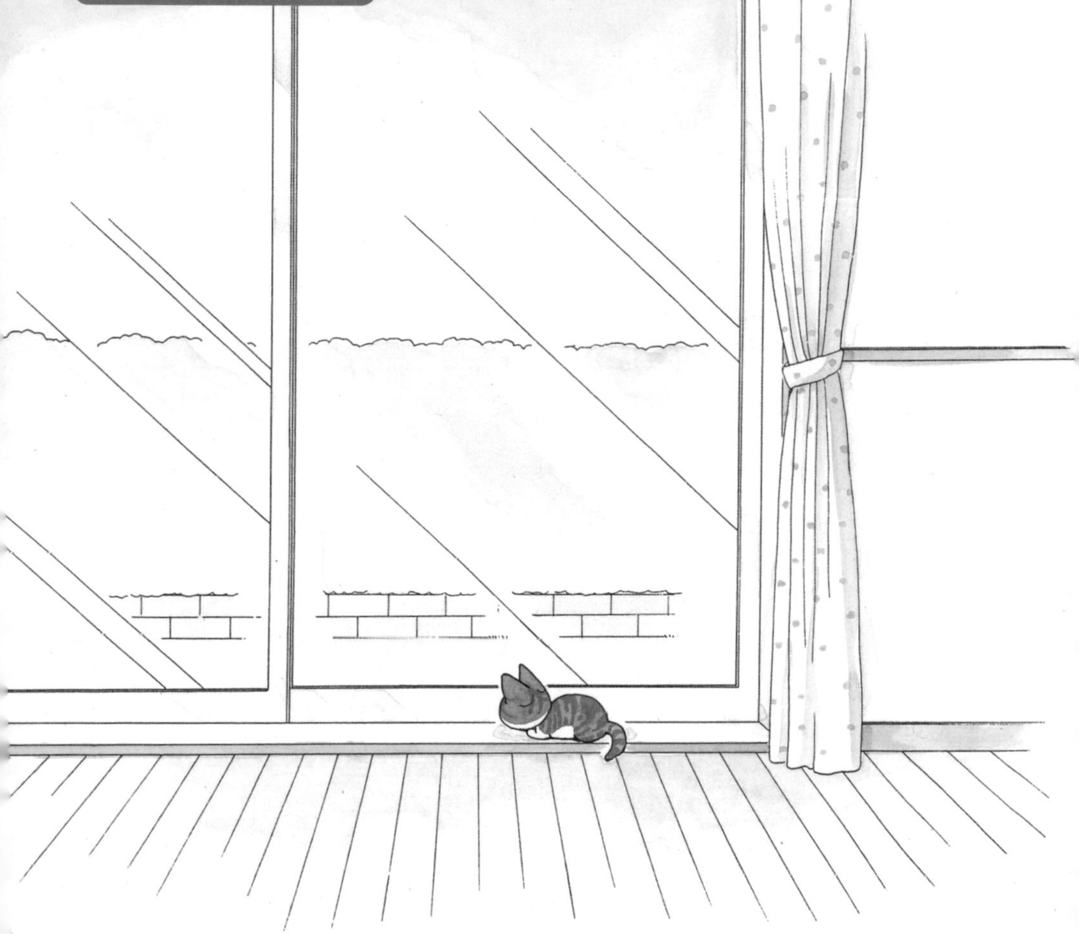

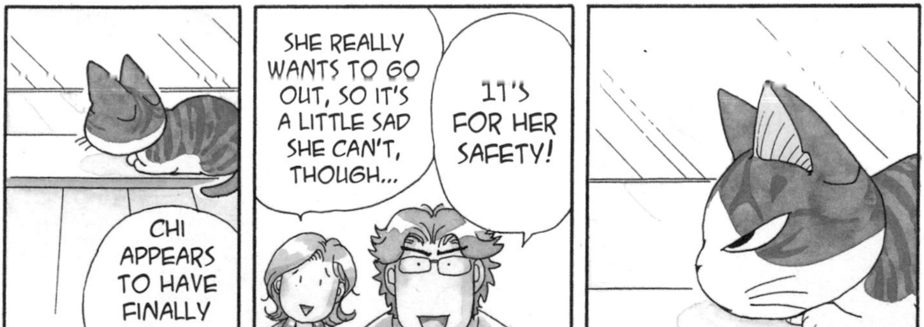
CHI APPEARS TO HAVE FINALLY CALMED DOWN.
SHE REALLY WANTS TO GO OUT, SO IT'S A LITTLE SAD SHE CAN'T, THOUGH...
IT'S FOR HER SAFETY!

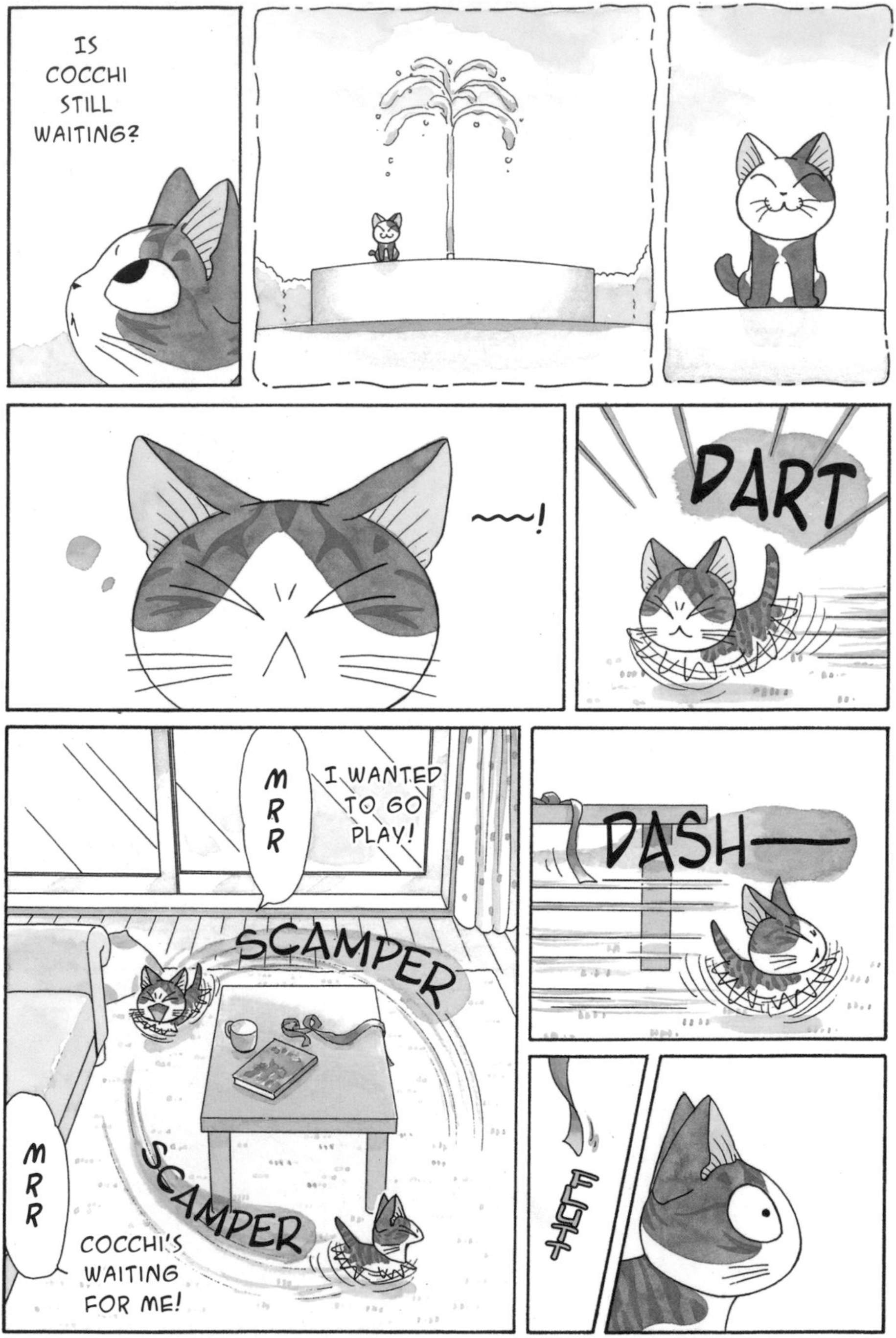
IS COCCHI STILL WAITING?
~~~!
DART
MRR
I WANTED TO GO PLAY!
SCAMPER
SCAMPER
MRR
COCCHI'S WAITING FOR ME!
DASH—
FLUTT
~~~

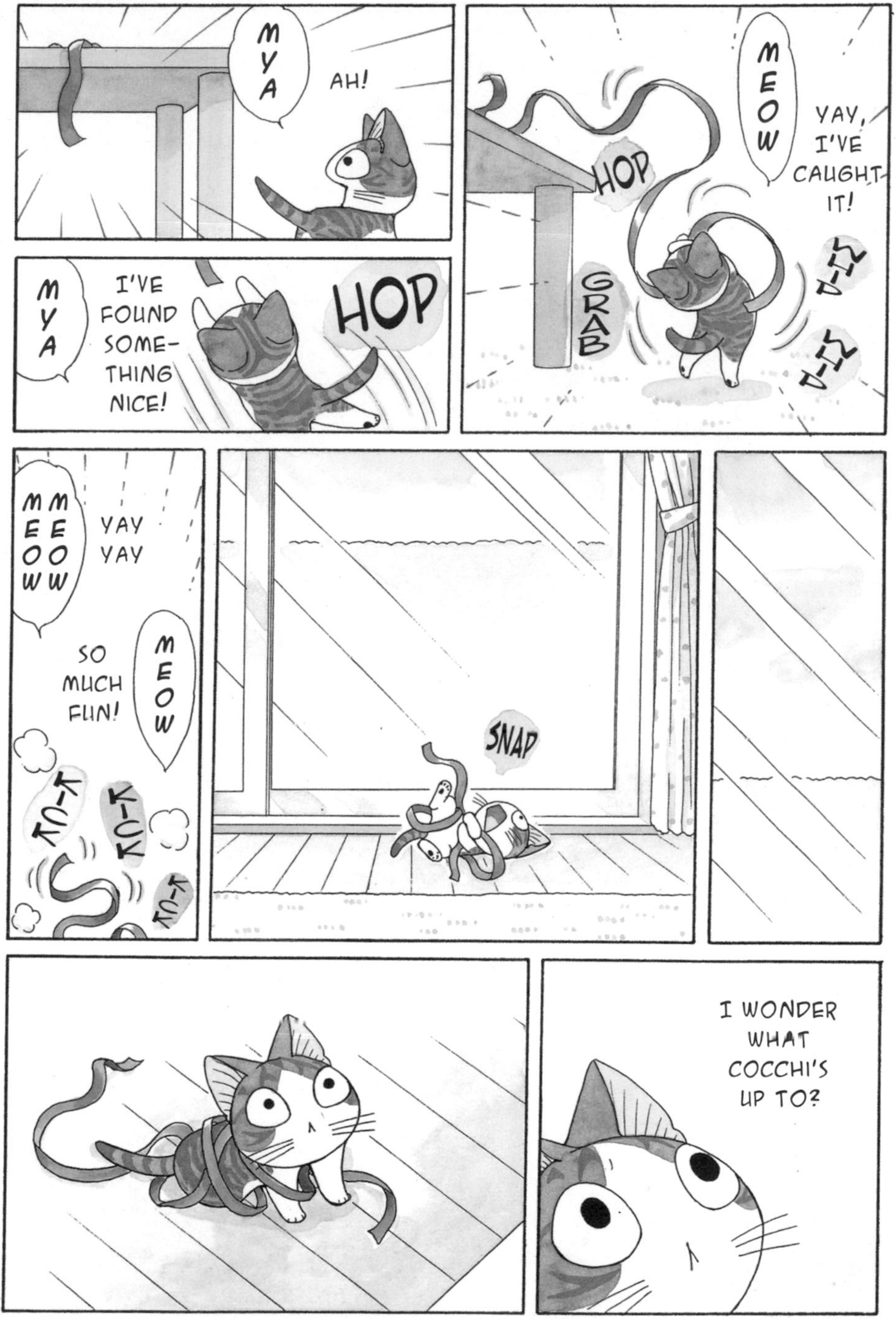
MYA
AH!
MYA
I'VE FOUND SOME-THING NICE!
HOP
MEOW
YAY, I'VE CAUGHT IT!
HOP
GRAB
WHIP
WHIP
MEOW MEOW
YAY YAY
SO MUCH FUN!
MEOW
KICK
KICK
KICK
SNAP
I WONDER WHAT COCCHI'S UP TO?

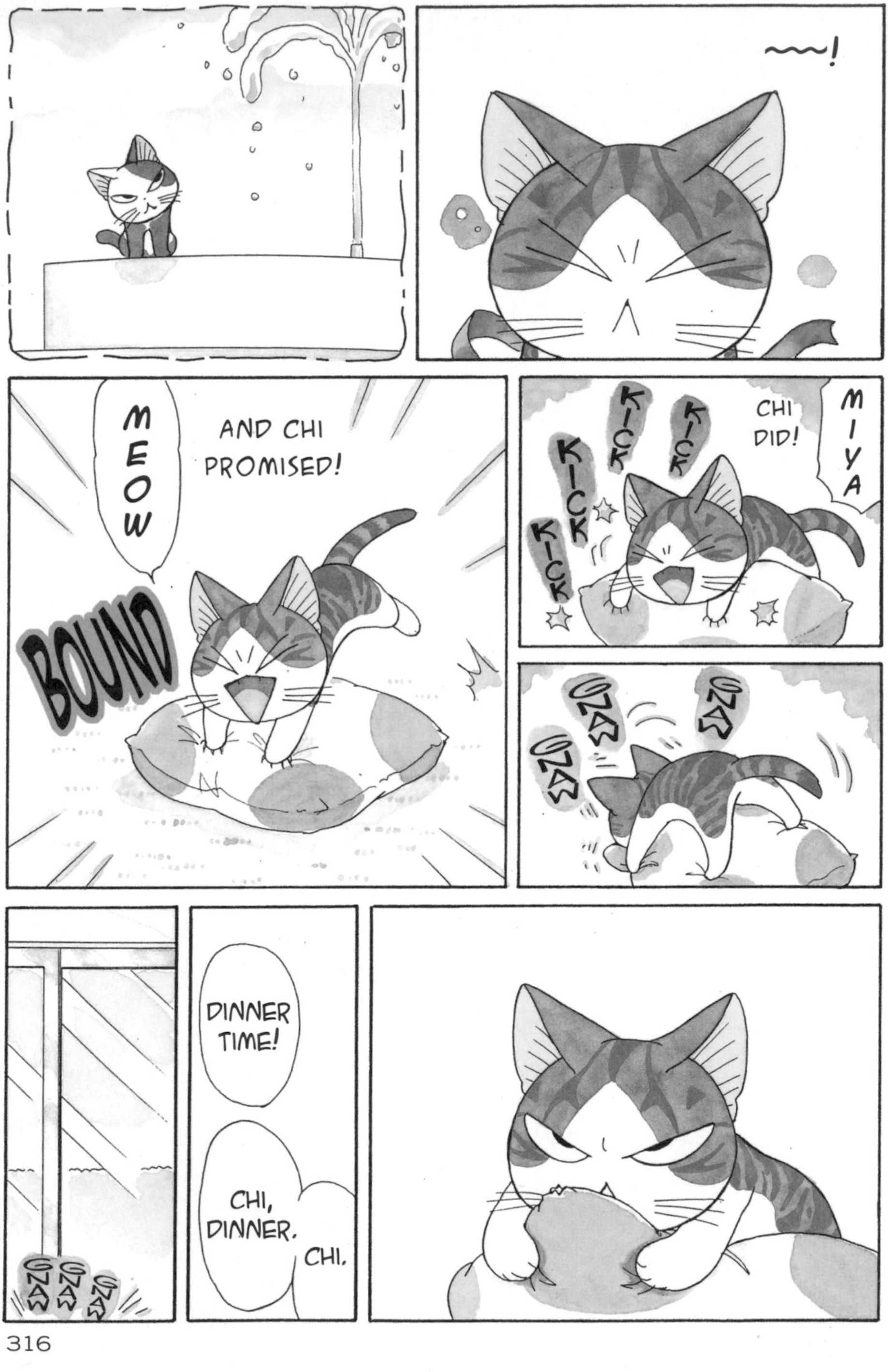

~~~!
MEOW
AND CHI PROMISED!
BOUND
KICK
KICK
KICK
KICK
CHI DID!
MIYA
GNAW
GNAW
GNAW
GNAW GNAW GNAW
DINNER TIME!
CHI, DINNER.
CHI.
~~~

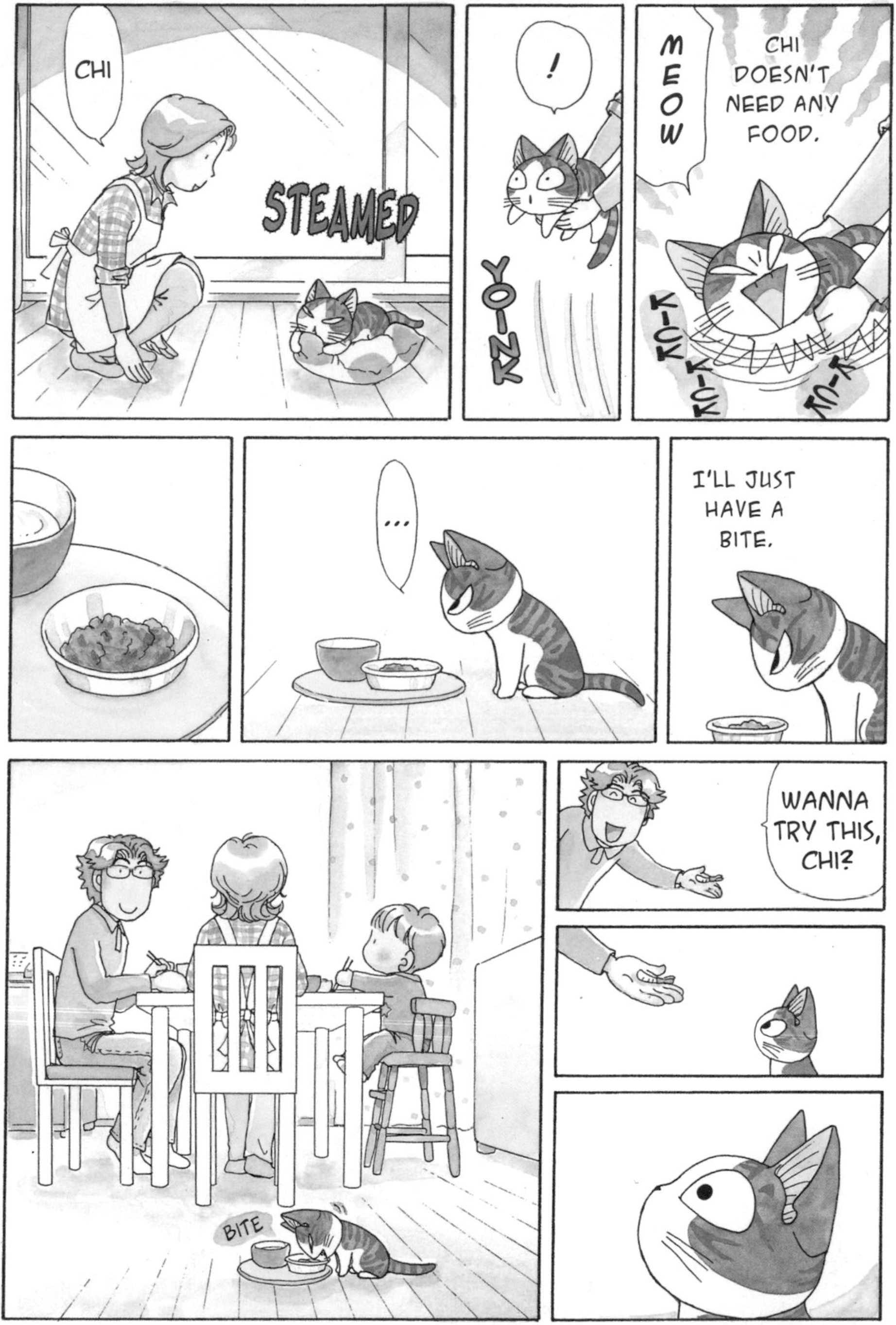
CHI
STEAMED
!
YOINK
MEOW
CHI DOESN'T NEED ANY FOOD.
KICK
KICK
KICK
...
I'LL JUST HAVE A BITE.
BITE
WANNA TRY THIS, CHI?

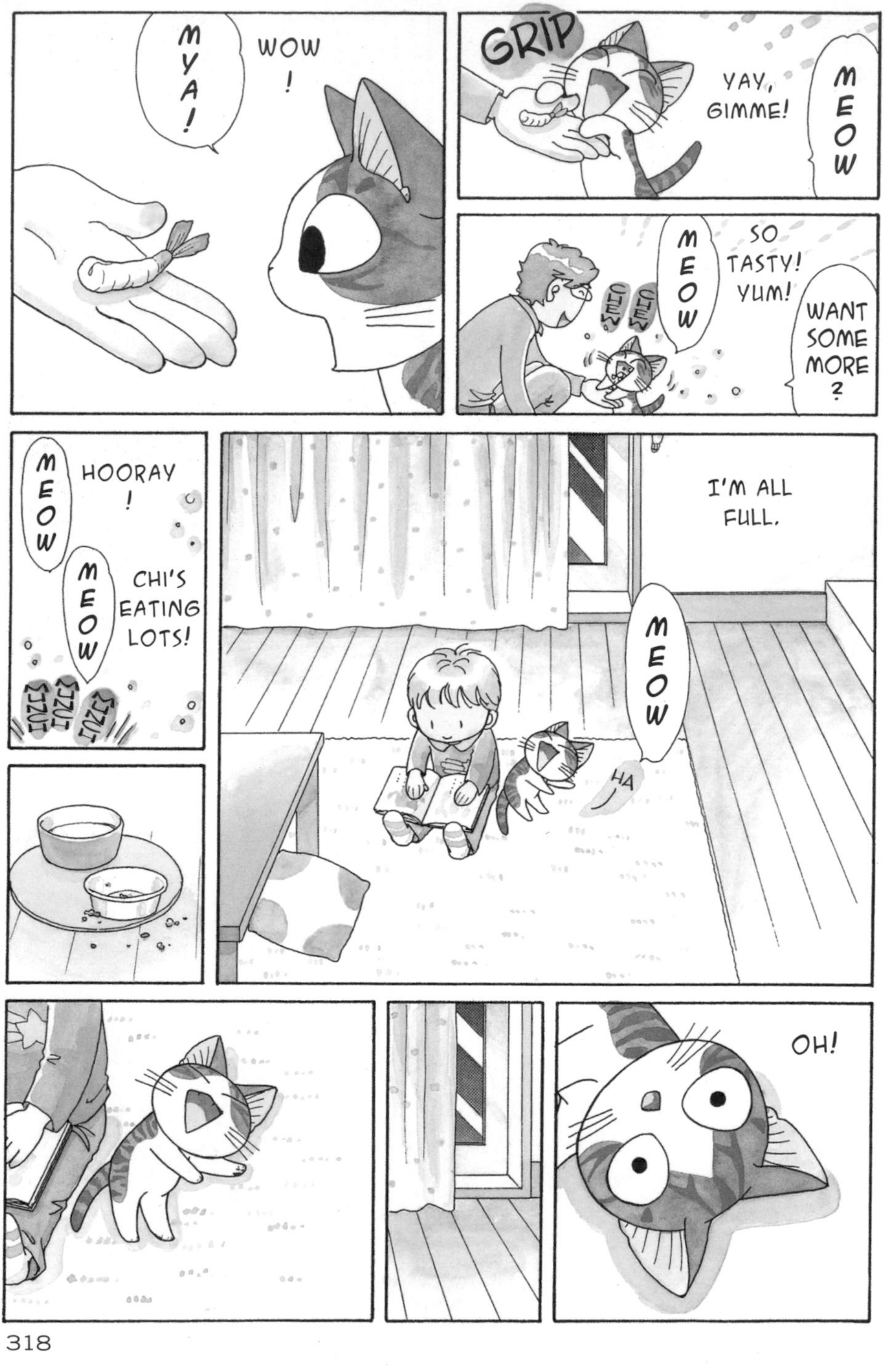
MYA!
WOW!
GRIP
YAY, GIMME!
MEOW
MEOW
SO TASTY! YUM!
CHEW CHEW
WANT SOME MORE?
MEOW MEOW
HOORAY!
MEOW MEOW
CHI'S EATING LOTS!
I'M ALL FULL.
MEOW
HA
OH!

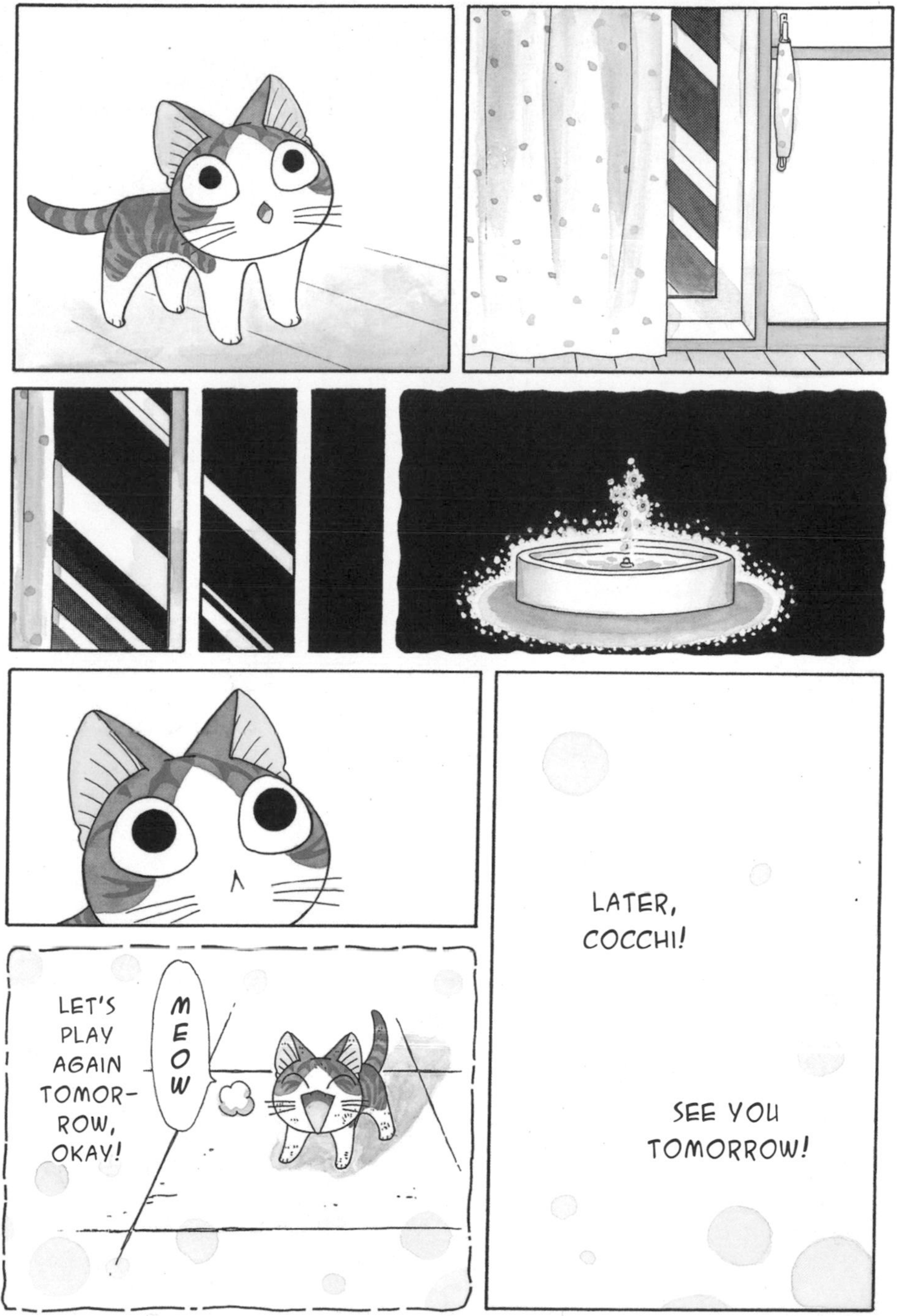

LET'S PLAY AGAIN TOMOR-ROW, OKAY!
MEOW
LATER, COCCHI!
SEE YOU TOMORROW!

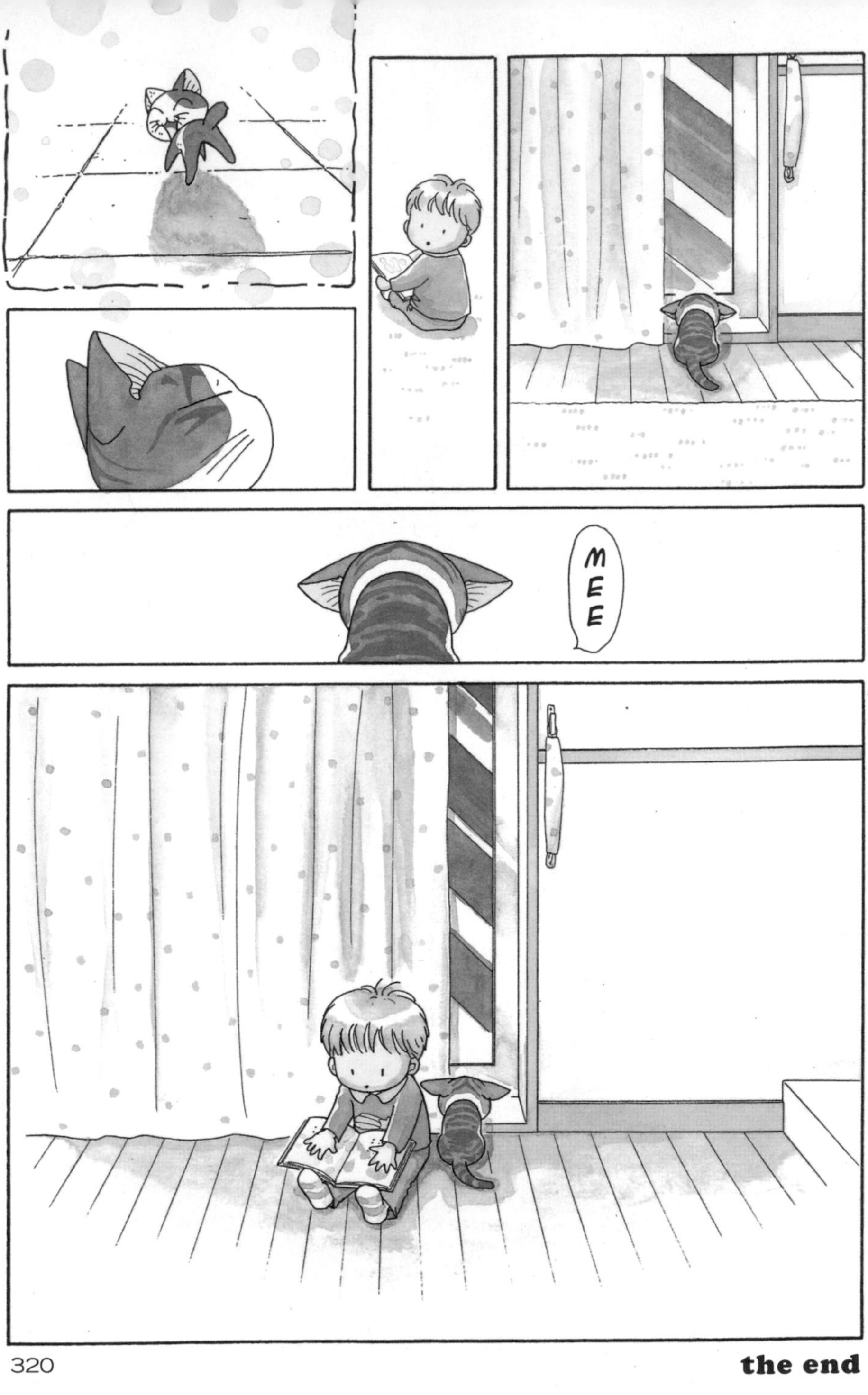
MEE



**the end**

# homemade 151: a cat is linked

KACHAK
WE'RE GOING NOW.
HAVE FUN, OKAY?
DO YOU HAVE YOUR SANDBOX SET?
YUP
OKAY!

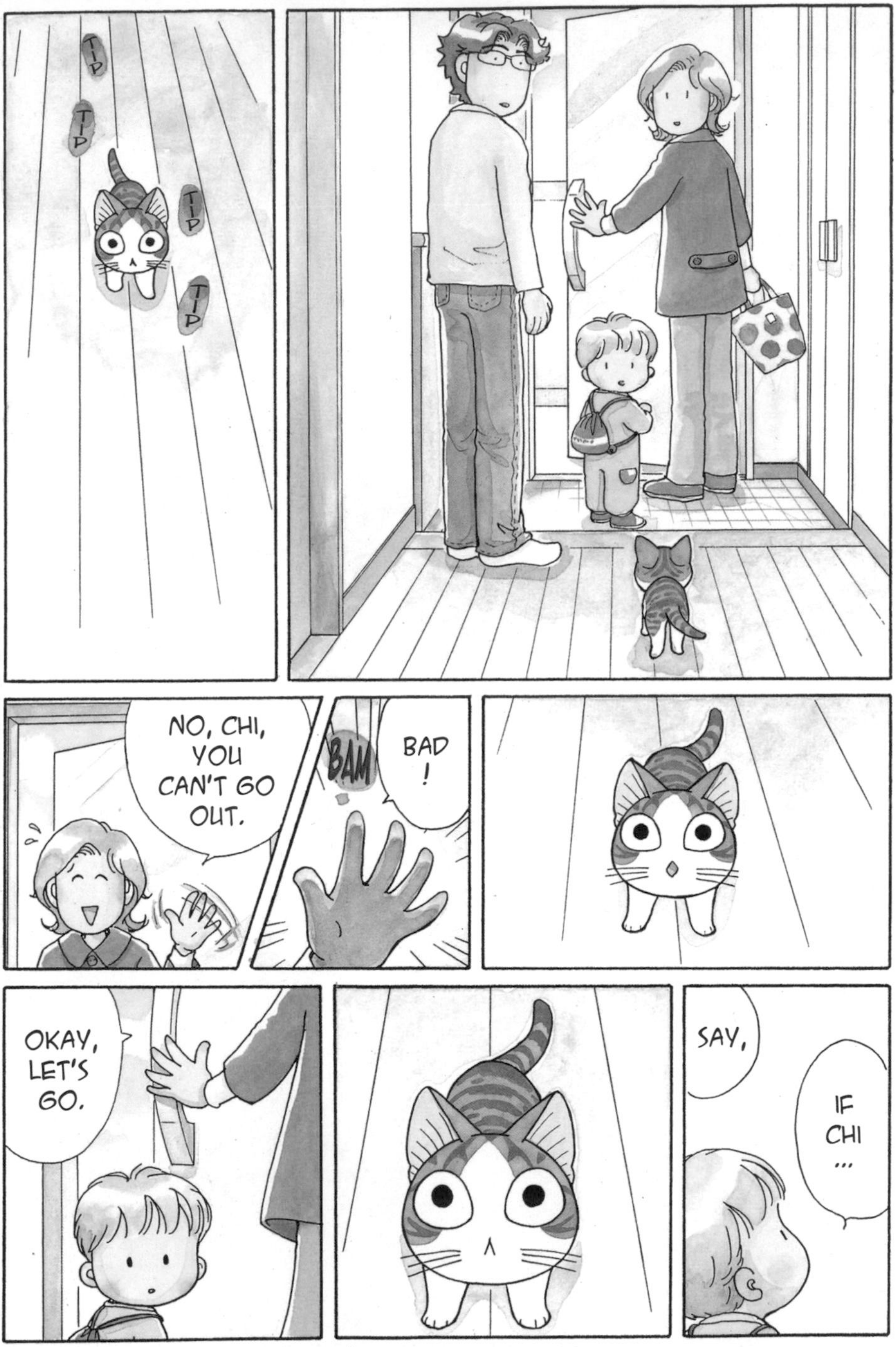
TIP
TIP
TIP
TIP
NO, CHI, YOU CAN'T GO OUT.
BAM
BAD!
OKAY, LET'S GO.
SAY,
IF CHI...

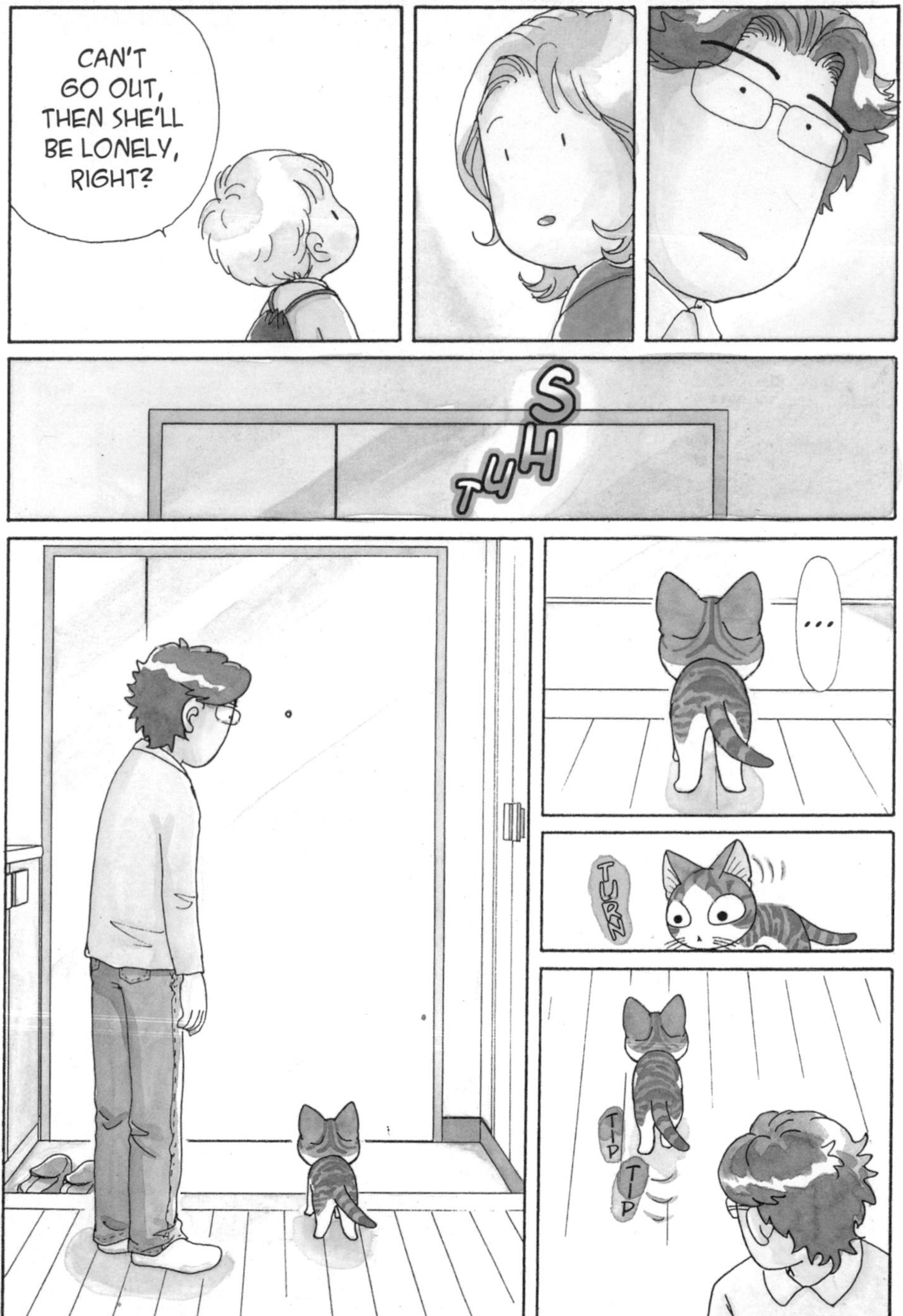
CAN'T GO OUT, THEN SHE'LL BE LONELY, RIGHT?
SHHT
...
TURN
TIP
TIP
TIP

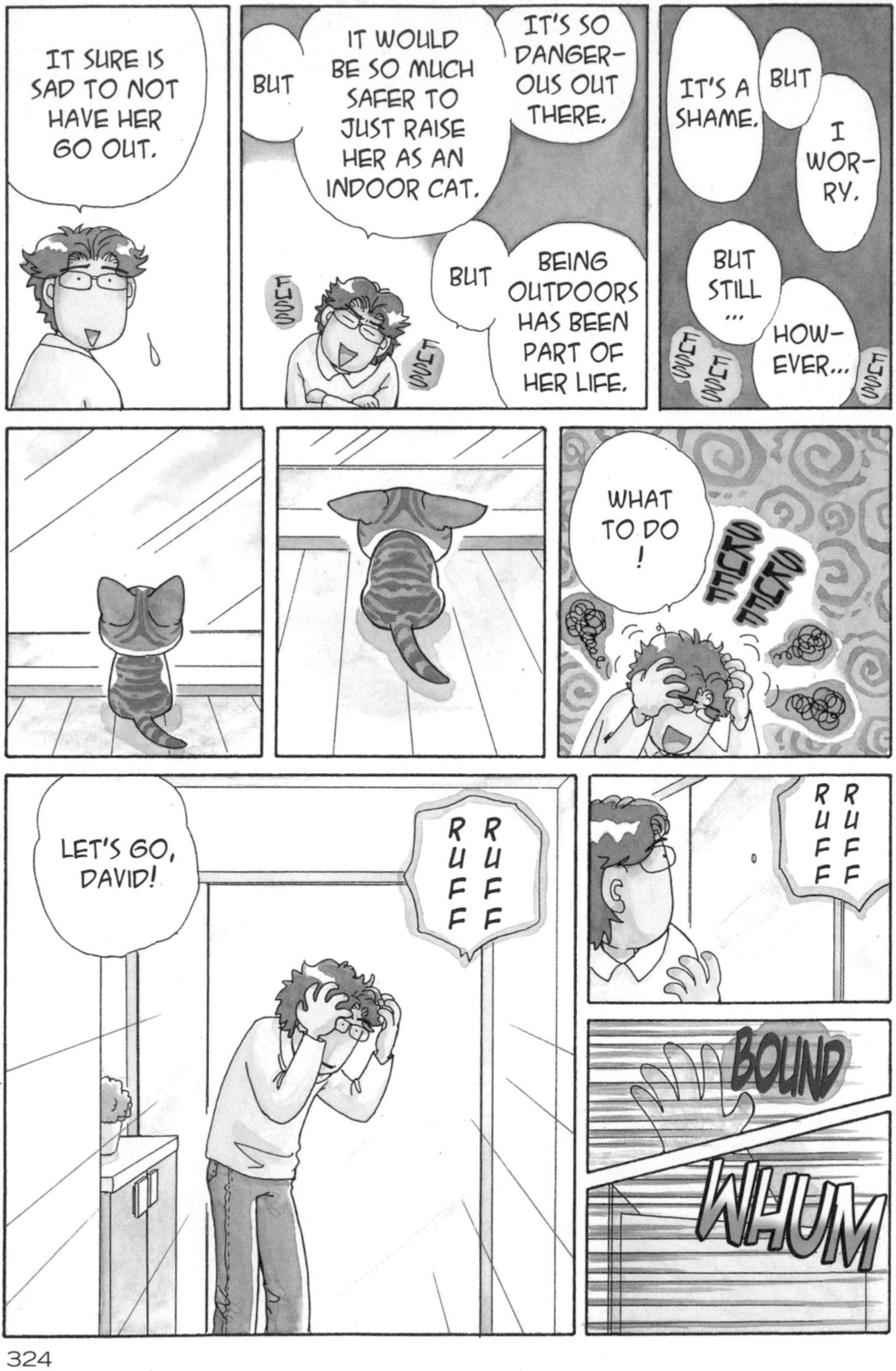
IT SURE IS SAD TO NOT HAVE HER GO OUT.
BUT
IT WOULD BE SO MUCH SAFER TO JUST RAISE HER AS AN INDOOR CAT.
IT'S SO DANGEROUS OUT THERE.
FUSS
BUT
BEING OUTDOORS HAS BEEN PART OF HER LIFE.
FUSS
IT'S A SHAME.
BUT
I WORRY.
BUT STILL ...
HOWEVER...
FUSS
FUSS
FUSS
WHAT TO DO!
SCRUFF
SCRUFF
LET'S GO, DAVID!
RUFF RUFF
RUFF RUFF
BOUND
WHUM

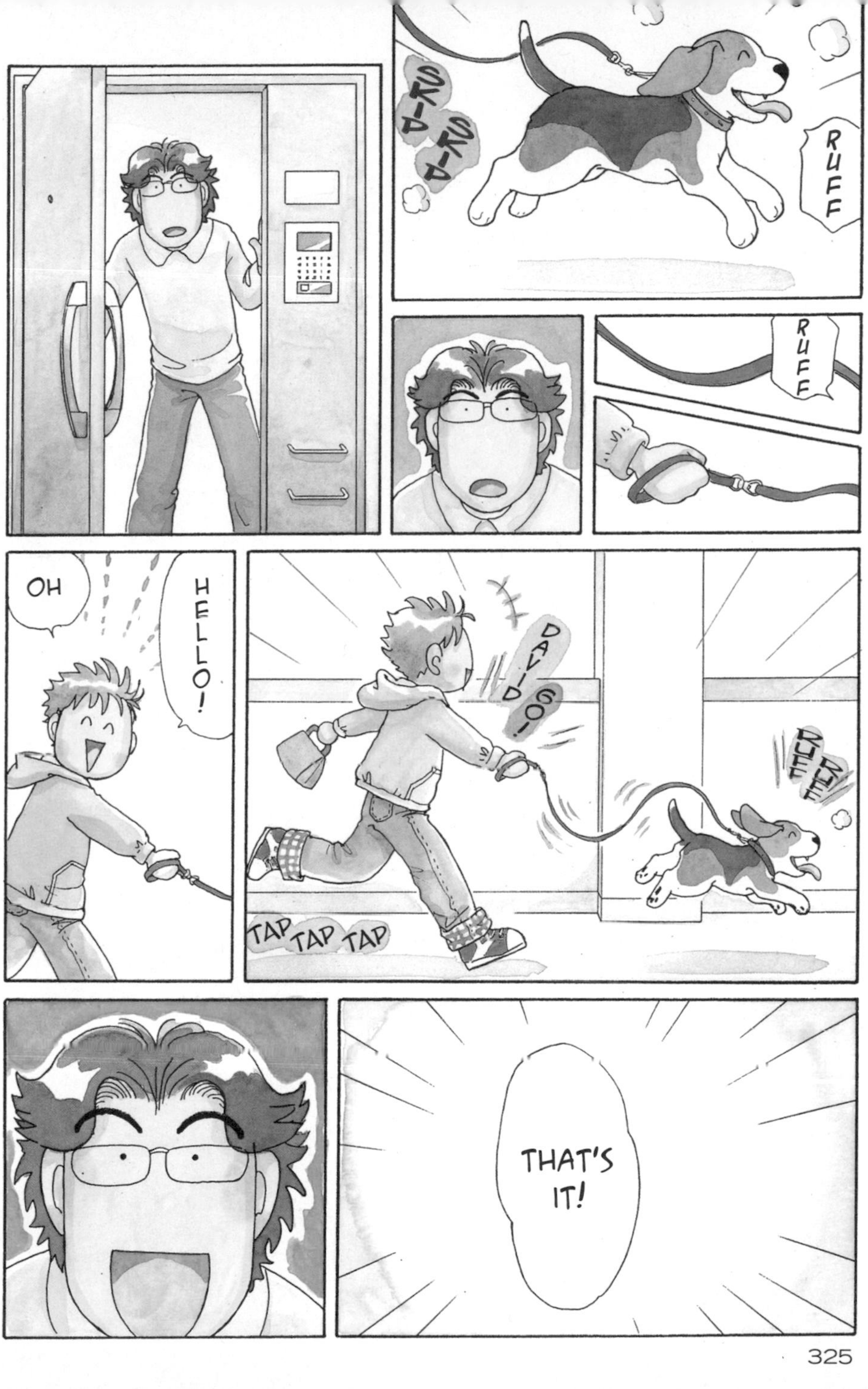
SKIP SKIP
RUFF
RUFF
OH
HELLO!
DAVID, GO!
RUFF RUFF
TAP TAP TAP
THAT'S IT!

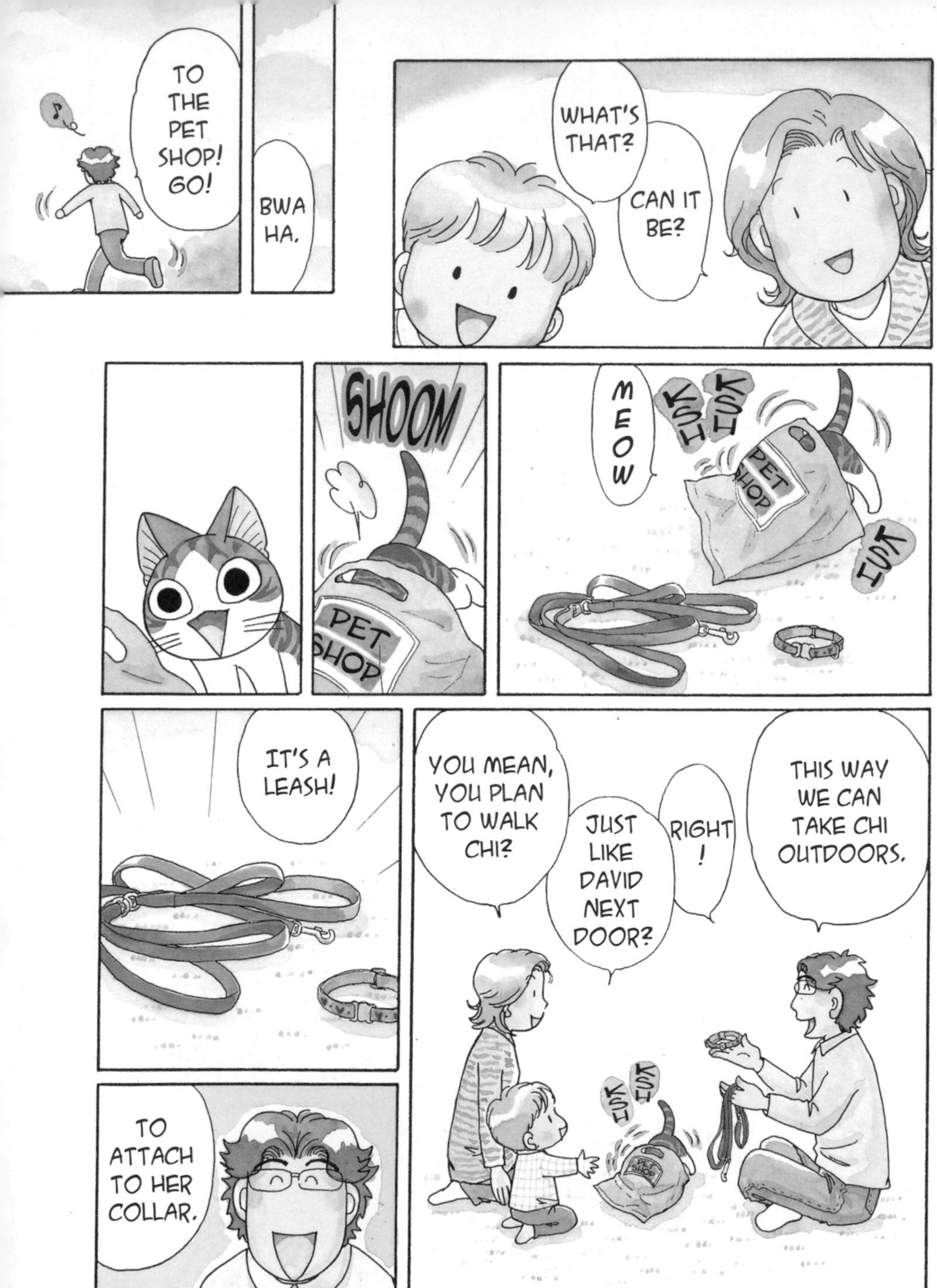
TO THE PET SHOP! GO!
BWA HA.
WHAT'S THAT?
CAN IT BE?
SHOOM
MEOW
KSH
KSH
KSH
IT'S A LEASH!
TO ATTACH TO HER COLLAR.
YOU MEAN, YOU PLAN TO WALK CHI?
JUST LIKE DAVID NEXT DOOR?
RIGHT!
THIS WAY WE CAN TAKE CHI OUTDOORS.
KSH
KSH
PET SHOP

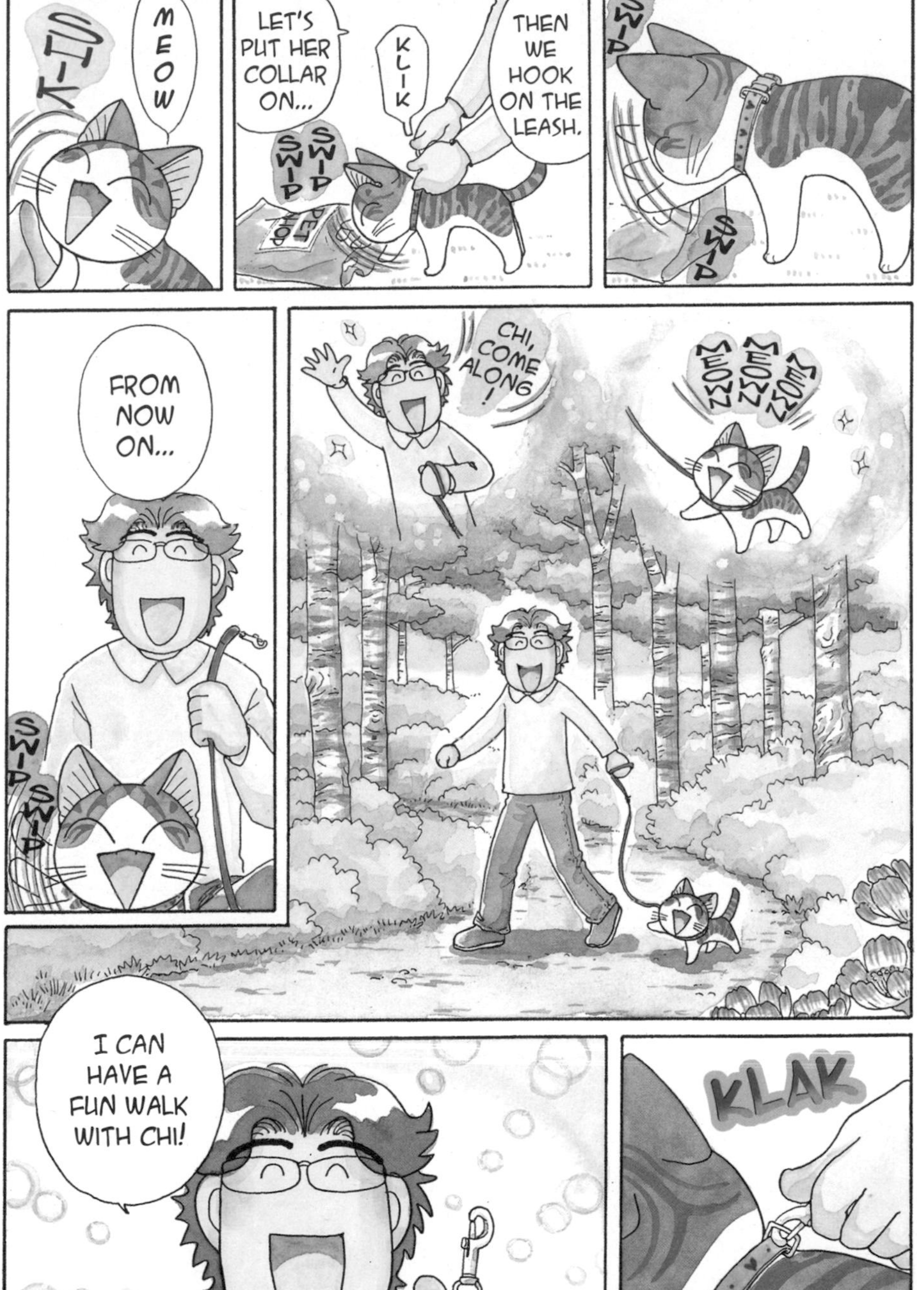
SHIK
MEOW
LET'S PUT HER COLLAR ON...
KLIK
THEN WE HOOK ON THE LEASH.
SWIP SWIP
PET SHOP
SWIP
SWIP
FROM NOW ON...
SWIP SWIP
CHI, COME ALONG!
MEOWN MEOWN MEOWN
I CAN HAVE A FUN WALK WITH CHI!
KLAK

HUH?

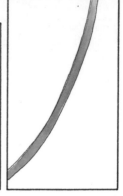

HEY?

...

...?

WHY AM I GETTING A BAD FEELING?

**the end**

## homemade 152: a cat is unleashed

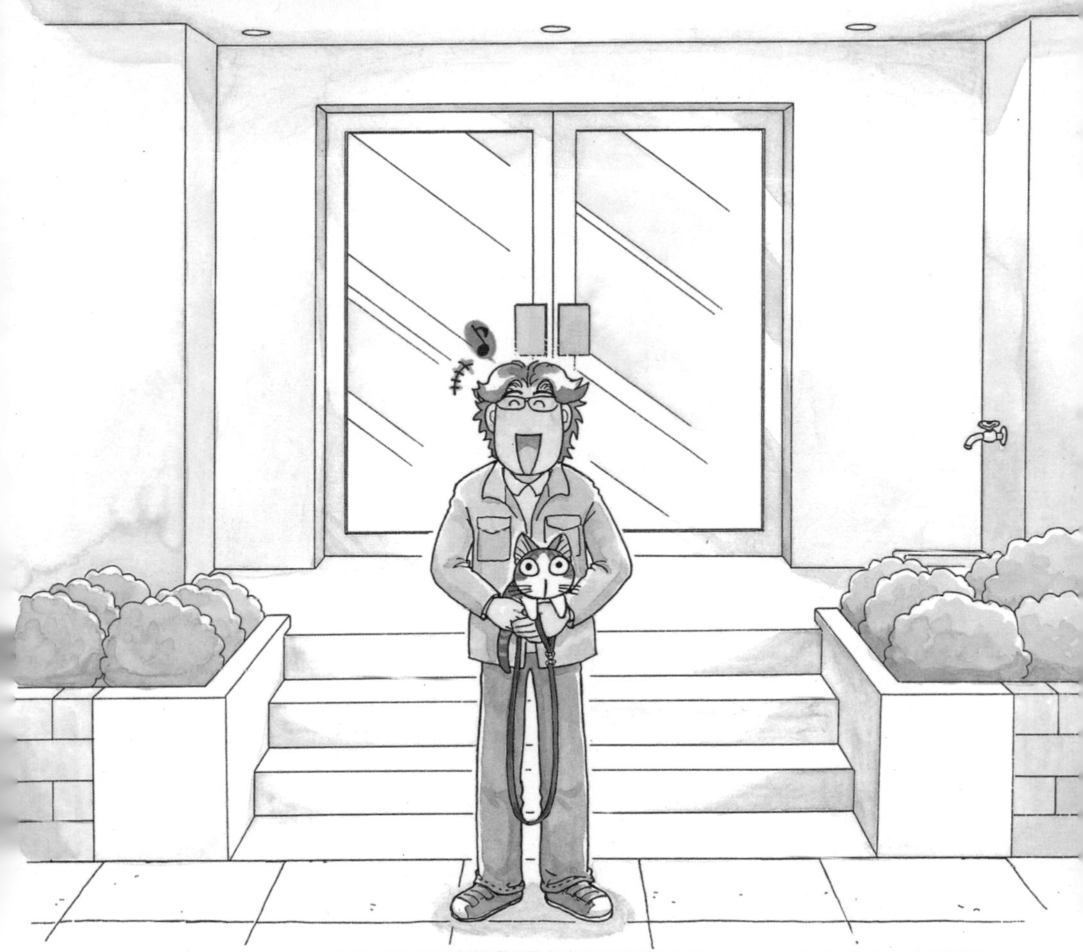

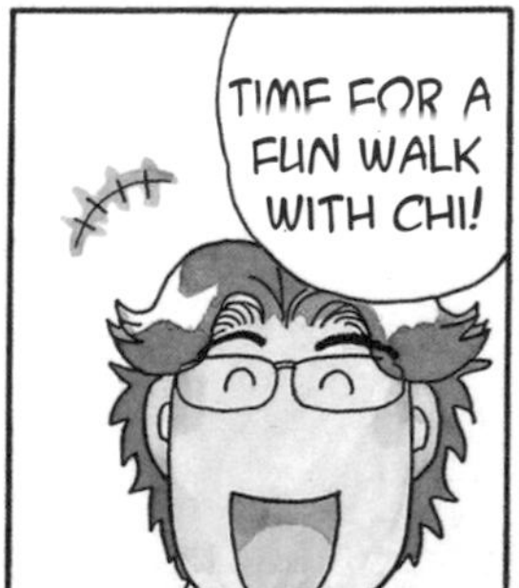
TIME FOR A FUN WALK WITH CHI!

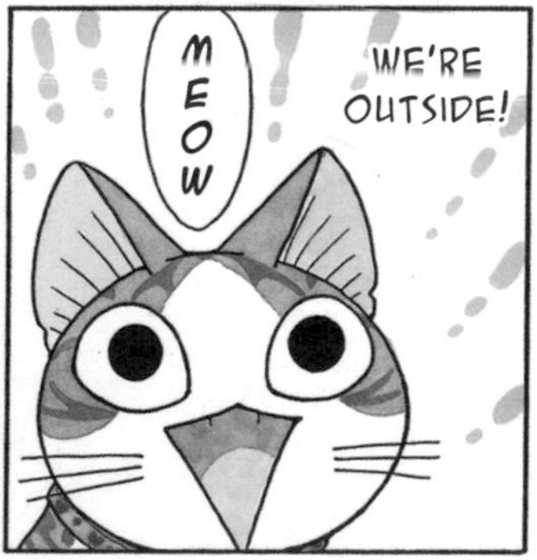
WE'RE OUTSIDE!
MEOW

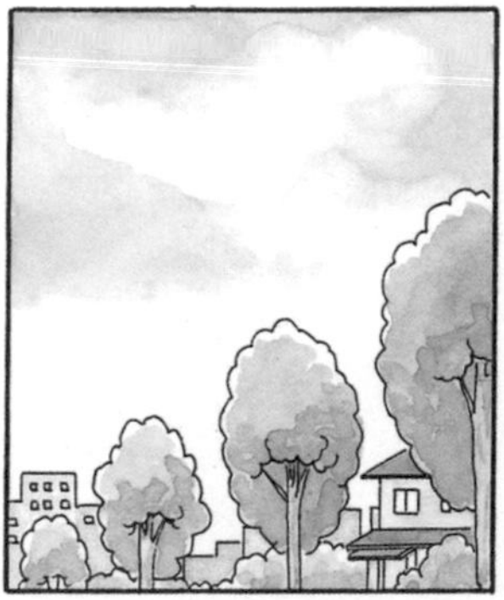

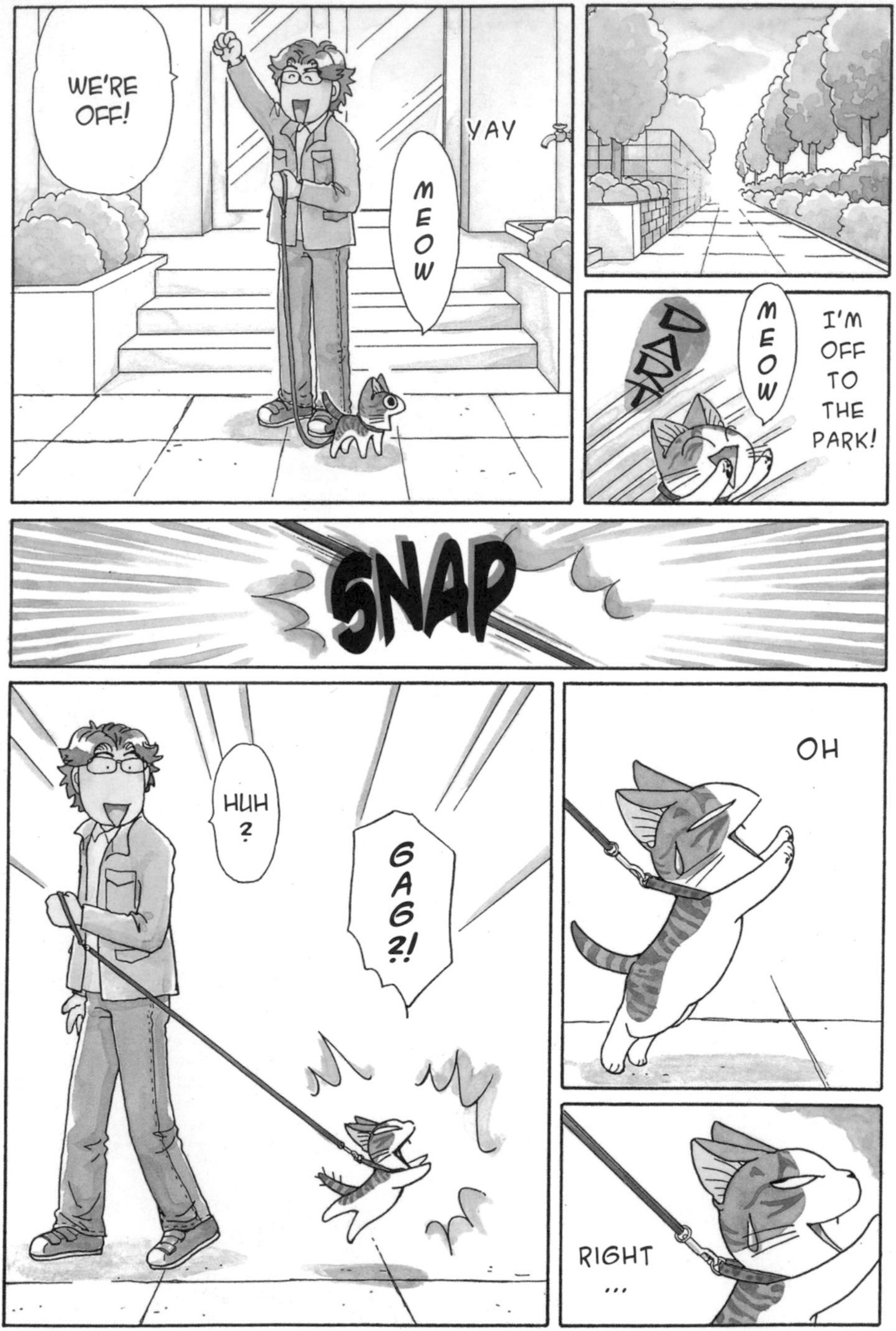

WE'RE OFF!
YAY
MEOW
MEOW
DART
I'M OFF TO THE PARK!
SNAP
HUH?
GAG?!
OH
RIGHT ...

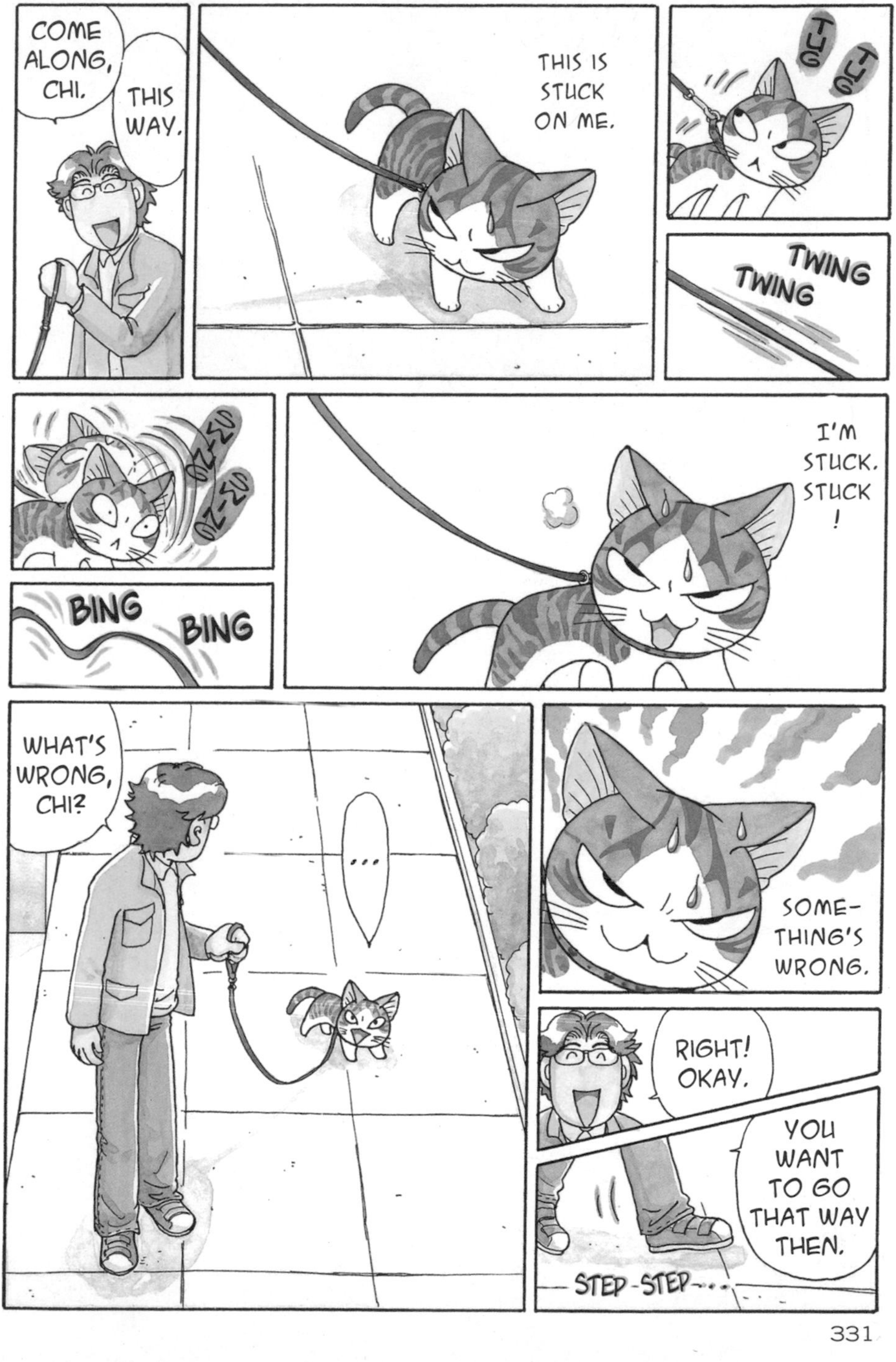
COME ALONG, CHI.
THIS WAY.
THIS IS STUCK ON ME.
TUG
TUG
TWING
TWING
BING
BING
I'M STUCK. STUCK!
WHAT'S WRONG, CHI?
...
SOME-THING'S WRONG.
RIGHT! OKAY.
YOU WANT TO GO THAT WAY THEN.
STEP-STEP...

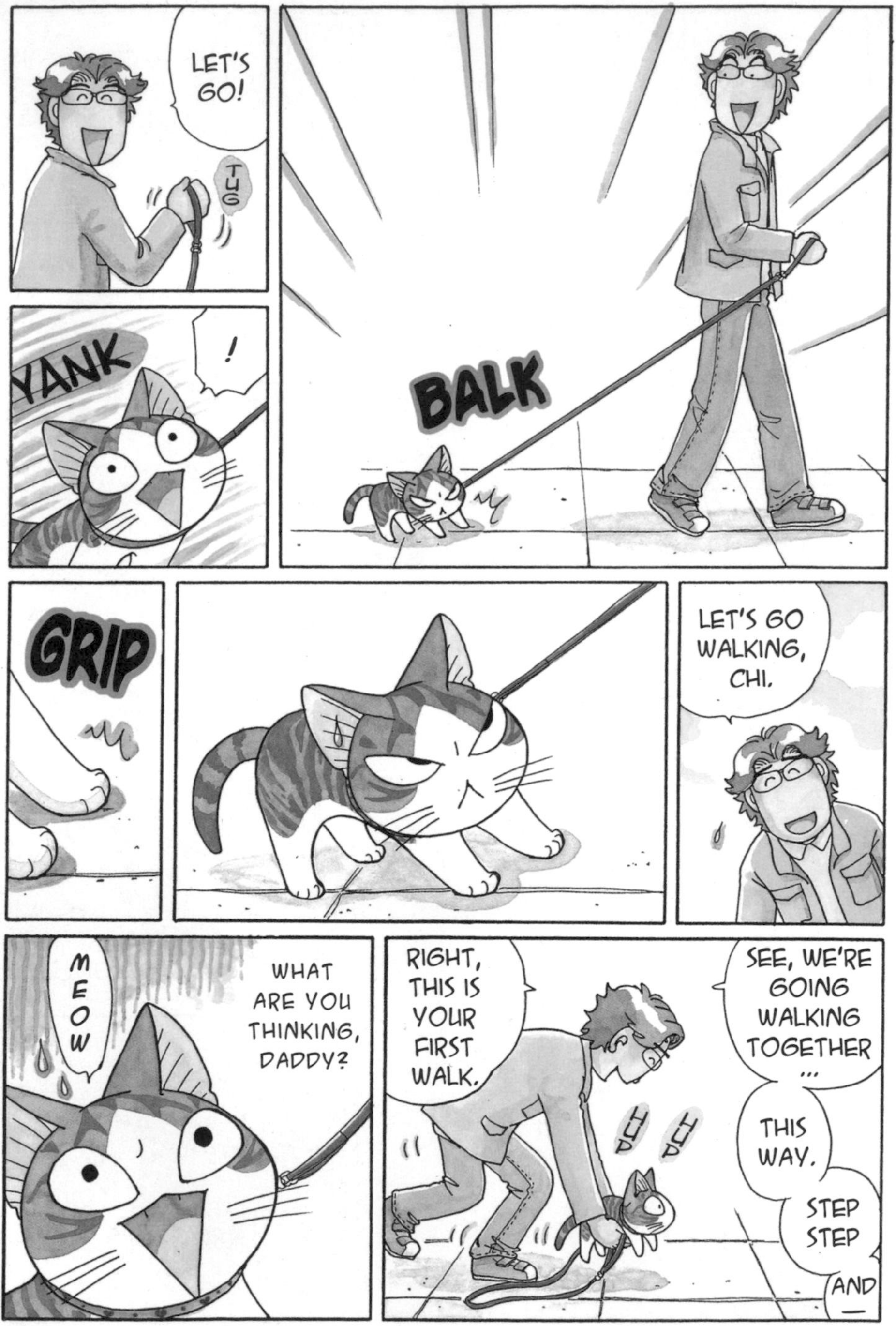
LET'S GO!
TUG
YANK
!
BALK
GRIP
LET'S GO WALKING, CHI.
MEOW
WHAT ARE YOU THINKING, DADDY?
RIGHT, THIS IS YOUR FIRST WALK.
SEE, WE'RE GOING WALKING TOGETHER ...
HUP
HUP
THIS WAY.
STEP STEP
AND

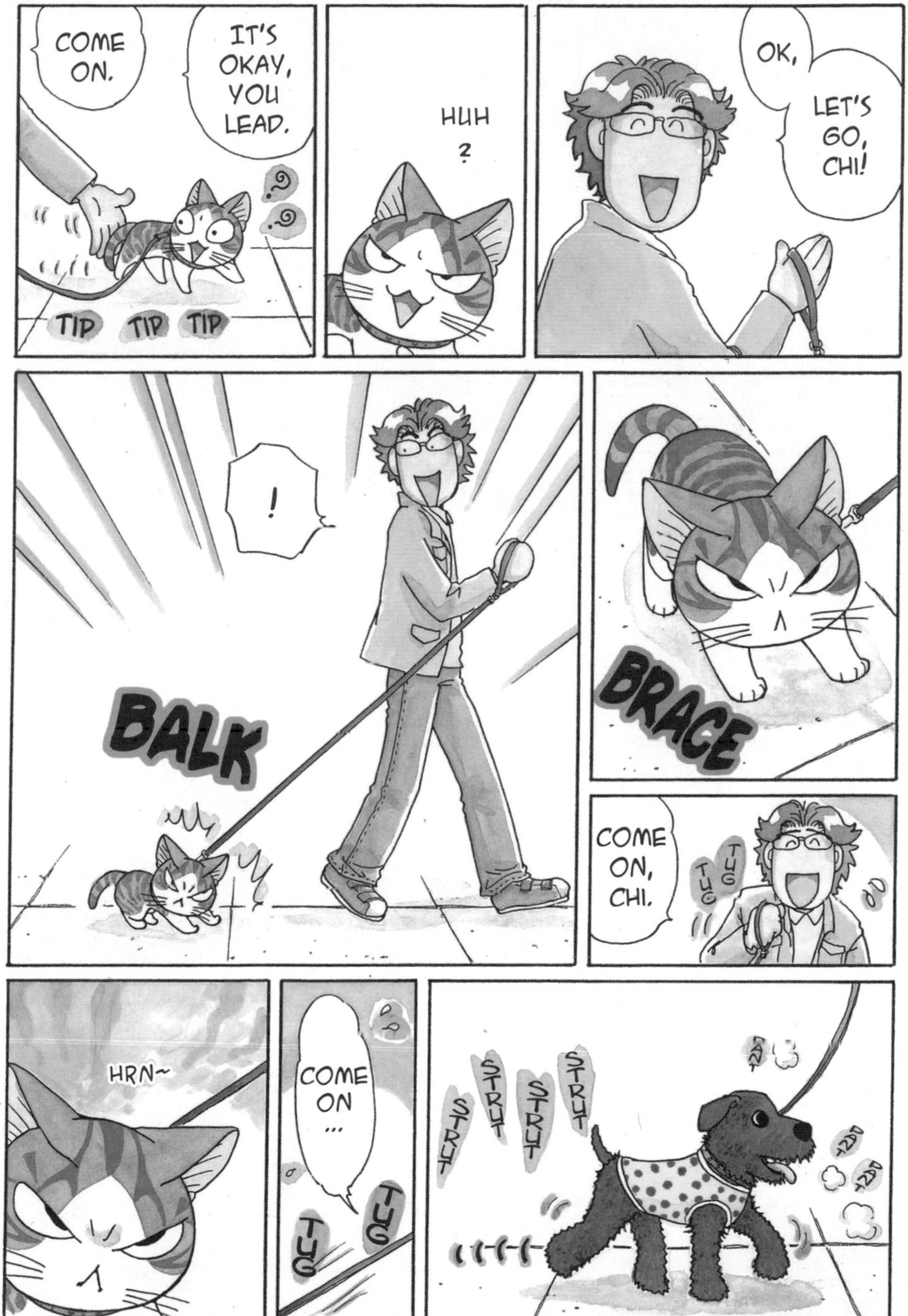
COME ON.
IT'S OKAY, YOU LEAD.
TIP TIP TIP
HUH ?
OK,
LET'S GO, CHI!
!
BALK
BRACE
COME ON, CHI.
TUG TUG
HRN~
COME ON ...
TUG TUG
STRUT STRUT STRUT STRUT

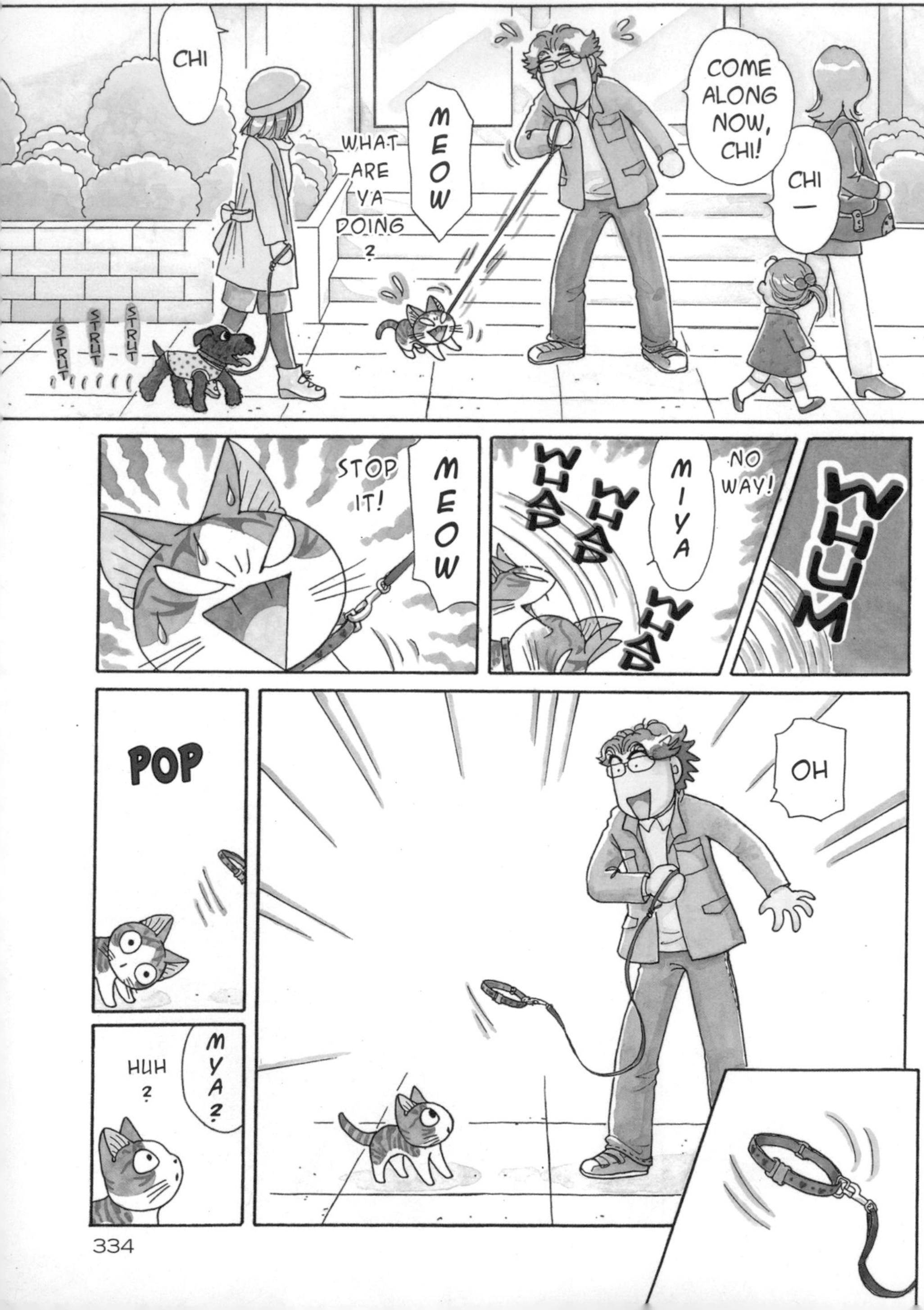
CHI
STRUT STRUT STRUT
WHAT ARE YA DOING?
MEOW
COME ALONG NOW, CHI!
CHI—
STOP IT!
MEOW
WHAP WHAP WHAP
MIYA
NO WAY!
WHUM
POP
HUH?
MYA?
OH

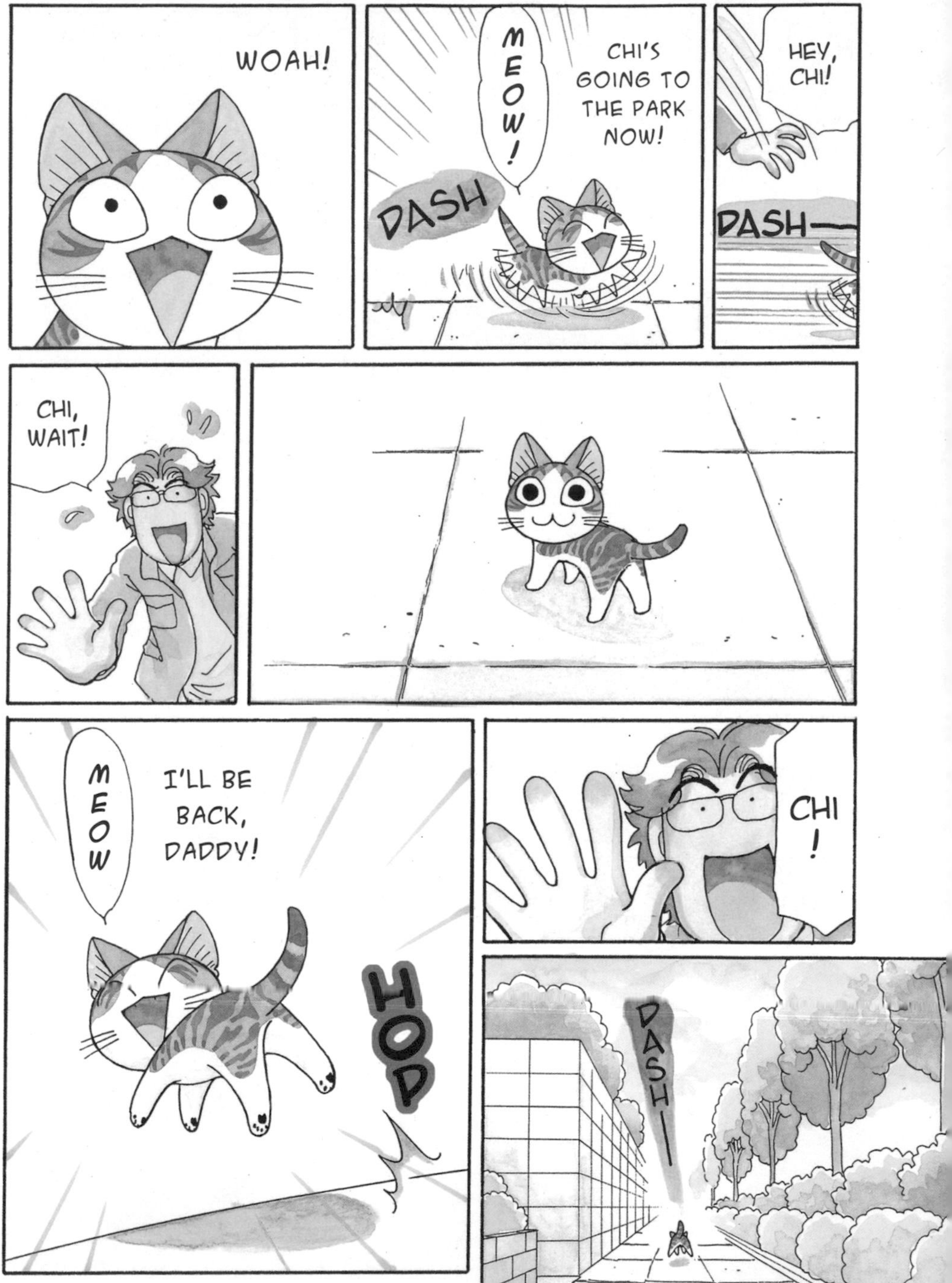
WOAH!
MEOW!
CHI'S GOING TO THE PARK NOW!
DASH
HEY, CHI!
DASH—
CHI, WAIT!
MEOW
I'LL BE BACK, DADDY!
HOP
CHI!
DASH

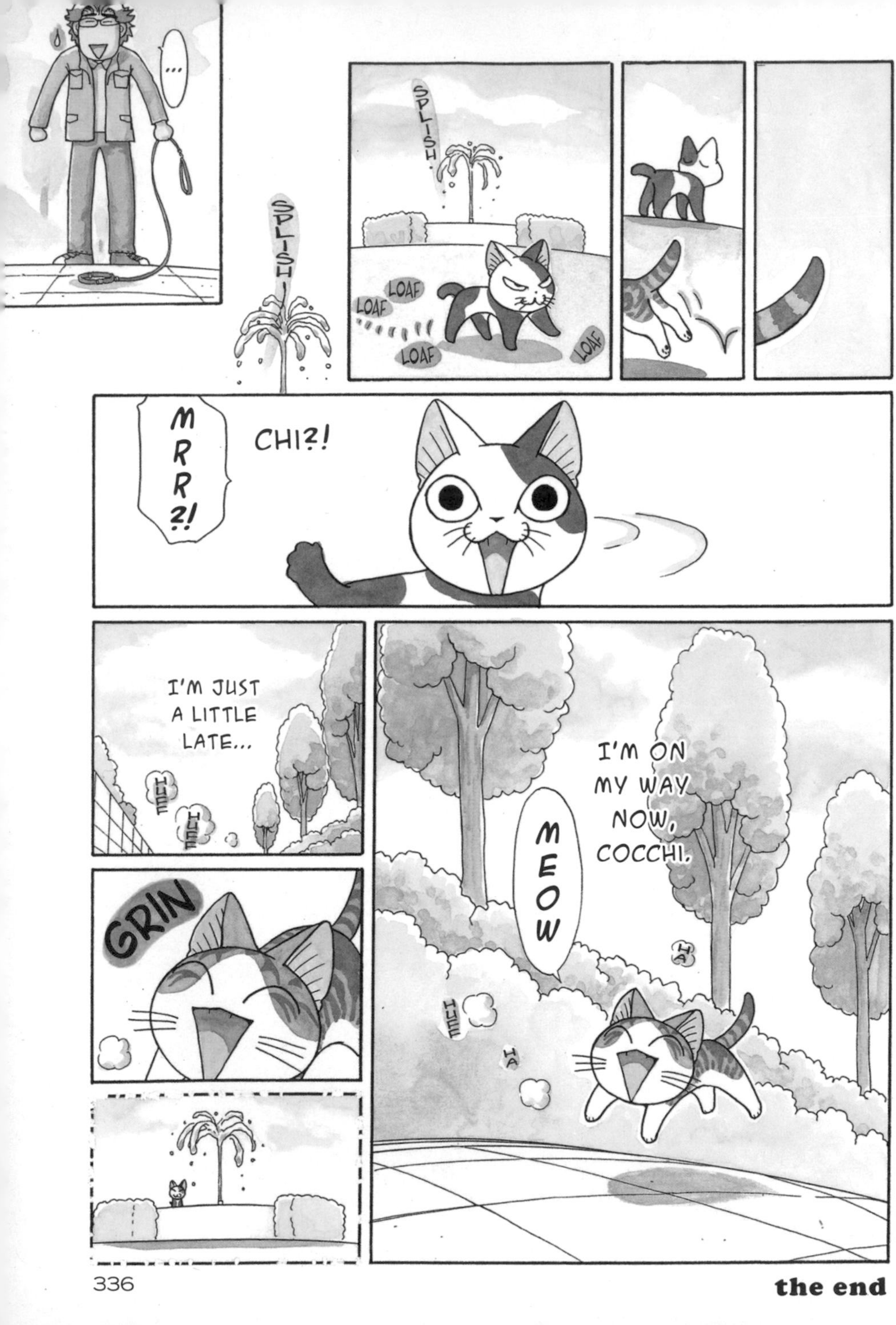
...
SPLISH
SPLISH
LOAF
LOAF
LOAF
LOAF
MRRR?!
CHI?!
I'M JUST A LITTLE LATE...
HUFF
HUFF
GRIN
I'M ON MY WAY NOW, COCCHI.
MEOW
HA
HUFF
HA



**the end**

## homemade 153: a cat hurries

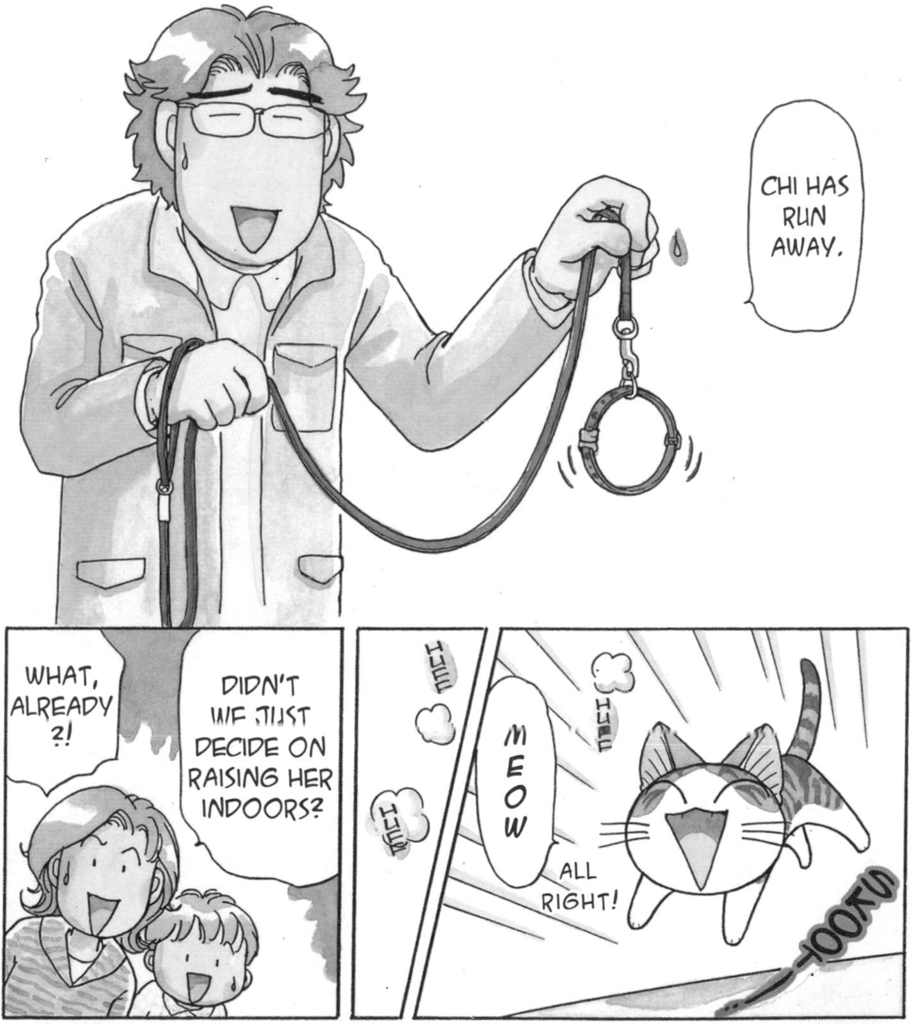
CHI HAS RUN AWAY.
WHAT, ALREADY ?!
DIDN'T WE JUST DECIDE ON RAISING HER INDOORS?
HUFF
HUFF
HUFF
MEOW
ALL RIGHT!

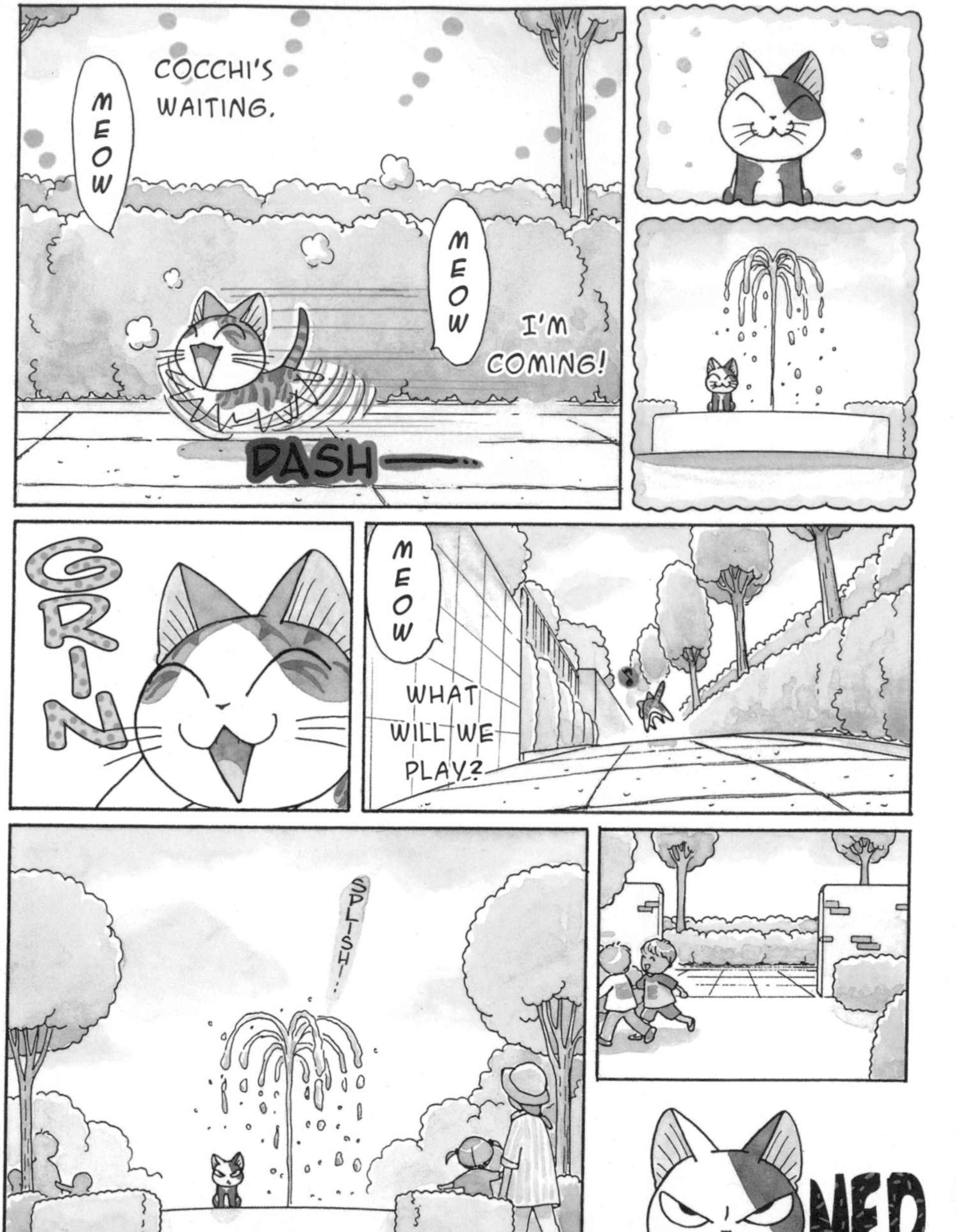
MEOW
COCCHI'S WAITING.
MEOW
I'M COMING!
DASH
GRIN
MEOW
WHAT WILL WE PLAY?
SPLISH...
STEAMED

TSK

MRR

MEOWN

SKIP

MRR

WELL, I AIN'T WAITING ANY LONGER.

TIP TIP TIP

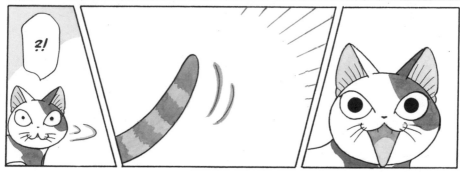

?!

IT'S CHI!

CHI, I'M OVER HERE!

MRR

YO, CHI!

MRR

HOP

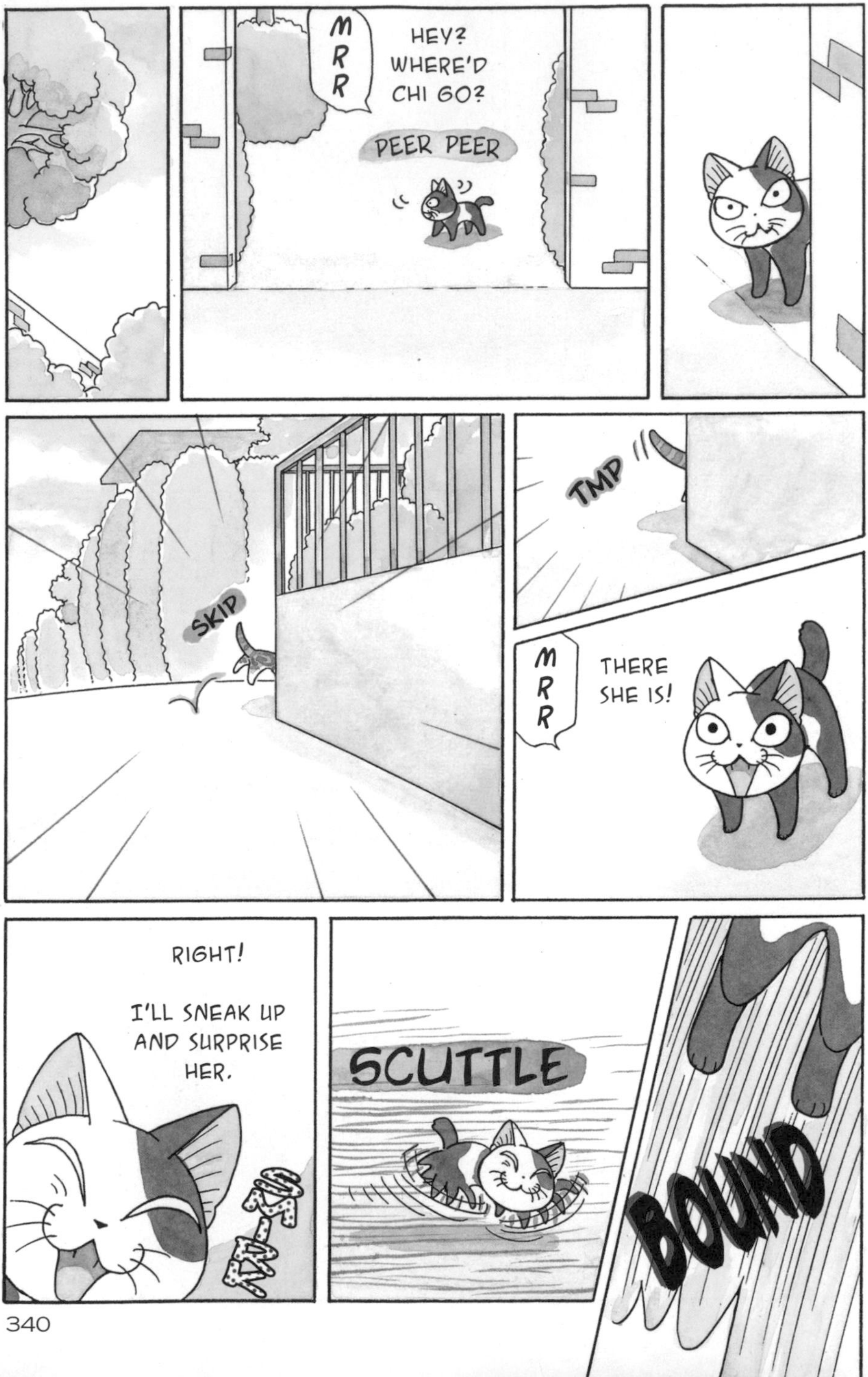
MRR
HEY? WHERE'D CHI GO?
PEER PEER
SKIP
TMP
MRR
THERE SHE IS!
RIGHT!
I'LL SNEAK UP AND SURPRISE HER.
SCUTTLE
BOUND

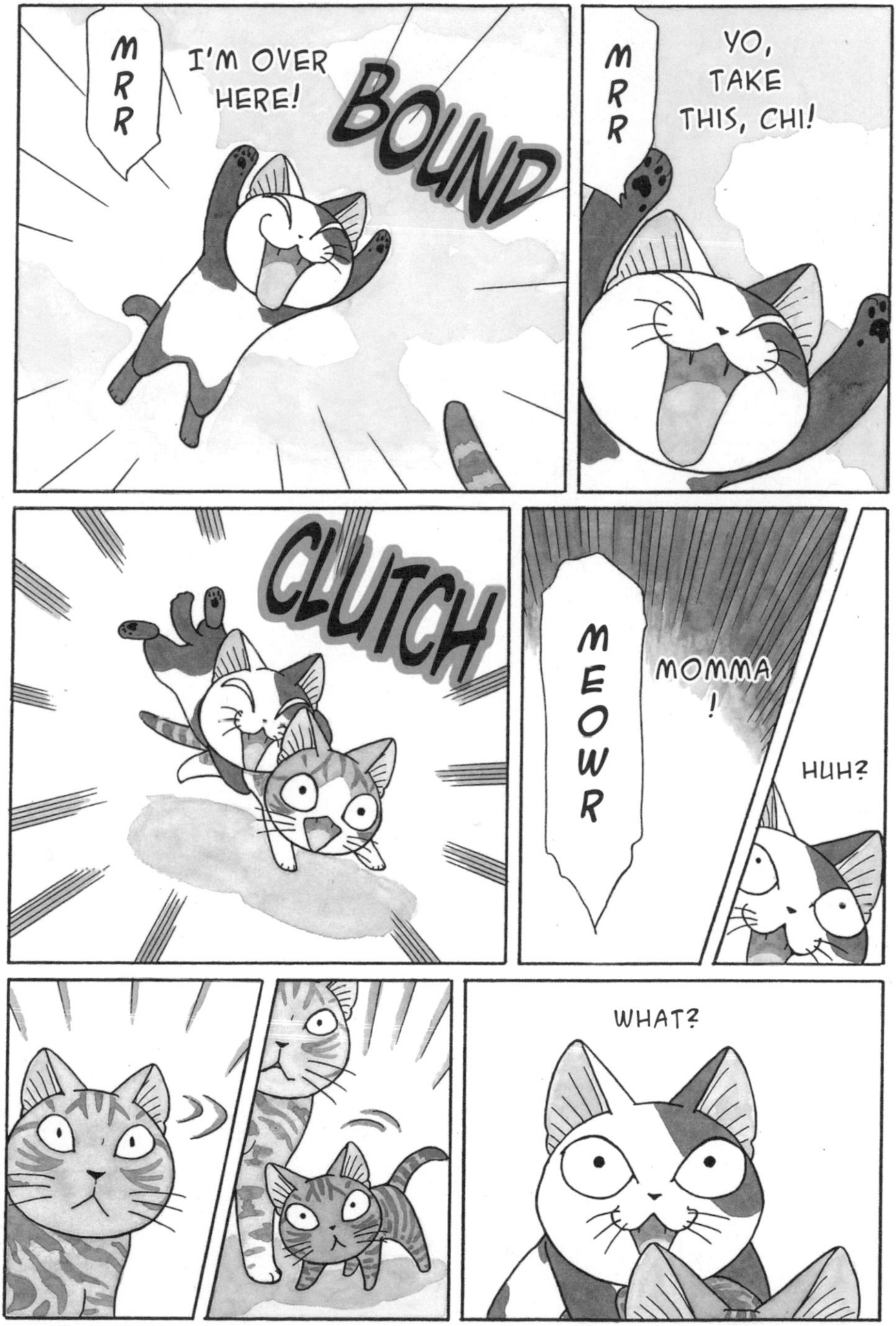
MRR
I'M OVER HERE!
BOUND
MRR
YO, TAKE THIS, CHI!
CLUTCH
MEOWR
MOMMA!
HUH?
WHAT?

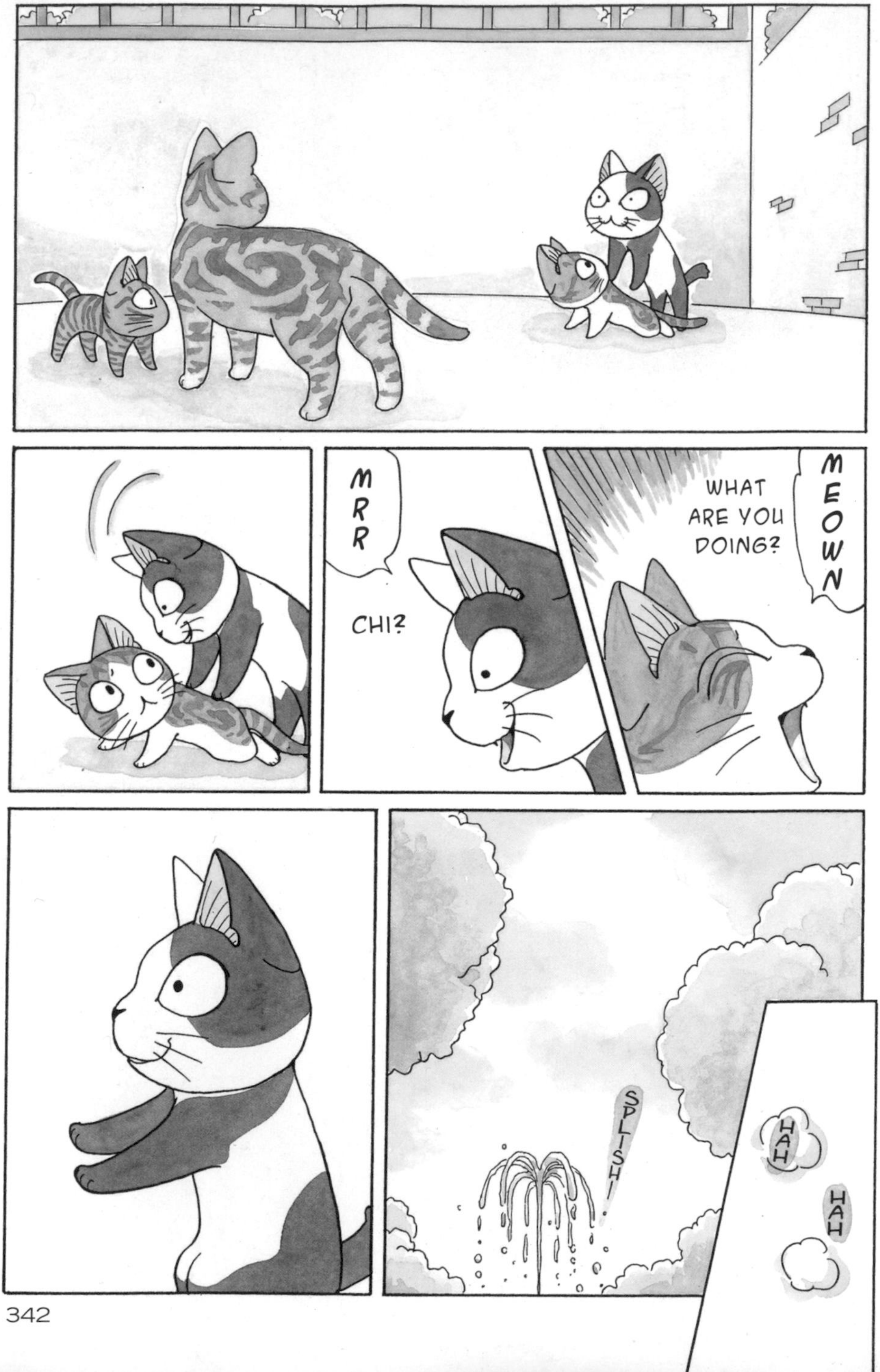
MRR
CHI?
WHAT ARE YOU DOING?
MEOWN
SPLISH!
HAH
HAH

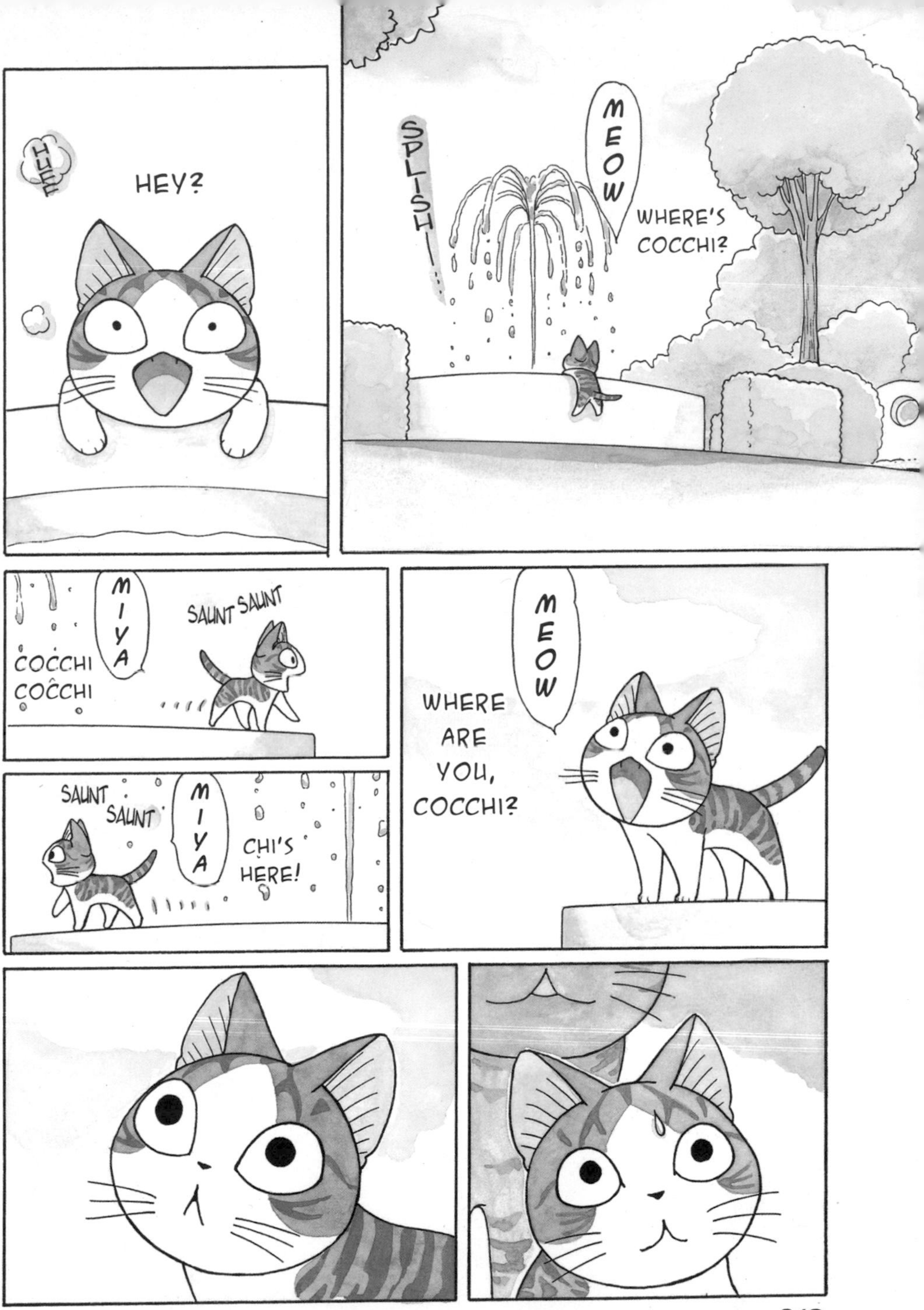
HUFF
HEY?
SPLISH
MEOW
WHERE'S COCCHI?
COCCHI COCCHI
MIYA
SAUNT SAUNT
SAUNT SAUNT
MIYA
CHI'S HERE!
MEOW
WHERE ARE YOU, COCCHI?

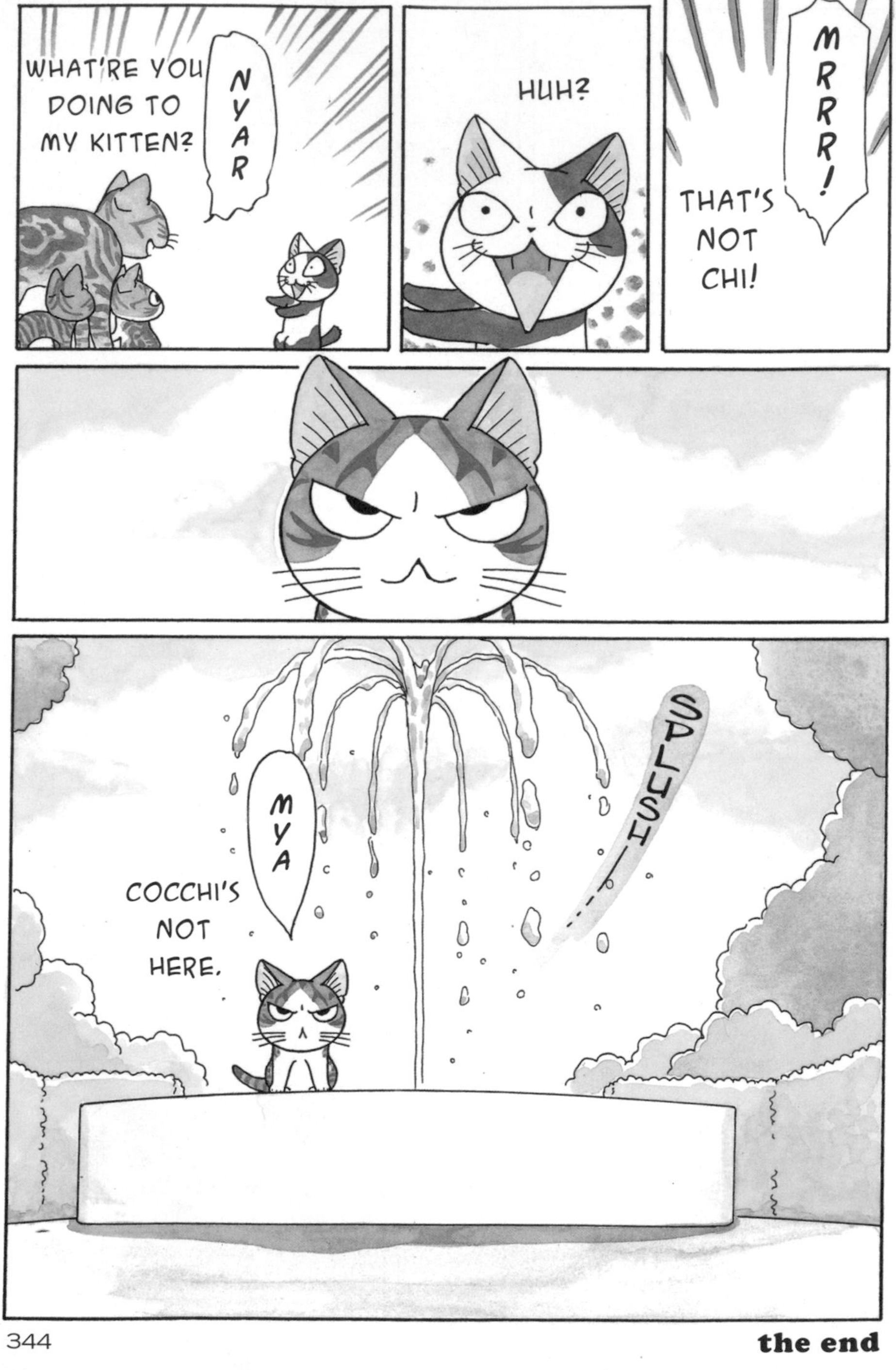
WHAT'RE YOU DOING TO MY KITTEN?
NYAR
HUH?
MRRR!
THAT'S NOT CHI!
MYA
COCCHI'S NOT HERE.
SPLUSH



**the end**

# homemade 154: a cat waits

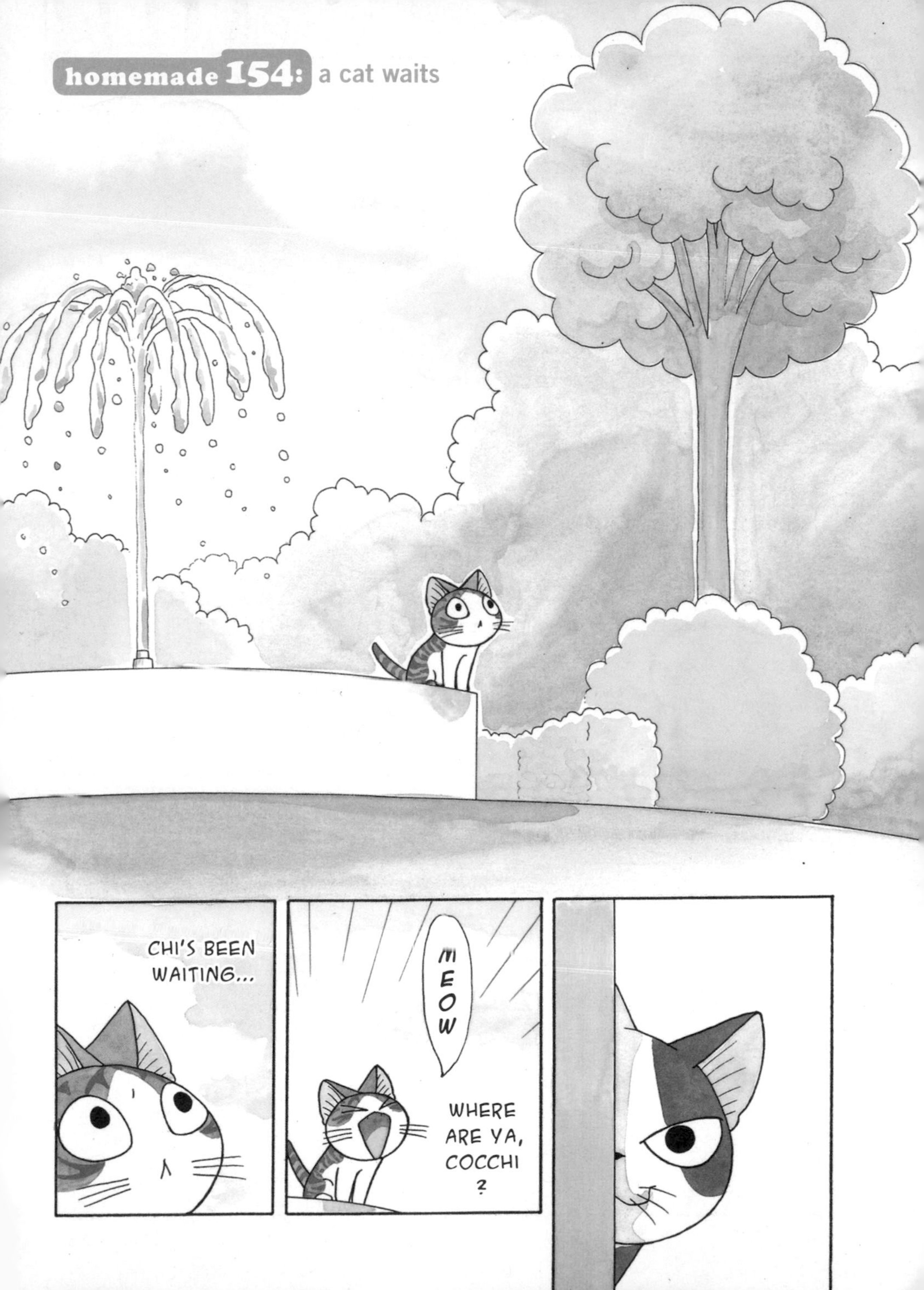
CHI'S BEEN WAITING...
MEOW
WHERE ARE YA, COCCHI?

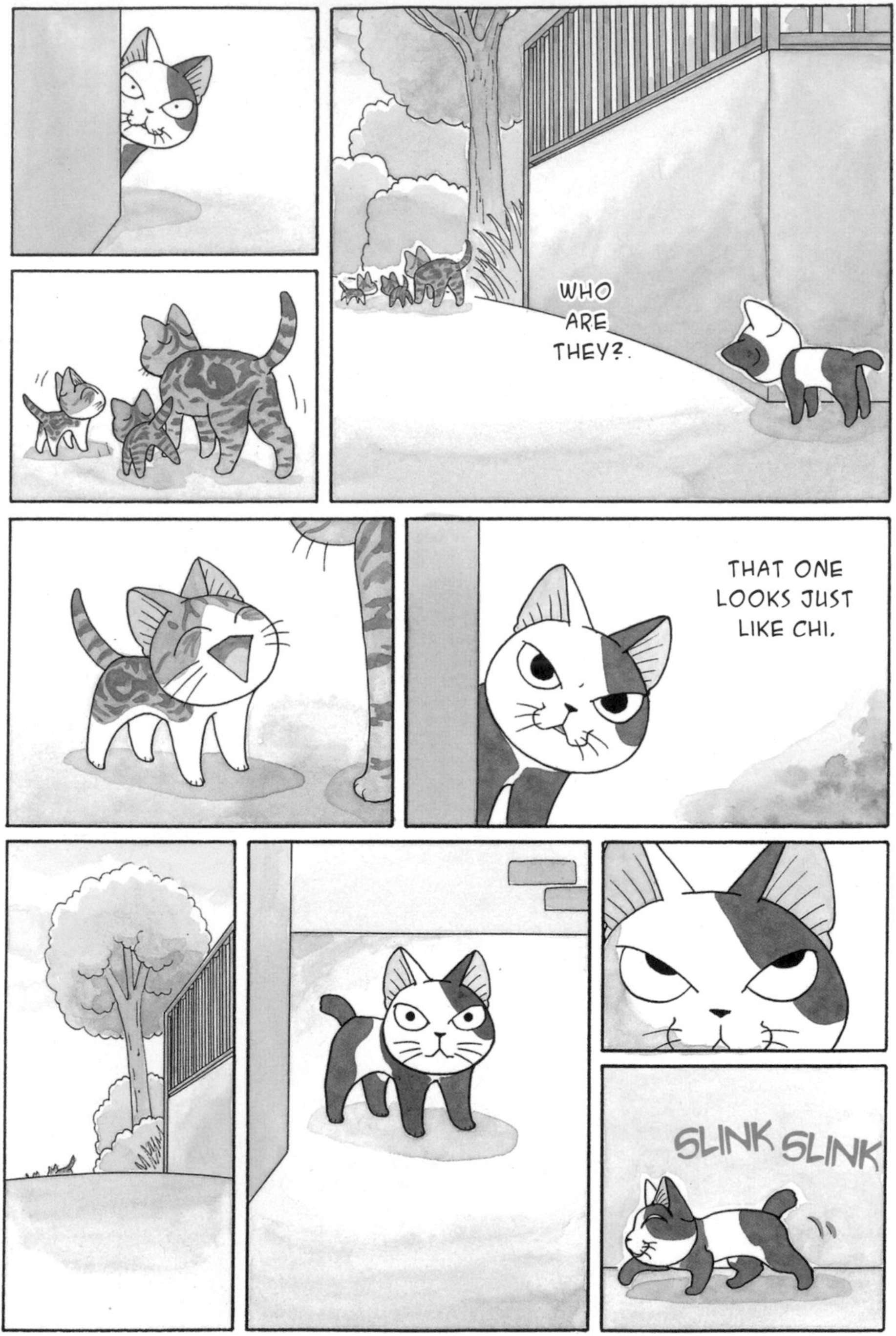
WHO ARE THEY?
THAT ONE LOOKS JUST LIKE CHI.
SLINK SLINK

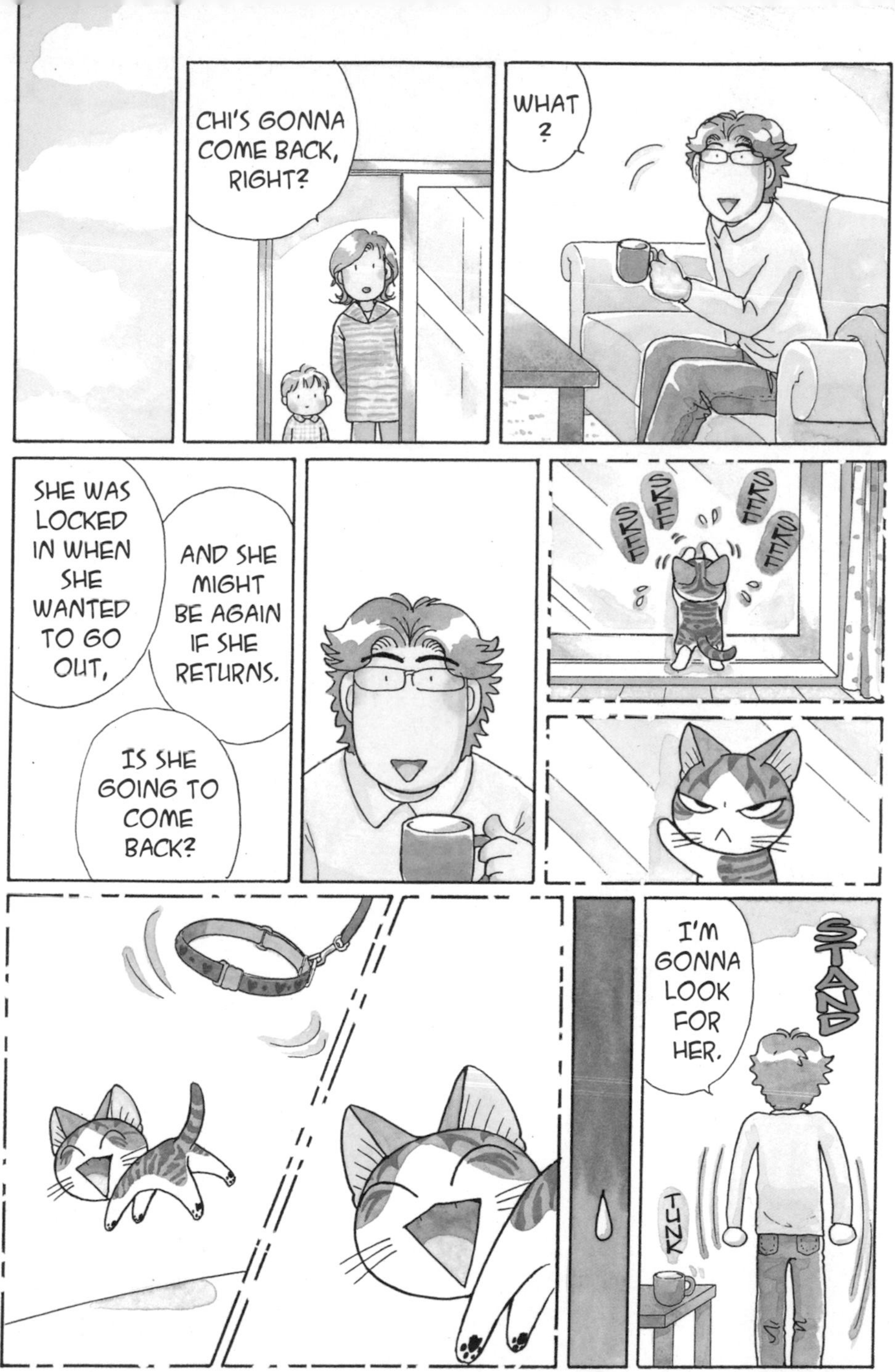
CHI'S GONNA COME BACK, RIGHT?
WHAT?
SHE WAS LOCKED IN WHEN SHE WANTED TO GO OUT,
AND SHE MIGHT BE AGAIN IF SHE RETURNS.
IS SHE GOING TO COME BACK?
SKEE
SKEE
SKEE
SKEE
I'M GONNA LOOK FOR HER.
STAND
TUNK

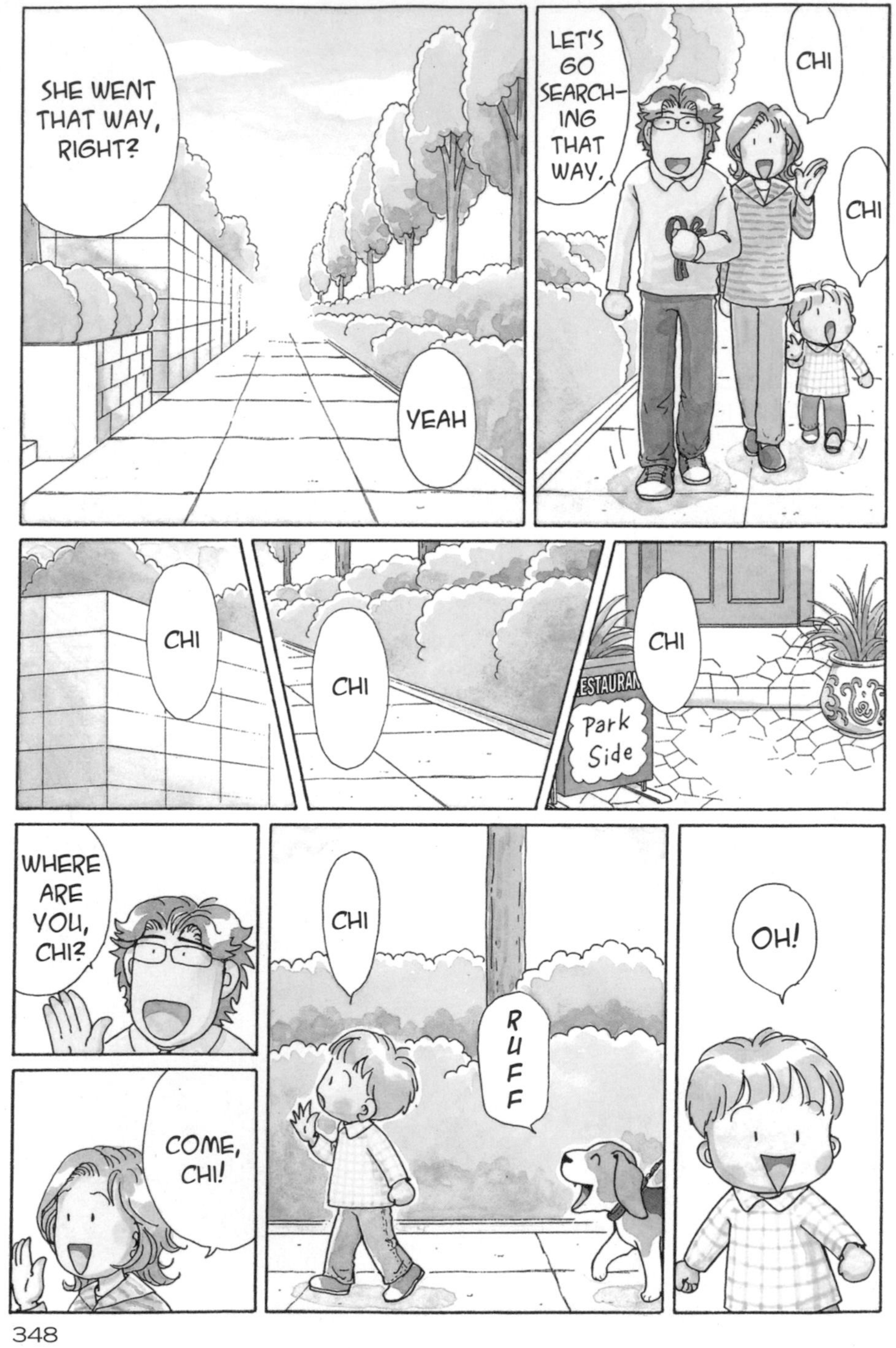
SHE WENT THAT WAY, RIGHT?
YEAH
LET'S GO SEARCH-ING THAT WAY.
CHI
CHI
CHI
CHI
Park Side
CHI
WHERE ARE YOU, CHI?
COME, CHI!
CHI
RUFF
OH!

HELLO

RUFF RUFF

OH, KU-SANO FROM NEXT DOOR.

A WALK, HUH?

YES

WHAT'S THE MATTER?

DAVID!

RUFF

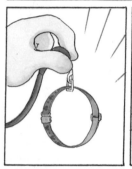

WE'RE LOOK-ING FOR CHI...

SNIFF SNIFF SNIFF

DAVID?

RUFF

SNIFF SNIFF

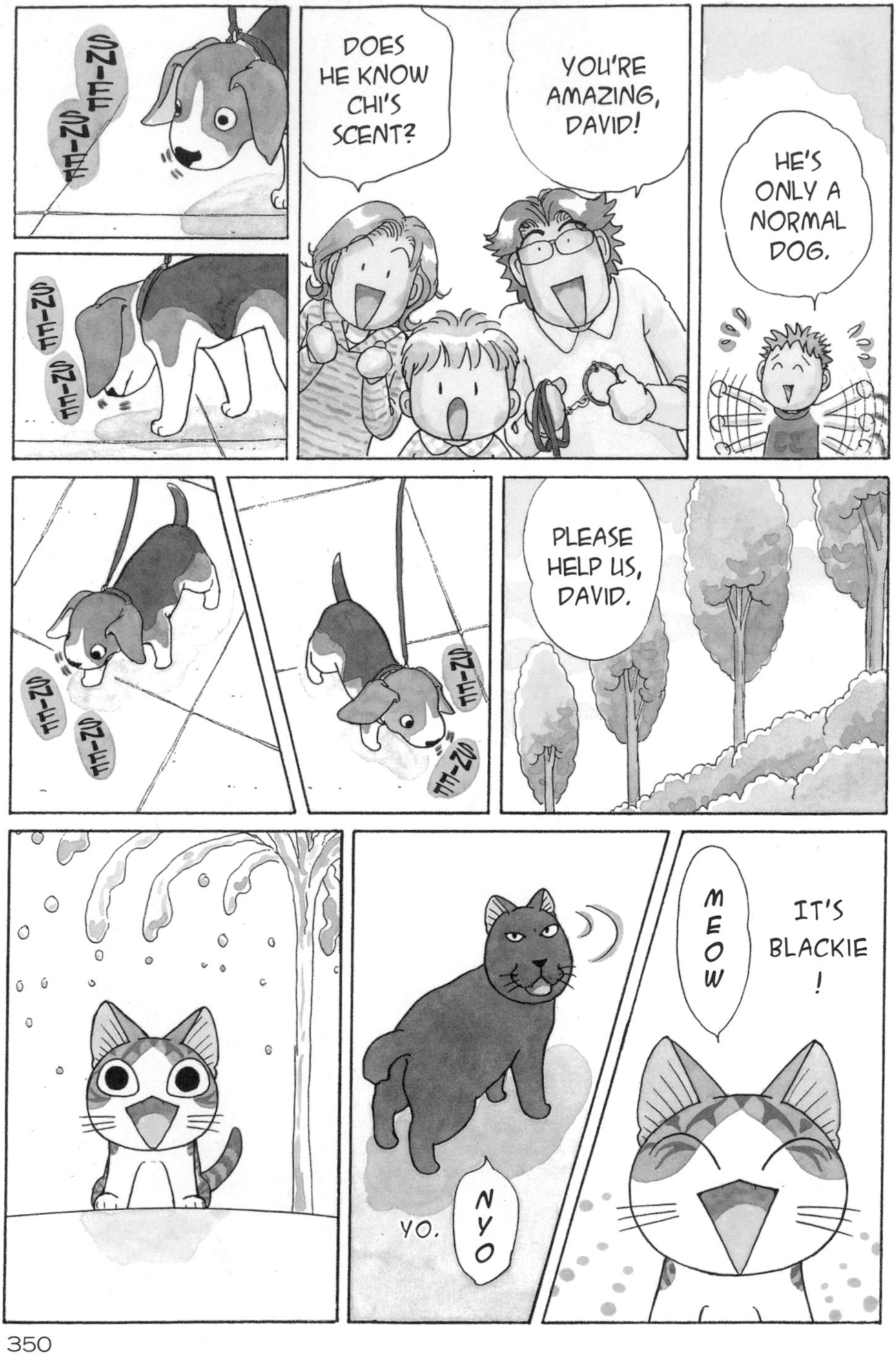
SNIFF
SNIFF
SNIFF
SNIFF
DOES HE KNOW CHI'S SCENT?
YOU'RE AMAZING, DAVID!
HE'S ONLY A NORMAL DOG.
SNIFF
SNIFF
SNIFF
SNIFF
PLEASE HELP US, DAVID.
YO.
NYO
MEOW
IT'S BLACKIE!

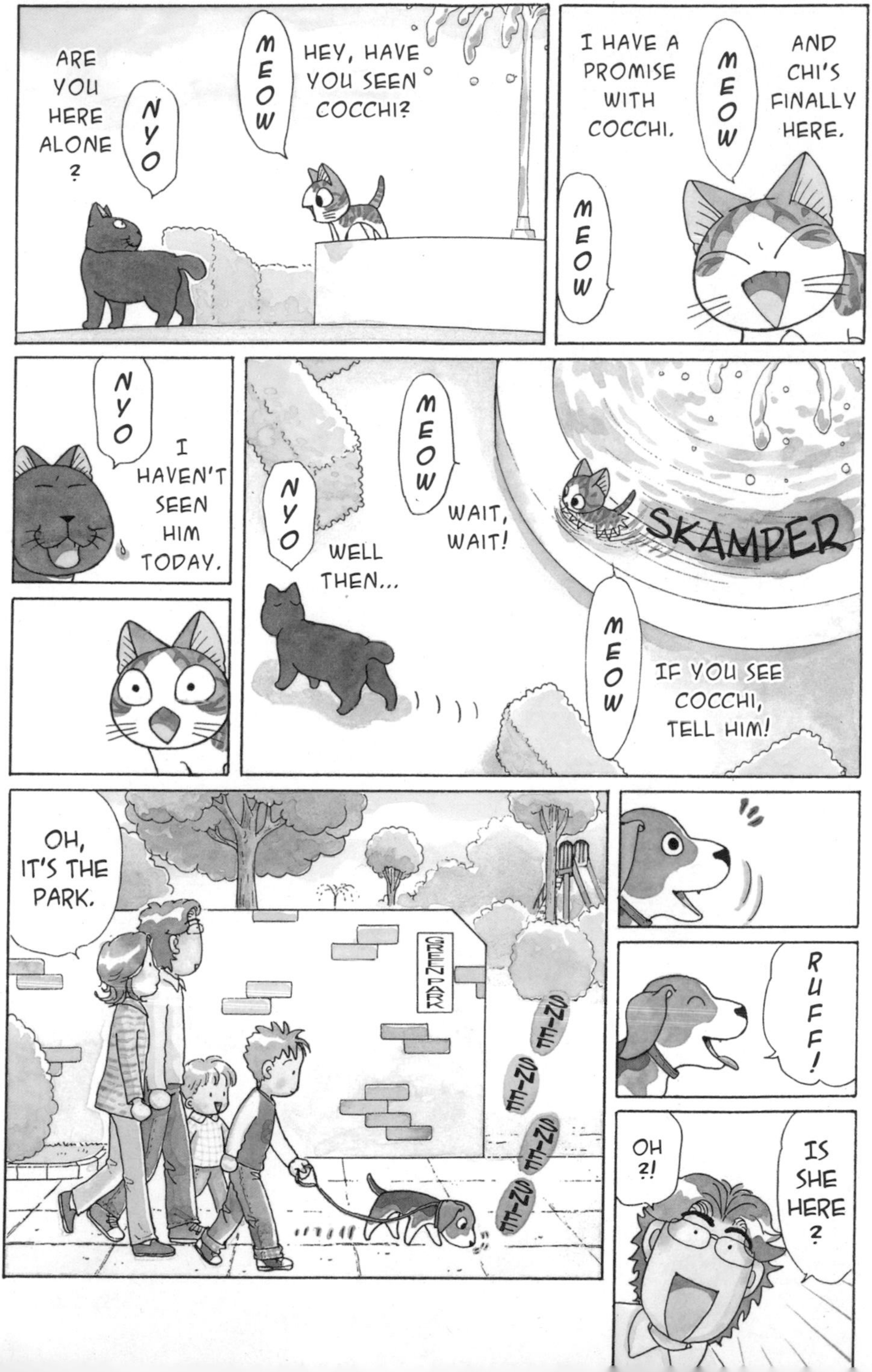
ARE YOU HERE ALONE?
NYO
MEOW
HEY, HAVE YOU SEEN COCCHI?
I HAVE A PROMISE WITH COCCHI.
MEOW
AND CHI'S FINALLY HERE.
MEOW
NYO
I HAVEN'T SEEN HIM TODAY.
MEOW
NYO
WELL THEN...
WAIT, WAIT!
SKAMPER
MEOW
IF YOU SEE COCCHI, TELL HIM!
OH, IT'S THE PARK.
GREEN PARK
SNIFF
SNIFF
SNIFF
SNIFF
RUFF!
OH?!
IS SHE HERE?

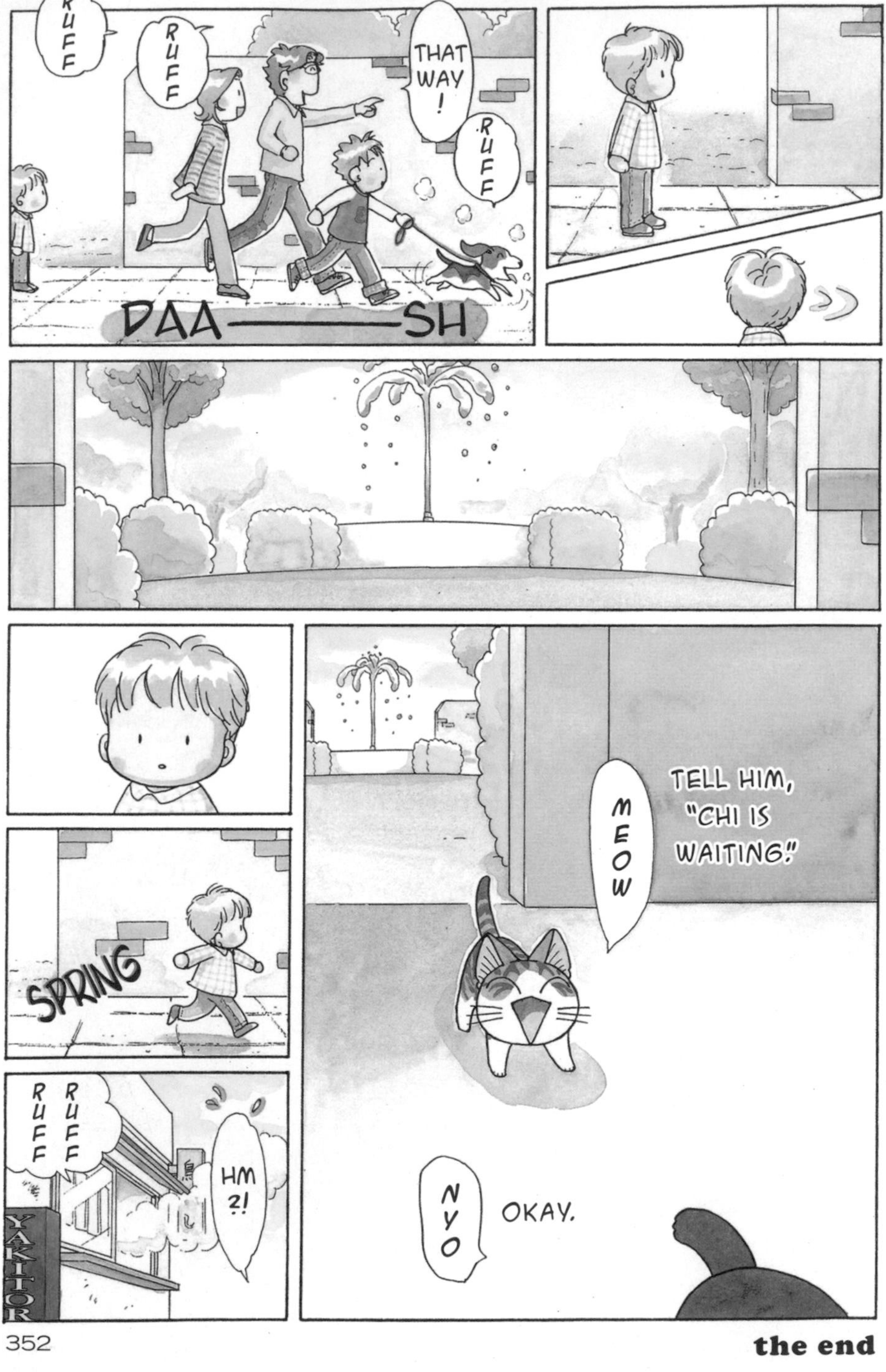
RUFF
RUFF
THAT WAY!
RUFF
DAA———SH
SPRING
RUFF
RUFF
HM?!
YAKITOR
MEOW
TELL HIM, "CHI IS WAITING!"
NYO
OKAY.

**the end**

# homemade 155: a cat is irritated

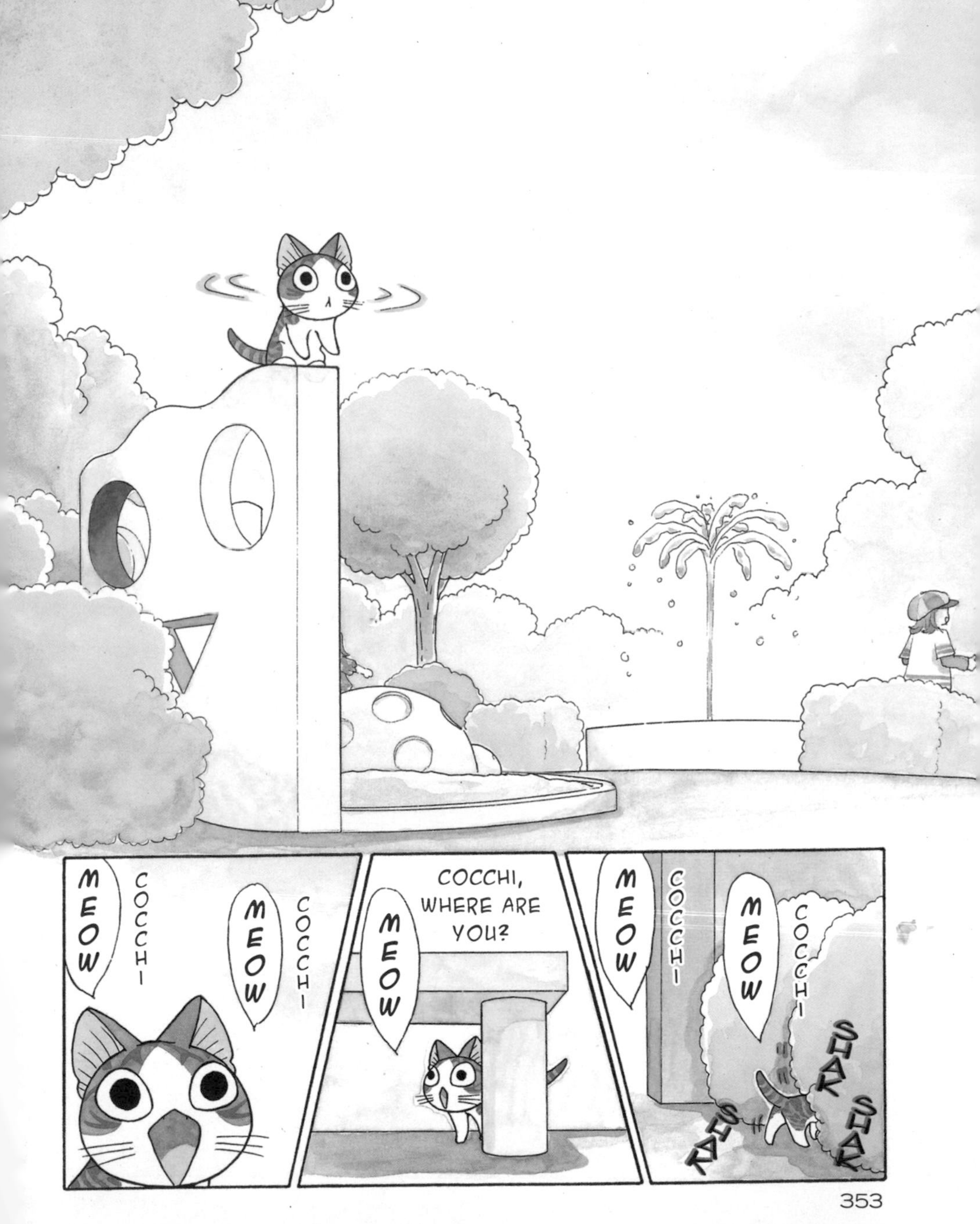

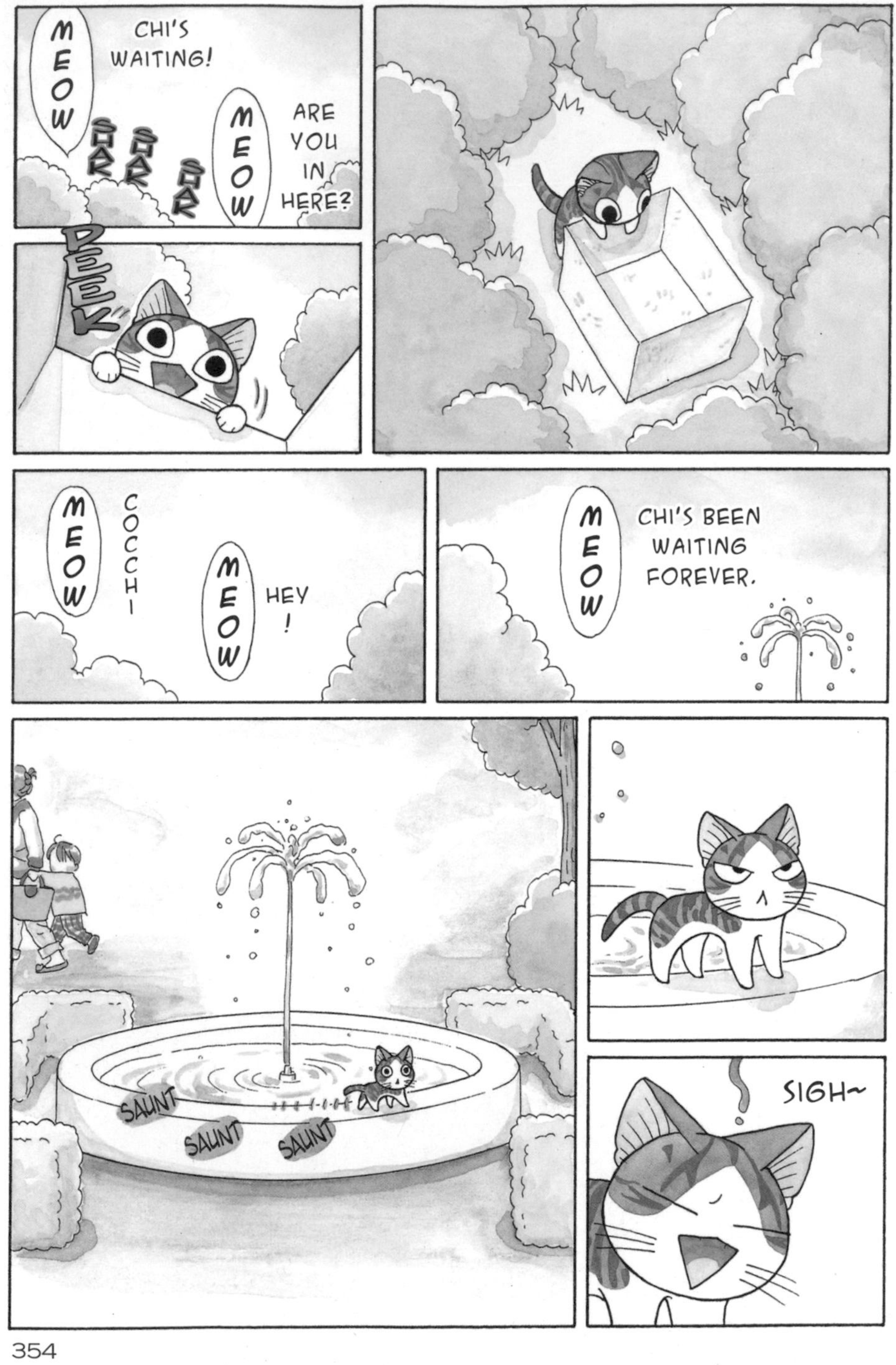
MEOW
CHI'S WAITING!
SOAR
SOAR
SOAR
MEOW
ARE YOU IN HERE?
PEEK
MEOW
COCCHI
MEOW
HEY!
MEOW
CHI'S BEEN WAITING FOREVER.
SAUNT
SAUNT
SAUNT
SIGH~

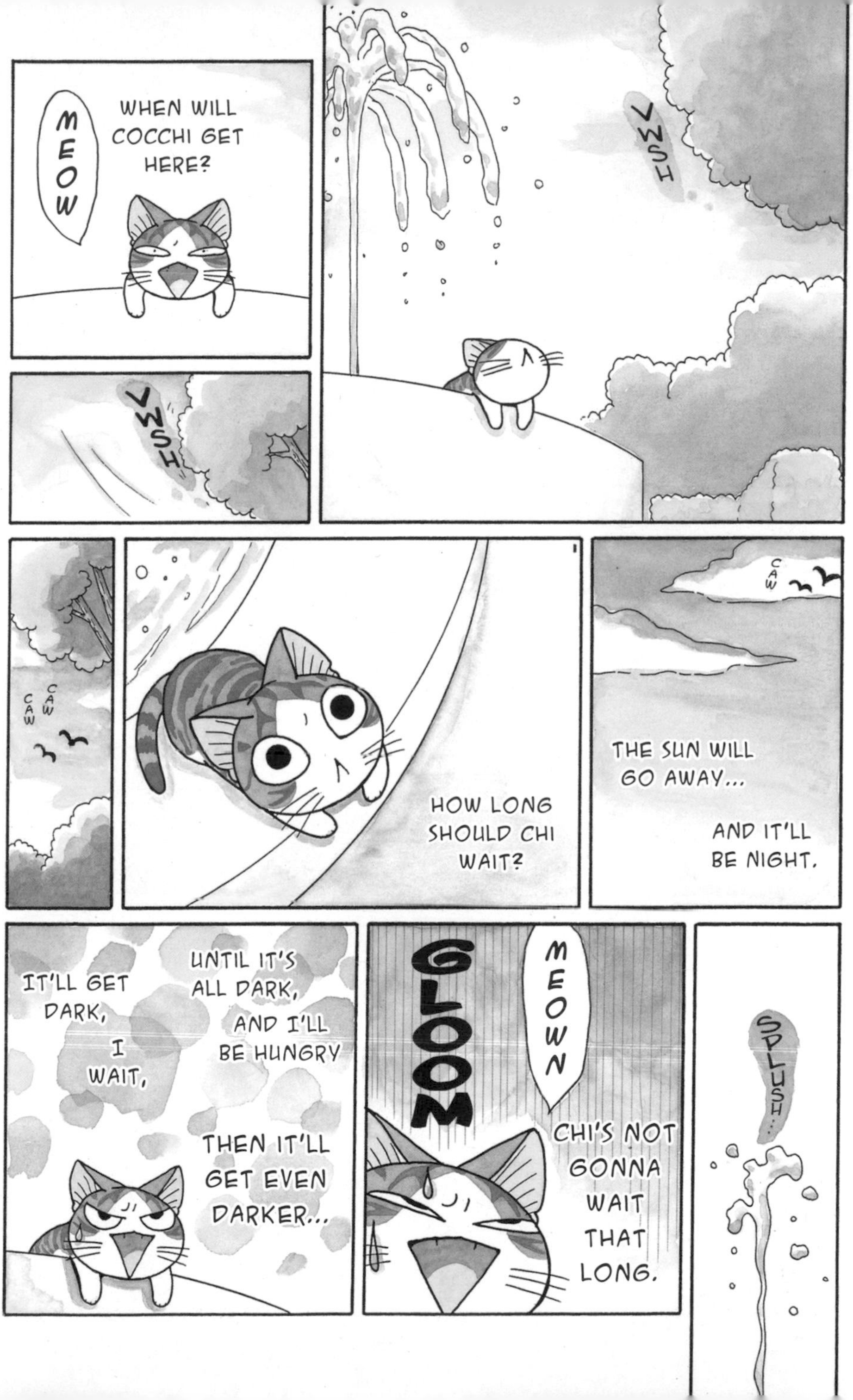
MEOW
WHEN WILL COCCHI GET HERE?
VWSH
VWSH
CAW CAW
HOW LONG SHOULD CHI WAIT?
CAW
THE SUN WILL GO AWAY...
AND IT'LL BE NIGHT.
IT'LL GET DARK,
I WAIT,
UNTIL IT'S ALL DARK,
AND I'LL BE HUNGRY
THEN IT'LL GET EVEN DARKER...
GLOOM
MEOWN
CHI'S NOT GONNA WAIT THAT LONG.
SPLUSH...

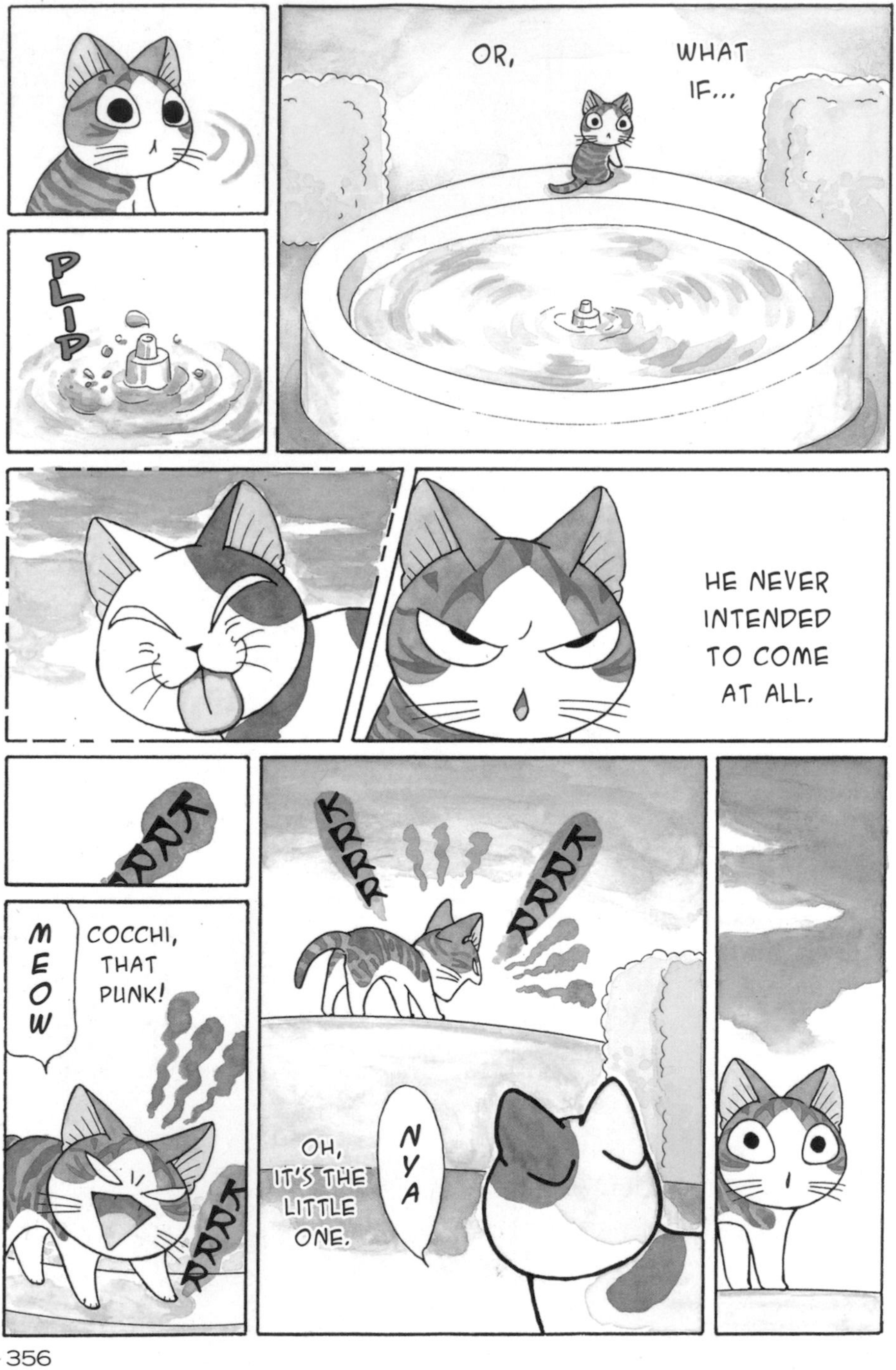
PLIP
OR,
WHAT IF...
HE NEVER INTENDED TO COME AT ALL.
RRRRK
MEOW
COCCHI, THAT PUNK!
RRRRK
KRRRR
RRRRK
OH, IT'S THE LITTLE ONE.
NYA

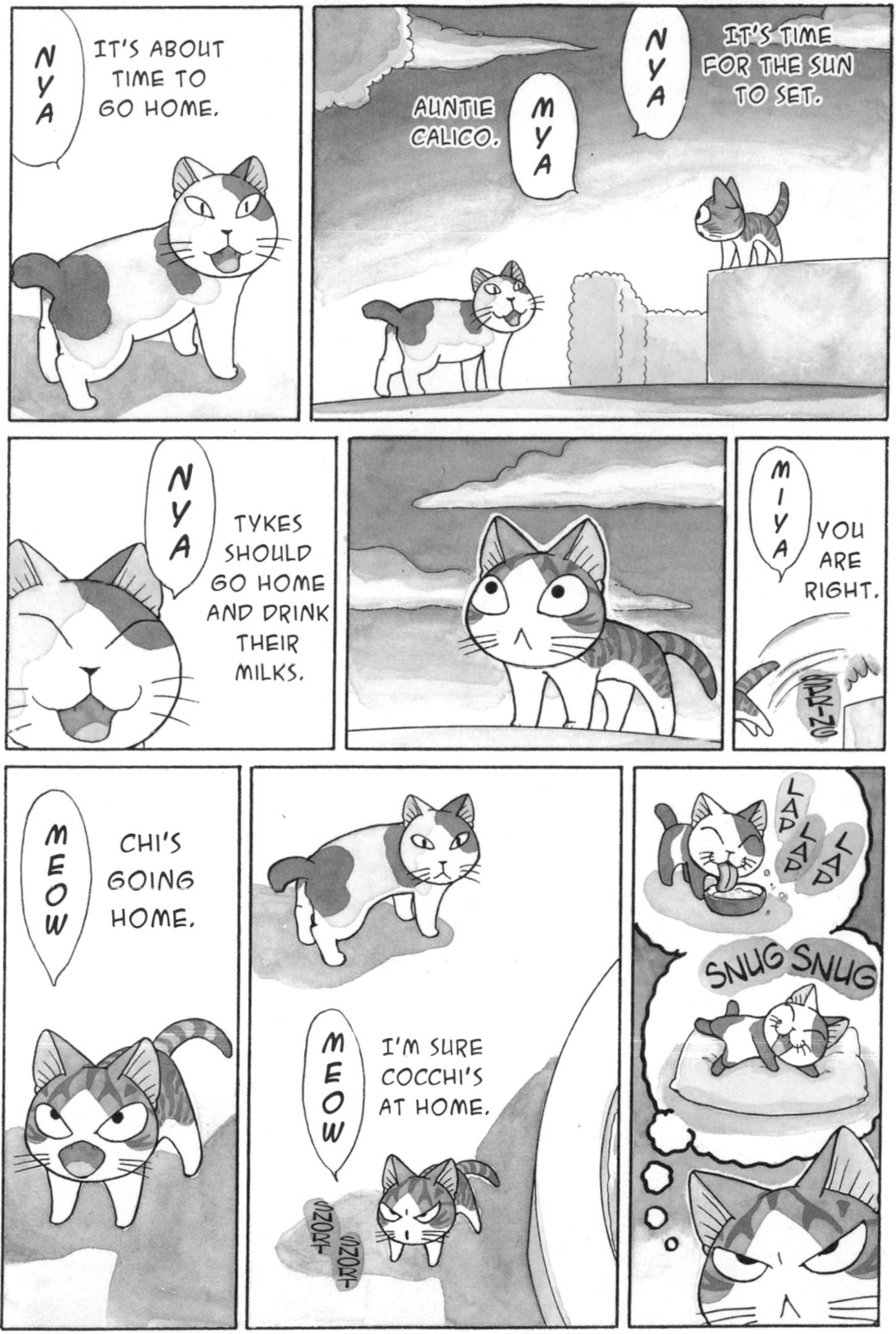
NYA
IT'S ABOUT TIME TO GO HOME.
AUNTIE CALICO.
MYA
NYA
IT'S TIME FOR THE SUN TO SET.
NYA
TYKES SHOULD GO HOME AND DRINK THEIR MILKS.
MIYA
YOU ARE RIGHT.
SPRING
MEOW
CHI'S GOING HOME.
MEOW
I'M SURE COCCHI'S AT HOME.
SNORT SNORT
LAP LAP LAP
SNUG SNUG

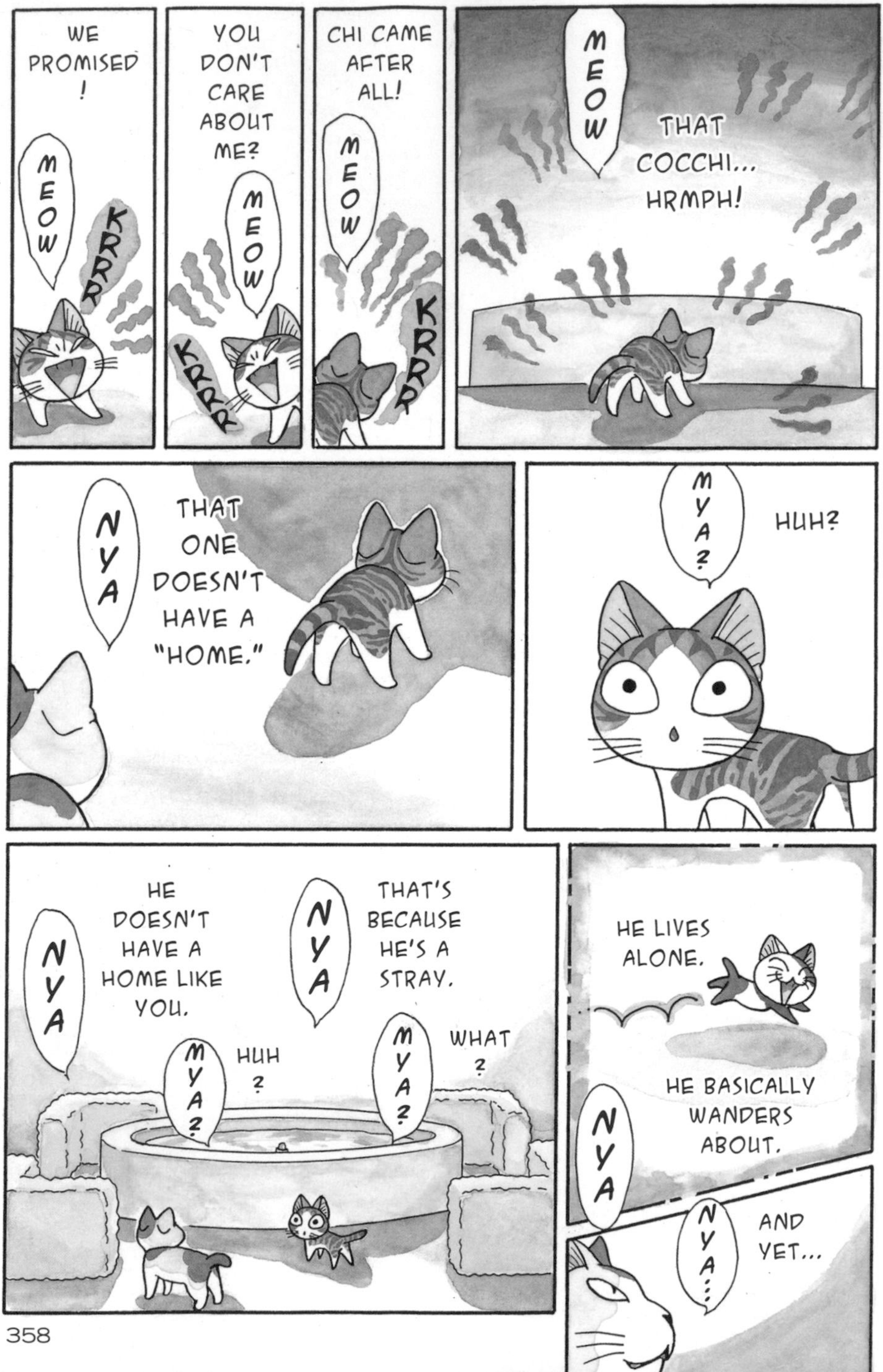
WE PROMISED!
MEOW
KRRR
YOU DON'T CARE ABOUT ME?
MEOW
KRRR
CHI CAME AFTER ALL!
MEOW
KRRR
MEOW
THAT COCCHI... HRMPH!
NYA
THAT ONE DOESN'T HAVE A "HOME."
MYA?
HUH?
NYA
HE DOESN'T HAVE A HOME LIKE YOU.
MYA?
HUH?
NYA
THAT'S BECAUSE HE'S A STRAY.
MYA?
WHAT?
HE LIVES ALONE.
NYA
HE BASICALLY WANDERS ABOUT.
NYA...
AND YET...

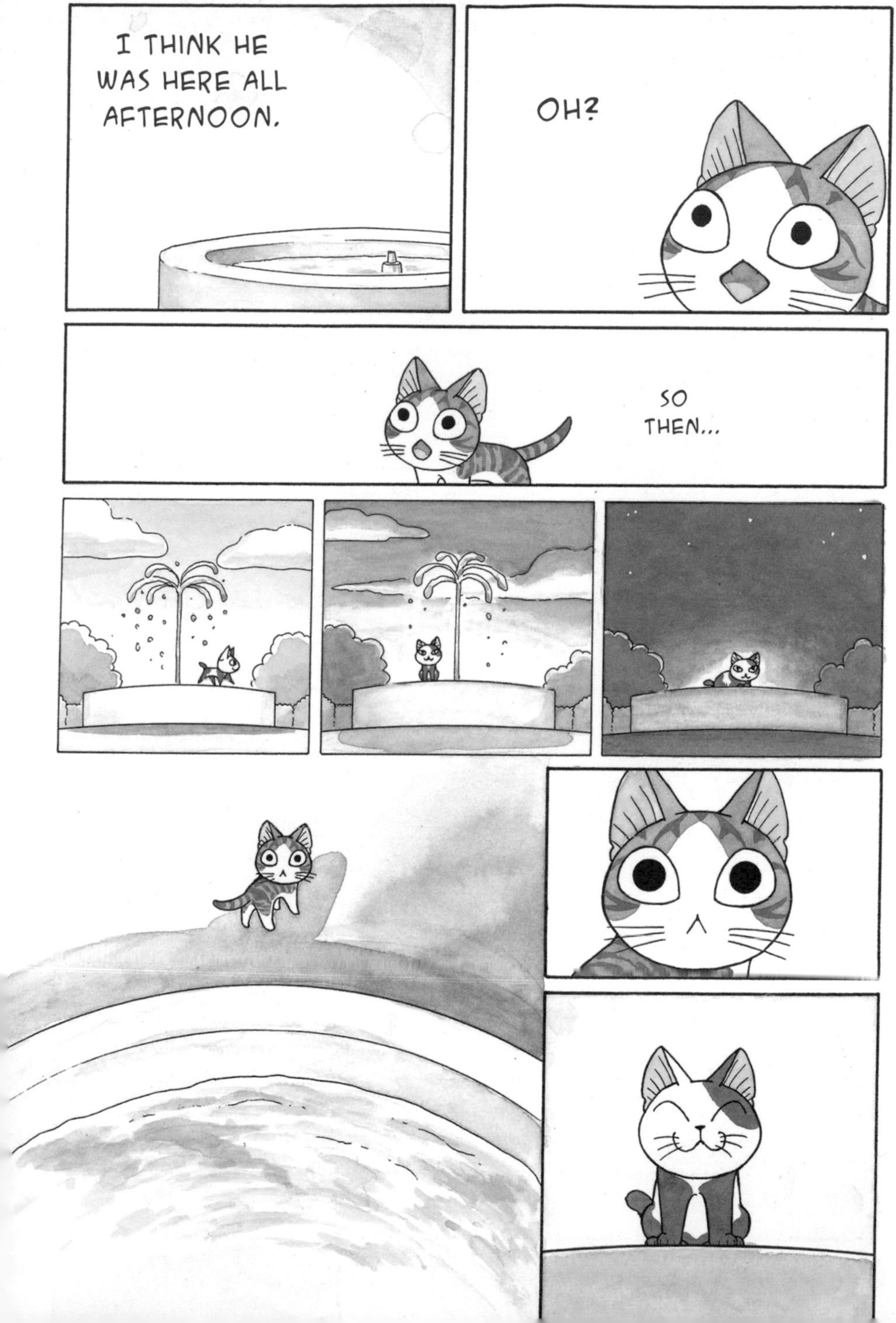
I THINK HE WAS HERE ALL AFTERNOON.
OH?
SO THEN...

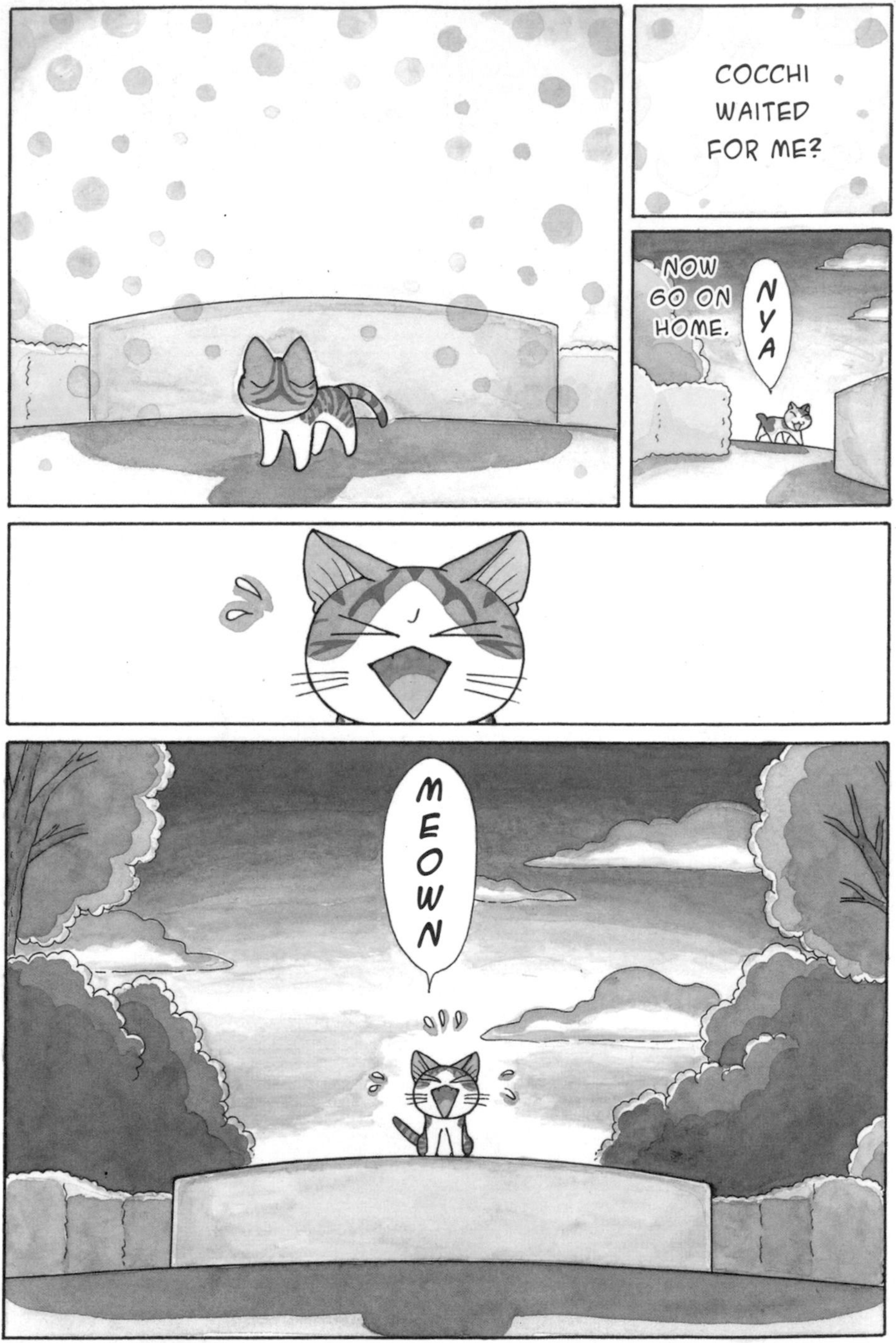
COCCHI WAITED FOR ME?
NOW GO ON HOME.
NYA
MEOWN



the end

# homemade 156: a cat is misunderstood

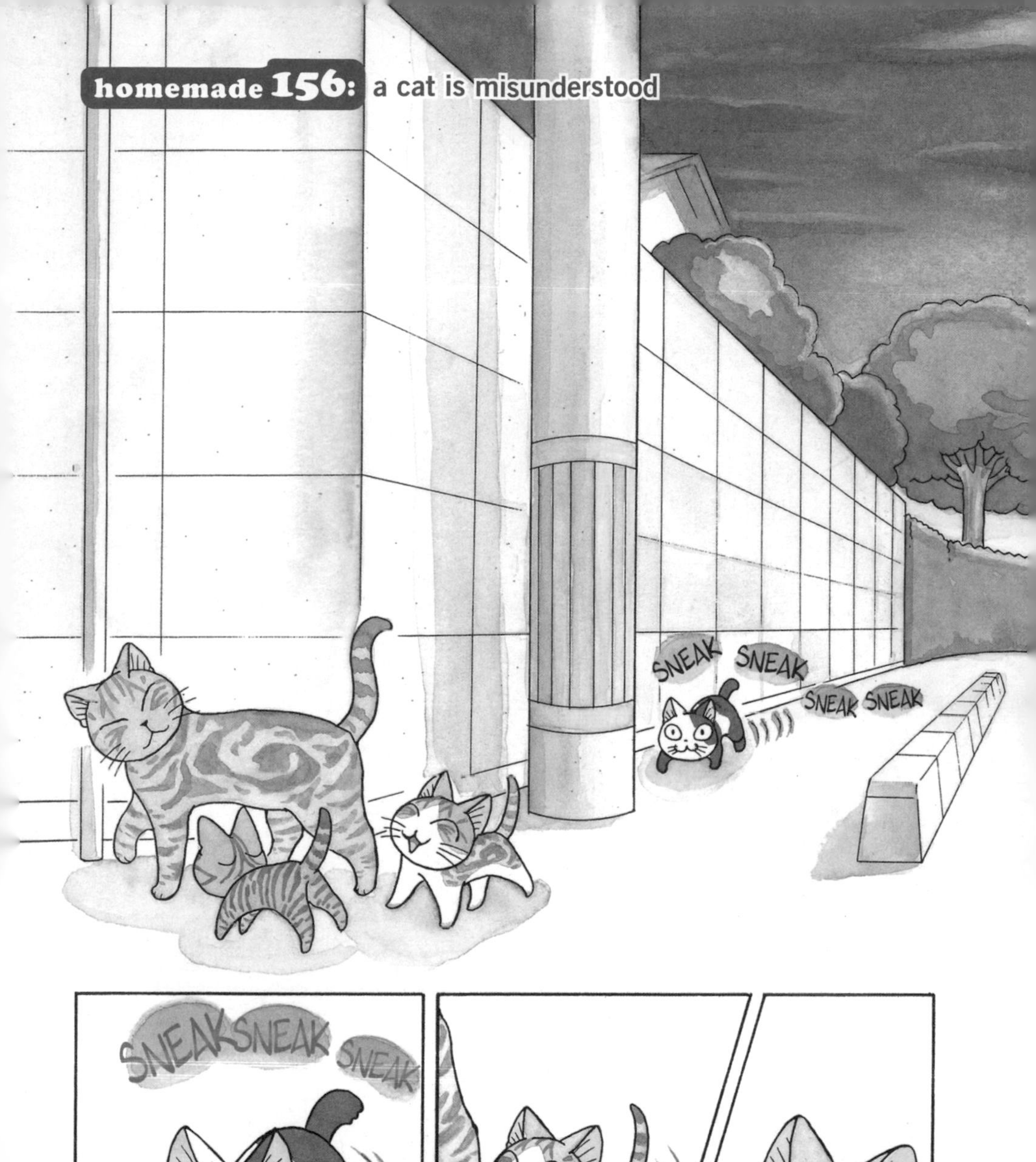
SNEAK SNEAK
SNEAK SNEAK
SNEAK SNEAK
SNEAK

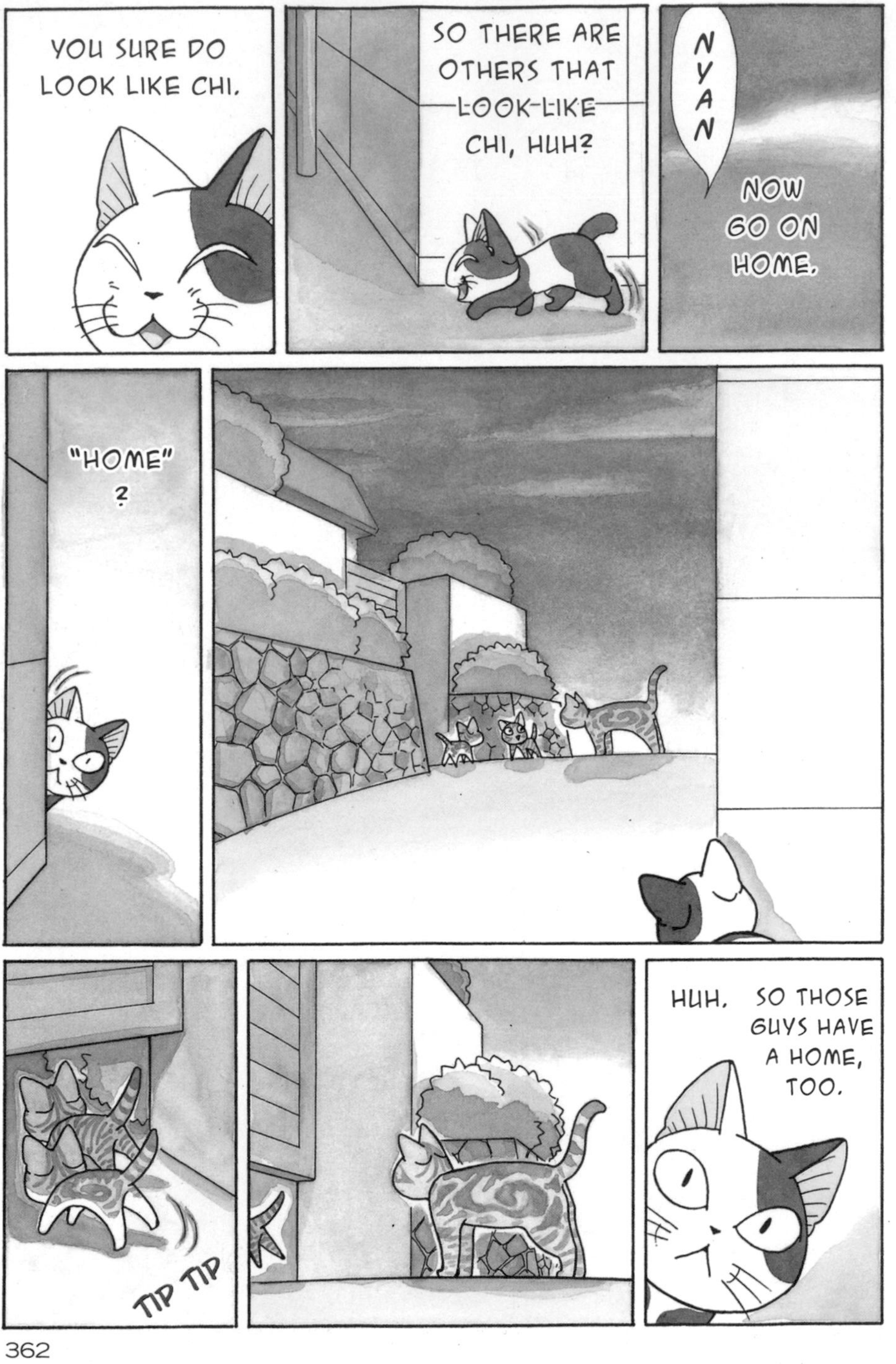

YOU SURE DO LOOK LIKE CHI.
SO THERE ARE OTHERS THAT LOOK LIKE CHI, HUH?
NYAN
NOW GO ON HOME.
"HOME"?
TIP TIP
HUH. SO THOSE GUYS HAVE A HOME, TOO.

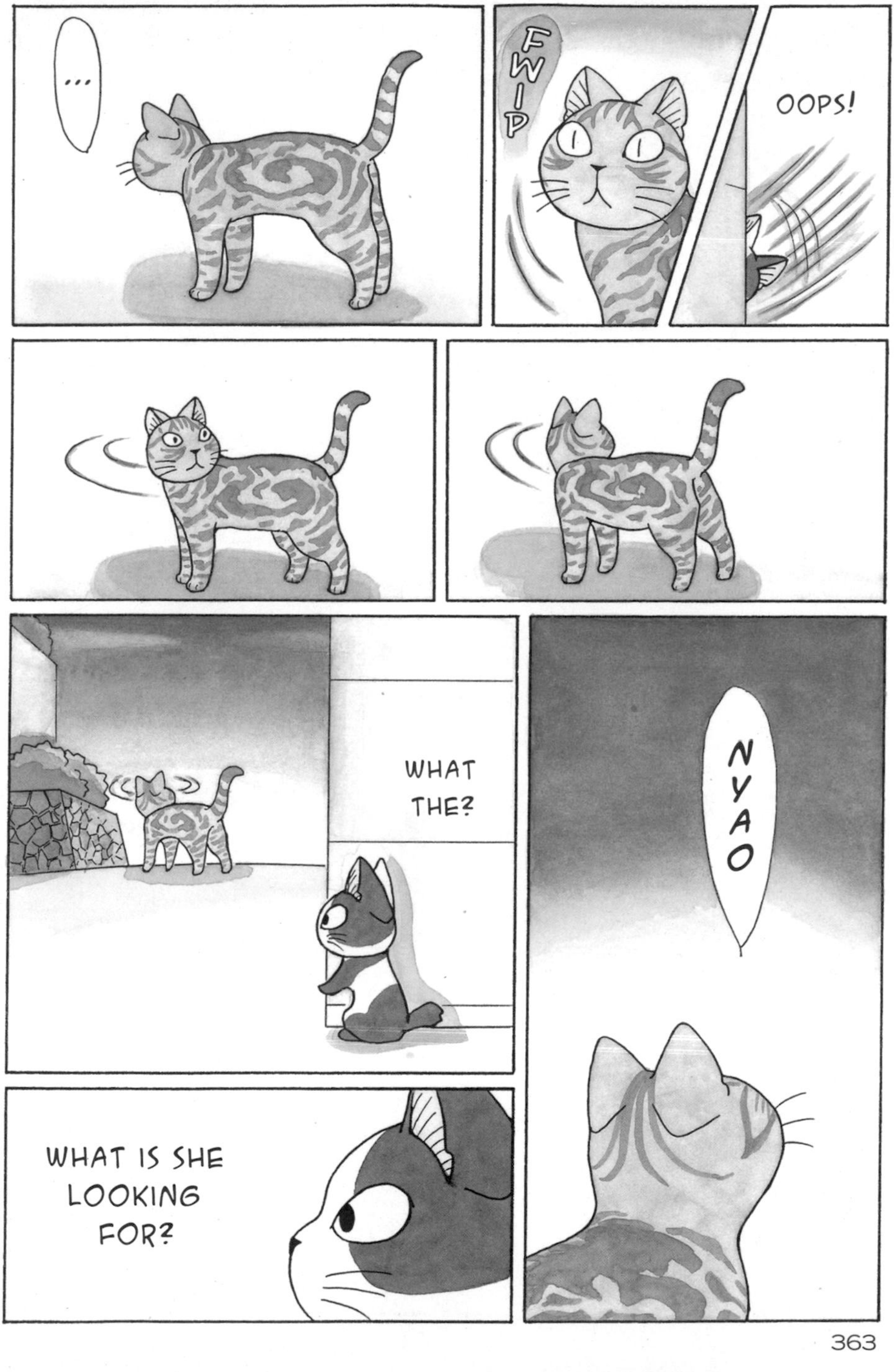
...
FWIP
OOPS!
WHAT THE?
NYAO
WHAT IS SHE LOOKING FOR?

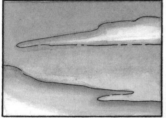

WHO WAS THAT CAT CALLING?

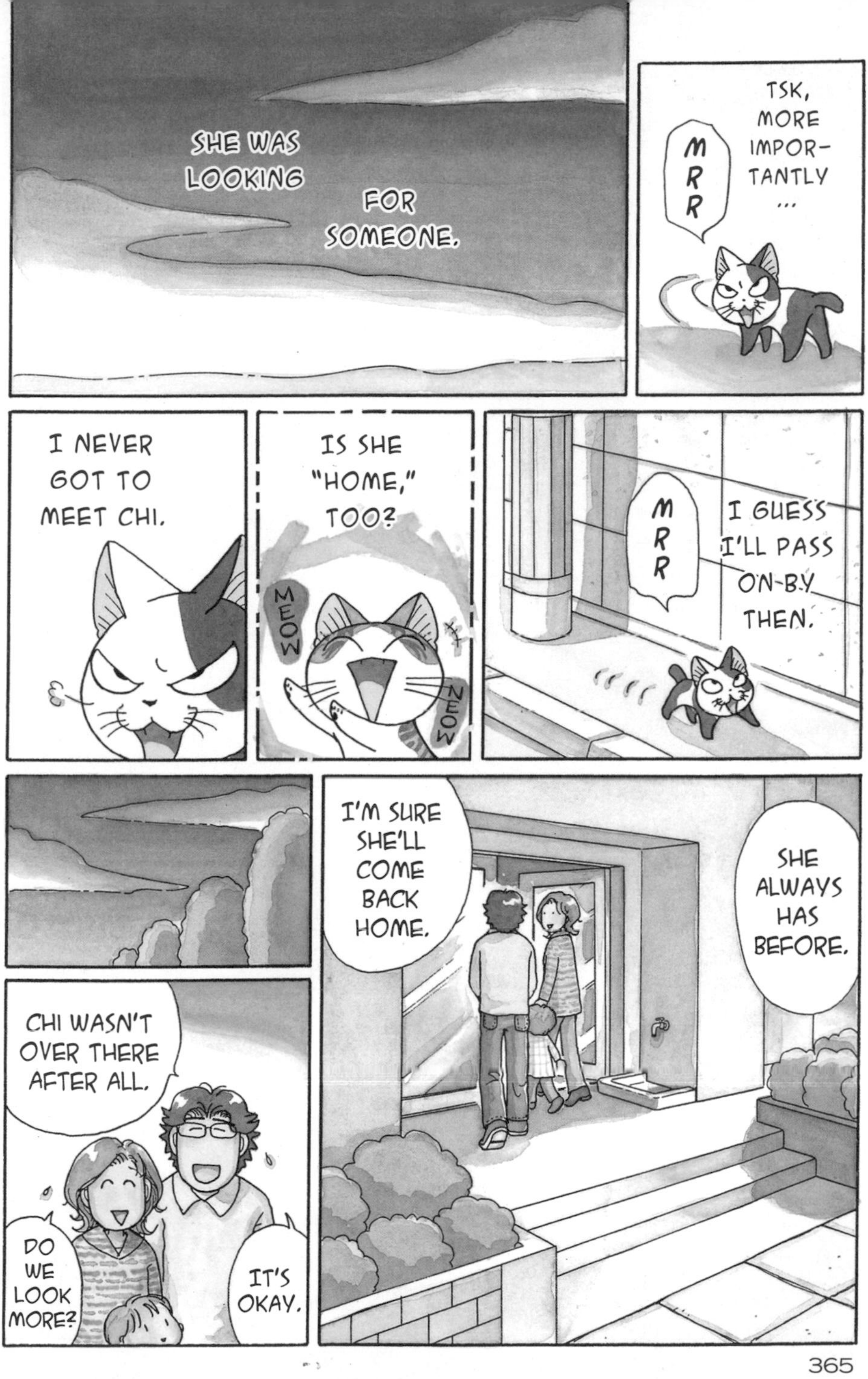
SHE WAS LOOKING
FOR SOMEONE.
MRR
TSK, MORE IMPOR-TANTLY ...
I NEVER GOT TO MEET CHI.
IS SHE "HOME," TOO?
MEOW
MEOW
MRR
I GUESS I'LL PASS ON BY THEN.
CHI WASN'T OVER THERE AFTER ALL.
DO WE LOOK MORE?
IT'S OKAY.
I'M SURE SHE'LL COME BACK HOME.
SHE ALWAYS HAS BEFORE.

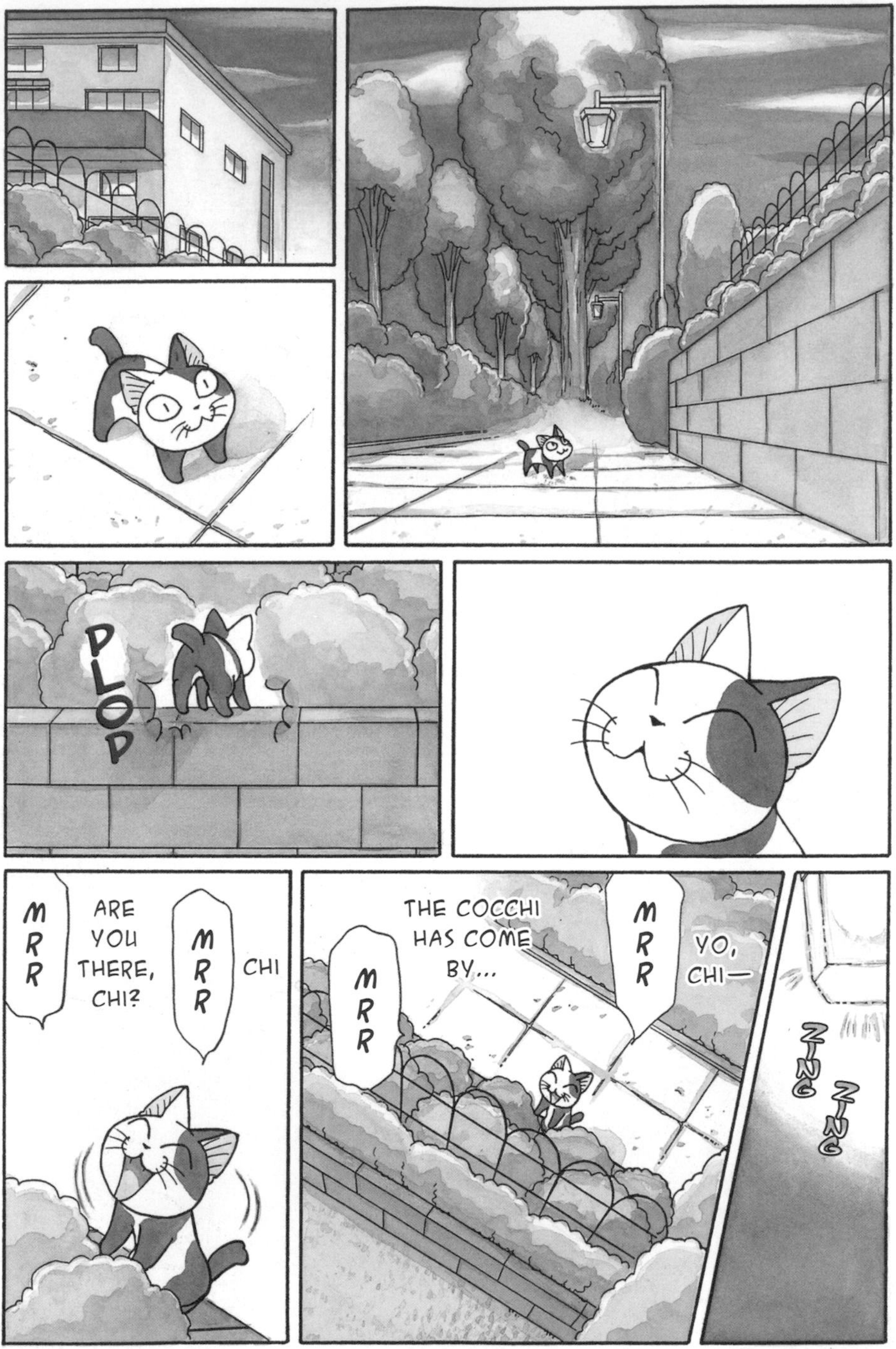
PLOP
MRR
ARE YOU THERE, CHI?
MRR
CHI
THE COCCHI HAS COME BY...
MRR
MRR
YO, CHI—
ZING ZING

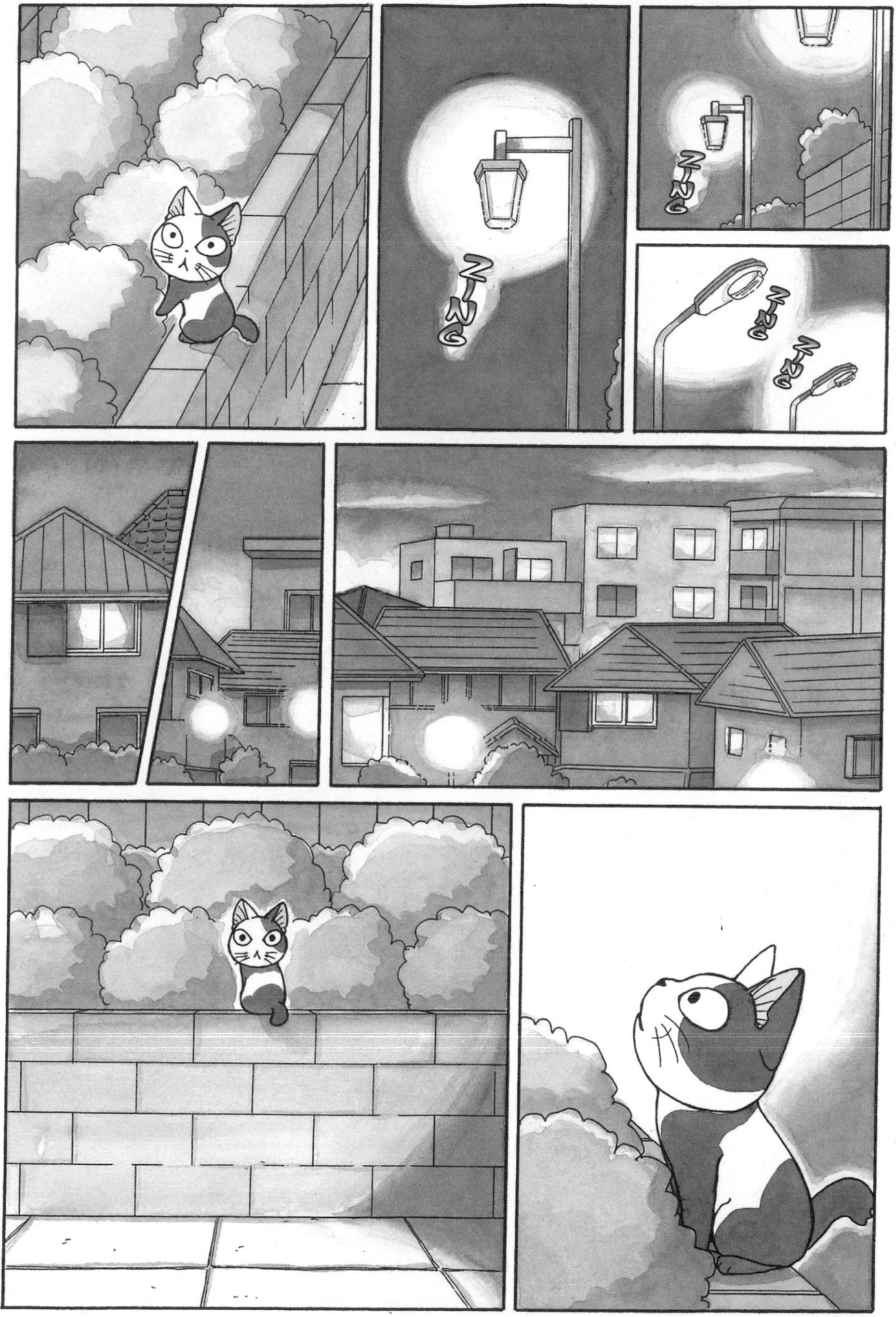
ZING
ZING
ZING
ZING

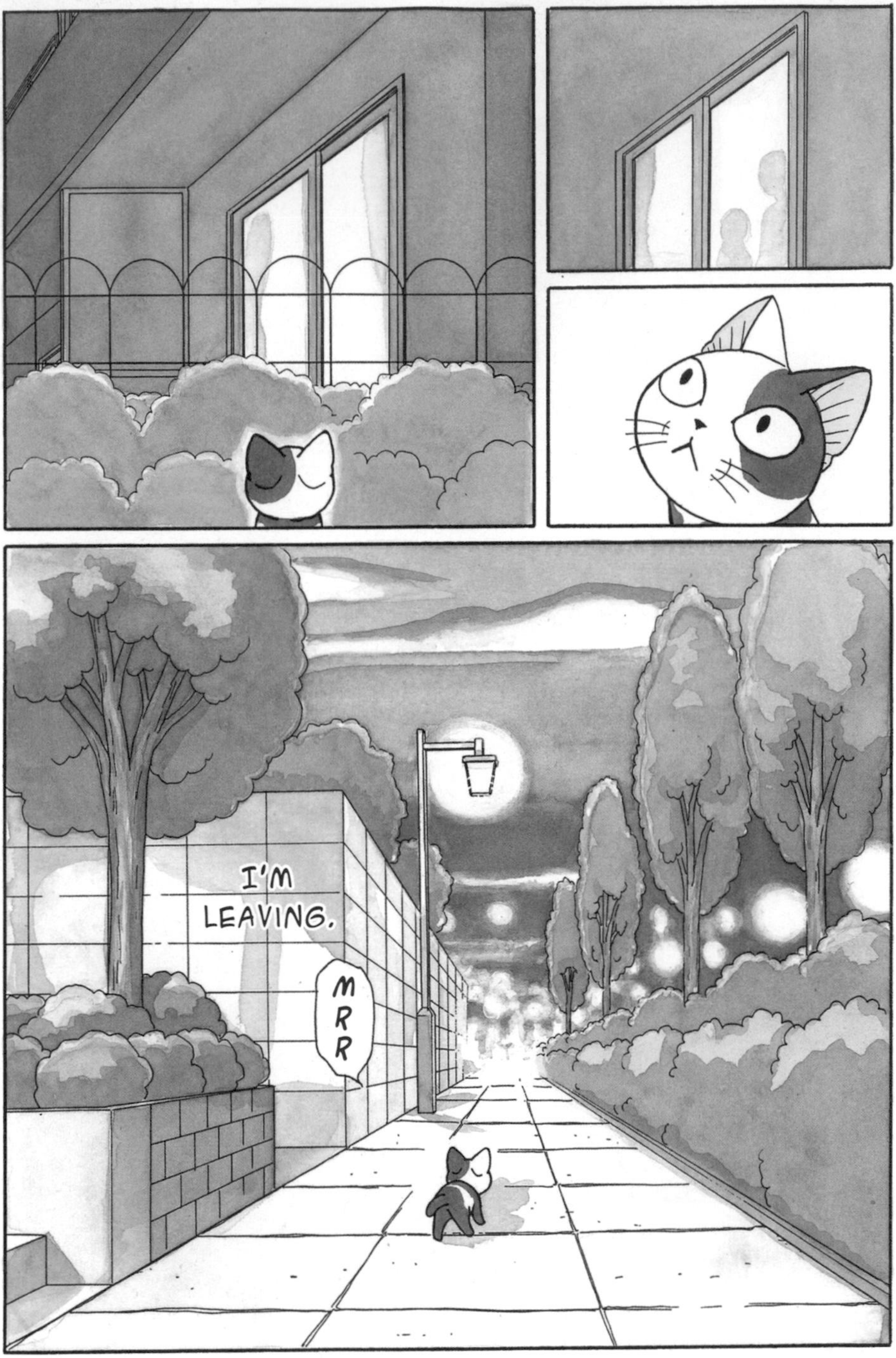
I'M LEAVING.
MRR



**the end**

# homemade 157: a cat yearns

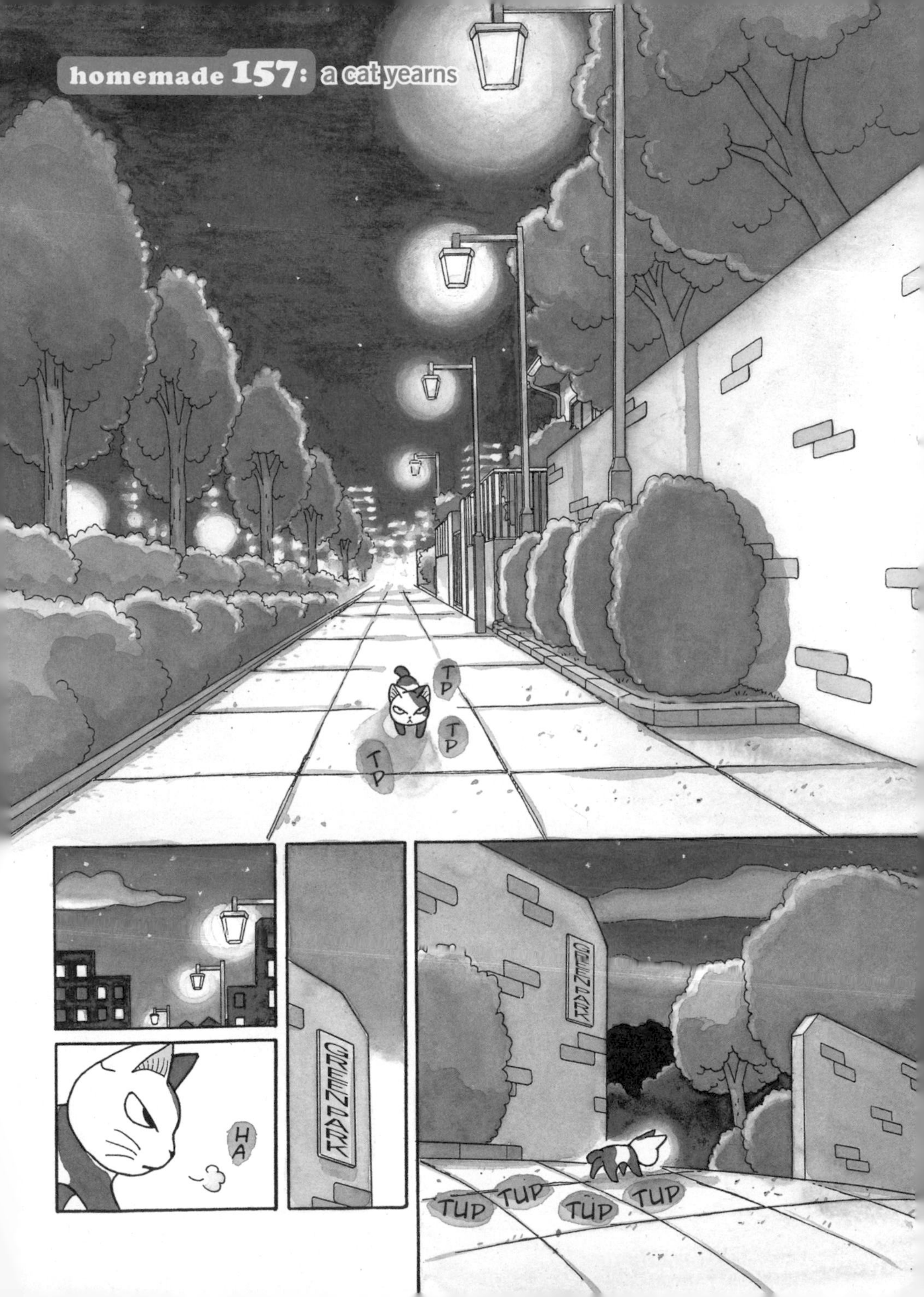
TP
TP
TP
HA
GREEN PARK
GREEN PARK
TUP
TUP
TUP
TUP

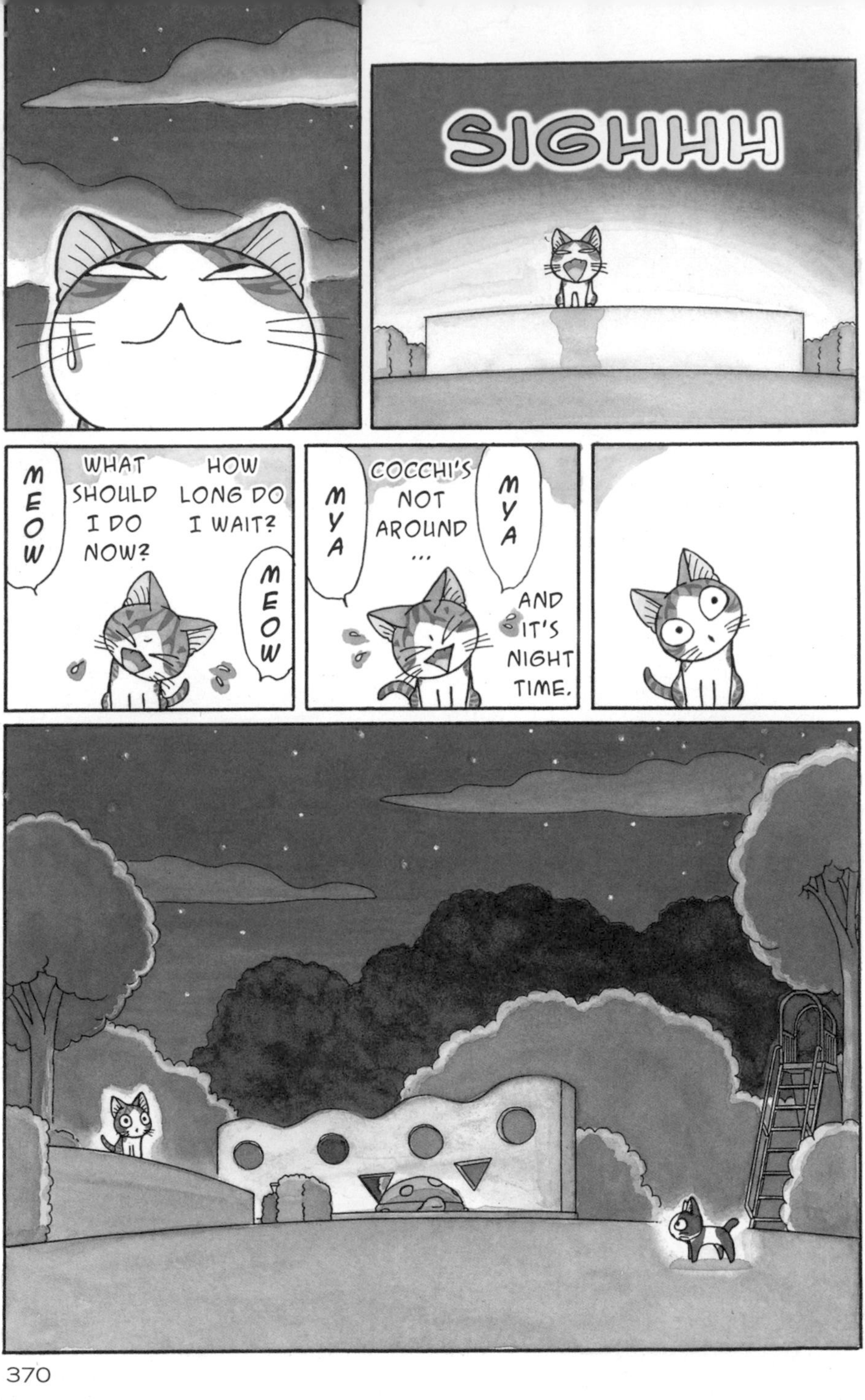
SIGHHH
MEOW
WHAT SHOULD I DO NOW?
HOW LONG DO I WAIT?
MEOW
MYA
COCCHI'S NOT AROUND ...
MYA
AND IT'S NIGHT TIME.

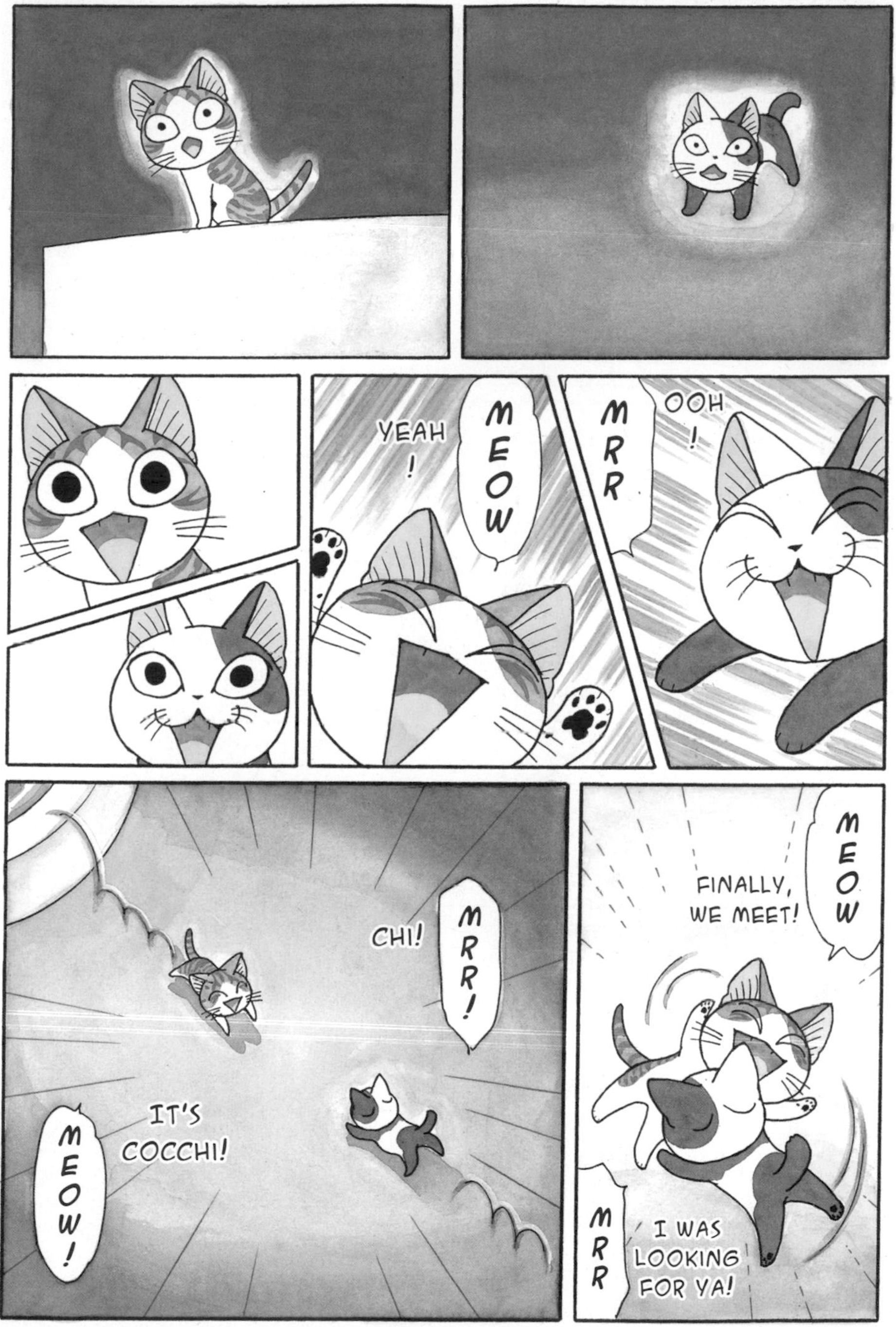
YEAH!
MEOW
MRR
OOH!
CHI!
MRR!
IT'S COCCHI!
MEOW!
FINALLY, WE MEET!
MEOW
MRR
I WAS LOOKING FOR YA!

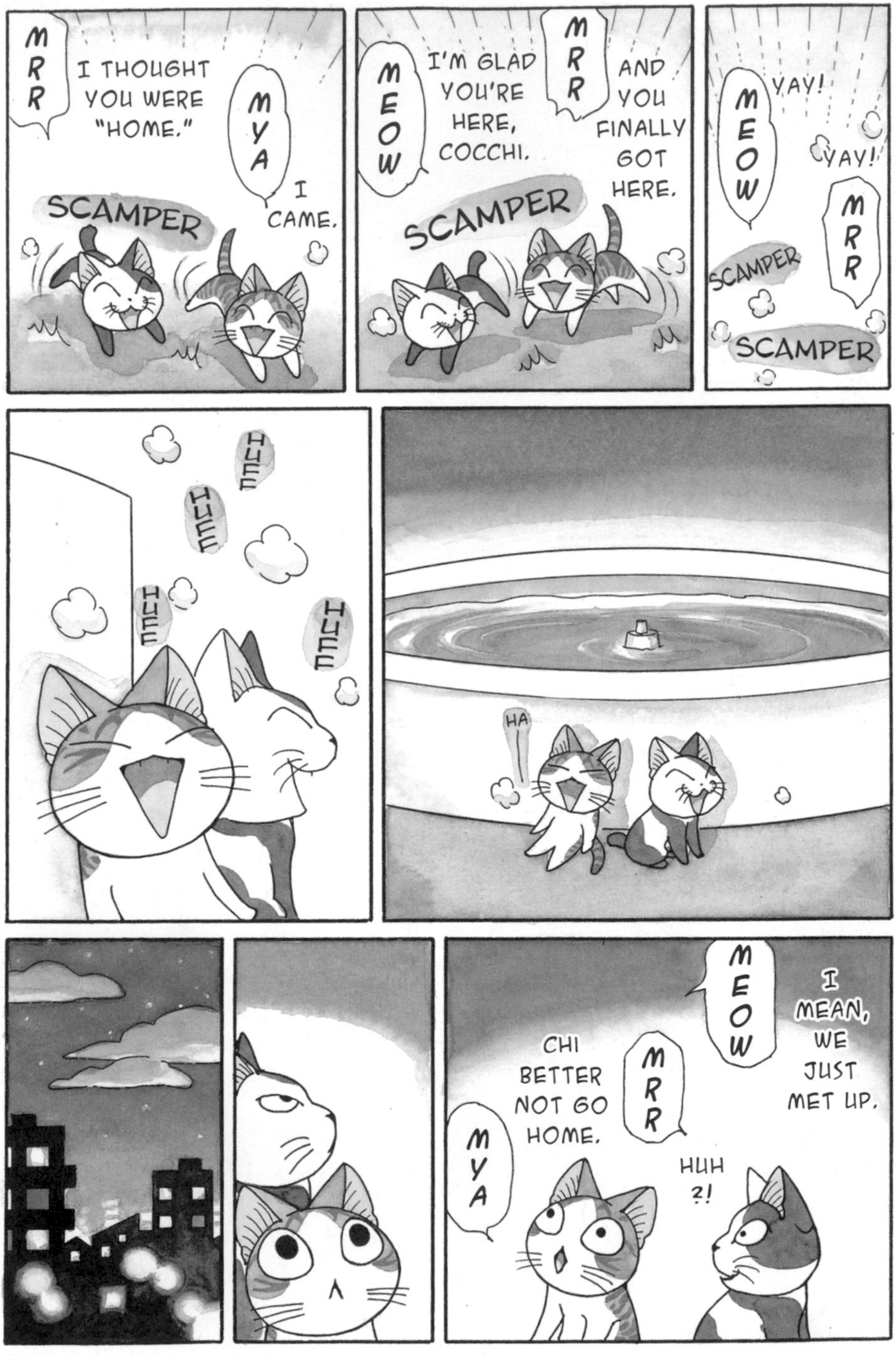
MRR
I THOUGHT YOU WERE "HOME."
MYA
I CAME.
SCAMPER
MEOW
I'M GLAD YOU'RE HERE, COCCHI.
MRR
AND YOU FINALLY GOT HERE.
SCAMPER
MEOW
YAY!
YAY!
MRR
SCAMPER
SCAMPER
HUFF
HUFF
HUFF
HUFF
HA
MEOW
I MEAN, WE JUST MET UP.
MRR
CHI BETTER NOT GO HOME.
MYA
HUH?!

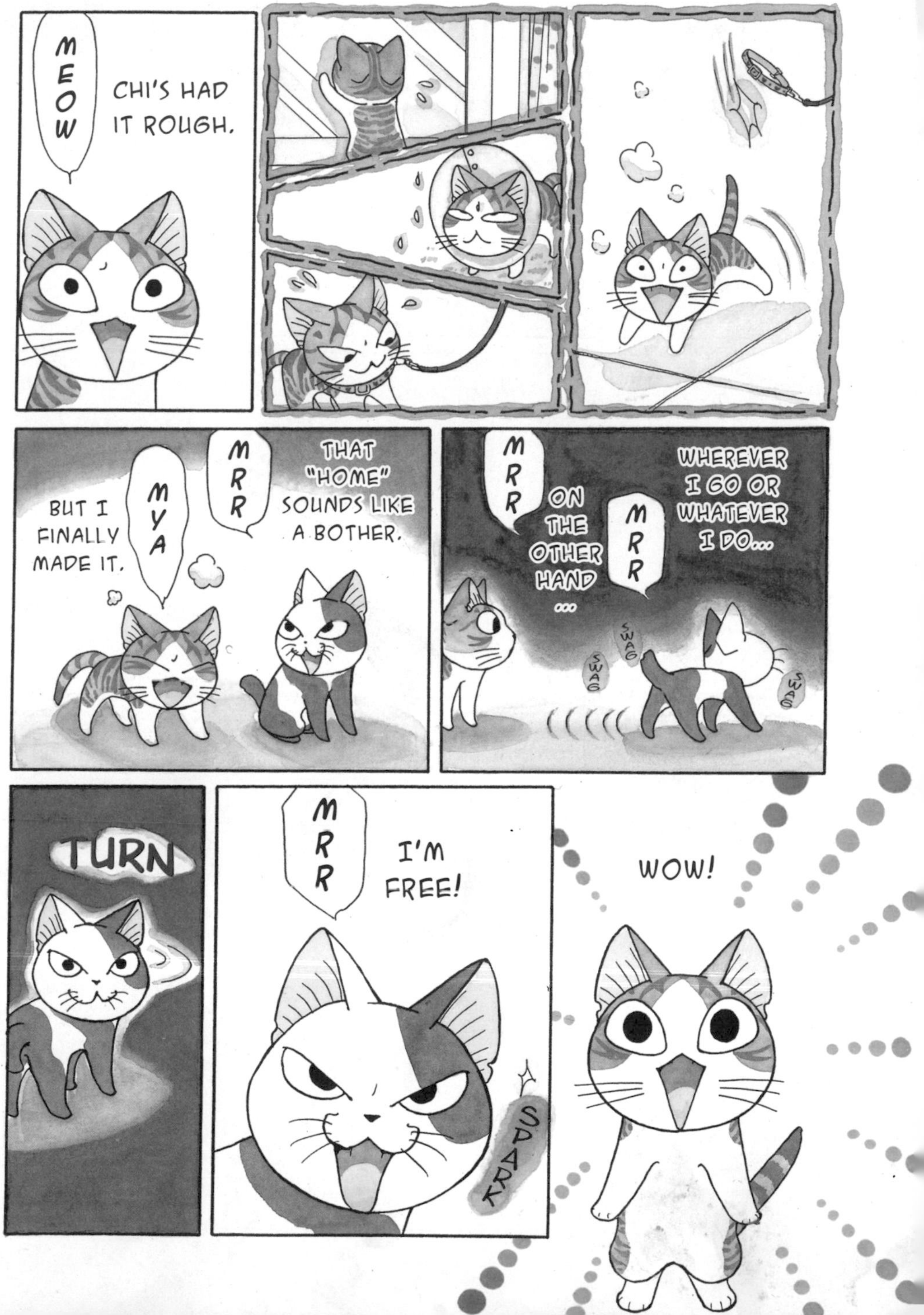
MEOW
CHI'S HAD IT ROUGH.
BUT I FINALLY MADE IT.
MYA
MRR
THAT "HOME" SOUNDS LIKE A BOTHER.
MRR
ON THE OTHER HAND...
MRR
WHEREVER I GO OR WHATEVER I DO...
SWAG
SWAG
TURN
MRR
I'M FREE!
SPARK
WOW!

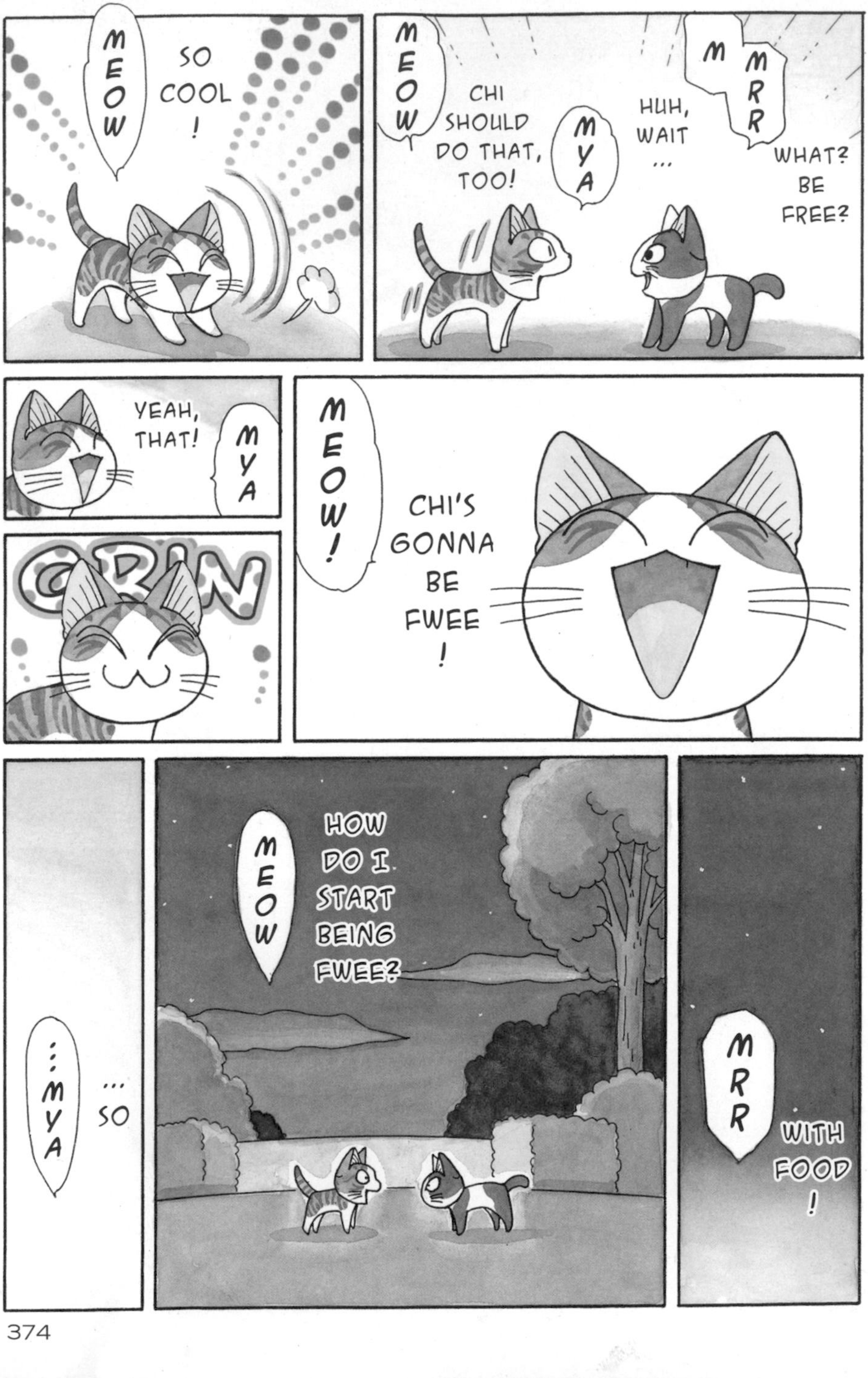
MEOW
SO COOL!
MEOW
CHI SHOULD DO THAT, TOO!
MYA
HUH, WAIT...
M
MRR
WHAT? BE FREE?
YEAH, THAT!
MYA
GRIN
MEOW!
CHI'S GONNA BE FWEE!
...MYA
...SO
MEOW
HOW DO I START BEING FWEE?
MRR
WITH FOOD!

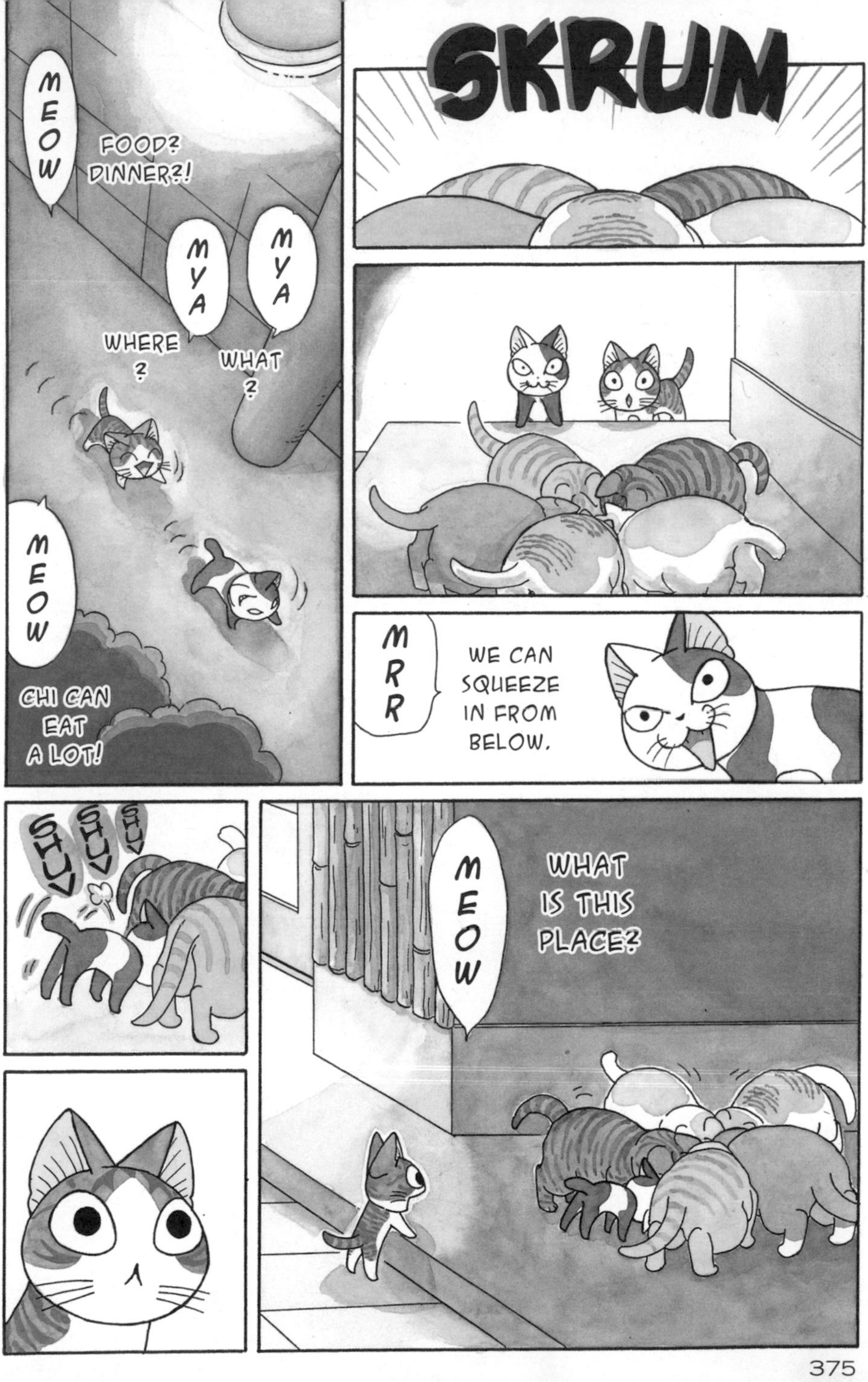

MEOW
FOOD? DINNER?!
MYA
WHERE ?
MYA
WHAT ?
MEOW
CHI CAN EAT A LOT!
SKRUM
MRR
WE CAN SQUEEZE IN FROM BELOW.
SHUV SHUV SHUV
MEOW
WHAT IS THIS PLACE?

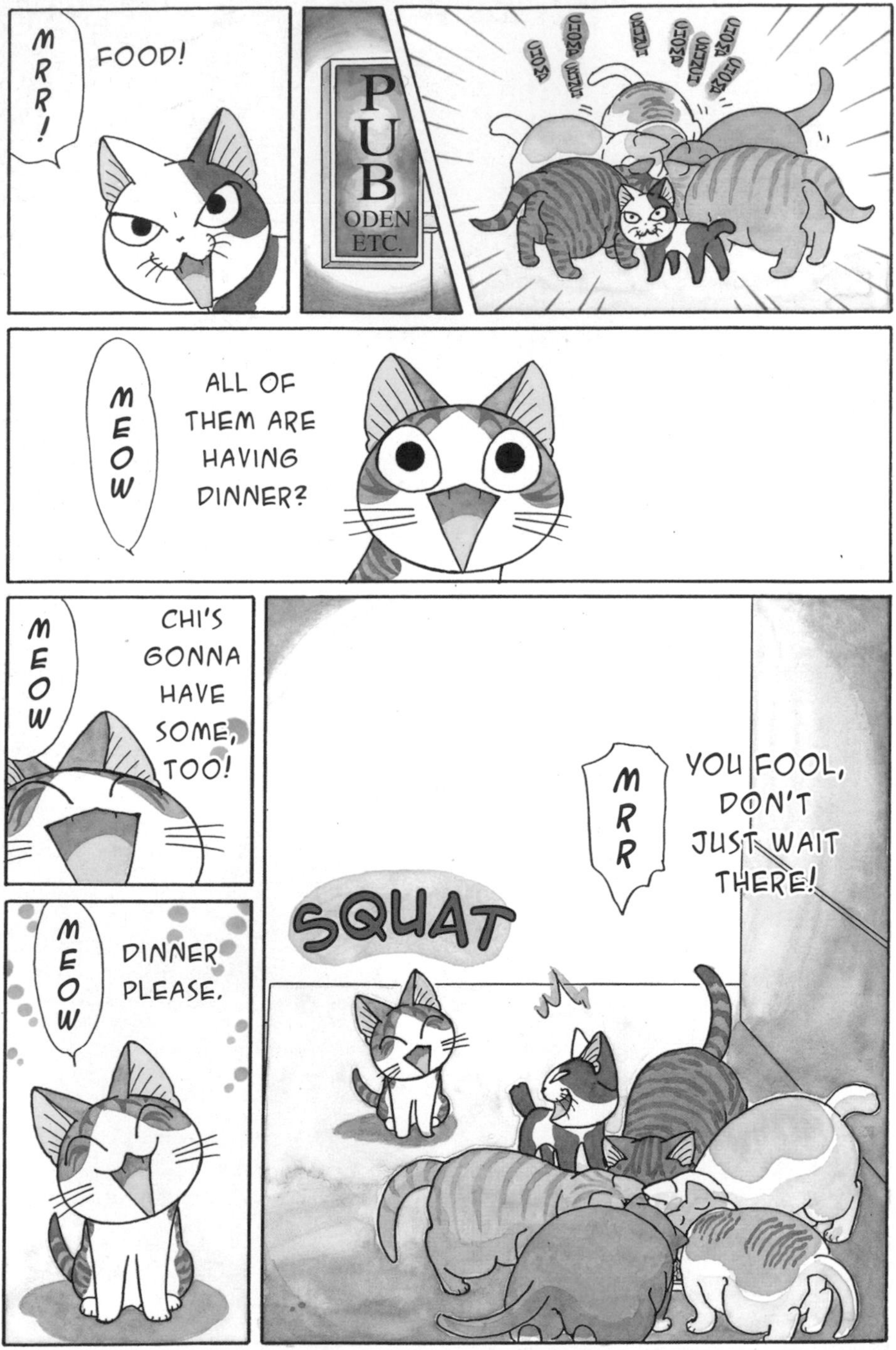
MRR!
FOOD!
PUB
ODEN
ETC.
CHOMP
CHOMP
CRUNCH
CRUNCH
CHOMP
CRUNCH
CHOMP
CHOMP
MEOW
ALL OF THEM ARE HAVING DINNER?
MEOW
CHI'S GONNA HAVE SOME, TOO!
MEOW
DINNER PLEASE.
SQUAT
MRR
YOU FOOL, DON'T JUST WAIT THERE!



the end

## homemade 158: a cat apprentices

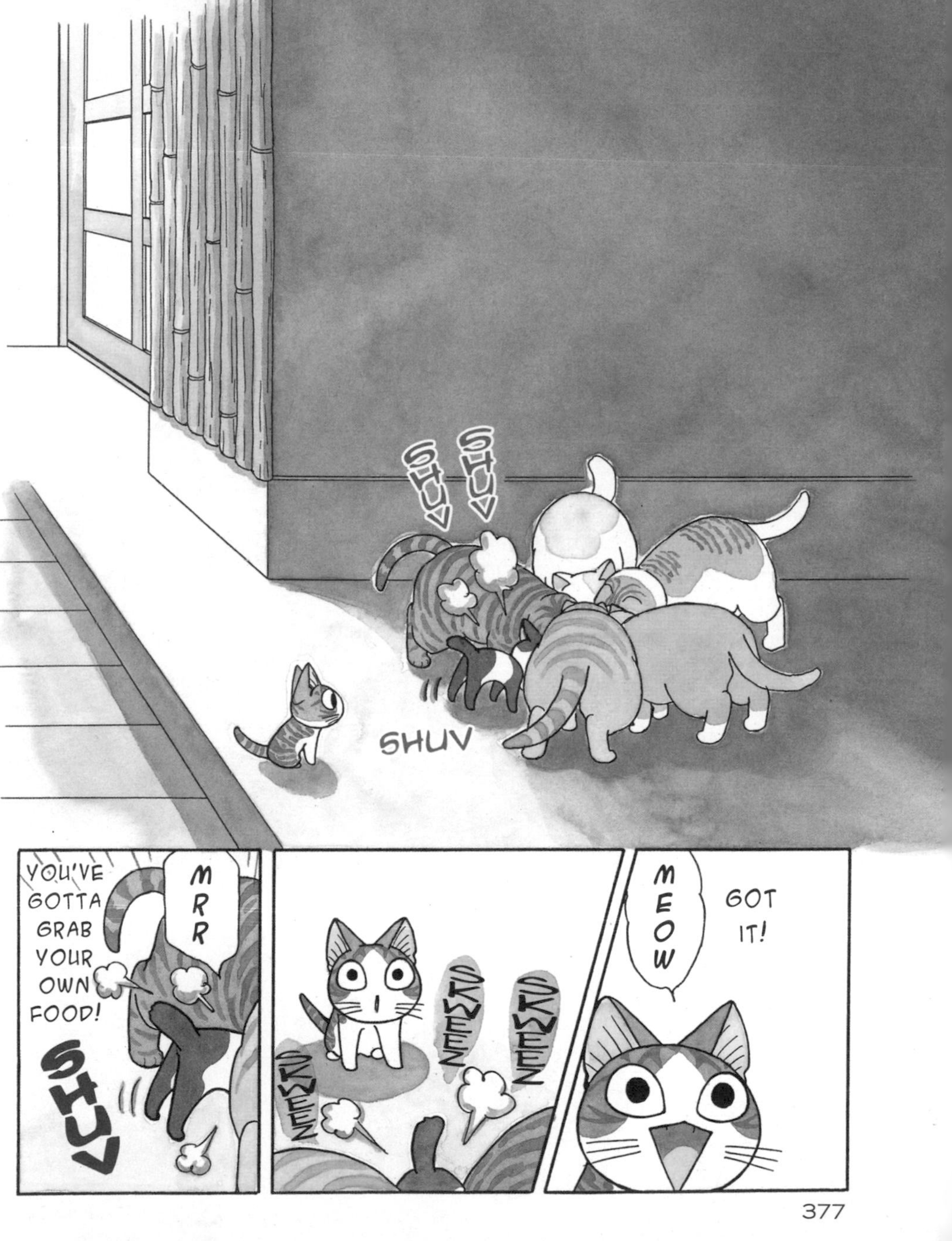

SHUV
SHUV
SHUV
YOU'VE GOTTA GRAB YOUR OWN FOOD!
MRR
SHUV
SKWEEZ
SKWEEZ
SKWEEZ
MEOW
GOT IT!

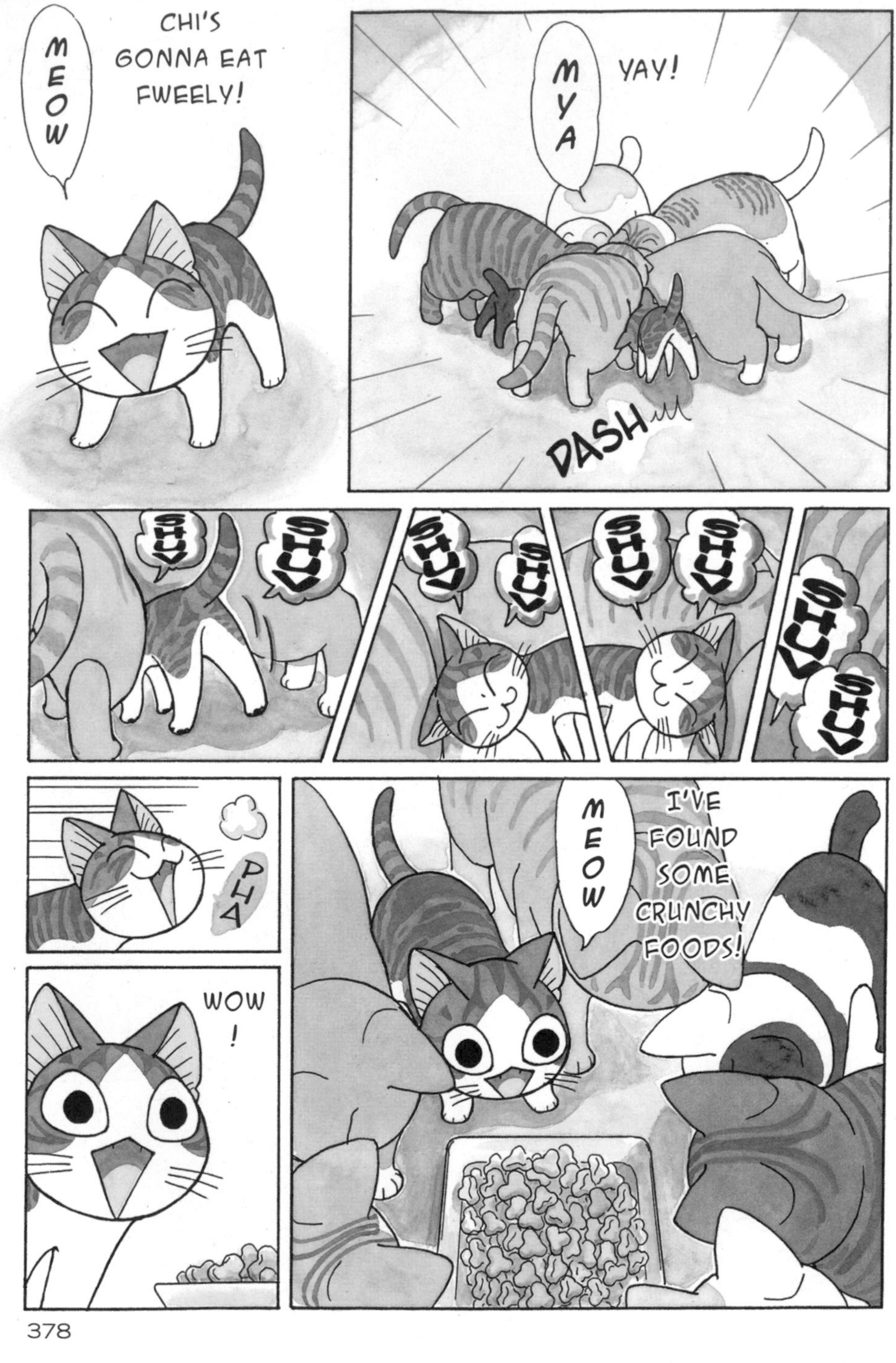
MEOW
CHI'S GONNA EAT FWEELY!
MYA
YAY!
DASH
SHUV
SHUV
SHUV
SHUV
SHUV
SHUV
SHUV
SHUV
PHA
WOW!
MEOW
I'VE FOUND SOME CRUNCHY FOODS!

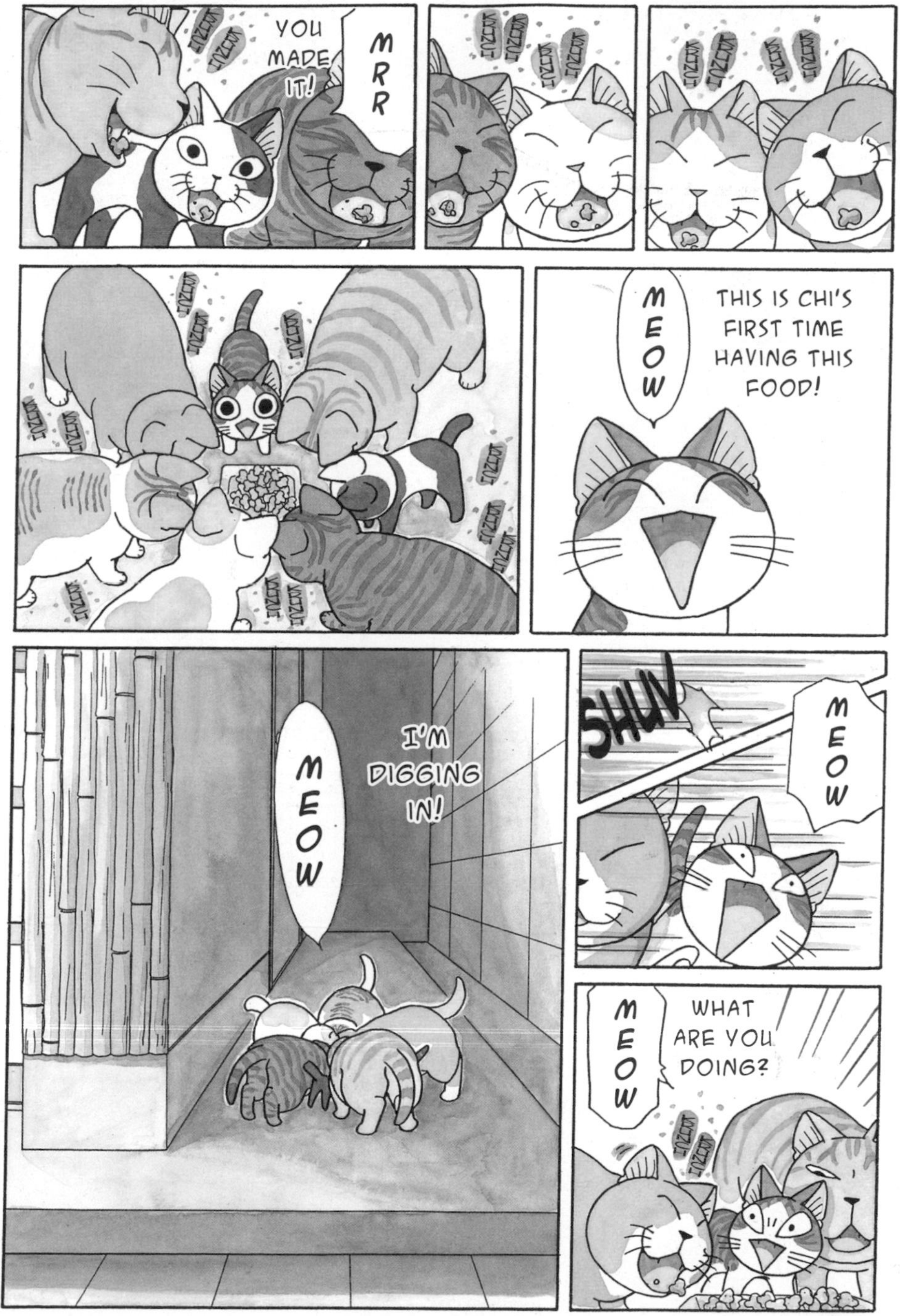
YOU MADE IT!
MRR
MEOW
THIS IS CHI'S FIRST TIME HAVING THIS FOOD!
MEOW
I'M DIGGING IN!
SHUV
MEOW
MEOW
WHAT ARE YOU DOING?

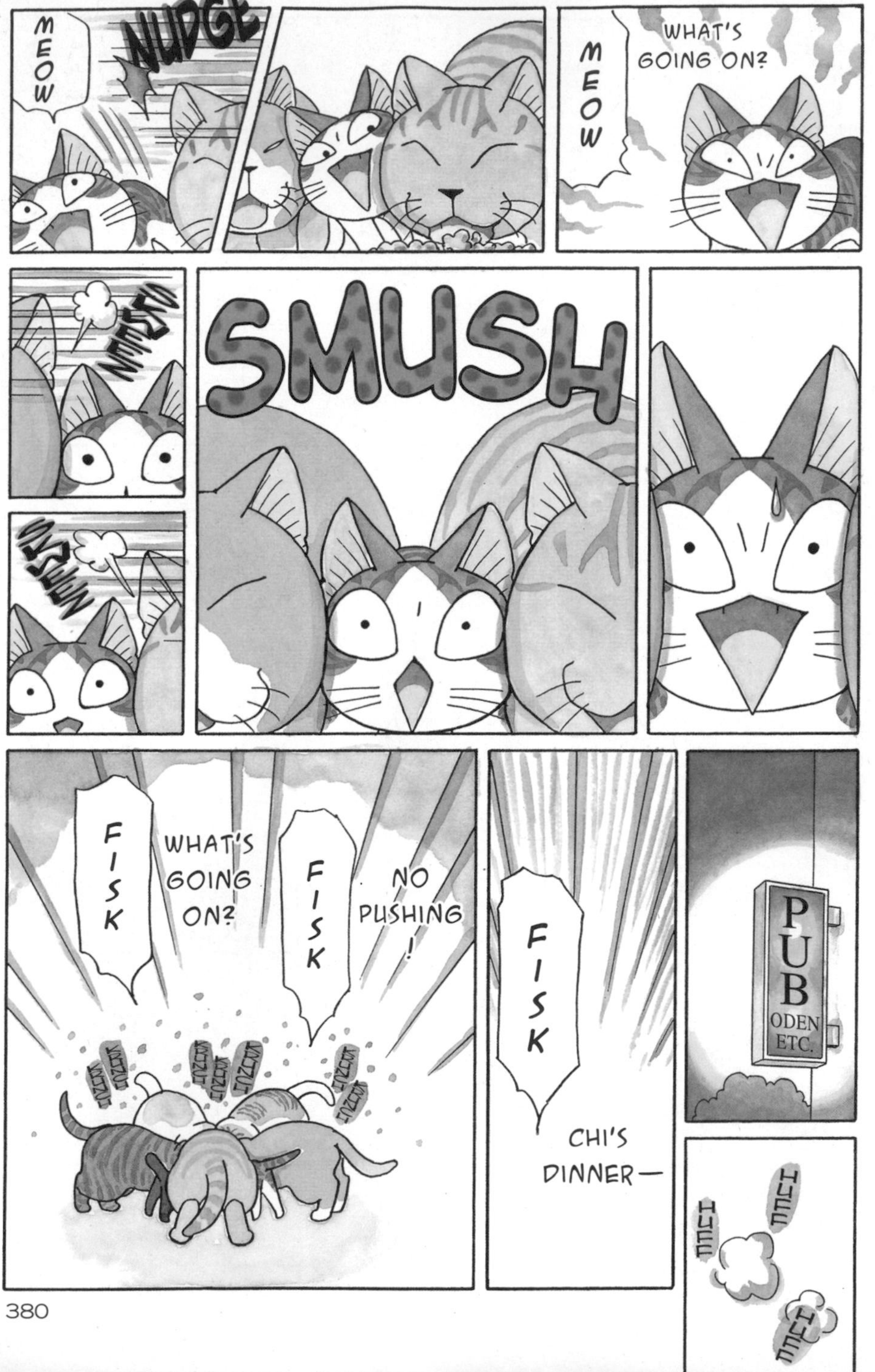
MEOW
NUDGE
MEOW
WHAT'S GOING ON?
SMUSH
FISK
WHAT'S GOING ON?
FISK
NO PUSHING!
FISK
CHI'S DINNER—
PUB
ODEN ETC.
HUFF
HUFF
HUFF

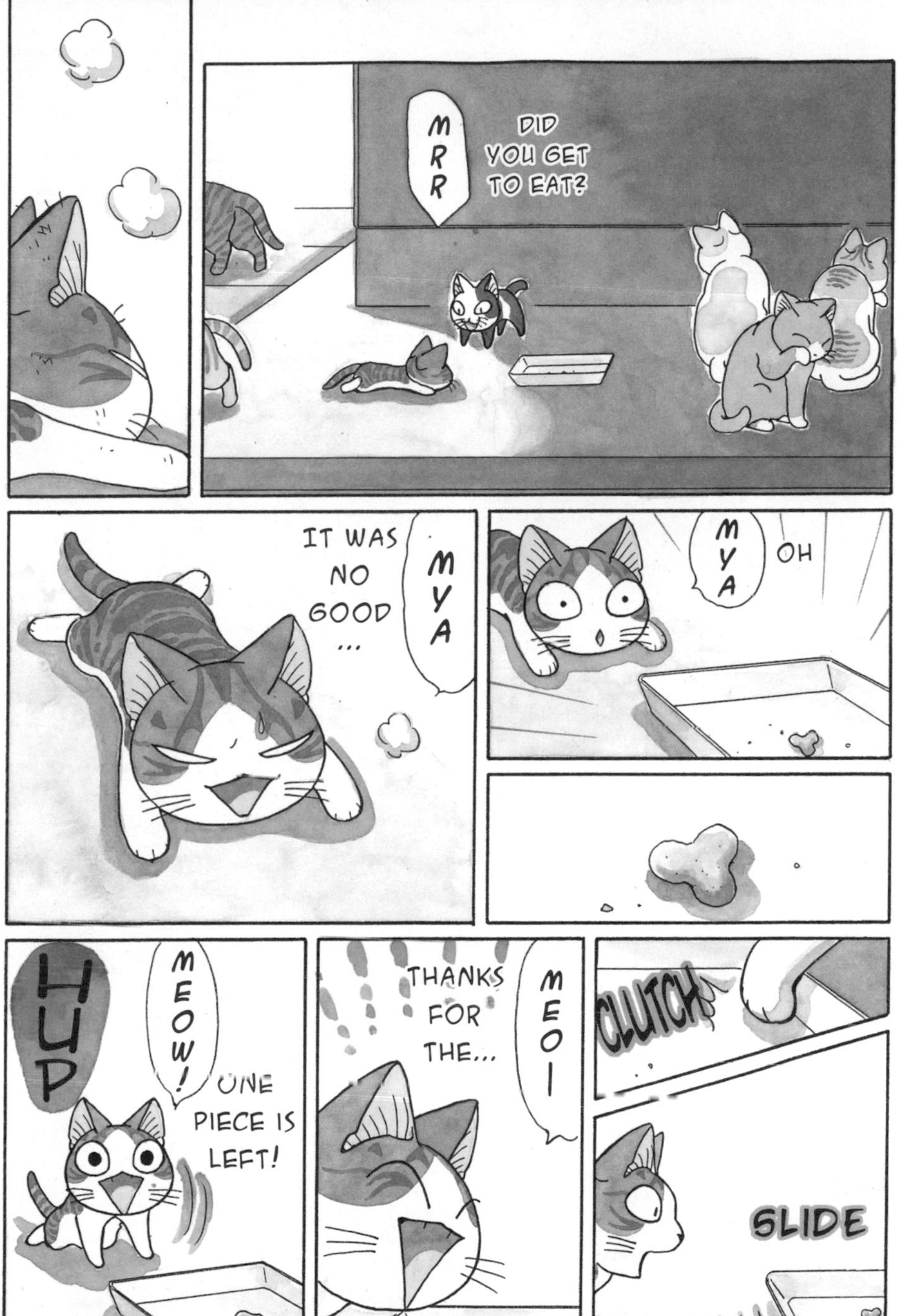
MRR
DID YOU GET TO EAT?
IT WAS NO GOOD ...
MYA
MYA
OH
HUP
MEOW!
ONE PIECE IS LEFT!
THANKS FOR THE...
MEOI
CLUTCH
SLIDE

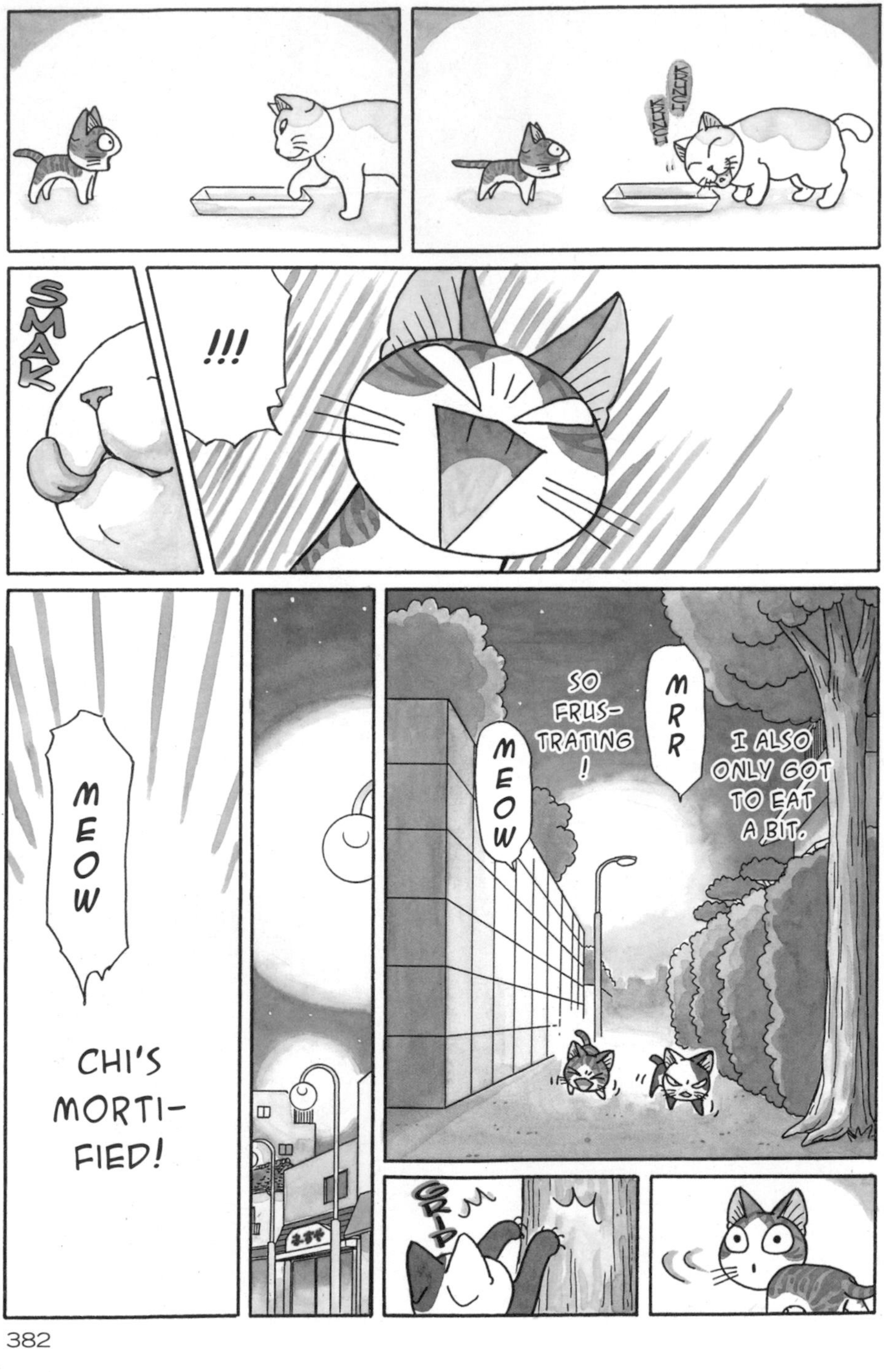
KRUNCH
KRUNCH
SMAK
!!!
MEOW
CHI'S MORTIFIED!
SO FRUS-TRATING!
MRR
MEOW
I ALSO ONLY GOT TO EAT A BIT.
GRIP

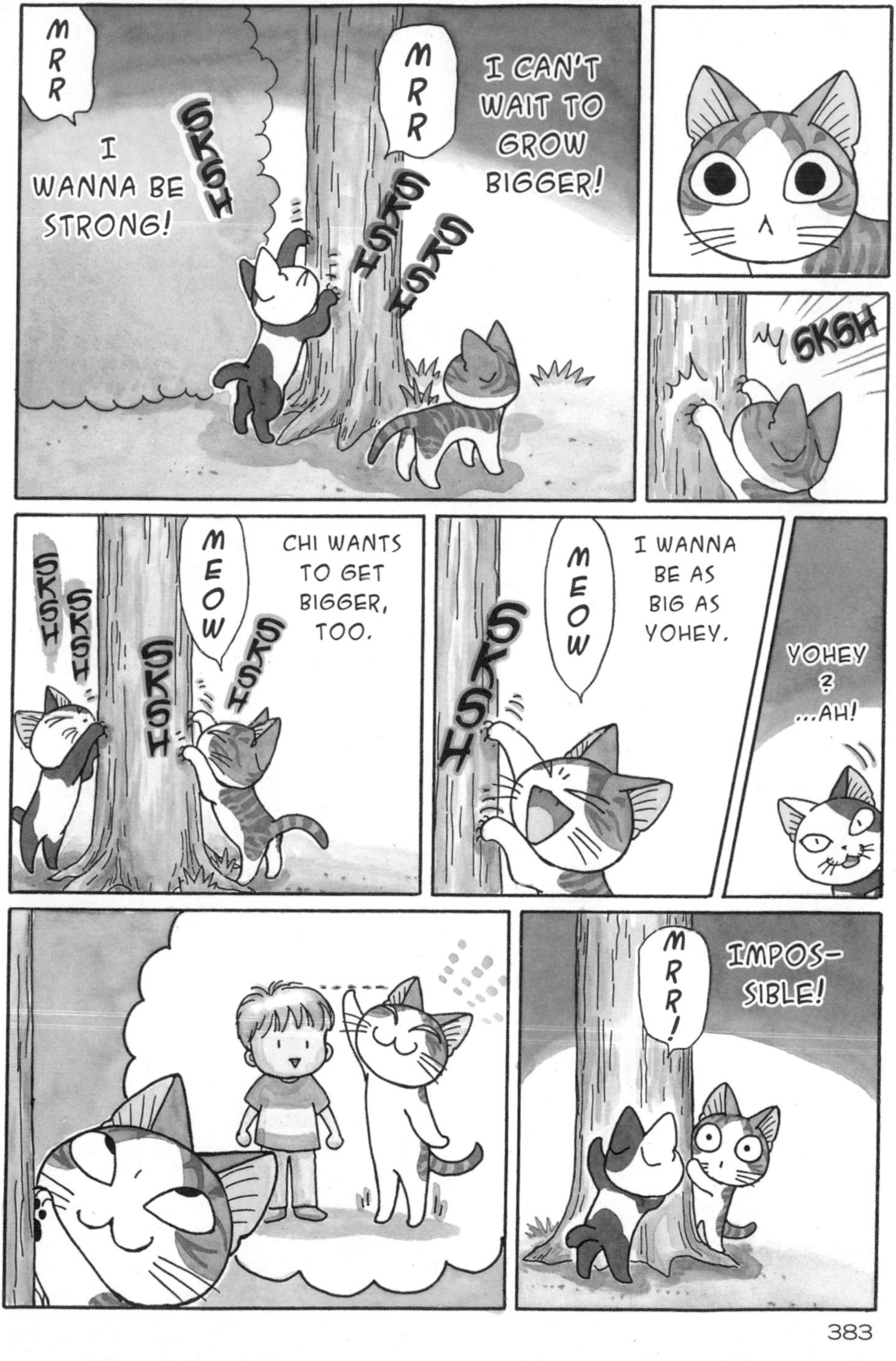
MRR
SKSH
I WANNA BE STRONG!
MRR
SKSH
SKSH
I CAN'T WAIT TO GROW BIGGER!
SKSH
SKSH
SKSH
MEOW
SKSH
SKSH
CHI WANTS TO GET BIGGER, TOO.
MEOW
SKSH
I WANNA BE AS BIG AS YOHEY.
YOHEY ? ...AH!
MRR!
IMPOS-SIBLE!

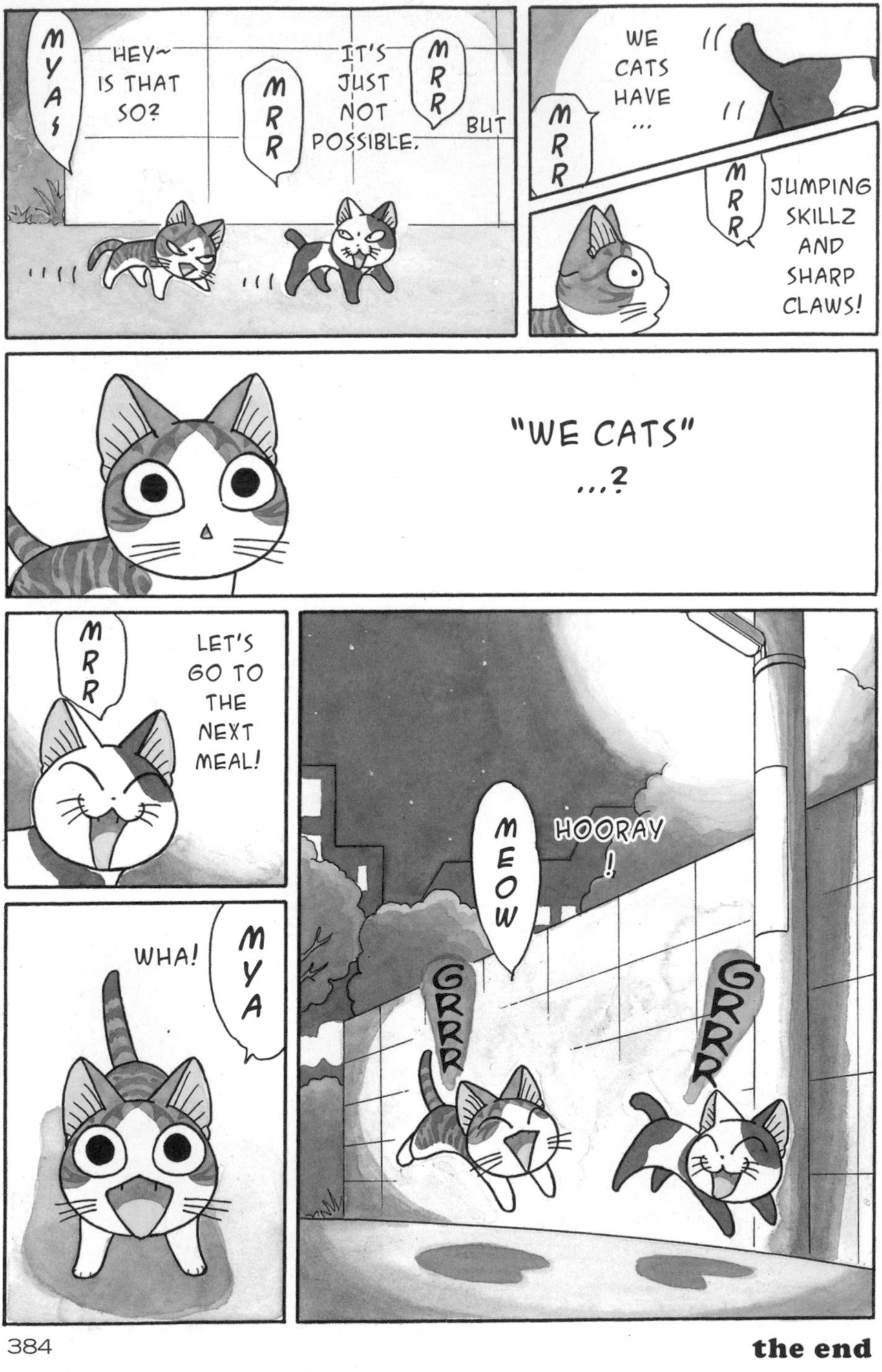
MYA~
HEY~ IS THAT SO?
MRR
IT'S JUST NOT POSSIBLE.
MRR
BUT
WE CATS HAVE ...
MRR
MRR
JUMPING SKILLZ AND SHARP CLAWS!
"WE CATS" ...?
MRR
LET'S GO TO THE NEXT MEAL!
WHA!
MYA
MEOW
HOORAY!
GRRR
GRRR

**the end**

# homemade 159: a cat practices

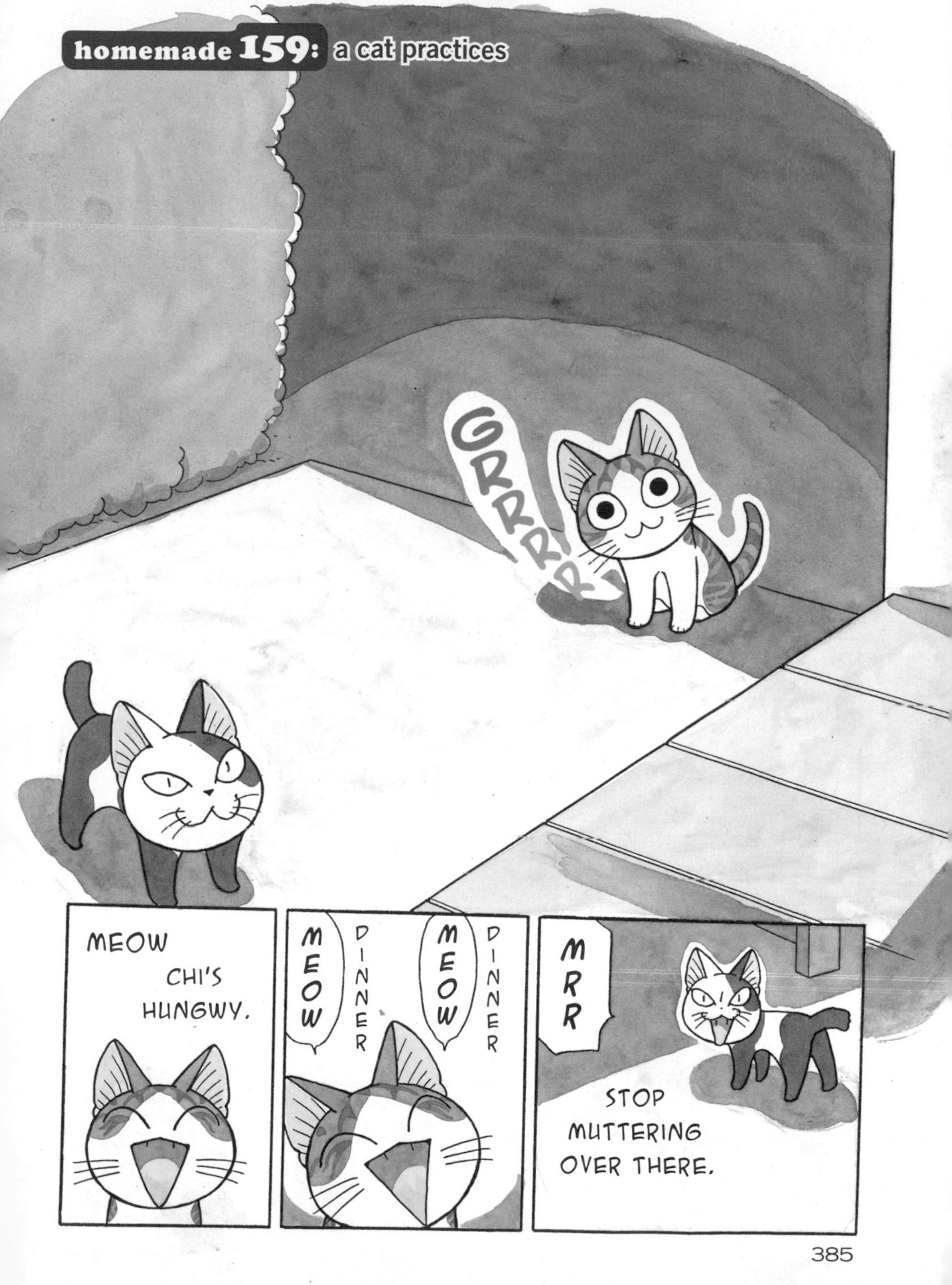
GRRRR
MEOW
CHI'S HUNGWY.
MEOW
DINNER
MEOW
DINNER
MRR
STOP MUTTERING OVER THERE.

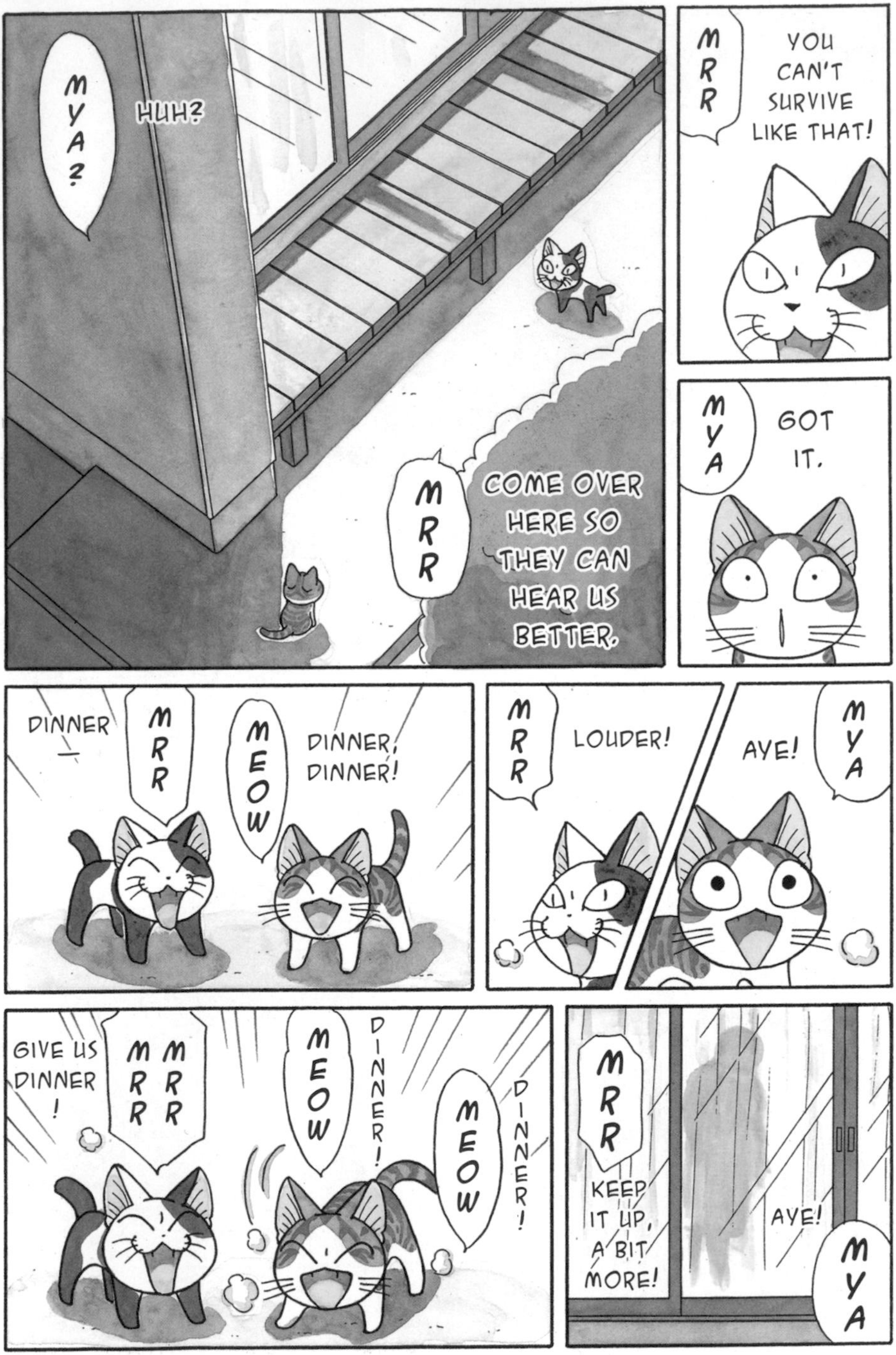
MYA?
HUH?
MRR
COME OVER HERE SO THEY CAN HEAR US BETTER.
MRR
YOU CAN'T SURVIVE LIKE THAT!
MYA
GOT IT.
DINNER—
MRR
MEOW
DINNER, DINNER!
MRR
LOUDER!
AYE!
MYA
GIVE US DINNER!
MRR MRR
MEOW
DINNER!
MEOW
DINNER!
MRR
KEEP IT UP, A BIT MORE!
AYE!
MYA

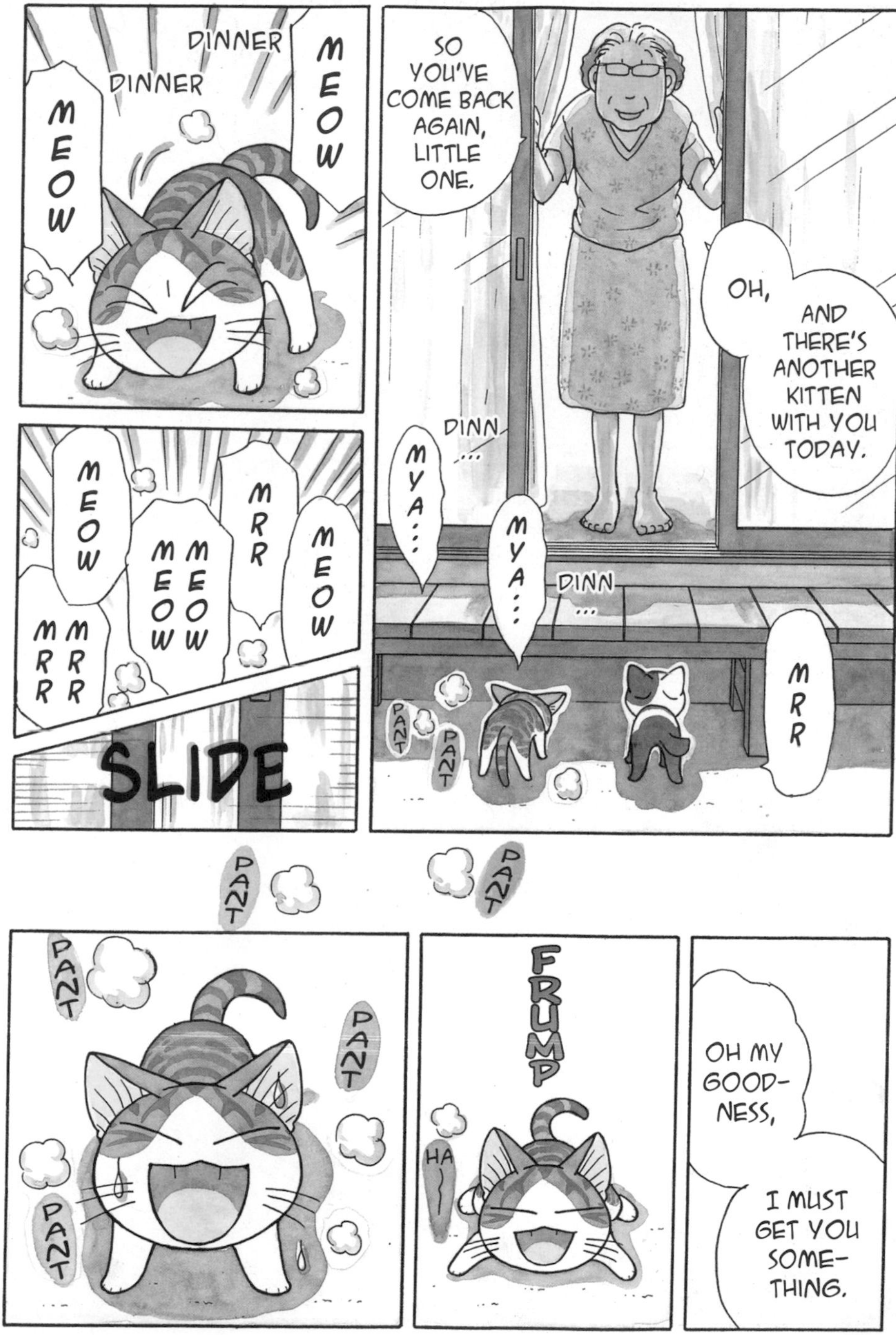

MEOW
DINNER
DINNER
MEOW
MEOW
MRR MRR
MEOW MEOW
MRR
MEOW
SLIDE
SO YOU'VE COME BACK AGAIN, LITTLE ONE.
OH, AND THERE'S ANOTHER KITTEN WITH YOU TODAY.
DINN...
MYA...
MYA...
DINN...
PANT PANT
MRR
PANT
PANT
PANT
PANT
PANT
FRUMP
HA
OH MY GOODNESS,
I MUST GET YOU SOMETHING.

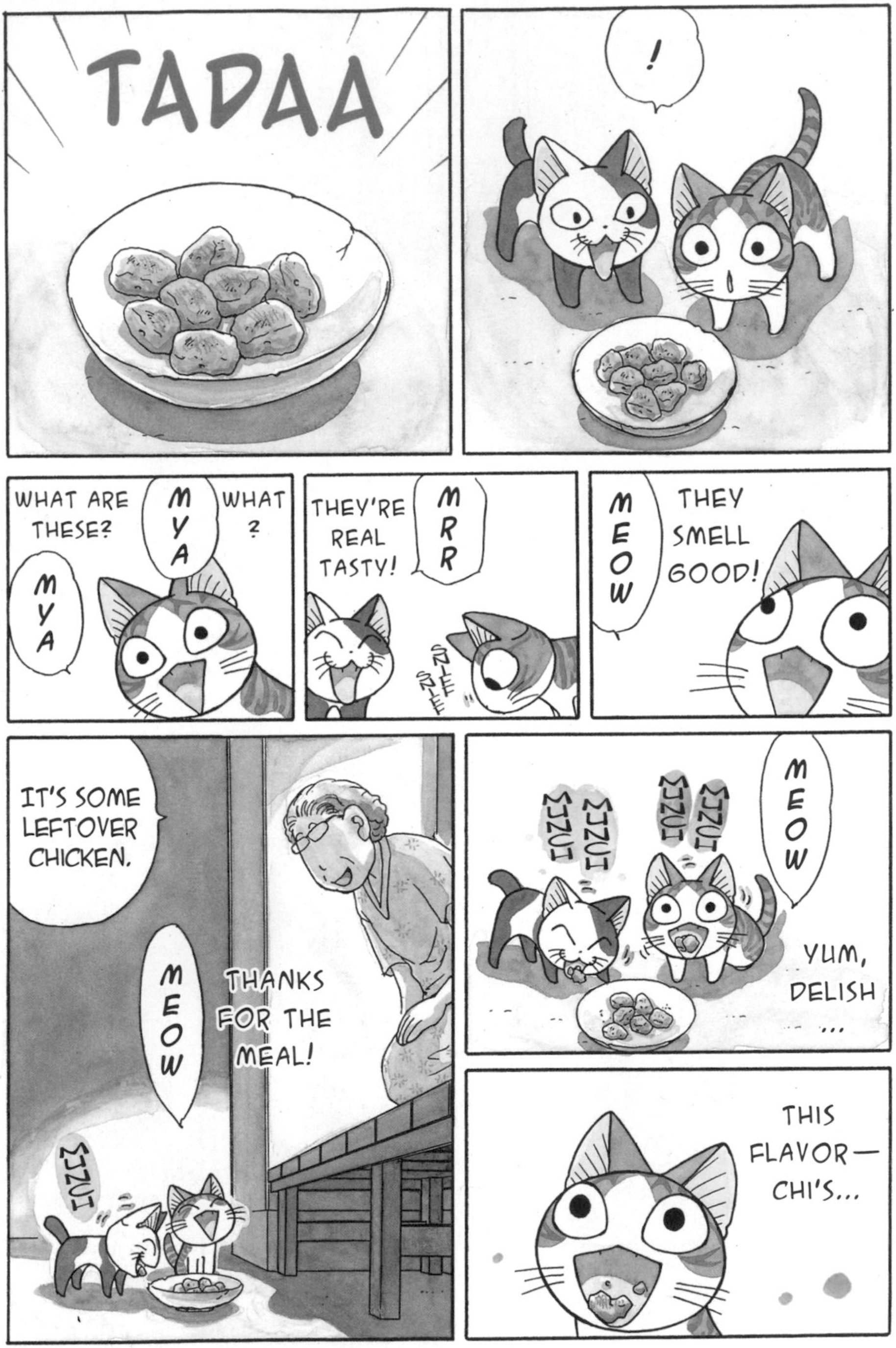
TADAA
!
WHAT ARE THESE?
MYA
WHAT?
MYA
THEY'RE REAL TASTY!
MRR
SNIFF SNIFF
MEOW
THEY SMELL GOOD!
IT'S SOME LEFTOVER CHICKEN.
MEOW
THANKS FOR THE MEAL!
MUNCH
MUNCH MUNCH
MUNCH MUNCH
MEOW
YUM, DELISH ...
THIS FLAVOR— CHI'S...

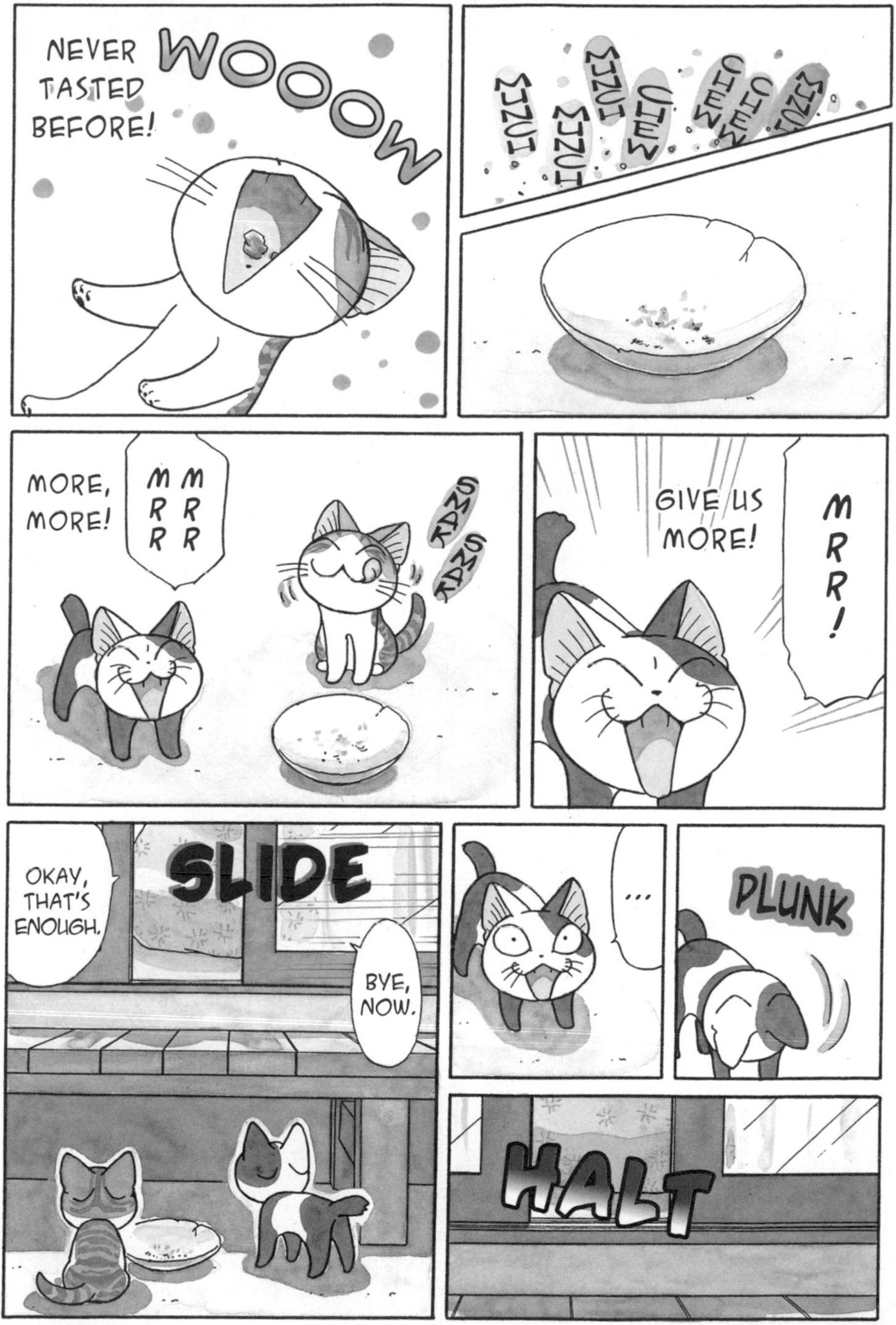
NEVER TASTED BEFORE!
WOOOW
MUNCH MUNCH MUNCH CHEW CHEW CHEW MUNCH
MORE, MORE!
MRR MRR
SMAK SMAK
GIVE US MORE!
MRR!
OKAY, THAT'S ENOUGH.
SLIDE
BYE, NOW.
...
PLUNK
HALT

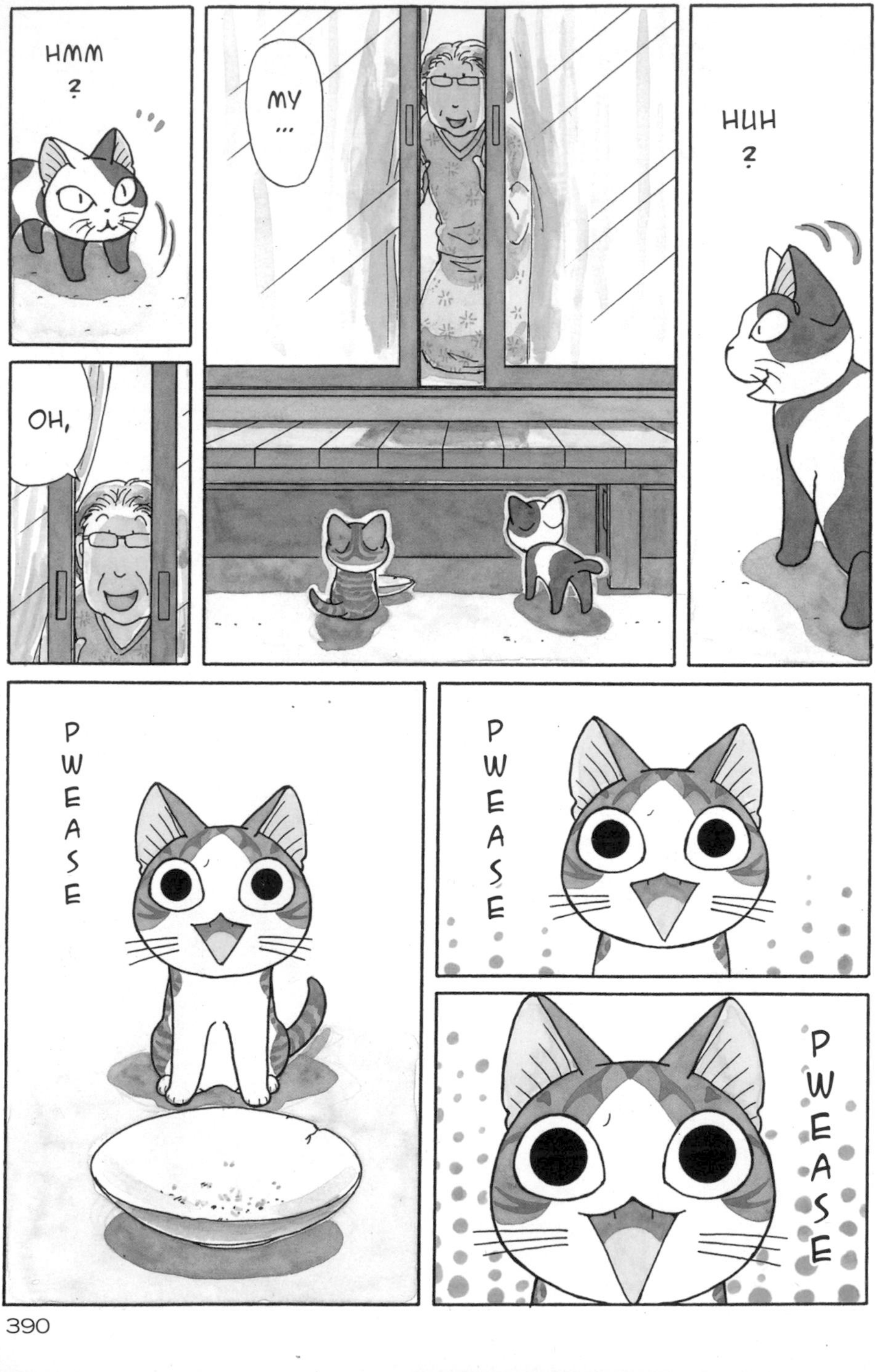
HMM ?
OH,
MY ...
HUH ?
PWEASE
PWEASE
PWEASE

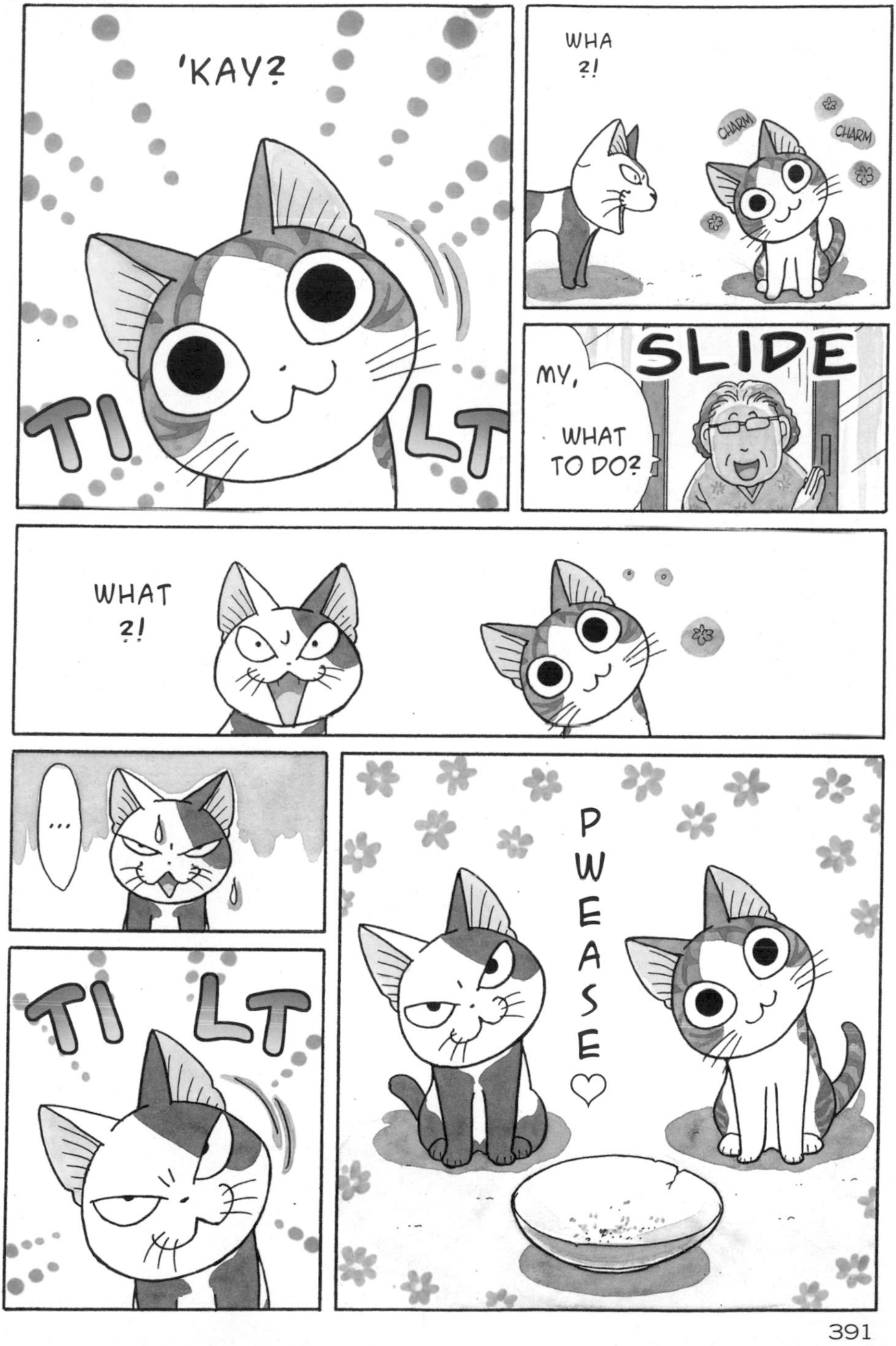
'KAY?
TILT
WHA ?!
CHARM
CHARM
MY, WHAT TO DO?
SLIDE
WHAT ?!
...
TILT
PWEASE♡

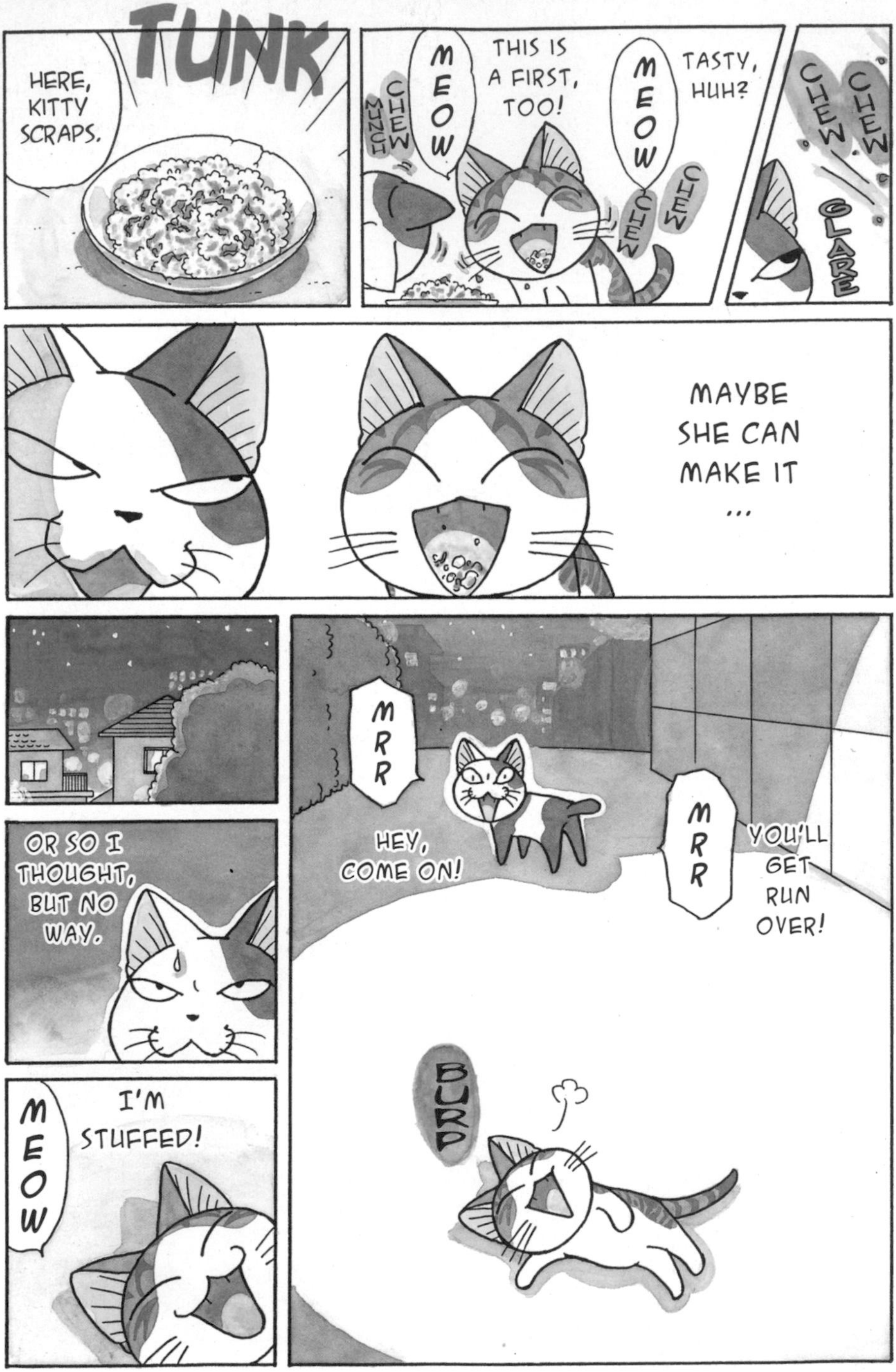
TUNK
HERE, KITTY SCRAPS.
MUNCH CHEW
MEOW
THIS IS A FIRST, TOO!
MEOW
TASTY, HUH?
CHEW CHEW
CHEW CHEW
GLARE
MAYBE SHE CAN MAKE IT ...
OR SO I THOUGHT, BUT NO WAY.
MEOW
I'M STUFFED!
MRR
HEY, COME ON!
MRR
YOU'LL GET RUN OVER!
BURP



**the end**

## homemade 160: a cat is sleepy

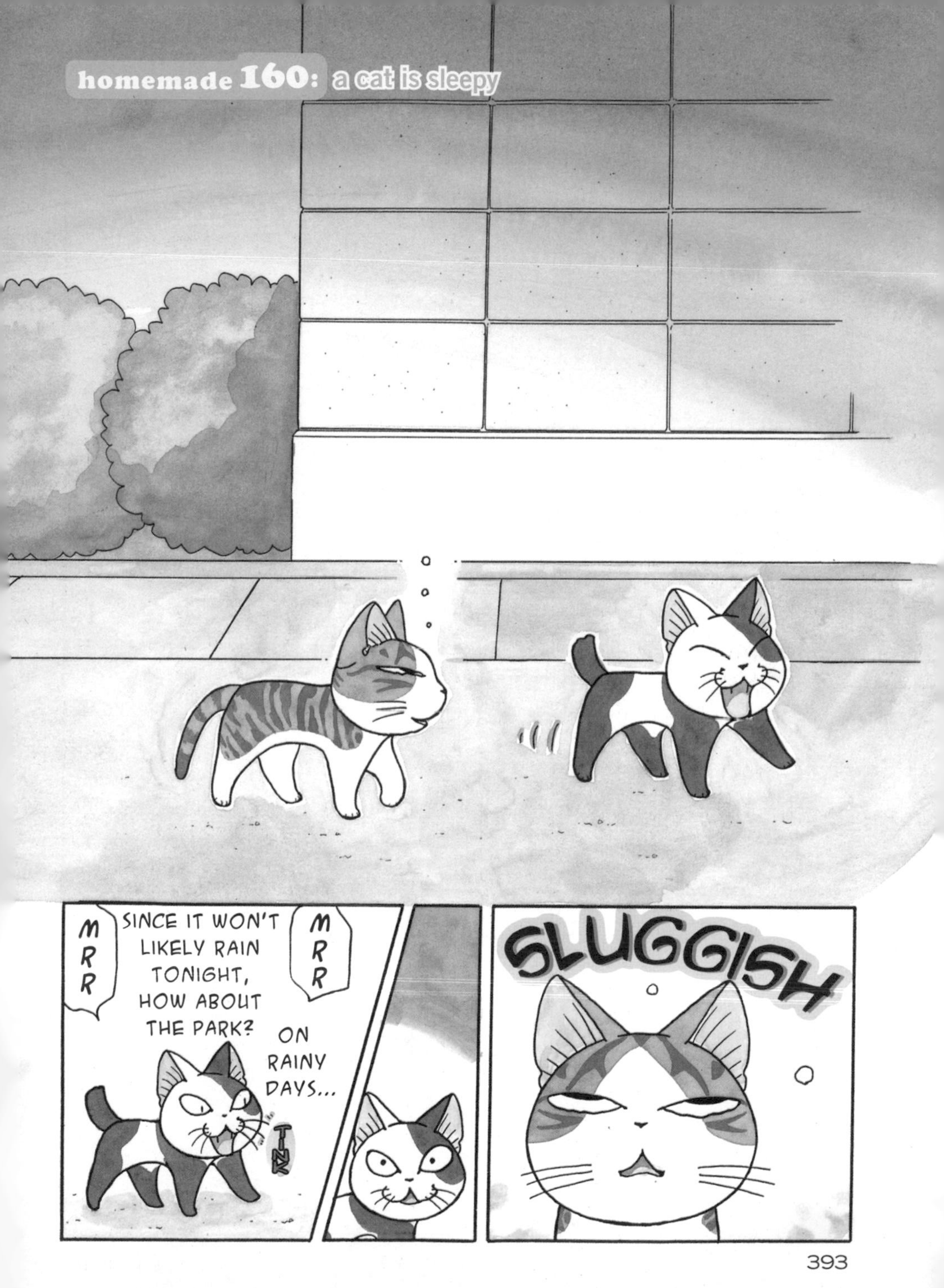
MRR
SINCE IT WON'T LIKELY RAIN TONIGHT, HOW ABOUT THE PARK?
MRR
ON RAINY DAYS...
SLUGGISH

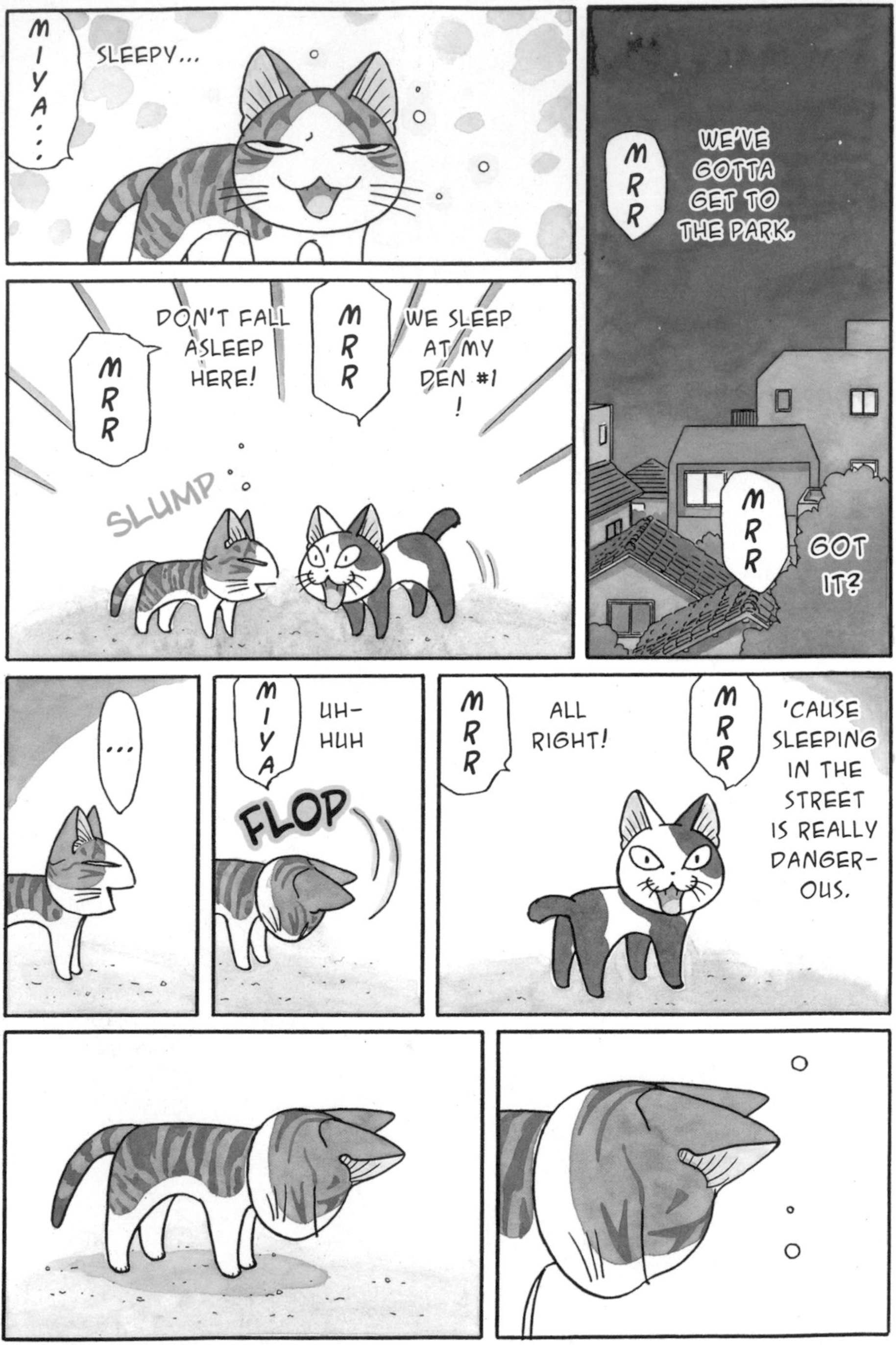
MIYA...
SLEEPY...
MRR
DON'T FALL ASLEEP HERE!
MRR
WE SLEEP AT MY DEN #1!
SLUMP
MRR
WE'VE GOTTA GET TO THE PARK.
MRR
GOT IT?
...
MIYA
UH-HUH
FLOP
MRR
ALL RIGHT!
MRR
'CAUSE SLEEPING IN THE STREET IS REALLY DANGER-OUS.

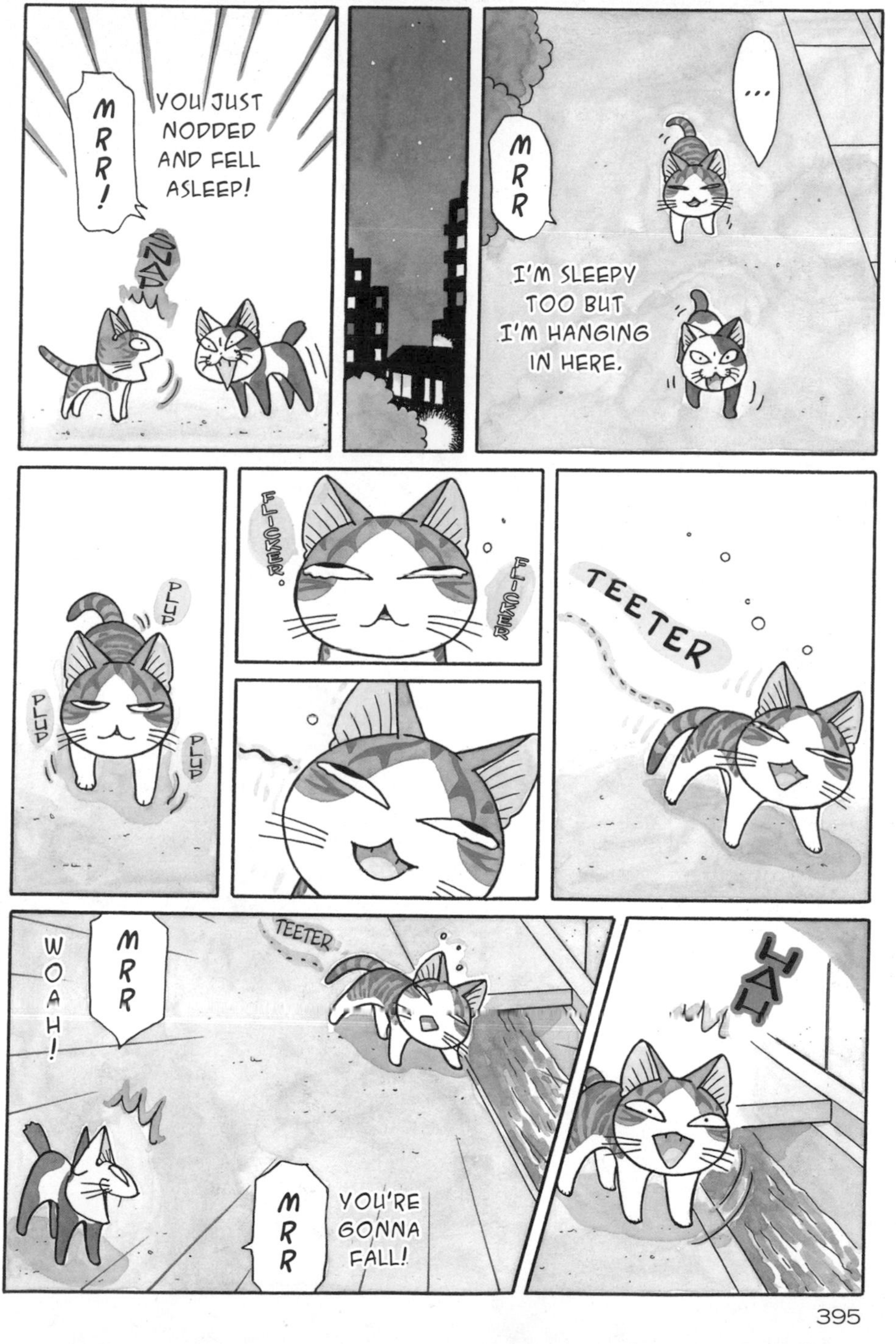
MRR!
YOU JUST NODDED AND FELL ASLEEP!
SNAP
MRR
...
I'M SLEEPY TOO BUT I'M HANGING IN HERE.
PLUP
PLUP
PLUP
FLICKER
FLICKER
TEETER
WOAH!
MRR
TEETER
MRR
YOU'RE GONNA FALL!
HAH

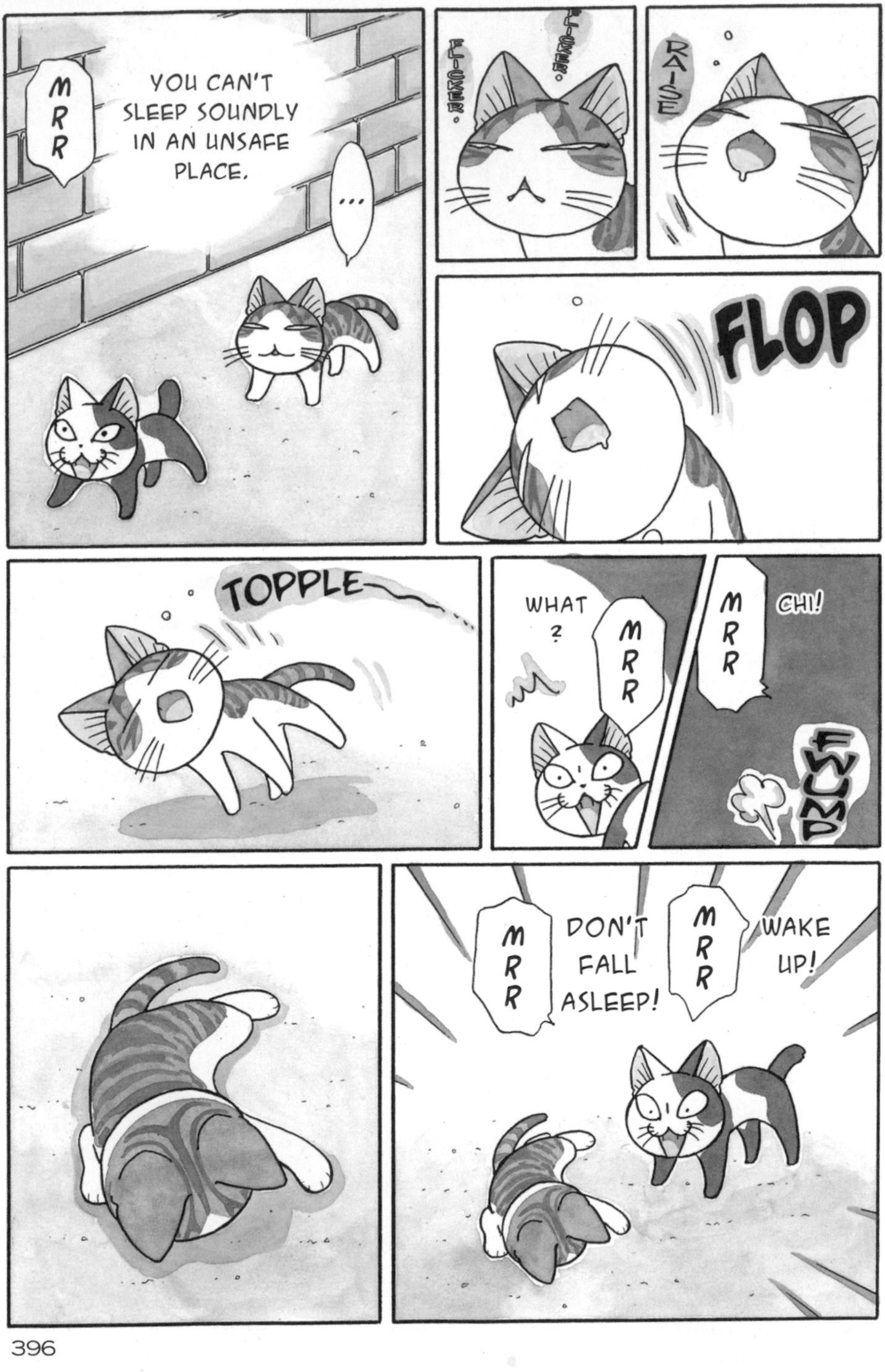
MRR
YOU CAN'T SLEEP SOUNDLY IN AN UNSAFE PLACE.
...
FLICKER.
FLICKER.
RAISE
FLOP
TOPPLE
WHAT?
MRR
MRR
CHI!
FWUMP
MRR
DON'T FALL ASLEEP!
MRR
WAKE UP!

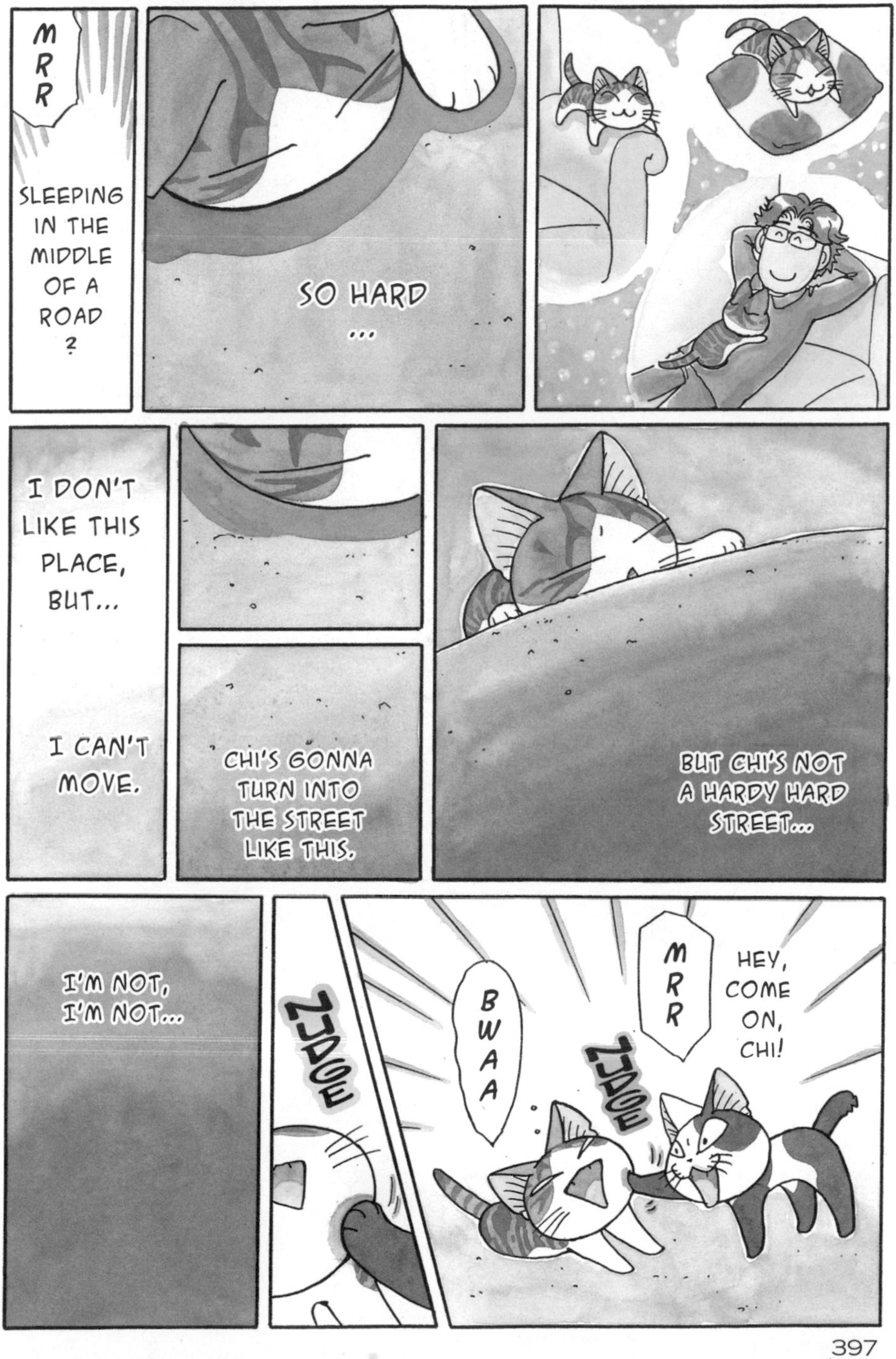
MRR
SLEEPING IN THE MIDDLE OF A ROAD?
SO HARD ...
I DON'T LIKE THIS PLACE, BUT...
I CAN'T MOVE.
CHI'S GONNA TURN INTO THE STREET LIKE THIS.
BUT CHI'S NOT A HARDY HARD STREET...
I'M NOT, I'M NOT...
NUDGE
BWAA
NUDGE
MRR
HEY, COME ON, CHI!

SLUMP

THUD

PUSH

SHUV SHUV

MRR

I'M SAYING, WAKE UP!

GIVE ME A BREAK~

MYA

WOAH

MRR

WOAH

MRR

G'NIGHT, COCCHI...

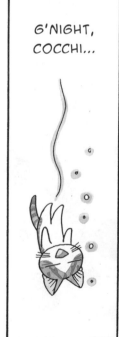

FLOP

THIS IS NICE.

OR DADDY...

IT'S NOT MY CUSHY CUSH...

IS IT LIKE CHI?!
IT'S NOT CHI.
THEN WHAT?
SMAK SMAK
MRR
WAKE UP, CHI!
CHI!
MRR!
IT MUST BE SOMETHING SIMILAR.

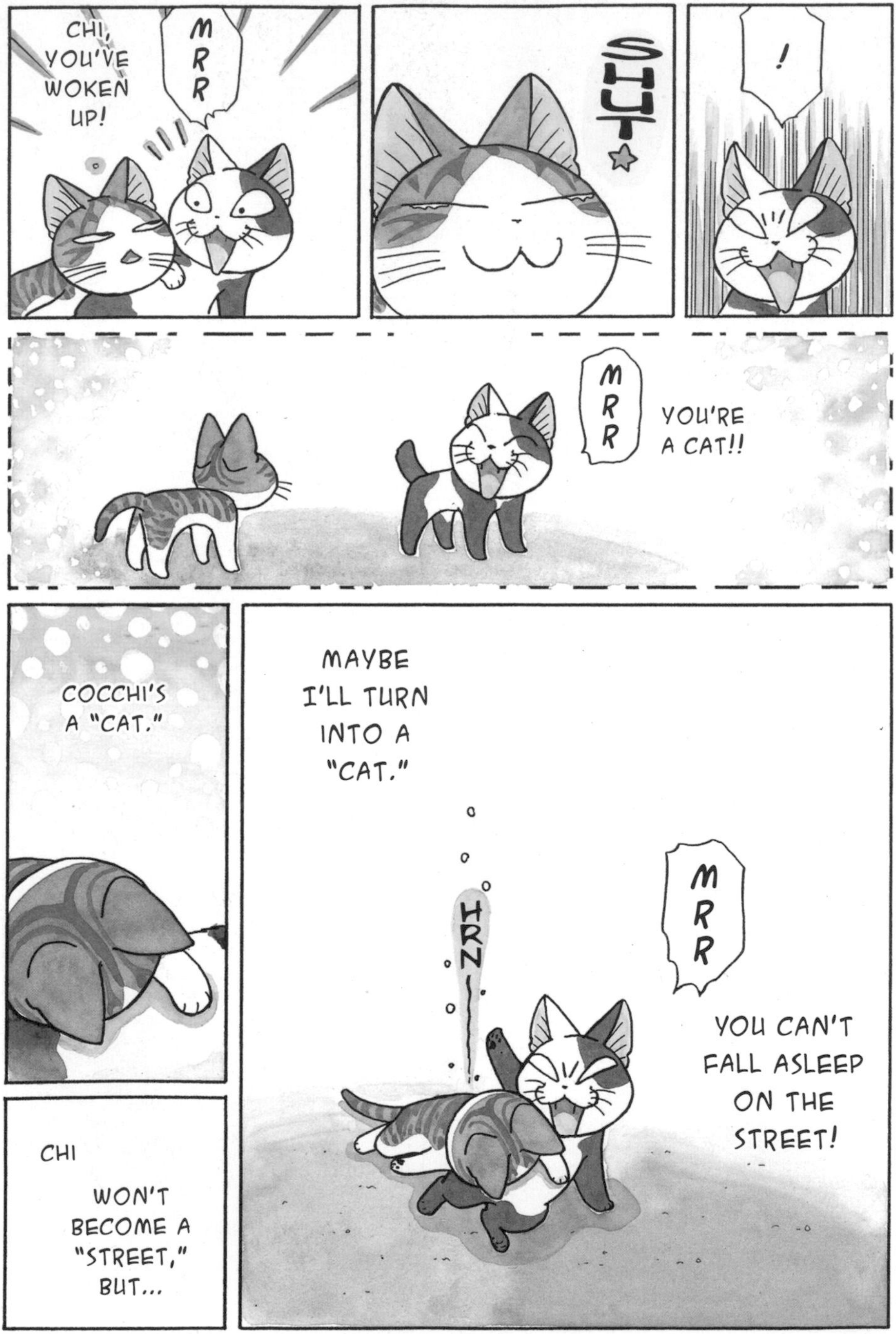
CHI, YOU'VE WOKEN UP!
MRR
SHUT☆
!
MRR
YOU'RE A CAT!!
COCCHI'S A "CAT."
CHI
WON'T BECOME A "STREET," BUT...
MAYBE I'LL TURN INTO A "CAT."
HRN—
MRR
YOU CAN'T FALL ASLEEP ON THE STREET!



**the end**

## homemade 161: a cat is hunted

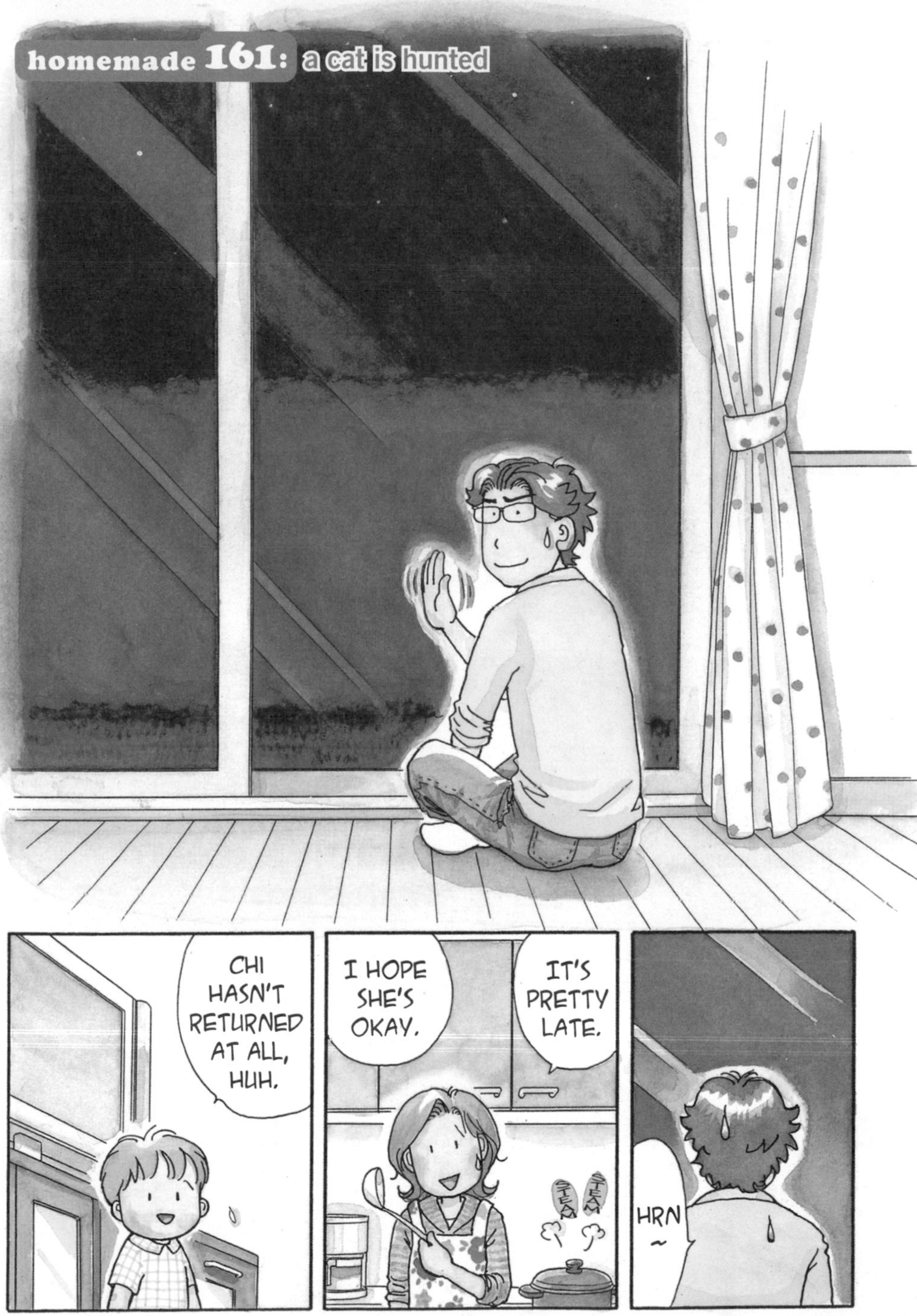

CHI HASN'T RETURNED AT ALL, HUH.
I HOPE SHE'S OKAY.
IT'S PRETTY LATE.
STEAM
STEAM
HRN ~

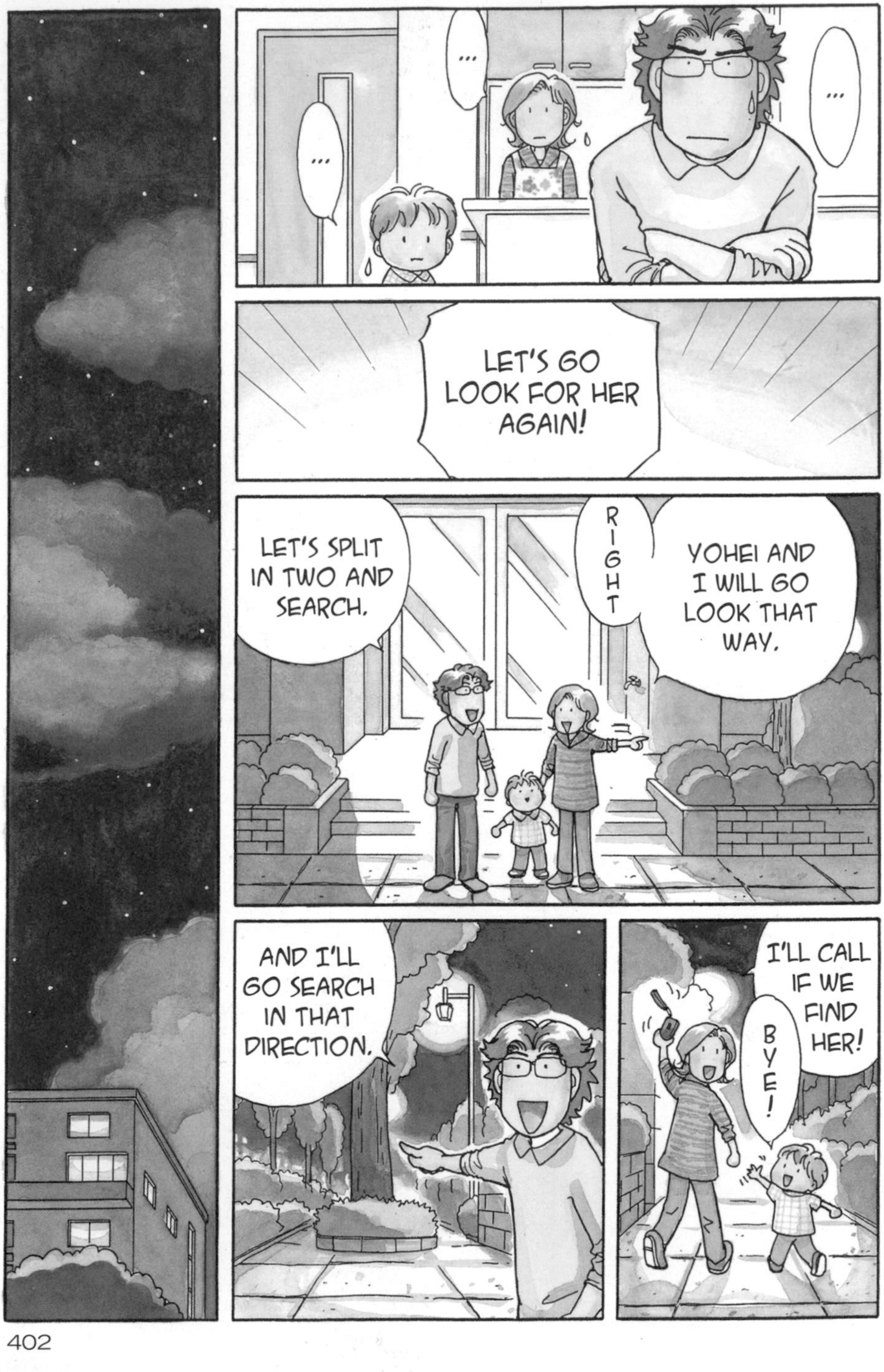
...
...
...
LET'S GO LOOK FOR HER AGAIN!
LET'S SPLIT IN TWO AND SEARCH.
RIGHT
YOHEI AND I WILL GO LOOK THAT WAY.
AND I'LL GO SEARCH IN THAT DIRECTION.
I'LL CALL IF WE FIND HER!
BYE!

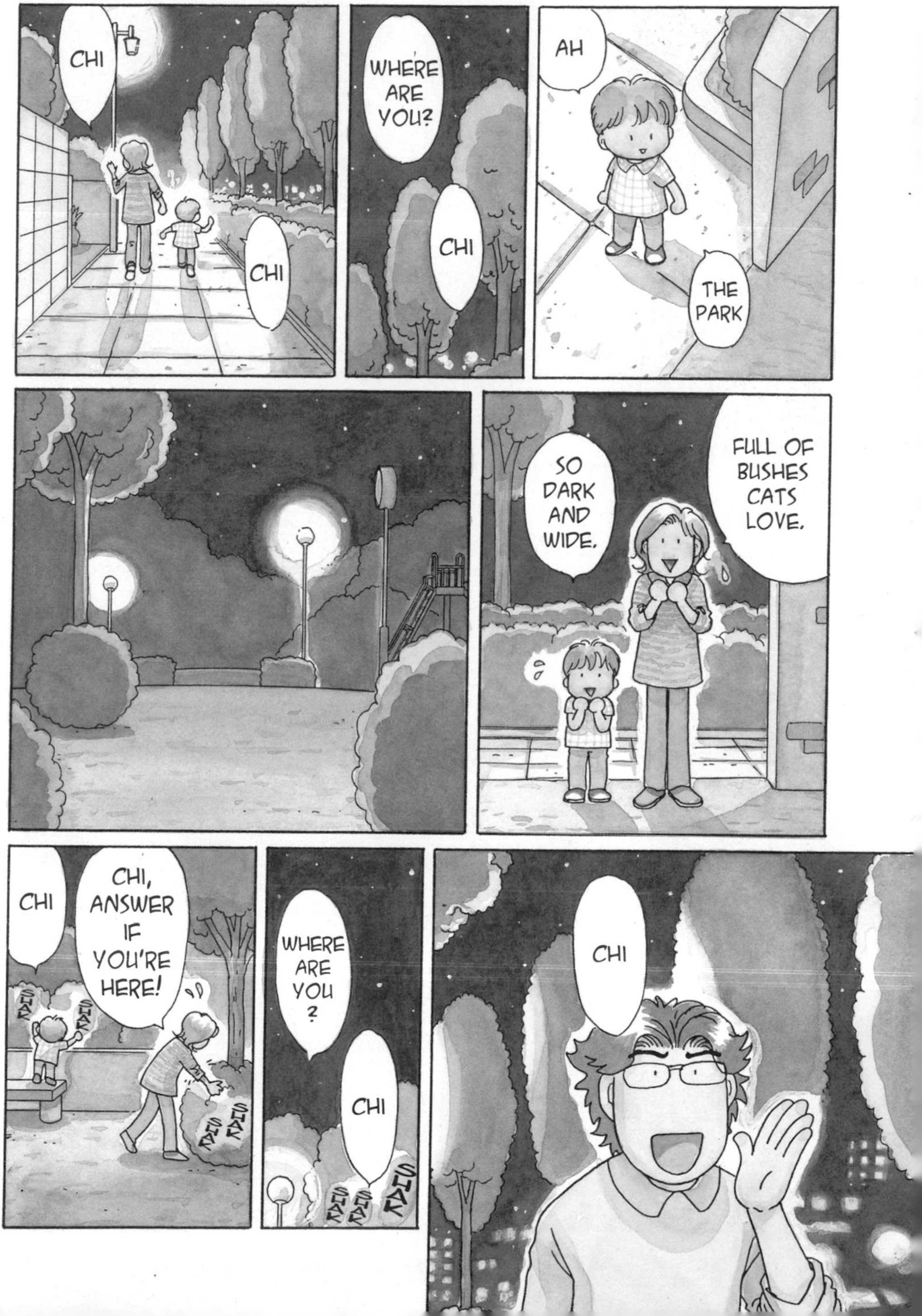
CHI
CHI
WHERE ARE YOU?
CHI
AH
THE PARK
SO DARK AND WIDE.
FULL OF BUSHES CATS LOVE.
CHI
CHI, ANSWER IF YOU'RE HERE!
SHAK SHAK
SHAK SHAK
WHERE ARE YOU ?
CHI
SHAK SHAK SHAK
CHI

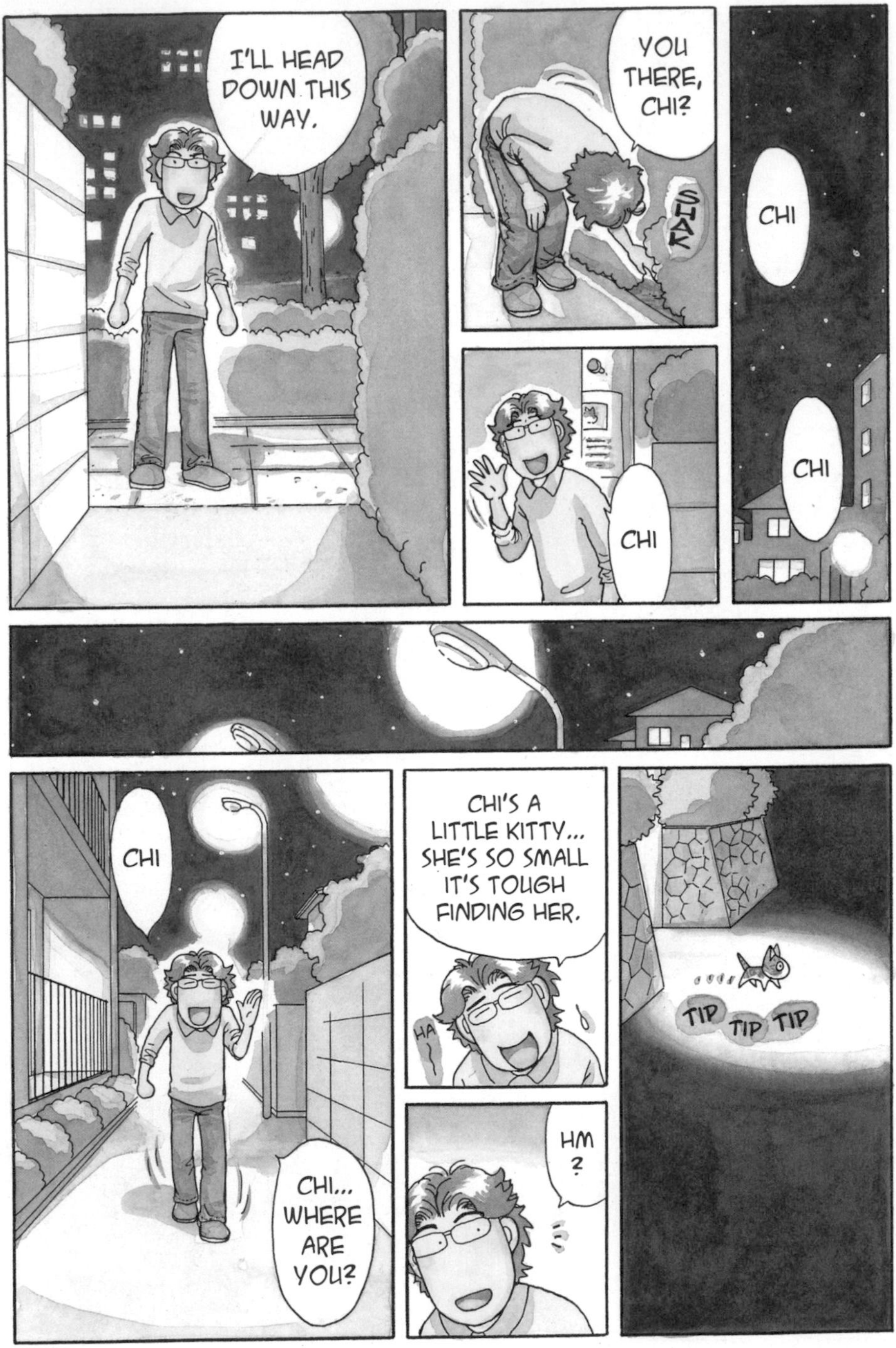

I'LL HEAD DOWN THIS WAY.
YOU THERE, CHI?
SHAK
CHI
CHI
CHI
CHI
CHI... WHERE ARE YOU?
CHI'S A LITTLE KITTY... SHE'S SO SMALL IT'S TOUGH FINDING HER.
HA
HM?
TIP TIP TIP

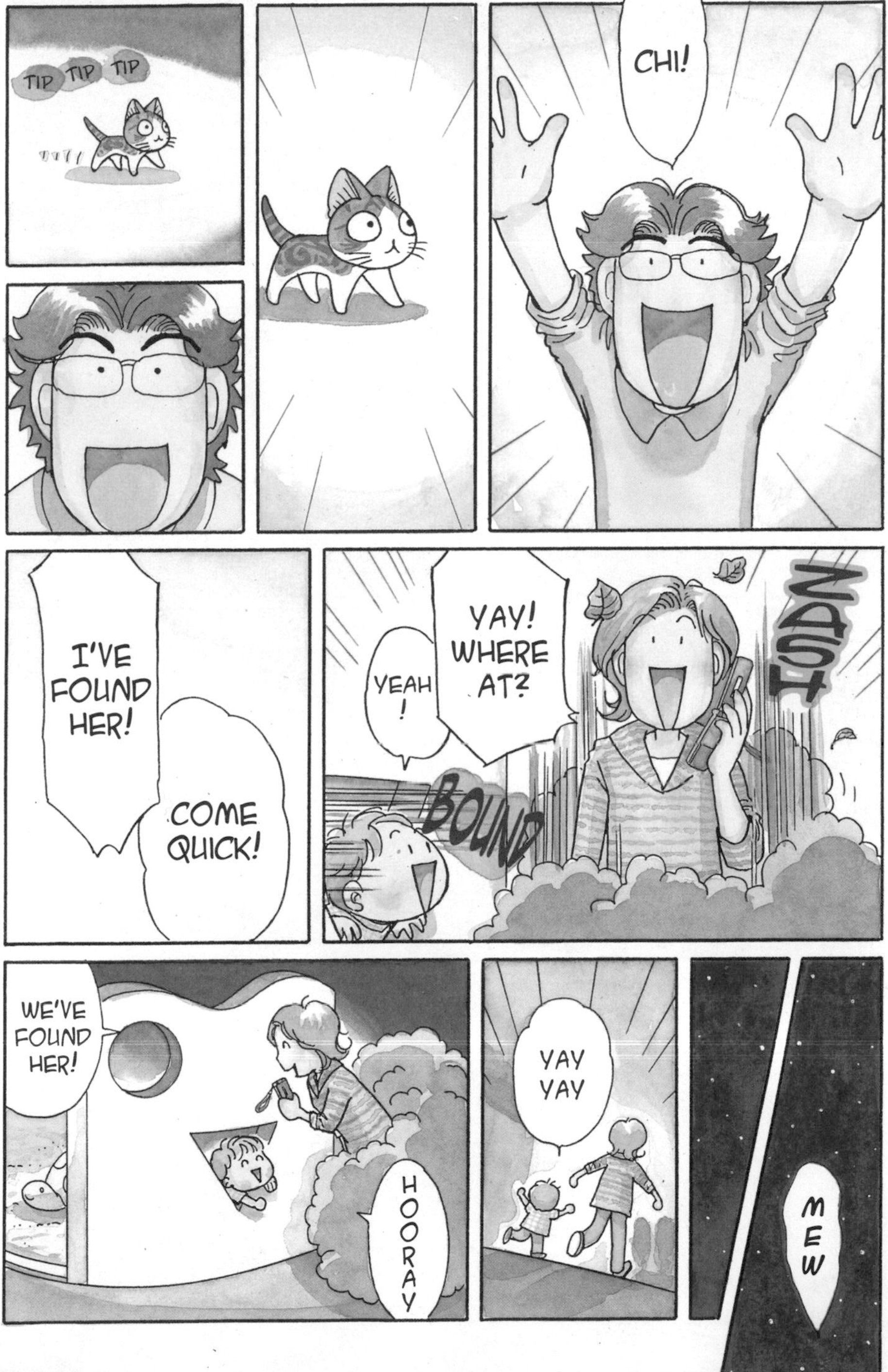
TIP TIP TIP
CHI!
I'VE FOUND HER!
COME QUICK!
YEAH!
YAY! WHERE AT?
ZASH
BOUND
WE'VE FOUND HER!
HOORAY
YAY YAY
MEW

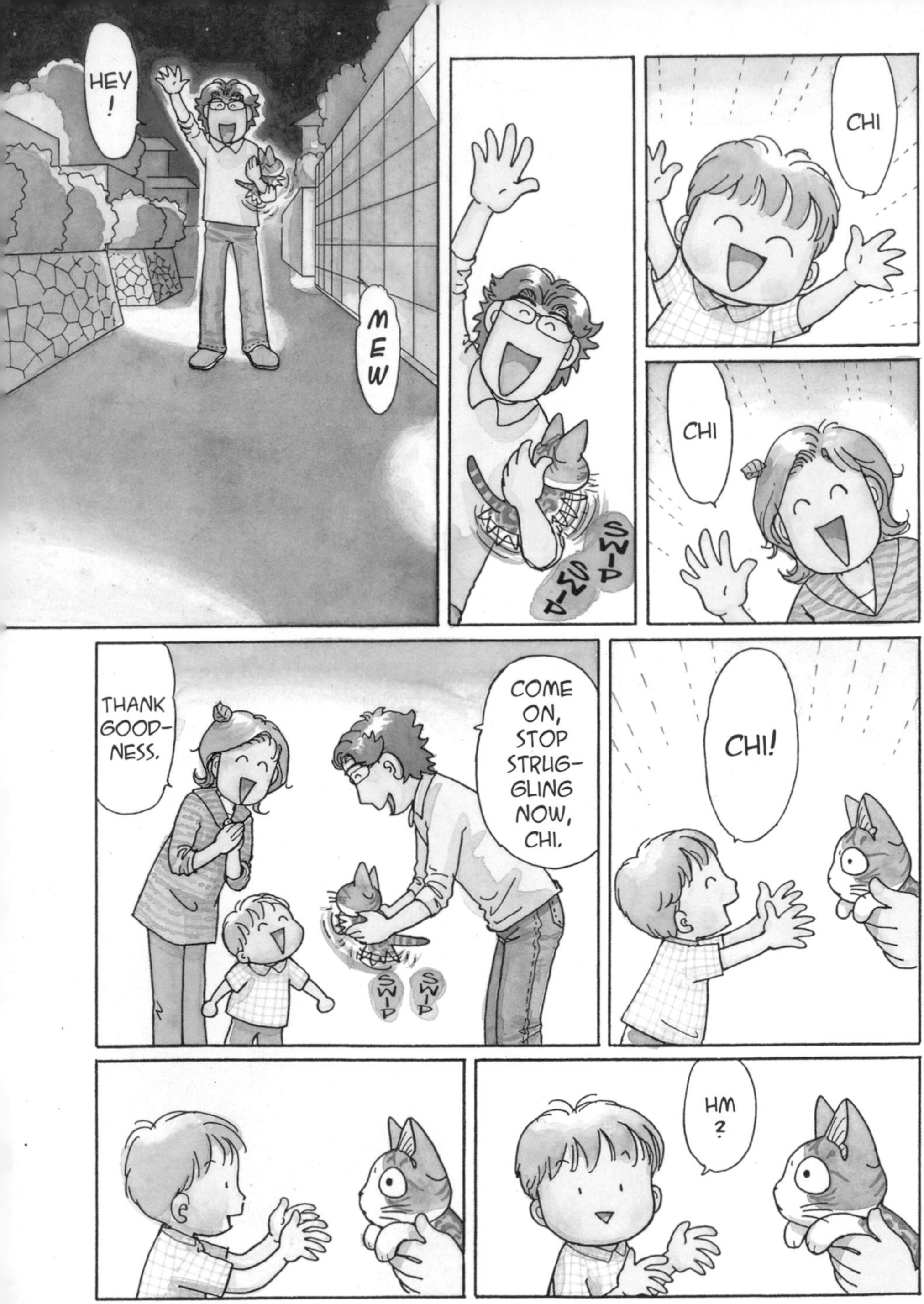
HEY!
MEW
SWIP SWIP
CHI
CHI
THANK GOODNESS.
COME ON, STOP STRUGGLING NOW, CHI.
SWIP SWIP
CHI!
HM?

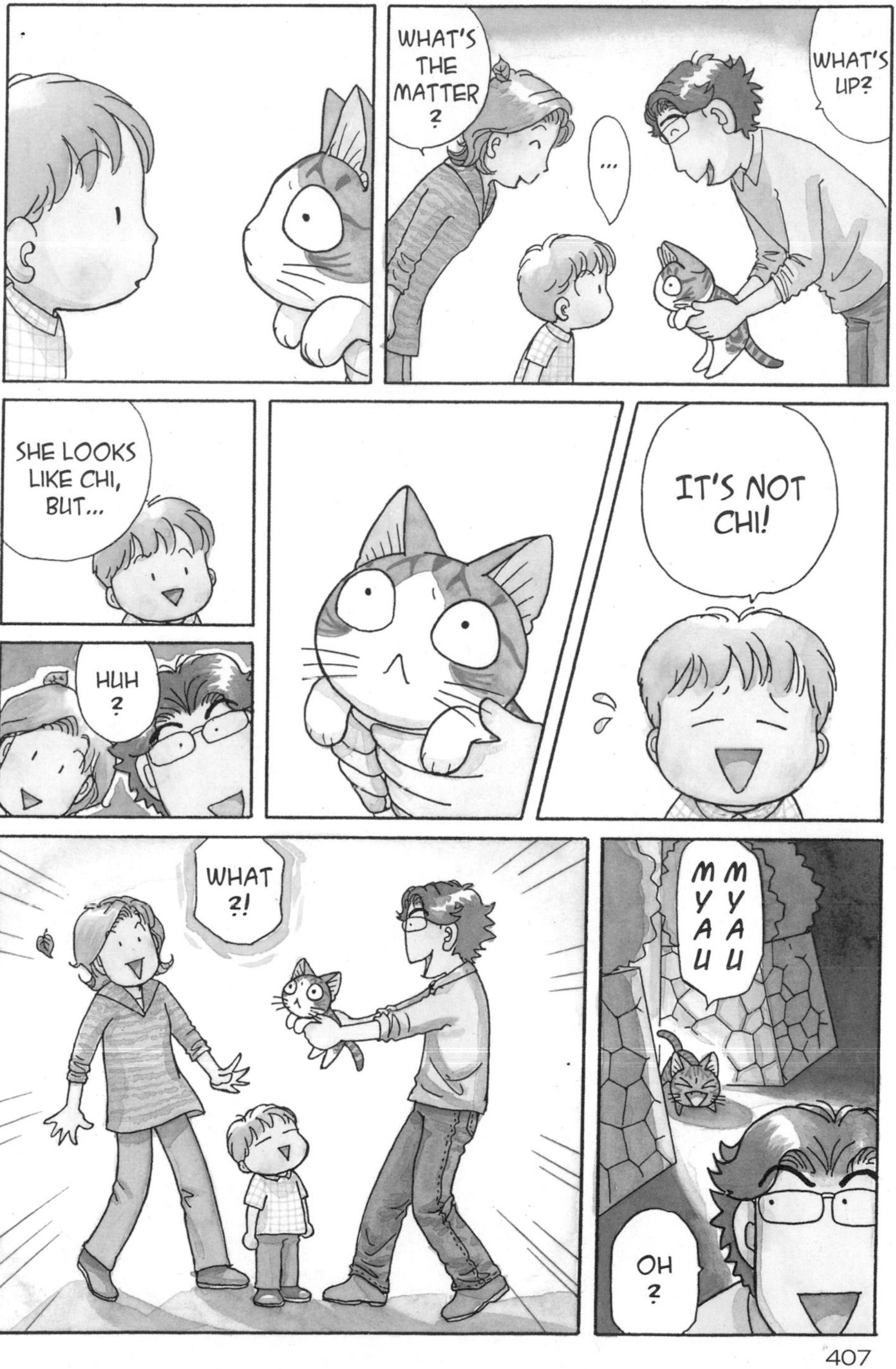
WHAT'S THE MATTER?
...
WHAT'S UP?
SHE LOOKS LIKE CHI, BUT...
HUH?
IT'S NOT CHI!
WHAT?!
MYAU
MYAU
OH?

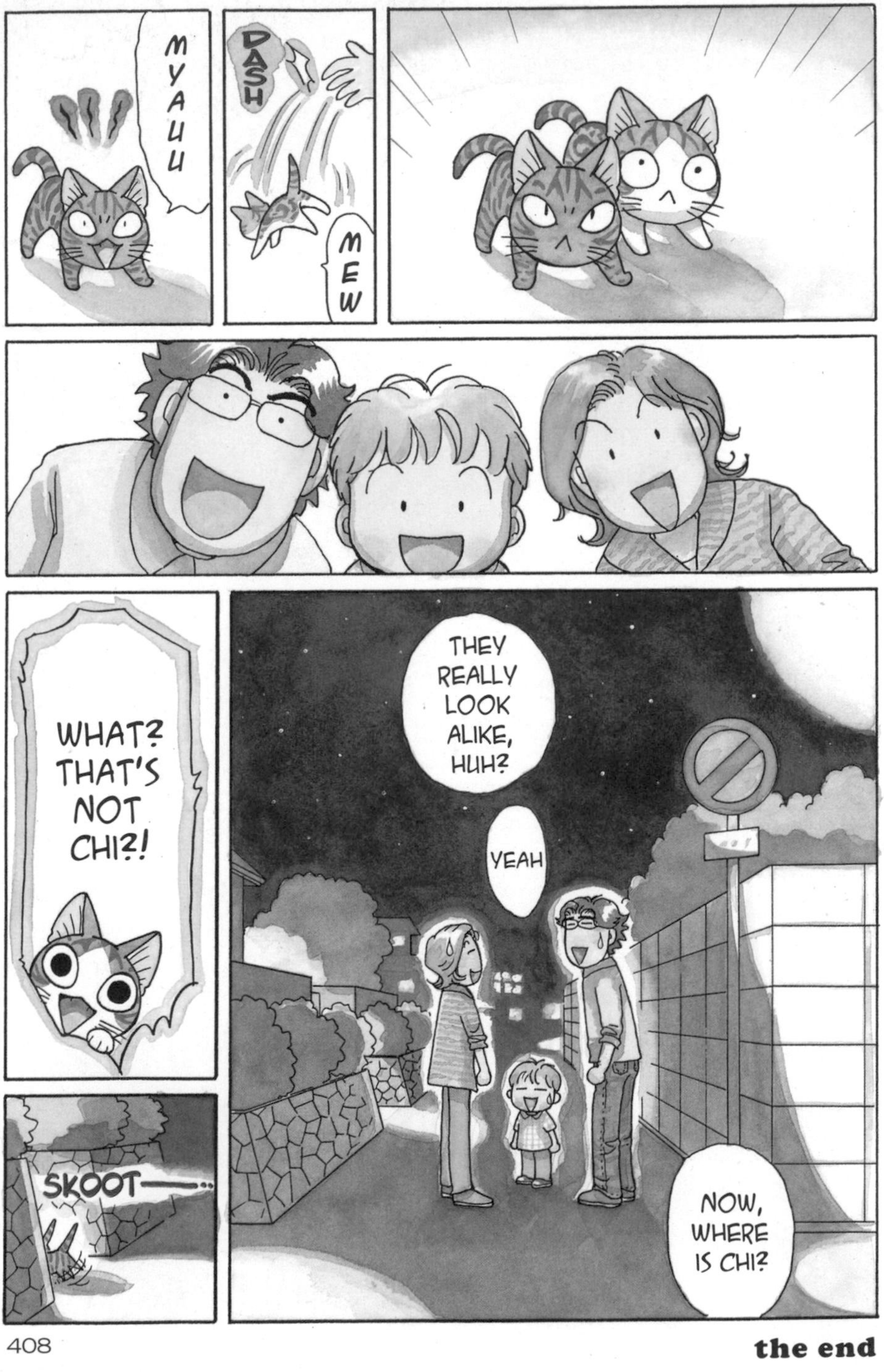
MYAUU
DASH
MEW
WHAT? THAT'S NOT CHI?!
THEY REALLY LOOK ALIKE, HUH?
YEAH
SKOOT—
NOW, WHERE IS CHI?



**the end**

# homemade 162: a cat is exhausted

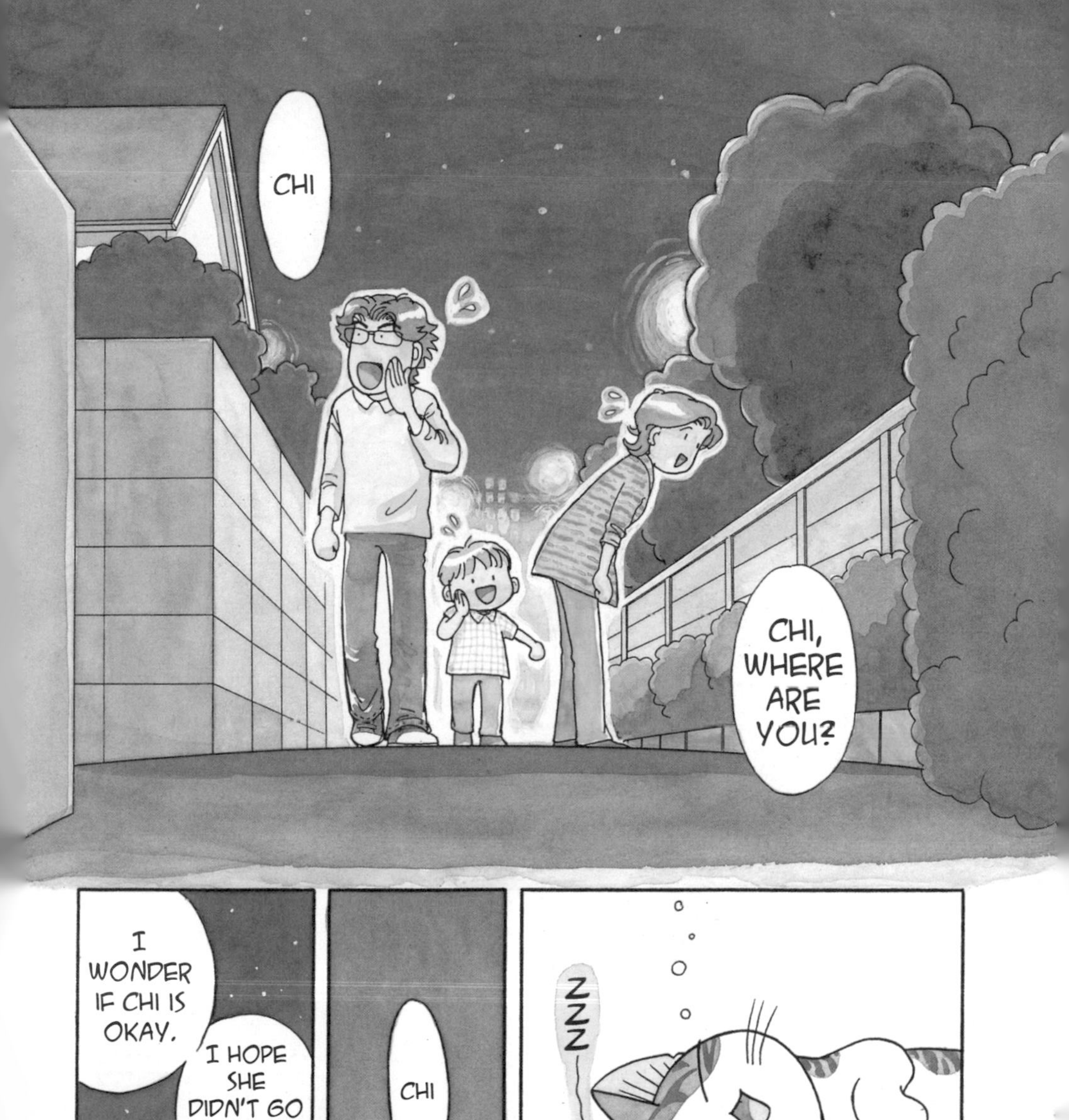
CHI
CHI, WHERE ARE YOU?
I WONDER IF CHI IS OKAY.
I HOPE SHE DIDN'T GO THROUGH SOME TROUBLE.
CHI
ZZZ

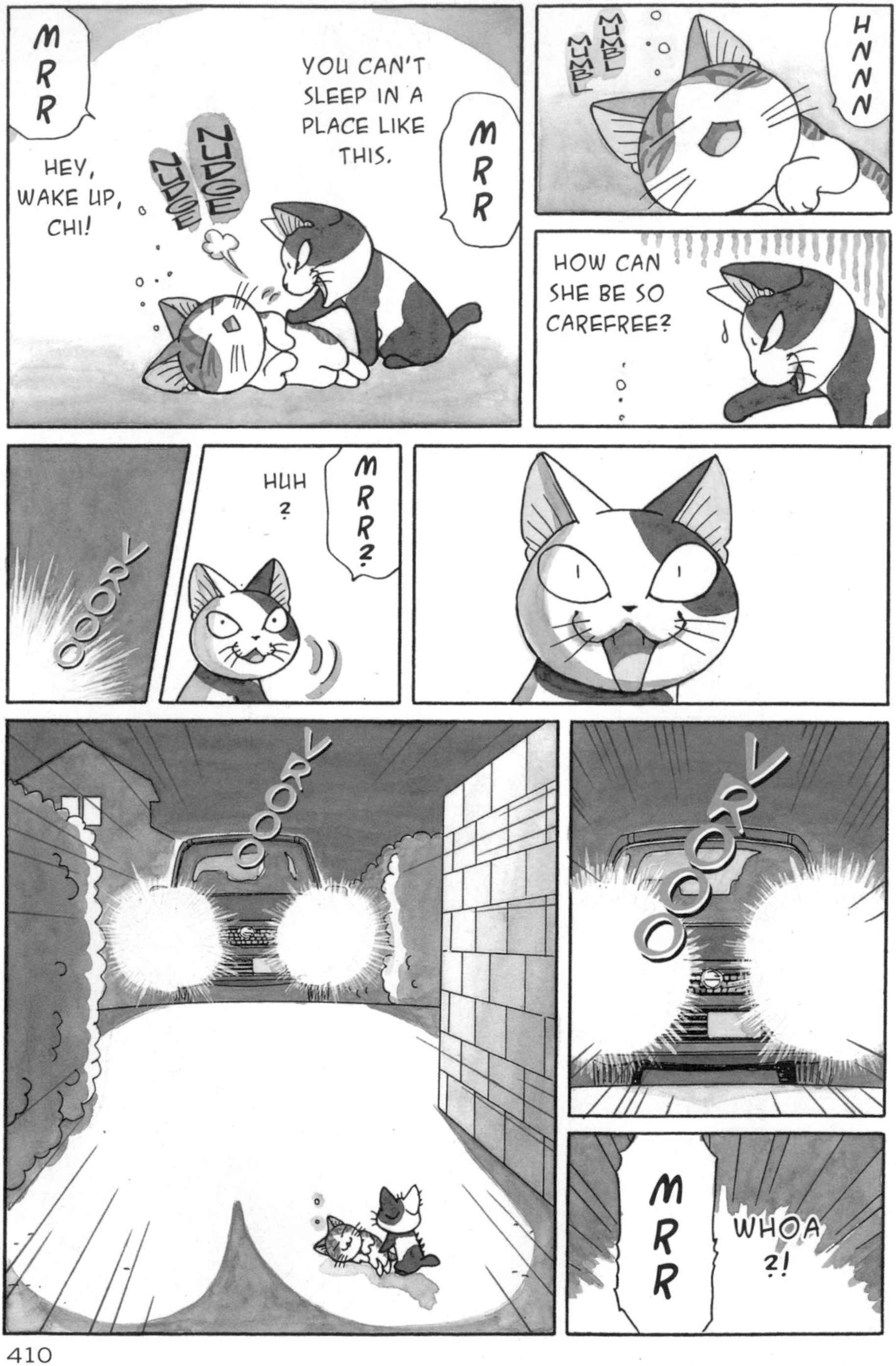
MRR
HEY, WAKE UP, CHI!
NUDGE NUDGE
YOU CAN'T SLEEP IN A PLACE LIKE THIS.
MRR
MUMBL MUMBL
HNNN
HOW CAN SHE BE SO CAREFREE?
OOORV
HUH?
MRR?
OOORV
OOORV
MRR
WHOA?!

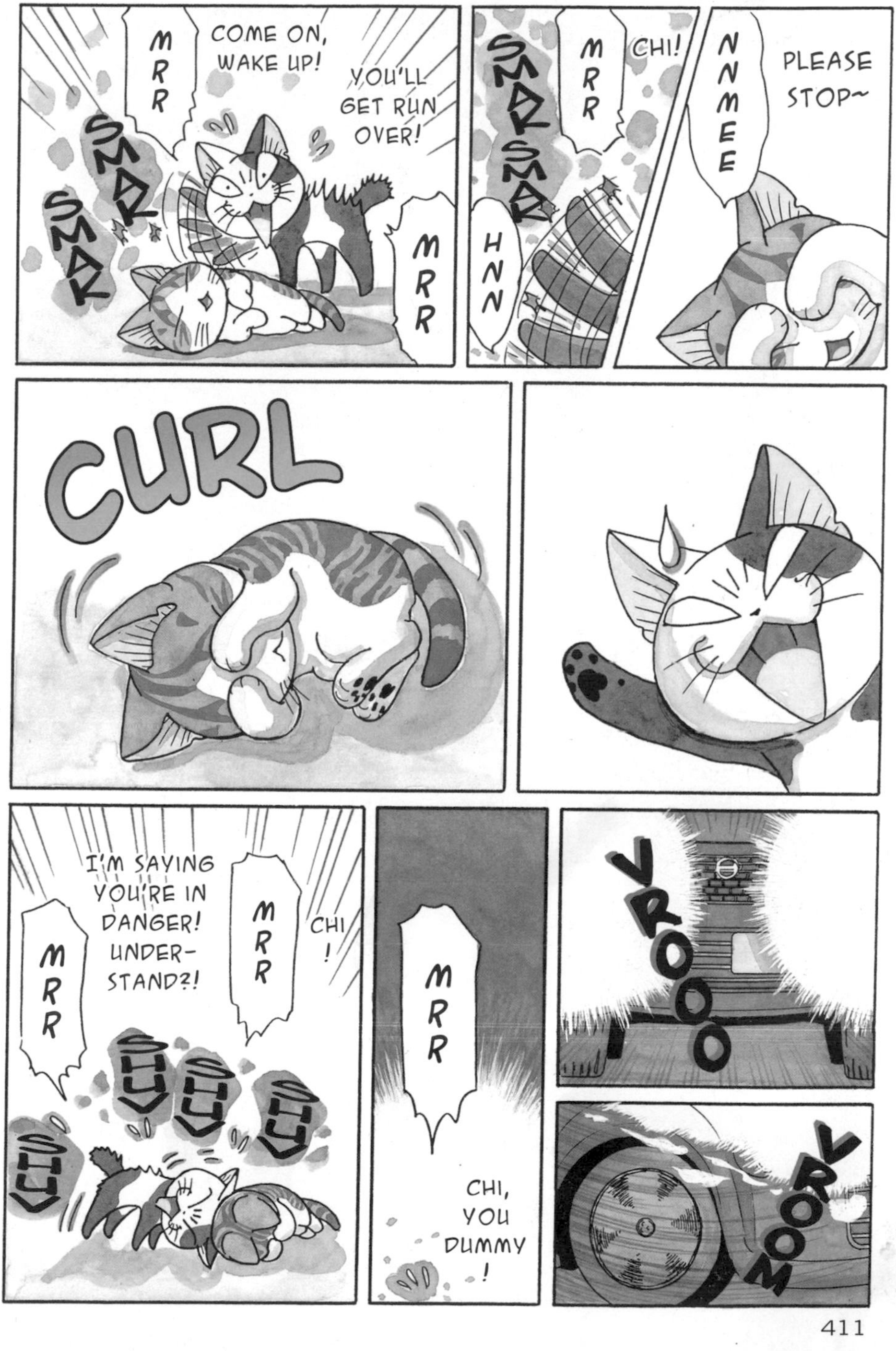
MRR
COME ON, WAKE UP!
YOU'LL GET RUN OVER!
SMAR
SMAR
MRR
SMAR SMAR
MRR
CHI!
HNN
NNMEE
PLEASE STOP~
CURL
I'M SAYING YOU'RE IN DANGER! UNDERSTAND?!
MRR
MRR
CHI!
SHU
SHU
SHU
SHU
MRR
CHI, YOU DUMMY!
VROOO
VROOM

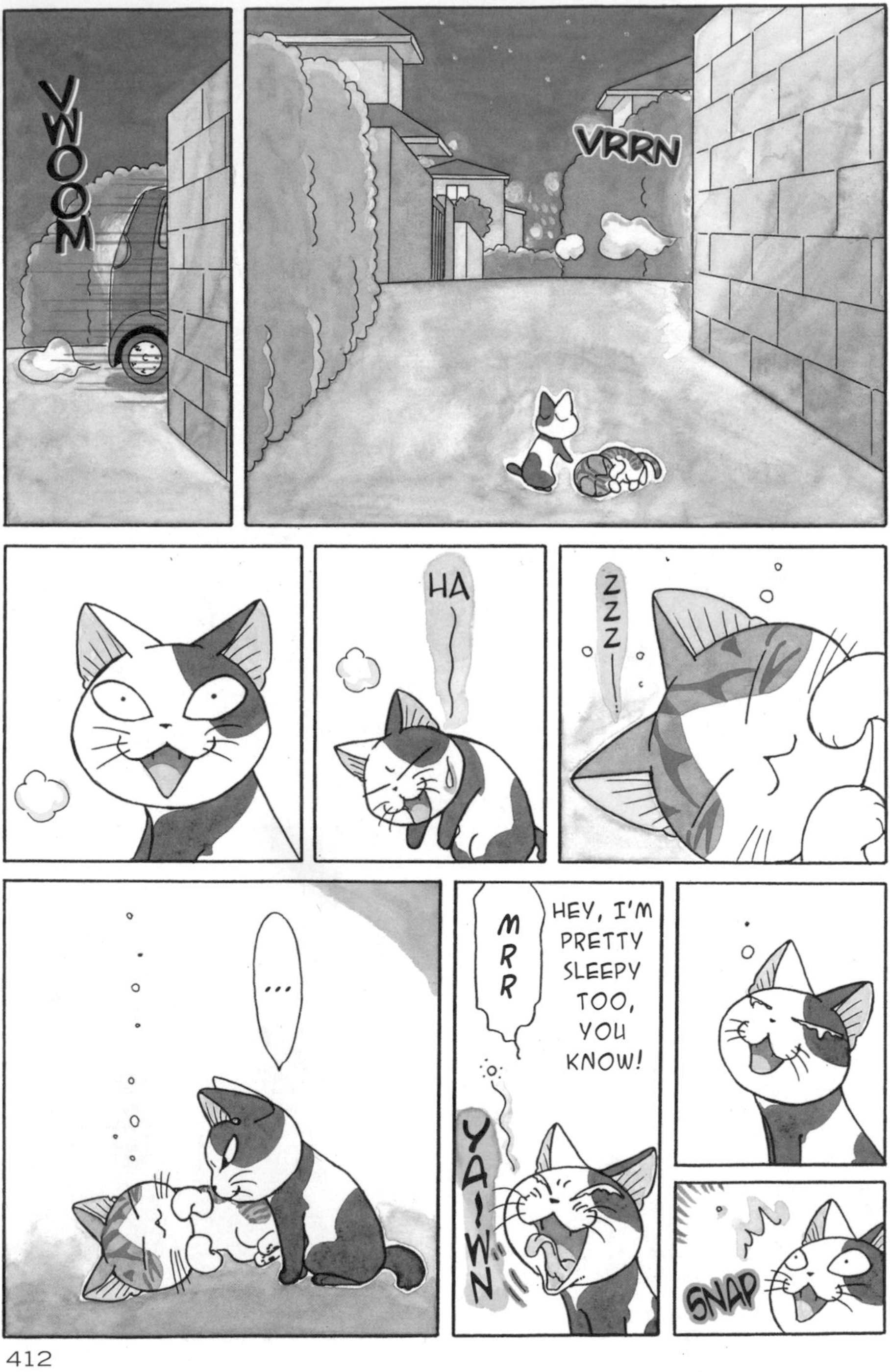
VWOOM
VRRN
HA
ZZZ
...
MRR
HEY, I'M PRETTY SLEEPY TOO, YOU KNOW!
YAWN
SNAP

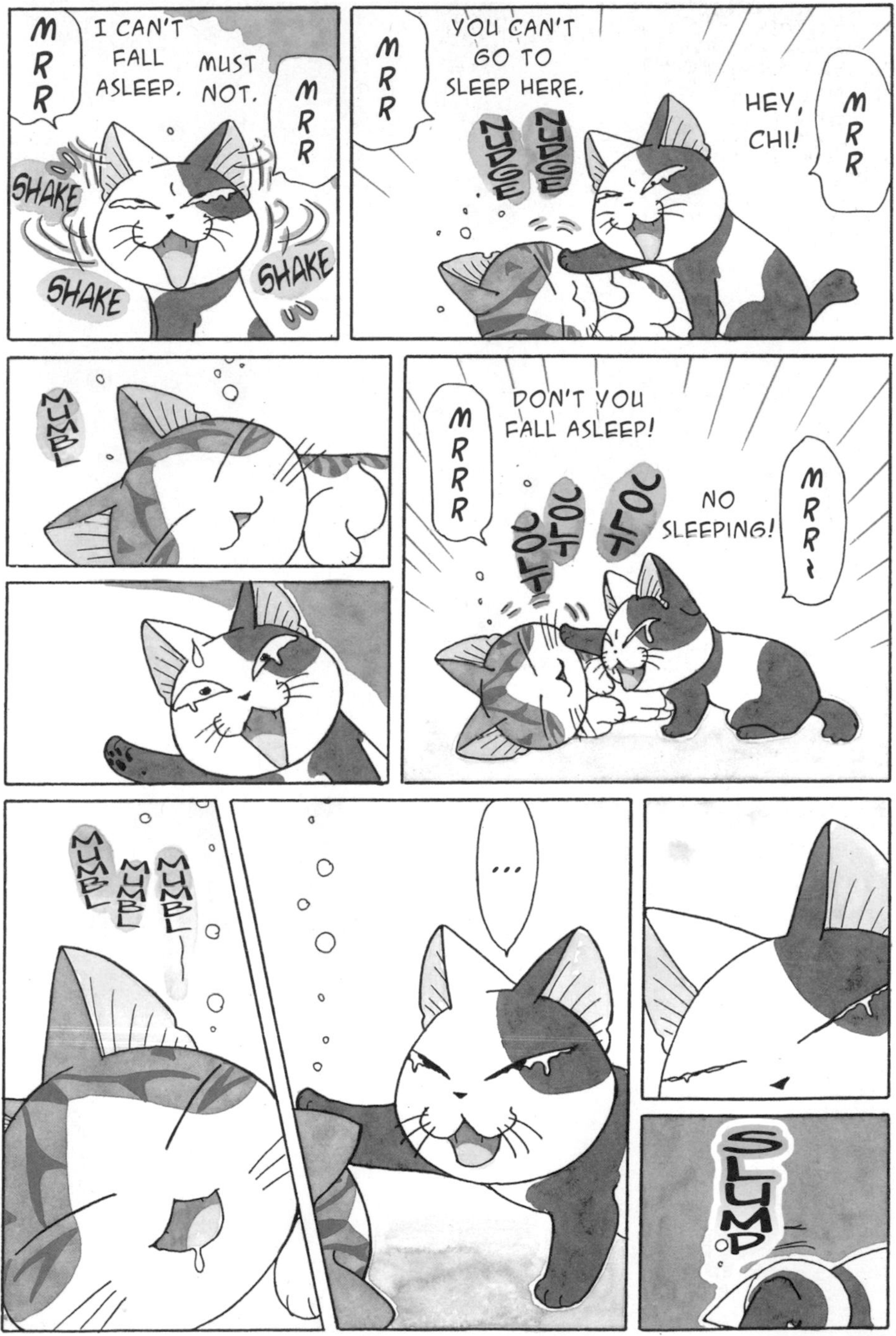
MRR
I CAN'T FALL ASLEEP.
MUST NOT.
MRR
SHAKE
SHAKE
SHAKE
MRR
YOU CAN'T GO TO SLEEP HERE.
NUDGE
NUDGE
HEY, CHI!
MRR
MUMBL
MRRR
DON'T YOU FALL ASLEEP!
JOLT
JOLT
JOLT
NO SLEEPING!
MRR
MUMBL
MUMBL
MUMBL
...
SLUMP

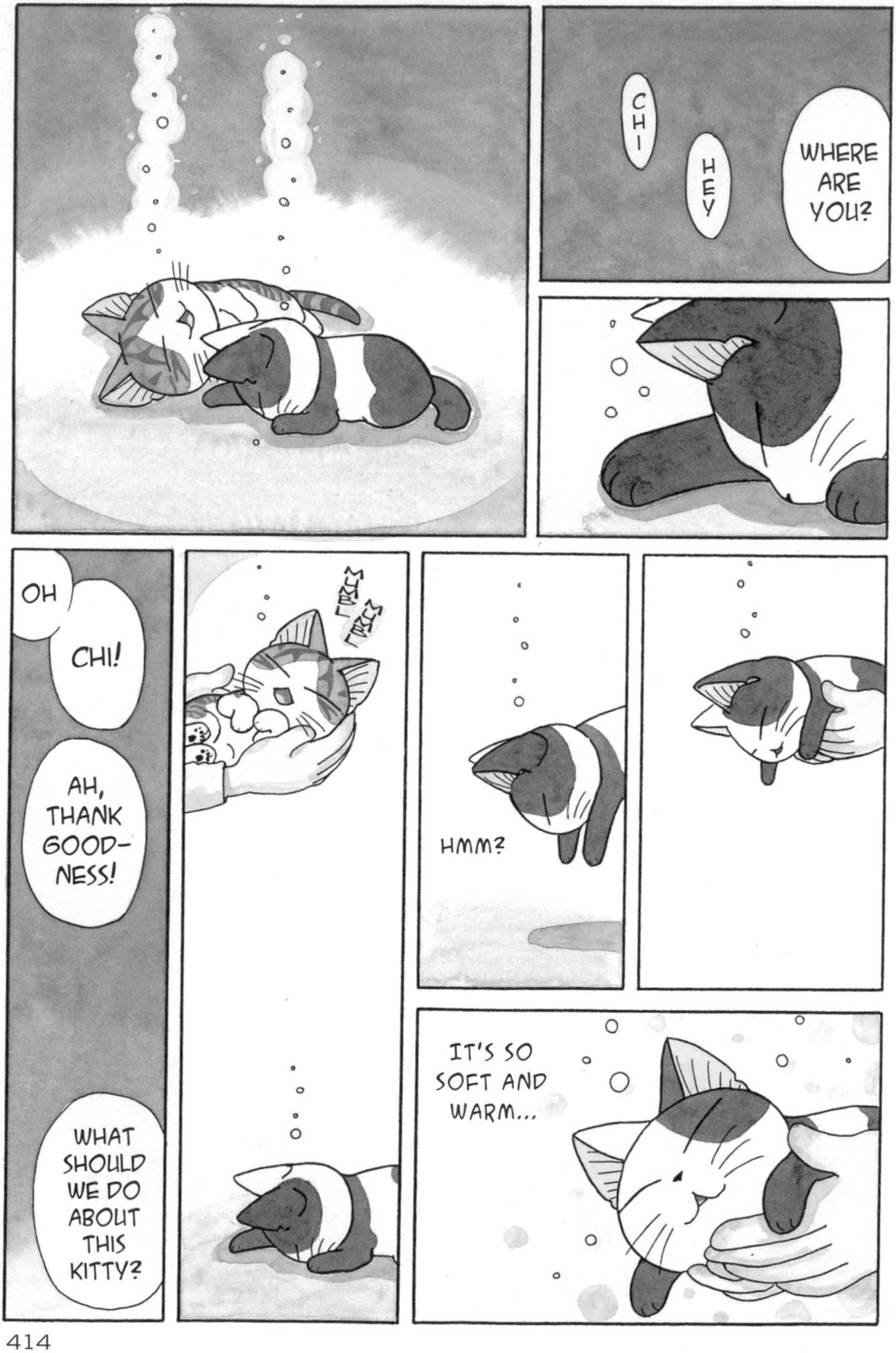
CHI
HEY
WHERE ARE YOU?
OH
CHI!
AH, THANK GOODNESS!
WHAT SHOULD WE DO ABOUT THIS KITTY?
MUMBL MUMBL
HMM?
IT'S SO SOFT AND WARM...

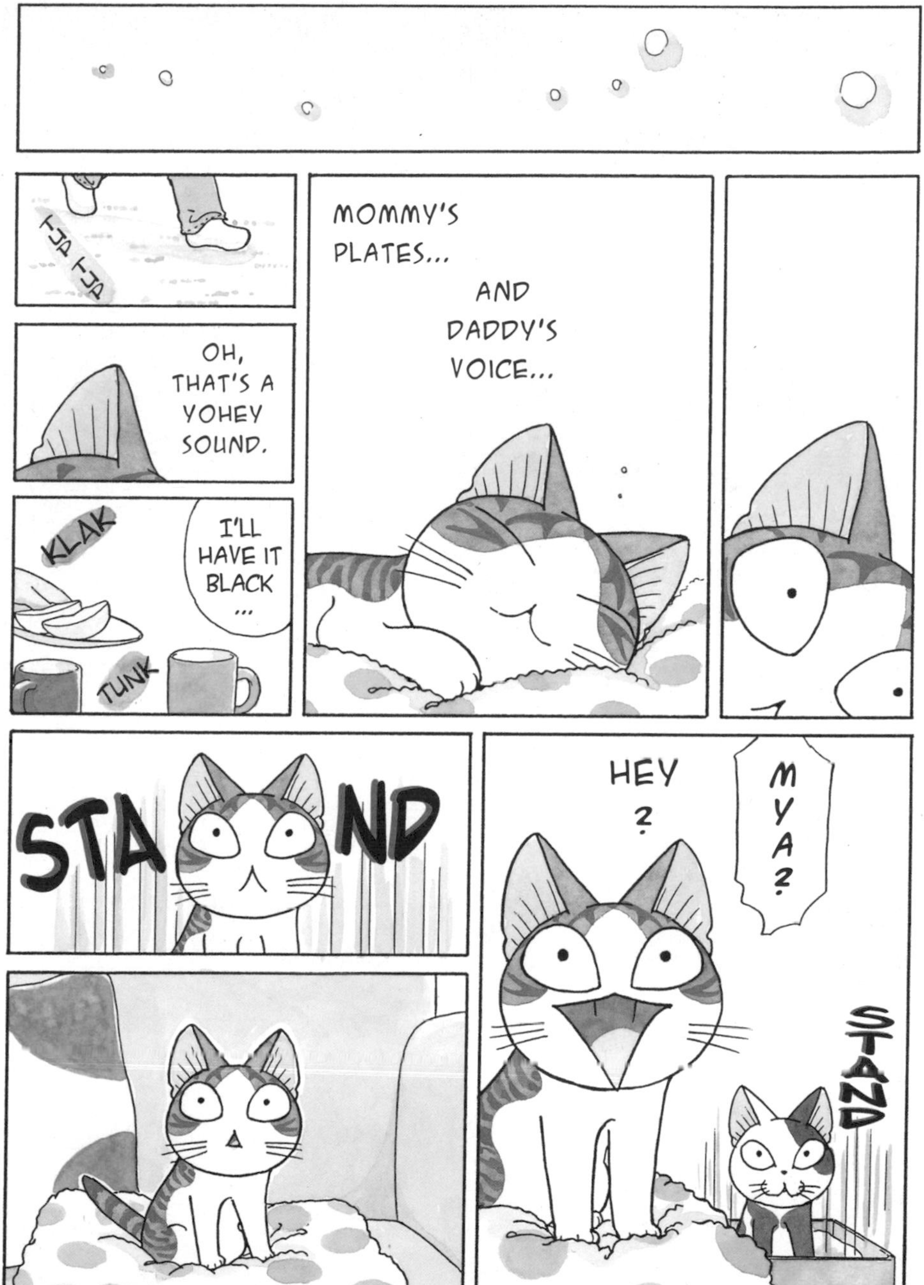
OH, THAT'S A YOHEY SOUND.
KLAK
I'LL HAVE IT BLACK ...
TUNK
MOMMY'S PLATES...
AND DADDY'S VOICE...
STAND
HEY ?
MYA?
STAND

MRR

HUH?

WHAT?!

MRR?!

MEOW?!

SHE'S WOKEN UP CONFUSED.

AND WE COULDN'T JUST LEAVE THE OTHER KITTEN BACK THERE...

WHERE IS THIS?

MEOW?

MRR?

WHY ARE WE HOME?

WHAT THE WHAT?

MRR?

**the end**

## homemade 163: a cat is the same as ever

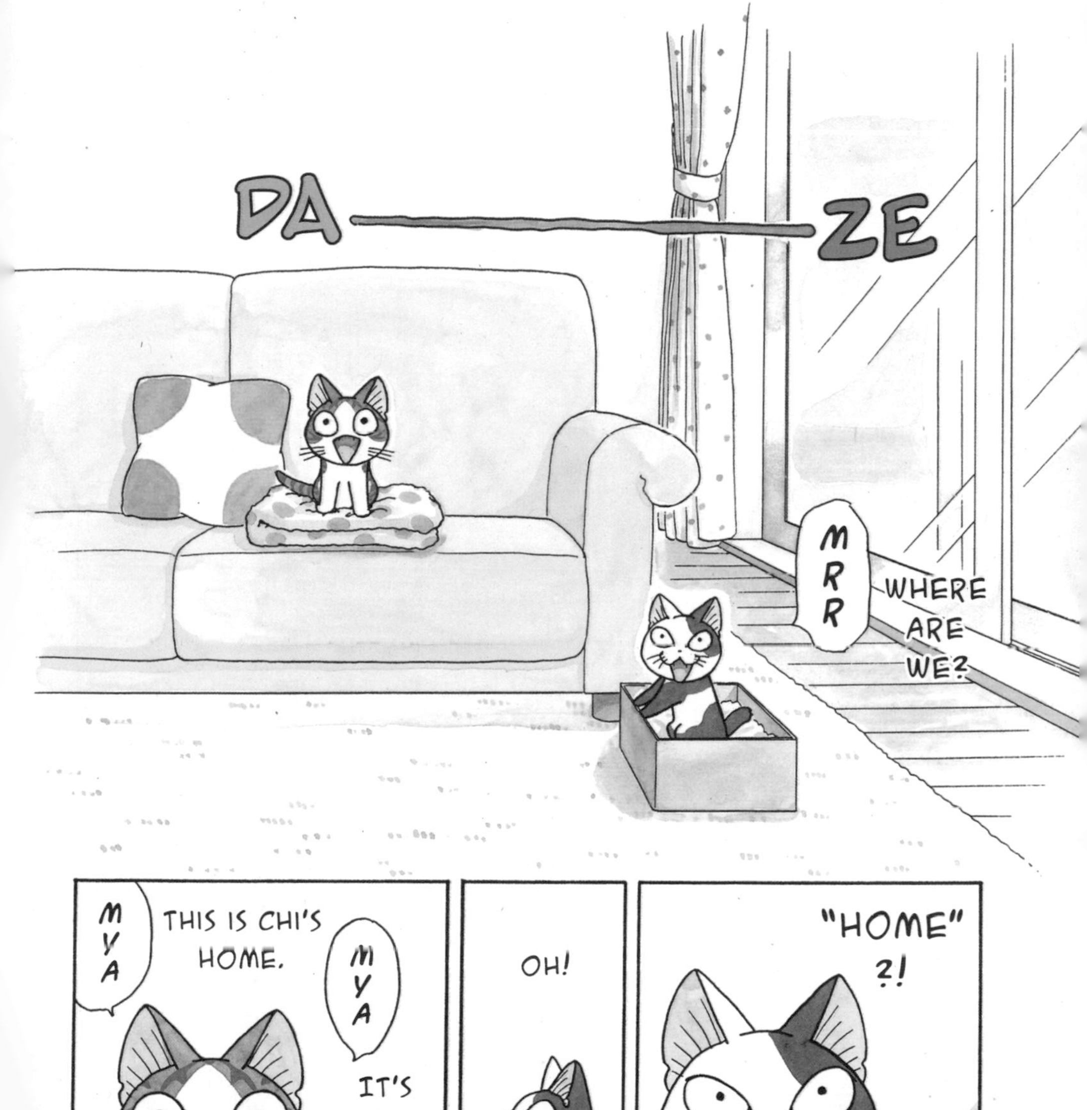
DA——ZE
MRR
WHERE ARE WE?
MYA
THIS IS CHI'S HOME.
MYA
IT'S HOME.
OH!
"HOME" ?!

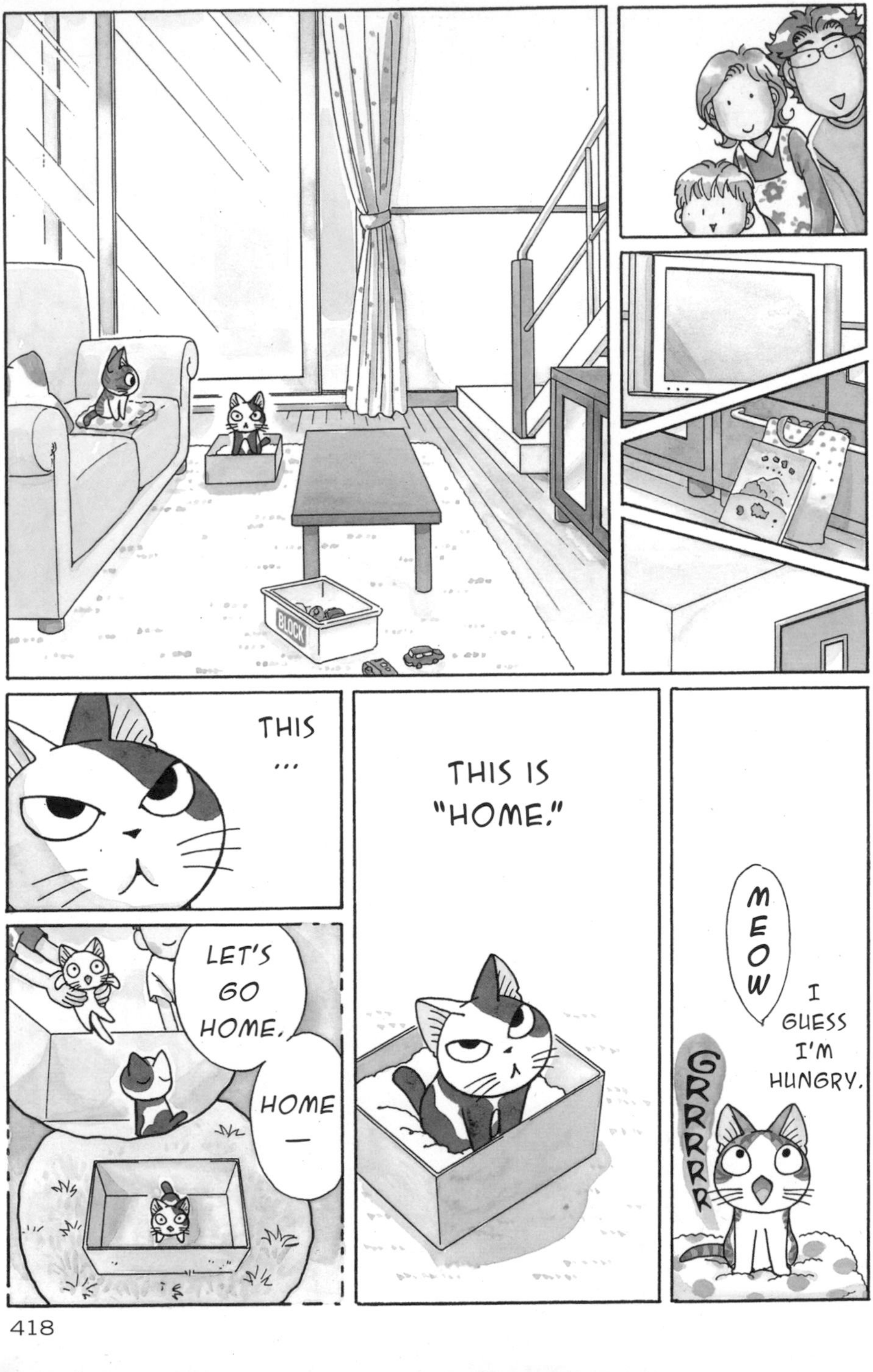
THIS
...
LET'S GO HOME.
HOME
—
THIS IS "HOME."
MEOW
GRRRRR
I GUESS I'M HUNGRY.

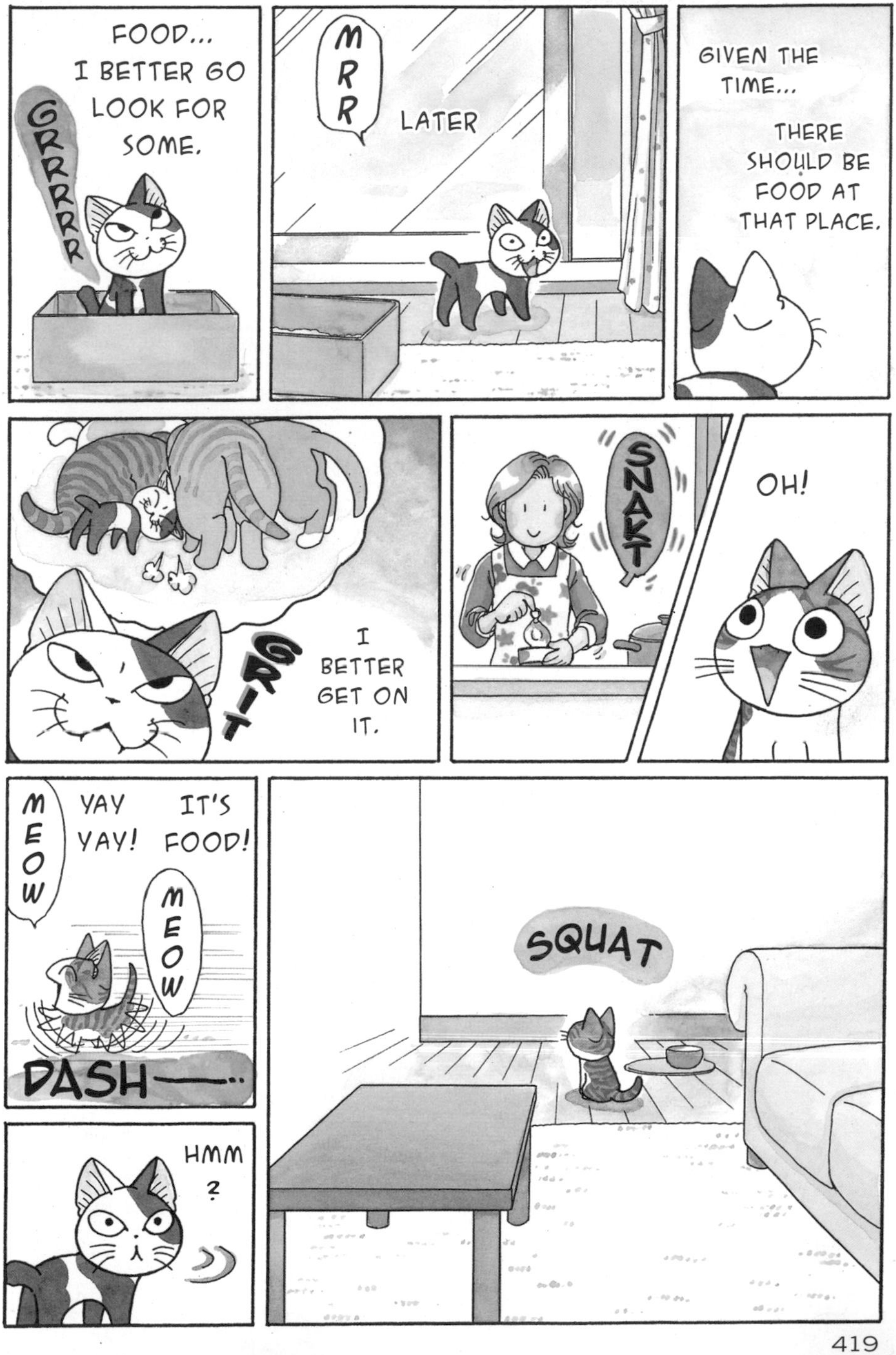

FOOD... I BETTER GO LOOK FOR SOME.
GRRRRRR
MRR
LATER
GIVEN THE TIME...
THERE SHOULD BE FOOD AT THAT PLACE.
I BETTER GET ON IT.
GRIT
SNAKT
OH!
MEOW
YAY YAY!
IT'S FOOD!
MEOW
DASH——..
SQUAT
HMM ?

STILL

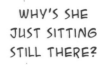

WHY'S SHE JUST SITTING STILL THERE?

HERE.

YAY!

MYA!

TURN

MEOW

IT'S BREAK-FAST, COCCHI!

MEOW

FOOD'S READY!

HUH ?!

WHAT ?!

420

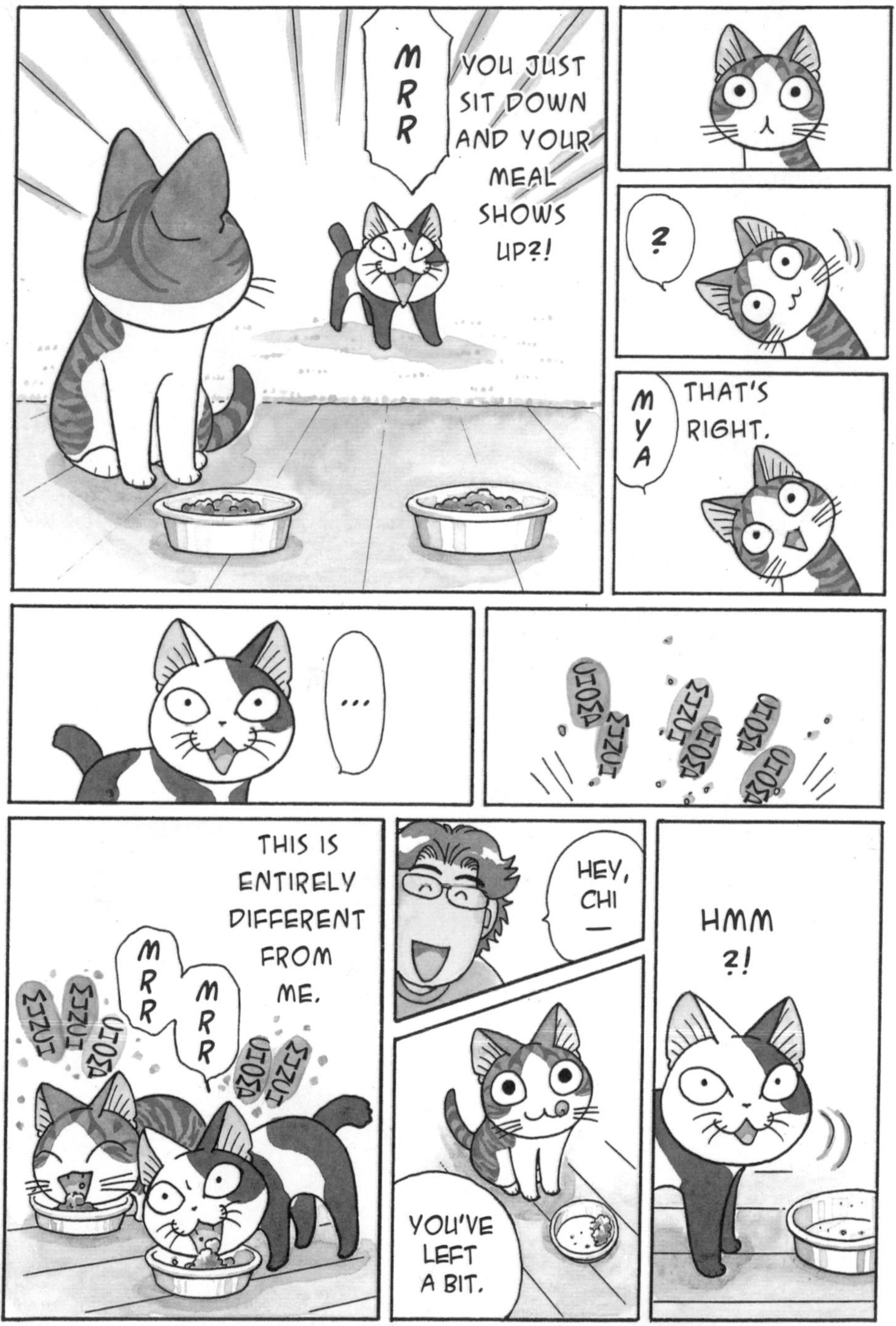
MRR
YOU JUST SIT DOWN AND YOUR MEAL SHOWS UP?!
?
MYA
THAT'S RIGHT.
...
CHOMP
MUNCH
MUNCH
CHOMP
CHOMP
CHOMP
THIS IS ENTIRELY DIFFERENT FROM ME.
MRR
MRR
MUNCH
MUNCH
CHOMP
CHOMP
MUNCH
HEY, CHI —
YOU'VE LEFT A BIT.
HMM ?!

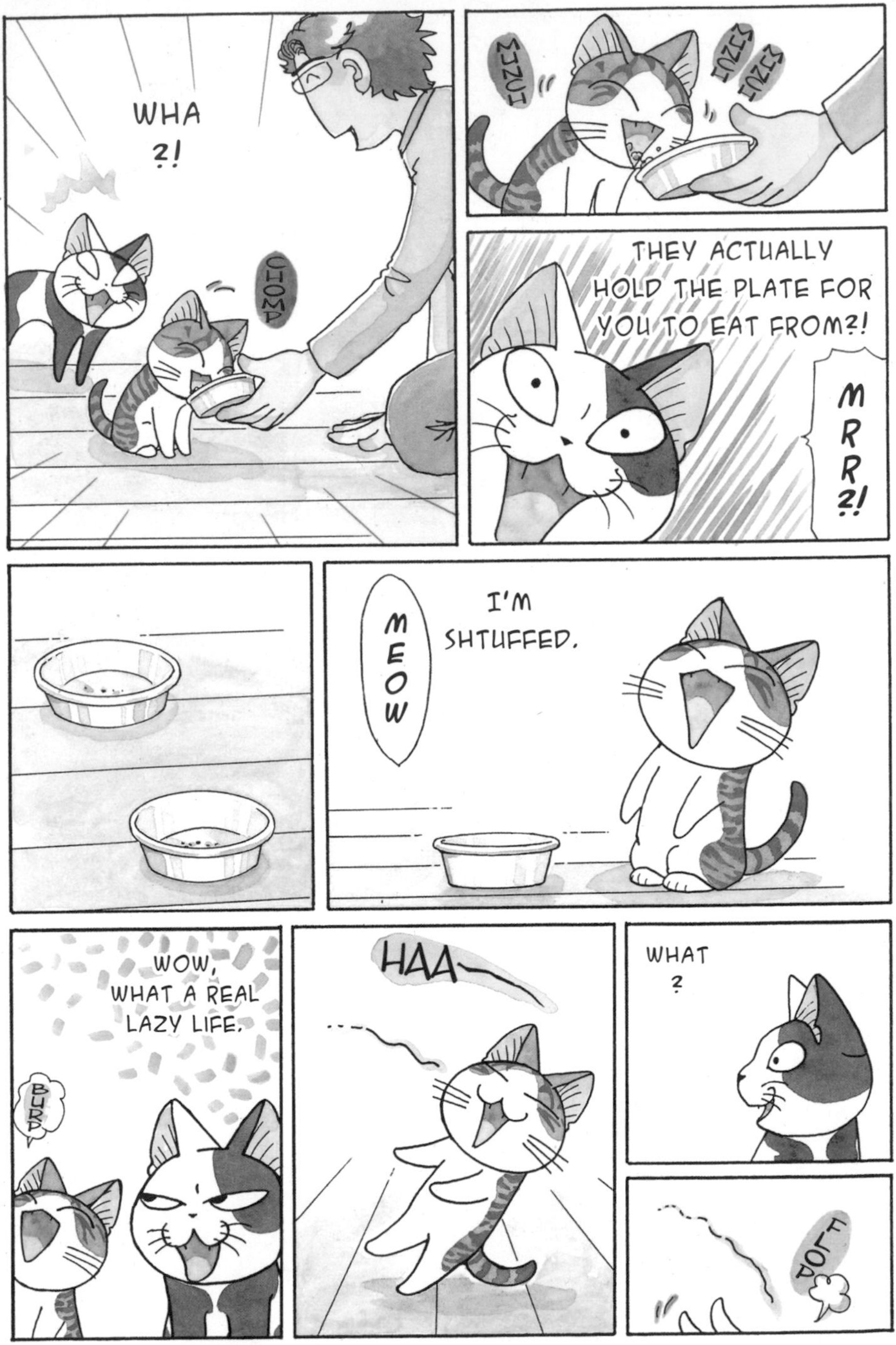
WHA ?!
CHOMP
MUNCH
SLURP SLURP
THEY ACTUALLY HOLD THE PLATE FOR YOU TO EAT FROM?!
MRR?!
MEOW
I'M SHTUFFED.
WOW, WHAT A REAL LAZY LIFE.
BURP
HAA
WHAT ?
FLOP

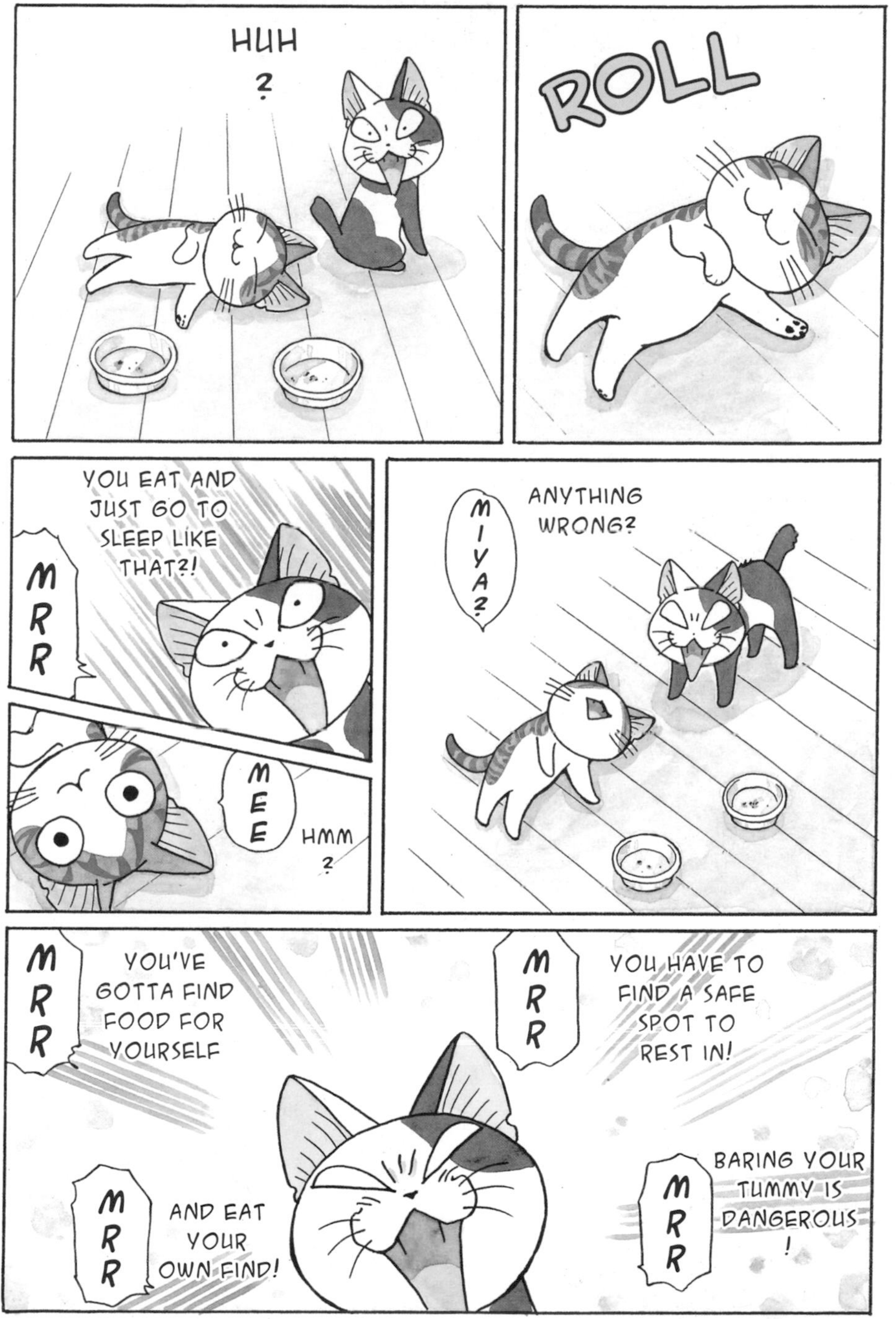
HUH?
ROLL
MRR
YOU EAT AND JUST GO TO SLEEP LIKE THAT?!
MEE
HMM?
MIYA?
ANYTHING WRONG?
MRR
YOU'VE GOTTA FIND FOOD FOR YOURSELF
MRR
YOU HAVE TO FIND A SAFE SPOT TO REST IN!
MRR
AND EAT YOUR OWN FIND!
MRR
BARING YOUR TUMMY IS DANGEROUS!

HAH
HAH
HAH
HAH
HMM?
MEE?
WHY?
MYA
...

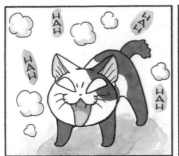

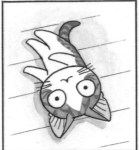

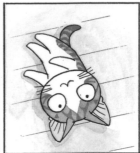

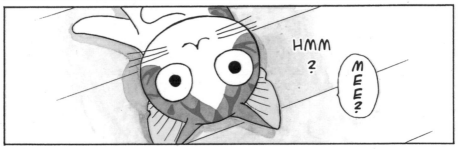

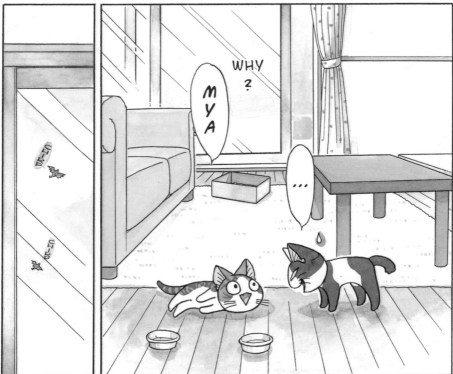

the end

## homemade 164: a cat feels at home

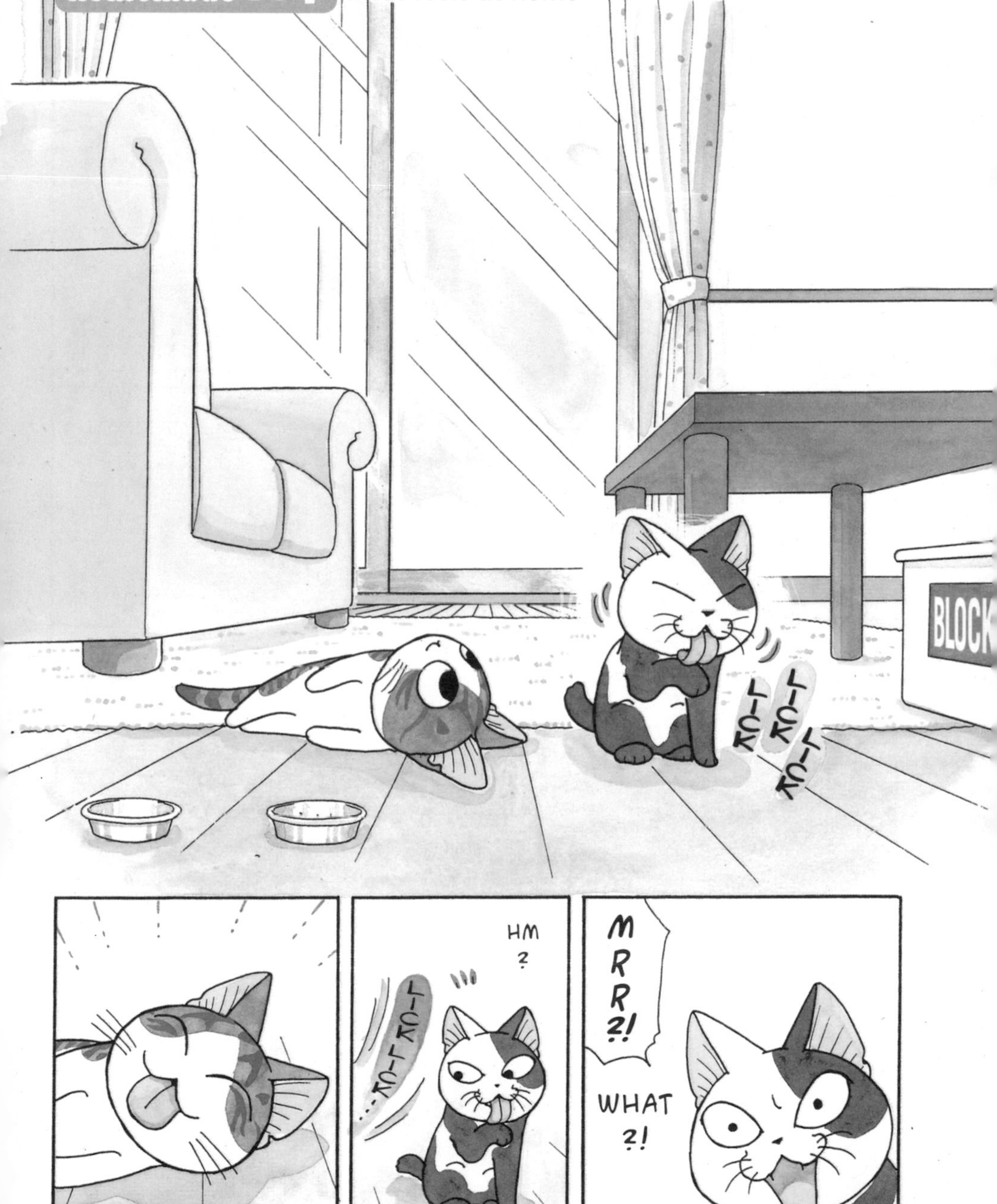
LICK
LICK
LICK
HM ?
LICK LICK...
MRRR?!
WHAT ?!

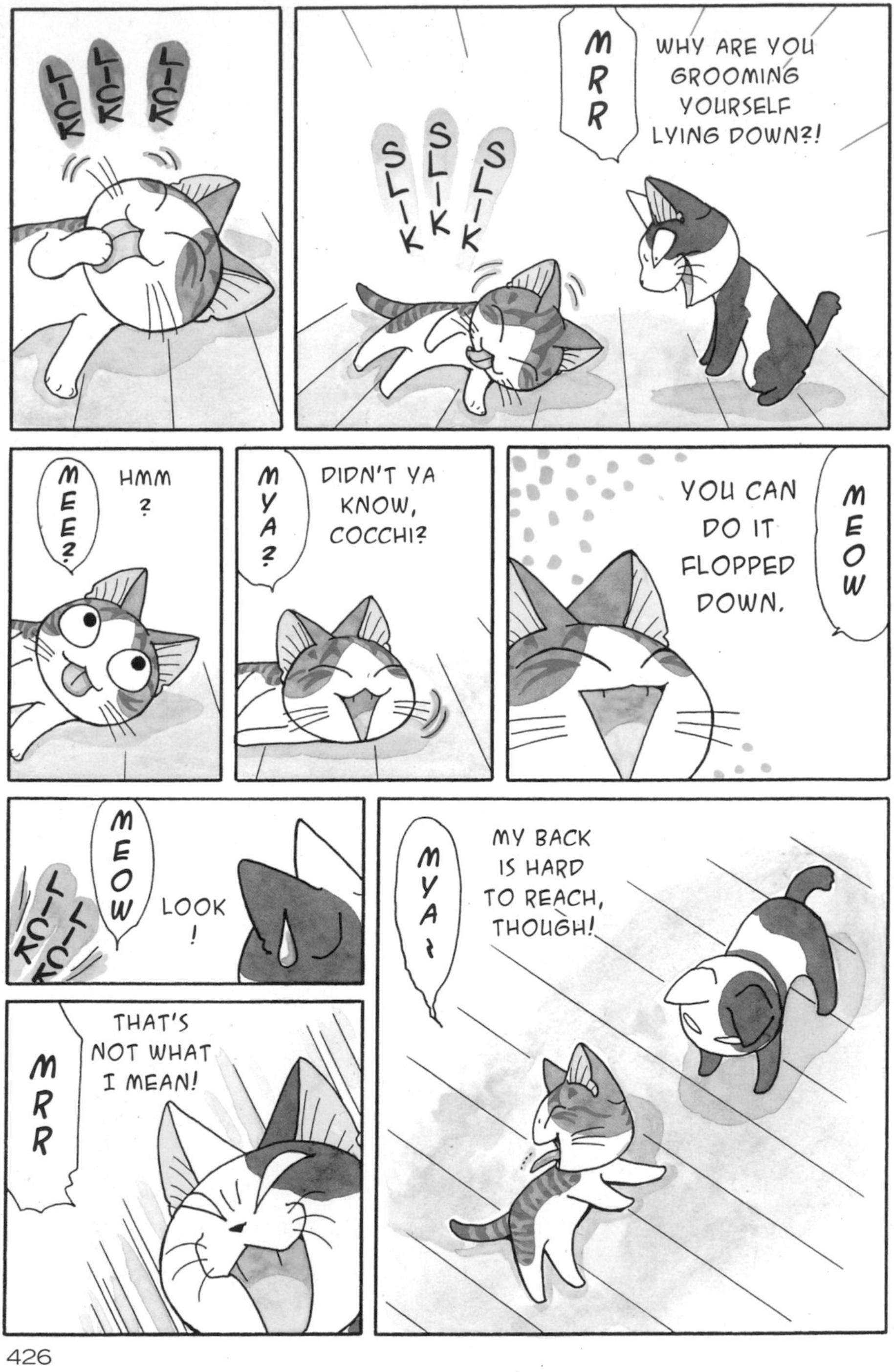
LICK LICK LICK
MRR
WHY ARE YOU GROOMING YOURSELF LYING DOWN?!
SLIK SLIK SLIK
MEE?
HMM?
MYA?
DIDN'T YA KNOW, COCCHI?
YOU CAN DO IT FLOPPED DOWN.
MEOW
LICK LICK
MEOW
LOOK!
MYA~
MY BACK IS HARD TO REACH, THOUGH!
MRR
THAT'S NOT WHAT I MEAN!

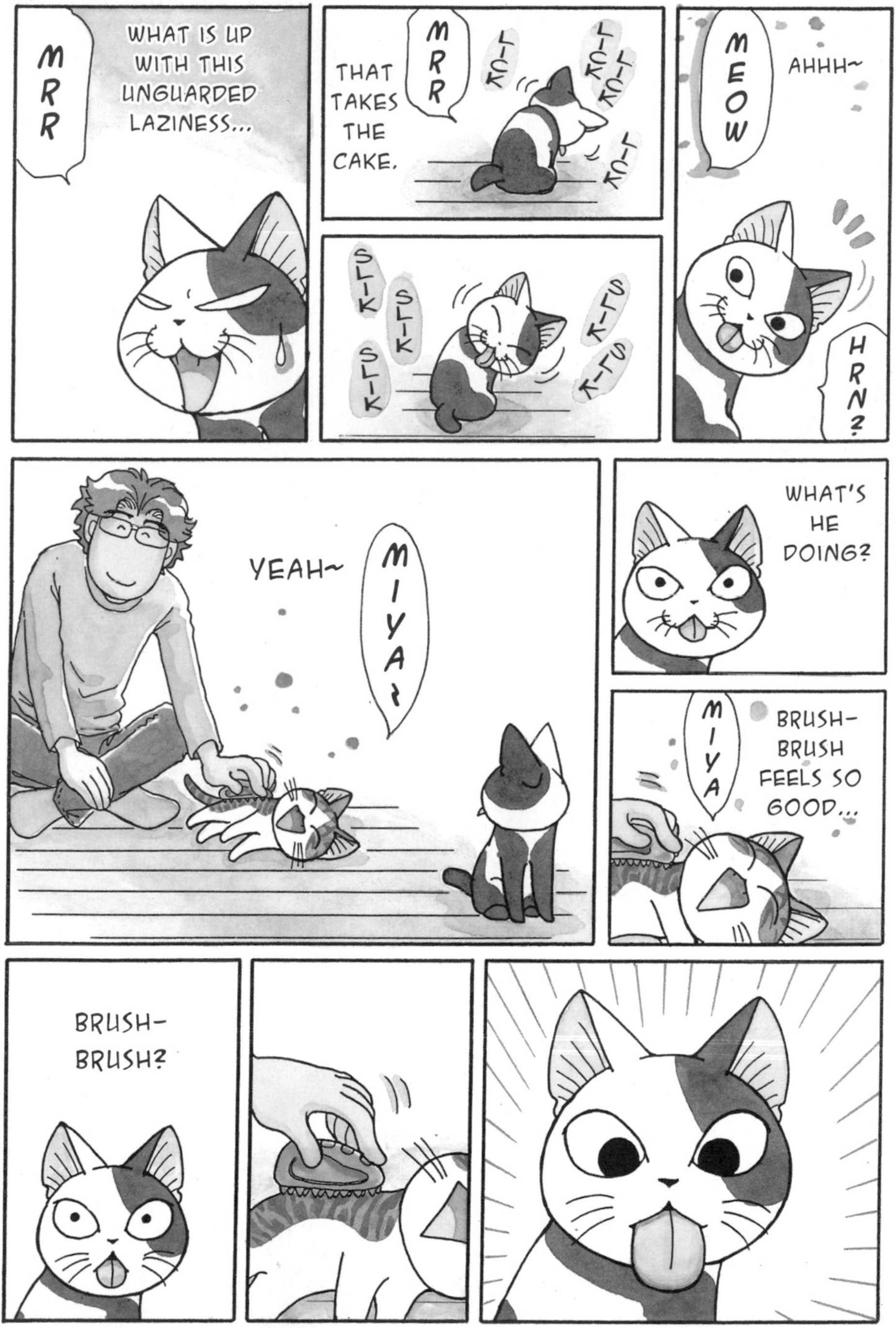
MRR
WHAT IS UP WITH THIS UNGUARDED LAZINESS...
THAT TAKES THE CAKE.
MRR
LICK
LICK
LICK
LICK
SLIK
SLIK
SLIK
SLIK
SLIK
MEOW
AHHH~
HRN?
YEAH~
MIYA~
WHAT'S HE DOING?
MIYA
BRUSH-BRUSH FEELS SO GOOD...
BRUSH-BRUSH?

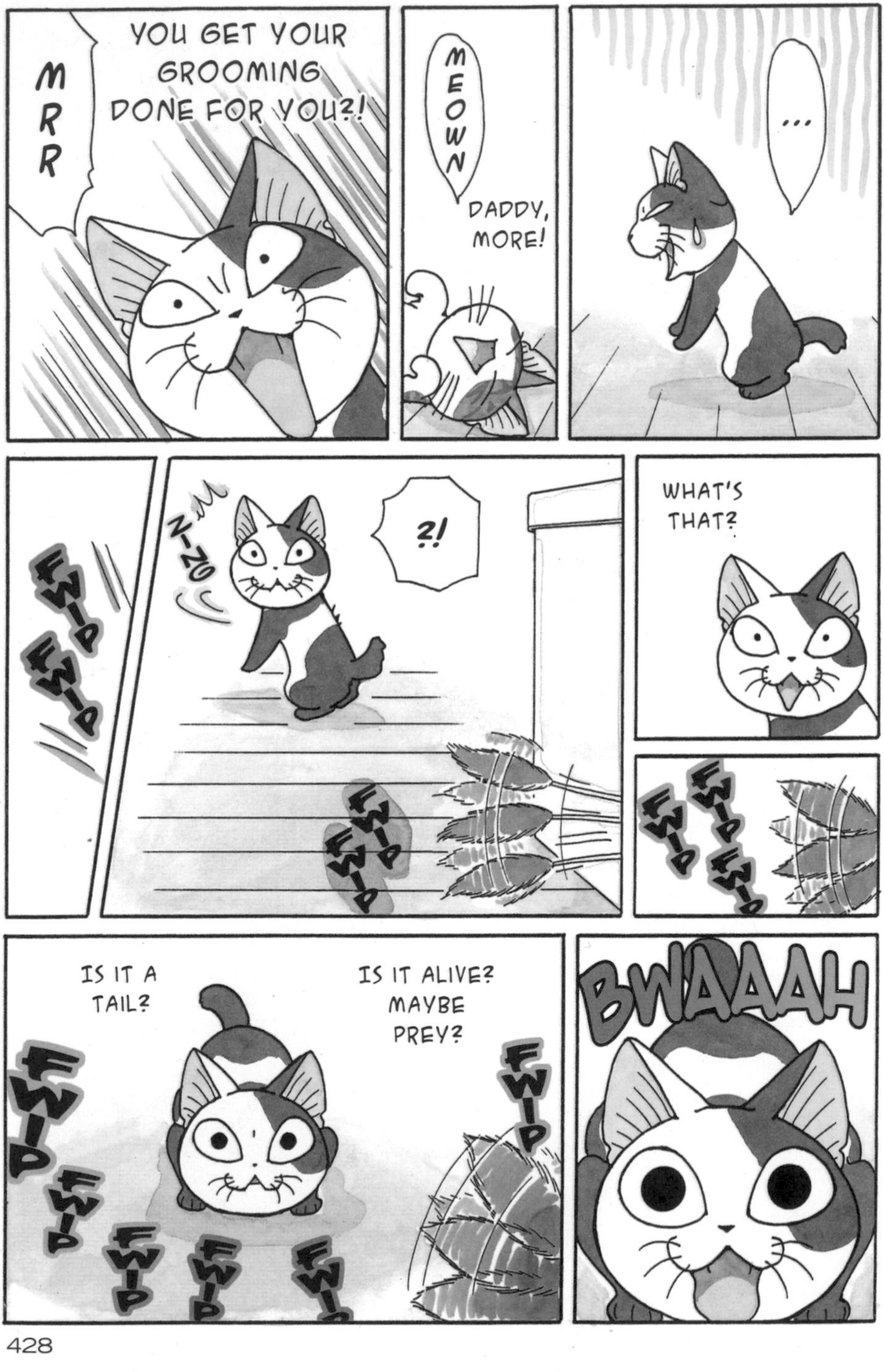
MRR
YOU GET YOUR GROOMING DONE FOR YOU?!
MEOWN
DADDY, MORE!
...
FWIP FWIP FWIP
N-ZO
?!
FWIP FWIP FWIP
WHAT'S THAT?
FWIP FWIP FWIP FWIP
IS IT A TAIL?
IS IT ALIVE? MAYBE PREY?
FWIP FWIP FWIP FWIP FWIP FWIP FWIP
BWAAAH

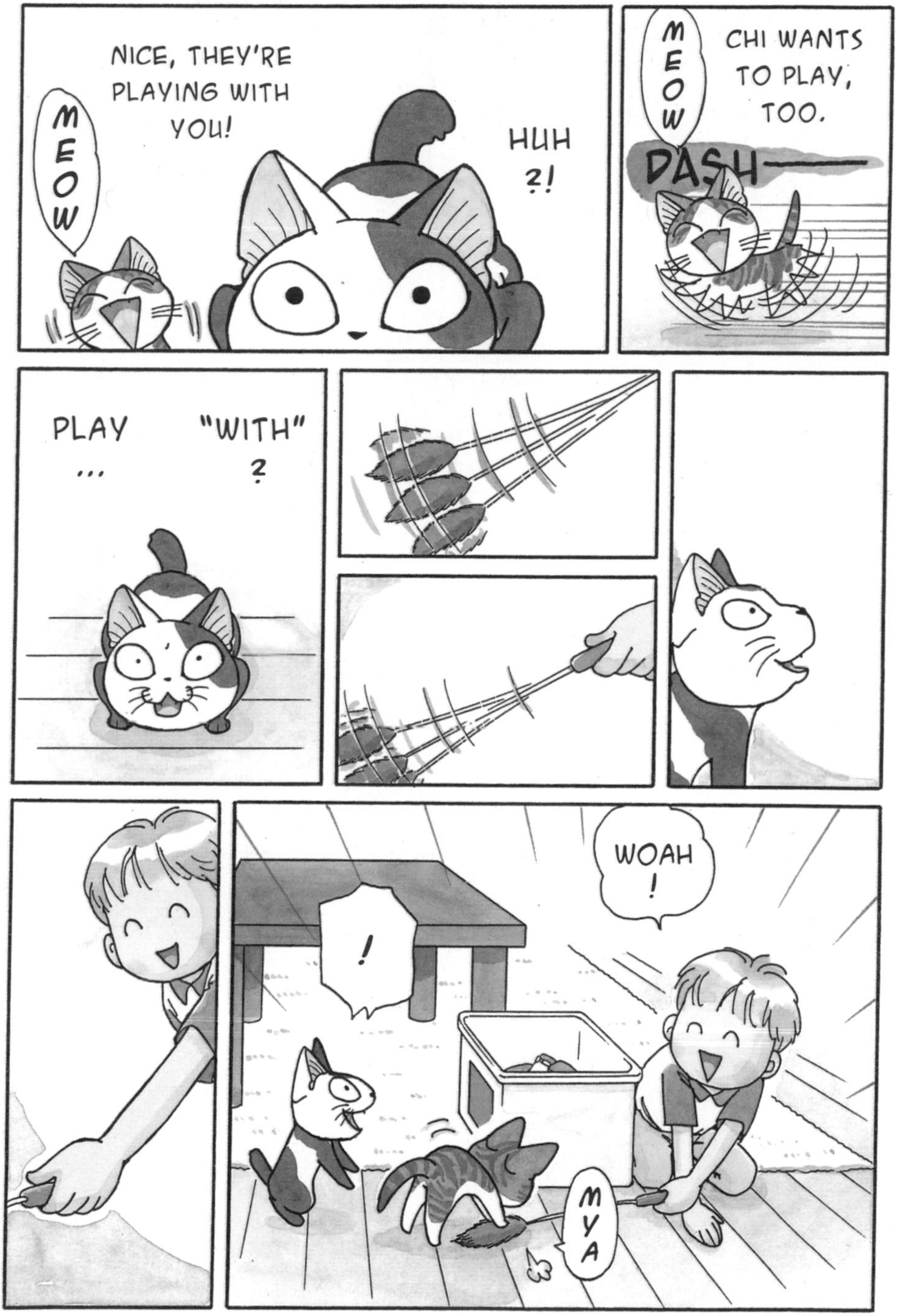
MEOW
NICE, THEY'RE PLAYING WITH YOU!
HUH ?!
MEOW
CHI WANTS TO PLAY, TOO.
DASH
PLAY ...
"WITH" ?
WOAH !
!
MYA

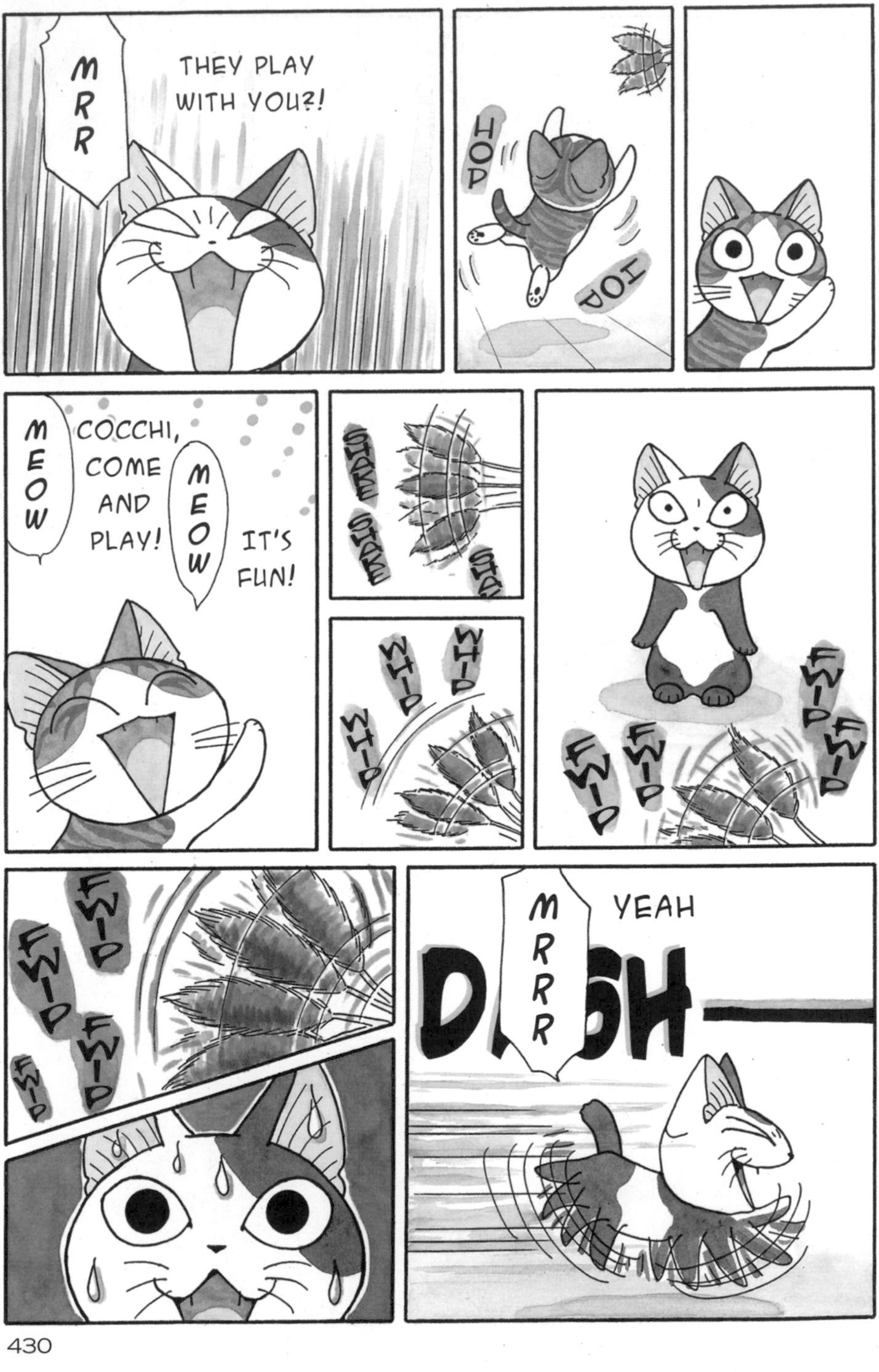
MRR
THEY PLAY WITH YOU?!
HOP
HOP
MEOW
COCCHI, COME AND PLAY!
MEOW
IT'S FUN!
SHAKE
SHAKE
WHIP
WHIP
WHIP
FWIP
FWIP
FWIP
FWIP
FWIP
FWIP
FWIP
FWIP
FWIP
MRRR
YEAH

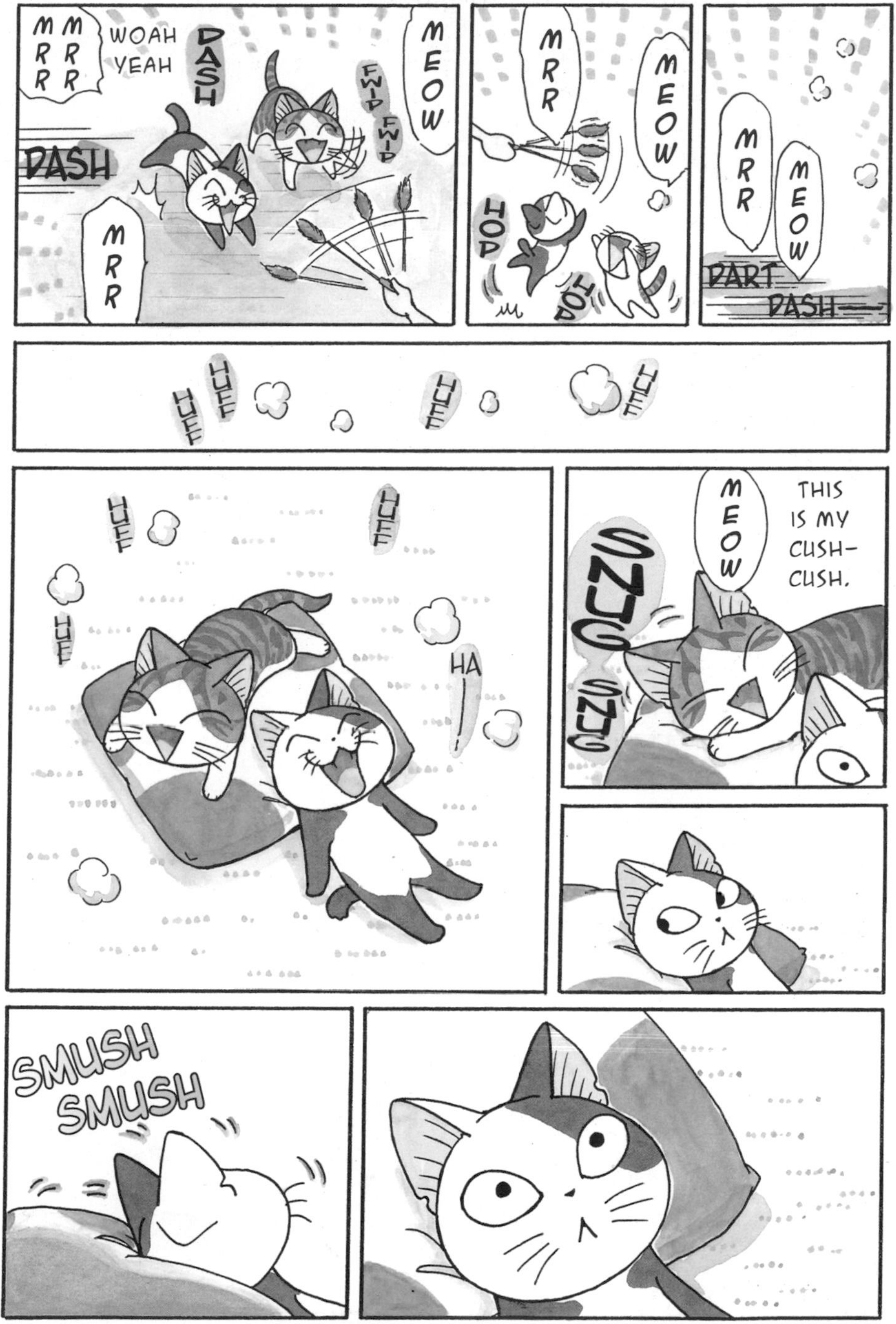
MRRR
MRRR
WOAH YEAH
DASH
DASH
MRR
FWIP FWIP
MEOW
MRR
MEOW
HOP
HOP
MRR
MEOW
DART
DASH
HUFF
HUFF
HUFF
HUFF
HUFF
HUFF
HUF
HA
MEOW
THIS IS MY CUSH-CUSH.
SNUG
SNUG
SMUSH
SMUSH

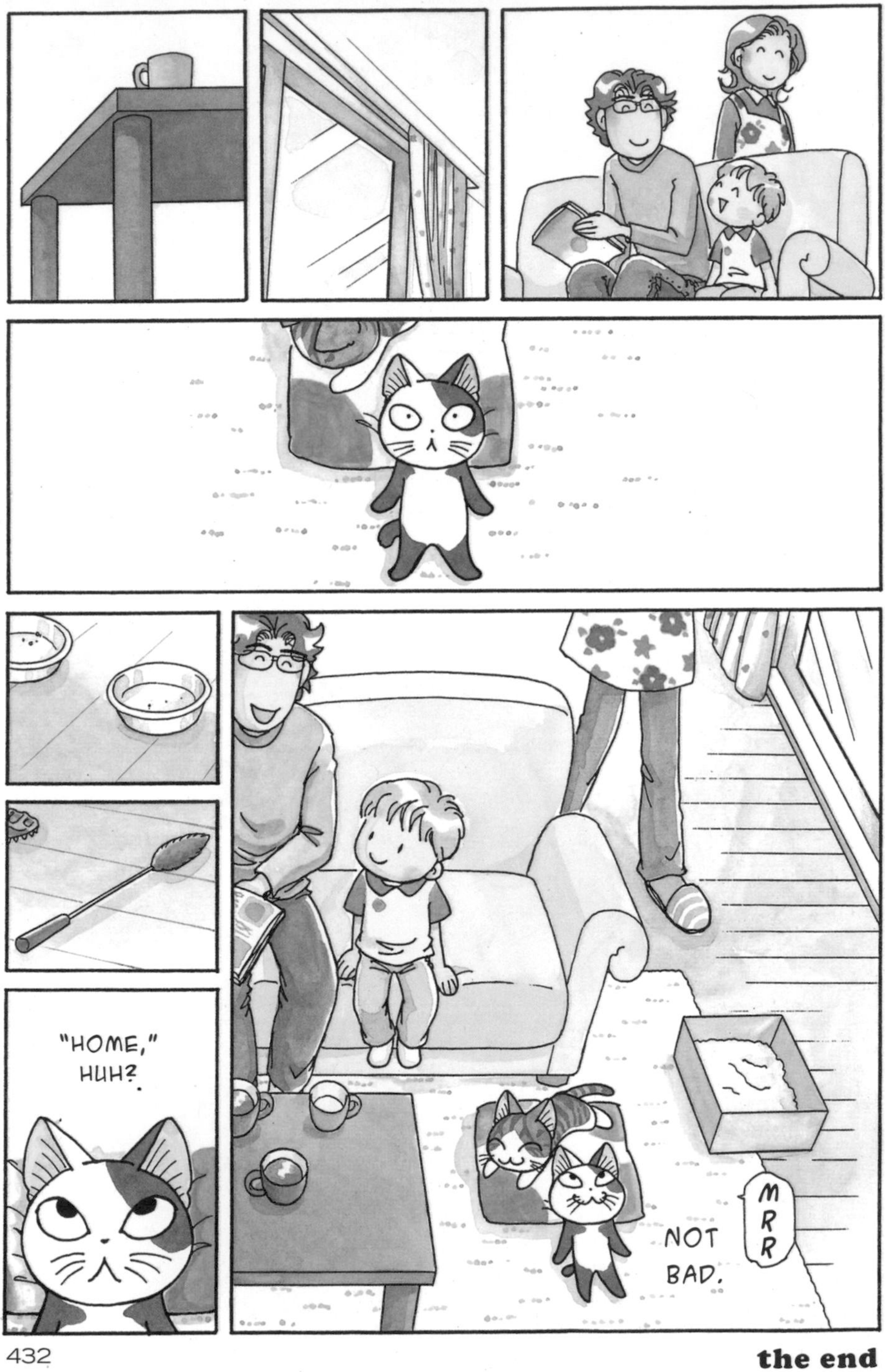
"HOME,"
HUH?
NOT BAD.
MRR



**the end**

**homemade special** a cat goes to China

Chi's Sweet Home

# 甜甜私房猫

Chi's Sweet Home

×

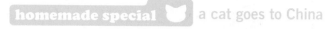

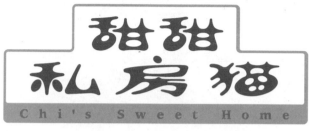

Kentucky Fried Chicken

# 肯德基

MRR
TOUGH CHARACTERS!
MYA
THE TITLE SAYS, "TIANTIAN SHII FANMAO."

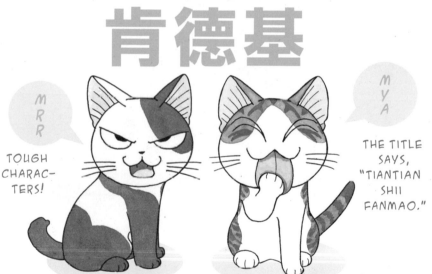

Meo-what! Chi was selected as a campaign character for Kentucky Fried Chicken in China!! From December 26, 2011 through January 18, 2012, KFC diners could select between three different combo meals for a chance to collect one of four Chi cell-phone straps. There were even television commercials broadcast. Saying "I want to collect all of them for her but I'm still one short," scores of people made repeat visits, and the campaign was a huge success! Apparently, 5,000,000 straps were made!

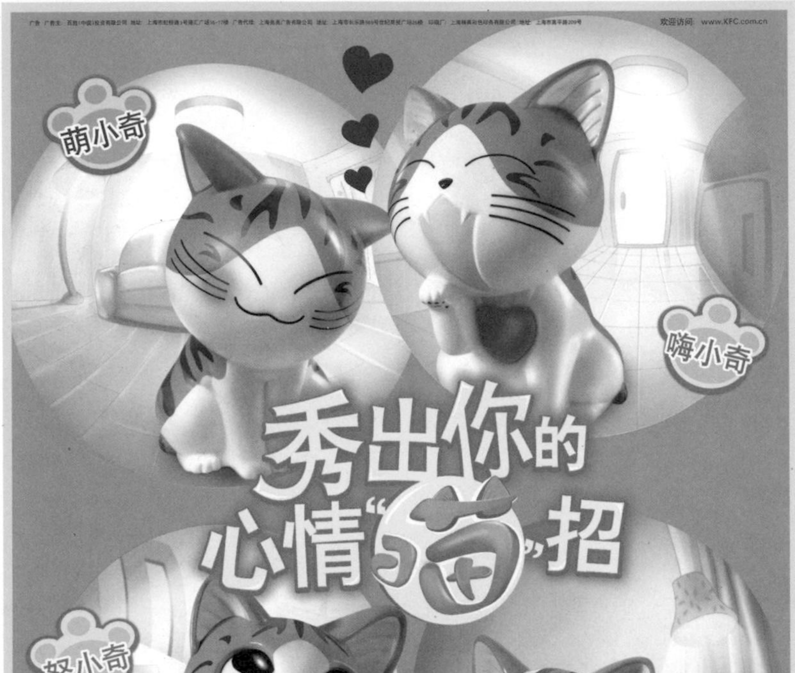
欢迎访问: www.KFC.com.cn
萌小奇
嗨小奇
秀出你的
心情"喵"招
怒小奇
怜小奇
甜甜私房猫
©K-K/TX-C
PEPSI
买"喵"招套餐，含小奇猫挂饰(一款)!
香辣/劲脆鸡腿堡
+ 美帽虾(4只)
+ 百事可乐(中)
+ 小奇猫挂饰
萌小奇
嗨小奇
怜小奇
怒小奇
生活如此多娇

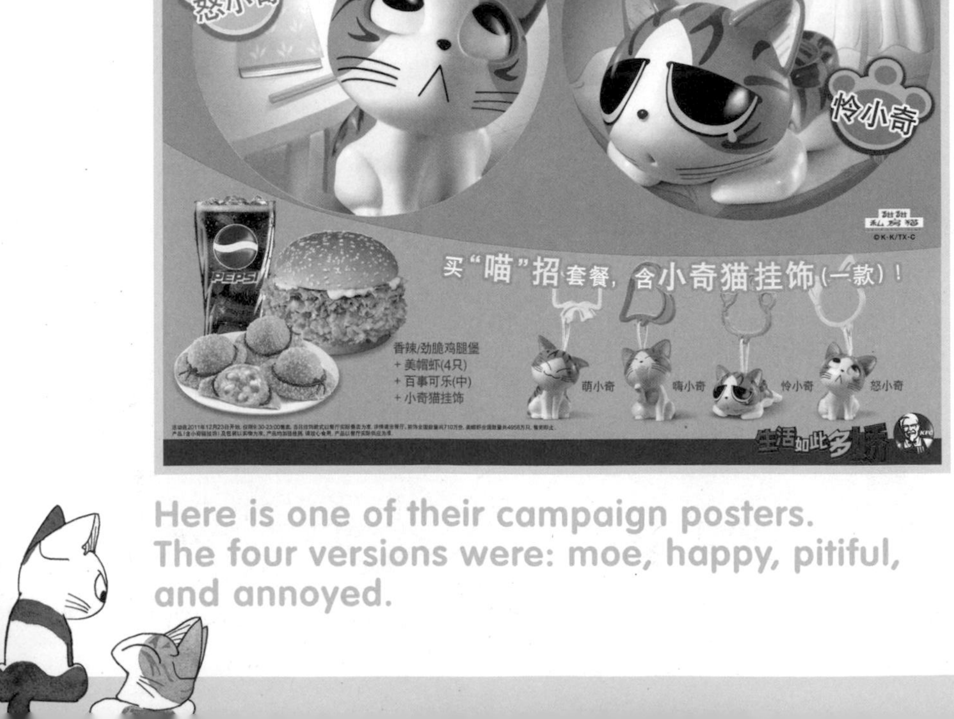

Here is one of their campaign posters.
The four versions were: moe, happy, pitiful,
and annoyed.

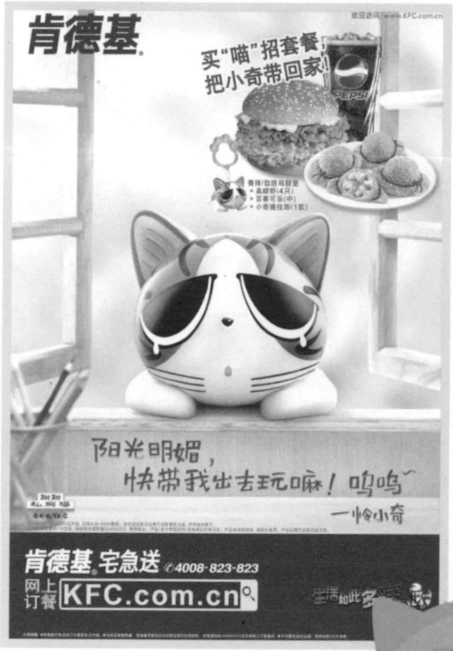
肯德基
欢迎访问www.KFC.com.cn
买"喵"招套餐，
把小奇带回家！
PEPSI
阳光明媚，
快带我出去玩嘛！呜呜~
一怜小奇
©K·K/TX·C
肯德基宅急送 ✆4008-823-823
网上订餐 KFC.com.cn

This is an in-store only backlit display poster.

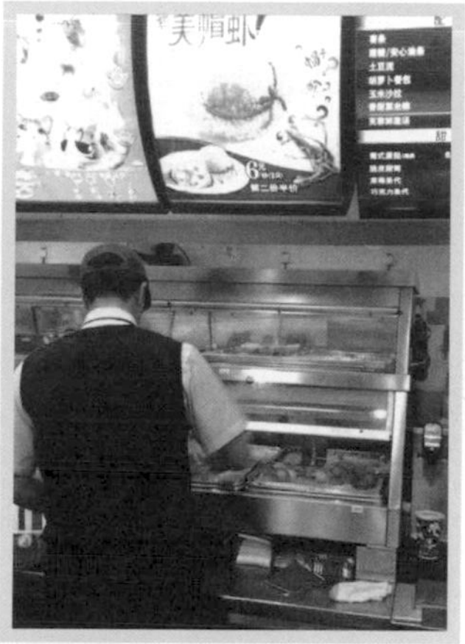

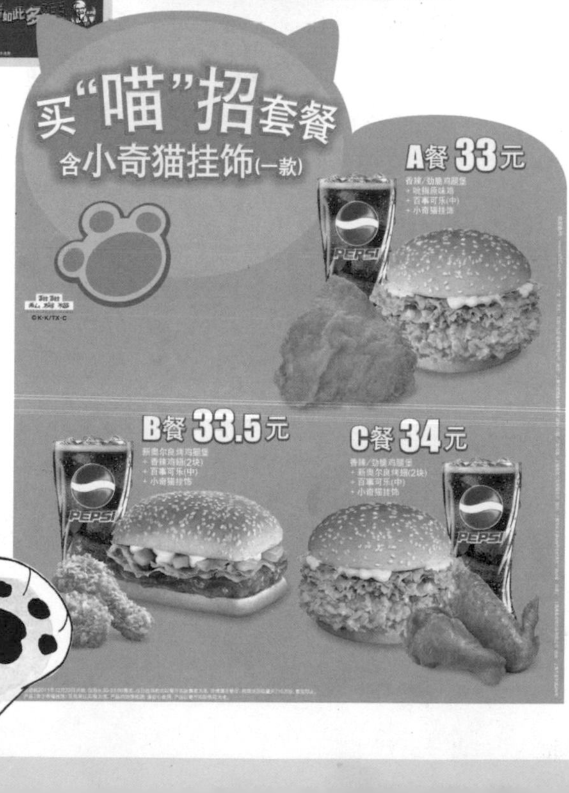
买"喵"招套餐
含小奇猫挂饰(一款)
A餐 33元
B餐 33.5元
C餐 34元
PEPSI
©K·K/TX·C

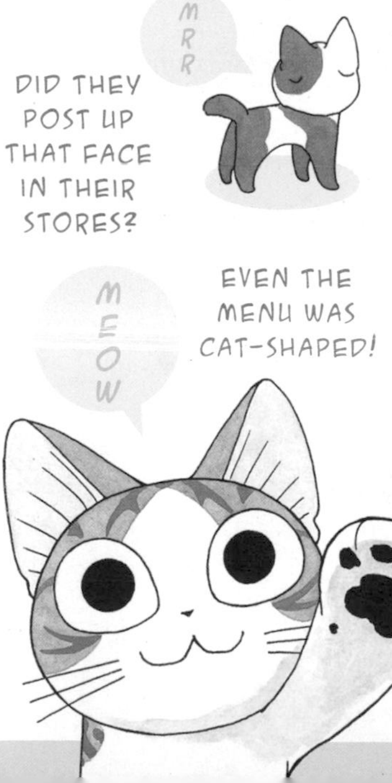
MRR
DID THEY POST UP THAT FACE IN THEIR STORES?
MEOW
EVEN THE MENU WAS CAT-SHAPED!

## And here are the special combo meal boxes!

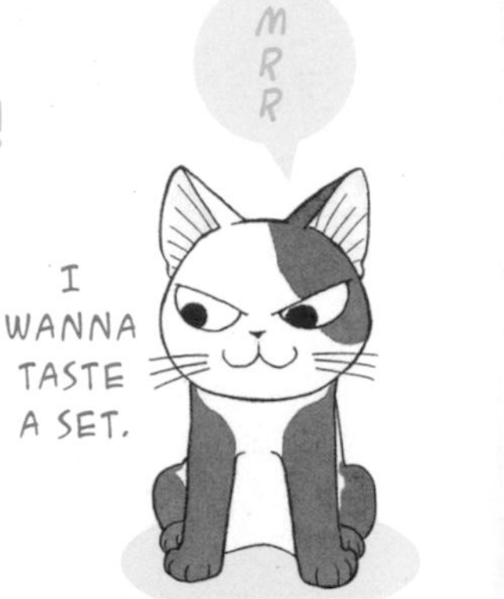
MRR
I WANNA TASTE A SET.

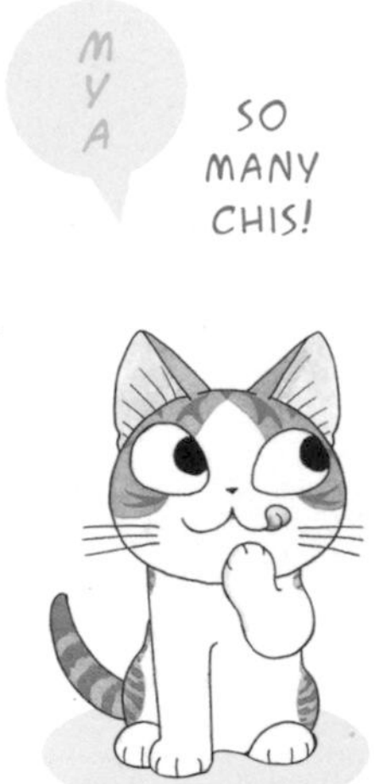
MYA
SO MANY CHIS!

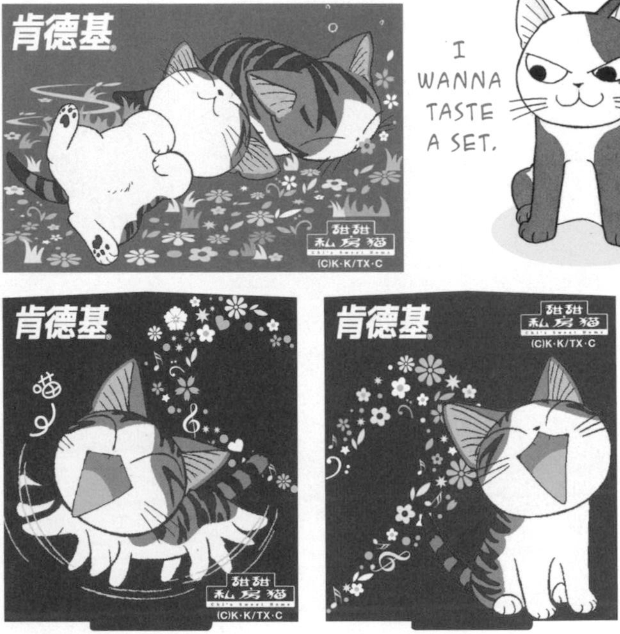
肯德基
甜甜私房猫
(C)K·K/TX·C
肯德基
甜甜私房猫
(C)K·K/TX·C
肯德基
甜甜私房猫
(C)K·K/TX·C

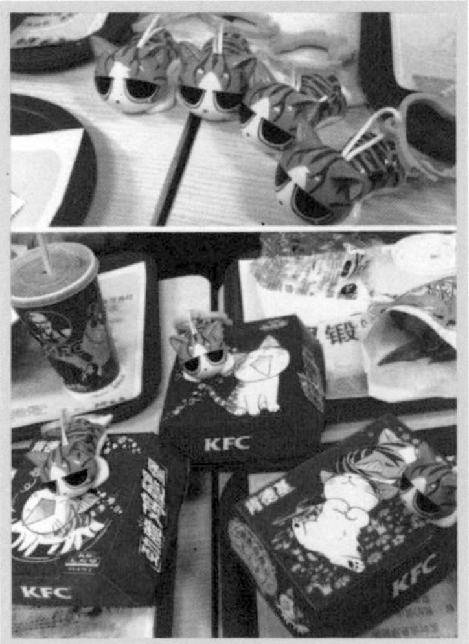
KFC
KFC
肯德基
KFC

**In Shanghai, many posters were seen in subway station platforms and in bus-stop shelters. At many stores, by the end of the campaign their warehouse was entirely out of the strap toys! To all of Chi's fans in China, we hope you continue to support her! Thanks!**

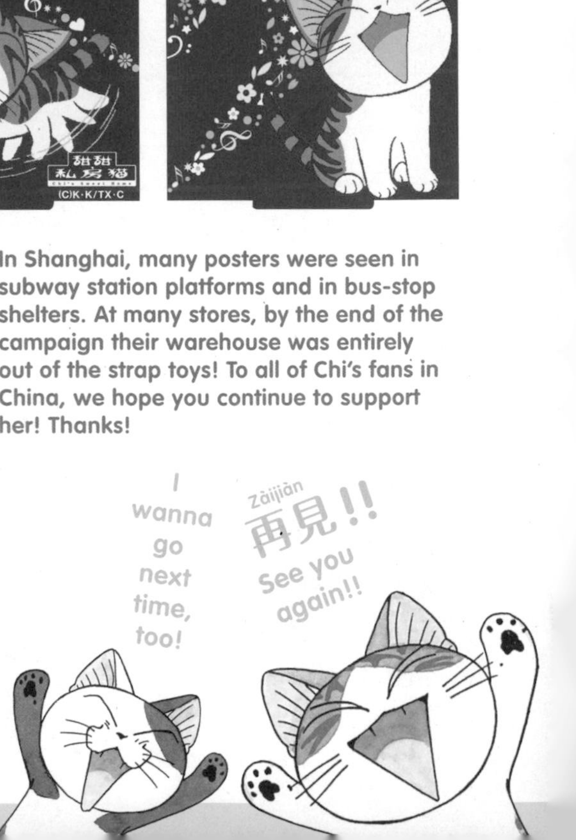
I wanna go next time, too!
Zàijiàn
再見!!
See you again!!

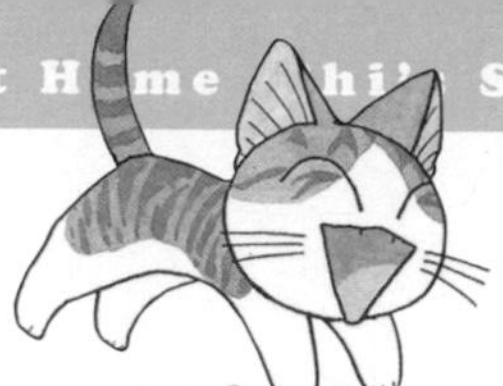

homemade special

# Chi goes global!

*Chi's Sweet Home* attracts not only the American and Japanese reader but is also widely read around the world. Editions released by each foreign publisher vary, though the comic's content always remains true to the original. So while one version may be in full color, others are in black and white; meanwhile, logos may differ and extras may change from those found in the original Japanese edition.

In this Homemade Special, reporters Blackie and Chi, having heard of such rumors regarding the various releases, visit a few of the many foreign publishers who have translated *Chi's Sweet Home* to interview them.

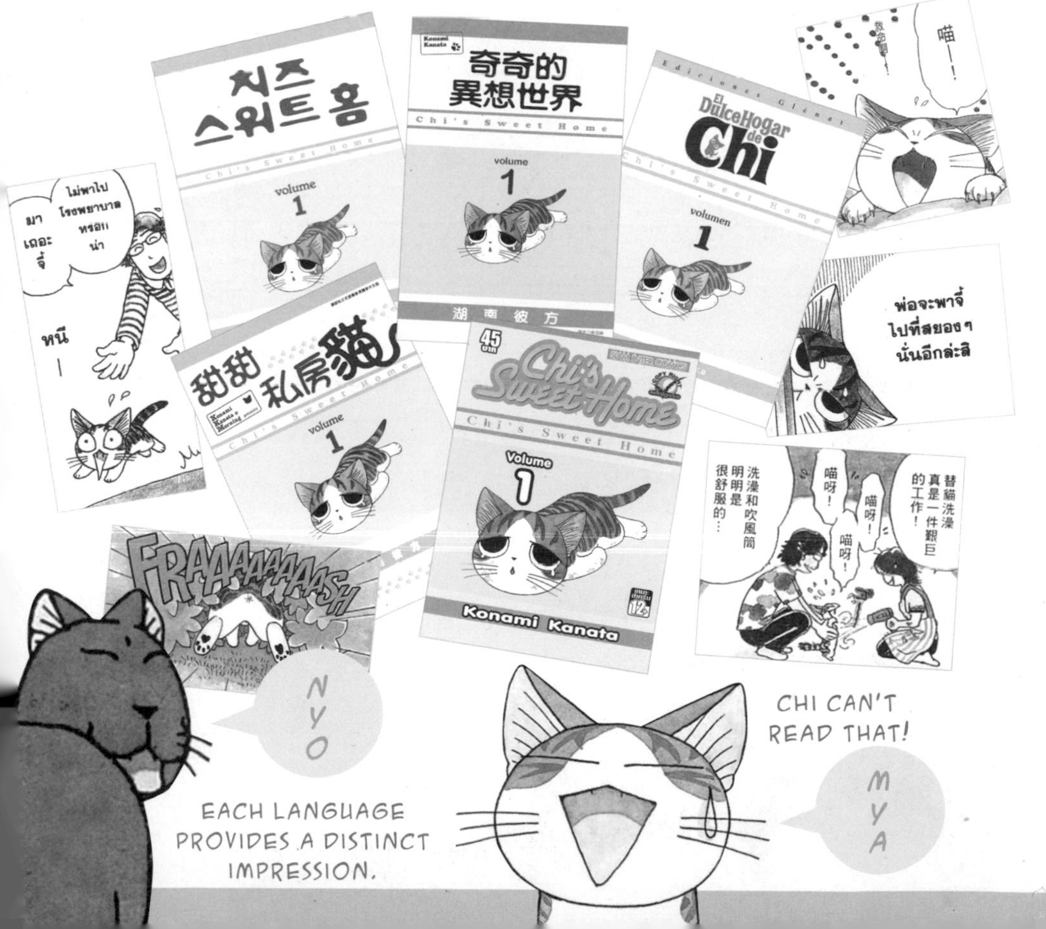
치즈 스위트 홈
Chi's Sweet Home
volume 1
奇奇的異想世界
Chi's Sweet Home
volume 1
湖南彼方
Ediciones Glénat
El Dulce Hogar de Chi
Chi's Sweet Home
volumen 1
喵—！
甜甜私房貓
Chi's Sweet Home
volume 1
Chi's Sweet Home
Chi's Sweet Home
Volume 1
Konami Kanata
FRAAAAAAAASH
替貓洗澡真是一件艱巨的工作！
喵呀！
喵呀！
喵呀！
洗澡和吹風筒明明是很舒服的…
NYO
EACH LANGUAGE PROVIDES A DISTINCT IMPRESSION.
CHI CAN'T READ THAT!
MYA

# It's Chi's Sweet World—a look at the

## SPAIN
### Ediciones Glénat

The Spanish version launched in 2009, and as the entire staff loves cats we soon became big fans of Chi. When we came up with the idea of presenting our readers' cats as a book extra, we first started off with our own cats. By the second volume we began sharing images of our readers' kitties. Everyone in Spain is crazy about Chi's adventures, and cat-lovers just cannot get enough of her. We'd like to thank the author for creating such a fascinating cat world. We're looking forward to Chi's next adventure!

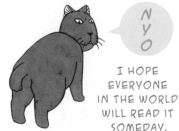

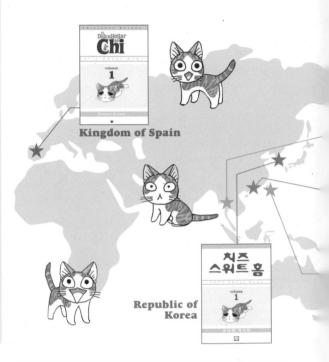

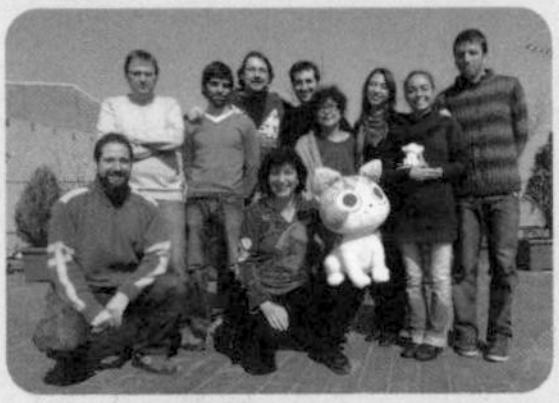

El Dulce Hogar de Chi
volumen
1
Kingdom of Spain
치즈 스위트 홈
volume
1
Republic of Korea

Other countries where *Chi's Sweet Home* has been published:

**China** **Finland** **France**

More countries across the globe are also looking to publish *Chi* as well!

NYO
I HOPE EVERYONE IN THE WORLD WILL READ IT SOMEDAY.

The world of *Chi's Sweet Home* will steadily expand as long as cats exist!

## South Korea
### Haksan Publishing, Co. (주)학산문화사

In South Korea more people tend to have dogs as pets rather than cats. But recently the number of cat-owners has been growing and an increasing number of cat-themed books have been published here. Among them *Chi's Sweet Home* we feel stands alone at the top. One reason for this is how it doesn't just emphasize cuteness but depicts a family story, where Chi and the Yamadas live together in harmony. While cat-lovers cannot resist grabbing a copy once they see Chi on the front cover, others find themselves attracted by the warm and fuzzy drama illustrated in this series' pages.

As the first volume debuted here in early 2010, we know there is a long road ahead for Chi, but we'll be watching over her until she finds her true sweet home someday in the next volumes. Fight on, Chi!

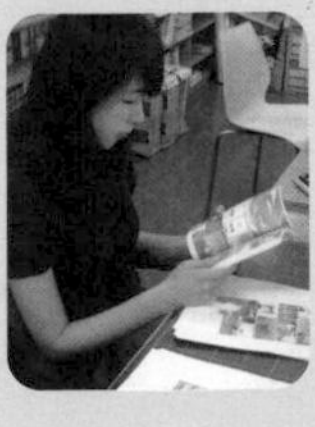

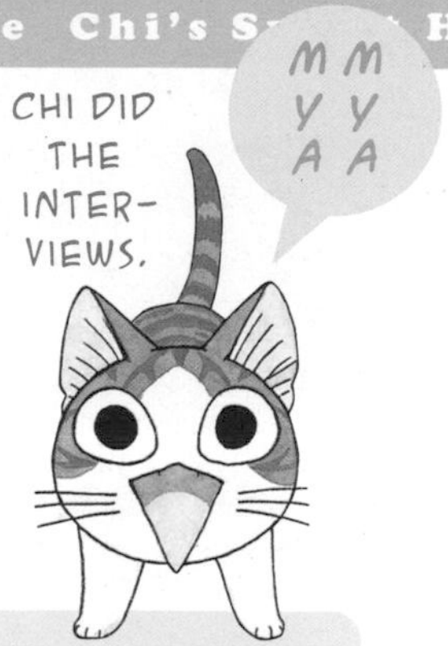
CHI DID THE INTER-VIEWS.
MYA MYA

## many publishers now releasing this comic.

**Red-hot interviews with the many foreign publishing houses who are releasing international editions of *Chi's Sweet Home*! What about Chi intrigues fans from other countries? Let's go ask them!**

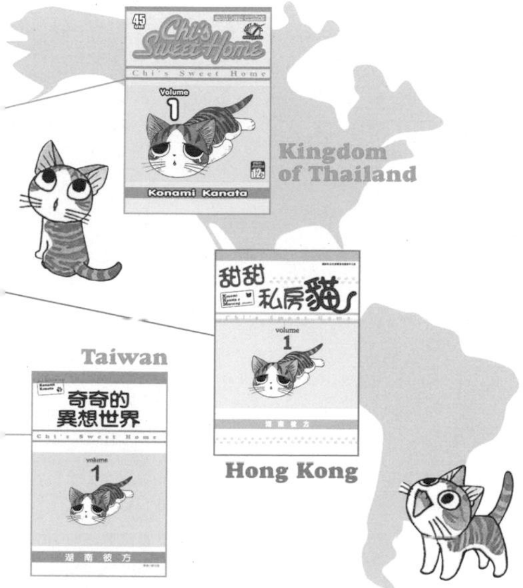
Chi's Sweet Home
Volume 1
Konami Kanata
Kingdom of Thailand
甜甜私房貓
volume 1
Hong Kong
Taiwan
奇奇的異想世界
volume 1
湖南彼方

### Thailand
### Siam Inter Multimedia, PLC.

SIAM INTER Multimedia

I wasn't much of a cat fan before, but upon reading this comic I came to the realization that, yeah, cats have all sorts of cute sides to them! To tell the truth, I was a little concerned about selling *Chi's Sweet Home* in Thailand. I mean, our heroine Chi is always nude! And she is almost too sexy on the covers of volume 5 and 6. (Laughs) Still, I desperately want to read the next install-ment.

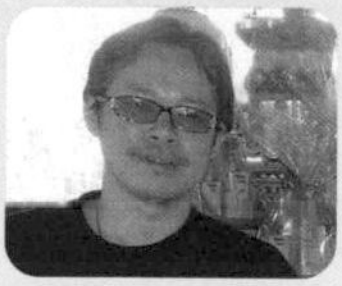

### Taiwan
### Sharp Point Press

尖端出版

Congratulations on the release of *Chi's Sweet Home* Volume 7! I am certain that anyone who experiences Chi's cuteness will shout out, "How cute!"
Taiwanese readers are also greatly looking forward to more of Chi's adventure. We hope Chi will gleefully continue to saunter on and give everyone who reads this comic joy!

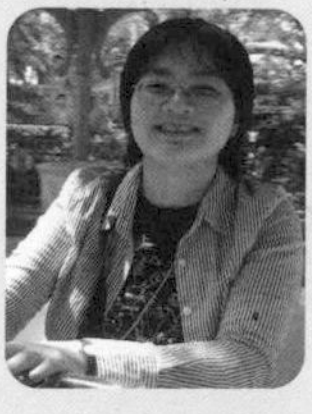

### Hong Kong
### Rightman Publishing, Inc.

正文社 www.rightman.net

I think I first ran into Chi in a toy store. At that time, I wasn't at all sure whose home Chi came from... And to think that I would eventually become a comic editor and would once again meet with Chi... I guess it was fate. (Laughs)
*Chi's Sweet Home* is very popular in Hong Kong. Men and women alike, everyone loves to read *Chi* because she is just so adorable! Cat-owners of course empathize with Chi's every movement. But we also feel readers who live cat-free lives also read the comic and find Chi's mildly hyper and occasionally sulky antics quite interesting.
I hope Chi will continue to be a bundle of cheer and that more people will come to love her. Good luck, Chi!

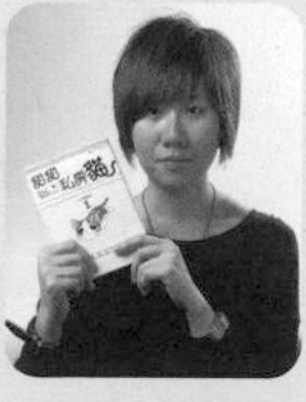

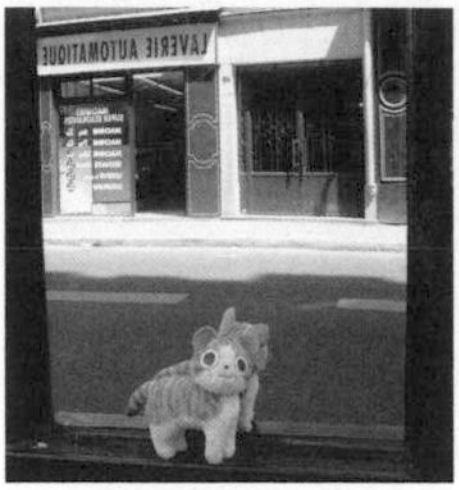
LAVERIE AUTOMATIQUE

## Our Humble Reporter Chi Reports from Paris!

**A French version of *Chi's Sweet Home* debuted in late 2010, published by Glénat Editions. So, Chi went on a business trip to France and was tasked to guide a tour of Paris after her meeting!**

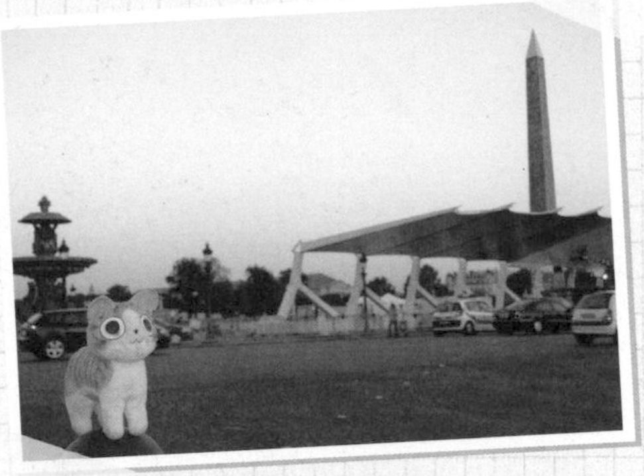

**1 Place de la Concorde**

Arrived in Paris!

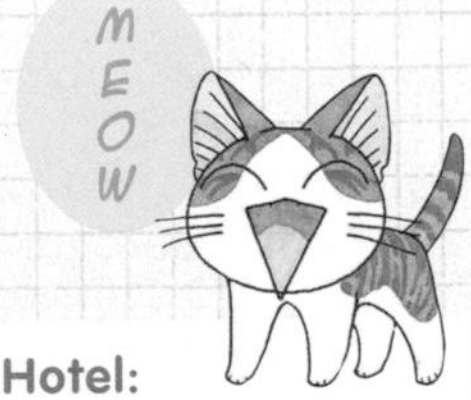
THE BUILDING BEHIND CHI!
MEOW

**2 5-Star Hotel: Hôtel de Crillon**

Chi wants to stay here, too...

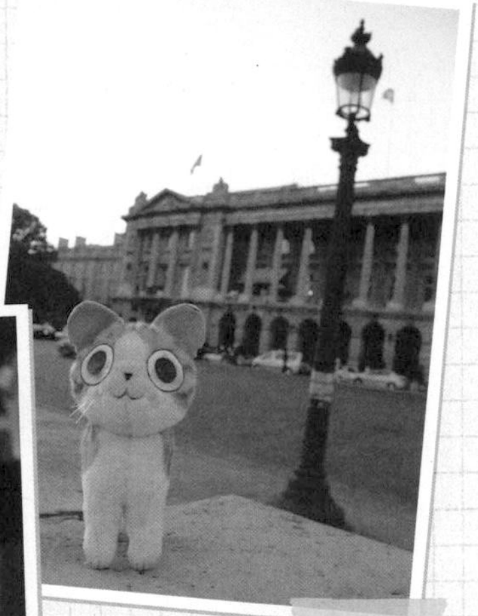

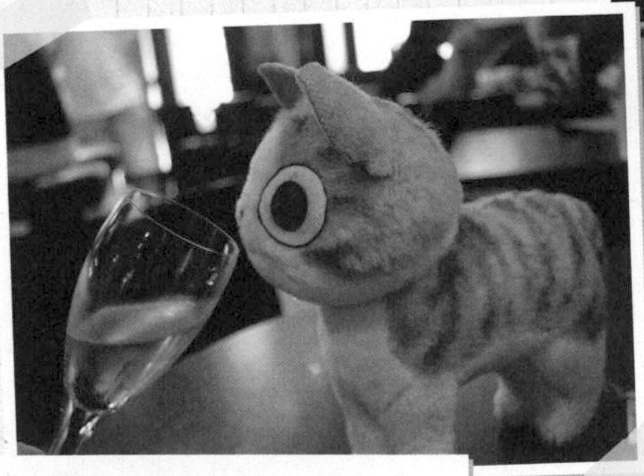

**3 At a restaurant. Chi's first glass of champagne!**

Smells good...? Hey, it's alcohol!

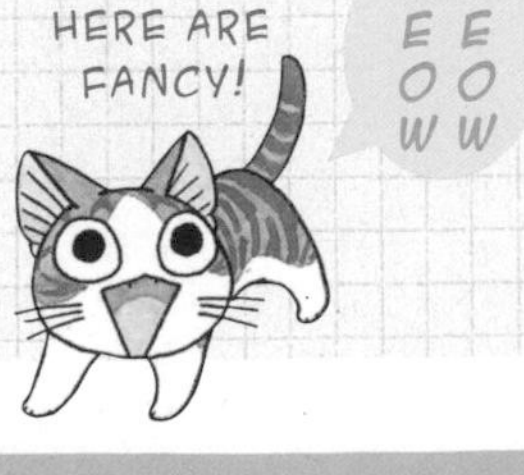
THE HOTELS AND FOOD HERE ARE FANCY!
MEOW MEOW

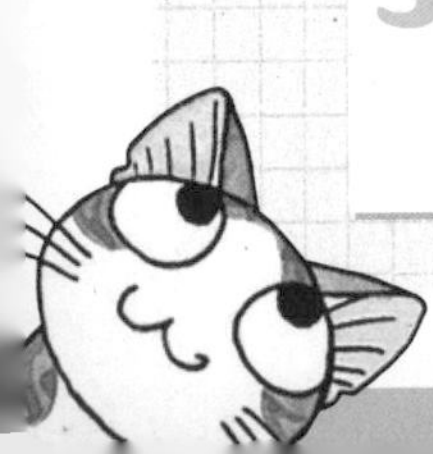

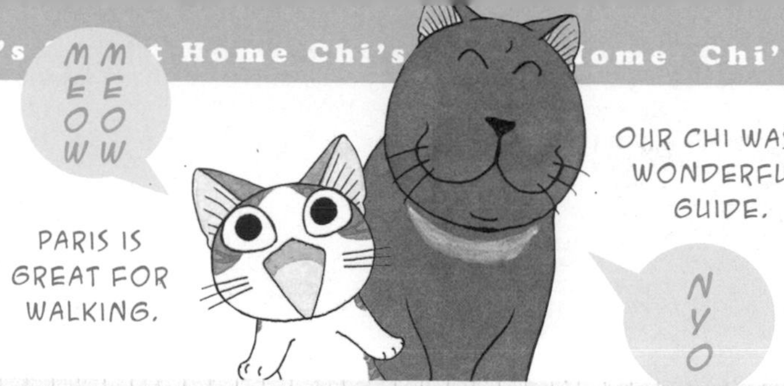
MEOW MEOW
PARIS IS GREAT FOR WALKING.
OUR CHI WAS A WONDERFUL GUIDE.
NYO

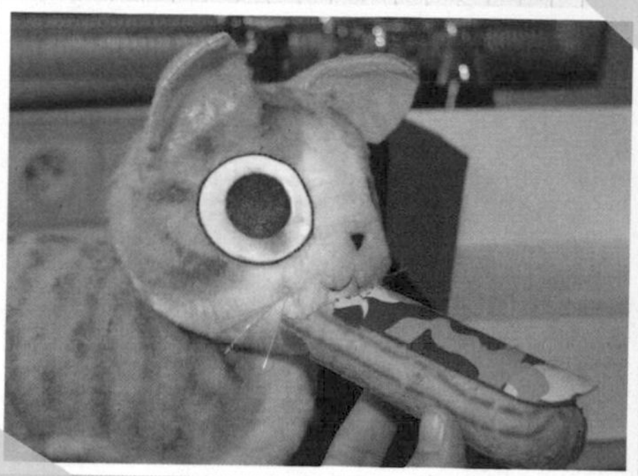

**4** **Eating a fauchon éclair**

What's this?! Delish!

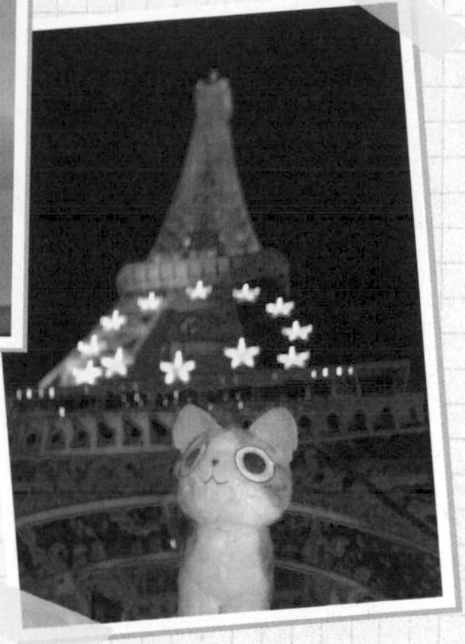

**5** **The Eiffel Tower**

It's beautiful. Paris sure is nice!

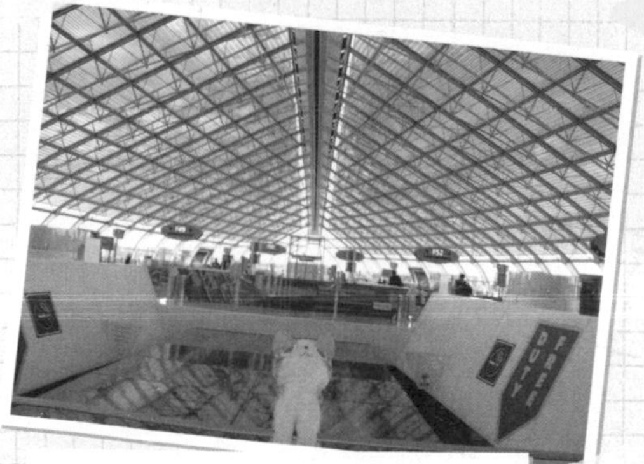

**6** **Charles de Gaulle International Airport**

What a huge airport! Okay, my business trip is all done!

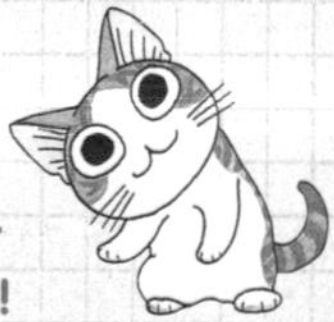

**Follow more of Chi's global adventures on her Japanese website!**
http://morningmanga.com/chisweetravel

**And find more Chi fun at her English language site...**
http://www.chisweethome.net

# Let's Make a Chi Face!!

Copy or cut out the image to the right and fold using the following instructions.

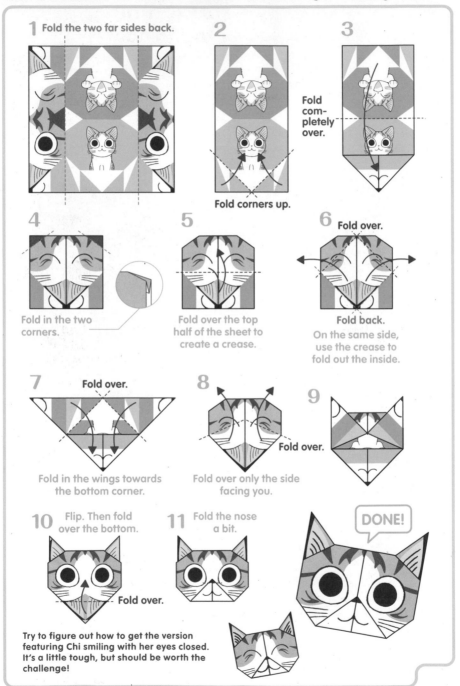

**1** Fold the two far sides back.

**2** Fold corners up.

**3** Fold completely over.

**4** Fold in the two corners.

**5** Fold over the top half of the sheet to create a crease.

**6** Fold over. Fold back.

On the same side, use the crease to fold out the inside.

**7** Fold over.

Fold in the wings towards the bottom corner.

**8** Fold over.

Fold over only the side facing you.

**9**

**10** Flip. Then fold over the bottom. Fold over.

**11** Fold the nose a bit.

DONE!

Try to figure out how to get the version featuring Chi smiling with her eyes closed. It's a little tough, but should be worth the challenge!

# Chi's Sweet Origami
## (instructions on facing page)

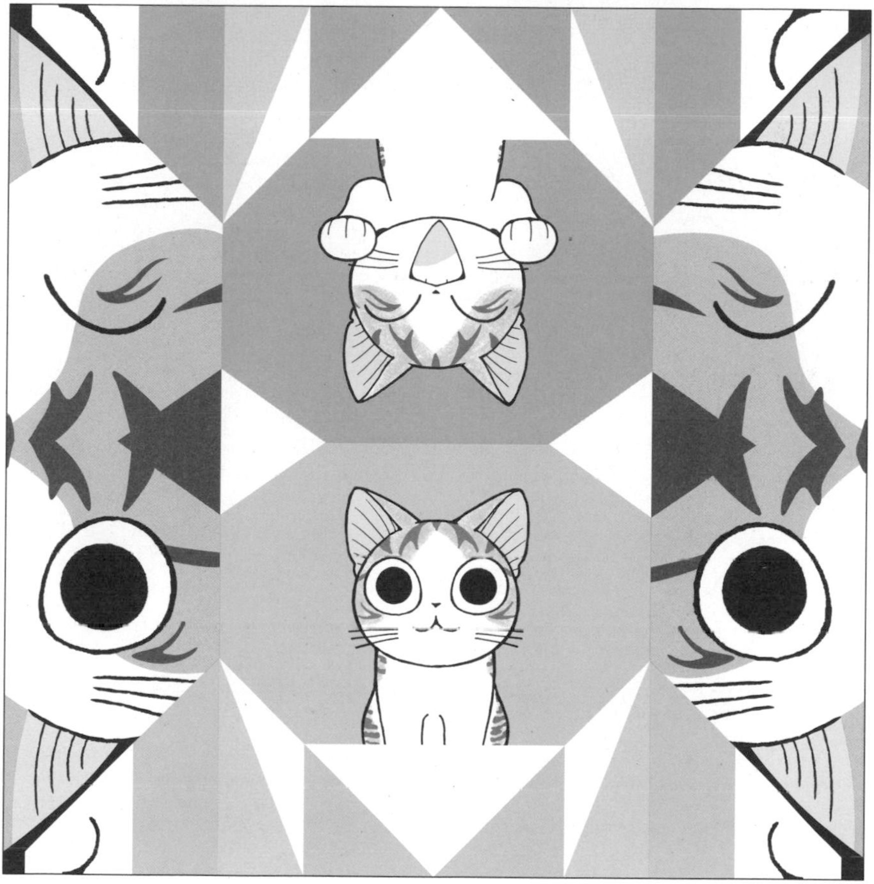

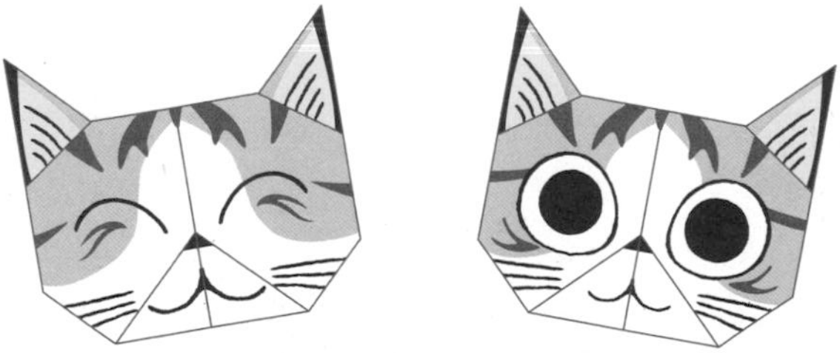

**Let's try to fold our way to both of Chi's origami faces!**

A recently discovered sheet of posted paper reveals an unexpected fact.

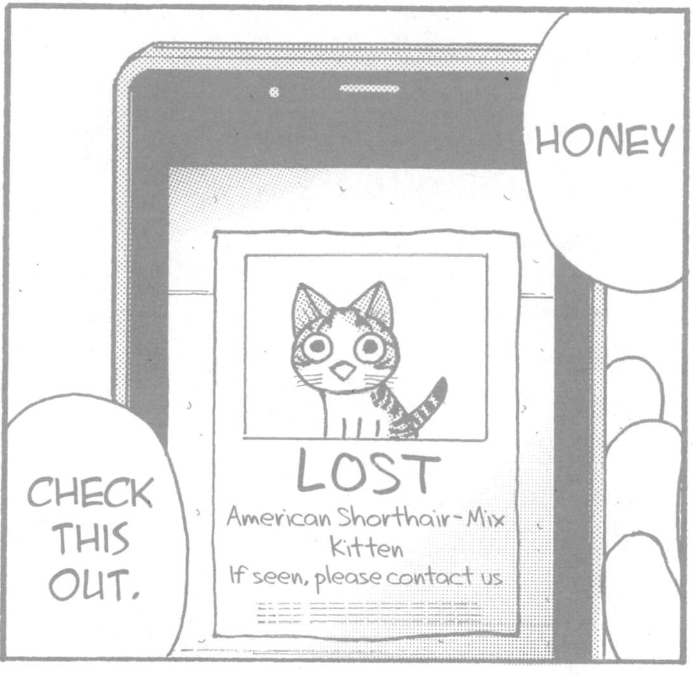
HONEY
CHECK THIS OUT.
LOST
American Shorthair-Mix Kitten
If seen, please contact us

The Complete
Chi's Sweet Home part 4

# ON SALE THIS WINTER!!

## Vertical Comics News

**Ten months after its heartwarming finale, Chi is coming back as an anime!**

**This Fall 2016, a brand new Chi animated television series will debut!**

**What meow?! Apparently the anime is going to be in 3DCG, too!**

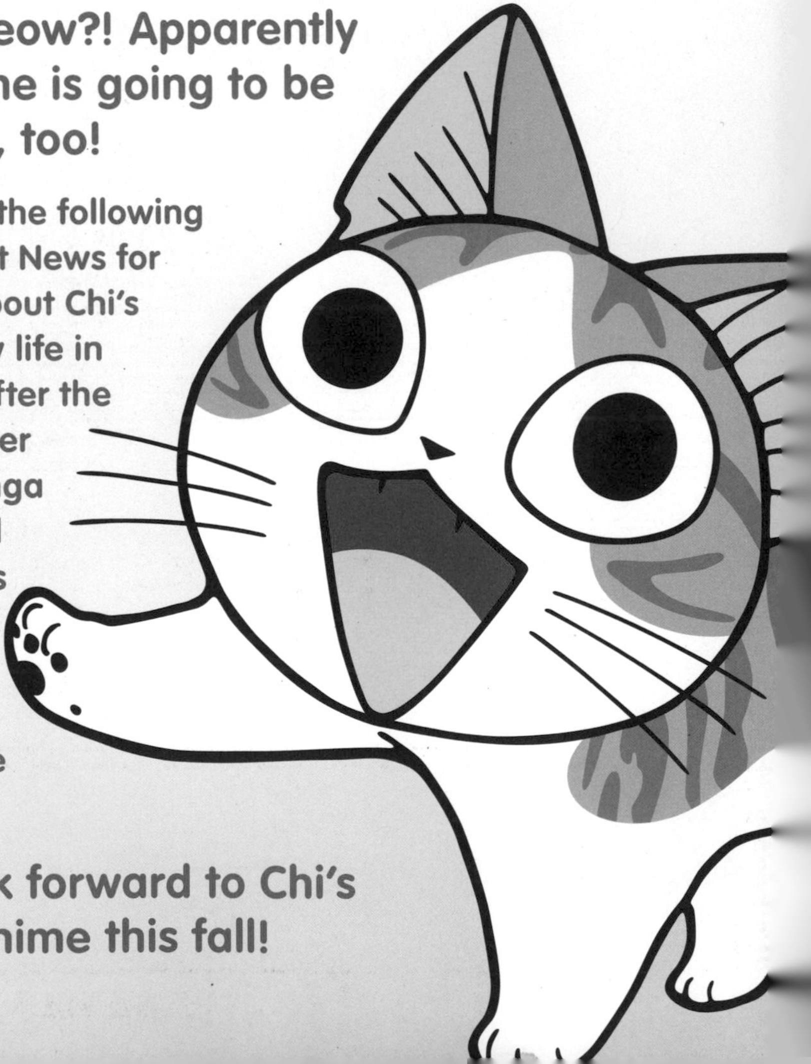

Check out the following Chi's Sweet News for a comic about Chi's happy new life in Paris set after the final chapter of the manga series, and some news on the making of her new anime series!

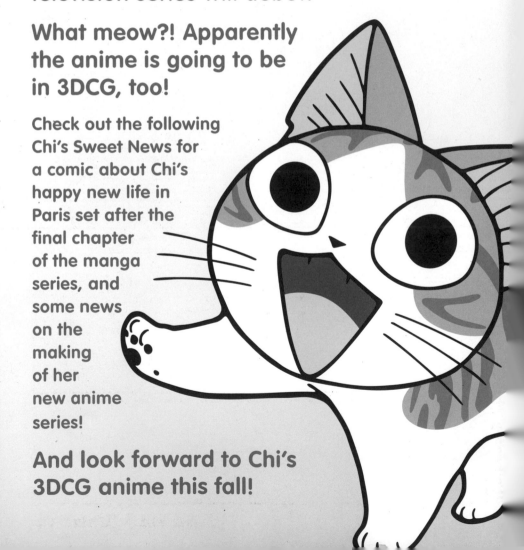

**And look forward to Chi's 3DCG anime this fall!**

Anime Adaptation Report!

Chi's Sweet Home Extra Edition

# Chi's Sweet News

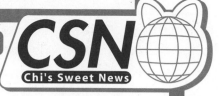

CSN Chi's Sweet News

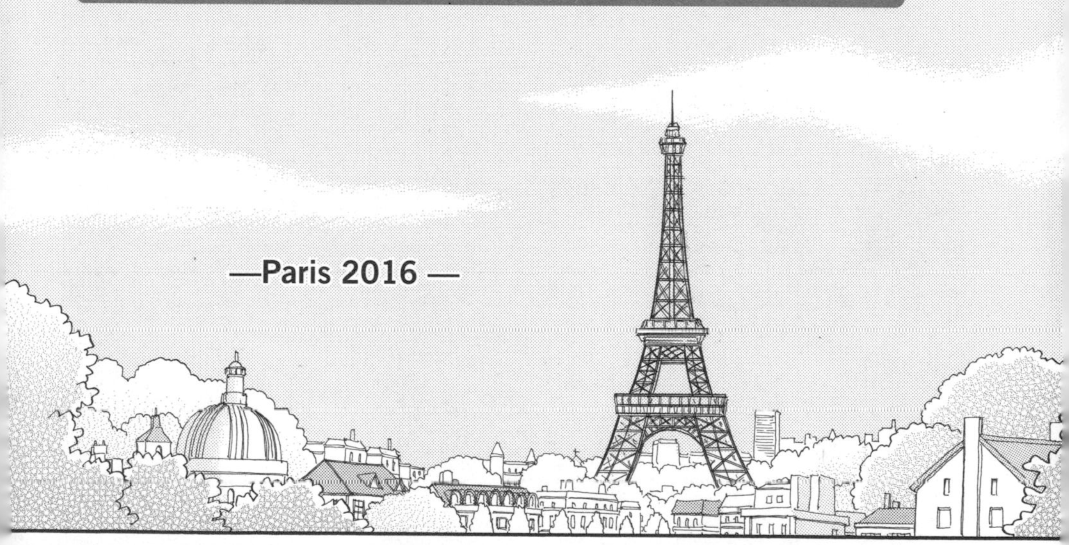
—Paris 2016 —

It's been a while, but Chi is back!!

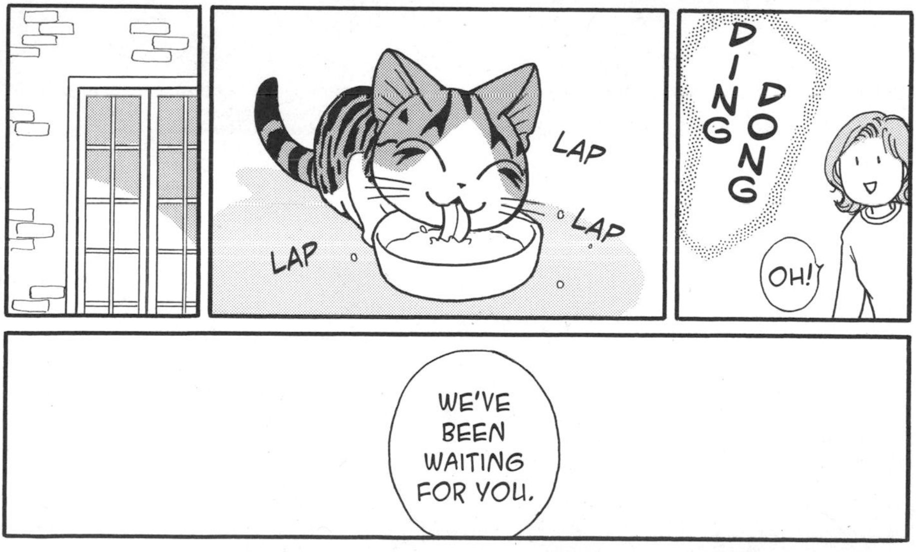
LAP
LAP
LAP
DING DONG
OH!
WE'VE BEEN WAITING FOR YOU.

**Konami Kanata**

CHI! IT'S A GUEST! COME

ARE YOU USED TO PARIS NOW, YOHEI?

AND YOU'VE GROWN, HUH.

SWOOP

SWOOM

?

!

SHUT

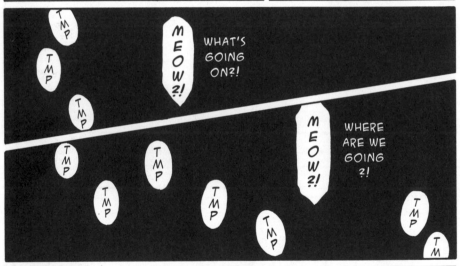
TMP TMP TMP TMP TMP TMP TMP TMP TMP TMP TMP TMP TM

MEOW?! WHAT'S GOING ON?!

MEOW?! WHERE ARE WE GOING?!

TP

POP

GASP

WHAT THE WHAT?

BEEN A WHILE, CHI...

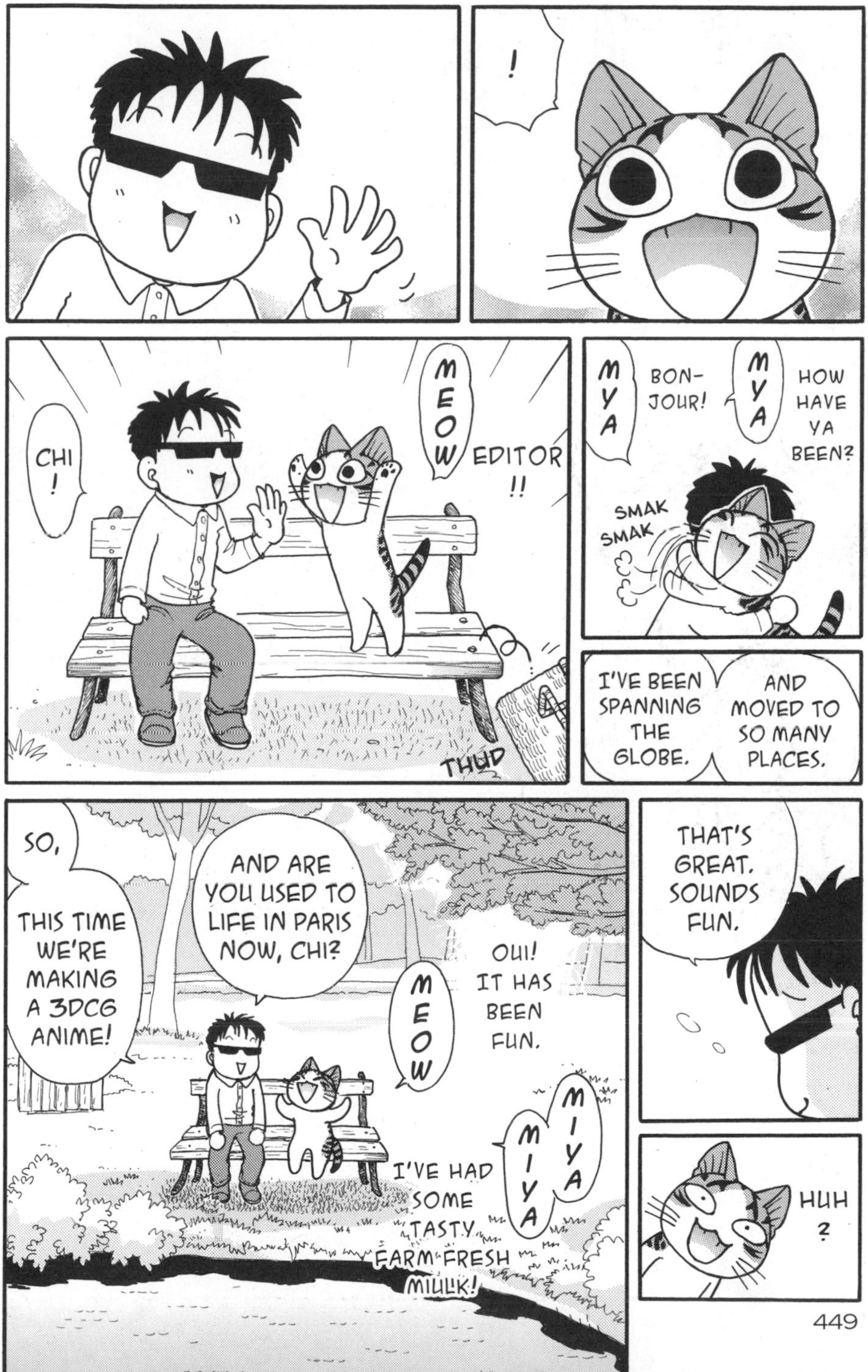
!
CHI!
MEOW
EDITOR!!
THUD
MYA
BON-JOUR!
MYA
HOW HAVE YA BEEN?
SMAK SMAK
I'VE BEEN SPANNING THE GLOBE.
AND MOVED TO SO MANY PLACES.
SO,
THIS TIME WE'RE MAKING A 3DCG ANIME!
AND ARE YOU USED TO LIFE IN PARIS NOW, CHI?
MEOW
OUI! IT HAS BEEN FUN.
MIYA
MIYA
I'VE HAD SOME TASTY FARM FRESH MIULK!
THAT'S GREAT. SOUNDS FUN.
HUH?

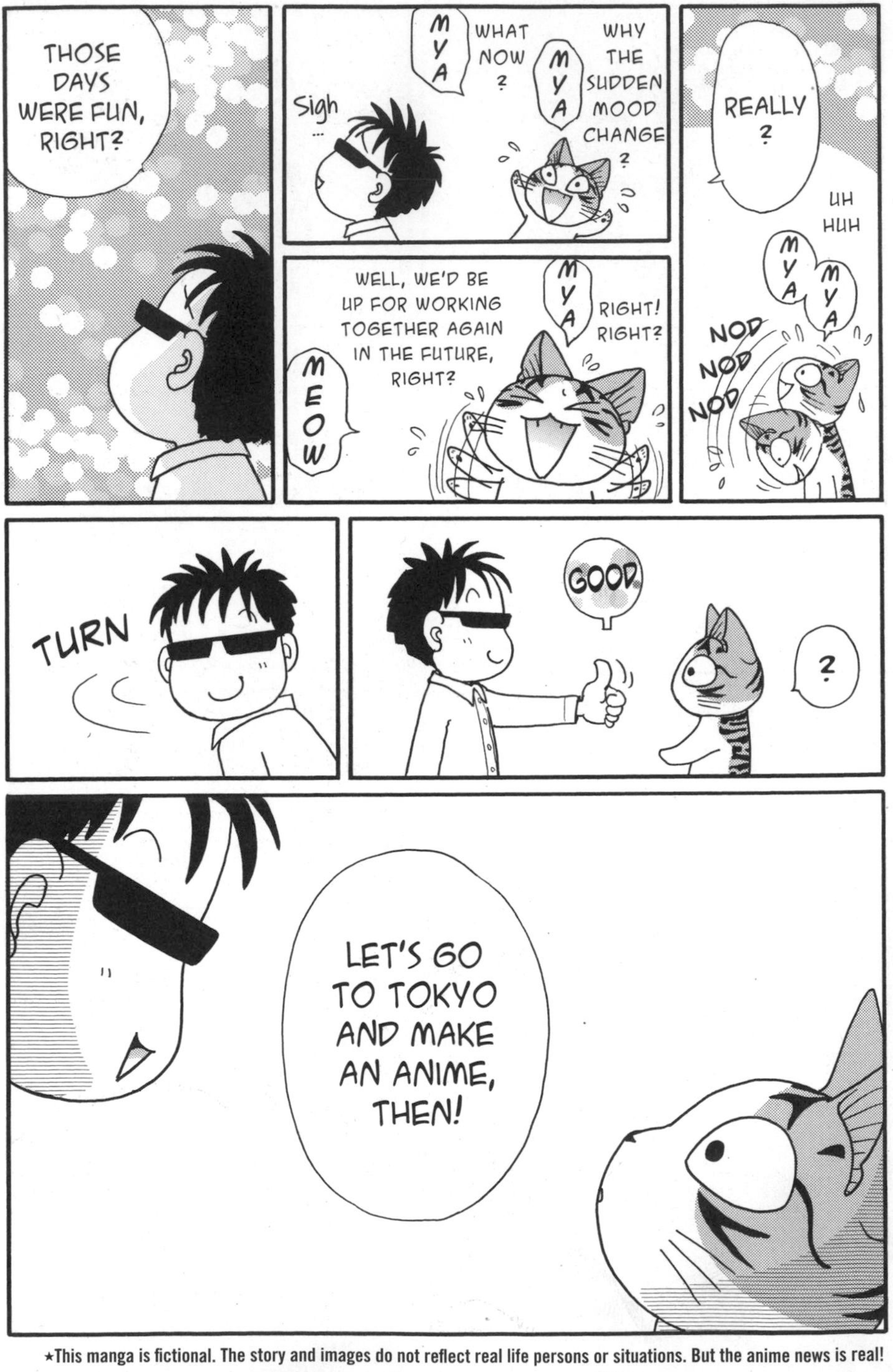
THOSE DAYS WERE FUN, RIGHT?
Sigh ...
MYA
WHAT NOW?
MYA
WHY THE SUDDEN MOOD CHANGE?
WELL, WE'D BE UP FOR WORKING TOGETHER AGAIN IN THE FUTURE, RIGHT?
MEOW
MYA
RIGHT! RIGHT?
REALLY?
UH HUH
MYA
MYA
NOD NOD NOD
TURN
GOOD
?
LET'S GO TO TOKYO AND MAKE AN ANIME, THEN!

★This manga is fictional. The story and images do not reflect real life persons or situations. But the anime news is real!

Twitter→@chi_ssweethome Facebook→http://www.facebook.com/chissweethomeofficial/

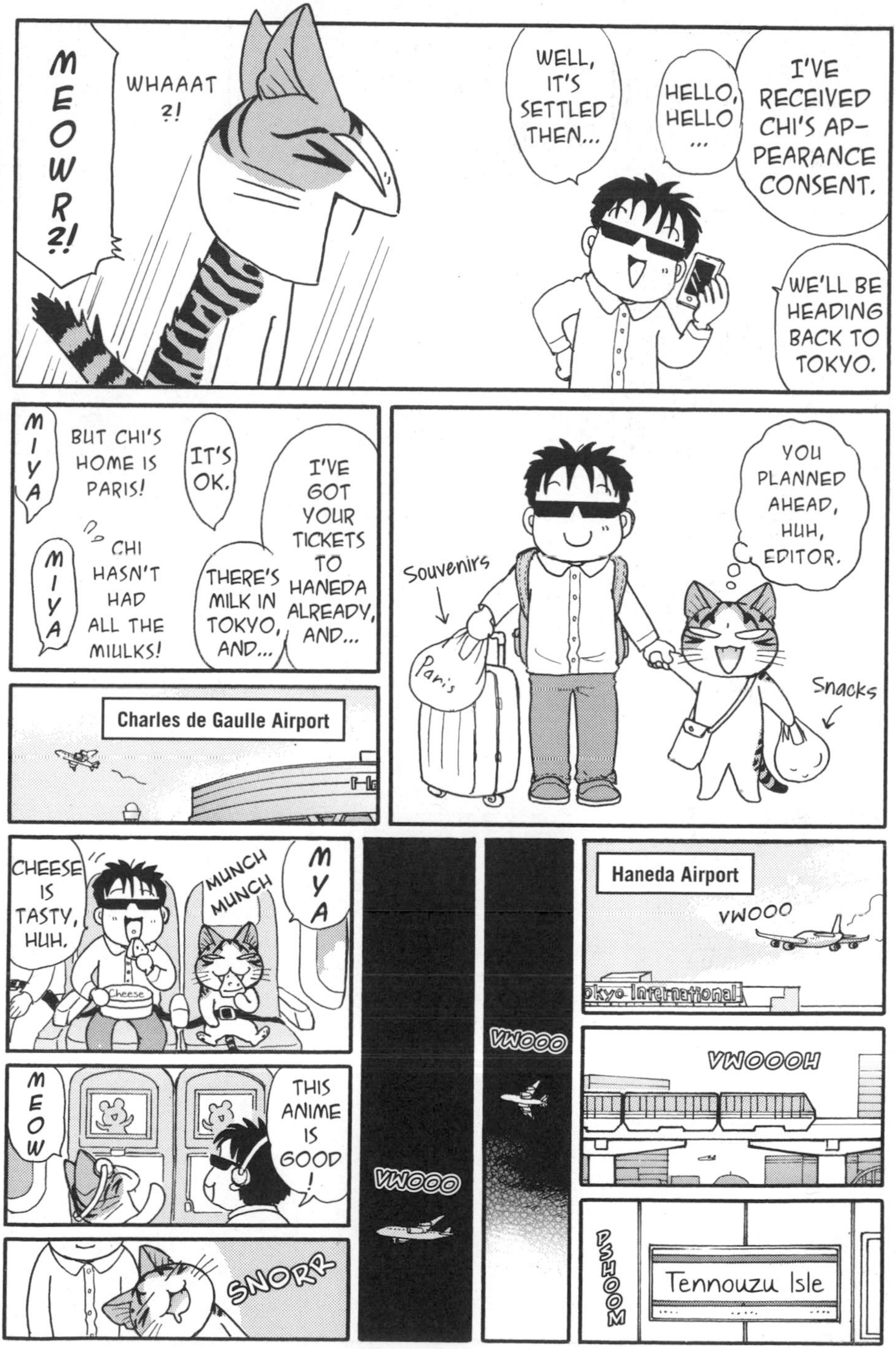
MEOWR?!
WHAAAT?!
WELL, IT'S SETTLED THEN...
HELLO, HELLO ...
I'VE RECEIVED CHI'S APPEARANCE CONSENT.
WE'LL BE HEADING BACK TO TOKYO.
MIYA
BUT CHI'S HOME IS PARIS!
MIYA
CHI HASN'T HAD ALL THE MIULKS!
IT'S OK.
I'VE GOT YOUR TICKETS TO HANEDA ALREADY, AND...
THERE'S MILK IN TOKYO, AND...
Charles de Gaulle Airport
YOU PLANNED AHEAD, HUH, EDITOR.
Souvenirs
Paris
Snacks
CHEESE IS TASTY, HUH.
MUNCH MUNCH
MYA
Cheese
MEOW
THIS ANIME IS GOOD!
SNORR
VWOOO
VWOOO
Haneda Airport
VWOOO
okyo International
VWOOOH
PSHOOM
Tennouzu Isle

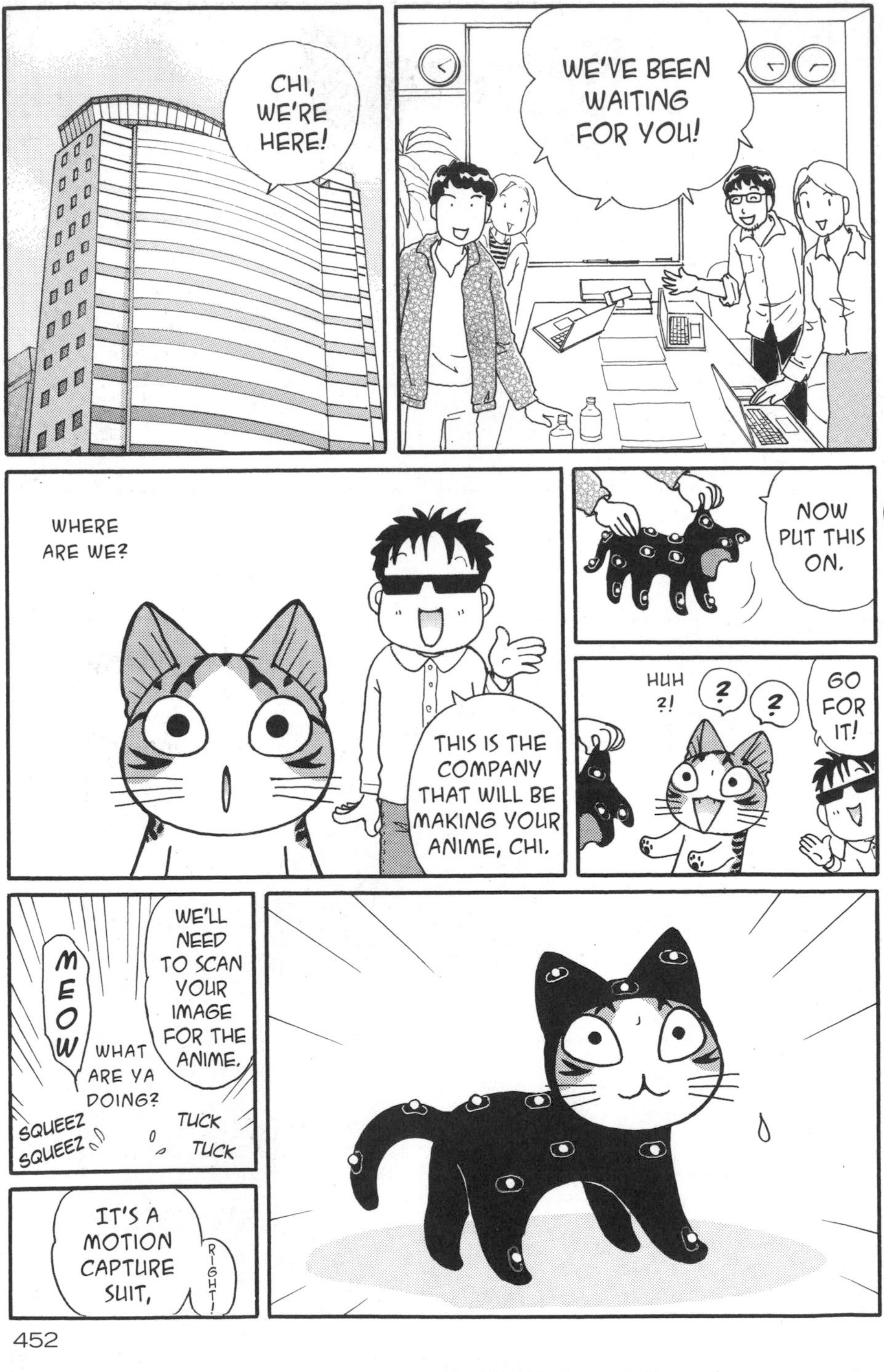
CHI, WE'RE HERE!
WE'VE BEEN WAITING FOR YOU!
WHERE ARE WE?
THIS IS THE COMPANY THAT WILL BE MAKING YOUR ANIME, CHI.
NOW PUT THIS ON.
HUH ?!
?
?
GO FOR IT!
MEOW
WE'LL NEED TO SCAN YOUR IMAGE FOR THE ANIME.
WHAT ARE YA DOING?
SQUEEZ SQUEEZ
TUCK TUCK
IT'S A MOTION CAPTURE SUIT,
RIGHT!

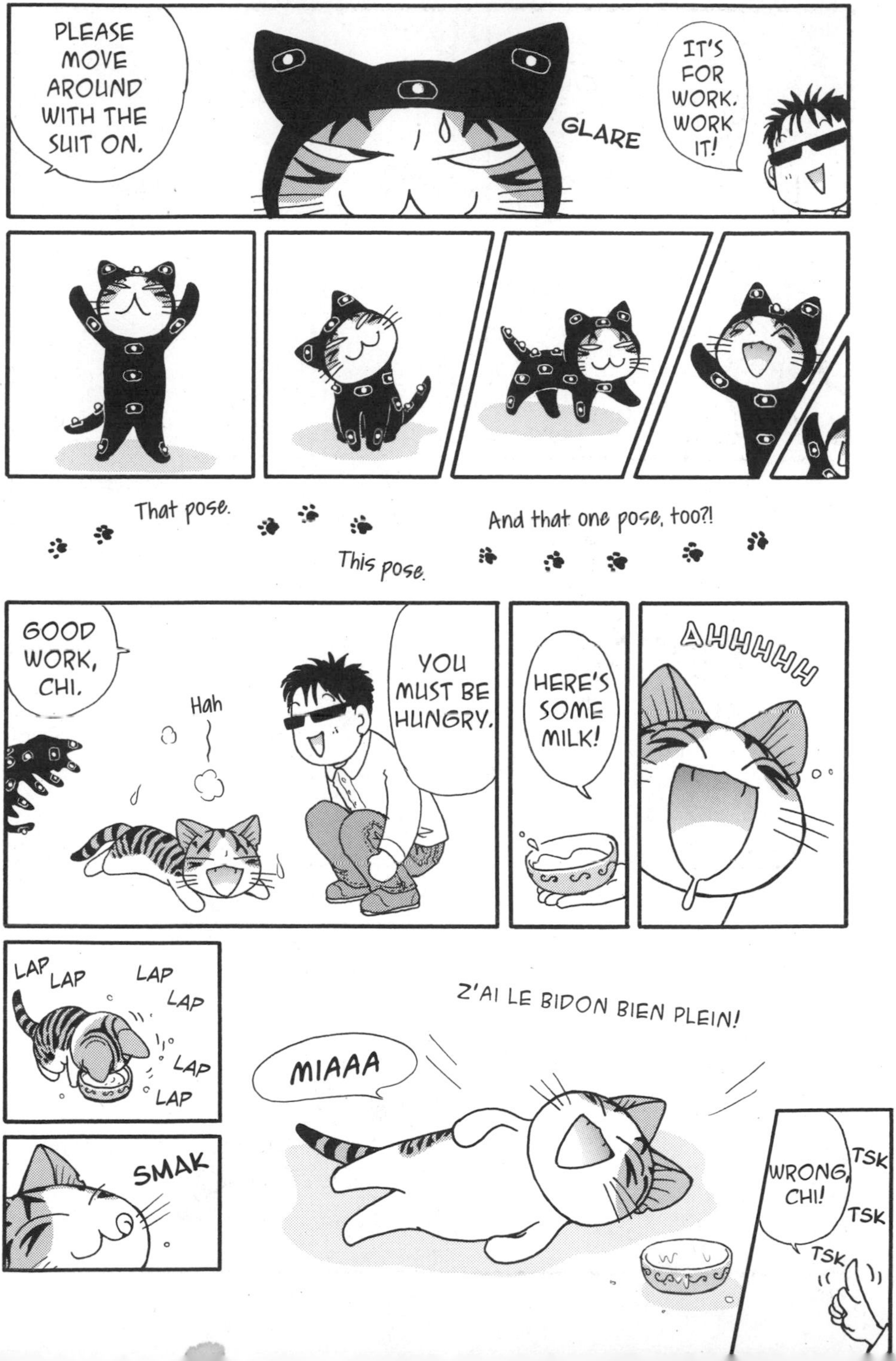
PLEASE MOVE AROUND WITH THE SUIT ON.
GLARE
IT'S FOR WORK. WORK IT!
That pose.
This pose.
And that one pose, too?!
GOOD WORK, CHI.
Hah
YOU MUST BE HUNGRY.
HERE'S SOME MILK!
AHHHHH
LAP LAP LAP LAP LAP LAP
SMAK
Z'AI LE BIDON BIEN PLEIN!
MIAAA
WRONG, CHI!
TSK
TSK
TSK

THIS IS TOKYO.
TRY AGAIN.
I'M SHTUFFED!
MEOW
MEOW
CHI WANTS TO GO HOME.
GO "HOME," HUH?
MYA
TO PARIS!
IS NEAR GAKUGEI UNIVER-SITY STATION.
MYA?!
GA-KU-GEI UNIVER-CITY?!
KTUK KTUK
YOUR ANIME HOME ...

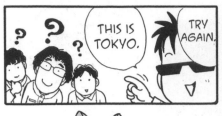

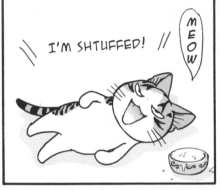

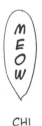

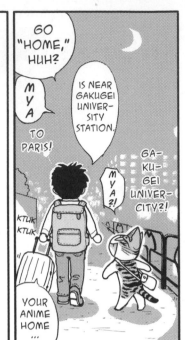

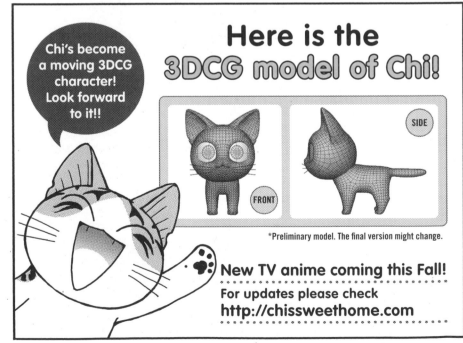

# Kitten in the Gap

FUKU FUKU

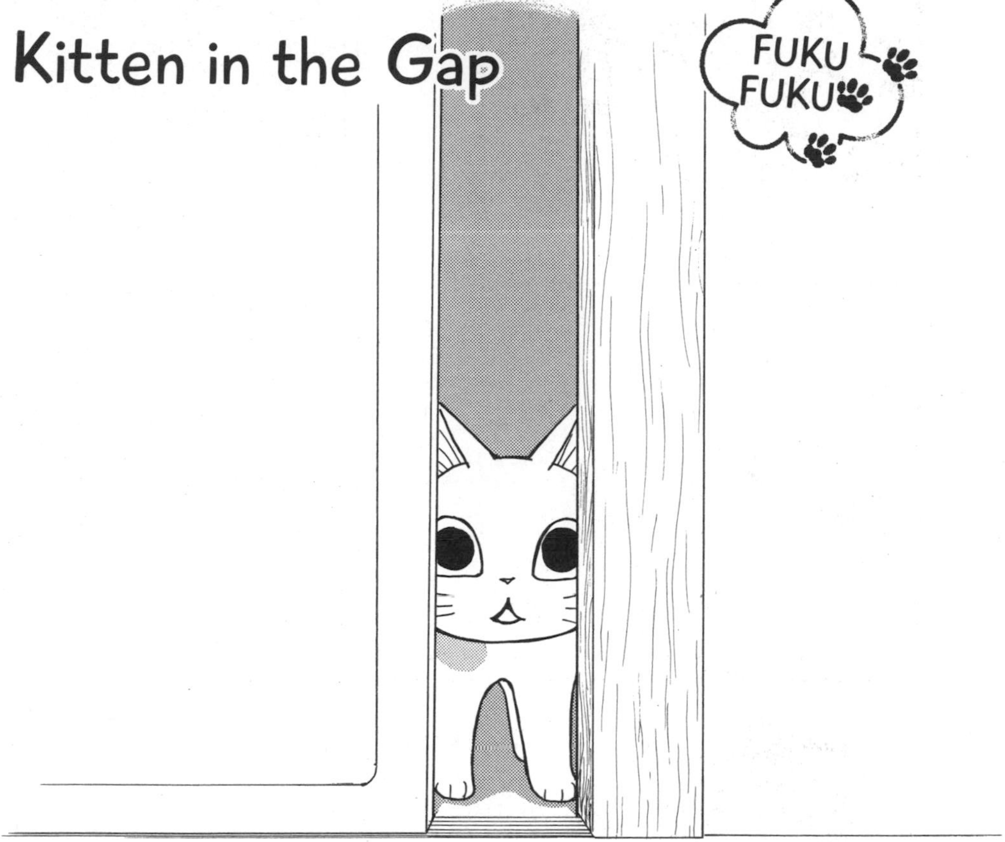

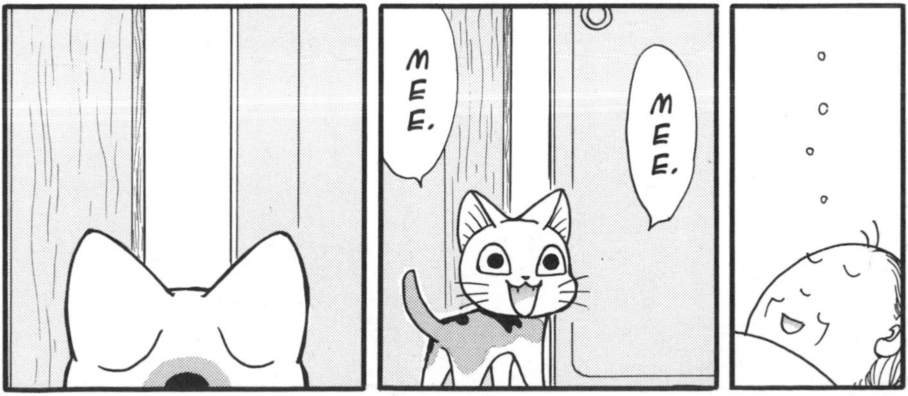
MEE.
MEE.

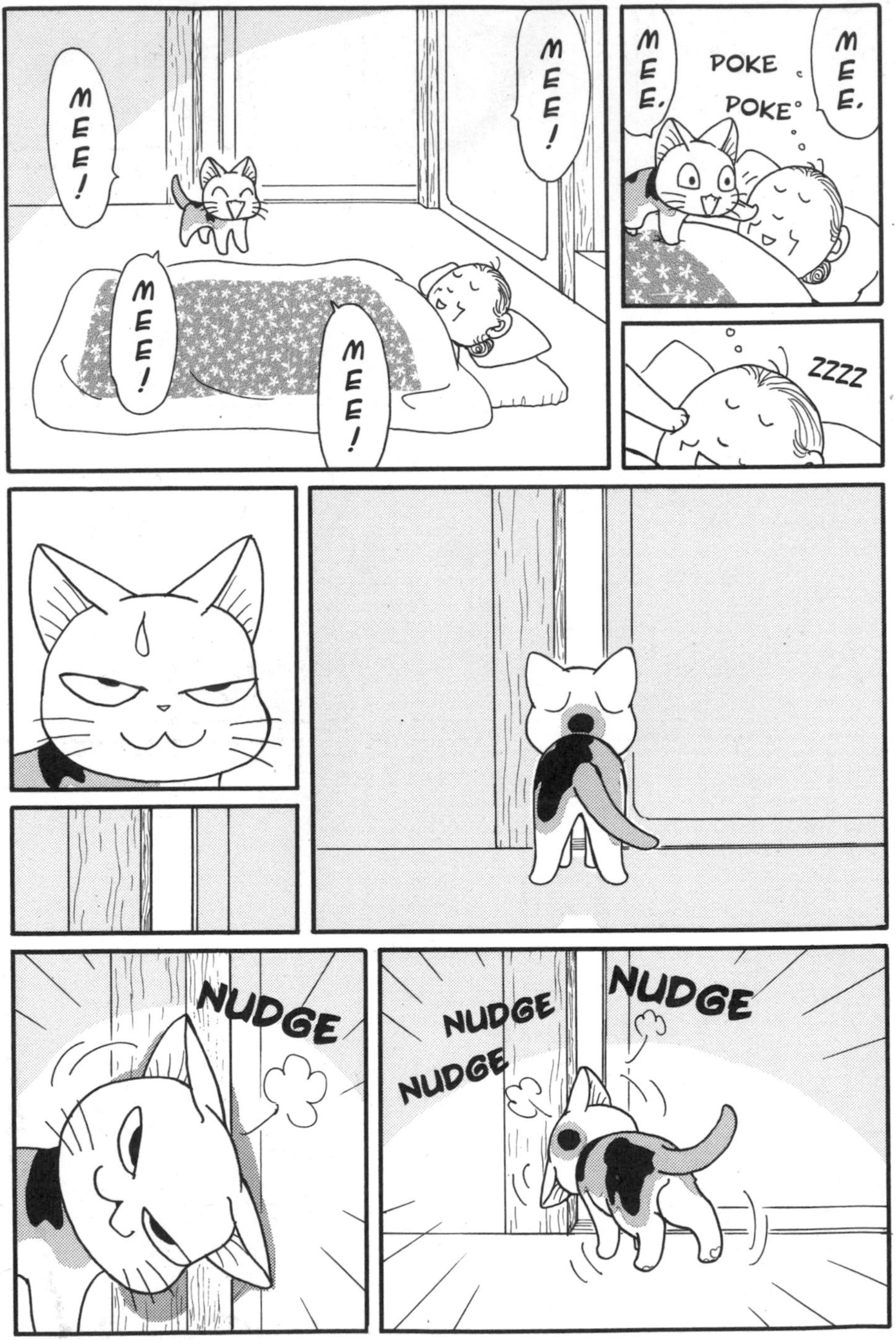
MEE!
MEE!
MEE!
MEE!
MEE.
POKE
POKE
MEE.
ZZZZ
NUDGE
NUDGE
NUDGE
NUDGE

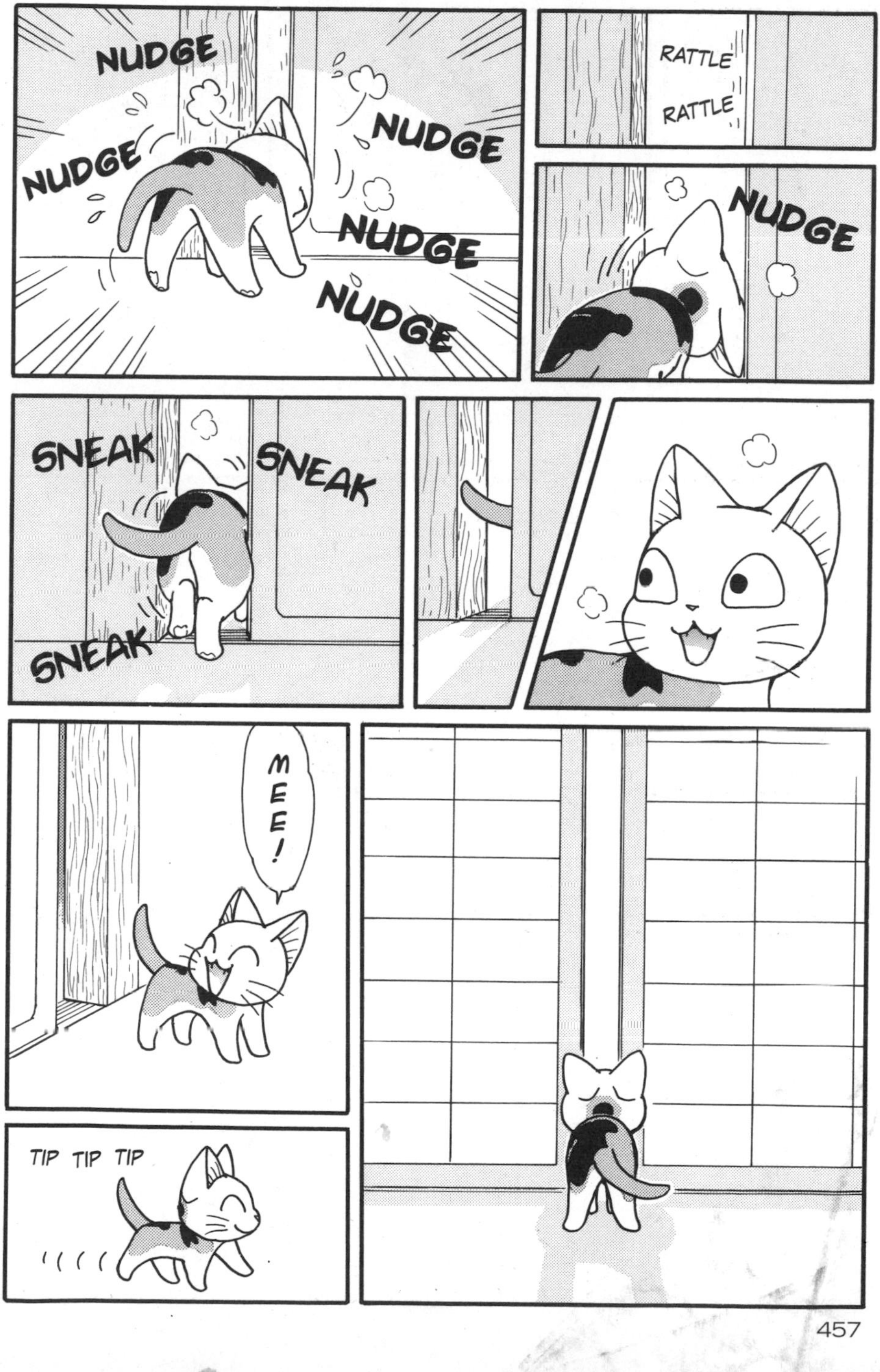
NUDGE
NUDGE
NUDGE
NUDGE
NUDGE
RATTLE
RATTLE
NUDGE
SNEAK
SNEAK
SNEAK
MEE!
TIP TIP TIP

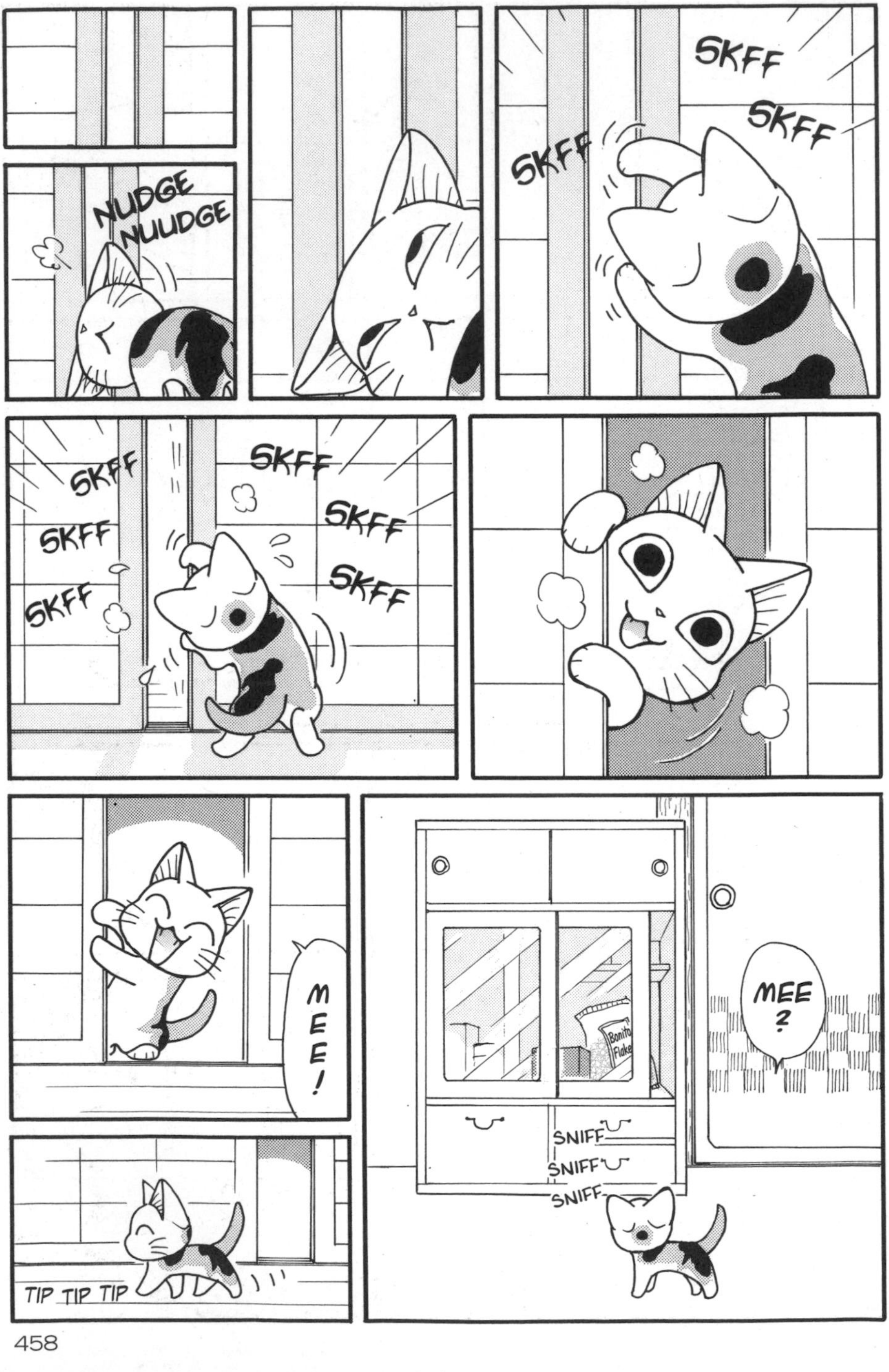
NUDGE
NUUDGE
SKFF
SKFF
SKFF
SKFF
SKFF
SKFF
SKFF
SKFF
SKFF
MEE!
TIP TIP TIP
Bonito Flakes
MEE?
SNIFF
SNIFF
SNIFF

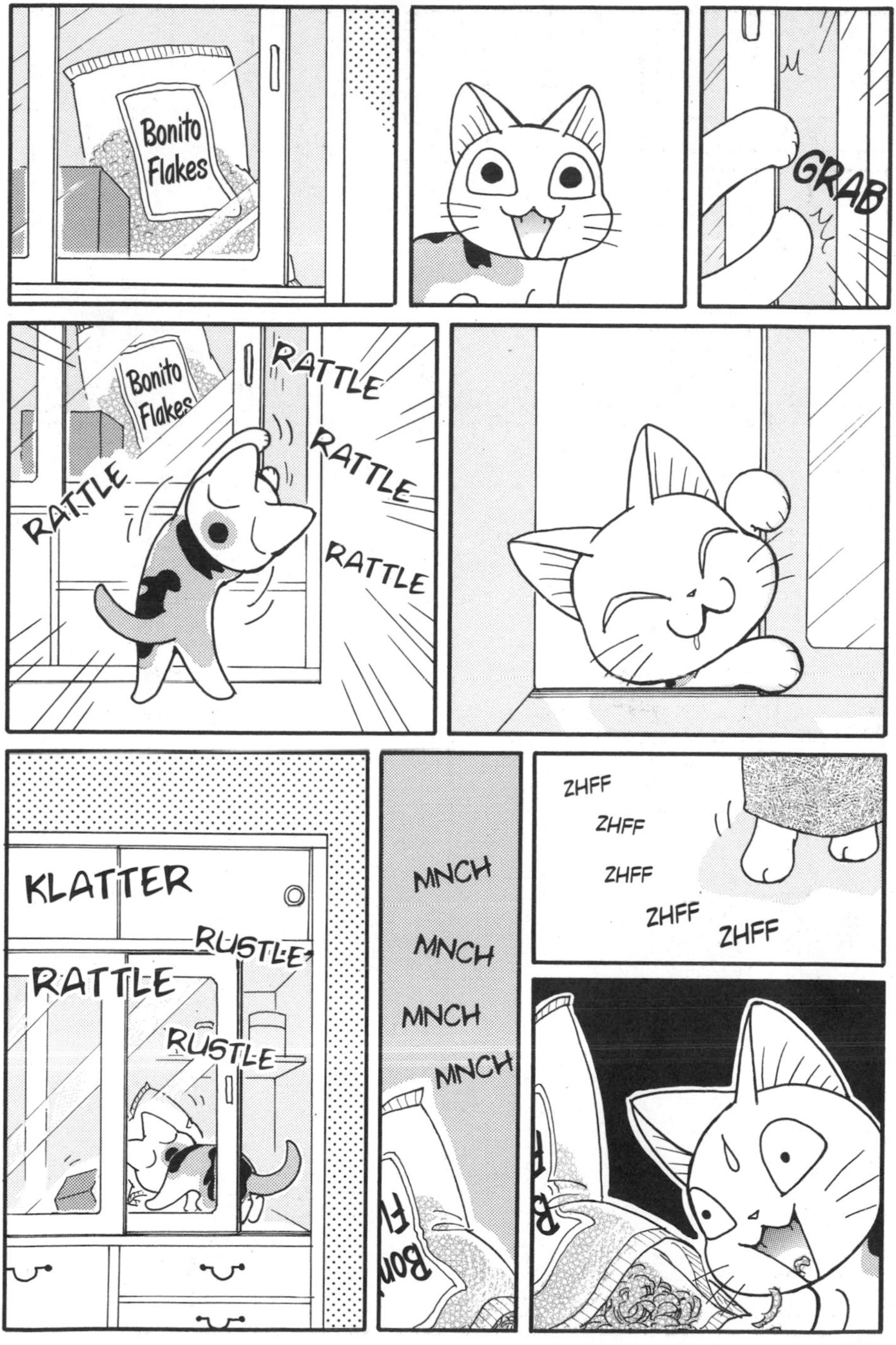
Bonito Flakes
GRAB
Bonito Flakes
RATTLE
RATTLE
RATTLE
RATTLE
KLATTER
RUSTLE
RATTLE
RUSTLE
MNCH
MNCH
MNCH
MNCH
ZHFF
ZHFF
ZHFF
ZHFF
ZHFF

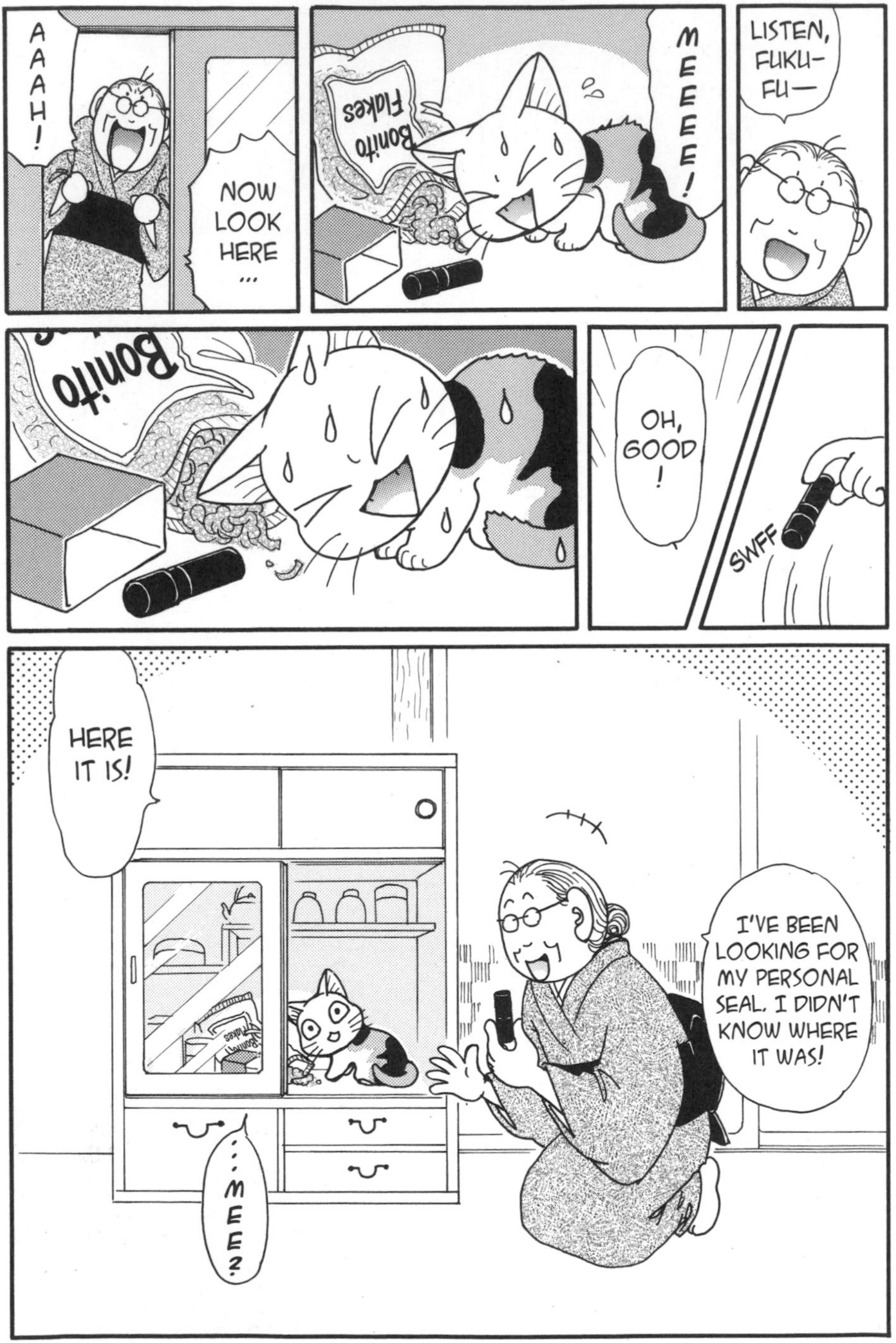
AAAAH!
NOW LOOK HERE ...
Bonito Flakes
MEEEEE!
LISTEN, FUKU-FU—
Bonito
OH, GOOD!
SWFF
HERE IT IS!
I'VE BEEN LOOKING FOR MY PERSONAL SEAL. I DIDN'T KNOW WHERE IT WAS!
Bonito Flakes
...MEE?

the end

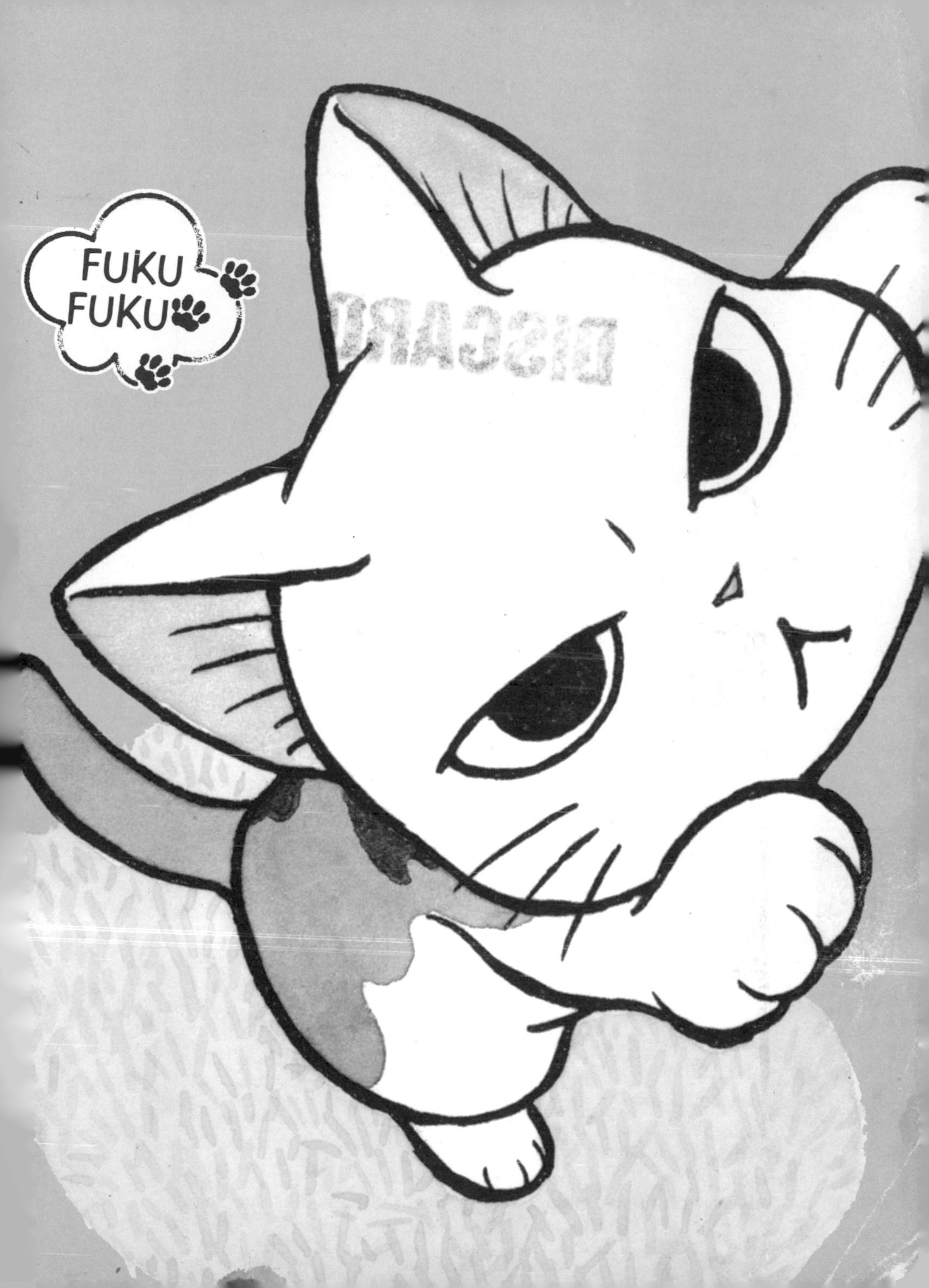
FUKU
FUKU

**The Complete**
**Chi's Sweet Home, Part 3**

Translation - Ed Chavez
Marlaina McElheny
Production - Grace Lu
Hiroko Mizuno
Tomoe Tsutsumi




First published in Japan in 2010, 2011, 2012 by Kodansha, Ltd., Tokyo
Publication for this English edition arranged through Kodansha, Ltd., Tokyo
English lan

Translatio
Published

Originally Ltd., 2009
*Chiizu S*

*FukuFuk* *Fuku Funya~n*
*Ko-neko*
*FukuFuk* ., 2013-2015

This is a

ISBN: 97

Manufac

First Edi

Vertical,
451 Par
New York
www.vert

Special t

Vertical ces.